NIGHTS OUT

NIGHTS OUT
LIFE IN COSMOPOLITAN LONDON

JUDITH R. WALKOWITZ

YALE UNIVERSITY PRESS
NEW HAVEN AND LONDON

For information about this and other Yale University Press publications, please contact:
U.S. Office: sales.press@yale.edu   www.yalebooks.com
Europe Office: sales @yaleup.co.uk   www.yalebooks.co.uk

Set in Arno Pro by IDSUK (Data Connection) Ltd
Printed in Great Britain by TJ International Ltd, Padstow, Cornwall

Library of Congress Cataloging-in-Publication Data

Walkowitz, Judith R.
    Nights out: life in cosmopolitan London / Judith R. Walkowitz.
        p. cm.
Includes bibliographical references.
ISBN 978-0–300–15194–7 (cloth: alk. paper)
1. Soho (London, England)—History—20th century. 2. London (England)—
History—20th century. 3. Woolf, Virginia, 1882–1941—Travel—England—London.
4. Cosmopolitanism—England—London—History—20th century. 5. Nightlife—
England—London—History—20th century. 6. City and town life—England—
London—History—20th century. 7. Cultural pluralism—England—London—
History—20th century. 8. Popular culture—England—London—History—20th century.
9. Political culture—England—London—History—20th century. 10. Social change—
England—London—History—20th century.   I. Title.
    DA685.S6W35 2012
    942.1'32—dc23
                                                                                2011041756
A catalogue record for this book is available from the British Library.

10 9 8 7 6 5 4 3 2 1

For Lucy

Contents

Illustrations

Figures

Plates

Maps

Acknowledgments

T HIS BOOK HAS BEEN MANY YEARS IN THE MAKING. OVER THE YEARS, IT has changed its thematic focus and expanded its temporal dimensions. Let me begin by thanking the granting agencies and institutions that supported its research: the Center for Advanced Study in the Behavioral Sciences, where I held a Mellon Fellowship; the Dorothy and Lewis B. Cullman Center for Writers and Scholars, New York Public Library; the Guggenheim Foundation; the National Endowment for the Humanities; and the Johns Hopkins University.

I am greatly indebted to a series of librarians and libraries. I would like to thank Alison Kenney of the Westminster Archives, Dave Smith and Jay Barksdale of the New York Public Library, Margaret Burri and Chellaminal Vaidyanathan of the Johns Hopkins University Alex Werner and Cathy Ross of the Museum of London, and Sarah Jillings of the Jewish Museum. Thanks additionally to the staff of the British Library and British Newspaper Library, the London Metropolitan Archives, the Theatre Museum, the National Archives, Selfridges Archives (now at the History of Advertising Trust), the William Andrews Clark Memorial Library, and the Harry Ransom Center.

Many students assisted me in the research and final preparation of the manuscript. Special thanks to Jessica Clark, Laurel Flinn, Michael Henderson, Ethan Miller, Constantina Papoulias, Katie Hindmarch-Watson, Ren Pepitone, and Jessica Valdez. I am also indebted to my graduate and undergraduate classes at the Johns Hopkins University for joining me on imaginative explorations of London's history.

Over the years, many individuals have shared their expertise and related research with me. Thanks to Pietro Dipaola, Brent Edwardes, Sally Fiber, Donna Gabaccia, Carol Helstosky, Louise Jackson, Samuel Roberts, Stefan Slater, Jerry

White, Richard Wright and Andrea Zemgulys. My thanks to other colleagues on both sides of the Atlantic who generously read and commented on portions of this book: Sally Alexander, Cora Kaplan, Toby Ditz, Diana Fuss, Becky Conekin, Patricia Crain, Deborah Gordon, Dorothy Hodgson, Peter Jelavich, Martha Howell, Margaret Hunt, Catherine Hall, Mary Ryan, Lara Kriegel, Sharon Marcus, Lucy McDiarmid, Mary Morissey, Ellen Ross, and Barbara Taylor. I owe a special debt to Martha Howell, who read the entire manuscript and provided analytic insights and organizational guidance. Frank Mort also read the entire manuscript, many times, and offered me a priceless combination of encouragement, intellectual rigor, and deep empirical knowledge of the subject. Christine Stansell and Seth Koven as readers for Yale University Press offered incisive, detailed commentaries designed to make this book more readable as well as more enlightening. I have tried my best.

A three-year NYLON seminar funded by the British Academy provided a stimulating context for me to advance my ideas about cosmopolitanism and cities. Other venues where I have presented my work include the Victorian Studies Association, the American Historical Association, the North American Conference of British Studies, the Berkshire Conference on Women's History, Johns Hopkins University, Villanova University, Rutgers University, University of Wisconsin, University of Utah, University of Pennsylvania, Stanford University, Texas A&M, University of Texas at Austin, Columbia University, University of Manchester, and the Institute of Historical Research, Goldsmiths College and Queen Mary College, University of London.

Earlier versions of three chapters have previously appeared in other publications. A portion of chapter 1 has appeared as "Emergence of Cosmopolitan Soho," in *The New Blackwell Companion to the City*, edited by Sophie Watson and Gary Bridges (Oxford: Blackwell, 2010), 419–30. An earlier version of chapter 2 appeared as "Cosmopolitanism, Feminism, and the Moving Body," *Victorian Literature and Culture* 38, no. 2 (2010): 427–9 (Cambridge University Press). A version of chapter 3 appeared as "The 'Vision of Salome': Cosmopolitanism and Erotic Dancing in Central London, 1908–1918," *American Historical Review* 108, no. 2 (2003): 337–76.

Many thanks to Heather McCallum, my editor at Yale, who embraced this project and offered wise counsel from the start. Rachael Lonsdale of Yale University Press provided great assistance with photographs and permissions. Many thanks to Candida Brazil and Ann Bone for their careful editing of the manuscript, to Stephen Kent for the book design, and to Jim O'Brien for his indexing. Special thanks to Charlotte Sheedy, my long-time literary agent, for her invaluable advice and faith in me.

Finally, my family, Daniel Walkowitz, Rebecca Walkowitz, and Henry Turner, all scholars in their own right, put up with me and lovingly encouraged me during the nearly two decades it took for this project to reach completion. Daniel and Rebecca read many portions of this book over the years, and I want to acknowledge my intellectual debt to these two experts of dancing and cosmopolitanism, respectfully. All our lives have been enhanced by the addition of Lucy Turner Walkowitz, and I dedicate this book to her.

Introduction

VIRGINIA WOOLF LOVED SOHO. IN THE EARLY 1920S, HER FAVORITE URBAN itinerary brought her to this old, foreign quarter of central London, located to the west of Bloomsbury. Her "usual round," as she put it, involved a journey from Gordon Square, where her sister Vanessa still lived, to the bookish fringes of Soho. While rummaging through the stalls of used books along the Charing Cross Road, Woolf might encounter Roger Fry with four or five yellow French books under his arms. Woolf would then cross Cambridge Circus, walk up Shaftesbury Avenue, and turn into Gerrard Street to visit the 1917 Club, a socialist establishment co-founded by her husband Leonard that brought intellectuals and political activists together under the banner of free speech. Some of the less high-minded members of her club availed themselves of Soho's dubious commercial attractions and popped across the road for an illicit drink at Mrs. Meyrick's notorious 43 Club.[1] Woolf's participation in Soho's nightlife stopped short of shady night clubs like The 43, but Virginia and Leonard often went behind the Palace Theatre in Cambridge Circus to meet friends at a Franco-Italian "Soho restaurant" in the area of Old Compton Street.[2]

Soho's appeal extended well beyond this bohemian cultural geography. Woolf frequently made detours north and west into Berwick Street Market, discovered by her on a trip to have her watch repaired in Rupert Street. The colors and the noise of the market roused in her vivid mental pictures, which she processed into fiction.[3] Woolf took pride in her ability to haggle over the price of slightly defective silk stockings with the Jewish stall-keepers and aggressive shop touts known as schleppers. Berwick Street Market's stocking stalls were chiefly kept by Jewish Londoners, but their patrons were more ethnically diverse.

According to one travel writer, they were decidedly "cosmopolitan—French, Swiss, Italian, Greek and suburban."[4]

Woolf was undoubtedly drawn to Soho's blend of old and new London. Soho was a physical remnant of the old Georgian city, full of "queer people" and "curious trades," its reputation for raffish nonconformity stretching back to the early modern period.[5] However, apart from her watchmaker, whose craft placed him squarely within Soho's long tradition of skilled artisanal trades, the Soho sites visited by Woolf were modern establishments. The Charing Cross Road, her point of entry into Soho, opened in 1887 as a late Victorian street improvement. Its secondhand booksellers were not traditional features of the locale but had settled there after 1906.[6] Berwick Street Market was also of recent vintage, only officially recognized by municipal authorities in 1892, even though there had been some street trading there for over two hundred years. Since the Great War, the market had expanded and diversified its merchandise to include up-to-date, ready-to-wear fashion, and acquired a mixed-class clientele. Its aggressive traders sold accessories and dance frocks to shop girls and clerks who dreamt of becoming actresses once they quit their desks and counters for the day.[7] The Soho dining places patronized by Virginia and Leonard Woolf were another sign of Soho's new consumer economy, most of them dating from the final two decades of the previous century and thereafter. Originally enterprises catering to immigrants, Soho restaurants like Roche's and Petit Riche went on to carve out a distinctive marketing niche in the metropolis by offering economical versions of haute cuisine in a quaint Old London setting.[8] By the 1920s, most of them had "deviated" from French to Franco-Italian cooking, as Italians established themselves as the "masters" of Soho and headquartered their "very active Fascism" in the Italian club on Greek Street.[9] But twenties Soho also served as a meeting place for other political tendencies. The 1917 Club chose a Soho address as much for its longstanding associations with radical and refugee London as for its relative cheapness and centrality.

Woolf's journey through the streets also signaled Soho's modern geography. She did not follow any established route, nor did she limit her rambles to the parish boundaries of St. Anne, which had established the traditional civic and ecclesiastical identity for Soho since the early modern period. Her usual round extended beyond St. Anne's western limits to the Berwick Street area, still officially part of the parish of St. James, Westminster, but informally annexed to Soho as a result of the building of Regent Street in the 1820s. In effect, her itinerary testified to the imaginative remapping of Soho in the nineteenth century as a parallelogram bounded by the heavily commercialized West End thoroughfares of Oxford Street to the north, Regent Street to the west, the

Charing Cross Road to the east, and Coventry Street and Leicester Square to the south.[10] Rather than segregate and contain Soho, the illuminated West End thoroughfares opened up Soho to commercial development and encouraged movement in both directions, even enabling middle-class women like Woolf to join the "republican" army of ramblers in Soho.[11]

This book revisits the clothing stalls, restaurants, clubs, and other spaces of encounter that formed the backdrop to Woolf's urban rambles in Soho. It poses the following question: how did this tiny space, no more than 130 or so acres on the eastern edge of the fashionable West End and never exceeding 24,000 residents in the twentieth century, become a potent incubator of metropolitan change?[12] To find the answer, it examines the modern commercial economies that linked Soho to its peripheries, and to the world beyond. It charts how these economies enabled Soho to gain fame as a relaxed zone of freedom and toleration, as the one place in the metropolis where the usual rules did not apply, while also producing a social scene marked by segregation, tensions, and inequalities. Featuring vivid characters and striking narratives, *Nights Out* retells London's story from the perspective of Soho residents and its habitués. It shows how people of different ethnicities lived together and apart, decades before this social heterogeneity became a commonplace of multicultural London. Despite its diversity, Soho was not so much a cultural melting pot as a space of intimate and sometimes tumultuous interaction between men and women of many walks of life: rich and poor, unschooled émigrés and Bloomsbury literati, moral purity campaigners and libertarian anarchists, undercover police and dance hostesses, fascists and anti-fascists, queers and heterosexuals, Italians, Jews, Greeks, Americans, Germans, Swiss, black GIs, and white Britons.[13]

Theories of Cosmopolitanism

This mobility and flux underscores another attraction of the locale and key theme of this book: Soho's cosmopolitanism. Between 1890 and 1945, Soho's porous geographic identity and borderlands, not to mention its doubtful commerce, politics, and "strange, outlandish population," contributed to its pre-eminence as London's "cosmopolis."[14] Its cosmopolitan reputation dated from the second half of the nineteenth century, when it became a multiethnic, polyglot settlement of many European diasporas. Close descriptions of its cosmopolitan population and customs abounded in fin-de-siècle print culture. The social scientist Charles Booth, whose investigators found five languages spoken in one house, declared Soho to be as markedly cosmopolitan as other London neighborhoods were "curiously insular and self-contained."[15] In an article in the illustrated travel guide *Living London* (1902), writer Count Armfelt introduced Soho as the center of "Cosmopolitan London," as the "cherished home of foreign artists, dancers, musicians, and singers . . . and the sanctuary of political refugees, conspirators, deserters, and defaulters of all nations."[16]

Nights Out makes a historical contribution to the lively, ongoing scholarly debate over the meanings and critical uses of cosmopolitanism. This academic conversation tends to bifurcate into two areas of concern. The first case relates to cosmopolitanism as an intellectual program, the second to cosmopolitanism as a social and cultural experience. In the first instance, literary critics, and philosophers debate the merits of cosmopolitanism as a privileged, ethical or aesthetic form of thinking and textual practice.[17] Philosophers such as Martha Nussbaum treat cosmopolitanism as a fixed, normative set of principles, while literary critics engage in more specific, historically based projects of exploring high cultural literary production. Critics Amanda Anderson and Jessica Berman, for instance, argue that cosmopolitanism enabled nineteenth- and twentieth-century writers to elaborate self-reflexive detachment, intercultural exchange, and critical thinking.[18] Rebecca Walkowitz also finds a usable past in the "critical cosmopolitanism" of modernist writers such as Woolf and Joseph Conrad who labored to produce a new kind of cosmopolitan literary style, using affect, posture, and modes of being to generate "specific projects of democratic individualism . . . antifascism and anti-imperialism."[19]

Outside of literary circles, a different discussion of cosmopolitanism has ensued among anthropologists and scholars of cultural studies, who have called for closer attention to less highbrow versions of the cosmopolitan project. James Clifford, for example, points to a kind of cosmopolitan thinking among transnational migrants—or "discrepant cosmopolitans"—based on the material knowledge gained through adverse daily routines.[20] Writing of "visceral cosmopolitanism" in the twentieth century, Mica Nava also identifies a more democratic form of everyday cosmopolitanism enabled by transnational modes of consumer culture that undercut gendered national norms.[21] Carol Breckenridge and Arjan Appadurai further dispute the notion that cosmopolitanism possesses any intrinsic normative meaning. Instead, these two writers have encouraged more historically specific studies to flesh out cosmopolitanism's shifting practices and discordant meanings. But to date, their call has resulted in limited efforts to produce historical ethnoscapes of urban cosmopolitan enclaves.[22]

To this end, *Nights Out* spotlights Soho, recognized in its own day as a practical laboratory of the cosmopolitan experience for both plebeian transmigrants and avant-garde devotees of cultural cosmopolitanism such as Woolf and

Conrad. It forcefully argues for the centrality of commercialized culture in shaping political formations, particularly during the interwar years. In contrast to neo-Kantian and Habermasian critics, I do not interpret the political reframing of Soho's cosmopolitanism as simply the expression of critical thinking and detachment; it was a broader cultural project indebted to new ways of seeing and performing the body, to new media outlets and innovative forms of musical culture and connoisseurship.[23]

Historicizing Urban Cosmopolitanism

Since the Enlightenment, cosmopolitanism has conveyed a set of competing meanings. In the nineteenth century it could signify disinterested humanitarianism as well as the accomplishments and worldly knowledge of cultivated individuals. However, it could also suggest the malicious/benign workings of the capitalist market.[24] In the late Victorian period, it gained new currency as a description of urban spaces and their cultural and social milieux. This spatial designation occurred during a moment of geographic turmoil at the worldwide and local level. Britain's global hegemony as an imperialist and capitalist power brought the "world qua world . . . into view," to quote critic Tanya Agathocleous, rendering visible the time/space compressions of globalization. In the heyday of Victorian imperialism, a New London took shape in London's West End thoroughfares that bounded Soho, devoted to cosmopolitan attractions and drawing in more and more cosmopolitan crowds.[25] The West End's commercial attractions seemed to ratify Britain's global reach and embody London's international status as the greatest city of the world, as an international finance center and tourist attraction with a range of urban and cultural amenities to support that claim.[26]

Popular print culture enabled new geographic imaginings by ascribing a positive, bourgeois version of cosmopolitanism to the department stores, variety theatres, hotels, and luxury restaurants built along Soho's imposing commercial peripheries. This positive version conveyed the West End's reputation for sensory indulgence, privileged mobility, and worldly command of goods, ideas, and bodies. Journalists and writers made special note of the dramatic materializations of foreign cultural artifacts along these commercial thoroughfares, linking them to a culture of visual pleasure featuring women as spectacle and increasingly as active spectators.[27] Throughout this period, however, cosmopolitanism in its glossy, pleasurable, privileged sense seemed to depend on close proximity to the dangers and enticements of a second set of associations also linked to cosmopolitanism.[28] When the same journalists turned their attention to the neighboring district of Soho in the 1890s, they produced a more ominous picture of cosmopolitanism's impact on London. With its foreign refugees and irregular economies of sex and crime, Soho represented the epitome of a bad or dangerous cosmopolitanism: a debased condition of transgression, displacement and degeneration.[29] Yet this land of lost causes and deterritorialized foreigners was intimately tied to major sectors of the metropolitan economy: it served as a back region of sweated labor, artisan production, and street prostitution for the front stages of pleasure along the boulevards.

By the first decade of the twentieth century, however, Soho became something more than an industrial hinterland for the commercial West End. Numerous commentators took note of Soho's improved commercial fortunes and publicized its tasteful as well as sleazy forms of cosmopolitan pleasures, centered on nightlife, fashion, and food culture. Its seedy environs served as a strategic location for the brokering of transnational goods, bodily display, politics, and appetites, even in forms that were heavily mediated for English consumption. Soho's commercial spaces also became sites of social exchange between elite social actors and first and second generation immigrants in Soho who honed their skills as providers of cosmopolitan attractions. Soho's cosmopolitanism was not static: it shifted over time between 1890 and 1945 in response to changes in population, economies, cultural novelty, insurgent nationalisms, governmental oversight, and, as important, the initiatives of Sohoites themselves. At the same time, media depictions of Soho were crucial to advancing the commercial appeal of the district. As Frank Mort has noted, successive waves of publicists and writers had to reinvent Soho for new habitués, even though these reinventions drew on the district's historically enduring associations.[30]

Cosmopolitanism and the Nation

Cosmopolitanism, as critics have shown, inevitably exists in tension with conventional norms and attachments to the nation.[31] These tensions were readily apparent in Soho's cultural and political life. Sohoites' disposition towards the English host culture varied widely, while Londoners reciprocated with their own mixed feelings about Soho. Between 1890 and 1945, crime reporters and social investigators figured Soho as a plague spot of foreign crime, disease, and vice, spreading its poison across the metropolis.[32] By contrast, urban travel guides presented a more reassuring account of this emblematic central space. In 1920, novelist John Galsworthy portrayed Soho as a benign enclave "remote from the British body politic": it was "full of Greeks, Ishmaelites, cats, Italians, tomatoes, restaurants" and "organs," not to mention "queer names" and "people looking out of upper windows."[33] But, even as a picturesque tourist attraction, Soho was never fully imagined to be outside of England. At the turn of the twentieth century, its new commercial allure partly derived from its provenance as a vestige of Old London. By plowing through and obliterating most of the urban fabric of Old London, Victorian street improvements inadvertently elevated Soho's status as an intact remnant of London Past and a repository of Georgian literary and historical memories. Thanks to the promotional efforts of local reformers, bohemian writers, and ethnic entrepreneurs, Soho acquired a reputation for being simultaneously safe and dangerous, securely English and enticingly foreign, sedately old-fashioned and scandalously modern. By 1914, Soho was a familiar attraction, not only for the cognoscenti but also for the respectable Londoner who wanted "to feel devilish" and swagger down Old Compton Street as if he or she were abroad.[34]

During the interwar period, Soho continued to evolve in tension with a British national temperament that had become more insular and suburban. Interwar Soho sustained a reputation as a foreign locale in a London that had "half-closed" its doors to foreigners through immigration restrictions.[35] Throughout the interwar years, Soho's ethnic entrepreneurs adapted their commerce to suit British tastes and travel fantasies. As social outsiders with considerable knowledge of the habits and viewpoints of the host culture, they demonstrated a form of self-reflexive "double consciousness" commonly ascribed to worldly, modern cosmopolitans.[36] The proprietors of Italian restaurants along Old Compton Street and Gerrard Street produced hybrid Franco-Italian cuisine for British palates, while they and their families performed the roles of genial, charming, "good Italians." The Jewish manager of the Windmill Theatre adapted French and American forms of erotic displays to showcase healthy, ordinary British girls. Berwick Street Market's Jewish traders hawked dance frocks purporting to come from Paris and New York that were actually produced locally in London; Jewish and black proprietors of black clubs advertised authentic hot American jazz performed by black musicians who impersonated Americans, but in fact hailed from Cardiff, Africa and the West Indies. As these examples demonstrate, adaptations to British taste not only involved a local refashioning of foreign imports; they also demanded a theatrical social masquerade by service workers and their employers.

Soho's cosmopolitans interacted with the British state and other polities in unsettling and unpredictable ways. In common with other petty shopkeepers and working-class denizens of the metropolis, Sohoites experienced the British state as a distant and unresponsive entity. Between 1887 and the Second World War, municipal and national authorities tended to leave Soho's old, unimproved built environment undisturbed. Apart from a few one-way streets and some new municipal services, they did not contemplate large-scale redevelopment of the area. As a result, local residents' encounters with governmental representatives were limited to interactions with police, state schools, and municipal facilities such as public baths, institutions warmly recalled by Jewish Sohoites.[37] Soho's businessmen often complained of too much police interference, except when a gang of ruffians arrived, at which point the local police constable would discreetly glide around the corner.[38]

Depending on their ethnicity, national loyalties among Sohoites could be "divided," to quote historian Lucio Sponza.[39] Jewish Sohoites evinced little nostalgia for their countries of origin, where they had suffered persecution, civil disabilities, and occupational restrictions, but northern Italian immigrants in Soho's catering industry learned to be patriotic Italians during their long exile in London. In the twenties and thirties, their nationalist fervor made them susceptible to the attractions of Italian Fascism, although most, like Peppino Leoni of the Quo Vadis on Dean Street, did not regard this allegiance as incompatible with a respect for the laws and institutions of Britain. Even Italian anarchists, Soho's most dedicated internationalists, were both nationalists and cosmopolitans. The anarchist and anti-Fascist Emidio Recchioni, owner of the King Bomba provision shop, might embrace the cause of international revolutionary solidarity, but his primary field of political interest remained Italy. As a sign of his attachment to his homeland, Recchioni used the profits of his Old Compton Street establishment to underwrite two assassination attempts against Mussolini. Outside the Italian diaspora, select commercial spaces came under the banner of the Popular Front, an internationalist movement that set itself against the fascist dictators of Europe and the appeasement policies of the British government.[40]

Interwar Soho emerged as a space of the right and the left, but unlike the East End at this time, political passions rarely spilled into the streets. For the most part, tensions were contained within interior spaces and within diasporas. While some habitués and residents used Soho as a staging ground for individual political expression and self-fashioning, others lived within enclaves heavily patrolled by communal ties. Ethnic communities had porous boundaries, as later discussions of Soho's streets, markets, nightclubs, and nearby mass leisure resorts will demonstrate. But the persistence of communal segregation and segmented spaces within Soho partially explains the notable absence of public disorder and violence in a district simultaneously occupied by anti-fascists and Italian Fascists, as long as anti-fascists were English bohemians, Jews, Africans, or West Indians, and *not* Italians.

Soho Histories

Nights Out is the first social and cultural history of Soho to detail Soho's cosmopolitan makeover in the fifty-year period prior to the First World War when it transmuted from a dingy, foreign, proletarian quarter into a commodified center of cultural tourism. It builds on Jerry White's presentation of Soho as a space of crime, sex, and cultural innovation on the part of immigrants and London's youth; it also anticipates key features of the postwar scene of sexual experimentalism and pleasure, recently chronicled by Frank Mort.[41] Other London historians, from Peter Ackroyd to Roy Porter, readily acknowledge Soho's distinctiveness as a heady cocktail of talent, eccentricity, style, and social diversity, but they tend to treat its special character as somehow embedded solely in its bricks, ignoring the dynamic processes that reinvented Soho's cultural nonconformity over time.[42] To date, only a handful of compartmentalized historical studies of this colorful "urban village" have materialized. Two books have paved the way to writing a new kind of history of Soho, one not solely dependent on the perspectives of bohemian journalists and memoirists: Judith Summers's *Soho: A History of London's Most Colourful Neighbourhood* (1989) and *Living Up West* (1994), by Gerry Black and based on the oral history interviews of the West End Jews in the project of London's Jewish Museum.[43] *Nights Out* is indebted to their work, as well as to gay histories of the metropolis by Matt Houlbrook and Matt Cook, who have highlighted Soho as a space of sexual nonconformity.[44] But it pursues a different strategy than many of the studies mentioned above.[45] Rather than focus exclusively on one group or another, this book highlights the places of encounter where diverse social actors engaged in commercial and political transactions that reshaped London and Londoners.

To capture this multiplicity, it has drawn on a wide range of sources, including print media, memoirs, fiction, municipal and business records, state archives, post office directories, and census manuscripts, as well as visual artifacts and oral history collections. Like cosmopolitanism itself, the written, visual and oral sources for this project are the product of cultural constructs and material processes. Later chapters make extensive use of oral histories of men and women who lived in or gravitated to Soho, based on the collections of West End Jews (Jewish Museum), the Hall Carpenter Archives, and the History of Jazz in Britain (both at the British Library Sound Archive). As with textual accounts, such as undercover police reports, travelogues, and restaurant reviews, oral narratives have a dual status as sources of historical data and cultural visions of urban practices. While they represent rare documentary evidence of historical reality from "non-hegemonic subjects," their factual veracity may be less important than their imaginative construction – through fantasy, symbolism, and desire—of historical and recollected states of mind.[46]

The vivid memories of Jewish informants of their nights out along Soho's peripheries at the Astoria Dance Salon or Lyons' Corner Houses are a case in point. Jewish ex-milliners and furriers remembered the massive Corner House restaurants as an extension of their Soho work and living space, a pleasure zone to which they repaired to order egg mayonnaise, the cheapest dish on the menu.[47] While crediting their stories as powerful interpretive devices that informed their practice and actions, I also assess them for telling silences, exclusions, and contradictions. And I set their spatial stories and perspectives against those enunciated by others, particularly the gay men who patronized Lyons', and the company's own waitresses, the smartly uniformed Nippies, who serviced the many publics of the Corner Houses and managed their sometimes strained interaction. Taken together, these multiple perspectives illuminate a complex social world subject to large-scale processes and intimate encounters, a scenario at odds with the idealized model of a contained urban village recollected many decades later in the Jewish Museum's oral narratives.[48]

Nights Out proceeds in roughly chronological order, beginning in the 1890s, with the consolidation of Soho's reputation as London's cosmopolis, and concluding with a chapter on wartime Soho's contribution to democratic nationalism, embodied by the "spirit of the Blitz." A brief conclusion and epilogue on postwar Soho follows. By continuing the story of London's cosmopolitanism beyond 1918, *Nights Out* offers a distinctive perspective on the period between the two world wars, famously described by Robert Graves and Alan Hodge as a static, escapist "long week-end."[49] To be sure, many of the same themes sketched by Graves and Hodge reappear in this volume: the explosive, hedonist nightlife of the twenties, the coming of the mass market and consumer democracy, interwar politics of the left and the right, and democratic nationalism. *Nights Out* chronicles how these different paths to modernity intersected in a single compressed locale, situated on English soil, but closely linked to other national territories. This heterogeneous environment contrasts sharply with Graves and Hodge's account of an insular Little England between the wars. Moreover, it presents a more continuous narrative of the first half of the twentieth century than the fractured periodization of interwar histories indebted to *The Long Week-End*.

Despite changes wrought by the Great War, interwar Soho sustained important continuities with its prewar past. Two material factors partially account for this continuity: the persistence of Soho's seedy urban fabric and its residential immigrant community. In this old environment, interwar Soho maintained a reputation as a cosmopolitan space of political exchange, ethnic heterogeneity, cultural innovation, and transgressive desire. It was certainly less foreign than it had been in earlier decades, in good part because of immigration restrictions and a falling off in international tourism. Between 1900 and 1939, Soho's population declined from 24,000 to 7,240.[50] Yet, it was still populated by first and second generation immigrant entrepreneurs eager to entice patrons into Soho streets with the promise of seeing life in an exotic locale. At the same time, Soho was subject to interwar redevelopments that drew more working-class Londoners to its streets. The construction of mass market leisure industries along Soho's borders established a new set of flows between Soho and its commercial peripheries. Lyons' Corner Houses, the Astoria dance hall and cinema, and Marks & Spencer's emporium on Oxford Street attracted working-class patrons into the center, some of whom made a detour into Soho. The racial mix of Soho also diversified as black jazz clubs gained popularity in the thirties.

Separate chapters track the shifting and overlapping fortunes of Soho's commercial economies of dance, food, fashion, music and sex, all of them marketed as foreign imports. Some of these transnational cultural forms accentuated expressive bodily practices and encouraged individual agency and desire, while others, such as chorus lines or haute cuisine standards of food service, ensured strict bodily management and discipline. These attractions were subject to various modes of economic and state management. Apart from disciplinary oversight, Soho's commercial spaces were further differentiated by social mix, technologies of visual display, social and theatrical performances, and political culture.

Dancing and its commercial tie-ins exemplify these multiple trajectories. A potent symbol of a modern urban kinesthesia, dancing was imaginatively aligned with Soho's cosmopolitanism and its radiating influence throughout the metropolis. But dancing was more than a cultural metaphor for urban flux and syncopated movement; it was also a commercial form integral to the leisure economy of central London. Tracking the new vogues of dancing from the commercial thoroughfares into Soho exposes the economic synergy between the West End thoroughfares and old Soho. *Nights Out*'s discussion of dance, which appears in five chapters of this volume, begins in chapter 2 at Soho's peripheries, in the late Victorian theaters of variety in Leicester Square and the Charing Cross Road. These palaces of pleasure featured spectacular ballets as leg shows for worldly men. The same theaters also staged novelty solo dances, including performances by female cultural innovators of a new expressive form of dancing. In 1908, the Palace Theatre of Varieties went so far as to recruit the North American dancer

Maud Allan, whose cosmopolitan performance delighted women as well as men. The theatrical performances of dancing celebrities like Allan set into motion a dance revolution in the early years of the twentieth century that would change nightlife and move respectable women, both as spectators and social partici- pants, into heretofore forbidden spaces of the nocturnal city. During the Great War and its aftermath, social dancing became a major attraction of Soho's after- hours nightclubs. In the interwar years, social dancing also encouraged boundary crossings in the other direction, propelling Jewish Sohoites to the dance halls along Soho's peripheries on Saturday and Sunday nights. Interwar dance forms and venues gave rise to different political effects. By the late 1930s, the progres- sive musical press celebrated the democratic and internationalist spirit of Soho's black clubs, epitomized by interracial couples on the dance floor.[51] A few streets away, the Windmill Theatre, a tiny variety theater specializing in dancing girls and gags, struck a different note of restrained middlebrow Englishness, despite its featured display of nude female tableaux.

Dancing was also interwoven with other local economies, particularly with Soho's catering trade. At the end of the nineteenth century, the foreign restau- rants of Soho expanded beyond their local immigrant clientele by offering after- theater suppers to metropolitan tourists. In the Edwardian period, both theater and dining engaged Londoners in public performances of gender, imaginative expatriation, sensory stimulation, and social distinction. Social dancing between the wars necessitated a set of props and costumes, including stockings and ready- to-wear dance frocks acquired by working-class women from Jewish traders of Berwick Street Market. Jazz dancing in commercial venues required live music, largely provided by Jewish dance musicians employed in dance halls, swank West End establishments, and Soho hot spots. Soho had long been a center of musical performance, instrument making, sheet music, and, in the twentieth century, musical recording. But its reputation for hot jazz dates from the thirties with the opening of black clubs. Jewish communist musicians, employed in the elite fleshpots of the West End, would repair to Soho dives after work, where they mixed with visiting black American "firemen" and West Indian players. Along with interracial dancing, these social exchanges between black and white musicians informally transformed black clubs into sites of progressive interna- tional politics.

One final service economy pervaded the local scene and contributed to Soho's liminality: commercialized sex. Throughout the late-nineteenth and twentieth centuries, moral purity advocates and the media repeatedly stigma- tized Soho as "London's vicious circle" and center of cosmopolitan vice.[52] These public campaigns periodically incited police crackdowns of Soho's streetwalkers, brothels, houses of assignation, and nightclubs harboring male and female sex workers. Despite sporadic police raids, however, the sex trade proliferated and altered, as sex workers moved on and off the streets and into massage parlors, theaters, dance clubs, cafes, and restaurants. It was a highly profitable local business and a potent source of police graft and corruption. Sex workers were linked to other licit and illicit businesses in the area, supplying revenue to Soho's restaurateurs with upper "rooms to let" and patronizing Jewish shopkeepers and milliners who sold them dresses and hats.[53] In the interwar years, sex workers were familiar street characters and figures of conjecture for both residents and tourists. They were part of the continuum of sexualized bodies on display in Soho venues as the ranks of "women of the painted class" swelled, and ordinary women embraced Hollywood glamour and enhanced their visibility and erotic allure through make-up, dress, and "personality."[54] According to historian Matt Houlbrook, the new eroticized look of heterosexuality also affected the self-presentation of men looking for "homosex" in and around Soho.[55] The edgy kaleidoscope of local street styles provoked boundary disputes over licit and illicit expressions of sexuality, impelling municipal authorities and commercial establishments to devise new social disciplines.

Thanks to dancing and sex, but also to food, fashion, and music, nightlife emerged as a defining feature of Soho and the inspiration for this book's main title. *Nights Out* underscores Soho's temporal as well as spatial geography and the movement of people in and out of the district. Memoirists and journalists commonly remarked on the magical transformation of Soho over the course of a day: from a grubby, foreign daytime scene, Soho by night acquired a "successful" air once it was taken over by metropolitan revelers.[56] Old stables in back alleys morphed into bohemian resorts attracting Bright Young Things and other patrons in evening clothes.[57] Soho's nighttime economy also blended with its daytime scene. Frances Partridge, a young member of the Bloomsbury set, remembered brushing past streetwalkers on Gerrard Street at 2:30 in the afternoon.[58] The Windmill Theatre, featuring nude posing, opened its doors to patrons at 2 p.m. for continuous performances. Alternatively, daytime commerce extended into the night: Berwick Street Market stalls, lit by gas flares as well as electricity, were open until 9 p.m., attracting thrifty housewives, girls in business, and local streetwalkers.

In 1902, Robert Machray, author of *The Night Side of London*, declared Soho to be the "district which in a sense holds more of the night side of London than all of the rest of it put together."[59] In other words, Soho not only possessed more night haunts than other districts, but more of the crime, danger, artifice, sexual transgressions, adventure, poetry, and mystery that he imagined to be associated with the night. Like many other chroniclers of London's night haunts, Machray positioned himself as a privileged male spectator who confidently moved across the divided social landscape of the metropolis.[60] Outside of venues he marked off as "In Society," Machray's world was occupied by men. The women he encountered on his jaunts were mere accessories to male pleasure, most of them Women of the Town. For Machray, Soho's pleasure zone epitomized this nocturnal masculine domain.

Twenty-four years later, in 1926, H. V. Morton offered a more optimistic, democratic, and heterosocial picture of London's nightlife. Morton introduced his sketches of Nights in London by first repeating some well-worn literary conventions of nightwalking. Night, he declared, was strange, sinister, and dramatic, and brought with it something "of the jungle." But modernity had conquered most of the dangers of "dark London." Nightlife was the last frontier, the "last social habit to be developed by a city." Morton credited the growth of the Victorian West End, the invention of gas, and the establishment of a police force, as well as the advent of cheap transport, with bringing commercialized London nightlife into existence, and enabling ordinary citizens the opportunity and the audacity to "plunge into the night." Thanks to these innovations, the nights of modern London were now "free to all men" and, by implication, all women. In twenties London, millions of Londoners could now extract a little more from life than nature intended, using the respite from the day to gain a "release from routine." Ordinary Londoners, male and female, joined the crowds gliding past in waves in the West End and became part of the mystery of the great metropolis.[61]

The attractions of Soho and its commercial peripheries heavily depended on the crowds and infrastructures enumerated by Morton. Artificial lighting represented a technology vital to the local atmospherics and cultural production of Soho's nightlife.[62] Although print culture consistently represented Soho streets as dark, they were, in fact, as brightly—or dimly—lit by public gas lamps as most of the other residential areas of Westminster, including Knightsbridge. But their darkness was accentuated by their close proximity to the "high power lighting" in the main streets. In 1910, Westminster Council contracted with the Gas Light and Coke Company to install lights of 1,800 and 3,000 candlepower along streets bordering Soho, while the district's own lampposts were fitted with 90 candlepower lamps. In 1926, the Council decided to increase these lamps to 180 candlepower in an effort to reduce the disparity between the main streets and the side streets.[63] Electric shop lights and signs, most of them located in the southeastern corner of Soho, provided Soho's streets with additional illumination. After closing, however, local shops tended to be shuttered, leaving restaurants as the sole bright spots in a gloomy urban landscape. The play of light and shadow not only created a mysterious atmosphere out of doors; it was also key to the transgressive ambience inside Soho's "shady" nightclubs. One elite female club habitué recalled that the "idea of the darkness was that you'd be dancing with someone else's husband and your husband was across the room with the man's wife."[64] Bright lights could be equally naughty: in her Silver Slipper Club off Regent Street, Mrs. Meyrick installed a glass floor lit from underneath that had a "strange effect on a dress of very thin nature."[65] These examples testify to the capacity of Soho's cosmopolitan venues to stimulate the imagination and to extend the promise of infinite possibility to men and women across the social landscape. The chapters that follow chronicle the political and cultural effects of this promise, and its incomplete realization.

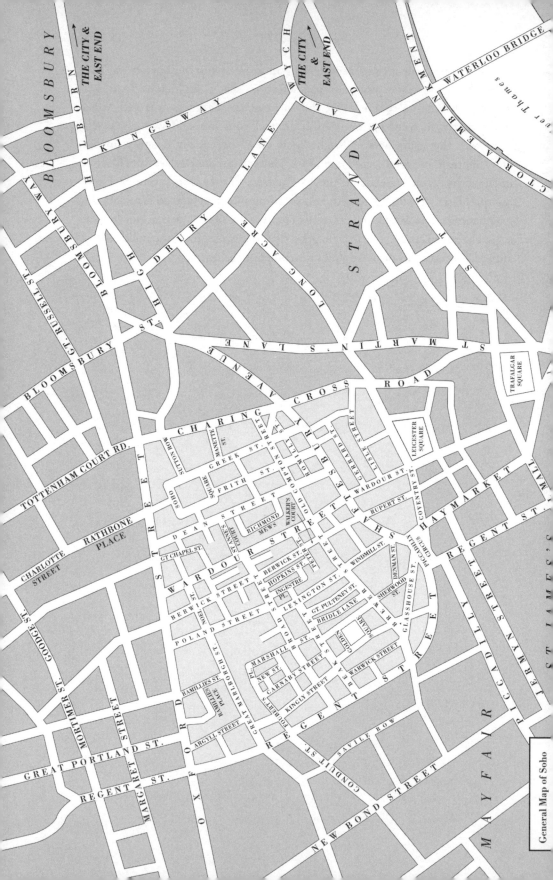

General Map of Soho

CHAPTER I

Cosmopolitan Soho

An EARLY MODERN PARISH MAP OF ST. ANNE, SOHO APPEARS ON THE FRONT of a postcard circulated by the Soho Society, a local amenities group organized in 1972 (Plate 1). Joe's Basement, a premier photographic shop on Wardour Street, Soho, produced the map in appealing green colors, suggestive of the pastoral origins of sixteenth-century Soho as open space and hunting ground between Westminster and the City of London. The caption of the postcard reads: "First published c.1690, this map shows the original pattern of Soho streets, still easily recognizable today."[1]

The Soho Society reproduced this artifact to defend the integrity of Soho's urban gridwork against the rapacious designs of late twentieth-century property speculators and municipal planners. The early-modern engraving also carried its own political design: its intention was to delineate the (1686) parish boundaries of St. Anne, Soho, and to mark its interior territory as readable, knowable, and clearly bounded. St. Anne appears as a manorial village, with parish church (designed by Wren's office), market, aristocratic residences, squares, and orderly streets. In this drawing, St. Anne stands alone, disconnected from the rest of London. Carved out of four aristocratic estates, the new parish was surrounded by ancient highways. To the north is Tyburn Road, the traditional name of Oxford Street, before it became a world-famous shopping street. Hog Lane, the top part of what is now Charing Cross Road, sets the eastern limits, while Wardour Street, a straight north-south line, forms the seventeenth-century western frontier of Soho. No sharp line delineates the southern boundary of the parish, which encompassed Leicester Fields (now Leicester Square) and what the *Survey of London* (1966) describes as the "higgledy-piggledy" development in the southeastern corner around Newport Market.[2]

In the seventeenth century, Soho was a fashionable but mixed neighborhood, home to aristocratic fashion, foreign ambassadors, and Huguenot Protestant artisans who were fleeing religious persecution in France after the revocation of the Edict of Nantes (1685). The map conveys very little of Soho's diverse social character: its two-dimensional ground plan obscures most of the private property and social distinctions in the parish, but highlights the legal and admin-istrative orders that preside over them. Only the public institutions—the great houses and the church—are noted by name and signaled with little house ideograms. In contrast, the map reduces private houses, with all their variegated shapes and sizes, to defined rectangular blocks along the street grid. In these structures resided artists, artisans, and aristocrats. One may, nonetheless, detect some social differentiation in the numbered alleys and courts that thread their way through the larger streets; these entities are keyed to a list located on the top right of the engraving. As evidence of a foreign presence, virtually coincident with the parish's foundations, the "French Church" on Hog Lane appears as no. 14 on this list.

Soho's seventeenth-century street patterns would persist into the twenty-first century, but Soho's geographic and social identity has always been more mobile, fluid, and contested than this orderly engraving or subsequent mappings of Soho would suggest.[3] Soho's "recognizable" boundaries have, in fact, been historically mutable, the result of changing and overlapping jurisdictions of governmental and philanthropic institutions, as well as new roadways and commercial devel-opment. They have also shifted in relation to changing social usages and informal annexations of contiguous spaces by Sohoites.

Material and imaginative forces converged to shape Soho as a cosmopolitan space in late Victorian and Edwardian London. This chapter first assesses the changing built environment and social geography of Soho and its West End peripheries in the nineteenth century. Then it turns its attention to the new mental mappings of cosmopolitan Soho by a series of key social actors, texts, and media events between 1894 and 1914. At the turn of the century, social surveys, fiction, and popular journalism figured Soho as a plague spot of international crime, subversive politics, and illicit sex, while also charting its new status as an attractive stage set for bodily pleasures, appetites, and modern technologies of the self. A new genre of Victorian local history was especially crucial to Soho's enhanced cachet. Soho reformers and ethnic entrepreneurs exploited books on Soho and its historical associations to advance contemporary Soho's reputation as the repository of memories of Old London and as a benign site of sophisti-cated, cosmopolitan pleasures.

Urban Cosmopolitanism and New London

In the last decades of the nineteenth century, a central district devoted to cosmopolitan consumption was assembled along the street improvements of Regent Street, Shaftesbury Avenue, and Charing Cross Road and the older environs of Oxford Street and Leicester Square. These West End boulevards cemented Soho's modern identity, but they also opened up the district for commercial and industrial exploitation. Nineteenth-century thoroughfares ripped through the central rookeries of Old London, displacing thousands of residents from the noisome slums that resisted police supervision. Simultaneously, they transported new social actors into the district, including legions of service and theatrical workers who assisted and entertained suburbanites and tourists descending on the West End to visit the shops and the shows.[4] By the first decade of the twentieth century, the electrified underground railways disgorged thousands of travelers along the entire circumference of Soho, at stations located at Oxford Circus, Piccadilly Circus, Tottenham Court Road, and Leicester Square.[5]

The rebuilding of Soho's peripheries began with the Regent Street project of the 1820s, a large canyon, 120 feet wide and two miles in length, fronted by palatial, six-story shops and residences. Built on Crown lands, Regent Street was the centerpiece of John Nash's renovation of the "court end" of London, providing a parade ground and shopping street for a fashionable neighborhood. The new street also connected the royal green space of Regent's Park at its northern end to the Prince Regent's palace at Carleton House in the south. It supplied a main sewer pipe under the surface and badly needed access for north-south traffic through central London.[6] Its sham-stuccoed facades and window displays of "female fripperies" immediately gave it a Parisian impression.[7] Regent Street became an elite shopping street catering mostly for ladies, as well as a gilded parade ground for high-class prostitutes.[8]

Regent Street was also a massive work of social engineering. It created an east-west spine that stratified the labor market, residential patterns, and consumer pleasures of central London for the next century and longer.[9] One of Nash's stated objectives was to provide "a complete separation between the Streets occupied by the Nobility and Gentry, and the narrower Streets and meaner houses occupied by mechanics and the trading part of the community."[10] The Regent Street project razed the streets around Swallow Street and displaced thousands of residents.[11]

The process of slum clearance and reconstruction of central London continued in the 1840s with the construction of New Oxford Street as an east-west thoroughfare through London's center that eliminated the maze of old rookeries of St. Giles. Once again, a metropolitan improvement resulted in the eviction of thousands of poor inhabitants, forcing them into the few poor areas that remained and intensifying the problem of overcrowding in the inner city.

Public uproar forced Parliament to require that future metropolitan improvements provide housing for displaced inhabitants. In the late 1880s, when the Metropolitan Board of Works undertook the construction of Northumberland Avenue, the Charing Cross Road, and Shaftesbury Avenue, it felt obliged to provide housing for some, but not all, of the 10,000 inhabitants displaced by the new streets. Its passion for economy led it to construct narrow thoroughfares with restricted vistas that carefully hewed to pre-existing roads. Opened in 1886 and running through eastern St. James and St. Anne, Shaftesbury Avenue became the center of late Victorian Theatreland, on which six theaters were constructed, as well as restaurants, shops, and mansion blocks. It was a nondescript roadway lacking vistas, "a story of a wasted opportunity," a street where pedestrians "hurry by."[12] The Charing Cross Road was equally undistinguished. Opened in 1887, it retained all the "pot-houses" of old Crown Street, while over time accruing a miscellaneous collection of theaters, dark, brooding tenements, secondhand bookstores, "rubber good stores," pornography shops, and governmental offices towards its southern end.[13] The Charing cross Road established the eastern boundary of modern-day Soho, hiving off an eastern part of St. Anne's parish around St. Martin's Lane. After the construction of these two thoroughfares, municipal agencies largely tended to ignore Soho as a built environment, despite periodic calls for the construction of wider roads linking Regent Street and the Charing Cross Road.[14]

Meanwhile the older sedimented landscapes of Oxford Street and Leicester Square underwent considerable renovation. A mile-long thoroughfare extending eastward from Park Lane to Tottenham Court Road, Oxford Street was already an ancient highway and turnpike before Nash's "New Street" materialized. Affectionately christened the "old Mediterranean" by Thomas de Quincey, the Oxford Road dated back to Roman times. It possessed an unsavory reputation as the site of Tyburn Tree, the location of today's Marble Arch, where public executions were held between 1171 and 1783. Once it was cleansed of the Tyburn association, however, it became a Regency shopping street and site of entertainments for residents of the newly fashionable quarters of Marylebone.[15] By the late Victorian period, it was the most popular shopping street in London, the center of a heavily capitalized retail trade in ladies' wear. It would always remain a less select, less uniform, less "Parisian" environment than Nash's "new" street. With its "expanding" shops, its "windows larger and more attractive," Oxford Street "grows busier every year for foot and carriage traffic," observed George Duckworth, one of Charles Booth's social investigators, in 1898.[16]

Following the lead of retailers in New York, Paris, and the north of England, Oxford Street drapers began to expand into department stores. Because they were not as constrained by Crown property management as their Regent Street counterparts, they could more easily renovate their fronts and interior spaces. Within a few years after the Great Exhibition, Oxford Street traders redesigned their shop fronts to accommodate large sheets of glass to exhibit "large-scale specimens" of their goods to passersby.[17] In 1909, this retail development culminated with the opening of Selfridges's grand emporium that added a "note of exclamation" to the otherwise humdrum architectural scene of Oxford Street.[18] Selfridges advertised itself as a magnetic social rendezvous and center of "cosmopolitan style" dedicated to female pleasure and notable for "change, variety, diversity, mutation."[19]

At Soho's southern border, Leicester Square, home of the "Shows of London," underwent its own late-Victorian makeover. The road expansion of Coventry Street, the rehabilitation of the Square's central "piazza," and the construction of elite variety theaters along the north and eastern part of the Square helped to spruce up a district that had gone into sad decline during the early decades of the nineteenth century. Calling themselves the "greatest cosmopolitan clubs in London," the Alhambra and Empire theaters of variety provided a range of foreign and native entertainments devoted to the exhibition of the "female form divine."[20]

Surrounded by these commercial peripheries, Soho became the dark, industrial back region that serviced the spectacular front stage of the West End pleasure zone. The bright, open boulevards did not sweep away all of the unsavory elements of vice, crime, and overcrowding associated with the nearby slums.[21] Nor did the street improvements fully erase the plebeian world of industrial labor and toil from the central district. In the streets north and south of Oxford Street, a vast, new industrial backstage arose to service the shopping and restaurant habits of metropolitan visitors. In his walks around Oxford Street, George Duckworth observed how Peter Robinson, the great Oxford Street emporium, had expanded its work operations into the side streets, with barrack accommodations for shop assistants and workrooms for the army of tailors and dressmakers who labored to produce the mantels, blouses, etc. retailed in the store. Cheek by jowl with these establishments, Duckworth and his accompanying policeman noted brothels, massage establishments, and apartments where women who walked Regent Street and Piccadilly resided with their general servants.[22]

West End commercial development refashioned old Georgian Soho into a modern site of doubtful commerce and industry, employing a new cosmopolitan workforce of immigrants. By the late nineteenth century, Soho had become decisively more proletarian than its early modern incarnation, and more ethnically diverse, filled with cosmopolitan masses. A new geography of Soho emerged from an informal amalgamation of St. Anne and the eastern part of St. James. Some internal differences between the two regions would persist: overall, St. Anne remained more Latin, more prosperous, its Georgian fabric more refined; the congested streets east of Regent Street in St. James attracted poorer trades and became the primary West End settlement of Jewish tailors. But increasingly observers treated the parallelogram between Regent Street and Charing Cross Road as a single district, accommodating 24,000 residents in 1901.[23] They expressed astonishment at its surprising array of occupations and ethnicities and the movement of outsiders through the streets. Rather than segregate and contain Soho, the late Victorian thoroughfares laid bare "the foreign quarter of the metropolis . . . for the inspection of the world at large."[24]

Into the twentieth century, Soho retained a French gloss, but its foreign population diversified in the post 1848 era, when tailoring workshops and culinary businesses attracted new settlements of Jewish, Italian, and other European immigrants eager to find employment.[25] At the same time, Victorian Soho became notoriously impoverished. St. James, Westminster and St. Anne, Soho were the most densely populated parishes in mid-century London and the epicenter of the cholera epidemic in the 1850s.[26] But the end of the century, overcrowding in St. Anne, Soho had abated. Plate 2 shows the state of St. Anne and the eastern part of St. James in 1889, according to Booth's "map of poverty." St. Anne's streets are marked pink (comfortable with good wages) or purple (mixed, some comfortable, some poor), but the winding streets in adjoining St. James, Westminster remained poor (uniformly marked on the Booth maps as below the poverty line, in purple and blue). As the cockney population began to desert Soho and environs, its streets were repopulated by Italian, French, and German immigrants, some of them refugees of failed revolutions, most of them economic migrants. By the 1890s, Eastern European Jews moved in and represented the last major diasporic settlement in Soho before the Great War. In 1900, the vicar of St. Anne, Soho declared that two-thirds of his parish (8,000 out of 12,000) were foreign.[27] Throughout the twentieth century, Soho would remain heterogeneous and polyglot, and no ethnic grouping exerted cultural or political predominance.[28]

"The Worst Street in London"

Events in 1906 brought Soho's reputation for dangerous cosmopolitanism into sharp relief, as a set of social actors competed to speak for and about Soho. At the center of the dispute were two representatives of official London. In October of that year, Inspector McKay of the Met's C Division vilified Greek Street, Soho, before the Royal Commission on the Police, which was investigating charges against the police for corruption and bribery related to prostitution, gambling, and the mistreatment of foreigners.[29] When asked about the character of the street, McKay denounced Greek Street as the "worst street in the West End of London." "Crowds of people gather there nightly who are little else than a pest. I will go further and say that some of the vilest reptiles in London live there or frequent it."[30] By the next day, the national dailies had reproduced McKay's testimony as banner headlines: "Worst Street in London," "Vilest Reptiles of London," and the "Dangers that Police Have to Cope with in Soho," including the "Risk of the Knife."[31]

McKay's negative testimony provoked Reverend J. H. Cardwell of St. Anne, Soho to mount a defense of the hardworking, foreign residents of Greek Street. Cardwell resided on Dean Street, only a few hundred yards from Greek Street. Along with some prominent businessmen and residents, he denounced McKay's testimony as an absurd calumny. "I will say that there is not a single disreputable character in Greek-street. I will even go so far as to say that there is scarcely one in the whole of Soho," a claim deemed sufficiently excessive at the time to provoke a disclaimer from the *Evening Standard*: "we should have thought disreputable characters were to be found everywhere."[32] Cardwell buttressed his defense of Greek Street by pointing to the moral improvements wrought by recent anti-vice campaigns that he had spearheaded: "Soho ... by no means perfect is a cleaner and purer place than it once was."[33]

Both sides of this dispute gestured to striking changes in Soho's fin-de-siècle population and social reputation. McKay's rendition of Greek Street's dangerous heterogeneity signaled a general demographic shift in the parish from French to cosmopolitan, as well as to the heightened presence of political refugees who owed no allegiance to any nation. For over a hundred years, French political exiles had followed the example of the Huguenots and found a dingy refuge in Soho. By 1848, a more diverse set of political émigrés began to arrive, including Karl Marx and his family, who rented two rooms on the fourth floor of 28 Dean Street from John Marengo, an Italian-born cook.[34] After 1871, Italian, Swiss, and Russians, many of them anarchists, swelled the population of political émigrés in and around Soho, spreading north of Oxford Street, where an overflow of Soho developed, as émigrés endeavored to remain as close to Soho's radical clubs, restaurants, and news shops as they could.

The intensive policing of these political dissidents in the 1890s helped to reconfigure Soho's status as a refuge for dangerous cosmopolitanism.[35]

Sensational news accounts pinpointed Soho as the refuge for the rejected of Europe after a wave of continental assassinations and bombings were traced back to émigré conspirators in London. In 1894, media coverage of the death of Martial Bourdin confirmed Soho's iconic status as the "rabbit warren of anarchism."[36] Bourdin was a Soho lady's tailor and anarchist of French descent, who was killed when he apparently tripped while carrying a bomb in the close vicinity of the Greenwich Observatory. The national press had a field day tracking Bourdin and his peripatetic associates around Soho and its environs. While localizing the anarchist danger in Soho and the contiguous streets north of Oxford Street, news stories also charted the links between Soho incendiaries and other anarchist cells throughout London and Europe. Readers were advised that anarchists never stayed in one place. Even within this delimited zone, they constantly shifted meeting places, as a precaution against a small army of spies and agent provocateurs who endeavored to insinuate themselves into anarchist groups by infesting the illegal gambling dens and foreign clubs of Soho.[37]

Compounding Soho's infamy as the "cosmopolitan home of arson and murder" was its equally unsavory reputation as a center of cosmopolitan vice. An anti-vice campaign in the 1890s amplified Soho's notoriety as a "perfect little paradise for pimps", and incited police supervision of the district by the likes of Inspector McKay.[38] Spearheading these campaigns was Reverend Cardwell, the defender of Greek Street's honor in 1906. Newly arrived in Soho in 1891, Cardwell found St. Anne's parish to be full of brothels, the police to be indifferent, and respectable workers being "literally driven out of house and home to make room for the traders in vice who can afford to pay exorbitant rents."[39] Cardwell claimed that one in six houses in Soho was a disorderly house. Some sex workers occupied the new mansion flats built along the adjacent thoroughfares, others lived in upper rooms of Georgian houses above "so-called" restaurants. He noted, moreover, that Soho's sex trade was largely controlled and staffed by foreigners. Statistics provided by the Metropolitan Police supported this assertion: in the C or St. James Division of the Metropolitan Police, encompassing Mayfair to Soho, foreigners accounted for 25 out of 32 persons charged with brothel-keeping in 1892, while foreign women also represented a significant minority of women apprehended as prostitutes in the C Division.[40] In addition, a quarter of the individuals prosecuted for living off immoral earnings in London were foreign.[41] By stressing the organized and foreign nature of Soho vice, both the police and social reformers such as Cardwell strengthened their case for a police crackdown.[42]

Cardwell's anti-vice campaign sprouted a second crusade against "bogus clubs" or nightclubs that featured illegal gambling and drinking and were the resort of criminals. Reporting on the raids, news media explained that these clubs catered to "the imported vice and rascality of the Continent"; they were owned by some "greasy, unprincipled fellow who, we may be pretty sure, has left his country for his country's good."[43] Tales proliferated of the foreign *souteneur*, the "London terror," who lounged around Soho, playing cards and dominoes in one of the foreign clubs.[44] Simultaneously purity groups pressured police to step up arrests of foreign news agents in Soho for selling cheap visual pornography, alongside revolutionary tracts, continental newspapers, and London foreign language publications catering to London's expatriate communities.[45] By 1896, Soho's infamy was so well-established that the *Sun* newspaper began a paragraph on a "Soho Incident" with the observation, "Soho seems determined to sustain its pre-eminence as a centre of disturbance."[46]

While targeting criminals, Cardwell energetically tried to "disabuse the public of erroneous [negative] impressions of Soho." To this end, he defended respectable Sohoites in all their ethnic heterogeneity. In 1900, when asked by a reporter from *Cassell's* if his parish was more "Continental than English," he catalogued his exotic flock as if they were a prized collection.[47] "Every European nationality is represented in this parish. We have Austrians, Belgians, Danes, Dutchmen, Frenchmen, Poles, Portuguese, Roumanians, Russians, Servians, Spaniards, Swedes and Turks, to whom may be added Armenians, Persians and Africans . . . the Italians alone number also 650." In order to allay anxieties over this dizzying array, Cardwell tried to contain Soho's diversity within hermetically sealed enclaves, stressing that "the members of the various nationalities keep pretty much to themselves."[48]

In an ecumenical spirit, Cardwell praised the Latin residents as well as the Jews of Soho, who had "invaded" the district close to Piccadilly and Regent Street. A better class of Jews settled in Soho after learning to "work and learn and save in the East End." Cardwell welcomed their cooperation, although he also added, "while we wish they were Christian, we do not make any direct effort for their conversion."[49] He even stood up for local anarchists. "One of our Soho Anarchists was the man who blew himself up," he conceded, while trying to "blow up the Greenwich observatory." "But our Soho anarchists are not what the public imagine." They are not desperadoes, nor "drinking, good-for-nothing fellows," but for the most part "decent, moral living people."[50]

Poverty Studies and Local History

Cardwell's efforts to "disabuse the public of erroneous impressions of Soho" led him to summon up the glories of Soho Past to counter the dark picture of contemporary Soho poverty and overcrowding circulated by his fellow philanthropist Arthur Sherwell, of the West London Mission. In *Life in West London* (1892), Sherwell presented Soho as an impoverished "Outcast London" located at the margins of the wealthy West End. Sherwell's ecological model aligned the weak, enervated, effeminate bodies of Soho's workers with what he described as the invertebrate and indeterminate nature of the district's industrial structure. The root cause of Soho's distress, from Sherwell's perspective, was the area's close proximity to the metropolitan luxury trades and the wasteful consumption of the West End. The dynamic commercial development of the leisure industries led to the expansion of workshops and warehouses into the district, and the subsequent contraction of available housing stock, resulting in overcrowding and high rents for residents. Sherwell reported that a larger percentage of families lived in one-room tenements in Soho than in any other district in London in the 1890s.[51] Sherwell identified a second structural weakness of Soho's industrial economy. Because no trade predominated, the district lacked industrial coherence and individuality.[52] Finally, the presence of food provision, clothing, and theatrical trades, dominated by sweated female labor, cemented his diagnosis of Soho's industrial vulnerability. Sherwell deemed the sex trade, which had provoked Cardwell's foray into civic reform, to be a secondary outcome of Soho's pre-existing invertebrate state.

While mindful of Soho's "terrible social evils," Cardwell challenged Sherwell's stark picture of poverty and overcrowding in Soho. When Charles Booth, the great social investigator of London poverty, interviewed Cardwell in 1898, Booth observed that Cardwell was "emphatic on the point that his parishioners are not poor", and that most of the disorder in Soho was the work of outsiders.[53] Cardwell, moreover, insisted that Sherwell's imperfect social statistics blackened Soho's reputation and confused Soho's geographical identity by blurring the boundaries between Soho and adjacent dark poverty spots (such as Drury Lane and Clare Market) to the east of the parish.[54] By contrast, Cardwell defended a geography of Soho that conformed to the historic limits of his parish, more or less as they were set in the early modern period. But this was only one of a number of imaginative mappings of Soho available at the time.[55] Whereas Sherwell aligned Soho with the jurisdictional boundaries of the Strand Sanitary District to the south and east, the police, London guides, and practically everyone else tended to push Soho's frontiers westward to Regent Street, encompassing the historic parish of St. Anne as well as the eastern part of St. James. Although Oxford Street traditionally marked the northern boundary of Soho, Special Branch and Scotland Yard detectives tended to incorporate streets north of this divide into their understanding of "Soho," as they tracked the resettlement of anarchists and other immigrants into the Charlotte Street area.[56]

Instead of assembling his own sociological profile of Soho, Cardwell opted for an alternative system of urban knowledge: a topographical history of Old Soho.[57] In other words, Cardwell used local history to counter public denigrations of Soho present as a low cosmopolitan space, a strategy that other contemporaries would follow. Compiled by St. Anne clergy and parish workers, *Two Centuries of Soho* (1898) detailed the rise and progress of Soho's firms, institutions, and amusements over two centuries. Rather than dwell on the present horrors of Soho, Cardwell later explained, the book's purpose was to stir up parochial patriotism, not only among residents, but among "those engaged in business, who spend their working days in the parish."[58]

As a work of local history, *Two Centuries of Soho* embraced the empiricist method and imaginative geography of Victorian topographical guidebooks, such as *Old and New London, London Past and Present*, and *Soho and Its Associations*.[59] Topographical guides interwove past history and geographic description, superimposing literary and historical associations on to streets and districts. Linking parts of London to bits of literature, celebrity biographies and significant historical events, such texts promoted a spectral sense of place. Building on the Romantic attachment to ruins as material memory, topographical guides exploited a paradigmatic Victorian ambivalence about the improving modern city. They registered London's past as extending into the present, just as that connection with an urban material past was on the verge of disappearing through street improvements.[60] They juxtaposed the cityscapes of old and new London, the meandering alley set against the straight, rational thoroughfare. These old spaces might serve as cautionary tales that revealed the historical principles determining the inevitable downward path of London districts. Or they might figure as potent repositories of disorderly fantasies, escape, fears, and pleasurable imaginings that transported the subject to an alternative state of being.[61]

By the late nineteenth century, Soho occupied a special status in this story of Old and New London. More than any other central district, declared the author of *Old and New London*, Soho revealed the past history and character of London: "we fancy that no city in Europe can more thoroughly tell the story of its own past than can Soho testify to the glories of other days which still surround its decaying and decayed houses with a halo."[62] Enhancing Soho's status as a physical vestige of the urban past was the renewal of interest in Georgian material culture. During most of the Queen's reign, Victorian writers tended to deprecate Georgian terraced houses as monotonous, unadorned brick walls with holes in them and deserving of demolition.[63] They found little visual delight in the regularity, monochrome facades, and symmetry of Georgian neoclassical decorative vocabulary. However, this negative view of the Georgian legacy began to abate as

Victorians felt dwarfed by purpose-built edifices of office towers, hotels, department stores, and theaters constructed along the West End boulevards.[64] The
destruction of Old London led to a new appreciation of the homely Georgian
material legacy that remained, including the urban fabric of grimy Soho.[65]

Two Centuries of Soho capitalized on these late Victorian recalibrations of
history and heritage styles.[66] Sir Walter Besant's prestigious preface to Two
Centuries introduced Soho as one of the most interesting districts in London
where "the solid and beautiful houses yet remain" and the associations of
the past still cling to its stately streets.[67] Cardwell's introduction also stressed
eighteenth-century traditions that continued into the present: the parish's record
of peaceful coexistence among religious denominations, its many medical institutions, and its "forwardness in ministries of healing", dating back to the eighteenth century, and, finally, its history of hospitality towards foreigners "who now
form one-half her population."[68]

Not surprisingly, St. Anne, Soho church and parish institutions, carved out of
St. Martin in the Field in 1677, took pride of place in the volume as an enduring
legacy of Old Soho. The religious diversity of Old Soho was also highlighted:
there was an entry for the French Huguenot church (founded in 1662), which
had already taken over a church for Greek refugees years before the Anglican
parish church had begun construction in 1685, and another for St. Patrick's
Roman Catholic Church, catering to the Irish poor of St. Giles, which opened its
doors in 1791.[69] Turning its attention to more recent charitable efforts, Two
Centuries paid tribute to the veritable army of Victorian philanthropists and religious missionaries who descended on Soho to look after an increasingly impoverished population. It presented the landscape of late Victorian Soho as studded
by hospitals, schools, missions, medical dispensaries, working men's clubs, trade
societies, churches, and clubs for working boys and girls.[70]

One novel feature of Soho philanthropy was the proliferation of new charities
targeting women in need. The Soho Bazaar opened in 1816 in Soho Square
under the supervision of businessman John Trotter to assist war widows whose
husbands died in the Napoleonic Wars by allowing them to sell merchandise at
stalls.[71] As the Soho Bazaar went into slow decline in the late Victorian period, a
new set of female philanthropies cropped up to advance the cause of women.
Two Centuries respectfully profiled the work of the Honourable Maude Stanley,
originator of the girls' club movement, whose first club opened in the old
Newport Market in 1880. It praised the new Italianate stuccoed club house at 59
Greek Street that opened in 1896 as "a veritable palace of delight for the young
women toilers of Soho" and acted as a "counter attraction to the coarse and
low pleasures of the Music Halls and Dancing Rooms."[72] Club members

were employed in the multitudinous trades of Soho; all told, twenty-seven different trades were represented. Miss Stanley's success, and exclusion of Jewish workers, led Lily Montagu to organize an institution along similar lines for Jewish women toiling in domestic workshops. Assisted by Jewish lady workers from Maida Vale and Kensington, the Dean Street club offered Jewish working girls a full range of rational recreations, from English classes to ambulance training, as well as placement in jobs and apprenticeships. A third reforming institution, the West London Mission's Sisters of the Poor, accommodated a district nursing center, a medical dispensary, and an orchestral practice space in its Greek Street house. Even more noteworthy, the sisters ran a crèche, meeting a great want in the neighborhood, where so many women went out to work.[73]

Workingmen's self-help societies also claimed a place in Mr. Cardwell's history. The St. James and Soho Working Men's Club inaugurated the workingmen's club movement in 1864, thus serving as a model for Stanley and Montagu's improving societies for women. Not surprisingly, *Two Centuries* was silent about the role of these central London workingmen's clubs in bridging the gap in radical politics between Chartism and the resurgence of socialism in the 1880s, nor did it mention their links to continental political refugees.[74] But it did recognize an Italian analogue to the self-help ethos of London workingmen in the Società Italiana Cuochi-Camerieri, founded in 1886 to provide a sick benefit club and social center for Italian waiters in London. At its quarters at 27 Soho Square, the "air is full of the language of Tasso, spoken with a central London accent."[75]

Cardwell's history of charities and religious agencies charted the dynamic convergence of Old and New London as Soho's institutions adapted to the changing social face of the population under their care. By comparison, the book's next section on business firms, occupying two-thirds of the volume, was more backward-looking, its entries restricted to those solid English firms already in existence at the beginning of the Queen's reign. Violin-making and silver-smiths were the "two arts inseparably connected with our parish from the period of its first foundation to the present."[76] By the 1890s, a few Huguenot silversmith firms persisted, but Cardwell acknowledged that scores of old establishments had disappeared, victims of successful competition by the Sheffield electroplate industry.[77] Nonetheless, Cardwell was able to enumerate the continuation of many other old-fashioned and substantial businesses catering to the carriage trade that had "carried on with little or no change in [their] character."[78] They included Hopkins and Purvis, the oil colormen in Greek Street, and Burroughs and Watts, the billiard makers in Soho Square whose ivory billiard balls required the "annual destruction of 1140 elephants." Then there were the six booksellers and printers specializing in medical and ecclesiastical publishing, pedigrees and gilt-embossed opera programs, seven leather sellers and saddlers, as well as the two pioneers in the provision of cheap music and books, Novello, the world-renowned music publisher of Wardour Street, and Bickers and Sons of Leicester Square.[79]

Despite Reverend Cardwell's publicist efforts, a story of displacement, fraudulence, and decay adhered to *Two Centuries* story of Soho's fin-de-siècle industrial production. On Wardour Street, where Thomas Sheraton once had his showrooms, the tradition of furniture-making persisted; but like so much else in Soho, this trade had acquired a shady, declining reputation. Soho artisans exploited their skills to produce fake antiquities for consumers who had developed a "new interest for old things," notably for old Georgian fittings and furniture, signified by "Chippendale," "Sheraton," and "Adam."[80] Not only did Wardour Street emerge as the hub of the antique and salvages trade for these items (as well as for older medieval and Renaissance artifacts imported from northern Europe); it simultaneously became the center of the production of "furniture of uncertain age" that was "probably not so venerable in years as in appearance."[81]

The changing fortunes of Soho's material fabric also yielded a mixed historical lesson, revealing a heterogeneous blending of high and low, sacred and profane, foreign and native-born, the world of letters, and the pleasures of the flesh. Readers learned, for example, that part of St. Patrick's Church had previously belonged to Carlisle House, an elegant, aristocratic residence before it was converted for commercial use in the 1760s. In these luxurious surroundings, Mme. Cornelys, a "foreign adventuress," presided over the Soho masquerade, where she attracted the cream of London society to her "Temple of Festivity." The bohemian social world of Georgian Soho also surfaced in the history of the Westminster General Dispensary. The dispensary occupied the same house on Gerrard Street previously tenanted by the Turk's Head Tavern, where Dr. Johnson, Boswell, Reynolds, and their friends assembled weekly for their renowned Literary Club.[82]

Material fragments hidden within the interiors of Soho's industrial buildings also evoked memories of a lost fashionable and cultivated past. A visit to the business premises of a Dean Street saddler, for instance, unearthed a fine painted staircase and some interesting chimney pieces in a good state of preservation.[83] The Society of Artists declared 43 Gerrard Street to have been the home of the poet John Dryden: as confirmation, *Two Centuries* recorded the presence of an interior "staircase with corkscrew banisters and a mahogany rail, characteristic of Dryden's time." The headquarters of Crosse & Blackwell, the jam manufacturers, in Soho Square once served as the aristocratic home of the Earl of Faucenberg. It still boasted ceilings "said to have been painted by Angelica Kauffmann", and a "beautiful chimney-piece" in the private office of Mr. Blackwell.[84] Finally, "Two

Centuries" drew attention to the beautiful mahogany staircase and mural wall to be found inside the premises of Wilson and Son, tin-plate workers at 75 Dean Street. The well-preserved wall painting was attributed to Hogarth. "Soho once abounded in beautiful specimens of wall painting, but for the most part they have been neglected or destroyed, and few now remain to tell of the faded glory of the past."[85]

The last section of *Two Centuries* was devoted to "Soho amusements" on the grounds that Soho had emerged as the modern center of amusements for the metropolis and the world, thanks to the presence of Theatreland and the northern and eastern part of Leicester Square within the parish.[86] Here the massive theaters of variety exerted a "demoralizing" influence on the girls of the neighborhood. This short segment, a mere eighteen pages, radically shifted tone as it moved forward in time: it began jocularly, with a racy account of Mme. Cornelys and the Soho masquerade, before moving on to the Regency panoramas and raffish shows of Leicester Square and to the mid-century founding of the Royalty Theatre on Dean Street. But it concluded with a disapproving nod at the late Victorian variety entertainments at the Empire and Palace theaters, both of which began as serious theaters but descended into glorified music halls.[87] "Soho amusements" celebrated the gay sophisticated attractions of the distant past, but disenchantment set in when it fixed its gaze on mass leisure industries of the present.

In *Two Centuries*, Cardwell showed himself more invested in Soho's sturdy past than in the cosmopolitan Soho of his own time. Apart from the extensive labors of philanthropists, and the persistence of artisan firms dating back to Georgian and Regency days, Cardwell could detect no signs of cultural energy or enterprise in the present-day Soho. Nonetheless, his local history proved to be a usable past for repackaging contemporary Soho. It provided journalists and ethnic entrepreneurs with exactly the kind of cultural capital to refurbish Soho's modern cosmopolitan reputation. For one version of this enhanced status, we turn next to contemporary reviews of Soho restaurants in the catering press.

Cosmopolitan Catering in Soho

In 1906, the *Caterer and Hotel-Keeper*, the main trade journal for the restaurant and hotel industry, exploited this romantic history in a food travelogue of Soho.[88] Amidst articles on refrigeration and kitchen labor-saving devices, it published a seven-part series on Soho's restaurants that presented Soho not as a parish, or part of a police or sanitary district, but as a bounded cultural zone dedicated to food. Mindful of recent media scandals, the *Caterer* acknowledged that "the darker social problems of Soho . . . are perhaps more complicated and difficult than in any other district," but it pronounced these problems to be "outside the scope of these articles."[89]

The first article introduced readers to this "fascinating district on the northern border of theatre land," and it delineated three distinctive features of Soho.[90] It highlighted its cosmopolitanism, signified by the profusion of foreign provision shops with French, German, Italian, and Austrian names above their lintel and by displays of gastronomic wares that were startling to British taste: huge, holey cheeses weighing down the counters or bulging sausages of "nondescript shapes and variegated colours."[91] It briefly noted a second feature, Soho's centuries-old history as a refuge for outcasts and rebels who provided the original clientele for the restaurants. But it quickly moved on to underscore Soho's distinction as the home of an English bohemia of the distant past. Surveying the contemporary street scene, the *Caterer* could discern no physical sign of Soho's former glory as a "noble Bohemia," apart from the picturesque little restaurants of various nations. Greek Street, so vilified by Inspector McKay, was "enlivened by the presence of about ten restaurants—French, German, Austrian, Italian, and English," the sole reminder of the street's commercial heyday when it was the site of Wedgwood's showroom.[92]

The *Caterer* praised the picturesque eateries along Old Compton Street that allowed playgoers to test out foreign food, especially French cuisine, in agreeable surroundings for "remarkably small cost."[93] Here it signaled an expanding market niche in Soho: the purveying of after-theater suppers for theatergoing couples, part of the expansion of middle-class heterosexual nightlife in the metropolis. As it moved on to other venues, it discerned the tendency of Soho restaurants to shift from French to Italian catering. In Soho the transalpine Italians jostled with the French on every street, trying to attract palates and purses by offering inexpensive, hybrid Franco-Italian cuisine.[94] Gerrard Street, once the home of such celebrated English literary artists as Dryden and Burke, was "now connected with Italian catering rather than with pictorial or literary art."[95]

The "wily" "intelligent aliens" of Soho, rather than Cardwell's tradesmen and philanthropists, became the protagonists of the *Caterer*'s narrative.[96] Mr. Uccelli of the Boulogne Restaurant in Gerrard Street was one such hero. A native of Italy, "he is better described as a Cosmopolitan than as an Italian, for he has spent far less time in Italy than out of it." His movements followed the well-established pattern of Italian catering workers who found their way to London after a probationary period in the international hotel circuit. Mr. Uccelli found his market niche in Soho by providing an economic version of the silver service and French haute cuisine available to wealthy patrons in West End establishments. Thanks to Mr. Uccelli's careful management, the Boulogne was able to use wholesome materials to make tasty, varied, well-cooked luncheons for 1s 6d and still turn a profit.[97]

The *Caterer* featured the Boulogne as an example of a new culinary practice in the heart of London. It printed its menu in French; it organized its meal in conformity to the standards—of service, order of courses, and assemblage of dishes—established by Escoffier.[98] It decorated its walls with engraved mirrors to create an atmosphere of greater spaciousness and bring light to dark corners. Its tables were covered with white cloths, its waiters wore evening dress. But the Boulogne departed from the reigning gastronomic orthodoxy by supplementing French fare with Italian specialties, such as macaroni.[99] The result was a hybrid cuisine, neither the ordinary peasant fare previously consumed by culinary workers in their native land, nor the international French cuisine available in grand hotels across Europe and in the West End.[100]

By profiling the rags to riches story of men like Mr. Uccelli, the *Caterer* strove to reshape Soho's reputation from a center of dangerous cosmopolitanism to a safe zone of tasteful, exotic, and economic consumption. Rather than threaten the integrity of the nation, the *Caterer's* version of Soho cosmopolitanism ratified London's capacity to master and contain unsettling multiplicity within a specialized enclave of cosmopolitan difference.[101] To domesticate Soho's eateries, the *Caterer* anointed them as the colorful inheritors of the splendid bohemia of the Georgian past. It cast Soho's ethnic entrepreneurs as the heroes of the story, as honest counterpoints to Soho's dangerous gang of international criminals and dynamiting anarchists. And it publicized their hybrid food culture as part of a campaign to modernize the conservative culinary taste of the "great British public."[102]

Bohemia in London

The *Caterer* was not alone in configuring Soho as a specialized zone of restaurant culture built over a sturdy Georgian cultural space. Arthur Ransome's semi-fictional, semi-autobiographical *Bohemia in London* (1907) offered a similar picture of cosmopolitan Soho as a haven of bohemian sociability. But it was less centered on Soho's immigrants than on its adventurous visitors. *Bohemia in London* was Ransome's first-person account of his own early years as a struggling writer, intended to evoke the "strange, tense, despairing hopeful and sordid life that is lived in London by young artists and writers." It joined with the *Caterer* against Cardwell in offering an optimistic account of Soho's commodity culture. Like the *Caterer*, Ransome sketched a topography of Soho's eateries, moving from street to street, but he had no interest in the cosmopolitan careers of catering workers and entrepreneurs, nor in the success of their businesses. Instead he adopted the more conventional point of view of the knowing urban traveler, offering readers an impressionist tour through an exotic terrain known only to the cognoscenti. As Frank Mort observes, Ransome's book was well received at the time of publication and became an extremely influential topographical guide to twentieth-century Soho, a classic roadmap, or *Bildungsroman*, for aspiring bohemians of future generations (including bohemian women like artist Nina Hamnett) who gravitated to Soho venues in search of self-invention and the collective life of art.[103]

To find Bohemia, Ransome set out in 1904 from his mother's suburban Balham, a "Columbus in search of the new world." He adopted a Parisian model of bohemia, derived from Henri Murger's *Scènes de la vie de bohème* (1845–9), as it was transmitted and modified over the century by Puccini's opera *La Bohème* (1895), and domesticated for English consumption by George du Maurier's bestseller *Trilby* (1895).[104] In keeping with this tradition, Ransome's bohemia was populated by adventurous young men "from conventional [middle-class] homes determined to live in any way other than that to which they have been accustomed."[105] Bohemians rejected bourgeois domesticity and embraced a voluntary life of poverty. They inhabited a decidedly male terrain, coming together in studios, cafés, pubs, and restaurants, where they treated immigrant service workers and female companions as props for their own self-fashioning.

Ransome directly challenged Murger's assertion that bohemia neither exists nor can exist anywhere but Paris. London, he admitted, had no Montmartre: it was so unwieldy that poets and playwrights "are scattered over a dozen districts." But artists and writers gravitated to certain districts possessing special atmosphere and a distinctive aura of literary reminiscence. Rather than slavishly imitate a foreign cultural transplant, Ransome and his friends determined to follow in the footsteps of a noble English bohemia, to be indebted to "the memoirs of famous artists and writers that contributed to make the poetry of the present."[106]

Soho occupied center stage in this picture of London's bohemia. Except for the cafés, where he observed "dark-eyes, dark skin, sallowed-skinned faces everywhere", and heard a babble of voices, Ransome made scant reference to Soho's foreignness, absorbing the immigrant residents into the grubby daytime scene.[107] By and large, Soho remained firmly grounded in English soil; haunted by decidedly English-speaking literary ghosts (we hear nothing of Rimbaud and Verlaine, who gave poetry readings in Old Compton Street in the 1870s). Nor was there any reference to Soho's notoriety as a dangerous cosmopolitan zone of crime and violence: only in the downstairs room of one café where "we brought our young women" did he note the brief appearance of a "grim Police Inspector and his important body guard."[108] Instead, Ransome focused on Soho's leisure economy by night, when it assumed a more successful air, attracting English pleasure-seekers, dressed in odd costumes, who ventured there to enjoy "merry dinners" in small eating places.[109]

Like the *Caterer*, Ransome began his travelogue by enumerating the literary bachelors and dandies of the Georgian and Regency years, who led gay and precarious existences in Soho and forged a communal life in public settings. He detailed the squares and streets where writer Pierce Egan lived and Hazlitt died, also noting the house on Greek Street where de Quincey was saved from starvation by a woman of the streets. He updated the story of the Turk's Head on Gerrard Street where Johnson and his friends held their Literary Club, casually mentioning that a similar collective life of art and writing was carried on by unnamed writers of his own day who met every Tuesday at the little Mont Blanc restaurant located on the same street.

Then he moved on to enumerate the many small restaurants where he and his anonymous friends enjoyed easygoing sociability and exercised "adventurous choice." A lean painter took him to his first Soho restaurant, Roche's in Old Compton Street.[110] Groping their way through the London fog from Cambridge Circus, the two stumbled into the "glamour and noise" of Roche's long room as they entered from the street. "This is bohemia," the painter said. "What do you think of it?" Ransome did not record his reply, but, as literary historian Hugh David observes, he left no doubt that it fulfilled every dream he had cherished when he left suburbia.[111] Roche's was a labyrinth of interconnecting rooms; beyond the long room was an inner room (where he would dine in subsequent visits) and downstairs a "hot little inferno." They returned to the long table in the front so he could see the "whole place, and observe the people who came in." Here he saw a "splendid old man," a throwback to the Romantic Age, whose hair fell down over the collar of his velvet coat, while his painter guide went on to identify "So and so" the painter, the journalist, the music critic, and the editor of a newspaper.[112]

Ambience, decor, conversation, seeing and being seen—these were the cultural attractions of dining out in Soho, rather than the gastronomy itself. Other London guides might detail the dishes and order of courses of Soho eateries as an economical version of international cuisine, but Ransome only described the food as excellently cooked and cheap. It was the atmospherics of dining, not physical consumption or taste, that stimulated the imagination. Ransome even took pleasure in kitschy restaurant art. He enjoyed eating at the Dieppe, a cheaper place near Piccadilly Circus, "not for the sake of the food so much as for the pictures." He and his friends were amused by wall murals inspired by Botticelli's *Primavera* in early Victorian costume. And they found it especially entertaining to dine among strangers and guess their identity or even to strike up conversations with them.[113]

Ransome stressed the haphazard existence of young men who dined in Soho, but their fleeting existence in no way portended a more general crisis of knowledge, or challenge to the social order. While engaging in his own act of self-invention, Ransome remained confident of his ability to assess social types and urban spaces through visual signs. Only once did his observational skills seem to fail him. This occurred when he visited a Leicester Square monster café on the edge of bohemia. Ransome struck up a conversation with a man sporting all the signifiers of bohemia: "a huge felt hat banged freely down over thick black hair," "an enormous black beard", and a magnificent manner. The man delighted his friends with impromptu poetry. But it turned out his beard was a disguise and that he was a clerk working in a bank who played the "wild Bohemian every night."[114] The boundaries between bohemia and suburbia, the life of art and the life of philistine commerce, were not as clearly demarcated as Ransome initially suggested.

The sham bohemian might lead us to question the reliability of Ransome's account of the bohemian life. What other misreadings and selective editing of bohemian sociability did he offer? Certainly reviews of the book at the time found his portrait of London bohemia to be surprisingly tame, a verdict endorsed by recent historians of literary culture.[115] Compared to Murger's boisterous and decadent bohemia, Ransome's account was cleaned-up and quaintly English, notes Peter Brooker. In his vignettes, "drink flows, but no one gets drunk, no one drinks absinthe," no one commits suicide, no man or woman has sex.[116] His anecdotal history pointedly edited out the transgressive activities of the recent bohemian past.

Unlike the ghosts of Johnson, Dryden, and even the opium eater de Quincey, recent scandals of bohemia seemed to have left no mark on Soho's special atmosphere. Ransome had nothing to say about the doomed writers and artists of the 1890s who "feasted with panthers" in Soho.[117] His anecdotes surgically bypassed Oscar Wilde, James McNeill Whistler, Arthur Symons, and other Francophile intellectuals who gravitated to Soho in that decade, where they drank absinthe, took drugs, discussed symbolism, made trysts with dancers and sailors, contemplated suicide, or pursued other doubtful practices. Readers find no mention of a key disclosure of Wilde's sensational "trial of the century," his habit of dining with young male prostitutes in private upper rooms above Kettner's.[118] None of these excesses darkened Ransome's cleaned-up version of Soho. Except for his anonymous friends, Soho's artists and writers were safely dead and gone, embedded in a sanitized Georgian and Regency past. But *Bohemia in London* did some important cultural work for the Edwardians. It not only helped to domesticate Soho as a mass tourist site of restaurant culture. As Brooker observes, its refiguring of bohemia also proved to be a double win for the expanding café society of the prewar years: it erased the icon of the degenerate aesthete of the 1890s and produced a jollier "bohemian more to its liking."[119] By publicizing a new image of bohemia, it enabled the formation of a new cultural elite achieved through the mingling of prewar avant-garde rebels with Slade art school socialites at the Café Royal, the Tour Eiffel, and Soho's bohemian prewar nightclubs.

The Soho of *The Secret Agent*

Nevertheless, despite the promotional efforts of Cardwell, the *Caterer*, and Ransome, negative associations still clung to turn-of-the-century Soho as a sleazy center of carnal appetite, cultural inauthenticity, social mixing, and political disloyalty. In *The Secret Agent* (1907), Joseph Conrad brilliantly satirized these themes. His novel about Soho anarchists operates as a counterpoint to Ransome's cheerful depiction of Soho bohemia. *The Secret Agent's* scenes of the pornography shop and the Italian restaurant would go on to have an afterlife in films, novels, and London anthologies where they are cited as the epitome of Soho sleaze.[120] While marketed to different reading publics and aligned to different aesthetic movements, *Bohemia in London* and *The Secret Agent* jointly cemented Soho's legendary status as a site of seedy pleasures and bohemian camaraderie.

Conrad's unruly, lazy, sham anarchists both echo and challenge the communal myth of male bohemian sociability purveyed by Ransome. Unlike Ransome, Conrad was anxious to maintain aesthetic distance from his story, even though, or perhaps *because*, he personally fitted the social profile so well of a cosmopolitan Sohoite.[121] Conrad was not only a continental émigré, like so many other residents of Soho, he was also a bohemian habitué of its restaurants. He was part of the Tuesday luncheon crowd of writers and artists (noted by Ransome) who dined at the Mont Blanc restaurant in Gerrard Street.[122] Yet *The Secret Agent* contains no reference to Soho as a grouping point for cultural bohemia, although the anarchist protagonists of his novel could well stand in as ironic signifiers of a bohemian coterie.

Instead of promoting a cleaned-up Soho, *The Secret Agent* revisits its reputation for dangerous cosmopolitanism. It returns to the 1894 true crime story of Soho anarchist Bourdin who met his death in the vicinity of Greenwich conservatory while carrying a bomb. But it considerably reworks Soho past and present.

The novel radically alters the contours of the chronology of the Bourdin incident by setting the events in the late 1880s, amalgamating them to other
anarchist news events and staging a fictional drama of domestic violence at the
center. Despite its pastness, *The Secret Agent* emphatically registers some features
of the contemporary landscape.[123] It highlights two up-to-date "temples of
commerce," the pornography shop and the Italian restaurant, that serve as
meeting places for Soho anarchists and others.[124] Both are traps for gullible
customers; their "special atmosphere" exuding a culture of fraud that calls into
question the political convictions of the motley gang of self-proclaimed revolutionaries who congregate there.[125] In keeping with Conrad's modernist perspective, these institutions of sleazy cosmopolitan Soho seem to encourage a culture
of "evil freedom," detached from local and national identity. They are at the
center of a mutable city of alienating changes, defamiliarized and unmoored
from stable associations of nation and self.[126]

Unlike Ransome's romantic portrait of the locale, Conrad's Old Soho is not
the repository of cultural memory and literary ghosts. It is a bleak wasteland of
unimproved London, a "muddy, inhospitable accumulation of bricks, slates, and
stones," yet strangely animate, frequently likened to a primitive jungle or
an aquarium, full of "strange fish."[127] There is no creative community or local
patriotism in this rendition of Soho. Whereas Cardwell, the *Caterer*, and
Ransome invoked a host of positive associations of Soho past and present,
Conrad strips the locale of well-meaning reformers, inspiring literary ghosts
of the past, artisan trades or industrious workers, friendly neighbors, merry
bohemians, or even, with a few exceptions, women.

The first page of *The Secret Agent* introduces readers to Mr. Verloc's pornography shop of "shady wares." It is one of those "grim brick houses which existed
in large quantities before the era of reconstruction dawned upon London."[128]
This version of Old Soho represents the district as inert and hidden in the
shadows, before it was ringed and opened up by street improvements and
subject to anti-vice clean-up campaigns and governmental crackdowns on alien
immigration. Although set in the past, the shop's shady wares paradoxically align
it to recent economic modernization, to the "reconstructed" zone of pleasure
and visual culture consolidated along Soho's peripheries in the last decades of
the nineteenth century.[129]

Verloc's house in Brett Street is replete with ambivalent, suggestive meanings.
It is both a home and shop; it sells two kinds of "shady" wares, political newspapers and sexual commodities.[130] Both are on display in the shop window,
arranged in the crowded, miscellaneous manner so deplored by modern experts
of window dressing. This cheap showcase contains badly printed newspapers

with rousing titles like the *Torch* and the *Gong*, and a range of sexual aids, including "more or less undressed dancing girls," French comic magazines with titles hinting at impropriety, and closed yellow envelopes suggestive of "French letters."[131] The shop attracts two kinds of customers: amateurs who are duped into buying shoddy goods, and more mature men, with their "collars up," whom we later find out might be Mr. Verloc's anarchist comrades.[132] The shop also has two sales persons, Verloc, family man, anarchist, police spy, and secret agent of the novel's title, and his attractive wife, Winnie, who produces "rage in the heart" of youthful customers. Silent and undemonstrative, exhibiting a "full bust, tight bodice, and broad hips," she offers the three-dimensional real thing, rather than the two-dimensional paper representations of the female form that patrons crave.[133] "Standing with unfathomable indifference behind the rampart," she references a full set of silent female bodies on commercial display in the West End, from shopgirls to prostitutes masquerading as masseuses, to the popular erotic entertainments known as tableaux vivants of Leicester Square and Charing Cross Road, where real women who were "more or less undressed" stood motionless and silent as pictures on a carefully lit stage.[134] One effect of the meshing of sex and politics in Verloc's shop is to suggest that the politics on offer appears to be as fraudulent as the sex, and as parasitic.

A visit to a second Soho establishment, the Italian restaurant, confirms this general impression of inauthenticity and fraudulent identity. The Assistant Commissioner, on the track of Soho anarchists, visits the restaurant to try out his disguise before he ventures to Verloc's shop in Brett Street. The Assistant Commissioner recognizes the little Italian restaurant as a cheap variant of the luxury restaurants of the West End. It is "one of those traps for the hungry, low and narrow, baited with a perspective of mirrors and white napery." Yet it has an "atmosphere of its own," because it purveys an entirely hybrid "fraudulent cookery" cuisine (called "Franco-Italian" by Conrad's contemporaries), unknown outside of Britain.[135]

Inside this "peculiarly British institution," the Assistant Commissioner feels the effects of this fraudulent ambience. He seems to lose "some more of his identity," to enjoy a lonely, "evil freedom."[136] Seeing himself in a mirror, he is "struck by his foreign appearance" and once again raises "the collar of his jacket" to emulate the "mature" male patrons of Verloc's shop.[137] But then he realizes that other patrons of the restaurant had also lost their identity: they had become "unstamped," "professionally, socially, racially." They are as "denationalized" as the dishes set before them.[138]

In *The Secret Agent*, Conrad ironically targets the cultural stereotypes that circulated about Soho. He mocks the romantic notion that restaurants could

serve as theaters of self-invention and public culture. He simultaneously challenges realist forms of urban knowledge that purportedly enable the skilled
observer to read the signs of the city and render it legible. He treats Soho as a
sleazy site of fraudulent, unaesthetic commodity exchange, lacking any stable
value and history of its own. Rather than inspiring creative freedom, Soho's
"temples of commerce" destroy identity, rendering all patrons indistinct,
unplaced cosmopolitans. No one is who he seems; everyone is both foreign
and native.[139]

Strayed Houses and the National Heritage

Soho is not the only London space marked by displacement and confusion in
The Secret Agent. In one of his walks through the West End, Verloc confronts the
topographical challenges of London's "strayed houses."[140] In search of the foreign
embassy in Chesham Square (in Westminster) that employs him as a double
agent, he notes that 1 Chesham Square is, in fact, located at least sixty yards
down a narrow alley, while 37 Chesham Square is similarly displaced, actually
belonging to "Posthill Street."[141] Verloc, we are told, is too much of a cosmopolitan to be confounded by these examples of "London's topographical
mysteries," too sophisticated to rely on surface impressions of human character
or conventional mappings of geography.[142] In this scene (and many others),
Conrad satirizes cultural anxieties over cosmopolitan urban flux, yet his satirical
fiction of "strayed houses" eerily prefigures a national debate in 1914 over the
literal transplantation of Soho houses across the Atlantic. The 1914 cause
célèbre brought into relief the global forces that sent immigrants to London, yet
threatened to destabilize London's own centrality as a powerful world city.

In 1914, national attention once again focused on a Soho street in peril. The
street in question was Dean Street, and this time the threat emanated from
the property market rather than from international crime or vice. On January 9,
The Times warned its readers that "London is in imminent danger of losing a
beautiful and most interesting old house of the early Georgian period." It identified the endangered house as 75 Dean Street, Soho, "believed to have been the
residence of Hogarth's father-in-law, Sir James Thornhill." The Times made its
case for preservation on two grounds: the building's historical associations with
Thornhill and Hogarth, and its intrinsic beauty. Mr. Mulliner, the new proprietor, had arranged for its cleaning and restoration (at a cost of £4,000), hoping
to attract a suitable institutional benefactor. As no civic-minded individual or
body of persons came forward, Mulliner was now negotiating with a commercial
buyer who intended to demolish the house.[143]

Between January 9 and January 23, *The Times* kept up a spirited campaign to prevent the destruction of "Hogarth's Soho House." The campaign gained support from correspondents and editorials in the *Spectator*, the *Daily Chronicle*, the *Manchester Guardian*, the *Observer* and the *Architectural Review*. In response, the Commissioner of Works issued the first preservation order under the Ancient Monuments Act of 1913, placing "Hogarth's Soho House" under protection for eighteen months, until Parliament could decide whether to purchase it for the nation.[144]

The landmark status of "Hogarth's Soho House" seemed to depend on the dual claim that it was a "beautiful house with Hogarth associations." Although a precious relic of the English past, its historical value also derived from the blending of English and Venetian artistic traditions: the mural painting was "one of the few relics of a time when the artists of our smoky city took their inspiration from [sunny] Venice."[145] Commentators also stressed the building's importance to the English arts and crafts tradition.[146] Much praise was lavished on the paneling and staircase, deemed to be an unparalleled example of dexterous joinery.[147] Campaigners won the support of May Morris and Walter Crane, leaders of the Arts and Crafts movement; like Cardwell, they believed that historical interest in old buildings and locales fostered social conscience and civic patriotism.[148]

Nonetheless, questions remained about the building's historical provenance, particularly about its Hogarthian associations. *The Times* acknowledged that research into the rate books yielded no evidence of Thornhill's residence on Dean Street, but defenders of 75 Dean Street turned to topographical histories as collateral evidence.[149] A second sticking point was the house's location in Soho. Familiar tropes of the district's seediness, its cosmopolitan population, and its vulnerable proximity to a rapidly changing West End, all featured in the debate. Preservationists might claim that Soho deserved their attention because it was an old district threatened by modern developments in the property market. But urban planners, such as Laurence Gomme, believed that Soho had lost its claims to being a historic area by allowing itself to become an over-crowded slum.[150]

Commentators felt obliged to negotiate the irony of preserving this "noble piece of Old London" in "one of the most curious and foreign districts in London" where it was an island of peace "hemmed in by a babbling sea of foreign tongues."[151] While defending the Venetian-inspired artistry of the staircase mural painting as a prized example of assimilated cosmopolitanism, *The Times* alerted its readers to the destructive impact of cosmopolitan capital on Old Soho of the present day. It would be a "thousand pities," it warned, if these stately chambers fell into "vandals' hands" and were "broken up and carried piecemeal to some foreign country with a stronger sense of tradition and beauty."[152]

This was indeed the ironic denouement and fate of 75 Dean Street. The attempt to preserve a building under the Ancient Monuments Act of 1913 proved to be "tragically abortive."[153] The building fell victim to the conflicting claims over national interest and private property, but also to the shady market in antiques and salvages that had evolved out of the Wardour Street trade. H. H. Mulliner, the building's owner, was a connoisseur and director of the decorating firm of Lenygon and Morant, the leading exporter of English "olde worlde" rooms across the Atlantic.[154] Between 1912 and 1914, Mr. Mulliner presented himself as a patriotic benefactor of Hogarth's Soho House, only desirous of finding a buyer who would cover his out-of-pocket costs. When he realized that the preservation order did not involve compensation or governmental purchase, he petitioned against the Bill. He also disputed the historic value of the building, notably the family association with Thornhill and Hogarth. The Lords Select Committee upheld his petition on both these grounds.[155]

The First World War temporarily postponed the destruction of the building, but, shortly after the Armistice, the transatlantic trade in antiques and period rooms resumed, and the building's treasures were carried off to America.[156] But the spurious "olde English" Hogarth association did not die; it continued to enhance the commercial value of the interior artifacts. In 1925, to great public acclaim, the staircase and paneling of the Hogarth House were donated to the Art Institute of Chicago and only de-accessioned as a fraud in 1997.[157]

Conclusion

The 1914 preservationist campaign to save Hogarth's Soho House provides a fitting bookend to the 1906 McKay-Cardwell dispute over Soho's dangerous cosmopolitanism. These controversies highlight competing meanings of cosmopolitanism and national heritage associated with the locale. On the one hand, Soho was imagined to be mutable and disorienting, filled with deracinated and questionable objects, bodies, and practices; on the other hand, it was a precious relic of a sturdy national past. Old world charm and contemporary exoticism combined to establish Soho's positive cosmopolitan reputation as a modern space of taste and refinement. But its historic urban fabric proved to be as unstable and transportable to other countries as the immigrant refugees and dubious commerce that arrived on English shores and settled in Soho. Old Soho, it seems, could be as inauthentic as Soho's Franco-Italian cuisine, as foreign and as English as the deracinated characters of *The Secret Agent*. It was the product of an earlier moment of assimilated cosmopolitanism and modern historic invention. And its new cosmopolitan migrants proved themselves as capable of enacting the strategies of ironic self-fashioning as the worldly, privileged connoisseurs of Soho's old English treasures.

Worldly connoisseurs did not fix their gaze exclusively on Soho's Georgian artifacts. The next two chapters spotlight their attraction to more kinetic objects of cosmopolitan consumption, notably the performing female bodies on display at the variety theaters that bordered Soho. These amusements, so deplored in Cardwell's *Two Centuries*, provoked a memorable conflict between British moral reform feminists and the Men of the World, a battle of words, bodies, and music hall turns that would transform metropolitan consumer culture, expand heterosocial nightlife in and around Soho, and even shift political identifications of gender and the national body.

CHAPTER 2

Battle of the Empire

In the 1890s, Leicester Square's raffish environment made it the "best known spot in London" prior to the Second World War. Foreigner, provincial, and exiled Briton all made a "bee-line for Leicester Square," located at the southern border of Soho, because of its "world-wide reputation for naughtiness."[1] Advertising themselves as the greatest cosmopolitan clubs of the world, the square's theaters of varieties, the Alhambra and the Empire, staged spectacular ballets as leg shows for a predominantly male audience. In 1894, the Empire's cosmopolitan entertainments came under attack from feminist purity reformers, determined to reshape the metropolis and the globe according to their own moral vision. A "Battle of the Empire" ensued between the theater's defenders and its opponents: it was, to quote *The Sketch*, a "great fight . . . waged with a war of words, a battery of correspondence, and a skirmish of sketches."[2] This dispute forced social constituencies to take sides and consolidated a negative reputation for Victorian feminists as puritanical kill-joys. But it also exposed the intricate links between the theater world and commercialized sex, and set into motion a partial reconfiguration of the "night side" of London, even in sleazy Soho.[3]

Hostilities commenced in October 1894, when Mrs. Laura Ormiston Chant, a feminist purity reformer, successfully challenged the music and dancing license of the Empire Theatre of Varieties, before the licensing committee of the London County Council (LCC). Mrs. Chant raised two objections to the management of the Empire: first, that "the promenade, an open space behind the dress circle in front of the bar," where 500 people circulated nightly, was used "as the habitual resort of prostitutes in pursuit of their traffic." Her second indictment was that parts of the performance on stage were exceedingly indecent, including the costumes of the ballet dancers.[4] Mrs. Chant had personally visited

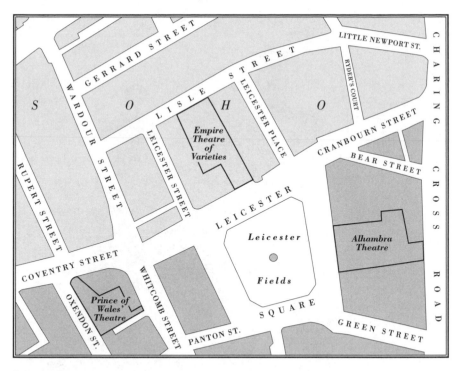

Leicester Square

the Empire's promenade five times, twice dressed in her best evening gown, and she had been herself accosted. On the basis of her testimony, her challenge to the Empire's license was successful.

Visually commemorated in the illustrated press and in numerous music hall spoofs, the "Battle of the Empire" was most extensively covered in the correspondence columns of the *Daily Telegraph*, under the heading "Prudes on the Prowl."[5] Following the *Telegraph*'s lead, *Punch* joined the fray. Its October 1894 cartoon of "Mrs. Prowlina Pry" (Figure 1) introduces its readers to the leading "prude."[6] "Mrs. Prowlina Pry" capitalizes on certain elements of Mrs. Chant's own appearance, notably her sartorial eccentricity and strong aquiline nose. But it mostly consolidates a well-recognized visual stereotyping of the strong-minded woman cum unattractive spinster.[7] Mrs. Chant is rendered visually ludicrous by her profile, long nose, bespeckled, lined face, and heavy chin, by her dowdy costume covering a shapeless uncorseted figure. A female of uncertain age, she comes equipped with opera glasses to spy on the proceedings, and she also sports a campy umbrella.[8]

Punch fixes Mrs. Pry as an outsider and oppositional figure. It captures her at the moment she endeavors to gain entrance to the Empire Theatre in Leicester

MRS. PROWLINA PRY.—"I HOPE I DON'T INTRUDE!"

THOUSANDS OF FELLOW-CREATURES FLUNG FROM WORK
   AT THE MERE PEN-STROKE OF A HASTY CENSOR!—
AN UNCONSIDERED TRIPLE ZEAL MAY SHIRK !
   BUT SENSE MAY NOT, NOR JUSTICE ! THEY ARE DENSER

THAN PUNCH IMAGINES, OUR NEW BUMBLE-BAND,
   IF MISTRESS PRY'S DECISION THEY ABIDE BY ;
BUT SHOULD THEY FAIL US, PUNCH THROUGHOUT THE LAND
   WILL WAKE THE PEOPLE PRUDES AND PRIGS ARE TRIED BY !

1 "Mrs. Prowlina Pry—"I hope I don't intrude!" *Punch*, October 27, 1894, p. 194. *Punch* lampoons Mrs. Chant as a strong-minded woman cum spinster as she tries to gain entrance to the Empire Theatre.

Square, but finds her way blocked by an enormous doorman/commissionaire.[9] Protected from the intruding gaze of female "prudes on the prowl," the gents in opera hats in the bright, electrically lit interior are free to enjoy their unspecified visual and sensory pleasures in complete safety—all with *Punch's* endorsement.

Unlike Mrs. Prowlina Pry, Mrs. Chant had, in fact, gained entry into the theater, and her observations about her visits to the Empire promenade had a decisive impact on the LCC. On the basis of her testimony, the Progressive-dominated LCC prohibited the sale of alcoholic drinks within the auditorium. It further insisted that the management of the Empire reduce the space of the two promenades by adding rows of seats and constructing a barrier between the bar and the promenades.[10] The management reluctantly agreed. It erected a canvas screen, but warned its 647 employees that this might spell the financial ruin of the Empire, as a substantial proportion of its profits derived from promenade patrons and their drink. Outraged by this compromise, the young aristocratic bloods and toffs who frequented the Empire used their walking sticks to destroy the barricade, sallying forth into Leicester Square carrying fragments of timber and canvas as trophies. The ringleader of the group was a young cadet from Sandhurst, Winston Churchill, who, in these "rather unvirginal surroundings," delivered his maiden political speech, calling for a Tory victory in the next election.[11] At the same time, many other groups and individuals joined the fray, including intellectuals and aesthetes such as G. B. Shaw and Arthur Symons. In 1895, the Licensing Committee reversed its decision against the Empire promenade because its inspectors reported to them that the change had made no difference in the class of persons attending the music-halls.[12] Music hall promenades would continue to operate as a zone of commercialized sex until 1916, when wartime exigencies forced their closure.

Cosmopolitanism and the Variety Theaters

Thanks to the media attention and the music hall parodies it provoked, the "Battle of the Empire" became an emblem of the Naughty Nineties. Scholars of Victorian studies continue to invoke the Battle of the Empire as a potent social drama and testing ground of urban epistemologies and body politics.[13] Overall, their accounts interpret the music hall/variety theater *either* as a space of economic and social determination, embodying the logic of capital and empire *or* as a laboratory for social change, establishing the expressive conditions of possibility for new social selves and even collective mobilization in the public sphere. Building on these studies, while disrupting their entrenched dichotomies, this chapter positions Mrs. Chant's campaign in relation to another analytic term: cosmopolitanism, a term widely deployed at the time to describe the fascinating but morally dubious cultural forms on offer at the Empire Theatre, particularly the spectacular displays of the female body.

As a system of distinction and taste, cosmopolitanism reordered the economy of the city, drawing new constituencies into expanding consumer markets and altering the social mapping of groups inside and outside the metropolis and the nation.[14] This process confirmed some existing hierarchies, but it disrupted others. Cosmopolitan entertainments of the Empire Theatre, for example, targeted an elite male audience of tourists and men about town; to appeal to this consumer niche, the theater's management substituted spectacular bodily displays of women for the homely comic singers who traditionally enjoyed star billing in the popular music halls of working-class districts. On the one hand, these new spectacles privileged male visual command of the female body, an argument advanced by Chant and her allies. On the other hand, female performers at the Empire—from novelty dancers to acrobats—publicized iconoclastic bodily idioms that troubled corporeal norms of nation, gender, sexuality, and class.

These kinesthetic and social remappings crystallized during Mrs. Chant's campaign against the Empire Theatre and its aftermath. Rather than leave Mrs. Chant out in the cold, as *Punch* and other historians have done, I want to put her back into the variety theater, not simply as the cool, detached observer of its cosmopolitanism, but also as the engaged insider susceptible to its expressive economy. Previous studies have tended to represent Mrs. Chant as a naive, provincial, staunchly liberal critic of the Empire's worldly, jingoist culture. I intend to show that she was more engaged with geopolitical alignments, imperialism, and kinesthetic fantasies of movement than has been previously assumed. Against the normative values of imperial masculinity and cosmopolitanism represented by the Empire Theatre, Mrs. Chant championed an alternative empire, a republican Anglo-American version of empire to be moralized by female activists.[15] As a dress reformer and physical culture advocate, she despised the licentious cancan, but she adored the strong, unfettered bodies of foreign female acrobats. Her own investment in transnational forms of female mobility helps us to appreciate the unexpected consequences of the Empire controversy for feminism, female bodily idioms, and cosmopolitan practices in London's West End.

Mrs. Chant and Body Politics

Although best known for her star turn in the Battle of the Empire, Mrs. Chant had already earned an international reputation as a charismatic, magnetic speaker, an ardent proponent of women's rights, a non-denominational preacher, and moral reformer, who regularly lectured across America and Britain in defense of "God, Home, and Humanity."[16] In 1888, the *Women's Penny Paper* profiled Chant as a model New Woman: active and mobile in the public domain and a partner in a successful companionate marriage.[17] She was interviewed, amidst her children and her pets, in her home at 49 Gower Street in Bloomsbury, just to the east and north of Soho, a district of snug middle-class life, modest hotels for foreign tourists, and headquarters of cultural enterprises associated with London's progressives, radicals, and New Women.[18] Her "experience in life," the interview went on to state, has been varied. For "some years she was a successful teacher; another period was spent as a nurse in the London Hospital; and for a year she was the manager of a lunatic asylum. About eleven years ago she became the wife of Mr. Thomas Chant, a surgeon."[19]

The unpublished memoir of her granddaughter emphasizes another side of Mrs. Chant's varied experience: her rebellious nature, her propensity for risk-taking and her struggles with authority. As a rebellious daughter, Laura ran away from home at twenty, to become trained as a nurse—originally as preparation for missionary work in India—to the great disapproval of her father, who regarded nursing as a degraded occupation and disowned her. Her marriage to Thomas Chant violated hospital rules and led to her dismissal. If she was a trial to her parents and to the administration of the London Hospital, she would also prove a trial to her children, particularly as she had their hair cut short and dressed them in artistic and sanitary costumes—short, knitted stockings and open-work sandals.[20]

Chant's activities, from dress reform, social purity, physical culture, temperance reform to the social gospel, embraced a wide range of liberal feminist causes that revolved around body politics in the late nineteenth century.[21] The late-Victorian "religion of health," to which Chant firmly subscribed, aligned health and morality as pathways to social and individual improvement and opposed them to the degenerative effects of unregulated sexual expression and wasteful consumption.[22]

This feminist body politics had considerable spatial implications. At the global level, it connected women reformers to transnational political networks and to imperial politics. As editor of the purity journal, the *Vigilance Record*, Chant denounced both the European corruption of colonial subjects as well as the persistence of indecent native customs.[23] On both sides of the Atlantic, she embraced a heterodox, syncretic, universalist religion closely aligned to theosophy. By so doing she refashioned the Nonconformist conscience into something more appropriate for a citizen of the world.[24]

New systems of communication and transportation enabled Mrs. Chant to be a woman on the move at many levels. Building on the old abolitionist alliance of the early nineteenth century, she participated in a set of transatlantic exchanges that cemented a tradition of Anglo-Saxon racial imperialism. This racial imperialism was founded on constitutionalism, racial purity, and the cherished freedoms and mobility of a liberal political heritage.[25] She juxtaposed this transatlantic connection of Old and New England to the denigrated traffic in bodies, objects, and cultural forms emanating from Europe and on display in London's West End.

Mrs. Chant's moral and cultural empire contrasted sharply with the imperial culture celebrated by the management of the Empire Theatre and the aficionados of its promenade. She disdained the rampant commercialism of the halls, and repudiated the kind of imperial man who visited the Empire to rendezvous with others returning from the "waste places" of the world.[26] To Chant, these men and their amusements embodied the negative elements of British imperial rule: aggressive militarism and jingoism, libertine capitalism, loose, undomesticated sexual morality, wasteful expenditure, and the sanctioning of continental and oriental—"foreign"—profligacy.

Mrs. Chant's attack on the Empire Theatre was not solely driven by her opposition to this imperialist ethos. As a metropolitan reformer, she judged erotic display and commercialized sex to be unhealthy, immoral, and practical impediments to women's free circulation through the metropolis, particularly the city center. This desire to transform that center, with its variety theaters, shopping, restaurants, clubs, and hotels, into an orderly heterosocial space illustrates what Mary Ryan has called a major "civic project" of the nineteenth century: the provision of public space for respectable women.[27]

In her metropolitan journeys, Mrs. Chant subscribed to the principles of movement, mapping, and circulation that broadly informed nineteenth-century urban planning and reform. As historians have noted, city planners and reformers tried to remake Victorian London into a city of constant motion, possessed of arteries and veins.[28] These commercial arteries enabled the production of the "Freeborn English Pedestrian," to quote historian Patrick Joyce's characterization of the self-regulating, disciplined urban denizen of the nineteenth century. According to Joyce, this urban type was a recent historic product of sociotechnical developments, of pavements, curbs, gutters, queues, train and bus tickets, and walking through the city in lines. A new culture of walking took form, one also indebted to discursive genres such as Wordsworthian "spatial stories" that encouraged introspective urban rambles.[29] These developments changed bodily and habitual modes of using the city and, according to Joyce, created a liberal body culture analogous to liberal political theory.

This liberal understanding of orderly locomotion informed Mrs. Chant's normative views on urban movement and governance. It also informed the LCC's failed effort to control prostitution in the Empire Theatre through the mandated construction of a barrier and fixed seating.[30] For Chant and her allies on the LCC, "the rule of freedom," to use Joyce's term, involved self-reflexive, self-watching, internalized disciplines, coupled with formal and reformed police structures and structural revisions of the material environment to ensure moral regulation.[31] Chant openly disparaged an unthinking celebration of "the liberty of the subject" as "a lot of nonsense." "The fact is that possession of liberty is relative," she declared in 1899.[32]

The prostitute remained a potent focal point for the tensions embedded in Chant's liberal body politics. During the late 1880s, Chant had engaged in a campaign to make the streets safer for "ladies" and working women. This meant ridding the commercial thoroughfares that bordered Soho of streetwalkers, so that respectable women like herself could traverse those public spaces without fear of attack or loss of reputation.[33] Her commitment to mobile and self-contained female embodiment also led her to support rational dress reform and physical culture. Mrs. Chant combined the circulatory model of the self-regulating body/machine with another, biblically sanctioned, image of the female body as the temple, or home, of the soul.[34] She heartily endorsed physical culture—gymnastics, competitive sports, bicycling—to promote a strong, robust female body that could move through space.[35] According to Chant, female muscle development, achieved through bicycling and other forms of physical culture, did not change female character, nor did it "unsex" women; on the contrary it aided reproduction and accentuated sexual differ-ence.[36] Similarly, she supported rational dress as a way for women to present themselves in public as natural, chaste and sexed bodies, unconstrained by inconvenient and constricting fashions, and protected from the intrusive eyes of men.

Rational dressers like Chant were closely connected to other emancipatory causes of women, but they also defended rational dress on geopolitical and aesthetic grounds. They denounced tight corseting as a threat to women's child-bearing capacities and condemned the domination of Paris fashion as detri-mental to national trade and industry.[37] They disdained spectacular ornamentation, especially the décolleté of fashionable evening dress, as another barrier to women's cultural evolution. "Women always feel themselves in the position of being looked at rather than looking," declared E. M. King, the presi-dent of the Rational Dress Society and early semiotician of the male gaze, and then noted, "the reverse is the case with men."[38]

In keeping with these sentiments, Chant idealized a fully draped female body that would move through the crowd unobserved. Chant endorsed an outfit that was useful, rational, and modern: it would safeguard privacy and health and protect the body from air and seal off draughts. Her reformed dress would, moreover, follow the contours of the natural body, as manifested in the "S" shaped lines of Greek statuary. The harsh, constricting curves of the corset would be replaced by the more flexible, serpentine curvature of the body of modernity.[39]

This mobile, female form could also circulate as a sentient body, an observing subject, who could safely interact with the slow-moving human traffic of the street to produce reliable social narratives. Like male social investigators of her day, Chant imagined her urban spectator to be a rational observer, who could establish a universal knowledge of man and his world. Yet, this rationalist tradition of urban spectatorship also harbored an unacknowledged propensity for fantasy, for voyeurism, and for social masquerades.[40] All these conflicting dispositions towards regimentation, expressiveness, and mimicry were realized in Chant's ambivalent response to the halls.

When Mrs. Chant visited the Empire Theatre in 1894, it was not the first time she had inspected a music hall. In the years preceding the Empire campaign, she had visited the halls in her capacity as key propagandist for the purity movement. Chant published a series of articles in the *Vigilance Record*, detailing her visits to the halls in 1888 and 1889.[41] Her assessment of music hall entertainments was not uniformly negative. She admired Cockney comic singers like Albert Chevalier as a harmless, domesticated popular entertainment.[42] She also praised acts of physical dexterity and strength. She waxed enthusiastic about a "delightfully clever Japanese juggler" and a woman athlete or acrobat who "performed marvels on a trapeze suspended to the roof of the lofty Theatre."[43] Chant's defense of the acrobat is especially worthy of note. It signaled her interest in unconventional forms of female embodiment as well as her assessment of theatrical spaces as showcases for new ways of seeing and imagining the female body.[44] Chant chose not to dismiss the acrobat as a low, mindless, popular attraction who exhibited fetishistic bodily distortions. Nor did she elect to represent her as the epitome of non-narrative abstract art, in the manner of some bohemian aesthetes such as Arthur Symons who regularly patronized the Empire Theatre. Instead, Chant incorporated the female acrobat into her own political project as a fine, healthy specimen of female physical culture. Although she approved neither of the sensational position of the female acrobat nor her scanty costume, she hoped that "the immense muscular power displayed by a woman must have dispelled from the spectators any pet theories as to innate physical incapacity in the weaker or more accurately speaking, the undeveloped sex."[45]

During the early tours of the halls in the 1880s, Mrs. Chant was outraged by the "indecency" of theatrical costumes, particularly the attire of the corps de ballet who wore "flesh-coloured tights" draped with "transparent gauze."[46] To her mind, the spectacular ballet exuded continental vice, as did the foreign novelty acts that increasingly featured in variety entertainments.[47] Chant was also disturbed by homegrown acts—the noisy jingoism of the East End halls and the exhibition of child performers in nautical spectacles.[48] But she judged the popular music halls, overall, to be vastly superior "in tone and decency" to the fashionable West End establishments that attracted sporting aristocrats, military officers, colonial bureaucrats, students, clerks, and tourists from the dominions.[49] These theaters boasted a spacious auditorium, a large proscenium arch, and a deep stage that could accommodate a large troupe of dancers. Patrons crowded into these spaces to watch spectacular ballets, featuring prima ballerinas from southern Europe and a huge cast of "native" English dancing girls.

Leicester Square and the Empire Theatre

Spectacular ballets were the latest in a series of sensational public exhibitions of the female body that were associated with Leicester Square, home to the great "Shows of London" and birthplace of the Panorama. According to Tracy Davis, the Leicester Square theaters were a focal point of "a vital nexus of West End immorality involving prostitutes, alcohol, variety theatres, supper clubs, dancing halls, and gambling houses."[50] The Empire gained its reputation for naughtiness from the staging of spectacular ballets as leg shows and from the "nightly ballet" of the Ladies of the Night, who executed their "peculiar, exaggerated swing of the body from the hips" in the promenade bar. The heavily mirrored walls of the promenade enhanced the doubling effect of these two performance sites.[51]

Leicester Square's stylized naughtiness dated back to the late Georgian period, when the square emerged as Soho's central entertainment zone, located at its southern periphery. Its commercial development was the cultural outcome of many structural developments, notably the break-up of aristocratic estates, proximity to a wealthy neighborhood, and the exploitation of local crafts and decorative arts for commercialized leisure. Laid out on the estate of the second Earl of Leicester in 1630–48 and presided over by Leicester House, Leicester Square began its history as an aristocratic neighborhood within St. Anne's parish possessed of a distinctly foreign ambience. Its Anglo-French character owed as much to the Huguenot artisans and craftsmen who took up residence in nearby Soho as to the ambassadors and foreign painters who lived along the square. Their collective presence set the scene for the square's second metamorphosis, as the residential home and workshop for luminaries of the stage, literature, science, and art.[52] These cultural resources helped to precipitate what theater impresario and historian John Hollingshead termed the "third act" of the Square, its transformation into a center of public amusements.[53] According to critic Richard Altick, the construction of the Panorama in Leicester Place in 1791 was the "decisive event" that transformed a neighborhood dominated by the residences of gentlemen, well-to-do artists and professional men into a "raucous center of commercial entertainment."[54] Coinciding with this commercial growth was the division of the Leicester estate in 1788, the subsequent demolition of Leicester House, and the social decline of the area. Successive landlords ceased to regulate the character of the buildings, while the garden in the center of the square declined into a dumping ground for noisome objects.

By the mid-nineteenth century, Leicester Square was one of most "neglected and woebegone" spots in all of London.[55] Its public amusements also tended increasingly towards sensationalism and charlatanry.[56] During the 1840s, Savile House, on the square's north side, offered a range of exhibitions and entertainments that captured the miscellaneous, anarchic energy of the place.[57] Most significant, for our story, Savile House was notorious for its tableaux vivants, including fleshly embodiment of such subjects as "A Night with Titian," or a full-color enactment of "Venus Rising from the Sea."[58]

By the 1870s, Leicester Square had received a physical facelift, thanks to the renovation of the central garden and the construction of heavily capitalized entertainment centers, notably the Alhambra and Empire theaters, whose oscillating fortunes epitomized the square's own ups and downs. Located on the eastern side of the square, the Alhambra started off in 1854 as the Royal Panopticon of Science and Art, an educational institution endeavoring to cash in on the popular enthusiasm for mechanical display generated by the Great Exhibition of 1851. Unfortunately, the Panopticon so failed to edify patrons that it was converted to more popular use as the Alhambra Theatre of Varieties, featuring ballets and novelty dances such as the cancan.[59] The Empire Theatre, which opened its doors in 1884, underwent a similar evolution. It also began with lofty cultural intentions as an opera house, then became a theater, and finally regrouped as a theater of variety that specialized in spectacular dance. The Empire ballets far exceeded the Alhambra performances in their elaborate staging, design, and costuming, and in their introduction of "up-to-date" or topical subjects, many of them celebrations of the military and the Empire.[60]

Sumptuous appointments, modern scale and comforts, and licensed order were the governing principles of the Empire Theatre. Its classical Renaissance exterior of marble and freestone imitated the dignity of financial institutions, but its interior was given over to wild eclecticism, summoning up continental and oriental excesses, with different rooms appointed in Persian, Egyptian, and Louis Seize designs. Order was guaranteed by giant commissionaires and by price-stratified seating for 1,300 (from three-guinea boxes to sixpenny seats in the gallery), with separate entrances for separate areas of the theater, and interior connecting spaces appropriately decorated according to the social character of the public destined for each part of the auditorium.[61] Seated in the dark, patrons remained still and silent, passively consuming the brilliantly lit moving spectacles on stage. But another order—one that involved greater interaction and physical intimacy—prevailed in the five-shilling promenade at the back of the second tier. Here, in a space adapted from certain features of the *café chantant*, men of a "good class" could sit at tables and spend "a good deal of money in refreshments and liquor" upon women who had entered the establishment "without the escort of a man" and slowly circulated through the promenade to attract attention.[62]

These amenities established the Alhambra and Empire as the greatest cosmopolitan clubs in the world. They were the places where French visitors made their home in London, and where Englishmen could sometimes forget that they were English, but never that they ruled the empire.[63] Leicester Square's proximity to Soho's back streets, where "lean and hungry conspirators from the four quarters of the globe" had settled, further enabled this imaginative expatriation.[64] This "partly-French, partly-theatrical" district became the center of the "Exile World of London," home to "the followers and understrappers of Continental conspiracy."[65] Arthur Symons recalled the neighborhood as a "sordid" but "irresistible reminder of Paris and Italy," a syncretic amalgamation of European urbanity with "something more indigenously English."[66]

The Empire's entertainments mimicked the hybrid artifice of the neighborhood, combining the homely and the exotic: Andalusian dancers succeeded Cockney comedy singers, followed by bohemian acrobats, Cossack horse-trainers, dancing dogs, etc. The up-to-date twenty-minute ballet, the evening's featured presentation, was also assembled from indigenous and continental talent. Under the direction of the theater ballet mistress, Kitti Lanner, the foreign-born prima ballerina "played little part in the action but represented an ideal."[67] The ballerina was separated by costume and by skill from the well-drilled corps de ballet, composed of English working women who were organized in strict linear format to provide a visual frame for the ballerina and to enhance the scenic effects of rhythm, line, and color.[68] In the Empire Theatre's advertisements, the dancing girl figured as a healthy, good-humored daughter of Britannia, akin to the Gaiety Girl (the featured attraction of George Edwardes's musical comedies at the Gaiety Theatre in the Strand), and readily transformed into an emblem of the nation.[69] For all its cosmopolitanism, the Empire was a belligerently British establishment: in addition to the smiling dancer, Britannia herself graced the Empire program covers, surrounded by banners, flags, and crests.[70] Sufficiently cosmopolitan to appeal to foreign tourists, many of whom would not have been able to follow the patter of Cockney comic singers, as well as to Londoners desirous of a touch of the Continent, the Empire reassured its national audience that it still remained on British soil.

Erotic Performances

In 1894, the Empire Theatre stood as a conspicuous bastion of male privilege in a central leisure and entertainment zone that was fast becoming heterosocial and populated by men and women of many classes. While other parts of the commercial West End were increasingly feminized as a daytime zone of female pleasure, Leicester Square and its establishments remained a distinctly masculine nighttime space, a venue for illicit homosexual and heterosexual encounters, and a nocturnal no-go area for unaccompanied ladies.[71]

In the Empire promenades, multiple forms of erotic performances contributed to the ambiguity and frisson of this sexually charged space. The book dealer Cyril Beaumont recalled his visits to the promenade as a young boy in the 1890s: he was bored by the ballet, but fascinated by the circulating traffic of seductive, mysterious, and sinister "hetirae" in the promenades. They reminded him of the hermaphrodite temptresses of Aubrey Beardsley's drawings of Wilde's *Salome*, whose aggressive sexuality was represented through phallic iconography.[72] Beaumont's memoir gestures toward the homoerotic encounters in the promenades that were open secrets. "To the *habitué*," insisted J. B. Booth, "the feminine lure of the promenade made small appeal." Instead, men went there for "the companionship of other men," to rendezvous with other Men of the Empire.[73]

In the promenades, one form of masquerade could shade into another. Female erotic display on stage and in the promenade could provide a pretext for sexual conversation between men and a prototype for homosexual prostitutes. These covert practices of sexual and social cross-dressing seem to have eluded Mrs. Chant's own field of vision, partially because "sodomites" could not always be visually distinguished from men who were conventionally masculine. In fact, flamboyant West End sodomites were in attendance and the subject of a protesting letter retained in the archives of the LCC.[74] They may well have contributed to the Council's readiness to close down the promenades, anticipating by one year the sensational repudiation of bohemian decadence during the trials of Oscar Wilde.[75]

Another form of erotic display did not escape Mrs. Chant's attention. They were tableaux vivants, also known as *poses plastiques*, or Living Pictures. Tableaux vivants exploited the technological innovations of spectacular theater. Presented in a colossal gold frame and attired in flesh-tinted tights, female performers would strike an artistic pose and stand silent and immobilized as a picture. The Palace Theatre of Varieties, located on the Charing Cross Road, revived this practice as a form of erotic entertainment in 1893 in order to edge out its competitors in Leicester Square. Following the triumph of tableaux vivants at the Palace, other variety theaters followed suit, including the Empire, whose pictures were considerably less daring than the Palace.[76]

Mrs. Chant's Challenge

The proliferation and elaboration of erotic display was a key factor in Mrs. Chant's decision to step up the campaign against the variety theaters of the West End. In 1894, Mrs. Chant and Mr. W. A. Coote, the paid secretary of the National Vigilance Association, unexpectedly challenged the dancing and music licenses of the Empire and Palace Theatres. Echoing contemporary discussions in the press concerning the salacious influence of French salon painting, Mr. Coote insisted that a demoralizing foreign influence was at work in the selection of original art works selected for reproduction on the Palace stage.[77] Despite his protest, the Palace license was renewed. When it came time to consider the Empire's license, Coote's place was taken by Mrs. Chant and six ladies and gentlemen she called as witnesses.

Mrs. Chant astonished members of the Council and the press by conducting the case against the Empire herself. She presented herself before the Committee and the public as a "citizen," a representative of the "women of England," and the "calm, steady voice of the Non-Conformist conscience."[78] Yet it was her transatlantic connections that set into motion her campaign earlier that year when some American friends had gone there, on her recommendation, to hear Albert Chevalier "sing his coster songs."[79] Instead of enjoying an evening of wholesome, popular entertainment, they complained that "they were continually accosted and solicited by women." Moreover, they were shocked at the "character and want of clothing in the ballet."[80] "For that reason I determined to visit the Empire, but I did not do so till the Living Pictures [at the Palace] had made so much stir in July."[81]

Finding the Living Pictures at the Empire to be unobjectionable, Mrs. Chant focused instead on the nightly ballets on stage and in the promenade. She went about making her case by detailing her investigative strategies, keen to show herself to be a skilled interpreter of the performing body who took careful notes and made observations. She was intent on presenting her case in a dispassionate, lawyer-like way, to offer credible evidence that the Empire management knowingly permitted its premises to become a habitual resort of prostitutes.[82] Nonetheless, Chant's testimony exposed her own blurred performances as spectator and spectacle, a blurring that moved her closer than she would have liked to the theatricality of other social actors in the hall.

Chant began her testimony with an account of her entry into the promenade. To investigate the promenade, Mrs. Chant adopted a form of impersonation. On the first three occasions that she had visited the Empire, she dressed "quietly," but for this very reason the uniformed attendant in the promenade recognized her "as a stranger." In cross-examination, she explained that on the fourth and fifth occasions, she dressed "gaily," wearing her "prettiest evening dress in order that she might get her information more readily." The disguise, she hastened to add, did not extend to "décolletage."[83] So disguised, she was accosted by a gentleman, who apologized "directly he looked into her face."[84]

Mrs. Chant observed the appearance and behavior of the young and attractive women who entered the theater, "very much painted," and all of them "more or less gorgeously dressed." These women did not enter the orchestra seats but chose to sit in the unreserved seats in the lounge or "walked round the promenade" on the lookout for men.[85] "She noticed that these women took no interest in the performance, and that during the necessary darkening of the theatre for the tableaux vivants their behavior was very objectionable indeed." She even saw women accost men.[86]

From these visual signs—gorgeous dresses, painted faces, carriage and bearing, indifference to the performance, constant circulation, accosting men, "intentional suggestiveness"—Mrs. Chant concluded that female patrons of the promenade were "prostitutes in pursuit of their traffic." She bolstered this visual evidence with bits of conversation she was able to catch as a member of the throng. She "heard men and women talking" behind her; "some words caught my attention and made me listen to what was going on." "The impression, in my mind, or rather the conviction, was that it was a case of offer to procure. I have not the slightest doubt in my own mind from various signs—from various things that were said."[87] She heard fragments of other sexual conversations when a "little later on I moved place again with another portion of the crowd." Mrs. Chant did not elaborate on these conversations, but other witnesses reported overhearing gossip about sexual bargains and descriptions of assignation places in Greek Street and St. John's Wood.[88]

As a participant observer, Chant partially mimicked the body idioms and licensed practices of the promenaders, by moving about and not attending to the performance.[89] Participating in her masquerade required her to engage in the same level of distraction as her neighbors. At one point in her testimony, she acknowledged that she momentarily forgot her role as undercover detective and started to pay too much attention to the performance:

> the words [of the singer] were completely drowned by the loud and exceedingly objectionable conversation of one very tall highly painted young woman who stood near the stalls . . . [Had I] been there for any other purposes than I was, I should have called "silence" at once. But I was there to take notes and make my observations, and did not wish to attract unnecessary notice.[90]

When she focused on the stage, Chant adopted a second form of impersonation. Her observations became more resolutely judgmental: she pronounced the dresses of the dancers in "La Frolique" and "The Girl I Left Behind" to "be conceived for the express purpose of publishing the bodies of the women to the utmost extent."[91] "There seemed not the least attempt to disguise that which common sense and decency required to be hidden." To confirm this impression of indecency she resorted to binoculars. "There was one dancer in flesh-coloured tights, and she had to use opera-glasses to see whether they really were tights at all."[92] By emulating the voyeuristic practice of the stage-door Johnnies, Chant departed from the position of transparent authenticity to immerse herself in the theatricality of the milieu.

Mrs. Chant's testimony evoked the dreamlike intensity of the urban adventure, marked by an abrupt discontinuity of time and space, a forgetfulness and suspension or confusion of identities.[93] Caught up in the crowd and the spectacle, Mrs. Chant became distracted, even momentarily forgetting to attend to her investigative mission. Chant's confusion did not escape the notice of her critics, who began to vilify her immediately following her testimony before the licensing committee. In the *Daily Telegraph*, "An Englishman" condemned the "self-advertising women" with "wizened faces" who opposed the Empire's license as "spies" and "prudes," and who failed to see the humor of their being accosted.[94] Within the space of one week, 170 letters appeared in the *Telegraph* under the banner of "prudes on the prowl." Other newspapers also took up the matter, public meetings were held, and dozens of petitions sent, pro and con, to the London County Council. While men of the world roundly condemned Chant, working-class spokesmen were divided. The handful of trade unionists elected to the LCC supported her challenge to the Empire, as did women's groups and temperance organizations throughout London. Conversely, the theatrical trade unions, the London Trades Council, and the radical clubs of central London vehemently opposed the new restrictions.[95]

George Bernard Shaw was impressed by Mrs. Chant's example of democracy at work yet critical of her intervention. "You can't have a better example of democracy than the Empire case . . . Here is Mrs. Chant . . . and she flounces in and floors the whole County Council."[96] Yet he mockingly rebuked her for slandering stage performers and for disclosing in an interview the enormous profits made by promenaders, as much as twenty–thirty pounds a week: "That single utterance of Mrs. Chant is calculated to make more prostitutes than the ballet and the Living Pictures make in ten years."[97] All in all, he recognized her as a Shavian heroine: a woman of the governing classes whose rebellious energies both enabled and undercut her zeal for social order and left chaos and disarray in her wake.

Bohemian poet and journalist Arthur Symons was particularly vocal in his defense of the liberties of the halls against Chant's assault. Unlike Shaw, he saw no overlap between his aesthetic/political practice and Mrs. Chant's campaign. He simply challenged Chant's reading of the Empire Theatre, countering her views with his own extensive knowledge as a journalist who regularly reviewed its dance offerings. Throughout the Nineties, Symons helped to circulate a cultural defense of dance that significantly altered its dubious reputation as sexually improper and debased. Symons was, to quote one critic, the leading "ambassador" for French poetry in London.[98] In his journalism, he introduced French symbolist theory that elevated dance as a vanguard cultural form. Following Mallarmé, he argued that the dancer was a living image, poetry in motion, the essence of art as distinct from ordinary experience. The dancer's art resided in her artifice, in her abstract and fluid transcendence of naturalist experience.[99]

This defense of dance found minimal expression during the Battle of the Empire, although, as we shall see, it considerably informed one of the striking long-term effects of the affair. Overall, Chant's critics offered little commentary about the actual performances on the stage or in the promenade. Instead they repeatedly caricatured Mrs. Chant's body image and performance.[100] One *Judy* cartoon, entitled "A Facer," summons up the moment when the roué who accosted Chant realized his mistake once he looked into her face.[101] A *Moonshine* cartoon imagines the reformed ballet costume that would pass Mrs. Chant's inspection: the Empire dancer appears, bespectacled, covered from head to toe, sadly lacking in sex appeal and glamour, a striking contrast to the smiling, leggy, dancing girl who regularly embellished the Empire program covers, or the decorative women who frequented the promenade.[102]

How do we assess the significance of Mrs. Chant's bodily adventures in the Empire Theatre? In many ways Mrs. Chant was the ideal liberal subject, seeking to create a hygienic, self-regulating, urban citizenry whose rule of freedom was ensured not only by discourse and formal policing, but also by the organization of the built environment. Yet she was herself clearly disorderly, and it is not difficult to see why Shaw recognized her as a kind of Shavian heroine: her dress, her intrusion into the male precincts of the promenade and the licensing committee, her engagement with kinesthetic forms of expression, her affinity for the assertive spectacular female body of the acrobat—all challenged the accepted conventions of femininity.

Mrs. Chant's disruptive performance forced diverse constituencies to articulate opposing views on metropolitan encounters and geopolitical alignments. She supported the traditions of the English music hall in the form of the sentimental, comic Cockney singer, but she opposed tainted foreign, that is, continental, imports. She and her supporters upheld a "rule of freedom" in accordance with little Englander notions of propriety and decency, appropriate to all classes. But this liberal rule of freedom had transnational dimensions. It was consistent with an expanded and republican ideal of Greater Britain, circulated by liberal politicians such as Charles Dilke and conceived of as consolidating a white Anglo-Saxon cultural diaspora of Old and New Englands.[103] This international context framed the Empire affair: it was, after all, Mrs. Chant's friends from America who alerted her to the indecent performances in the Empire Theatre. Against Chant and her allies, the most vocal patrons of the music hall asserted a more elite, male privileging of sexual license and pleasure defended at the time as simultaneously imperial and cosmopolitan. They condemned Chant and her friends as "nobodies" from the provinces or from North London suburbs, who threatened the cosmopolitan pleasures of Men of the World in the center. Yet Mrs. Chant, a denizen of the West End, had worldly ambitions of her own. She championed an alternative empire, a space to be moralized by female activists.

The Battle of the Empire not only registered competing imaginative geographies at the heart of the late Victorian metropolis; it also precipitated some long-term political consequences for feminism. Its legacy illuminates how tastes, codes, and skills of the cosmopolitan attractions of variety entertainments could be appropriated and deployed as tactics by women. Feminists used these codes to mobilize women in the public sphere, while female cultural innovators showcased transnational bodily forms to refashion women's bodies and desires.

Despite Mrs. Chant's stagy performance, the Battle of the Empire consolidated a negative reputation for feminists as puritanical, anti-fashion, and anti-theatrical—a reputation that the next generation of Edwardian feminists felt obliged to challenge and revise. To advertise feminism, the Edwardian suffrage movement appropriated the technologies of spectacular theater, involving the massing of bodies, sumptuous set designs, and elaborate costuming. Suffragists also recruited attractive actresses to their cause. One of their prime recruits was the American actress Elizabeth Robins, whose performances and independent production of *Hedda Gabler* in 1891 marked the successful arrival of a stylishly dressed Ibsenite heroine on the London stage. Robins's 1907 play, *Votes for Women*, rewrote the story of Hedda Gabler, so that, instead of choosing suicide, an embittered and passionate woman-with-a-past told her story before a London crowd in Trafalgar Square and incited a political movement (Figure 2). *The Sketch* took note of the juxtaposition of popular burlesque and feminist melodrama. It judged the Trafalgar Square crowd scene to be the "finest stage crowd of recent years:" uproariously funny, chaotic, full of crowd patter, of burlesque, comic bodies who interrupted the melodrama of the public orator.[104] It was as if Mrs. Ormiston Chant, with a new fashion consultant, had vindicated herself amidst the Prude correspondents or the devotees of the Promenade.[105]

2 "The Finest Stage Crowd of Recent Years: 'Votes for Women,'" *The Sketch*, May 15, 1907. This stage photograph depicts a funny, chaotic stage crowd as it interrupts the melodramatic speech of a feminist orator. The juxtaposition of a popular burlesque and feminist melodrama recalls the earlier discursive contest between Mrs. Chant and the Prudes correspondents and the devotees of the Promenade.

Other productive consequences occurred *within* the precincts of the music hall. Although Mrs. Chant's campaign against indecent performances in the variety theatres failed in the short term, music hall managers had learned an important lesson: the need to mollify licensing authorities who were sympathetic to the complaints of "the Non-Conformist conscience."[106] These concessions increased managerial control over the verbal and gestural performances of music hall stars. But censorship codes also made managers receptive to cultural innovations in theatrical dancing, opening the way to the performances of North American interpretive dancer Maud Allan when Living Pictures were decisively banned by the LCC in 1907. As we shall see, Allan's performances strikingly melded the contending cultural forces at work in the Battle of the Empire.

Conclusion

The Empire Theatre reminds us, once again, of the imaginative resonance of the prostitute and the crowd in middle-class women's fantasies of sexual danger. Specifically, it shows us how a liberal feminist like Chant, with her strong commitment to women's free, disciplined movement through city spaces, energetically marked herself off from grotesque female bodies while she also made a spectacle of herself that partially blurred those differences. Second, the case illuminates how a spatial story of the metropolitan center exercised a hold on the national imagination and highlighted contested systems of empire and transnational networks. As a citizen and Englishwoman, Mrs. Chant challenged the legitimacy of the Empire, because it signified the normative values of imperial masculinity: easy access, total possession, complete sway over the pleasures of the globe.[107] These were also the values the Empire Theatre in Leicester Square underscored when it advertised itself as the greatest cosmopolitan club in the world. Against this version of cosmopolitanism, Mrs. Chant's championed a set of transnational values (Anglo-American) to fashion an alternative vision of empire and metropolitan order. Finally, Mrs. Chant's story teaches us that cultural politics rarely possesses a coherent, driving logic or single trajectory.[108] Mrs. Chant's "rule of freedom" might have supported a puritanical regime of bodily discipline, but, as the story of Maud Allan will demonstrate, Chant's feminist body politics also precipitated some of the conditions for the staging of more expressive, feminist forms of cosmopolitan embodiment.

CHAPTER 3

The "Vision of Salome"

"A NEW CLASSICAL DANCER HAS MADE HER APPEARANCE IN LONDON," declared the *New Jersey Telegraph* on March 23, 1908.[1] This "artistic sensation of the hour" was Maud Allan, an interpretive dancer from North America who made her debut on Soho's eastern border in a theatrical space that combined material luxury, sexual license, and cultural hybridity. Her dance program largely consisted of Greek-inspired classical numbers, in the mode developed by Isadora Duncan.[2] But it was her final dance of the evening, the orientalist "Vision of Salome," that drew crowds to the Palace Theatre of Varieties, in Cambridge Circus, at the juncture of Charing Cross Road and Shaftesbury Avenue (see Figure 3). "So enthusiastic are her audiences that the English claim her as a Canadian," explained the *New York World*, which then proceeded to set the record straight. "Although she was born in Toronto, she was reared in San Francisco, and considers herself an American." According to the newspaper, Allan's North American roots only partially accounted for her appeal: "Her art and seductive grace, however, are cosmopolitan," for Allan "learned the 'poetry of motion' in Berlin" and "has studied old Greek and Assyrian manuscripts and tablets" to absorb all she could of "ancient dance lore."[3] At the Palace Theatre, Maud Allan appeared as a superior embodiment of Anglo-Saxonism, a daughter of Greater Britain, who called "open the gates of the World" to "all London." The "dance revolution" that Allan helped usher in not only contributed to the cosmopolitan élan of prewar London; it also regendered cosmopolitanism, traditionally coded as masculine, and rendered it a cultural practice widely available to women.[4]

When the North American dancer Maud Allan introduced the "new," "expressive" dancing into London in 1908, her "nude exhibition" before an audience of "richly clad" Londoners and foreign visitors incited fantasies of escape and

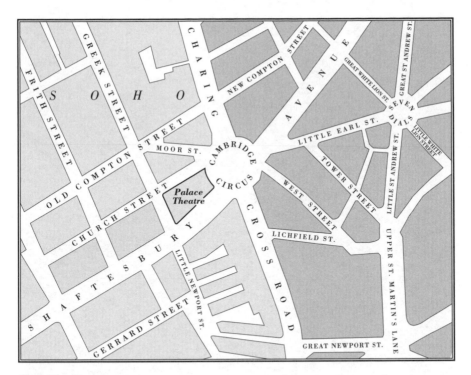

Cambridge Circus

pleasure, while simultaneously provoking anxieties of dislocation and unease.[5] Let me summarize the striking features of the body idiom performed across Allan's repertoire: a solitary, autonomous, unfettered, mobile, weighted, and scantily clad female body whose movements delineated emotional interiority, shifting states of consciousness, and autoeroticism. To be sure, Allan's gestural system built on available constructions of corporeality and subjectivity, but it gave unusual status to a self-pleasuring, embodied, and expressive female self and to the staging of the internal process of consciousness in public. Her dance gained an added charge from the raffish performance space in which it was staged, as well as from the diverse audience attracted to it, who transported Allan's interpretive dancing to other social spaces in the city.[6]

As the toast of London in 1908, Maud Allan was part of a wave of interpretive American dancers who arrived in Europe at the turn of the century and helped upgrade the status of theatrical dance. In 1895, Allan traveled to Berlin to study at the Royal College of Music, where she immersed herself in the experimental culture of aesthetic modernism, learning about symbolism, photography, and stage lighting. While studying the piano in 1900 and 1901, Allan became interested in the kind of barefoot dancing initiated by Isadora Duncan. Realizing that

3 "Maud Allan as Salome." From J. E. Crawford Flitch, *Modern Dancing and Dancers* (1910; repr. London, 1913). The purity campaigns against West End variety entertainments had the unintended effect of leading to the recruitment of Maud Allan to fill the sex appeal slot by the Palace Theatre in 1908.

she would be unable to make a living through music, she abandoned her studies and tried to prepare herself for a career in dancing. With no formal training in dance, she was initially dependent on artist and musician friends who taught her how to stage her art. In need of money and on the advice of a sculptor friend, she began to give public exhibitions of classical dancing, where she interpreted the music of Mendelssohn, Beethoven, Chopin, Schubert, and Anton Rubinstein. She subsequently diversified into the "Vision of Salome," performed to an orientalist musical score arranged by a friend, the Belgian composer Marcel Remy.[7] By 1906, when Allan made her debut as Salome in Vienna, the field was already crowded: Mata Hari was performing a version of the dance before Allan could even assemble her costume, consisting of beaded chains and not much else.[8]

In 1907, Maud Allan performed her Salome dance in Marienbad, that renowned site of cosmopolitan encounters and political intrigues, to the delight of the king of England, Edward VII. On the basis of his patronage, she was recruited by Alfred Butt, the manager of the Palace Theatre, to perform at his establishment in 1908. For two years, Allan enjoyed top billing in evening programs that also included jugglers, illusionists, character vocalists, Scottish comedians, animal acts, synchronized dance troupes, and the bioscope. For a nightly appearance in which she provided twenty minutes of classical and orientalist dancing, she received £250 a week, a top salary for a music hall star.[9] Her performances broke all box office records, and the shareholders of the Palace enjoyed profits exceeding 30 percent.[10] Allan's dancing appealed to a wide cross-section of Londoners and visiting tourists, but her most important female patron was Margot Asquith—wife of the Liberal prime minister, a cultural trendsetter in elite social circles and known for her sharp tongue, advanced taste, rebellious modernity, opposition to women's suffrage, and propensity to make a spectacle of herself.[11]

In 1910, when Allan toured the United States, the American press exposed Allan's family secret, a story that she had managed to suppress for close to fifteen years by changing her name. Shortly after her arrival in Berlin, her brother Theodore had been arrested in San Francisco for the murder of two young women; he was convicted and executed for these homicides in 1898. According to Allan's biographer, this personal tragedy and the shame it caused would haunt her for the rest of her life, but in the prewar years, details of what would later be termed her "degenerate" family history appeared publicly only in the United States. In London, where she returned in 1911, it was still not public knowledge, nor did it shadow her on her tour of Asia in 1913 and 1914.[12]

In 1918, however, her family past caught up with her. During the last months of the war, theater impresario J. T. Grein announced that he had recruited Allan for the feature role in a private presentation of Oscar Wilde's play *Salome* in London at the Royal Court Theatre. He also stated that he intended to export the production to neutral nations as a war aim, to enhance British intellectual prestige.[13] This announcement precipitated the startling denouement of Allan's career. Notices of this upcoming role initially appeared with no adverse comment in the London press, but they were followed by a vicious attack on the production in the right-wing press. The *Vigilante*, an anti-Semitic and xenophobic publication, called attention to the forthcoming presentation in an article that appeared under the bold-type heading, "Cult of the Clitoris." Members of the London audience, the author asserted, would be drawn from a list of 47,000. An article published three weeks earlier in the journal had already introduced readers to the list: it was allegedly held by the Germans, and it contained the names of English men and women who were open to German blackmail because of their "sexual perversions." Supposedly included in the list were the names of "wives of Cabinet Ministers, dancing girls, even Cabinet Ministers themselves."[14] After Grein brought the article to the attention of Allan, she sued the editor, Independent Member of Parliament Noel Pemberton Billing, for libel, her legal counsel insisting that the "cult of the clitoris" could only mean "lesbianism," a term reprinted in *The Times*—indeed, the first time it had appeared there in print.[15] As in the libel case of Oscar Wilde twenty-three years earlier, Allan became the person on trial, not her libeler. Allan lost her case and never recovered her career. Everyone else associated with the trial was also tainted by the affair.

Allan's life has been chronicled by biographers and cultural critics. Memoirists of prewar London allude to the "Maud Allan boom" as one of the media-driven fashions of the gay, pleasure-seeking Edwardian period, before the Great War Changed Everything.[16] A somewhat different body of literature produced by historians of performance has focused on Allan's prewar career, assessing her role in avant-garde dance and in the Salomania of the turn of the century.[17] The preponderance of scholarly attention, however, has concentrated on the later story of Allan's libel suit in 1918. Infamous in its own time, the libel suit has resurfaced in many post-1970s re-evaluations of the cultural, social, sexual, and even political consequences of the First World War.[18]

Given their focus on the war and its consequences, most studies of the libel suit ignore the prewar history of Maud Allan or treat it briefly as a prelude to the 1918 trial. Overall, they are inclined to treat Allan as a passive object, a cultural fraud who was made into a prewar icon of advanced taste by a worldly coterie of society ladies and homosexuals, only to be transformed by the radical right into a whipping boy for Asquith and his supporters in 1918. Moreover, scholars who have treated the 1918 proceedings as a cultural watershed have tended to concentrate on the transformative power of enunciated words and texts—the disputed evidence at the trial—at the expense of non-verbal performances such as Allan's embodied dance.

Allan was an iconic figure of fantasy, but she was also an active agent in the production of this fantasy. She was the bearer of the Wildean decadent legacy, but that is not all she stood for in the prewar years. By combining Greek neoclassical dance with her own original composition, the "Vision of Salome," Allan introduced a set of codes for female bodily expression that disrupted the Victorian conventional dichotomies of female virtue and female vice and pushed beyond such dualisms. She accomplished this shift by positioning herself outside a single national framework. Allan used the Orient as a register for female sensual expression, but she also built her dance from a range of other cultural forms, including American physical culture, theatrical posing, and modernist strategies of representation. Her hybrid display accounts in part for her capacity to attract an audience of men and women of radically different, even mutually exclusive, social constituencies, who were also participants in her creative enterprise. An exclusive focus on the 1918 trial obscures this wider cultural dimension of bodily expression, its interaction with prewar regulatory systems, as well as the implications of Allan's "boom" for the remapping of urban space. Not only did Allan's performances materialize a new femininity; they also facilitated the entry of respectable women into what one turn-of-the-century writer termed the "Night Side of London": the cosmopolitan spaces of the commercial West End.[19]

The Palace Theatre

In the Palace Theatre of Varieties, the built environment where Maud Allan danced, two meanings of cosmopolitanism were spatially and concretely expressed. Opened in 1891, and first launched as the Royal English Opera House in Cambridge Circus at the juncture of Shaftesbury Avenue and Charing Cross Road, the Palace was located in the center of late Victorian Theatreland (Figure 4). An exuberant expression of Victorian commercial enterprise, featuring a terracotta facade in the Northern Renaissance style, the building remained the only structure of "distinction" and "beauty" along the Charing Cross Road, a Victorian street improvement that opened in 1887 to facilitate the flow of London traffic between north and south.[20] While its ornamental facade and interiors blended a wide range of European and orientalist historical styles, the Palace also distinguished itself by its modern American steel-frame construction, electric lighting, and air filtration system.[21] Built by the impresario Richard

4 Facade of the Palace Theatre of Varieties, formerly the New Opera House. From "The New Opera House," *Illustrated London News*, January 31, 1891, p. 131. Decorated in a Northern Renaissance revival style, the Palace Theatre was part of the expansion of a sophisticated heterosocial nightlife in London. First launched by theater impresario Richard D'Oyly Carte as the New Opera House in 1891, it sought a wider public and eventually became a variety theater in 1893.

D'Oyly Carte for £150,000 to seat 2,000 spectators, who were spatially demarcated by class, the Royal English Opera House was part of the expansion of a sophisticated heterosocial nightlife in London. It was a luxurious analogue to another D'Oyly Carte enterprise, the Savoy Hotel Restaurant, the apex of gracious haute cuisine dining in London, a highly theatrical place to go to see and be seen, where men could be expected to dine with their wives.[22]

The official illustration of the theater's facade presents the Palace as a free-standing edifice, untarnished by any local street associations. Yet commentators frequently observed something dubious about the Palace Theatre's physical location, constructed as it was at a social crossroads along the eastern boundary of Soho. For the next century, the Palace Theatre would preside majestically over the southeastern entrance into Soho's labyrinthine streets (one of the two main entrances into Soho), surrounded along the avenue by industrial dwellings, secondhand bookstores, undistinguished-looking theaters, and pornography shops.[23]

This spatial liminality may have contributed to the commercial failure of D'Oyly Carte's theater as an opera house in 1891. Even more troubling than the physical location was the fact that the first year exhausted the supply of commercially appealing English operas. In 1892, under its new name, the Palace Theatre turned to international attractions: it featured a season devoted to the divine Sarah Bernhardt, whose enactment of Wilde's drama of *Salome* in French was banned at the last minute by the Lord Chamberlain, the theater censor, on the grounds that it depicted biblical characters on stage.[24] The following year, 1893, the Palace sought a wider public for its entertainments by transforming itself into a variety theater, thus repositioning itself within the leisure market as a site of gentlemen's entertainment.[25]

As a variety theater, the Palace no longer fell under the supervision of the theater censor but was instead subject to the restrictions of the London County Council and its inspectorate. This marked an important shift in political control, for the Progressives on the council were more responsive to the complaints of temperance and purity reformers than the Lord Chamberlain's office. Refused a liquor license by the council, the Palace management felt obliged to promote erotic display even more strenuously than its competitors in Leicester Square, the Empire and Alhambra theaters, which, as we have seen, advertised themselves as as "cosmopolitan clubs," populist extensions of the West End gentlemen's clubs.[26]

To compete with these attractions, the Palace revived tableaux vivants, also known as *poses plastiques* or Living Pictures, as a form of erotic entertainment in 1893.[27] Presented in a colossal gold frame and accompanied by music, female performers attired in flesh-tinted tights, their breasts often encrusted in plaster of Paris to evoke sculptures, would strike an "artistic" pose and stand silent and immobile for the delectation of the patrons of the music halls. Sometimes, the tableaux vivants would take their inspiration from genre and history paintings, but the most notorious ones were based on ancient Greek statuary, mythological subjects, or recent orientalist representations of the nude.[28] Despite the sensational exploitation of the genre in the music halls, female posing would also continue to be a respectable form of amateur entertainment, highlighting dramatic effect, emotional tension, and incipient action. As amateur theatrics, it would lead to developments from which early modern dance would emerge by the end of the century.[29]

Inspectors sent out by the London County Council to monitor Living Pictures in the variety theaters had difficulty evaluating the exhibits.[30] However, representatives of the National Vigilance Association, a social purity group with a strong feminist constituency, had no such qualms. In 1894, as we have seen,

Mrs. Chant and W. A. Coote challenged the dancing and entertainment license of the Palace Theatre before the licensing committee of the council.[31] Echoing contemporary discussions in the press concerning the salacious influence of French salon painting, Coote insisted that a demoralizing foreign influence was at work in the selection of original art works selected for reproduction on the Palace stage.[32]

Eventually the Palace license was renewed, but the Palace directors were cautioned to be more careful in the future. Despite these warnings, the Palace continued to promote Living Pictures throughout the 1890s and sustained a reputation for "candour concerning the human form."[33] However, in 1907, under renewed pressure from feminist social purity groups, the London County Council finally banned Living Pictures.[34] The Palace manager, Alfred Butt, looked for an act that would provide that candor yet escape the blue pencil of the censor. He invited Maud Allan to perform, as a kind of mobile substitute for Living Pictures, who would satisfy the cultural distinctions of high art but also manifest disturbing signs of animated modernity and sexuality.

Salome

As the star of the Palace Theatre, Allan achieved a much greater success in London than her North American competitors, Loie Fuller and Isadora Duncan.[35] Whatever the relative merits of their dancing, all three North Americans adopted similar strategies of self-advertisement as cultural innovators who engaged in discourse about their own art. They repudiated the ballet as mechanized technique, with low associations. Each projected herself as a freestanding artist, who managed her career, performed and choreographed her own dancing, made her own costumes, and danced to concert-grade Romantic music. Duncan and Allan enthusiastically embraced the trappings of international stardom, including sumptuous residences and world tours with elaborate retinues. Unlike Duncan, who only appeared in elite performance spaces with a simple curtain backdrop, Allan was willing to appear on the music hall stage, where she still relied on the decorative effects of stage furnishings and set design, particularly for her "Vision of Salome." Unlike Fuller, who covered herself up in billowing waves of cloth, Allan was willing to strip down to a diaphanous costume. Finally, in choosing the "Vision of Salome" as her featured number, Allan allied herself with the spirit and enterprise of Sarah Bernhardt, who had gained international renown twenty years earlier in London by impersonating exotic princesses bent on manipulating their sexuality for political ends, and by shamelessly engaging in self-promotion as a mobile, serpentine, modern woman.[36]

Fashioning Salome as her star role was a move that gave this American enter-tainer her credentials in exoticism and sexual display. It also linked her fortunes to Oscar Wilde, convicted of gross indecency in 1895, and to his *Salome* (1893), the part of Wilde's corpus most implicated in his "trial of the decade."[37] But Allan revised Wilde's play in ways that were at once more shocking than Wilde's rendering yet more accessible to a broad social constituency.

Wilde's *Salome* was a quintessentially cosmopolitan product: written in French and banned in England, it had made Wilde "a household word wherever the English language is *not* spoken."[38] It served as the libretto for the opera by Richard Strauss, who was attracted to the "inherent musicality," the incantatory and repetitive structuring of Wilde's text, as well as to its erotic possibilities.[39] Wilde's play differs from the biblical version in that it centers the story on Salome, who is less the instrument of her mother's revenge against John the Baptist than a desiring subject with a will of her own. Salome's dance is a pivotal element in the drama, but Wilde offers no description of it other than to state, in parentheses, "Salome *dances the dance of the seven veils*."[40] After dancing for her stepfather, Herod, Wilde's Salome demands the head of John the Baptist, who had rejected her erotic overtures. Herod orders John's head to be chopped off and delivered to the dancing princess on a silver plate. Salome makes love to the severed head, kissing it and declaring her love for it. Outraged, Herod orders his soldiers to kill her. Wilde's realization of the story clarified and highlighted a number of perverse sexualities associated with Salome, most notably her sadism, voyeurism, and fetishistic attachment to the head of John the Baptist.

Wilde's *Salome* was performed for 200 nights in Berlin in 1901, where Maud Allan claimed to have seen Max Reinhardt's highly visual and modernist produc-tion. Allan was clearly influenced by Reinhardt's staging: she seems to have lifted the sartorial idea of a transparent costume from his production while borrowing the conceit of jewel-encrusted breastplates from Mata Hari.[41] But there were striking innovations in her reassembling of this material. Allan performed Salome's dance not as the dance of the seven veils but as a dream sequence in which Salome re-enacts the events leading up to the beheading. "Drawn by an irresistible force," Salome "in a dream" descends the steps of Herod's palace to the strains of "weird" oriental music. She relives her dancing "triumph" before Herod when the head of John the Baptist appears to her as a phantasm. By all accounts, including Allan's own memoirs, the appearance of the head precipi-tates a "wild desire" in the virginal young Salome, a sensation "hitherto unknown to her." She caresses the head and then swoons in remorse, "a huddled—but still graceful, still beautiful—mass" (Figure 5). The dream conceit allowed Allan to collapse two of Wilde's scenes into one, the dance and the encounter with the

5 Salome with the head. "Is the Head Necessary?" asked *The Sketch* (March 25, 1908, supplement 3). The visual juxtaposition of Allan's mobile female body and the immobile, trunkless male head of the "Prophet" was the most shocking and climactic element of Allan's Salome performance.

head, thus eliminating Herod from the scene. The visual juxtaposition of a mobile female body and a very immobile, trunkless male head (a head without a heart) was the most shocking and climactic element of the performance.[42]

The well-oiled publicity machine of the Palace Theatre consolidated Allan's reputation by blurring aesthetic and erotic meanings attached to her dancing, but cleverly incorporating their traces in their promotions.[43] Overall, the British press response to Allan was quite restrained, to the effect that, yes, the dress was daring, the head of John the Baptist was a bit startling, but "the performance is absolutely free of offence."[44] It was here that Allan's "origins"—her Anglo-Saxonism—were displayed to great effect. Reviewers defended the artiste and her superior background against imputations of impropriety. Blame was attached instead to the provocative turns of her many foreign, commercial imitators, who proliferated on both sides of the Atlantic and who seemed to have copied her costume down to the last beaded fringe.[45] Reviewers also contrasted Allan's expressive dancing to the overly disciplined bodies of the well-drilled, precision dance troupe, the Palace Girls, who preceded her in the evening's program. Part of the John Tiller organization, the Palace Girls were recruited from the factory towns of the north of England; they specialized in prettiness, good teeth, and marvelous clockwork-like regularity of action.[46]

According to cultural critic Amy Koritz, this kind of publicity enabled Allan to get away with her Salome dance through a successful recategorization of the meanings and practices of her craft, enabling her to transform what was "Eastern" into something "Western" and what was "erotic" into something "spiritual."[47] From this recategorization, reviewers drew a political lesson. Because Allan could enact the art of the "East" without the "slightest suggestion of the vulgarity" so familiar to Cairo or Tangier, she could teach the British public about their own empire.[48] "We have the largest Eastern Empire the world has ever seen," declared a journalist. "[We have] to thank Miss Allan for beginning our education in a branch of art which we have persistently neglected."[49]

These comments point to Allan's insider/outsider role within the Imperial Nation. The polyvalent meanings of Allan's dancing entailed a more complex positioning within imperial culture than Koritz allows. Allan's dance united the empire and at the same time called attention to the multiple positions within it. Allan's identification as a Canadian Californian was critical to this revaluation. Her American body seemed to embody many of the qualities associated with Anglo-Saxonism: innocence, racial purity, and the cherished freedoms of a liberal political heritage, all values embraced by Chant and social purity feminists.[50] Approving testimonials to her American body and spirit appeared in press notices that drew attention to her wholesome upbringing in California, to "her natural litheness never ... checked or hampered by the wearing of a corset."[51] Similarly, it was her superior version of cosmopolitan Anglo-Saxonism that established Allan as a "piquant contrast" to the mechanized Palace dancers of the industrial North.

Allan both highlighted and obscured her North American identity when she defended her art in interviews and published memoirs.[52] She insisted that her Californian upbringing brought her close to nature and to the healthful simplicity of the Greeks, but she also asserted her status as an international star, unconstrained by local affiliations and indebted only to individual genius and the inspiration of the great art of the centuries. Like Duncan, she drew on the French symbolist formulations of dance as the "poetry of motion" to legitimate her own artistic practice. She celebrated dance as the "spontaneous expression of the spiritual state," a transcultural expression of some higher, less material realm, in which her body became an instrument for translating music and emotions into movement through a series of stationary poses and rapid movements.[53] Although up-to-date on contemporary aesthetic theory, she claimed to know nothing of the dance "technique of the day," the ballet. "I have sought all my attitudes and movement in the art galleries of Europe, on Etruscan vases and Assyrian tablets."[54] From all accounts, Allan's historical research translated into torso spiraling, rhythmic footwork, undulating arm gestures, and book-derived body postures, a set of movement techniques on display in both her classical and orientalist dancing. Discerning observers also noted that her dance was not drawn simply from the inspiration of the classical past, from the museums of Europe, and from French symbolist theory, but from American popular dance and physical culture, particularly the precepts and expressive strategies of François Delsarte.

Delsarte

Allan's Delsartean technique, underappreciated by historians, was key to her appeal for women. It linked her to the American women's health reform movement and to the amateur tradition of tableaux vivants. Her use of Delsarte was one way in which critics recognized her as an American dancing body, even though Delsarte itself was a cosmopolitan product, an aesthetic and performance theory for expressive movement developed by a French movement teacher, François Delsarte, and imported to the United States during the late nineteenth century. It was enormously popular in North America; it was taught in drama schools but also as an exercise program in women's institutes, the kind of venues visited by Mrs. Ormiston Chant on her American tours. Delsarte technique enabled middle-class women and girls to remake their bodies into noble bodies, into the "bodies of the best type."[55]

There is little doubt about Delsarte's influence on Allan. Delsarte's theories, Allan wrote, "teach us that every fibre, every vigorous impulse, every muscle and every feeling should have its existence so well defined that at any moment it can actually assert itself."[56] "Freedom through dance" was accomplished through "great strides, leaps and bounds, uplifted forehead, and far spread arms."[57] J. T. Grein, manager of the Independent Theatre and the music reviewer of the *Sunday Times*, recognized the Delsartean heritage:

> Good old Delsarte . . . forgotten in Europe, is having his day. For the Duncans and Maud Allans, *what else are they* but Delsartians. If proof were needed it would be easy to harmonize their every movement with the doctrines of the French aesthete and the fact that both ladies hail from the American continent where the Delsartian theory is taught in many girls' schools.[58]

Although Grein recognized an aesthetic vocabulary in Allan's dance, other newspaper critics were at a loss to discern any technique in her dance. Reviewers were alert to her dramatization of feeling and to her self-presentation as "unconscious of all save her dancing," but they were unable to mobilize any critical vocabulary to describe her movements in different parts of her repertoire.[59] Despite their respectful praise, reviewers subjected her body to an obsessive scrutiny. They took the occasion to comment on Allan's "beautiful sinuous movements," her "well-knit muscles," and her "uncompromising spine."[60] When they compared her dance to the "provocative posturing" of Eastern dancing from which it arose, they pitted one set of anatomical parts against another.[61] The languor and the sensuousness of her orientalist dance was mostly suggested "in the motions of the dancer's truly marvelous arms and hands, rather than by any writhings or sinuosities of the torso," explained one newspaper account.[62] To drive the point home, pictures of her arms, hands, as well as legs, not to speak of her bare feet, were reproduced in the magazines, where journalists countered Salome's fetishism with their own fetishism of the Salome dancer.

Visual artifacts of the period convey Allan's hybrid effects and allow us to fill in some of the documentary gaps about her performance. These photographs capture her dramatic expression; they also record the sensation of her "transparent" Salome costume and the highly realistic head used as a stage prop. In Figure 3 above, she is clad in an undulating, jangling costume, consisting of breastplates of pearls and jewels above her waist and a transparent black ninon skirt with chains of pearls strung around her hips. The costume did not so much

clothe her as "serve as ambient air wherein she floats," declared *The Times*.[63] And
the jangling costume must have accentuated any motion by establishing an
audible after-effect. Even in this still image, her movement is nonetheless
encoded in her body. The history of her performance is still visible in the
strained neck, the oppositional position of the arms, the twisting of the torso.[64]
Despite the orientalist costume, the pose echoes her portrait in classical garb
(Figure 6), suggesting the overlapping techniques and movements throughout
her dance program.[65]

These techniques derive from her Delsartean heritage. The kinesthetic expressiveness of Allan's dancing is powerfully conveyed by the sketches reproduced in
Figure 7. These newspaper illustrations of her classical repertoire adhere to an
Art Nouveau, Aubrey Beardsley style: they present an elongated, slender "S"
shaped body, dense hair juxtaposed to decorative squiggles at the bottom of her
draped costume. They delineate her mood changes in four classical dances that
interpret Romantic music from Mendelssohn's "Spring Song" to Grieg's "Peer
Gynt Suite." These illustrations testify to her ability to dramatize a range of
emotional states and personas. They also express the concept of freedom
through dance, described by one reviewer as a "wild Baccante intoxication of
joy."[66] Allan appears as a spiraling torso, head thrown back, in vigorous contrap-
osto. Finally, the sketch on the left of Figure 7 captures her will to power: it
pictures her as a force of nature hurtling through time.

Allan and Her Audience

In its cosmopolitan hybridity, its mobilization of a range of aesthetic theories
and representations of empire at home, Allan's "poetry of motion" appealed to
and reworked a range of gendered fantasies and sexual predilections. Photographs
of Allan document her rejection of the "stereotyped dancer's smile," her self-
absorption and disconnection from the audience. At the same time, they offer a
full frontal view and assert a boldness and assuredness about Allan's desirability.
One widely circulated photograph of Allan as Salome goes even further: it
captures Allan's trance-like state, evocative of the hysteric, the mystic, and the
autoerotic (Plate 3). She is dancing to please herself, yet encouraging and
enabling a voyeuristic gaze.

A wide range of women were drawn to her performance. These included well-
off ladies who had already made central London their trade route for daytime
shopping and who had begun to combine an evening visit to the Palace Theatre
with dinner or supper at the Savoy Hotel.[67] To accommodate demand, the
Palace also ran matinee shows devoted exclusively to Allan's dancing, where

6 Maud Allan in classical costume. From Maud Allan, *My Life and Dancing* (London: Everett, 1908). In classical costume, Allan repeats a Delsartean body posture that she assumes in her Salome theatrical photographs.

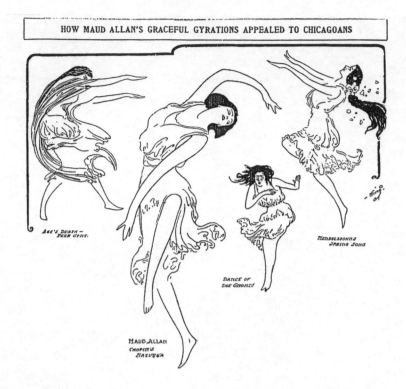

7 "How Maud Allan's Graceful Gyrations Appealed to Chicagoans," 1910. In this illustration, Allan appears as an elongated "S" shaped body who performs a range of mood changes in four classical dances. The sketch at the left strikingly captures her will to power.

smoking would not be permitted.[68] At these events, press commentators observed attending celebrity socialites, whose faces appeared in the photo-illustrated press. The press also noted humbler members of the consuming public, "girls in business" as well as suburban matrons and their daughters, out for a shopping day, equipped with their own binoculars.[69] An overlap with a female political public was also discerned. Commenting on one occasion, the liberal *Daily Chronicle*, which supported women's suffrage in 1908, estimated that at least 90 percent of the audience were ladies. "It might have been a suffragist meeting . . . the ladies were of all ages, well dressed, sedate."[70]

Lady Diana Cooper remembers going along to these ladies' matinees when she was a young girl, sent by her mother, the Duchess of Rutland, an aesthetic lady of heterodox taste. For Lady Diana, enthusiasm for Allan was part of an avant-garde passion for all things Greek, including Paul Poiret's Directoire fashions, newly imported from Paris, the opening gambit of Poiret's "war on corsets."[71] The uncorseted Allan was in tune with this fashion trend. "Maud

Allan had made a sensation at the Palace Theatre," Cooper wrote. "Greatly daring, she had appeared in a wisp of chiffon and bare legs with pipes and cymbals. My mother who despised the art of ballet [as practiced] by second rate dancers, was enthusiastic about this new Grecian frieze form of movement. She sent us weekly to watch and learn."[72]

Lady Diana also remembers another aristocratic admirer of Allan, Lady Constance Stewart Richardson, who went on to perform classical dancing on the London and New York stages in 1910, attired in her own wisp of chiffon.[73] Inhabiting what Diana Cooper later described as a "Greek boy's body," Lady Constance captured the exhibitionist edge of Allan's performance.[74] In Lady Constance's hands, Salome became not a means of advancing cosmopolitanism but of protesting the infiltration of Jewish cosmopolitans into elite London society. The actress Elizabeth Robins was present when Lady Constance arrived at a house party in London, dressed in the exact replica of Maud Allan's Salome costume.[75] To the king's great displeasure, she proceeded to demand the head of Sir Ernest Cassel, the king's Jewish personal financier, on a plate. By her gesture, Lady Constance highlighted the anti-Semitic components of Salomania that otherwise remained subdued in prewar Britain.[76] The intelligibility of Lady Constance's pantomime depended on a set of Jewish associations surrounding Salome, notably Salome's status as a historical Jewish princess and as a theatrical role long associated with Sarah Bernhardt, as well as the involvement of contemporary German-Jewish impresarios and financiers with stage and operatic productions of Salome in Great Britain and Germany.[77]

Allan's performance may have inspired an earl's daughter to take to the music halls (even as this same performer endeavored to restrict social access to other cosmopolitan bodies), but it also encouraged less privileged members of her adoring public, such as the schoolgirls who exchanged picture postcards of her and wrote of their "crush," to try out Allan's movements in the privacy of their own abodes.[78] When she serialized her memoirs in the Weekly Dispatch, a popular Sunday paper, Allan received bags of fan mail, which demonstrates how her performance broke down the distinction between dance as performance and dance as a participatory activity. A careful selection of the letters was republished in her newspaper column.[79] One letter, penned in a "girlish handwriting," stated, "I saw you and thought your dancing perfect. I tried to move my arms like yours, but they seemed to have much fewer joints."[80] This testimonial acknowledges recognition, stimulus towards body awareness, identification, emulation, and, of course, a failure to measure up to the international star's performance. It highlights dance's power of kinesthetic identification, clearly one source of pleasure attached to observing dance performances. Since Allan's technique was dominated by very familiar and recognizable movements, it was possible to return to a private space, take off one's stays, stockings, and shoes, and, with the help of a phonograph, combine "pleasure and physical culture."[81] Recommending her performance to its trade union supporters as a way to build "the Body Beautiful," the *Woman Worker* noted that Allan's "beautiful movements are the results of a series of regular and simple exercises."[82]

Allan also received a strange letter from a young man, part of another constituency drawn to her dancing, "who was earning his living in a City office":

> Madam ... I am a dancer (a natural dancer) of rather an exceptional nature, having met with great success privately or rather at private concerts on many occasions. I dance always as *a lady*. I am sure you will say at once what an extraordinary thing for a man to do; but, believe me, I am not effeminate.[83]

Published in a popular Sunday newspaper as an amusing, and slightly naughty, example of a cultural misreading, this letter signaled a particular constituency for her dance that the Palace Theatre had assiduously kept under wraps. Allan was a magnet for men who used the standing room in the back of the theater as a cruising ground to pick up other men. Cruising men may have been drawn to Allan's performance because of its association with Wilde's *Salome* but also because the variety theaters were well known to be spaces where "sodomites" circulated in the back with the "ladies of the night" and contributed to the frisson and ambiguity of this sexually charged environment.[84] Homosexual prostitutes often modeled their effeminate performance on sexually aggressive rough girls, including prostitutes.[85] The fact that Salome and Maud Allan were popular nicknames for transvestite "queens" and female impersonators of the Edwardian era further confirms Salome as a historical icon of sodomite subjectivity.

Ignoring the cruising in the back, the Palace Theatre used Allan's performance and image to recruit ladies as theater patrons. This strategy clearly paid off. The printed programs introduced in 1911 removed the ballet girl, the Palace's traditional house icon, from the cover and replaced her with Impressionist studies of a respectable and heterosocial audience. In a program cover from 1913, ladies and gentlemen in evening clothes pass a portrait of a scantily clad Maud Allan in the lobby; in a second cover, a man and a woman in the audience watch a stage where the figure of the female performer is barely visible. This image highlights the public intimacy and vital expressiveness of the couple. They have become the show itself, habitués of a new kind of heterosexual nightlife.[86] As part of a continuation of this strategy, the Palace next recruited Anna Pavlova, of the

Russian Imperial Ballet, who combined "the older traditional method" of the ballet with "the freedom that is demanded for the expression of emotional ideas."[87] With the appearance of Russian dancers in the music halls and the triumph of S. P. Diaghilev's company Ballets Russes at Covent Garden, a whole new epoch of dancing arrived in London. Expanding to meet the female demand inspired by Allan and Pavlova, dancing schools opened in unprecedented numbers, offering classes in social and theatrical dancing.[88] By this process, elite women and girls were incorporated into the world of dance; they in turn certified dancing's social respectability and authorized women of more modest means to take up theatrical dancing as a respectable occupation. Not only did dance move women into new metropolitan spaces; it also promoted British dancers as a "charming" export industry.[89] Thanks to the opening up of all those dance schools, British dancers became the primary staple for chorus lines throughout Europe—including the Folies Bergère.[90]

The elite female constituency that adored Allan and Pavlova also embraced a new form of social dancing, when the tango craze spread from Paris to London in 1913. Like ragtime dancing, tango was first performed on stage in 1912 as a dance number in *The Sunshine Girls*, and then refined, polished, and presented in a sophisticated form appropriate for social dancing, under the supervision of professional dance instructors.[91] Department stores like Selfridges lost no time in promoting new commodities associated with the tango—tango accessories and tango dresses in yellow and reddish-orange that required women to remove their steel-boned corsets.[92] Some newspaper correspondents denounced the tango and "the rag" as "horrors of American and South American negroid origin", and as threats to English moral fiber. These denunciations called forth a public defense of "modern dancing" as a display of a vital female individuality, the same expressive qualities, now aligned to heterosexuality, that enthusiasts had earlier discerned in Allan's dancing.[93]

Other Performances and Performance Sites

Allan's dancing had a cascading effect on other performance spaces. It set a new standard of high cultural performances of *Salome*, which provoked more controversy than Allan's own variety turn. In 1910, a production of Strauss's opera was staged at the Covent Garden Opera House, but only after the impresario Thomas Beecham persuaded Prime Minister Asquith to intercede with the theater censor.[94] The Lord Chamberlain permitted the performance on the condition that *Salome* appear in an abridged form. Consequently, a bloody sword was substituted for the decapitated head, and the character of John the

Baptist was renamed "The Prophet." Strauss's opera sold out less than an hour and a half after tickets went on sale. The production attracted a "distinguished audience," left "limp" by the performance.[95]

As a live production of Wilde's decadent, banned play, the opera met with a mixed critical reception. To convey their disgust, critics resorted to a medical lexicon of degeneration, dismissing *Salome* as the glorification of "erotomania," a "pathological study of a most unhealthy specimen."[96] Reviewers of the production were particularly disturbed and intrigued by the new importance attributed to Salome's dance. Thanks to Allan and the Salomania she had helped incite, Salome's dance had become vital to the expression of this modern female sexual subjectivity. Mme. Acté followed the example set by Mary Garden in New York at the Manhattan Opera House in 1909 and insisted on performing the dance herself, attired in a costume closely resembling the outfit adopted by Allan and her imitators: "barbaric" jewels, diaphanous skirt, breastplates, and snake bracelets.[97]

The success of Strauss's opera at Covent Garden clearly emboldened another group of Edwardian women, feminist actresses, to enact the modernity of Salome and her dance, this time along lines more compatible with militant feminism, and this time provoking an even more critical response from the press. On February 27 and 28, 1911, a private matinee production of Wilde's "banned" play was staged at the Court Theatre by a group called The New Players. This was the third time a private production of Wilde's play had been staged in London, but the first time it had been produced in a "real theatre."[98] The performance was organized by Adeline Bourne, the honorary secretary of the Actresses' Franchise League, who assumed the leading role.[99]

In reviewing the play, the press emphasized the illicit status of the production. A society within a society had arranged for its members to "evade the Censorship by giving private performances of unlicenced plays in public places" and to "wallow in sufficient sensuality to last a lifetime."[100] Reviewers also noted that mostly women were in attendance, including a large contingent of society ladies and well-known actresses. Turning their attention to the performance, critics dismissed Bourne's acting as strident and overwrought and her dancing as "not seductive enough."[101] "It was a sorry spectacle," declared the *Penny Illustrated Paper*, fit only for "sexless women and pussycat men."[102] The critics, moreover, associated the sexual aggression of her performance with the militant spirit of the suffragettes. *The Bystander* condemned Bourne's conception of the part as absurdly contemporary and a distortion of its fin-de-siècle spirit: Wilde's Salome, it declared, was "not a twentieth-century suffragette attempting an entrance into the House of Commons or asking for Mr. Winston Churchill's head on a charge sheet."[103] Conversely, the militant *Votes for Women* defended her contemporary rendition of a modern political princess: "Miss Bourne, who looked very charming in her Eastern dress, was terrible as an army with banners."[104]

Bourne's performance challenges conventional historical understandings of the kind of iconography then available to feminism. Like Allan, suffragists made a public spectacle of themselves and tried to control the terms of that spectacle, but they significantly differed from Allan in their desire to forge a civic body, "an army," out of the ornamental, expressive bodies of women.[105] Suffragists wanted to modernize women by making them into healthy, rights-bearing, national subjects, not, like Allan's Salome, sensuous, desiring selves, free of territorial constraints. Allan, avowedly no suffragist, aligned herself with the rebellious cultural modernism of Margot Asquith and her set, who celebrated a mobile, expressive individualism but disparaged the aims and methods of political feminism.[106]

The feminist production of *Salome* in 1911 unsettled these divisions.[107] By appropriating Salome, feminist actresses not only transformed her morbidity into a feminist war cry; they also detached her from the anti-suffragist milieux of the music hall and smart society circles that patronized Allan. While feminist actresses may have had a number of professional motivations for staging this performance, they brought Salome under the sign of Militant Woman, rendering her a new icon for the expanding militant operations of the Women's Social and Political Union, which had stepped up its campaigns of window smashing, arson, and political disruption in the streets of central London.[108]

The New Players' engagement with Salome signaled a new formation within feminist ranks. A younger generation of feminists was drawn to Salome's dance, because women could embrace it as their own cultural form and use it to claim possession of their own erotic gaze, albeit a hostile and aggressive one.[109] This marked a significant departure from the prevailing agenda of social purity feminists, such as Mrs. Chant, who labored to control and expose male vice but not to expand the opportunities for female sexual expression.[110] Sensing a cultural alteration, critics wasted no time in denouncing Bourne's Salome as an incitement to female sensual excess: witness the press condemnation of the Court production as "strident," "hysterical," and "crazily erotic."[111]

The Cult of the Clitoris

Ultimately, the female dancer's association with disorderly sex and politics, with cultural deceit and political treason, began to collect around the figure of Allan herself. An international traffic in rumors started on the Continent even before her visit to London in 1908.[112] But in 1910, different allegations of sexual misconduct began to percolate in the American press. The rumors emphasized the homoerotic overtones of her female following in London. In 1908, the *New York Times* reported on "Salome Dinner Dances" in Mayfair, restricted to ladies only, all of whom dressed up in a Maud Allan costume and performed for each other, as if they were women in a harem.[113] The American news media also exposed Allan's family secret, the fact that her brother was a murderer.[114] Finally, during the months she toured the United States in 1910, the American press discussed Allan's relationship with Prime Minister Asquith and his wife, noting the unseemly entry into the higher echelons of society and politics that Allan had gained through Mrs. Asquith and this lady's excessive attachment to the dancer. News coverage and illustrations even implied that Allan had participated in a *ménage à trois* with the Asquiths (Figure 8).[115]

In the prewar period, these rumors seemed to have been largely contained, at least in the public media, on one side of the Atlantic. But they prepared the ground for a frontal assault on what was perceived to be the perversity,

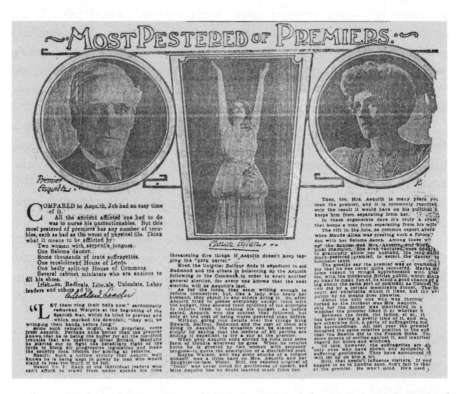

8   Allan and the Asquiths: "Most Pestered of Premiers," in which the prime minister is compared to Job. American news coverage of Allan in London included rumors of Allan's involvement in a *ménage à trois* with the Asquiths.

degeneracy, and political danger of Maud Allan's cosmopolitanism during the last days of the First World War. In 1918, J. T. Grein announced that he had recruited Allan for the lead role in a private performance of Wilde's *Salome* in London at the Court Theatre. The *Vigilante* responded with its infamous "Cult of the Clitoris." Its attack on Allan as a member of a coterie of sexual perverts, vulnerable to German blackmail, and hence potentially traitors, implicated other prominent individuals, notably Grein, a nationalized citizen of Jewish Dutch descent, and the Asquiths. The article, Allan wrote in 1921, was "part of a campaign to get rid of Asquith"; particular "venom" was "manifested against his wife," who had been accused of fraternizing with German prisoners of war. "The whole was a subtle suggestion that anti-British influences had surrounded the wife of the prime minister, and that I was mainly responsible."[116] Although Grein warned her against taking legal action, Allan persisted in bringing a libel suit that ended in disaster for herself and her friends.

The courtroom drama at the Old Bailey occupied the attention of the press for six days in June 1918 after the initial proceedings at Bow Street Police Court. Interest focused, first of all, on the elite coterie of society and political leaders "whose names were bandied about" at the trial and whose presence in the courtroom was signaled by newspaper descriptions of the "fashionable queue waiting outside Bow-street."[117] Acting for the prosecution, Hume Williams declared that the editor, Noel Pemberton Billing, "maliciously published a false and defamatory libel concerning Maud Allan." Williams introduced Allan as the "pioneer of the kind of classic Grecian form which was intended to have a meaning and express a poem" and cited her "Vision of Salome" as an example of this dignified art form. Williams allowed that Wilde's play was "unpleasant" and "unattractive," even "horrible," but denied that it contained any suggestions of the "Lesbian or Sodomite practices" that formed the basis of Billing's slanderous allusions to the "Cult of the Clitoris."[118]

Following Williams's opening remarks, Allan entered the dock. Under his questioning, she recounted the history of her performance and insisted that her dance had nothing "to do with Wilde's Salome."[119] Acting in his own defense, Billing proceeded to cross-examine her. Through innuendo and scandalous revelations pertaining to her private life, most notably her "degenerate" family history and her ambiguous relations with Margot Asquith, Billing set about building a case for Allan's perversion and for her participation in a cult of high-ranking "moral perverts." He further tried to discredit her by questioning her about her German education, her knowledge of sexological terminology, and her immersion in symbolic expression. At the trial, Billing was able to expose secrets of Allan's private life that had been publicly suppressed in prewar Britain. He was even able to defy strict wartime censorship codes and present what many newspapers described as "promiscuous innuendoes" about the disloyalty of important personages. Billing clearly benefited from a growing public distrust of wartime censorship and propaganda; the strict control of information fed the flames of gossip and made spy stories, including this one, thinkable (as did the execution of Mata Hari as a German spy in France in 1917).[120]

Ironically, Allan was punished for seeming to possess too much knowledge, particularly knowledge of a dangerous cosmopolitan variety. In particular, Allan was faulted for her familiarity with foreign medical knowledge—even though her opponents themselves heavily depended on the authority of continental sexology to make their case against her. The sexological tradition informed the specific accusation that Allan was catering to a "cult of the clitoris." Sexology treated an enlarged clitoris as a conventional symptom of lesbian anatomy, associated with female "hypersexuality" and a masculinized, degenerate condition. The fact that she understood what clitoris meant was cited as proof of Allan's own complicity in the "cult of the clitoris."[121]

In this way, Allan came to personify a tainted cosmopolitanism, one associated with disease, rootlessness, and the unplaced. *Salome*, declared the *Morning Post*, was a drama of "disease" and deracination. "These perversions have no home in the healthy mind of England . . . Far from being a typical English work it is abhorrent to every English instinct . . . They have, like scum on water, a floating root in the international population which drifts between capital and capital."[122] A similar line of argument was used against Allan's training in Germany and her introduction of "German" dancing into England, a type of dancing, Billing insisted, that "was quite foreign to the British public" before her performance.[123] To the jury, this reasoning seemed to justify Billing's charge of perversion.

At this time of national scandal, Justice Darling, the sitting judge, rather surprisingly invoked British feminism as the antidote to dangerous cosmopolitanism. After the jury delivered their verdict, Darling took the occasion to deplore the kind of dances and the kind of costumes worn by Allan. He then noted that in "a short time women will be able to have their influence upon legislation, and . . . I hope they will make it their business to see that much more purity is introduced into public representations than is the case at present."[124]

Previous critics have seen the trial as a simple repudiation of cosmopolitanism, but the picture is more complex. Billing's critique of Allan's cosmopolitanism detached her performance from one set of geopolitical associations—the cultural work of a noble, modern Anglo-Saxon body—and highlighted another set, her participation in a perverse fifth column of cosmopolitan, elite traitors in thrall to

German interests. This version of cosmopolitanism not only pushed her outside the boundaries of the nation; it even alienated her from her North American roots. It made her "foreign," as foreign as her Jewish predecessor, Sarah Bernhardt, and aligned her racially to what Billing described as the "German-Jewish" interests who promoted Salome productions and who were protected by the present government.[125]

However startling they appeared at the time, the trial proceedings actually reproduced some of the prewar meanings attached to Allan's performance, while giving them a new political salience. The trial limited the dynamic effects of her dance to a private, elite cult, whereas her performance had promoted a new body idiom to a diverse metropolitan audience. Allan's prewar cultural status depended on a blurring of multiple meanings of cosmopolitanism. The mass illustrated press was complicit in this blurring. It promoted Allan's dancing as art, while still conveying, in words and images, the multiple sexualities it put on display and its titillating effects on men and women. In other words, Allan's "perversion" was always in the air, attached to the dark side of her performance, but was held in check by other elements of her Delsartean performance. The ambiguities of Allan's cultural effects would further intensify, as diverse social constituencies took up her style, including vulgar, voluptuous commercial imitators, schoolgirls who emulated her Body Beautiful, young men who danced as ladies. Allan's performance set a precedent for high cultural productions as well. Allan's solo performance paved the way for Pavlova as a prestige turn at the Palace, while it also shaped and incited the operatic and theater productions of Salome at Covent Garden and the Court Theatre, condemned by critics in sexological terms as degenerate and crazily erotic.

Besides narrowing the set of meanings that Allan helped promote, the trial also repositioned feminism in the field of body politics. Billing and his cohorts usurped the role played by liberal feminist campaigners such as Mrs. Ormiston Chant in attacking vicious foreign entertainments; his right-wing journal, The Vigilante (renamed from The Imperialist) even pirated its title from the National Vigilance Association.[126] Darling undoubtedly had this strong feminist tradition in mind (as well as the hyper-patriotism of leading suffragists like Emmeline and Christabel Pankhurst during the war) when he expressed his hopes for the salutary effects of women's suffrage on public morality.[127] As disciplined members of the nation, he implied, mature women could be expected to police the unruly young women who had been part of Allan's following.

When he counterposed Allan to the suffragists, Darling obscured how feminist purity efforts were part of the deep background to Allan's story in London. Feminist purity opposition to Living Pictures precipitated the Palace Theatre's interest in Allan in the first place, as the management sought a form of female bodily display acceptable to a municipal government strongly responsive to purity interests. The judge's endorsement of women's suffrage, moreover, ignored the degree to which feminists and Allan shared many cultural values: a commitment to female self-expression and mobility, an engagement with a theatrical culture of female spectacle, an ideal of female bodily health and physical culture, but also a capacity to represent female anger and hostility to men. Also passing unnoticed by Darling was the 1911 feminist performance of *Salome*, signaling the emergence of a radical feminism devoted to individualist sexual expression and to disrupting the categories of virtue and vice that sustained Victorian womanhood.

Besides registering a selective memory about feminism and its discontents, Darling's remarks tell us something about the class and cultural logic governing female enfranchisement in 1918, when the Representation of the People Act extended the national franchise to adult men and to women over thirty who were householders or the wives of householders.[128] The law distinguished responsible matrons from the disenfranchised adult, a young woman between twenty-one and thirty, who came to be designated as "the flapper"—with all the allusions to dancing and to a new female body image, "overexposed" and "underdeveloped," that this catchword conveyed in the 1920s. Justice Darling may have anathematized Allan as representative of an elite group of idle, disloyal, pleasure-seeking women, but he simultaneously endorsed a law that disenfranchised ordinary, young women—the female munitions workers central to the war effort—as giddy, unthinking devotees of unseemly dancing.[129]

Conclusion

As the 1918 trial and the disenfranchisement of the "flapper" amply demonstrate, dance was a vehicle for shifting cultural and political identifications of gender and the national body in the early twentieth century. The story of dance is the story of avant-garde cosmopolitanism in the metropolis, but it also the story of the domestication of transnational cultural forms into a national culture. In 1918, the flapper, with her new body image of youthful, sexual ambivalence, signaled the domestication of the modern kinetic female body and its cosmopolitan subversion.

Besides transforming gendered bodily idioms, the dancing revolution set into motion by Allan and other international stars also reordered the metropolitan leisure economy and contributed to a new kind of nightlife for women as well as men. In prewar years, it sent elite women to the tea dances and dinner dances at the Grand Hotels, where they danced publicly amid tables of seated diners and even hired male partners employed by the establishment.[130] Dancing also moved respectable women into heretofore forbidden spaces of the nocturnal city.[131] When the new dancing culture came under wartime siege, some of it relocated from the publicly licensed venues to more circumscribed and clandestine arenas, to new social spaces outside the law, most of them sited in liminal, cosmopolitan Soho. A raffish nightlife emerged, where social elites mixed with lowlife types, heterosexual and homosexual couples bumped up against each other, and drugs and alcohol were readily available.[132] As these dancing establishments prolifer-ated, they forged links with other nighttime commercial spaces, encouraging dining out and other bodily appetites that advanced the local careers of Soho's ethnic entrepreneurs.

CHAPTER 4

The Italian Restaurant

DURING THE "MAUD ALLAN BOOM", MANY OF THE RICHLY CLAD LADIES and gentlemen who had attended Allan's "nude" performance went on to dine at sumptuous West End restaurants. Or they opted for after-theater suppers at the more intimate "little places" located behind the Palace Theatre in Soho. Both theater and dining engaged Londoners in public performances of gender, imaginative expatriation, sensory stimulation, and social distinction. The bodily rituals at table depended on the supporting roles of wait staff who were themselves savvy practitioners of cosmopolitan taste. They were increasingly composed of northern Italians who had migrated to London in hopes of moving up the hierarchy of the catering trade and ultimately opening a Soho restaurant.

Soho's Italian entrepreneurs, the main protagonists of this chapter, helped to sustain Soho's reputation as "London's escape from English cooking."[1] They moved between the decorous front stages of Soho's food industry and its gritty back regions. Soho's catering establishments may have provided stage sets for English fantasies of travel and escape, but they were also places of hard work and strict regimentation for the immigrants employed there. Subject to global market conditions, economically exploited by their own countrymen, working under modern militaristic systems of labor to produce foreign food for English consumption, immigrant catering workers seemed to embody the "discrepant cosmopolitans" described by anthropologist James Clifford.[2] Alternatively they could also lay claim to a second, worldly, knowing connotation of cosmopolitanism. They were skilled in the demands of display, decor, and performance required by the international portable food culture they supplied. Their immersion in the world of food subjected them to intense work discipline, but it enabled some individuals to become entrepreneurial purveyors of good taste.

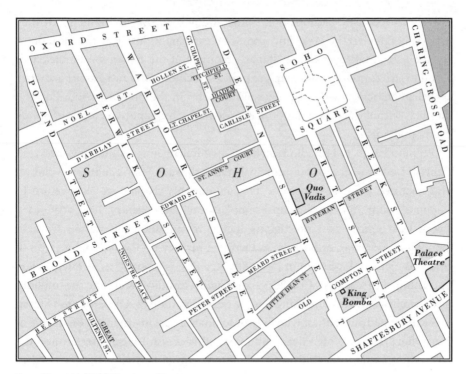

Dean Street and Old Compton Street

Soho's culinary trade manifested durable features that persisted well beyond the Great War. For the most part, interwar proprietors of Soho's eateries were prewar immigrants who had made their way up the catering trade. They still exploited the winning combination of old world charm, economical menus, and Soho's Georgian architectural quaintness to attract Londoners to the district as they had prior to the war. During the Roaring Twenties, however, Soho's restaurateurs also adapted to a new set of trends, involving decor, clientele, culinary styles, and shifts in immigration patterns. Proprietors of Soho eateries additionally faced the challenges of competing forms of nightlife, commercialized sex, and corrupt policing.

Equally significant, Soho's restaurateurs accommodated the penetration of the catering trade by Italian Fascism. Italian migrants to London were not merely imbedded in an international market of bodies and goods, but in nationalist and internationalist politics, intimately linked to the catering industry. Like other émigrés from the Italian peninsula, Soho's Italians learned to be Italian in exile, creating a nationalist politics out of their diasporic experience.[3] Food systems were especially important in forging this national identity. During the interwar period, Fascists used the portable food culture of Italy as a vehicle to solidify a fiercely nationalistic patriotism at home and abroad. Beginning in 1921, they especially targeted the West End and Soho catering industry as the focal point for the Fascist takeover of the "Italian colony." But the Italian food industry of London also supported other émigré politics, including the anti-Fascist activities of Italian anarchists who had migrated to Soho in the prewar period. Political conflicts within the Italian diaspora exposed the divergent trajectories of Soho's cosmopolitanism.

Peppino Leoni and Emidio Recchioni, two Italian émigrés and long-time residents of London, serve as our principal guides through Soho's culinary evolution and fractured political landscape. Throughout this chapter, we shall return to Peppino Leoni's life story as an exemplary migrant's history. For forty years, Leoni was Soho's most prestigious Italian restaurateur. He started work in London as a *commis*, or busboy, and worked his way up the restaurant ranks to open his own establishment in Dean Street, and was interned as an enemy alien and nominal Fascist in 1940.[4] Our second guide, Emidio Recchioni, the "millionaire anarchist" owner of the King Bomba provision shop on Old Compton Street, was a dedicated anti-Fascist who helped to finance various attempts on the life of Mussolini.[5] The two men lived and operated successful businesses around the corner from each other in the southeastern corner of Soho. Both arrived in London from northern Italy before the Great War. Both chose London because of their connection with Italian émigrés who were already established there. Together their histories shed light on Soho's burgeoning catering industry, its production of hybrid, mimetic Italian cookery, and the political conflicts that erupted within the Italian diaspora in this compressed space.

The Boy from Lake Maggiore

In 1907, Peppino Leoni arrived in London as a penniless boy of fifteen from his native town of Cannero, near Lake Maggiore in Italy. By the time he was twenty-seven he was headwaiter at the Savoy Hotel, the apex of luxurious, gracious international dining in London. In 1926, he opened Quo Vadis on Dean Street, Soho, with seven tables in one room. His first day's takings were only 12s, but within two years, he had built up a loyal and highly distinguished clientele sustained throughout the Depression. Over the next decade, Leoni conducted a successful "one-man show" that enabled him to expand his restaurant over four houses and to accommodate upwards of 200 patrons.[6] Leoni's Quo Vadis became famous for its elegant silver service, its appealing cuisine, its celebrity guests, the art exhibited on its walls, and the charming manners of its host.

Leoni's autobiography, *I Shall Die on the Carpet* (1967), presents a rags-to-riches story, a narrative of hard work and material success recounted by a catering entrepreneur who intended to work until he dropped. In this life history, family, and personal attachments take a back seat to the story of the restaurant. To explain his culinary ambitions and migratory wanderlust, Leoni returned to his peasant boyhood in Cannero, located in a "borderland" between Lombardy and Piedmont in Italy and Ticino in Switzerland. A depressed economic backwater, Cannero was also a destination site on the Grand Tour, an international contact zone between English tourists and mobile Italian workers.[7]

While working in the bottom rung of Cannero's tourist economy as a dishwasher and galley boy, Leoni encountered two representatives of the modern world of gastronomy. One group consisted of well-dressed strangers, with thick, gold chains spanning their well-fed stomachs, who greeted people in the local dialect.[8] They were natives of Cannero who had gone to England, prospered as restaurateurs and returned.[9] A second group of strangers also broadened young Peppino's horizons and made him dream of London. They were English tourists on holiday who impressed Peppino with their calm, polite, and cultivated ways. Peering into the windows of the hotel, the peasant boy was astonished to see the elaborate ritual of the British at table. These strangers always dressed for dinner: the men in evening jackets, the women in evening gowns and sparkling jewels. Peppino watched the progressive, hierarchical sequence of dishes unfold, accompanied by an intimate silver service of silent, deferential waiters who assisted the guests in their bodily performances.[10] The silver service required an extraordinary output of labor: plates were filled and brought to table by a slow progression of waiters emerging out of the kitchen. "What a job the washing-up must be I thought, as course followed course and the carefully aligned parade of cutlery on the tables diminished." And then there was the question of where the guest managed to put so much food, as fish followed soup, to be followed by poultry and then meat, a sweet, savory, and finally fruit.[11]

Hotel dining was completely removed from Leoni's own food habits. At home, and in most restaurants catering for ordinary Italians (such as the one where he had cleaned glasses), "we just had a knife, fork and spoon and if there happened to be more than one course, wiped the used implements with a piece of bread."[12] His one-dish meal would consist of polenta, flavored by herbs, with onions, peppers, or sardines as condiments. Pasta, legumes, wine, dairy products, or fresh produce would be consumed less frequently, while meat and wine only appeared at most on special occasions.[13] This food regime was monotonous, constrained by poverty, and nutritionally inadequate. After the Second World War, a more generous and balanced version of this peasant diet would gain popularity as the Mediterranean diet of choice among the English middle classes, but it would take some strategic supplements of dairy, meat, and fresh produce, pioneering food journalism, and an age of abundance to render it fashionable.[14]

Produced by intensive kitchen preparation and devoted to ostentatious consumption, the dinner at the Cannero hotel was premised on an entirely different cultural and economic logic. The luxurious hotel cooking was undoubtedly a hybrid gastronomy heavily indebted to French haute cuisine that set the standard of international fine dining.[15] With its long connection to the House of Savoy, Piedmont was the region where French cuisine first penetrated the Italian peninsula. The meal may have included some regional specialties—such as grissini, fonduta, or truffles—but other ingredients would have been imported from international food supplies.[16] Indeed, the young Leoni did not interpret this elaborate production to be French so much as it was foreign. He looked on the intricate ritual as an import to satisfy British taste and whose prototype was to be found in London, not Paris.

Peppino was able to find out more about London's cuisine when he rowed the English gentlemen out on the lake in his father's boat. He started off by asking them about England, and particularly London; they responded with tales of the big city—its teeming population, congested traffic, its streets brilliantly lit by gas. Then he asked them about the hotels and restaurants. They reeled off a list of luxurious and expensive establishments, many of them with Italian names. They may well have mentioned Gatti's in Adelaide Gallery in the Strand, which introduced the fashion of the Swiss-Italian restaurant, or Romano's in the Strand, a favorite haunt of theatrical people and clean-shirted Victorian bohemia, or Pagani's in Upper Regent Street, initially catering to visiting Italian singers and musicians but soon attracting metropolitan patrons with its "artist's room," lined with panels signed by painters, writers, and musicians.[17] Their conversation could have turned to the monster marble palaces in Piccadilly Circus owned by the Monico brothers and by Auguste Oddenino, establishments that were magnets for demi-mondes and young bloods on the town. All these places were "cosmopolitan" in their social mix: "you could meet everybody there if you chose. You could dine, lunch or sup in an atmosphere of complete respectability; but in and around it were crooks, con men, racecourse gangs and tough characters of all sorts."[18] Most of these restaurants purveyed French cuisine; only Pagani's was especially known for Italian cuisine.[19] These stories of Italian restaurateurs fired up Peppino's dream to open up a fashionable restaurant in London.

To realize his dream, Leoni joined the regional chain migration of transalpine Italians who set out to try their fortunes in London. Every year, wrote travel writer Mrs. Eliza Cook in 1902, Alpine peasants, most of them from the Ticino canton in Switzerland, underwent a "cruel and comfortless expatriation."[20] Emigrating from "their romantic valleys to our foggy shores," they hoped to prosper in the "golden land" of England.[21] In London, Mrs. Cook saw the new arrivals, "worn and shabby," waiting in the "pitiful black line of seedy applicants" outside the big London establishments, such as Monico, Gatti's, or Oddenino's.[22] Gatti and Monico were both *padroni*, employers who recruited young Italian boys to come to London, paid their passage, found them accommodation, and employed them as contract labor.[23] Mrs. Cook also noted that the metropolitan destination of these nomads was not the old Italian quarter of Clerkenwell, where an earlier generation of Italian migrants in itinerant trades had settled and built their church, but Soho and the West End, the center of the catering trades.[24]

Leoni's entry into London was shaped by material and social factors, but also by an imaginary version of the city. Like many transalpine migrants arriving after 1900, Leoni traveled directly to London, passing over France and Germany (he would later feel compelled to return to Europe to learn languages and gain experience). He did not seem to have been recruited by a *padrone*, but his journey was punctuated by strategic encounters with cosmopolitan representatives of Cannero's diaspora. Family connections were key elements of his migration. The young boy had persuaded a relative to loan him the £6 necessary to migrate to London. He then wrote to another distant relative in London, who assured him that there was no problem about accommodation or work possibilities once he arrived in the metropolis.[25] Arriving at Charing Cross station, Leoni went in search of a residence, equipped with an "address" and the visual memory of a map of central London drawn for him by a Cannero chef with a stick on a dusty road. The map showed him how to get from Charing Cross station to Whitfield Street, off Tottenham Court Road, where lodgings had been arranged for him.

Outside Charing Cross station, Leoni quickly learned to negotiate the menacing street traffic of the Strand and Oxford Street. He realized he could successfully protect himself by keeping in the middle of the crowd and crossing over with it when it surged forward. A migrant worker and not a tourist, he was so intent on reaching his destination that he ignored the London sights along the way that organized the cognitive map of most visitors. Yet his ability to traverse the imposing Strand by "staying in the middle" and merging with the crowd demonstrated a keen adaptation to metropolitan forms of mass self-regulation.[26]

Once he reached his lodgings in Whitfield Street, Leoni's depression vanished when he was greeted with "Italian voices", and the lodging-house keeper from Cannero offered him a cup of tea. Despite the reassuring welcome, Leoni soon discovered that he had not found a refuge in a heartless world. The tea, interpreted by him as an act of hospitality, was charged to his weekly bill. The cash nexus structured daily life and social relations within the Italian colony of London even more completely than it did in Cannero. The landlord arranged for him to go to Canterbury to work for a Swiss Italian from the Locarno area, but this first entry into the catering world turned out to be a disaster. Instead of offering Leoni 10s in wages, as he had been promised, the Canterbury restaurant owner insisted on paying him only 5s, barely enough for lodgings. Leoni returned to London and started over again, this time applying to one of the Soho employment exchanges, which sent him to another Swiss Italian restaurant in suburban Streatham, where he was again employed as a *commis débarrasseur*, a busboy.

London's Restaurant World

Leoni thus began his movement up the hierarchy of the restaurant world, a journey that would take him to suburban cafés, the monster restaurants of the West End, and the miniature foreign places of Soho, not to speak of grand ocean liners and resort hotels around Europe. Each of these metropolitan spaces represented distinct but overlapping market niches in London's catering world, offering different conditions of labor. In his survey of the victualing industry, Charles Booth was struck by the enormous earning differentials in West End catering, a consequence of skills, training, and experience as well as the status of the employer. Cooks and cellarmen earned from £2 to £20 a week ("it goes without saying that the majority of chefs are French," Booth reported).[27] For waiters, the figures were £1 or £2 to £20, while kitchen and scullery boys received 6s to 12s.[28]

Leoni's first place of employment, where he earned 5s a week, was a typical Swiss café that offered English fare with continental service—a "chop, a steak, or plate of meat . . . for 1s 6d to 2s."[29] Mrs. Cook credited these Alpine Italians with the "vast reform" in moderately priced dining places in London.[30] These eateries dotted the major thoroughfares throughout London and even spread to the suburbs.[31] They were interchangeably decorated with "pink and green glasses, silver slabs of plat[ed] ware, marble-topped tables, windows of coloured glass, sharply folded linen napkins, a mural design of an Alpine scene."[32]

Before long, Leoni entered a second market niche: the luxury restaurants of the West End. He moved on to the Savoy Hotel Restaurant, again as a *commis*, starting work each day at 6 a.m. and finishing by 11 p.m. According to Leoni, a lowly job like this was the ambition of every Italian who came to London, even if one went temporarily down in rank, because it allowed him to gain experience in elite catering, while slightly increasing his income from tips.[33]

Whereas Swiss cafés served versions of British cooking for moderate prices with continental service, luxury establishments like the Savoy overwhelmingly purveyed French haute cuisine. The British, food historians tell us, were the primary audience outside of France for this elite form of dining during the nineteenth century.[34] By 1890, there were 5,000 French chefs involved in elite cooking in England. For the cultural elite, the "standard set piece fancy meal was French in language, French in organization, prepared by Frenchmen, and basically French in taste."[35] Haute cuisine abandoned the strong flavors of Renaissance cooking in favor of food characterized by "lightness" and "refinement," achieved through the advance preparations of stocks and sauces, knife skills, and the use of heat sources such as reduction and braising. The diffusion of French haute cuisine in England, begun in the eighteenth century, gained momentum during the Napoleonic era and restoration, when noble households and the gentlemen's clubs of London regularly employed French chefs as a sign of membership in a cosmopolitan elite. Four celebrity chefs, Careme, Ude, Francatelli, and especially Soyer, the chef at the Reform Club, gained public fame through cookbooks and press coverage of their grand banquets.[36] But it would take a later generation of émigré chefs and hoteliers led by the theater impresario Richard D'Oyly Carte to establish the "restaurant habit" in London for mixed dining in public.[37]

In 1889 D'Oyly Carte built the Savoy Hotel and Restaurant over his theater in the Strand to encourage a link between eating and theatergoing. At the time of its construction, the Savoy was the most deluxe hotel in London, the most celebrated of grand hotels constructed in the central district.[38] With an eye towards the lucrative American tourist market, D'Oyly Carte incorporated all the modern comforts, such as electricity, elevators, bedrooms with en suite baths, as well as steel and concrete construction, into the hotel's design. Once it became successful, the Savoy inspired massive competitors such as the Ritz, Cecil, Berkeley, and Piccadilly, built along Green Park, Piccadilly, and the newly constructed Northumberland Avenue. No longer resting places for the weary traveler, these hotels were cosmopolitan destinations of pleasures that built their reputation around their restaurants.

D'Oyly Carte succeeded in attracting American visitors, but he had to work hard to persuade London society ladies to dine in public and even organize their own private parties in his restaurant. As a theater impresario, he constructed the restaurant like a stage set to show off the costumes and carriage of the guests.[39] He also recruited the Swiss hotelier César Ritz and French chef Auguste Escoffier as celebrity caterers who had a loyal cosmopolitan clientele. In César Ritz, D'Oyly Carte had a hotel manager keenly alert to the needs and demands of female patrons. As for Escoffier, women loved his nuanced cooking, the combination of simplicity and complexity of his version of haute cuisine, his active cultivation of ladies at table, as well as his novelty creations, such as "Pêche Melba," named after a noted theatrical personality of the day.[40]

As the epitome of the Belle Epoque in London, the Savoy became a place where fashionable society, plutocrats, and American visitors went to see and be seen: "the view of one's neighbours and their wives is no unimportant part of the Sunday dinner."[41] The Savoy management oversaw every detail essential to dressing a room and to creating a theatrical effect of luxury, repose, and intimacy in public, from flattering soft table lamps to delicate china and crystal, from soft carpets, scented flowers, to the spacing of small tables and the attractions of orchestral accompaniment.

In 1908, when he arrived for his interview in the empty restaurant saloon, Leoni was struck by this theatrical display of snow-white napery and glistening silverware. Most remarkable was the Savoy's plush carpet, so thick that one moved silently as if one was disembodied. This was a necessary feature of the silent service expected of the waiters, who had to go quietly and quickly about their jobs, unobtrusively removing finished plates.[42] At the same time, the top service staff of the Savoy energetically tried to establish a verbal rapport with the guests. Escoffier had reorganized the kitchen in order to accommodate à la carte service, so that vast numbers of guests could select their own dinners. However, he soon found that English patrons, faced with a French menu sprinkled with novelty dishes with fantastic names that were incomprehensible except to the already initiated, frequently asked the maître d'hôtel to order for them.[43]

In stark contrast to the tranquility of the saloon's warm front stage, Leoni found the kitchen to be "a steaming hell," a dazzling cacophony of noise and seeming commotion.[44] It was a warren of interconnected rooms, a backstage of mechanized labor, organized into militaristic lines of command. Here French chefs reigned, each with his own "brigade," and assiduously followed the culinary techniques introduced by Escoffier that broke down craft organization to ensure that no single chef prepared an entire meal or even an entire dish.[45] The *abailleur*, the "nerve center" of kitchen production, would receive a copy of the patron's orders from the waiter and relay them to the vast army of chefs and *sous chefs* assigned to different kitchen workstations. These workstations closely approximated the set of dishes (hors d'oeuvres, fish, roasts, grills and vegetables, sauces and sweets, and in Italian establishments, pasta) that followed a well-established sequence of courses on the menu. Kitchen communication entailed the ethnic and linguistic collaboration of Italian waiters and French kitchen staff. French chefs reigned supreme in the kitchen; the Italian waiting staff had to learn "kitchen French" to communicate with the chefs, engendering a tense relationship that would undergo further strain in the years to follow.[46]

Besides West End luxury restaurants and modest Swiss cafés, Soho's foreign restaurants formed a third market niche where an Italian waiter like Leoni became a fixture. "Little places" like Roche's on Old Compton Street, and Kettner's on Church Street, originally serviced local immigrants, but by the turn of the century the enclave entrepreneurs who first opened them had successfully expanded their business to attract well-heeled English patrons, mostly theatergoers and bohemians.[47] Soho restaurants offered an economical version of the international dining style of French cuisine and silver service available at far greater expense in the luxury restaurants of the West End. The work history of Soho proprietors, such Azario of the Florence, or Baglioni of the Restaurant de l'Italie, regularly included stints at West End venues, such as the Monico, Cavour, Romano's, and the Savoy, where they made business contacts and saved up their tips to buy a Soho freehold.[48]

The peripatetic careers of Italian caterers provided aspiring restaurateurs like Leoni with a blueprint for self-advancement. In the three years preceding the Great War, Leoni's culinary nomadism took him to many watering places in Europe and Britain, sandwiched in between a stint in the Italian army during the Italian Libyan war of 1911. It was a journey that would instruct him in the practices of international haute cuisine, provide him with the necessary credentials and professional connections to move up the ranks of elite service in London, and enable him to learn French and German. While his extensive journeys did not inspire him to expand his culinary repertoire beyond Escoffier and some Italian specialties, they enabled him to build up relationships with international patrons who might become clientele for some future restaurant of his own.

In the summer of 1914, Leoni entered the Soho restaurant trade as manager of Gallina's Rendezvous in Dean Street. The Rendezvous was a prosperous Franco-Italian restaurant, praised by the *Caterer* for its clean kitchen, economic cookery, and tasteful interior. Its proprietor Peter Gallina, described by restaurant critic Newnham-Davis as a "great personality," took the lease of the building in 1907, gave it an "Old-English window", and decorated it inside like a country inn.[49] His fortune was assured when bohemian "scouts" such as journalist G. R. Sims discovered the Rendezvous and told the general public of its existence. By 1913, Gallina undertook other forms of publicity to attract a broad English public. He inserted advertisements in theater programs, inviting theatergoers to sup after the theater: "The cooking is perfect/ the prices are moderate/ the service is quick and quiet/ you are in Bohemia."[50] Like the celebrity chefs of the past, he gave public cookery classes to ladies and published a booklet of menus. The Rendezvous expanded to become one of the "landmarks" of Dean Street, with the business annexing the house next door and capable of serving 200 people.[51]

"Intelligent," "handy" Italians of Soho such as Gallina drew praise from food writers in the *Caterer*, but these "alien" caterers came under harsh scrutiny from other media outlets and the law in the decade before the Great War.[52] One persistent line of criticism centered on kitchen hygiene. Soho's reputation suffered from exposés of adulterated food, prepared in unhygienic settings and served by deracinated foreigners. Reports of filthy staff lavatories, neglected food storage containers, and rat-infested underground kitchens, blackened with smoke and flies, signified Soho's "bad cosmopolitanism" and its alimentary threat to the British body politic. Journalists, politicians, and fiction writers returned again and again to the doubtful mysteries of the "cheap" table d'hôte, emblematic of the "devious, vicious, dirtily-pleasant, exoticism" of the district.[53] In the face of these exposés, Kettner's opened its kitchens for public inspection, an openness that was intriguingly matched by its promise of privacy in its first floor *cabinets particuliers*, long used for sexual trysts by the likes of Oscar Wilde and H. G. Wells.[54]

Besides illicit sex and dirt, Soho also gained a doubtful reputation from the ethnically indeterminate cuisine of its Franco-Italian establishments. Metropolitan journalists tracked the "deviation" of Soho restaurant food from French to Italian, or Franco-Italian, as Italians came to dominate the Soho market niche as proprietors. Retaining French names and French menus, sometimes "printed in a mongrel French," such restaurants purveyed hybrid "French" dishes "with a British accent," while also integrating one or two Italian pasta dishes into the bill of fare.[55]

Exploitative labor practices of the West End catering trade further compounded the local catering industry's association with dangerous cosmo-politanism. The "foreign waiter" question, mostly focused on German workers, figured prominently in debates over alien labor and the displacement of British workers. During the debate on the Aliens Bill in 1905, one MP declared, "We have heard in this debate about the aliens in the East End—what about aliens in the West End? (Cheers)."[56] At the same time, stories proliferated about the foreign "Teutonic" waiter as an insidious spy for foreign powers, further stoking nationalist fears. "Is the Foreign Waiter in England a Paid Secret Servant of His Own Country?" headlined one *Daily Mirror* article on "Spy Waiters" in 1905.[57] One result of this xenophobic resentment was the formation of the Loyal British Waiters Society in 1910, aimed at the "displacement of the foreigner and re-instatement of the Britisher."[58]

When Charles Booth tried to account for the displacement of English labor from the luxury end of West End catering (except in clubland, where waiters were exclusively British), he too framed the question in terms of national character and manliness. Booth noted that maître d's and chefs "understandably want to work with their own" and thus push forward their own countrymen.[59] Employers, he added, also preferred the foreign waiter to his English counterpart because the former is cheaper, "completely master of his business, having worked his way up through all grades," and in command of many foreign languages. On these latter grounds, the Englishman suffered from his own deficiencies. But Booth also thought that the Englishman "could reasonably object" to many conditions of the trade: servile reliance on tips, long and incessant toil extending over twelve hours exclusive of breaks, and the "heavy tax" the employer "imposes on his industry"—all of them offensive to manly traditions of English independence.[60] "Unlike his English 'confrere,' the German, Swiss or Italian waiter receives no wages" and even had to pay his employer a percentage amounting to 6d or more in the pound.[61]

Soho's Italian Anarchists

Between 1905 and 1909, one group, Soho anarchists, actively challenged the negative estimation of Soho's immigrant labor force. Instead of distrusting cosmopolitan food workers, anarchist organizers lauded their deterritorialization as grounds for organizing them into an international union, the Caterer Workers Union. Leaders of this union came from the Italian, German, and French anarchist émigré community that had settled among catering workers in Soho and in the Charlotte Street area north of Oxford Street. Between 1870 and 1914, every street in southeastern Soho was honeycombed with anarchist clubs, restaurants, and meeting places. Historian Pietro Dipaola has identified about 300 Italian anarchists in residence in London during this period; he further estimates that about fifty–eighty Italian anarchists, mostly artisans, shopkeepers, and catering workers, were centered in London at any given time.[62] Among them were Emidio Recchioni, our exemplary anarchist owner of a provision shop, Pietro Guadacci, a decorator, Silvio Corio, a compositor, and Francesco Galasso, a medical doctor. Most of them had left Italy to join forces with the exiled anarchist Errico Malatesta, residing in exile in North London. A leading exponent of Bakunin's "propaganda of the deed," Malatesta supported violent insurrection, political assassination, and the forcible appropriation and redistribution of wealth. In London, Italian anarchists churned out an extraordinary amount of political propaganda for export to the continent. Whatever their beliefs about the violent overthrow of the state, however, they maintained a low profile and law-abiding presence in England. Besides their own clubs, anarchists also frequented the friendly societies and clubs of the Italian colony, including the waiters' Club Cooperativo on Greek Street, where in 1915 they went so far as to stage an anarchist drama.[63]

To strengthen their connection to the Italian catering community, anarchists reached out to waiters and kitchen workers of different nationalities who were "subject to a harsh sweating system."[64] Their journal, *The Revue* (1905–9), published in French, German, and English, especially targeted the *tronc* system used by employees for pooling tips and the registry offices "that rob and swindle" vulnerable migrants.[65] *The Revue* also exposed unsanitary conditions: it noted that the restaurateur Oddenino, where Leoni had worked briefly before the war, had been knighted by the King of Italy, despite the fact that "this good gentleman actually provides his waiters with a dressing-room, which is described as 'a damp, dirty hole,' just high enough to stand up in which has not been swept for two years."[66]

According to Dipaola, Italian anarchists abruptly curtailed their organizing efforts among catering workers in 1909 when their attention was diverted elsewhere.[67] However, a resurgence of internationalist syndicalist activity in 1913 (partially emboldened by the passage of the Shop Acts of 1912 and 1913) resulted in renewed labor unrest in the catering trade, including impromptu strike actions of foreign kitchen and wait staff in West End and Soho restaurants, publicized as "downing of dishes."[68] These lightning strikes managed to wrest concessions from hotel and restaurant managements that included a minimum wage, abolition of fines, and recognition of a national *Kartel* of ethnic benefit societies (including the Club Cooperativo) representing waiters.[69] But these gains do not appear to have been permanent. The organizing effort ended in 1914, when, according to one postwar source, "the outbreak of war produced national animosities between members which broke up the movement."[70] In September 1914, the *Catering Worker* protested "the wholesale firing of Austrian and German workers"; by 1915, it had ceased publication.[71]

The Great War exposed some of the divisions among members of London's Italian diaspora. Many Italian anarchists became vocal opponents of the war, concentrating their activities on the youth who had to register for conscription with the Italian army, even though Italy declared itself to be neutral until 1915, when it entered the war on the Allied side with France, Britain, and Russia. This anti-war stance not only placed anarchists at odds with Italian and British officials, but also in direct conflict with leaders of London's Italian catering trade.[72] Prominent among these anti-war organizers was the well-heeled

9 Emidio Recchioni. From Alfio Bernabei, "The Plot to Kill Mussolini," *History Today* 49, no. 4 (1999): 2. A dedicated anarchist, successful businessman, and Italian resident of Soho, Recchioni used the profits of his provision shop on Old Compton Street to underwrite two assassination attempts against Mussolini. Special Branch reports described him as "fairly well-educated and of good appearance and dress."

anarchist Emidio Recchioni (Figure 9), whose activities among "Austro-Italians" brought him to the attention of the British authorities in July 1915, when the Italian embassy requested his deportation.[73]

By 1915, Recchioni was a successful businessman, owner of the King Bomba provision shop on Old Compton Street, and long-time resident of London. He arrived in Soho in 1899 from Italy, a seasoned anarchist, journalist, and political refugee who had been embroiled in an assassination attempt against Prime Minister Crispi. Sent to one of Italy's prison islands, he managed to escape and make his way to London to join forces with Malatesta. Like many other revolutionaries, Recchioni viewed his London asylum as a temporary place from which to organize continental plots and publish propaganda destined for export. His London exile would last thirty-five years until his death. During that time, he wrote extensively for many anarchist periodicals published in the Americas and France under the pseudonym of "Nemo." Although Recchioni made his livelihood from the sale of food, he tended to regard Italian caterers and catering workers with contempt. A 1915 report from the Special Branch, Britain's political police and intelligence service, highlighted his hostility to the trade. Reporting to the Home Office, James O'Brien, Chief Inspector of Special Branch, detailed Recchioni's long anarchist history and his present efforts to persuade Italian reservists not to take up the colors. He drew particular attention to the following incident:

> A few weeks ago when the Italian residents in London marched in procession from the Embankment to the Italian Embassy, Recchioni and a few of his followers took up a position on the line of route and the language he made use of towards the organizers and leaders of the procession was of a very insulting nature. He described the procession as a "Brothel Keeper's Circus" and remarked that things had come to a pretty pass when such men as they could influence public opinion.[74]

At the same, O'Brien acknowledged Recchioni's influence within the Italian colony as cause for concern. "He poses as a leader and man of importance. . . . He is fairly well educated and of good appearance and address, which gives him a decided advantage over his associates who are chiefly Waiters and *Plongeurs*."[75] In the end, the Italian government decided not to pursue the deportation because they did not want to have him on their hands in Italy.[76] A 1917 follow up by Special Branch noted his continued anti-war activity and the use of his King Bomba shop as a "centre of anti-Allied propaganda", and again recalled his "abominable language" towards the Italian recruitment procession.[77]

Leoni may well have been among the crowd of catering workers who marched to the Italian embassy to join up, much to the derision of Emidio Recchioni and his friends, who condemned the war as an imperialist and capitalist enterprise. Leoni did not wait to be called up, but volunteered for action. In his autobiography, he explained his action as an expression of a well-developed patriotism, already demonstrated by his earlier volunteer service during the ill-fated Libyan war in 1911. He did not state how he acquired this nationalism, not a standard affiliation for peasants of his generation, but it was certainly encouraged by the two local prewar Italian newspapers, *Londra-Roma* and *La Gazetta*, both of which traded on nationalism and the Italian fantasy of empire.[78] The 1914 war additionally played on Leoni's regional antipathy towards Austria.[79] In the years that followed, reflecting on Italy's poor military performance during the war, he came to think that his patriotism "was sadly misplaced" and that he would have been safer "in the ranks of the better equipped British army."[80] Whatever his criticism of the Italian army, he had no sympathy for the anti-war disturbances by "socialist infiltrators" in the Italian army and in the Chamber of Deputies itself, not to speak of radical agitators like Recchioni who tried to stir up dissent in central London.

Wartime Soho

Even before he left London, Leoni must have witnessed the departure of French kitchen workers and chefs for the Front, as well as the wholesale firing, deportation, and internment of German nationals from the trade (estimated at 10 percent of the waiters in Britain). The declaration of war sounded the knell for the German hotel waiter "who has long held sway in our chief hotels and restaurants," declared the *Caterer* in its September 1914 issue.[81] Anti-German sentiment found more violent expression on London streets: rioters and looters attacked German bakeries and delicatessens (as well as other shops), at a rate far exceeding the incidents of personal violence and property damage against Italians in 1940.[82] In Soho and elsewhere, anti-German riots soon turned into anti-alien riots; Jewish shopkeepers and provision shop owners selling foreign imports felt obliged to put up signs declaring themselves to be Russian or British, and not German.[83] The departure of European kitchen and service workers coincided with the arrival of Belgian refugees in Soho, who took their place and led to a diversification of the wartime culinary scene with the opening of patisseries and café bars.[84]

London caterers also had to deal with other wartime conditions that "knobbled" the trade: food scarcities, the absence of "cosmopolitan patronage," cessation of large public dinners, and increasing governmental restrictions on food and drink.[85] During the first two years of the war, when there was no food rationing, the submarine blockade of imported goods drastically affected food markets. Newspapers reported long queues, scarcities of basic goods, escalating prices, and extensive distress. Food scarcity forced popular caterers like Gallina to curtail their menus, print them in English, and reduce the size of their portions, because it was impossible to recover the full cost from the customers. Meanwhile high-class restaurateurs were severely hit by the 10 p.m. rule, the so-called "Beauty Sleep Order," that prohibited the sale of alcohol to servicemen after 10 p.m., which all but eliminated after-theater suppers, the most lucrative

part of the Soho trade.[86] By December 1916, the government had finally introduced the first stage of food rationing. "A Public Meals Order" restricted the
number of courses to two in the day and to three at evening, but it was not until
1917 that full-scale rationing restricted the amount of sugar, meat, and fats in
each portion. As historian John Burnett observes, the limitation of courses
allowed for creative accounting, since fish, soup, poultry, and game were only
rationed as half-courses and cheese was off rations altogether.[87]

How did this affect Soho? "The gloom of war invaded Soho," recalled writer
Stephen Graham, as food became scarce on the market stalls of Berwick Street.[88]
In the early months, press reports observed an emptying out of Soho's foreign
workforce and its cosmopolitan restaurant clientele. The *Caterer* reported slack
business in a number of restaurants, but noted that Pinoli's had not yet lost any
of its staff, who were Italian and Swiss.[89] But within a year, after Italy joined the
Allied side, Soho had been largely denuded of Italian service personnel. When
Italy entered the war in May 1915, the "Rambler" in the *Daily Mirror* recorded
"Little Italy and Soho's delight"; a Soho restaurateur had assured the reporter
that "Italy is going to give Austria a good hiding."[90] Four months later, *The Times*
reported a "Changed Soho." The streets were less crowded, the restaurants had
fewer customers, the old waiters had disappeared. Over 700 Italians left, no
fewer than 14 from one restaurant alone. Only old men remained. Of the women
and children left behind, "one hears of little or no distress," declared *The Times*,
insisting that French and Italian housewives were so thrifty that they could make
money go further than the average English housekeeper.[91]

Some businesses in Soho seemed to have had a good war and attracted new
clientele. During the war, Soho restaurateurs managed the "manpower" shortage
by following the example of teashops and hiring women as servers, most of them
Belgian.[92] Business began to pick up by December 1915, when the *Caterer*
reported more dining out and an increase in restaurant business.[93] Thanks to the
troops, nightlife intensified. Graham recalled that theaters and music halls
enjoyed a boom time, while restaurants depended on "the farewell dinners of
men returning to the trenches."[94] The foundations for the "after war prosperity"
of the restaurant were being made as Soho became "less disreputable."[95]

A female memoirist, Mrs. C. S. Peel, also dated Soho's apotheosis from the
war and identified a second new clientele: "dining-out girls," the vast army of girl
clerks employed in government offices in and around Whitehall.[96] Well-paid
shorthand typists, whose wages had increased from £1 pound (20s) to 35s a
week, frequented the moderate-priced restaurants of Soho, either going alone or
with a friend.[97] Travel writer Thomas Burke was less enthusiastic about these
new patrons. He held women accountable for Soho's crass commercialization, as

well as for the "idiotic" fashion of dancing and dining in the large West End restaurants of the twenties. Although Soho still possessed a "scent of adventure," its once cozy and memorable cafés had become "uncomfortably English." This feminized English clientele transformed Soho into everybody's territory. Instead of "cold-eyed anarchists," or "petty bourgeois and artisans of the locale," or members of London's male bohemia like himself, swarms of couples from the suburbs now descended on Soho's eateries.[98]

Of the restaurant fare of wartime Soho, the *Daily Mirror* commented in 1921, "The less said the better."[99] Mrs. Peel, who advised the Ministry of Food Control, recalled how Soho's provision trade tried to adapt to the cessation of food imports: behind their shops on Old Compton Street, Gennaro and Recchioni churned out macaroni, while a Belgian horsemeat shop appeared, with "unpleasant looking joints in the window," a sight that lingered on after the war.[100]

Soho memoirists, from Mrs. Henrey to Stephen Graham, believed that Soho's entrepreneurs had, in the end, enjoyed a "good war." Restaurateurs profited from Soho's burgeoning nightlife as the center of the wartime pleasure zone. Mrs. Henrey, whose stepfather was a French chef, remembered the "garish, feverish, money making of Soho in the middle of the war." "In spite of the blood baths of the trenches and Verdun, just now at their bloodiest, business in Soho, behind a veil of hypocrisy, was very brilliant." Everyone had what he called his "business"—an evocative English word adopted by Italians, French and Belgians who could not "find an equivalent in their mother tongue."[101] The big winners from the war, Henrey insisted, were the Italians. They initiated the system of closed shops during the Great War, which enabled them to take "the best places in the hotel and restaurant world." "Numerically, the strongest and individually the wealthiest," they lorded "over Soho."[102]

The Postwar Scene

Peacetime London witnessed a booming restaurant culture in the West End and Soho, but also some unsettling changes.[103] Catering workers participated in a new wave of strikes that convulsed Britain in 1919 and 1920. Servicemen returning from the war, some of them inspired by the revolutionary "Red Dawn" in Russia, found a postwar Britain in an economic downturn, with massive unemployment, high prices, and a government that failed to live up to its wartime promises of social reconstruction. A wave of strikes in 1919 ensued, totaling 1,532 across the nation (and another 1,607 in 1920).[104] Northern miners and shipyard workers were the first to strike; industrial action spread to London transport and electrical workers, eventually mobilizing short-term strikes among a dizzying array of trades, from tailors and chorus girls, to bakers and the police.[105] Restaurant workers also took part in strike actions that were short-lived. On February 5, the *Daily Express* reported on the "lightning strike" of 7–8,000 catering workers in London that brought temporary "chaos" to London's most prominent hotels and restaurants, but these strikes soon abated.[106]

Meanwhile, Soho consolidated its status as London's cosmopolitan center of culinary delights. Its ethnic diversity appeared all the more singular as tighter immigration restrictions resulted in an England that had "half closed" its doors to foreign workers and was increasingly turned inwards, isolationist, even pastoral.[107] Soho's open borders, declared the *Soho Gazette*, a short-lived local newspaper published by Silvio Corio, who was the Soho anarchist lover of Sylvia Pankhurst, made it different from other districts which tended to develop a life of their own and remain isolated from the rest.[108] Home to Jews and Turks, French, Italians and Greeks, Soho remained "a perpetual attraction to the countless Londoners who having spent holidays in France and Belgium, Italy and Spain, love the sound of foreign languages and the sight of foreign ways."[109]

Throughout the twenties, Soho retained and extended its reputation as a "permanent exhibition of foreign cooking."[110] Historians have noted that in this decade the distinctive cuisines of "foreign restaurants" began to be disaggregated and prized.[111] Interwar Soho could boast "restaurants of all nations," including Spanish, Chinese, Hungarian, Greek, and Japanese eateries. Along the straight and narrow streets between Oxford Street and Shaftesbury Avenue, restaurants by the dozen were to be found, owned by foreigners, staffed by foreigners, but patronized by Londoners. Chicken played an important role in the menu of the modest establishments, as well as economical hors d'oeuvres, such as beetroot and potato salad.

Despite this apparent diversity, keen observers noted that Italians were the owners and wait staff of the most prosperous restaurants in the West End and Soho. A few years ago, wrote German travel writer Paul Cohen-Portheim in 1935, London's foreign restaurants sported French names; "now they are all Italian."[112] Other writers reported that Old Compton Street and surrounding streets had become an Italian village. "The Germans did not return after the war, and the French failed to return in the same numbers as Italians," explained one French travel writer.[113] According to *The New Survey of London Life and Labour* in the early thirties, foreigners still accounted for 90 percent of the kitchen staff and 70 percent of the waiting staff in West End hotels and restaurants of the "expensive type."[114] In luxury venues, the appointment of an Italian chef or headwaiter resulted in the hiring of Italian staff.[115] At the lower end of the trade, Cypriots, Maltese, and Hong Kong Chinese substituted for Europeans; described by the *Survey* as "technically British citizens" and not subject to immigration restrictions, they took the "lowest duties at the lowest wages" in Soho.[116]

Besides these demographic changes, alterations in Soho's local economy also affected the restaurant industry. The district's lunchtime trade benefited from Wardour Street's burgeoning film industry, dominated by Jews. To a certain extent, restaurants also profited from an expanded nightlife. By 1921, Soho restaurants were able to revive their after-theater suppers, as a new licensing law extended drinking to 11 p.m. and, provided some food was served, to 12:30 a.m.[117] Too small to offer dancing, Soho restaurants vied with nightclubs for space along Old Compton Street, Gerrard Street, and Frith Street. The new vogue in late-night dancing and drinking led a string of Italian restaurateurs to diversify into club ownership themselves, while others accommodated the expanding sex trade in the clubs by allowing their upstairs rooms to be used for "immoral purposes" by prostitutes and their customers.

One final feature drastically affected Soho's postwar scene: the Fascist invasion of Soho. During the 1920s, the mainstream press and restaurant guides benignly noted the link between Fascism and Soho's catering industry. A decade before the British Union of Fascists (heavily financed by Mussolini) took to the streets to protest unemployment and Jews, *The Times* reported the march of the *Fascisti* in 1922 as they celebrated Italian Armistice day at Westminster Abbey; upon their return eastwards, it noted that the marchers swung up Whitehall and into Noel Street, Soho (where their first headquarters were located in the early twenties), while "singing their wonderful marching song."[118]

Restaurant critics also observed the Fascist tendencies of West End and Soho caterers with bemused detachment.[119] During the twenties, they tended to treat caterers' political enthusiasm for Mussolini as a histrionic component of the Italian personality, the flip side of the "genial Italian."[120] In 1924, the food critic "Diner-Out" praised Luca Martini as the "ruling spirit" of the Rendezvous on Dean Street, where he managed a staff of two headwaiters, fifty waiters, and a full complement of 150 service workers.[121] "Diner-Out's" lightly satirical sketch of the "fiery" Martini credited him with the same propensity for operatic self-aggrandizement as his political idol, Mussolini. Thanks to Martini, patrons receive the same "swift and efficient service" whether they ordered the "cheap table d'hôte" or the expensive "à la carte." And if anything "should not please, you send for Martini, and watch him in his best 'Fascistic' manner put things right."[122]

French commentators pointedly noted the Italian culinary and Fascist mastery of Soho. "Greek Street, Wardour Street, Frith Street, Dean Street" were "once the meeting ground of all the [undercover state] police in Europe," observed writer Paul Morand in 1934.[123] Now these streets were the hub of the Italian restaurant trade and of its Fascism. "The Italians learnt their profession of chefs and waiters from the French and the Swiss: now they are the masters of Soho. Most of the little restaurants, Kettner's, the Rendezvous, Mars . . . are Italian under a French label."[124] "Their very active Fascism has its headquarters in Greek Street," he added, while also noting that anti-Fascism "has very much diminished as it has all over the world."[125]

During the twenties, government officials seemed to have been equally indifferent to this new political formation. Until 1935, the British government maintained friendly relations with the Fascist state and paid little attention to the Fascist penetration of the Italian diaspora in its midst. In the previous decade, the "loudest protest against Mussolini's government was raised by English democrats," observes historian Lucio Sponza, who identifies Sylvia Pankhurst, Silvio Corio, and their English friends as instrumental in the organization of anti-Fascist sentiment in Britain. In the mid-twenties, Pankhurst and Corio founded the Friends of Italian Freedom, whose English contingent included George Lansbury, Bertrand Russell, and Rebecca West.[126] Italian anti-Fascist activity was limited to the anarchist group centered around Emidio Recchioni and the publication of the weekly *Il Comento*, the only Italian anti-Fascist publication of London. Published from 1922 to 1924, its columns exposed Fascist atrocities abroad and denounced the Fascist takeover of Italian associations in London, including the Italian Hospital, the Dante Alighieri Society, and eventually the Club Cooperativo.[127] By 1924, however, local anti-Fascists had lost their public battle against a heavily financed campaign by the Italian Fascist government to win the consent of the London colony (and, according to Sponza, they were too quarrelsome and divisive to lead a successful anti-Fascist offensive).[128] When *Il Comento* folded, Recchioni's opposition to Mussolini took a more covert individualist and conspiratorial approach.[129]

Leoni in Dean Street

Meanwhile, in Leoni's Dean Street restaurant, high bohemia, Fascism, and Italian regional cooking politely coexisted. Leoni accommodated himself to all the new trends of the 1920s when he opened the Quo Vadis restaurant in 1926. Returning from the war in 1919, he regained his place on the international circuit, working first on an ocean liner, the *Majestic*, and then returning to the Savoy as headwaiter. He continued to save up money for his dream restaurant from his wages and tips. His plans for a family business took a step forward when his mother arranged for him to marry the girl from the next village. First settling in Bloomsbury, the Leonis subsequently moved to a house in Whitfield Street, north of Oxford Street, where they occupied the basement and ground floors. All their residences were in small pockets of the West End and Soho, remembered as "very Italian" by Anglo-Italians interviewed in the new millennium.[130] The rooms in the top floors were furnished with two or three beds and let to Italian waiters.[131] By 1926, Leoni had saved up almost enough money, £800, to buy a restaurant, with the help of a bank loan. He selected Soho as the site of his future restaurant, close to Theatreland, where it would be possible to attract patrons for after-theater suppers and expand horizontally along the street.[132]

Leoni was able to buy a property on Dean Street, with an eye to extending the restaurant over time to two adjacent houses, as Gallina had done with the Rendezvous. The property, 27 Dean Street, had been a disreputable Italian café whose owner had died before he could open it, while the adjacent houses were still occupied by humble immigrant businesses. Leoni chose a Latin name, Quo Vadis, for his restaurant, after seeing a huge hoarding on Leicester Square advertising a film by that title. Translated as "Where art thou going?" the name constituted a personal existential joke about Leoni's risk-taking in opening up a restaurant, but it also promised an opulent, fine Italian cuisine, in the form of a Roman-style feast. Leoni moved his family into the top floor. In partnership with an Italian chef, whom Leoni would soon buy out, Quo Vadis opened with seven tables in 1926, and the first day's taking was a paltry 12s 6d, the weekly earnings of a scullery hand.

Leoni hoped to entice the world of fashion into his establishment, but first he had to confront two unpleasant features of the Soho scene: corrupt policing and the burgeoning sex trade. During the Great War, Soho's sex trade vastly expanded. Vigorous police surveillance of the West End thoroughfares pushed streetwalkers into Soho's dark, narrow streets, where the mushrooming of late-night entertainment venues created an atmosphere conducive to transgressive practices and cross-class erotic encounters.[133] Even after the war, many streetwalkers seemed to have remained in Soho; police identified Gerrard and Lisle streets as principal spots for street solicitation in London.[134] Sex workers also found the all-night cafés and shady nightclubs on these streets to be useful spaces to pick up clients.[135]

Soho's Italian restaurateurs were linked to this booming sex trade, both as participants in an interconnected commerce in bodily appetites and as landlords with upper rooms to let. In 1920, journalist Sidney Moseley, for instance, claimed that Piccadilly demi-mondaines "made their headquarters on the upper floor of 'bohemian restaurants.'" Moseley went on to insinuate that police turned a blind eye to this practice, or worse, offered protection in return for bribes.[136] Leoni was certainly aware of these dubious rentals even before he opened his own Soho restaurant. He recalled a conversation with his friendly bank manager, Mr. Amey, who praised Leoni for regularly depositing his small, hard-earned, weekly savings in the bank, instead of following the example of his compatriots who daily deposited "large wads" of banknotes gained from "vice."[137]

Westminster Council reports from 1919 to 1928 tend to confirm Moseley and Amey's impressions.[138] Italian restaurateurs conducted many, but not all, of the ground floor businesses, letting out upper rooms to prostitutes. Some of these restaurateurs were well-known figures, including Old Compton Street's Antonio Rubaino of the Dieppe Restaurant and Angelo Molinari, later described in Home Office reports as the proprietor of "doubtful restaurants."[139] The local police were implicated in this expanding trade. Suspect houses tended to be "watched" for long periods, first by an agent of the Public Morality Council, the moral purity organization focused on central London, and then by the police who were under the supervision of the C division's Sergeant George Goddard. For almost a decade, authorities remained clueless about the police protection racket operated by Goddard.[140]

As a new Soho restaurateur, Leoni soon found himself a target of Goddard's extortion system. In a chapter of his autobiography, entitled "A Date in Soho Square," he offers an account of his adventures with this corrupt policeman. Business at the new Quo Vadis was slow. Bills were piling up, and customers were scarce. One day, Leoni's partner and chef arrived with a business proposition from a policeman: Leoni and his partner should "keep the restaurant going as a blind but there are two rooms upstairs which are wasted and we could use them for another purpose."[141] Outraged, Leoni refused to cooperate with "a bunch of crooked policemen operating a protection racket." But a few days later, a man came into the restaurant and told Leoni to meet him "in Soho Square tonight at eleven-thirty, at the bench which faces Oxford Street." Leoni showed up to find a man seated with a hat shadowing his face, who threatened to "shop" him if he didn't cooperate. He knew Leoni sold wine without a license, bought from a pub down the street. "These villains missed nothing," Leoni thought, and said he would think about it. Before there could be any further visitation from bent coppers, Leoni recalled, a "Detective Inspector [sic] was arrested and one of Soho's greatest scandals became public knowledge."[142] The "Detective Inspector" turned out to be Sergeant Goddard, the most notorious "bent" copper of the 1920s and apparently the same policeman who had threatened Leoni in Soho Square. In 1928, Goddard was arrested along with his assistant, Constable Wilkins, Mrs. Kate Meyrick of the 43 Club, and Ribuffi, an "alien" restaurateur, for "perverting the cause of justice" and participating in a protection racket that allowed Meyrick and Ribuffi to sell alcohol after hours. Angelo Molinari, the Old Compton Street restaurateur, was also named in the proceedings.[143]

When the "Police Inspector" was arrested, Leoni remembered that he breathed a "sigh of relief." His restaurant was saved. The scandal of Goddard's arrest "gave Soho an undesirable publicity" and attracted a certain number of sensation-seekers into Leoni's restaurant. But they were casual trade, not the sophisticated, regular patrons he craved, and presumably not the kind who knew "how to handle their knives and forks" or who could appreciate Leoni's cuisine.[144]

Famous for Art and Food

To attract discerning patrons, Leoni understood that he had to create a distinctive atmosphere. But he did not have the funds to underwrite an elegant refurbishment. Enter Edward Carrick, a young artist who came to his assistance by turning Quo Vadis into a "permanent exhibition of modern art."[145] Son of theatrical designer Edward Craig and grandson of the great thespian Ellen Terry, Carrick was twenty-one years old, a penniless artist, but well-connected in the world of art, journalism, and the theater. Leoni turned a chapter of his memoir over to Carrick to tell his own version of the founding of the Grubb Group of artists who exhibited at Quo Vadis and whose aesthetic and political tendencies ran the gamut of native and cosmopolitan styles.

Leoni and his restaurant realized Carrick's fantasy of Italian charm and hospitality, exuding a "simple warmth" that was "endearing."[146] Carrick arrived in London in 1928 on a professional errand for his father, who was residing in Italy. He was feeling nostalgic for Italy when he passed by the Dean Street restaurant and was enthralled by its name emblazoned in "large gilt letters."[147] He could not resist going into the restaurant, where Leoni provided a meal that was "well-cooked and excellently served" and cost 1s 6d. Carrick continued to lunch regularly at Quo Vadis until he became so poor that he could not even afford to pay the small amount Leoni had charged him for a meal.[148] Leoni insisted on giving him lunch even without payment.

The following year, Carrick proposed that he and his friends use the restaurant as exhibition space, just like they did in Paris, "where the walls are decorated with artists' paintings," and that he, Carrick, select the pictures.[149] Leoni thought it was a good idea, attracted by the promise of free publicity. Mindful of the new standards of restaurant chic set by Marcel Boulestin when he opened his stylish art deco restaurant in Covent Garden in 1927, he was also happy to depend on Carrick's artistic eye to ensure that his simple decor was "right."[150]

Within twenty-four hours Carrick produced a prospectus of the group, with Carrick as president. With "youthful flippancy," they named themselves the "Grubb Group" and broadcasted their motto as *Ars Longa, Grub Fugit*. The first exhibition was a tremendous success, with sixteen artists contributing a hundred pictures that covered every wall in Leoni's tiny establishment. Both the Grubb Group and Quo Vadis gained wide publicity in the art magazines and daily and evening papers.[151] Intrigued by an art exhibition in the "purlieus of Soho," the *Daily Express* proclaimed that "Soho has its own Academy", and dispatched a "special representative" to view the exhibition and to interview Carrick, who explained, "Many of these paintings have been done for food—for grub, if you like!"[152] By 1935, Leoni had sold 156 paintings (averaging about £5), including one by a Quo Vadis waiter.[153] The group was able to stage an exhibition every year until the war, only disbanding when Leoni was interned. Their show and attendant publicity gave "an annual impetus" to Leoni's business (see Plates 4 and 5) and enabled him to open the top two floors. By the late thirties, Quo Vadis extended across three houses on Dean Street, including one earlier tenanted by Karl Marx in the 1840s.[154] When Carrick offered to pay a commission on the work sold, Leoni refused on the grounds that "we were all artists, each in our different way."[155]

The Grubb Group extended and transformed the link between restaurants, artists, and the commercial public sphere already developed before the war.[156] In the 1890s, London artists had adopted the Parisian fashion of treating restaurants as their social headquarters. The Café Royal became a special favorite as a place of business for writers, seated on the red banquette seats, who exchanged contracts with publishers across the marble-top tables.[157] In the last years before the war, members of the avant-garde also began to mark their presence with their art in Soho's "small places," including Au Petit Savoyard, Tour Eiffel, Isola Bella, and the Cave of the Golden Calf (a cabaret). Restaurant art encompassed interior furnishings, wall decorations, and menu design, with an eye to establishing a demarcated bohemian environment that provided the proprietor with a commercial edge on the restaurant down the street. Even though wall decorations tended to appear in a restaurant's upper room reserved for the cognoscenti, they nonetheless lent an air of distinction to the whole establishment.[158]

The Grubb Group built on these established strategies of restaurant art exhibition, while introducing some innovations. To begin with, it displayed its art in Quo Vadis's main salon, open to public view even from the street, and marked the artwork for sale. Compared to earlier artistic coteries, the Grubb Group represented a broader representation of artistic styles, combining national as well as European traditions. It included a more diverse class and gender mix of

British artists, although none of the artist members were outsiders from America and Europe. As significant, the group accommodated divergent political views, serving as a paradigm of Soho's dual status as a political space of the right as well as of the left.[159] George Bissell's "vorticist" portrait of miners toiling in oppressive, claustrophobic underground spaces is a reminder of the era's labor unrest and radicalism, culminating in the General Strike of 1926, the year that Quo Vadis opened its doors. But exhibitors also included Tory members of café society who were more likely to have served as civilian strikebreakers than as supporters of the General Strike. "Mr. Gossip" of the *Daily Sketch* made special note of the participation of Oliver Messel, theater designer and host of "madcap" parties for the jazz-age socialite coterie memorialized by Evelyn Waugh as the "Bright Young Things."[160] Meanwhile, the Grubb's leading figure, Claude Flight, championed a political middle ground of democratic "art for all." Flight adapted continental and Japanese art practices to craft a specifically English form of modernism that was heavily indebted to the Arts and Crafts movement. His art displayed a cultural blend in many ways analogous to the hybrid food culture on offer at Quo Vadis.[161] Flight's linocuts pursued Futurist preoccupations with speed and movements, but, like London Transport posters, they displayed a more optimistic view of collective modern life than most continental modernists.[162] By contrast, Edward Carrick represented a more extreme right-wing political tendency. Carrick shared his father Gordon Craig's love of Italy and admiration for Mussolini as a "man of genius and a man of power . . . who controlled everything," and who epitomized the ideal stage director, moving Italy onto the world stage.[163] An Italian Fascist reviewer praised Carrick's painting exhibited in the restaurant, *Revolution*, that depicted the death of a sixteen-year-old Genoese "martyr" to the Fascist cause during one of the "saddest episodes in the war against communism."[164]

An Italian Experience

Thanks to the Grubb Group, Quo Vadis became famous for its art as well as its food, its walls full of witty signs of modernity, punctuated by a strident note or two of political outrage and distress. "Everyone who is anybody in the theatrical and artistic worlds" may be seen dining in one of the four rooms at Quo Vadis, declared *Town and Country* in 1932. In the thirties, Quo Vadis soon became a popular "haunt" of "smart bohemia," attracting writers Max Beerbohm, H. G. Wells, and Storm Jameson, film star Moira Shearer, West End actress Evelyn Laye, and cabaret star Delysia.[165] The political commitments of Leoni's clientele were as diverse as the artists who exhibited on the walls of the restaurant.

Jameson, for instance, was a prominent English anti-fascist who apparently did not mind dining in the same space as Fascist diplomats. From the outside, its green, glossy, neon-lit facade made it look slightly Parisian (Figure 10). Reviewers praised the interior for its "quiet simplicity," a tribute to Edward Carrick's decorative eye.[166] They also commended its air of restrained bustle, noting that the swift service was "a bit more friendly than usual." Quo Vadis offered a subdued version of the Italian experience that was more exuberantly performed at the Taverna Medicea, where the staff dressed up in Renaissance costume, or at Gennaro's, an "astonishing place" consisting of "room after room, all furnished in the most extravagant manner with mirrors, lamp-shades shaped and coloured like birds."[167]

Apart from the ever-changing pictures, the main draw at Quo Vadis was Leoni himself, who personally bridged the front and back stages of the restaurant. Reviewers praised Leoni as a good Italian, noting his rise to fortune in Soho and sketching his progress through the catering trade, a story line repeated at length

10 Exterior of Quo Vadis. From Thomas Burke, *English Night-Life: From Norman Curfew to Present Black-Out* (London: Batsford, 1943), opp. p. 135. Soho restaurants like Quo Vadis provided added illumination to Soho's dimly lit streets at night. This photograph captures the slightly Parisian impression of Quo Vadis's glossy, neon-lit facade.

in his later memoir. Readers learned that Leoni took the orders himself and made himself responsible for every detail of service and food production. His oversight began with personal visits to the markets at 5 a.m. to ensure that only fresh ingredients would be used in the kitchen and extended to the kitchen preparations: he invented novelty dishes and oversaw the preparation of each dish.[168] Like many other Soho establishments, Quo Vadis had "no chef in a strict sense in these kitchens. The corps of cooks work under Leoni."[169] Working alongside Leoni was his wife, Erminia, who managed the cash-desk, and his son, Raffaello, who commenced work as a *commis* at age twelve, attending night school until he was fourteen.[170]

London Week commended Quo Vadis for providing "some of the best Italian cooking in London."[171] Its Italian offerings were geared to the aspirations of a discerning British clientele. Its menu consisted of refined Italian dishes "which originated in Italy, but are adapted to the universal taste by the elimination of strong flavours." Other reviewers hedged their bets, describing the cuisine as "International" or "Franco-Italian," "the hybrid product begotten in Italy and France and flourishing in London."[172] By the end of the millennium, after Elizabeth David had wrought her transformation in taste, restaurant critics would look back at Quo Vadis and dismiss it as inauthentic.[173] Valerio Calzolari, who worked there as a waiter in the 1950s, found the food strange, coming as he did from a village near Bologna: "It was not Italian, it was not French. He [Leoni] used to take French dishes and put an Italian name, like *Pollo alla Principessa* instead of *Poulet à la Princesse*. That was not Italian food at all to me . . ."[174] To be sure, the food and service at Quo Vadis adhered to a portable food culture that incorporated French preparatory techniques and even blended French and Italian in the fancy titles of its dishes. Its menu differed markedly from Italy's *osterie* and *trattorie* that were emerging as food destinations as early as the thirties, when adventurous middle-class Italians sought out alternatives to the "insipid and monotonous internationalism" of dishes served up in elite Italian hotels and tourist restaurants.[175]

Authentic or not, Quo Vadis's sumptuous Italian cuisine appealed to the worldly members of the Wine and Food Society. Founded in 1933, the Society was dedicated to raising the "standard of cooking in the country" and rooting out the "pretentious dullness" in English hotels and restaurants.[176] Proud to be "food snobs," the high bohemians of *Wine and Food* exhibited a distinct preference for French regional cuisine, and an equally pronounced disdain for Soho Italian cooking: members tended to condescend to Italian cooks as more instinctive than French cooks, more dependent on fresh produce that lost its flavor "when they cross the sea."[177] But the Society treated Quo Vadis as an exception to the

rule.[178] Writing about "personality" and food, *Wine and Food* journalist
Christopher Dilke noted the "Napoleonic rise" of Leoni: "His restaurant, the
Quo Vadis, is bigger every time you go there but Leoni retains his control of
the *cuisine.*" The keynote of dining at Quo Vadis, he added, was "surprise": the
sole is served with bananas, the pigeon with pineapple.[179]

Fascism, Gastropolitics, and Leoni's Soho

In 1935, *London Week* observed "a strong wedge from the Italian Embassy"
among the mostly English clientele of Quo Vadis.[180] The patronage of Mussolini's
daughter, on top of Leoni's entrepreneurial success in London, may account for
the decision by the Italian Fascist government in 1936 to award Leoni the title of
Cavaliere del lavoro.[181] Whereas in Italy, Fascists used food ways to control
consumption, restrict imports, and forge a strong national identity, in London
they adapted their gastropolitics to the centrality of the restaurant trade in the
local émigré economy. In their propaganda campaign in London, Leoni would
emerge as a model Italian entrepreneur, a Fascist patriot who supported the local
Fascist newspaper, and one of Fascist Italy's most prized ambassadors of Italian
culinary culture.

In Italy, Fascists supported a rich food literature aimed at educating ordinary
citizens to consume less. They also celebrated regional dishes as a national
treasure that would unite the nation through popular cooking. They insisted on
"linguistic purity" and the elimination of French titles from Italian dishes and
kitchen preparation. Food propaganda of this sort was part of a "non-political"
strategy of compliance that allowed Fascist culture to penetrate daily life by
social and cultural means, rather than by direct coercion.[182] Along with simplicity
of preparation and pride in regional cooking, they encouraged a parsimonious
diet based on grains, with very restricted amounts of meat and oil, supplemented
by legumes, fresh produce, citrus fruit, and wine.[183]

In London, Fascists tried to encourage the diaspora to import goods from
Italy, and to take pride in the "civilizing mission" of Italian gastronomy. Most
importantly, Fascists identified the catering trade as fertile recruiting ground for
supporters and financial contributors. By 1931, 20,000 out of 29,000 Italians
living in Britain had been born in Italy. London was the largest Italian colony of
Britain, with 15,000 first and second generation Italians, most of them emigrants
from Piedmont and Lombardy, and heavily concentrated in the food and
catering trades.[184]

Despite the small size of the Italian colony (relative to cities of North and
South America), London emerged as a showcase of the Italian Fascist imperial

plan: the London Fascio (founded 1921) in Soho's Noel Street was the first to be organized outside of Italy, and it remained a beneficiary of considerable Fascist largesse over the next two decades. Why did London merit this attention from the Fascists? Historians cite Mussolini's respect for Britain as a model for Italy's own imperial aspirations, Fascist support among prominent Italophile British Conservatives, and the Fascist desire to maintain a prominent outpost in Europe.[185] The small numbers of Italian anti-fascists in London reflected both a cause and effect of this Fascist penetration.[186]

When the Fascist regime came to power in 1921, it expended considerable resources to transform Italians abroad into what historian Terri Colpi describes as "Mussolini's greatest fans and propagandists."[187] They only enrolled a minority of Anglo-Italians into the Fascio, but the London membership rate of 9 percent surpassed participation rates in all the other 487 Fasci of the Italian diaspora, and was even higher than in Fascist Italy.[188] To appreciate the relative success of the London Fascists, it is useful to note that Fascist membership significantly exceeded the Labour Party's membership rates in the UK at the same time.[189] Historians agree that the London Fascio's most fervent supporters were recruited from entrepreneurs and professionals, who were pressured to join the Fascio, donate money, and restrict employment to Fascist sympathizers.[190] As we have seen, Fascists also co-opted pre-existing emigrant societies, including the ex-soldiers and the waiters' union. From 1932 to 1936, the Fascist headquarters was located on the second floor of the waiters' Club Cooperativo on Greek Street. Fascist tentacles extended to other cultural institutions, philanthropies, and civic associations such as the Dante Alighieri Society and the Italian Chamber of Commerce. Fascists enjoyed the wholehearted support of the Catholic Church in London, including the local parish priest of Soho.[191] By 1928, the only weekly London news publication printed in Italian was *L'Italia Nostra*, the official Fascist publication of London, with offices within the Club Cooperativo on Greek Street.[192]

Simultaneously, the Fascists created new associations and social services, duplicating the associational network they had established in Italy: Italian schools following a strictly Fascist educational regime, women's organizations, leisure or *dopolavoro* clubs, youth organizations, and Fascist summer camps in Britain and Italy where children from the British Isles were sent at the regime's expense.[193] When Count Dino Grandi was appointed Italian Ambassador to Great Britain in 1932, his stated intention was to become the "father" of the Italian community and to turn London's Italian colony into a Fascist enclave through its radicalization and extension of social services. To that end, Grandi exhorted local Italians to reserve their primary allegiance for the Fatherland, but he also exhorted them to remain law-abiding residents of Britain, to distance themselves from, and not to interfere with, local politics.[194]

Historians of Anglo-Italians remain ambivalent about the effects of this Fascist penetration of London's Italian colony. While conceding that Fascists successfully enrolled large numbers of Italians in its social programs and organizations, Terri Colpi and Lucio Sponza question the depth of support for Fascist ideology among "ordinary" emigrants. Anglo-Italians, they argue, generally embraced Fascism out of "simple patriotism."[195] Or they point to the sober pragmatism of petty entrepreneurs and restaurateurs: joining the party made it easier to conduct business with the Italian government regarding property in Italy or imported goods. Membership in the Fascio also enhanced the social status of successful businessmen within the diaspora. More modest Italian workers were enticed by the entertainment facilities made available by the Fascio: the bar, the billiard rooms, the cinema, and dancing events. Until 1940, historians conclude, Italian emigrants did not regard an allegiance to Fascism to be incompatible with a respect for the laws and institutions of Britain. They had "divided loyalties."[196]

This historical judgment has been hard to test, as very few oral histories or personal memoirs of ordinary Anglo-Italians existed until the new millennium. The paucity of evidence was compounded by resisting historical subjects: until the past ten years, surviving Italians were reluctant to revisit the question of interwar Fascism and wartime internment, given the shame and trauma they experienced after Mussolini declared war against Britain in 1940. In June 1940, they were shocked to find themselves condemned as enemies of Britain and traumatized by the wholesale internment of men aged between eighteen and seventy who were Italian nationals. This trauma was almost immediately compounded by the death of 446 relatives and friends on July 2, 1940, when the *Arandora Star*, a transport ship carrying 1,570 "enemy aliens" to Canada, was sunk by the Germans. Faced with this evidentiary void, historians have tended to focus on the high political history of Fascism in Britain: on the response of British state actors, the collusion of British Italophile Conservatives during the thirties, and the disastrous British policy of indiscriminate wartime internment.[197]

A notable exception to this high political focus is Richard Wright's 2005 Ph.D. dissertation of Anglo-Italians during the period of Italian Fascism. Between 2001 and 2003, Wright interviewed 130 individuals who had been children or youth during the interwar years in Glasgow, Manchester, and London. He asked informants about their involvement in Fascist social and educational activities as well as about their parents' political sentiments, evidence he acknowledges to be somewhat problematic. Wright finds that many Anglo-Italians remained outside the orbit of the Fascio, particularly in Manchester. He also notes that support for

Fascism varied according to social status, national citizenship, and regional backgrounds. Thus southern Italians were more inclined to join the Fascio in the UK than northerners (except for those from Tuscany), Italian nationals more than British citizens, businessmen and professionals more than humbler workers. But in the end, he tends to endorse the generalizations earlier advanced by Sponza and others concerning those Italians who were sympathetic to Fascism: except for the political vanguard, most of them claimed to regard Fascism as synonymous with patriotism, nationalism, and communal attachments. Some of Wright's sample also included individuals who recalled parental opposition to Fascism, but none of them summoned up instances of public opposition to Fascism or participation in the forms of anti-Fascist institutions that developed among the Italian diaspora in other countries. Their parents' anti-Fascist sentiment seemed to be personal and familial.[198] Recently, historians Wendy Ugolini and Gavin Schaffer have respectfully taken issue with some of his findings. While appreciative of Wright's efforts to disaggregate the experience of Italians in the UK, these historians believe that many of Wright's witnesses replicated a communal myth that critically underplayed the propaganda and controlling functions of the Fasci in favor of its social aspects.[199]

From these studies, a picture of Fascist activities in interwar Britain has emerged, but the political subjectivity of ordinary immigrants remains elusive.[200] Fortunately, the Soho story presents one opportunity to go beyond this scholarly impasse. It allows us to descend below the level of political history to consider the material and social consequences of Fascism on London's urban spaces. The internalization of Fascist creed is not the sole test of the efficacy of Fascist activities on the ground. Italian emigrants like Leoni may have been nominal supporters of Fascism and naive in their understanding of the Fascist regime, but they were still implicated in an extensive strategy of compliance that allowed Fascism to operate a zone of influence in Soho. Fascist penetration of Soho did not eradicate Italian anti-Fascism, but it forced anti-Fascists to operate in secret and hindered their ability to build opposition to Mussolini.[201]

Mussolini's enemies could expect no support from the British government, which tended to be far more hostile to left-wing émigrés than to Fascists. British authorities largely ignored the Fascist presence in London's Little Italys until the Abyssinian war of 1935, when the government interpreted Mussolini's imperialist ventures in East Africa as a threat to Britain's own empire. Leoni recalled the Abyssinian war as a turning point in Anglo-Italian relations: the British, who "never had a high regard for the Italians," saw Italians as "belligerent" rather than as "servile," and condemned their use of poison gas.[202] In November 1935, the United Kingdom joined other members of the League of Nations in imposing economic sanctions on Italy. This geopolitical threat in turn prompted Special Branch to focus on the organization of Italian Fascists in London.

A March 1936 report by the intelligence agency MI5 on Italian Fascist penetration in the United Kingdom underscored the place of Soho and the catering trade in Fascist activities. Out of 11,000 Italian nationals, membership in the London Fasci stood at approximately 900 men, plus 100 members of the women's organization. Special Branch interpreted these numbers as a sign of the limited success of Fascist leaders "to control Italian nationals resident in this country which they claim to possess." But it did not report any active dissent from the Fascist presence in London. Special Branch further estimated that 1,000 young people were members of a paramilitary organization. Finally, MI5 noted that 1,300 children were enrolled in fourteen Italian schools in London, all "controlled from Greek Street," while about 500 children were sent annually to summer holiday camp where they were subject to a form of "semi-military or Fascist discipline."[203]

M15 pinpointed the Italian Club Cooperativo on Greek Street as "the centre from which the Italian Fascist party in Great Britain has spread."[204] Subsequent reports in 1936 and 1937 stressed the extent of Fascist surveillance of local Italians. "It is generally believed among London Italians that reports of any anti-Fascist utterances by Italians are made to [Party] authorities and to the Embassy."[205] According to MI5, the Fascists had enrolled about 150 of 700 café owners in "inner London" into an association to pressure proprietors to invest their business profits in land in Italy and to purchase all their supplies from Italian houses in England or directly from Italy.[206]

At the same time, the Abyssinian war and sanctions provoked the middle-market London press to cover Fascist activities in Soho that highlighted the loyalty of local Italians to Mussolini's regime. In 1935, the *Daily Express* reported on "moral mobilizations" organized by the London Fascio at the Club Cooperativo, where emigrants showed their loyalty to the cause by volunteering for service or donating money and gold. Mussolini's call to arms was heard in "Greek-street, Soho, headquarters of the *Fascio*," declared the *Express* reporter, who went on to describe men assembled in black shirts, breeches, and black top boots who listened intently to Ambassador Grandi as he exhorted them to rally around Il Duce.[207] A month later, another *Express* reporter visited the Soho headquarters; he saw a pile of letters, a bundle of cheques, rings, bracelets, cuff links, all of them "personal treasures" given by Italians on "Sanction day" to aid compatriots who "may suffer from sanctions by England."[208] Similar press reports of Fascist secret meetings in Soho appeared throughout the British Isles, the Empire, and North America.[209]

Non-Italian residents of Soho also recalled the Fascist presence. Mrs. Robert Henrey, who grew up in the French catering community of Soho, remembered the bombastic self-regard of elite Italian caterers who wore "the most expensive suits, drove the fastest cars and did all the talking."[210] As a society columnist, Mrs. Henrey was able to observe the higher echelons of Italian caterers in unguarded moments.[211] Italian establishments were at the center of the West End glamour scene, patronized by the Prince of Wales and his brother George, Duke of Kent, who danced their way from haunt to haunt, fawned over by Italian restaurateurs like the Quaglino brothers (described by *What's On* as "Men of Mussolini"), Sovrani, and Luigi of the Embassy Club.[212] According to Henrey, the Italian Fascist regime only compounded these men's delusions of greatness and made their hearts swell "with pride."[213] "I used to find them in the early hours of the morning, when the supper rush was over, having a quick meal in a screened off part of their restaurant discussing politics above the distant rhythmic roar of the dance band."[214] They looked forward to their weekly invitation to Grosvenor Square to drink champagne with Ambassador Grandi.[215] Another postwar writer, Stanley Jackson, recalled a similar scene of political grandiosity involving waiters and kitchen help at the Fascist headquarters in Greek Street. "The Italian Club was full of cigar smoke and Imperialism," remembered Jackson in 1946. "Waiters from the Café Royal, Quaglino's and other West End places would stride into Soho, their wallets crammed with tips from the decadent Anglo-Saxons. *Il Duce's* newest speech was hailed with rapture; pencils whizzed deliriously over maps."[216]

But the Fascists did not simply count on the spontaneous enthusiasm and bloated self-importance of local patriots; they stepped up surveillance and pressure on immigrants to join Fascist organizations.[217] The Italian Fascist press assumed a more aggressive and hostile stance towards Britain, no longer reminding local Italians to be law-abiding residents of Great Britain. The 1936 opening of the Casa del Littorio, the new Fascist headquarters on the Charing Cross Road, symbolized Fascism's more explicit political and imperial ambitions in London. Both in scale and prestigious location, argues Colpi, the Casa represented a material accomplishment, "never before been achieved by the British Italian community."[218]

L'Italia Nostra asserted its authority to speak for the interests of the Italian catering trade. When a Communist-organized demonstration of the unemployed protested against Italian waiters in London, the Italian Fascist press came to their defense. During the Abyssinian crisis, British waiters in Hyde Park, carrying placards bearing slogans like "War on Soho Front," demanded that "sanctions should begin at home."[219] *L'Italia Nostra* dismissed the protesting

English waiters as part of a Communist front and as just a "gang of unemployed," who "deceived themselves by thinking they would be able to replace our fellow countrymen in activity which requires skills the English have never demonstrated they possess."[220] It pointed out that Italians spent hard-earned money and paid taxes "in this country"; as important, they had "civilized the customs of this people, teaching them to eat in decent places, replacing old, dark, filthy inns with modern hotels furnished with all the refinements of continental civilization."[221]

L'Italia Nostra publicized the civilizing mission of Italians in a series of articles on Italian gastronomy, lauding Italian cuisine as an ancient art originating in the food ways of imperial Rome. So-called French cooking was "nothing but an adaptation of ancient Italian cooking", modified for service in restaurants.[222] The series chronicled the recent ascent of Italian cooking in London: although briefly interrupted by the war years when the "lights went out," Italian cuisine, it claimed, had regained its momentum with the birth of Fascism. As evidence, *L'Italia Nostra* ticked off a list of forty-five leading Italian chefs and managers of restaurants and grill rooms of London who contributed glory and financial support "for the nation": Bianchi at Café Royal, De Giuli at Monseigneur, Vergan at Quaglino, Calderoni at Maison Lyons', etc.[223] Finally, it reminded ordinary readers of their own patriotic obligation to buy Italian. "Every province, every city, every village of Italy has a gastronomic specialty worth exporting."[224]

As part of this gastropolitics, *L'Italia Nostra* drew particular attention to the culinary achievements of Leoni, who in turn amply rewarded the newspaper by buying extensive advertising space. Between 1932 and 1940, Leoni advertised his regional specialties in every edition of the weekly *L'Italia Nostra*, even shifting his advertising space in 1938 from page six to the prime advertising location to the right of the masthead (Pirelli advertised to the left). In return, *L'Italia Nostra* provided Leoni with a considerable amount of unpaid publicity. "Gastronomical Masters," for instance, reported his forthcoming demonstration of economical and healthy Italian dishes such as Zuppa alla Pavese at the Good Housekeeping Institute in 1938.[225] Leoni also garnered praise from the newspaper for hiring Mario Fulchiero, an unemployed chef from Turin, loyal Fascist, and culinary prize winner (see Plate 5), whose plight had been described in *L'Italia Nostra*. "Comrade Fulchero is now in London where he works fast and quietly between the pots and the ovens of the Quo Vadis."[226]

Anti-Fascism and Soho

While the Italian Fascio extended its control over Soho's Italians, the district's enduring reputation as a left-wing "land of lost causes" also made it a fitting site of anti-Fascism and Popular Front activity. Italy's invasion of Abyssinia in 1935 catalyzed political resistance on the British left, much of it taking place in Soho. The Comintern's revocation of its "class against class" policy in 1934 paved the way for the Popular Front, a broad-based political alliance of British left-wing groups to fight Fascism.[227] The Abyssinian war became the first international *cause célèbre* of the newly mobilized Popular Front. Popular Front activities tended to avoid direct street confrontations with the police and Fascists and be held in more contained spaces, such as Soho. The Abyssinian campaign provided an impetus to Pan-Africanists and English anti-fascists who met in Soho's black jazz clubs.[228]

In 1935, as a show of anti-fascist solidarity, the Artists International Association took over a Georgian mansion at 28 Soho Square intended for demolition, redecorated it themselves, and hung their pictures in "spacious and well-proportioned rooms."[229] The 1935 Artist International Exhibition attracted 6,000 visitors, including a "great number of people who are not in the habit of visiting art shows."[230] It was "something between a demonstration and a national gallery," noted the reviewer for the *Left Review*.[231] Under the banner of Artists against Fascism and War, the exhibition displayed the work of 350 artists, photographers, cartoonists, and designers, representing all shades of political commitment on the left, from liberals to communists. The exhibition was a "kind of Popular Front of artistic styles," as eclectic as the Grubb Group's exhibitions at Quo Vadis.[232] Next door, the Cambridge Anti-Fascist Exhibition used documents, photography, charts, and maps to track the Fascist rise to power and to energize resistance to it.[233]

But what about the Italian anti-Fascists of Soho? Their activities were so covert that they barely surfaced in the public media. One sign of their influence may be found in *New Times and Ethiopia News*, first published in May 1936 by the feminist and radical Sylvia Pankhurst. This weekly publication extensively covered the Ethiopian, or Abyssinian, war as well as Fascist activities in Italy. Pankhurst's biographers agree that her championing of anti-Fascism and anti-colonialism (as well as other ultra-leftist European causes) emanated from her connection to her lover Silvio Corio and his Soho anarchist friends.[234] The newspaper was predominantly a vehicle for the British anti-colonialist left, but a few Italian anti-Fascists could be found among its contributors. Corio, for instance, published articles under a pseudonym that focused on Fascist violence and misdeeds in Italy. Pankhurst also solicited articles from Italian anti-Fascists residing outside the UK, such as Gaetano Salvemini, who settled in the United States because the Fascist presence made London inhospitable. Corio's Soho comrades may not have appeared as interlocutors in Pankhurst's newspaper, but in 1940 she drew attention to their persistent harassment by Fascists in Soho, dating back over a decade. She summoned up the example of the then deceased Emidio Recchioni, "a giant among anti-fascists," who "traded under the sign of King Bomba in Old Compton Street," to illustrate the Fascist reign of terror in Soho left unchecked for nearly two decades by the British authorities. In 1932, "Old Recchioni":

> won an action for libel against the "Daily Telegraph" under the following circumstances: Two men were being tried before the Fascist Special Tribunal in Italy for an alleged attempt on the life of Mussolini. It was stated in a Fascist newspaper that Recchioni had been concerned in the attempt. The "Daily Telegraph" repeated the allegation. Recchioni was easily able to prove his innocence. The Court here awarded him £1,500 damages. Whilst his libel was pending, two brothers among these Fascist bullies went to Recchioni and threatened to kill him. The veteran faced them with a revolver; they beat a retreat.[235]

Pankhurst dramatically highlighted Old Recchioni's unflinching resolve in the face of Fascist thugs, but she incorrectly (or disingenuously) exonerated him from any complicity in assassination attempts against Mussolini. Thanks to the release of Home Office documents in 1999, historians now confirm that Recchioni did indeed underwrite two assassination attempts against Mussolini between 1929 and 1931. And he did so thanks to the Italian food industry, using the profits of his provision shop business on Old Compton Street.[236]

Recchioni's London life in food and politics extended from 1909 to 1934. He purchased his Italian vegetable shop in 1909 (renaming it King Bomba), ultimately moving his wife and two children to its upper floors. Like Quo Vadis, King Bomba was a family enterprise: Special Branch reports on Recchioni noted that both Costanza Recchioni and her daughter regularly worked there.[237] The shop had been in existence since 1892 and was already famous for being the first "macaroni factory" in Britain (Figure 11). Recchioni took advantage of the canned food industry in Italy, in large part developed to meet the demands of a huge international market for Italian goods generated by millions of Italian émigrés. His shop became "legendary" for the quality of its imported Italian products, representing both the nationalization of the Italian food economy and the commercial exploitation of its regional specialties: Parmesan cheese, Bel Paese, Gorgonzola, Panforte di Siena, Torroni di Cremona, "sublime Lucca oil," Salami di Milano, and cases of canned tomatoes.[238] King Bomba also sold "international" specialties, such as Spanish and French olives, French and Italian wine,

11 King Bomba shop window. From Alfio Bernabei, "The Plot to Kill Mussolini," *History Today* 49, no. 4 (1999): 2. Like Leoni, Emidio Recchioni participated in the civilizing mission of improving British culinary taste. His King Bomba provision shop was legendary for its fine quality of imported Italian products and displays of gastronomic wares startling to British taste.

even Indian chutney.[239] Like Quo Vadis, King Bomba participated in the civilizing mission to improve British taste, advertising its wares in the *Soho Gazette* and elsewhere as the "the best only for the table and the kitchen."[240] Its gastronomic influence was felt throughout London as discerning diners ate the salami, *paste*, cheese, and *funghi*, and drank the Chianti provided by Recchioni's provision shop on Old Compton Street. During the twenties and thirties, King Bomba became the setting for other kinds of exchanges and networks: it functioned as a literary salon, social retreat, and political space for radical clandestine activity.[241]

After the First World War, Recchioni and his small group of Soho comrades, including Decio Anzani, Silvio Corio, Francesco Galasso and a few others, shifted from anti-war work to anti-Fascist organizing in London's Italian colony. After their anti-Fascist newspaper, *Il Comento*, ceased publication in 1924, they became more secretive, bonding together into a Masonic order as a cover for anti-Fascist activities. King Bomba became a social center for anti-Fascists, including English and American intellectuals such as Sylvia Pankhurst, George Orwell, and Emma Goldman. Meanwhile Recchioni organized secret plots to assassinate Mussolini, convinced that popular support for Fascism rested on

Il Duce's cult of personality. When his role in these plots was purportedly exposed in 1932, the vehemence of local reprisals against him seems to confirm his views on Mussolini's political charisma. But for eight years previously, he was so discreet a conspirator that even his son had no inkling at the time of his father's "double life."[242]

Access to a passport to pursue his covert activities abroad may well have prompted Recchioni to apply for British citizenship in 1928 (granted in 1930). His application once again brought him to the notice of the Home Office and MI5, whose personnel were deeply divided about him. Recchioni's Special Branch file provides useful biographical details about the man, but even more so, it reveals the class and ethnic prejudices of the British political class, the degree to which Special Branch officers colluded with Italian Fascists, and the role of political patronage in naturalization proceedings. A 1929 Special Branch report declared Recchioni to be a "reformed character," no longer propagating anarchist views or maintaining connections with "British extremists." He had altered his views or "at any rate now refrains from expressing them."[243] Despite an extramarital liaison that resulted in a daughter out of wedlock, the Special Branch report emphasized Recchioni's respectable habits and enterprise. It cited Recchioni's English referees, including a Tory Westminster councillor, who testified to his respect for the constitution and praised him as a law-abiding person of strict business rectitude who enjoyed the esteem of local Italians.[244] Recchioni's application gained additional support when, in 1930, a Labour MP forwarded the request by Robert Williams, editor of the *Daily Herald*, who also pressed the Home Office to grant Recchioni's application.[245]

Only Superintendent O'Brien, who had been the inspector in charge of his investigation in 1915, dissented from this view, tacking on an addendum to the Police Report: "I have known applicant since he came to London. He is an intriguer of the first order and always willing to subsidize any movement which is out to create anarchy."[246] But John Pedder, Permanent Under-Secretary to the Home Office (who had handled the Recchioni case in 1915), believed that O'Brien's opposition to Recchioni showed personal animus. Recchioni impressed Pedder as a man of refinement, untainted by corrupt Soho associations. Pedder noted that a prominent reason put forward by the police in 1915 for deporting Recchioni was his denunciation of a "certain procession as a 'brothel-keeper's circus.'" In light of "subsequent events" (i.e. exposés of Italian restaurateurs' complicity in police graft in Soho) this action "tells in his favour rather than against it." "That circus contained many of the Italians prominent in Soho and possibly some of the Italians who have been deported in the last two years."[247] With the Home Office reeling from the Goddard police corruption scandal involving Italian restaurateurs, Pedder thought all the more of Recchioni for having distanced himself from the "Soho game."[248] The Home Office had another reason to overrule the "bad report" by O'Brien: according to a communication sent by a Colonel Carter of the Special Branch to the Italian secret police, Recchioni had developed "a personal friendship with the [Labour] prime minister Ramsay MacDonald."[249] Recchioni's long-term connection with trade unionists and the British left had evidently paid off.[250]

In 1929, Carter also tipped off the Italian police that Recchioni was rumored to be involved in recent failed assassination attempts against Mussolini and forwarded Recchioni's photograph to them. When Angelo Sbardellotto was arrested for a failed attempt against Il Duce in 1932, he identified the person in the photograph as "Nemo," the organizer who directed and financed the plot.[251] Within a few days, the Daily Telegraph, quoting Italian papers, named Recchioni as a conspirator in the failed assassination. As a result, Recchioni was physically endangered his shop boycotted. Not only did he receive the threatening visit of the two Fascist caterers later described by Pankhurst; he was entirely repudiated by the immigrant institutions penetrated by Fascism. A June 24 edition of L'Italia Nostra, whose back page contained an advertisement for Leoni's Quo Vadis, soundly denounced Recchioni as a renegade, to be "excluded from the community of the Italian colony of London." A week later it published letters from the Club Cooperativo and the Italian Chamber of Commerce rescinding his membership. The president of the Italian Hospital returned his donation. The paper also published what it regarded as an infuriating response from Recchioni, who denied the charge but stated, "I am truly surprised at the insolence [directed towards me] by someone who identifies with a regime and a man who has constantly propagated and practiced the worst forms of violence, barring none."[252]

On the brink of bankruptcy, Recchioni sued the Daily Telegraph for libel.[253] He denied any complicity in the assassination attempts. His complaint detailed the various forms of intimidation to which he had been subject as a result of the Telegraph's article about him: he received "black looks" from everyone on the street; he was insulted at the cinema; "things were scrawled on the shutters of his shop"; business people dropped their accounts; money was returned from charities. "I lost many customers, both British and Italian, and my credit was shaken."[254] The Home Office did not permit Carter to testify, presumably to protect MacDonald, now Prime Minister in the National Government. As a result, Recchioni received £1,177 in damages. He died two years later in 1934 while under medical treatment in Paris. "Had he lived longer," speculates historian Alfio Bernabei, "there is little doubt that he would have used the money extracted from one of the pillars of the British Establishment to finance further attempts against his enemies in Rome."[255] After Recchioni died, his son Vernon Richards carried on the provision shop business, published the first London weekly newspaper devoted to coverage of the Spanish Civil War, and became a major figure in British anarchism.

Following Recchioni's 1933 libel suit, the news media began to report stories of other anti-Fascists also victimized by local *squadristi*. Their stories underscore the malignant effects of Fascism's presence in Soho's streets, only realized by the British government very late in the day when, during wartime, they tried to culti-vate Italian anti-Fascists in Britain.[256] In 1934, Recchioni's friend Dr. Francesco Galasso successfully sued the *Daily Sketch* for libel on similar grounds to Recchioni, having suffered abuse on the street and loss of patients after the newspaper exposed him as an Italian anti-Fascist conspiring against Mussolini.[257] But, as Pankhurst would later show in 1940, this was the tip of the iceberg of Fascist intimidation in Soho. Writing in the *Soho Clarion* in 2009, Roger Squillario recalls that his anti-Fascist, socialist father, who owned a club a few houses down from Quo Vadis, was victimized by "Oswald Mosley's fascists from the East End, joined by the Italian fascists living in the vicinity."[258]

The Battle of Soho, 1940

Soho's notoriety as a center both of Fascism and Italian food peaked on June 11, 1940, one day after Mussolini declared war on Britain and the Allies.[259] "When Mussolini declared war from the Palazzo Venezia, he struck a grievous blow for [sic] the Italian colony in London," reported the the *Observer*. "For a few hours, on that unhappy night of divided loyalties, racial riots [between Greeks and Italians] disordered the maze of Soho."[260] On June 11, the *Manchester Guardian* also reported the breaking of windows, noting that "later still one or two noses shared the same misfortune, but for the most part the crowd was silent and puzzled and a little disconsolate." But the next morning, on June 12, its "London correspondent" reported a thicker crowd of curiosity seekers, attracted by news boards advertising the "Battle of Soho." Observers from the voluntary social survey Mass Observation also recorded the media manufacture of the news in Soho, exemplified by photographers arranging pictures of the crowd.[261]

Not everyone on the street was hostile. Mass Observers "overheard" Soho women express their animosity towards Italians, only to be reprimanded by a third woman from the neighborhood.[262] Interviewed in the early 1990s by writer Judith Summers, Zinna Bulmore remembered that her Jewish mother "tore into" two Soho women who were about to smash some restaurant windows: she "reminded them what the war was about and that most of those Italians had been living in England for several generations and weren't responsible for Mussolini."[263]

Historians no longer regard the anti-Italian riots by rowdies and hooligans as spontaneous reactions to Mussolini's speech.[264] To explain the disturbances in London, Liverpool and Scotland, they blame a sensational media campaign against Italians as potential Fifth Columnists. This campaign began in late April 1940, when, for the first time, the daily press leaked the statistics of Anglo-Italian participation in Fascist organizations collected earlier by MI5.[265] Popular anger was further exacerbated by government officials, notably Winston Churchill, the new prime minister, who ordered the wholesale internment of Italian men under seventy as "dangerous characters," and Duff Cooper, Minister of Information, who lambasted Mussolini and Italians as cowards.[266] Within twenty-four hours, police had detained 1,600 men, including 600 in London, of whom 45 were British-born Italians deemed to be "active members of the Fascist party in London."[267] Historian Tony Kushner interprets the bellicose actions of Churchill and Duff Cooper towards resident Italians as an effort to demonstrate a "tough masculinity" in the face of very bad political and military news (troop losses in Norway, Dunkirk, the resignation of Chamberlain, the imminent fall of Paris).[268] Sponza also asserts that Churchill's instructions to Special Branch to "collar the lot" gave legitimacy to rioting hooligans, while at the same time restricting the number of visible human targets they could attack.[269]

But historians still continue to speculate why Soho became the primary target of anti-Italian hostility in London, rather than Clerkenwell, the traditional home of Little Italy, or the Italian embassy in Grosvenor Square (where Sylvia Pankhurst staged a one-woman protest, throwing a copy of the New Times and Ethiopia News on the embassy steps), or the imposing Fascist headquarters on Charing Cross Road.[270] They point to the iconic role of Soho's Italian restaurants and food shops: "In the eyes of the people who indulged in violence and looting, the Italian shops were the quintessence of the Italian presence in Britain," Sponza argues.[271] To this explanation we might want to add the perception of Soho as a space pervaded by Fascism.

Soho's eateries responded to this high political crisis by mutating into a new set of national cuisines. "The maze of Soho" proved to be more syncretic than any stable "quintessence" of Italy would signify. Overnight, businesses changed hands. Café proprietors put up signs: "This is a British concern. We are not Italian."[272] Even the Spaghetti House in Old Compton Street carried the notice, "A British Restaurant."[273] The Observer ticked off a disorienting blur of cryptic messages: "Business as usual: French"; "This is a Belgian Concern"; "Swiss-owned and managed restaurant," while other newspapers identified even more exotic transformations.[274] Hannen Swaffer found "Cyprus" chalked over a café and "Iranian" written over another, to which was added "a French *protégé*."[275] At another establishment, *Parla Italiano* was erased from a list of languages spoken that included Turkish, Arabic, Russian, Serbian, etc.[276] Visitors to Soho found this linguistic Babel matched by a confusing display of foreign bodies: Mass Observers reported on a racially mixed Soho crowd of "dark-skinned men, Africans and negroes, and a great variety of Jews."[277]

Reporters also used the "Battle of Soho" to reflect on their own mixed feelings about their romance with Italy and Italians. Some invoked the longstanding sympathy between Britain and Italy, the British support for Garibaldi and Italian freedom. Historian George Trevelyan declared "June 10" to be "the bitterest day" he had yet known in his life, a betrayal of the *Risorgimento* liberal tradition that British people had always supported.[278] It was left to Sylvia Pankhurst's *New Times and Ethiopia News* to state that the Italian Fascists had betrayed the radical political heritage of Soho as well. Apart from politics, most of the press associated Soho with the purveyance of food and with "kindly, sympathetic" Italians they encountered in catering establishments, "too easy perhaps, but not for that less lovable."[279] The *New Statesman* speculated why laughter was the commonest reaction to Italy's entrance into the war: apart from Italy's dismal military record in the Great War, it blamed the "silly British convention" that "Italy suggests macaroni and ice creams and is funny."[280]

In search of charming, likable, and peaceable Italians, some reporters visited their favorite Soho restaurants. The *Express* man spoke with Signor Bertorelli of Charlotte Street who was pinning up a notice on the wall of his restaurant, stating "The proprietors of this restaurant are British subjects and have sons serving with the British Army."[281] Sympathetic to the fate of interned caterers, reporters rarely inquired into the situation of wives and children left behind, although later memoirs recall the poor, sad "women in black" straggling into St. Patrick's Soho and endeavoring to keep their little shops and restaurants, while their husbands were behind barbed wire.[282]

Interned on June 11, Leoni became part of the story line of the "Battle of Soho" when a reporter visited his restaurant in his absence. In the June 12 edition of the *News Chronicle*, Lionel Hale reported on how "life goes on" among the "*Signori* of Soho." Almost all the shifting sentiments of reporting the Soho riots appeared in his account. Hale began with the atmospherics of the previous night's "mild and muddled riot." "Whack. Whack. Boarding up windows in Soho shops. Stupid hooligans make windows dangerous hereabouts." He noticed "two gaping windows in Old Compton Street," where damage was done to "two French cafes," because "anyone cowardly and childish enough to break windows isn't likely to be able to distinguish between French and Italian names." Like other sympathetic journalists, he tried to console old restaurant friends. He went to Dean Street to "Leoni's restaurant, to shake hands with him. He is well known in London. He should be: he has been working in London for 33 years, since 1908. He wasn't there. Two detectives arrived yesterday morning and took him away." Instead he found his headwaiter Chiesa, who was "taking it hard." "I have been with him for 10 years. We have worked together, quarreled together—just like brothers. We have always said: Do nothing against the English law. And the English law is your friend. In 19 years I have never heard him say a word of politics."[283]

Out on the street again, Hale surveyed the hastily stuck-on slips on shops and restaurants declaring themselves to be "British since 1919" and the "large aimless crowd" wandering round Soho in the afternoon. Hale abruptly ended his sympathetic travelogue through Soho to focus on the demands of total mobilization. "There are Fascist Italians in London, plenty of 'em. Let them be left to the police; and, if the police round up for a day or two peaceful and innocent cafekeepers and ice-cream sellers, well, that's the fortunes of war."[284]

Fascists at Large, Anti-Fascists Interned

But this internment did not last two or three days, either for the 446 Italian internees who drowned on the *Arandora Star* in July 1940 en route to Canada, or for the other 1,100 Italians who were detained in camps in Britain. Officials had originally planned to exchange the interned Italians for the 2,000 Britons residing in Italy, but while that plan was pending, the government looked for a "suitable ship" to deport internees on the MI5 list of "dangerous characters." Special Branch seems to have targeted individuals who were members of the Fascist Party or visitors to the Fascist Club on the Charing Cross Road. Bernabei and others believe the round-up was deliberately mishandled by MI5: despite having received a detailed list of Italian anti-Fascists from William Gillies, the head of the Labour Party's International Division, MI5 included twelve of these names on its "dangerous" Fascist list.[285] More than bureaucratic incompetence doomed Decio Anzani, a close friend of Recchioni, Pankhurst, and Corio, and one of the anti-Fascists who drowned on the *Arandora Star*. A Home Office report described Anzani's drowning as a "tragic mistake," due to a "mechanical" error, but Anzani's earlier attempts to gain protection through British citizenship had met with deliberate Special Branch resistance: lacking Recchioni's connections, his requests for naturalization papers had been denied since 1935, on the grounds that he was connected to foreign associations, the Paris-based Rights of Man, anarchism, and, of course, anti-Fascism![286]

By the end of the month, some journalists and politicians began to protest against the indiscriminate internment of anti-Fascists, anti-Nazis and Jewish refugees. Numerous observers complained that none of the interned Italians had been "classified" according to a three-tiered system established for Germans and Austrians (and even this classification did not prevent the internment of anti-Nazi and Jewish émigrés). The sinking of the *Arandora Star* on July 1, with the catering celebrities of London on board, put an end to any further plans to send Italians abroad. The Home Office took over responsibility for the internees from the War Office, as it had made a "mess of deportation." By August, a procedure for evaluating internees by tribunals was put in place, so that those who did not appear to be dangerous could be released. Very slowly, a number of internees were freed: between 1940 and 1942, the number of Italian internees in Canada and Britain declined from 4,000 to 2,000; another 500 were released in 1942–3; by the time of the Armistice with Italy in September 1943, 1,000 men were still interned, but they returned to families in the ensuing fifteen months.[287] A substantially larger number of first and second generation Anglo-Italian men and women served in the armed forces and performed war work.

Most of the Italian internees from Soho, including the Camisa brothers and Leoni, were taken to the Lingfield racecourse in Surrey and then crammed into a disused cotton mill in Bury. Those who were not sent on the doomed *Arandora Star* were imprisoned in makeshift barracks on the Isle of Man. On the day of the round-up, the Camisa brothers were told that they were being taken to the police station for questioning, but they did not return for four years.[288] Leoni did not return to Dean Street until 1945, by which time his restaurant, which had been rented out to Indian caterers, was in shambles.[289]

Leoni's internment narrative detailed his "enforced holiday" on the Isle of Man. Moving beyond the self-presentation of a good Italian, he recalled his anger at the peremptory way in which a law-abiding resident could be caught up in a wholesale sweep, only escaping drowning on the *Arandora Star* because a "strange premonition" caused him to hide when his name was called in the detention camp.[290] He keenly felt his loss of identity as prosperous restaurateur and imperious employer: "I was no longer Mr. Leoni, owner of a thriving restaurant, whose waiters didn't dare contradict him. I was now Mr. Leoni, perhaps even only a number, an Italian internee . . ."[291] The interned Leoni fretted more about the fate of his restaurant than about the survival of his family in London, as he knew that his wife, a frugal peasant like himself, had "tucked away" her salary as cashier in the restaurant in the case of emergencies.[292]

Leoni presented his interrogation by a wartime tribunal as an affront to his hard-won, manly independence. Unlike Loretto Santarelli, manager of the Savoy

Hotel Restaurant, whose internment file noted that he claimed to be have been "forced" to subscribe to the Italian Fascist Club, Leoni refused to state he was coerced into supporting Fascism.[293] To the tribunal, he "pigheadedly" defended and normalized his Fascism with the statement, "The King is a Fascist, Mussolini is a Fascist, most of the Italian people are Fascists. I am a patriotic Italian. Therefore, I am a Fascist."[294] He did not see himself as a "real enemy" of England, although he did acknowledge that some of his interned countrymen fell into this category: they were angry southern Italians, "the gangsters, the Al Capones of our restricted world," who tried to bully him and spread malicious rumors.[295]

Leoni was more candid than many other Anglo-Italians about his attachment to Fascism, but his account was still confused and misleading. To be sure, he was not a regular habitué of the Fascist Club, or a member of the political vanguard. Although he stubbornly refused to deny he was a Fascist before the War Tribunal, he also insisted to readers of his autobiography that he had never at any time "directly subscribed a penny towards the Fascist Party." But this effort to distance himself from local Fascist operations was disingenuous. As we have seen, between 1932 and 1940, Leoni did indeed contribute more than "a penny" to the Fascist Party by regularly advertising his regional specialties in L'Italia Nostra, even occupying the prime advertising location to the right of the masthead. In return, L'Italia Nostra singled him out as an exemplary ambassador of Italianità in London, and he became the recipient of a knighthood from the Fascist Italian government.

Leoni had nothing to say about Italian anti-Fascists in the camps, where tense interactions erupted between Fascists and their opponents.[296] For Leoni, Italian anti-Fascism represented an unimaginable political choice, or perhaps a challenge to the culture of uncritical compliance of which he was a part. But in June 1940, Soho's anti-Fascists gained heightened visibility, thanks to Sylvia Pankhurst's New Times and Ethiopia News. Let us now return to the other side of this political denouement and consider the Italian anti-Fascists who were coming out of the shadows.

On June 22, 1940, Pankhurst published a front-page article, "Fascist and Nazi Spies and Propagandists in London," warning that "there are still numbers of Fascists and Nazis at large, while numbers of convinced opponents of the Mussolini and Hitler dictatorships have been interned."[297] Between August and November 1940, Pankhurst kept up the pressure on the authorities in a weekly series, "Fascists at Large, Anti-Fascists Interned," summoning up the example of Old Recchioni and documenting more recent examples of continuing Fascist terror in Soho, much to the annoyance of government officials who later remembered her as making "somewhat of a nuisance of herself by attempts to interfere with the policy of interning Italians."[298]

Unlike Trevelyan and other Liberal Italophiles, *New Times* greeted Mussolini's declaration of war with elation. "At last! The long agonising vigil is over. The Fascist regime is to-day an open and declared enemy," wrote Silvio Corio in "A Call to Italian Anti-Fascists."[299] Not only did Mussolini's entry into the war make the liberation of Italy and Ethiopia possible; it enabled Pankhurst and Corio to expose the "Fascist penetration" of Soho, including the sustained intimidation of Italian anti-Fascist residents.[300] And ultimately it allowed Pankhurst to bring the Italian women of Soho into the picture. Pankhurst blamed the British press for failing to inform the British public about the vulgar and oppressive aspects of Fascism. She deplored the outbreak of violence against Italian shopkeepers and exonerated the "small fry" of any responsibility for "the doings of Mussolini and his gangsters," noting that many Italians abroad, confronted with threats to their family and property in Italy, had been blackmailed into joining the Fascio.[301] Like other progressive observers, she acknowledged that many interned Italians deserted Mussolini as soon as he declared war on Britain. Instead, Pankhurst trained her sights on the powerful catering elite, the maître d's, restaurant managers and proprietors, who had refused to employ Italians unless they were members of the Fascio. These people were "easy prey" to the title of "Cavaliere" bestowed on them by Mussolini.[302] Fascism was particularly attractive to Soho's restaurateurs "with rooms", who were eager to be decorated as "honorary members of the militia."[303] Many of these individuals remained at large, she insisted, in part because they were naturalized or born citizens, while "true men and good comrades" of Britain's fight against the dictators drowned on the *Arandora Star* or remained interned.[304]

"Fascists Abroad, Anti-Fascists Interned" pinpointed Soho as the scene of conflict between anti-Fascists and Fascists. Early installments of the series mentioned street names and shops but were circumspect about identifying the dramatis personae.[305] By August 24, after her life had been threatened by two anonymous letters from the "Italian fascists in London," Pankhurst grew bolder.[306] Openly naming the anti-Fascists interned—Veneis, Molino, Gatti, Petrone, etc.—she also set out to expose the most prominent "rabid supporters of Mussolini" at large. On August 31, she identified the Orsi brothers of Stafford Street as the assailants of Luigi Molina, a socialist café owner on Macclesfield Street who had been interned on the Isle of Man. She further denounced these brothers as the bullies who had earlier threatened Recchioni in 1932.[307] She highlighted Rosenda, a militant Fascist and manager of the buttery at Claridge's, as an example of a Fascist manager who "arrogantly" refused to employ Italians unless they were members of the Fascio.[308] She named Peter Pini, café owner of St. James Street, as the Fascist official who initiated young boys into paramilitary associations; on September 28, during the Battle of Britain, she mentioned Pini again as one of the London Fascists who is "cheering the bombing planes which work destruction in London streets."[309]

Pankhurst was even more explicit in an unpublished "The Big Why in Soho," where she asks: why do "Fascists still stalk Soho"? Writing in a novelistic vein, she pulled together all the anecdotes from her "Fascists Abroad" series while fleshing out characters and locations. The individuals named in *New Times* reappeared here, but the ranks of Fascists expanded to include "unconcealed Fascists," most of them far less prominent than the celebrity caterers trumpeted in *L'Italia Nostra*. They included Cimati of Gennari's on Old Compton Street, Dosi of the Mars Hotel in Frith Street, Capitelli of Shelton Street, Furio of Newport Buildings, Cura brothers of Beak Street, Roveda the Barber, the poultry merchant in Peter Street, and Mazza, the pastry cook, who boldly stood on the corner of Old Compton Street with Fascist friends, "staring in the face whoever passes by."[310]

One of Britain's most prominent feminists, Pankhurst was especially attentive to the plight of Italian women, who, like Erminia Leoni, had always worked alongside their men in Soho's shops, restaurants, and cafés. The women left behind narrate the story of Fascist intimidation in "The Big Why in Soho." Francesca Molina recounts how "one of the terrible Orsi brothers" attacked her man and complained to the police that her Gino was holding secret anti-Fascist political meetings in the cellar. Another woman, Mrs. Farma, has a little restaurant on Greek Street, where she can hear the Fascists singing the "Giovinezza" every night at the Roma, the meeting place for local Fascists after the Italian club was closed. Her husband, a staunch anti-Fascist, is interned. For years, a discreet notice hung in their premises, "Please do not converse in politics." To Pankhurst, this notice stood as a sign of the Fascist terrorism that long cast its shadow over Soho. Their husbands interned, their sons conscripted, women like Mrs. Farma were left to run the Soho family businesses, or else see them redistributed and sold by the custodian of enemy property for next to nothing.[311]

Soho in Wartime

In the face of bombs and broken windows, new proprietors, customers and wait staff, scarce foodstuffs and stringent food regulations, and shifting political alignments, Soho still carried on its mission as "London's escape from English cooking."[312] Apart from parts of Dean Street and Berwick Street, Soho did not suffer very heavy damage in the big bombings of the autumn Blitz of 1940.[313] And the Italians would return. In September 1940, "open for lunch only" had begun to appear as a sign in Soho. Even so, diners had to be prepared to eat behind blackout curtains or with "tar paper replacing the window glass blown out in the blitz."[314] Slowly, after the worst of the bombing was over in November 1940, restaurants opened for dinner to accommodate the Free French and "cosmopolitan members of the BBC." Their offerings were constrained by food controls, rationing, and shortages. Price controls and rationing accelerated the streamlining and democratization of dining out in Soho and elsewhere. Meals were limited to three courses and were to cost no more than 5 shillings, except in some luxury restaurants that were allowed to add a "house charge." Ironically, price controls placed luxury eating within the reach of some diners for the first time. As *London Off Duty* told its readers, "you" can now "dine and wine like a lord, without the purse of a millionaire."[315]

Given food shortages, restaurants had to be inventive about their dishes.[316] They repeated some of the strategies adopted by eateries in the Great War. Horsemeat and chips were staples at Chez Rose and other Soho places. On Old Compton Street, Café Bleu, formerly the Spaghetti House, served American GIs spaghetti and Escalopes Bruxelles, consisting of a "couple of slices of spam dipped in reconstituted egg powder and bread crumbs and then fried."[317] Some foreign restaurants fared better than others when confronted with food restrictions. According to the *Manchester Guardian*, the French showed themselves to be the most ingenious in making potatoes, carrots, and sprouts interesting. "Far more acute are the problems confronting the more exotic restaurants—Spanish, Hungarian, and above all, Chinese and Indian."[318]

After the collapse of France in June 1940, wartime Soho assumed a more cosmopolitan and continental air than it had in decades. Soho's restaurant clientele and proprietors reflected the broad range of nationalities in London at the time. "There were soldiers in the Free French and Polish uniforms; there were people working for the exiled Allied governments or broadcasting to occupied Europe on BBC wavelengths, there were Austrian and German refugees."[319] Once again, the French appeared to be ascendant in Soho. Along with old bistros such as Greek Street's L'Escargot and Wardour Street's Chez Victor, new French restaurants sprung up to accommodate the Free French: Montparnasse, opened by a "Free Frenchman" on Piccadilly Circus (and soon closed for violation of the licensing laws), Chez Auguste on Old Compton Street, Restaurant des Alliés on Rupert Street, or Chez Rose on Greek Street.[320] The *Caterer* also reported that six famous French chefs provided meals to the followers of General de Gaulle in the basement of the Swiss Club on Gerrard Street.[321] Meanwhile, the York Minster pub on Dean Street, popularly known as the French House, became the "unofficial headquarters" of the Free French.[322]

Non-Italian caterers exploited the wartime displacement of Italians to expand their place in the catering trades. The *Manchester Guardian*'s "London correspondent" noted a range of imperial and European eateries in Soho. At least one of the new Spanish restaurants was "notoriously Republican," its atmosphere "Bohemian and Bloomsburyish," as distinct from the "West End-like Spanish places [i.e. Martinez and Majorca restaurants] nearer Regent Street, with their 'Franco tone.'" "But the rice is much the same in both camps."[323] In 1943, on the occasion of the Italian Armistice, the same reporter declared that Soho was "going Greek." Having earlier recorded that "Soho turned Swiss in a single night" when Italy entered the war, he now observed a second transformation: "many of the old Italian restaurants" were now owned by Greek Cypriots, who were able to migrate to Britain as imperial subjects. There were the Greek brothers Pitta, jubilant over the news of Italy's defeat in a café that was formerly owned by an Italian in Old Compton Street. In "Victory Café" down the road, a smiling elderly waiter explained to American "doughboys" that he was Greek, not Italian. David Bertorelli of Charlotte Street summed up the situation: after the last war, "the Italians had their chance. Now the Greeks are coming up, and I am not surprised." A naturalized citizen, Bertorelli went on to state that he "thinks Soho may never become as Italian again as it was before the war."[324]

This pessimistic forecast was premature. As early as 1943, "The London Correspondent" reported that many Italian restaurants persisted as "British-owned" enterprises. As a sign of change and continuity, he cited the example of the Spaghetti House on Old Compton Street. Before the war, the Spaghetti House sold 200 plates of spaghetti at 10 pence a helping. When the war broke out, it advertised itself as British-owned. It was now Café Bleu, under the control of a Swiss-born Italian, Mr. Bossi, who was happy to hear the news of the Italian defeat. Identified by Special Branch as a leading anti-Fascist, Mr. Bossi went into partnership with Mr. Paccini, newly returned to Soho from internment on the Isle of Man.[325]

New wartime conditions organized the dining and work experience at Café Bleu. Whatever its advertised nationality, Café Bleu still featured Italian pasta, prepared by Italian chefs. Instead of waiters, Mr. Bossi now employed waitresses, "a wartime innovation in Soho," according to Elena Salvoni, who started work at the Café Bleu in 1944 as a waitress and would emerge as a celebrity maître d' in postwar years. Growing up in Clerkenwell as a teenager, Salvoni went to Fascist holiday camps and participated in sports events at the Edgware Sports Arena, marching past Dr. Rampagna "with our right arms raised and fists clenched," unaware that she was performing a "Fascist salute."[326] At the beginning of the war, she worked as a seamstress in a small firm in Marylebone, but it had been forced to close down when clothing rationing was introduced. Salvoni happily accepted the job at Café Bleu, a "pretty restaurant," decorated with royal blue tiles, white tablecloths, and bentwood chairs, even though she initially received no wages and had to survive on tips.

In her memoirs, Salvoni nostalgically remembered a good war, unmarked by diasporic tensions or insurmountable obstacles. At Café Bleu, Salvoni rapidly accommodated herself to a work situation that required constant improvisation and management of a raffish social mix. The Café Bleu was renowned for its informality, for its singing wait and kitchen staff. Victor Berlemont of the York Minster sent over Free French soldiers to dine on the Café Bleu's sixteen tables. Salvoni befriended the homesick Italian-American GIs who missed their spaghetti and meatballs and had to make do with the aforementioned Escalopes Bruxelles. Café Bleu's customers included gangsters and bookies like Albert Dimes, "queers" and "poofs" who arrived in couples from the Helvetia after the pub closed at 2 p.m. And then there were the "ladies of the street," the French "Fifi's," dressed in sheer black stockings, who used the rooms above shops to conduct business during the day but returned to luxuriously appointed flats further west at night. Salvoni readily adjusted to the bombs and food shortages as well. When the bombs were coming down, she "turfed" everyone out midway through their meals. They all went to Leicester Square tube station where everyone had a "pitch."[327]

Conclusion

The Spaghetti House's transformation into the exuberant Café Bleu exemplifies the adaptive cosmopolitanism of Soho's Italian caterers, who weathered changing fashions in food and dramatic alterations in geopolitics. From the 1890s to 1940, Italian immigrants dominated Soho's catering, carving out a niche between the haute cuisine of the West End and the modest Swiss cafés spread across the metropolis. During this period, they purveyed a hybrid cuisine that served "Italian" food under a "French" label to suit metropolitan taste. Many features of Soho's prewar food culture, personnel, and restaurant names endured into the interwar years, although its restaurants also accommodated new trends in food fashions, decor, and market niches. Some restaurateurs like Leoni pursued the new vogue for regional Italian cooking as an enticement to discerning British diners. But they also adopted it as an expression of their own growing nationalism and patriotism, a political enthusiasm that rendered them susceptible to the attractions of Fascism. Tolerated and ignored by the British political elite and by the mainstream press until 1935, the London Fascio penetrated the local émigré community via the catering industry. To be sure, many of the Italians in London who enrolled in Fascist programs and organizations were nominal Fascists. But the Fascist colonization of Soho's urban space was not *nominal*, nor benign, as the harassment of local anti-Fascists, first exposed in libel suits of the early 1930s and later detailed in the pages of *New Times*, revealed.

Peppino Leoni and Emidio Recchioni's histories illuminate the political divisions within London's Italian diaspora that marked Soho's cosmopolitanism. One man supported the rule of order, hierarchy, and imperial ambitions; the other embraced international solidarity, anti-statism, and anti-imperialism. Even across the political divide, these two Italian émigrés exhibited some similar trajectories. Both made their living by running family businesses devoted to food. Both saw themselves as men of action and enterprise, pushing their families into the background of their life's work. Both were cosmopolites and nationalists, whose attachment to Italy endured and intensified over a long period of exile. Both engaged in the civilizing mission of improving British culinary taste, winning the affection and patronage of members of London's intelligentsia and some politicians. Both had strategic encounters with the British state and its police: as a Soho restaurateur, Leoni had to navigate the corrupt policing in Soho, but he proved far less successful at negotiating his own release from internment through the tribunal system. By contrast, Recchioni, "the born conspirator," managed to charm and hoodwink Home Office officials, even though Special Branch agents reported his covert actions to the Italian Secret Police. We could say that his Special Branch file exposes the cosmopolitan political activities of the British political police as fully as it does Recchioni's own transnational networks.

Except for some explosive moments, political tensions between Italian Fascists and Italian anti-Fascists in Soho were more or less contained indoors, in demarcated social and commercial spaces. Unlike the pitched battles in the East End between Mosley's British Fascists and Jews and Communists, the simultaneous presence of anti-Fascists and Italian Fascists in Soho's narrow streets seemed to have generated little public tension, as long as anti-Fascists were English bohemians, Africans or West Indians, and *not Italians*.[328] Despite this containment, Soho could boast one public space where public citizens mobilized their opposition to the dictators of Europe: Berwick Street, in the heart of the Jewish settlement of St. James, Soho. For writers and artists of the Popular Front, this "street of silk stockings" presented the ambivalent example of a modern urban space that could be mobilized in the fight against Fascism.

CHAPTER 5

Schleppers and Shoppers

"BERWICK MARKET, SOHO, ON A SATURDAY" APPEARS IN A TRAVEL BOOK on London in 1927 (Figure 12). Photographed from above, Berwick Street Market materializes as an extraordinarily compressed, bazaar-like space, completely dominated by commerce. Men and women, stylishly modern in their attire, are crushed together in the middle of the road, surrounded by a range of undergarments on public display. The photograph captures a kinetic, pushing, pulling multitude, but the accompanying caption works to disaggregate the crowd: it identifies the "prudent housewife" and the fashion-conscious working woman who visit the market in search of bargains. Bargain hunters such as these, it warns, need to keep their wits about them if they buy goods from a "foreign-looking stall holder." On Berwick Street, women may purchase anything from beef to basins, lace to lettuce, but their main object of desire, particularly for the expanding ranks of female clerical workers, seems to be the "so-called silken hose" that "twinkles up and down the City streets."[1]

Street markets like Berwick Street Market have long occupied a prominent place in the literary and visual panorama of London life. Messy, unhygienic, crowded obstructions to the free flow of traffic, they have been historically defended as the shopping center for the poor and culturally prized as liminal, carnivalesque places where journalists and writers can find good copy about the pulsating social organism of "Living London." As a sight of London, the attraction of street markets depends on nostalgia for an older form of urban sociability, and hostility to a new kind of planned urban modernity. Located in "run-down parts of London," they continue to be described as the cockney's natural habitat. Here "chaos reigns", and "the dead hand of the city planner seems far away."[2]

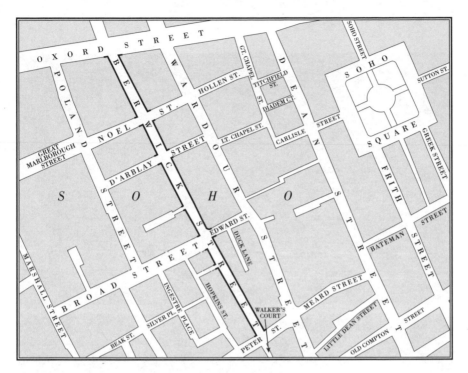

Berwick Street

Static images such as these tend to obscure the fact that London's street markets are not unchanging relics of the past. On the contrary, in the interwar period they vastly expanded their numbers and custom, at the same time that they diversified their merchandise and acquired a mixed-class clientele. The interwar career of Berwick Street Market in the heart of London's West End exemplifies this development. Its retail form was more kinetic, youth-oriented, physically interactive, and less class stratified than either the department store or the multiples.[3] Located in the old, proletarian, and foreign quarter of Soho, just behind the glitzy modern shopping streets of Regent Street and Oxford Street, Berwick Street Market was not simply an economic backwater. Its rapid expansion in the second and third decades of the twentieth century follows the general dynamic trend of street marketing in London.[4] Intimately tied to shifts in the highly capitalized sectors of retailing, it emerged, for about eighteen years, between 1918 and 1936, as a cutting edge retail space for mass market ready-to-wear fashion in the West End.

Berwick Street Market both supports and complicates Erving Goffman's concept of a bifurcated spatial ordering of business environments into front and back stages. Historians of London have drawn on Goffman's spatial metaphor to

12 "Berwick Market, Soho, on a Saturday." From Alec Waugh, " Round about Soho," in Arthur St. John Adcock, ed., *Wonderful London: The World's Greatest City*, vol. 1 (London: Educational Book Co., 1927), p. 131. On Berwick Street, women could purchase anything, from fish to fashion, but their main object of desire was the "so-called silken hose" that "twinkles up and down the City streets."

explain how the great shopping streets of the West End – Bond Street, Regent Street, and Oxford Street – functioned as decorous front regions for an ever-changing array of commodities and leisure services, while the workshops of the garment trade were relegated to the hidden back regions of small streets located to the north and south of Oxford Street.[5] In these back regions, the impression fostered by the front stage performances was "knowingly contradicted" by rigid time discipline, economic vulnerability, and hard labor.[6] But Berwick Street Market's evolution as a retail fashion street disrupts this social divide of fashion's "front and back." When Berwick Street Market traders opened gown shops in the northern end of the street in the last years of the Great War, their retail spaces still displayed expressive features of the rag trade usually relegated to its hidden back stage. In the market, the extreme pressures of physical exertion, time, and money were not occluded from the shopper's view, as they were along the great thoroughfares that surrounded it: they were open and explicit, and even a compelling tourist attraction.

Many of the risky features of this urban space coalesced around a figure closely identified with the retail culture of Berwick Street Market – the aggressive shop assistant or tout, locally known as the schlepper.[7] Let me clarify the local usage of this Yiddish term in Soho. According to the *OED*, schlepper is the nominative form of the verb to schlep, which means "to haul, carry, drag."[8] The traditional schlepper was a beast of burden, closely related to the figure of the Jewish pedlar, particularly to the "old clo' man" or woman, weighted down by the heavy sack of soiled, secondhand garments that he or she schlepped through the streets of London.[9] Since the eighteenth century, the Jewish old clothes' pedlar appeared in literary texts and illustrations as an iconic symbol of ethnic difference and degraded commerce.[10] By the 1920s, however, the pedlar-cum-schlepper had transmogrified into a smartly dressed, fast-talking, Jewish shop tout, sometimes identified as male, sometimes female, who schlepped or pulled customers into "guinea gown shops" surrounding Berwick Street Market.

Urban journalists and photographers paired the market's schlepper with a new kind of shopper in the 1920s, the dress-conscious working woman, imagined to be lipsticked, silk-stockinged, self-confident and looking like an actress, as historian Sally Alexander notes. These women were a subject of considerable interest to writers and social commentators of the period. Like the schlepper, the fashion-hungry modern working girl unsettled middle-class contemporaries who were compelled by her energy but disconcerted with her social aspirations, her "cosmopolitan appearance", and her "synthetic Hollywood dreams."[11] Even left-wing observers remained ambivalent about Berwick Street Market, deploring the vulgar invasion of the capitalist mass market into a Georgian space while marveling at the popular dynamism of the street.

Berwick Street's success as a fashion street depended on five overlapping historical developments. First, it was shaped by the industrial economy that accompanied the building of Regent Street in the early nineteenth century, which in turn attracted a second determining factor, the Jewish settlement of tailors around Berwick Street Market. A third historical feature was the mass culture of shopping that emerged on its doorstep along Oxford Street in the years prior to the Great War. A fourth development was Jewish traders' refitting of the market into a retail space for stockings and ready-made gowns purveyed to fashion-conscious working women. A fifth and final factor involved the performative street style of the Berwick Street neighborhood, where the retailing of food and fashion cohabited with a world of commercialized sex, crime, and entertainment. These five histories coalesced and reshaped Berwick Street into a Jewish, cosmopolitan market, with an unrivaled reputation for the assertive selling of modern, putatively "foreign" female fashions.

Old Berwick Street and New London

By the time that Berwick Street Market took off as a fashion street, it was already an old region of inner London. Laid out in the eastern edge of St. James parish in the turbulent years of 1688–9, the street was named after the speculative builder's patron, the Duke of Berwick, the illegitimate son of James II.[12] In 1720, the geographer Strype described Berwick Street "as a pretty, handsome, strait street with new well built Houses, much inhabited by the French, where they have a Church."[13] It may have been "handsome" and "strait," but it was already surrounded by a series of maze-like streets reflecting the uneven and uncoordinated development of the district, in sharp contrast to the gracious western parts of St. James or the orderly sequence of streets radiating out of Soho Square in neighboring St. Anne. Even so, Berwick Street was respectably inhabited in the early years of the eighteenth century, and was still home to artists and musicians by mid-century. However, by 1820, Berwick Street and its environs had been, to quote Fanny Burney, "left in the lurch," its plain, sturdy Georgian houses of fifteen rooms deserted by all but artisans and tradesmen, many of whom were ardent political radicals.[14]

Accelerating Berwick Street's social decline was the building of Regent Street to its west. The Regent Street project created a physical boundary that stratified residential patterns and labor markets in central London, and firmly established the western boundary of Soho. It isolated the eastern edge of St. James parish, where Berwick Street was located, from the wealthy residential area of the West End, and amalgamated it to St. Anne as an industrial hinterland for Savile Row and Regent Street firms. The subsequent transformation of Oxford Street drapers' shops into grand department stores further intensified the inward pressure of a vast industrial system of dormitories and workshops into the back streets surrounding Berwick Street Market.

In 1866, Harry Jones, the vicar of St. Luke's, Berwick Street, described Berwick Street as "crammed with artisans of all kinds" who belonged to "high-class workshops" servicing Regent Street. With tremendous enthusiasm, he detailed an industrial area extraordinary in its artisanal diversity: there were seamstresses, diamond cutters, sweeps, pianofortes, jewelers, artificial teeth men, pearlstringers, bookbinders, printers, sausage makers. There were makers of blinds, billiard balls, and explosive projectiles. The list seemed inexhaustible. "I could go on," he told the readers of *Macmillan's*, but merely added: "There are more tailors and shoemakers than I ever found together."[15]

Because they had to reside close to workshops, artisans were obliged to live in "places not fit for them." "Here in the west, houses built for a well-to-do class had been deserted by their original tenants, and then filled from cellar to garret by families of artisans compelled to live near their work in Regent Street."[16] As a result, the Berwick Street area was the most densely populated district of London, the epicenter of the cholera epidemic of 1854, where Doctor Snow was able to map the spread of the disease by measuring death rates in relation to proximity to the nearby Broad Street pump. While deploring these living condi-tions, Rev. Jones believed that his parish also demonstrated how "decent lives could be lived under unpromising conditions."[17] And he energetically tried to convey to readers the dynamic hive of industry created out of this density. "You can, or cannot, imagine the simmer of intelligent work which goes on, especially in the 'season,' in a district of three hundred yards square containing thirty streets, or parts of streets, and courts, all stuffed full of these busy people."[18] This intelligent work extended to a strong interest in radical politics. "We speak all languages" and "unite all nations," Jones explained. Within his parish dwelt a Pole who was with Napoleon at the "burning of Moscow", and a "Chartist dema-gogue finishing a dressing case, with a gold key, for a Russian potentate."[19] Historians of radicalism confirm Jones's account: they tell us that Chartist master tailors used the Three Doves on Berwick Street as one of their houses of call, and that O'Brienite Chartists, much admired by Marx for their forward-looking views on the nationalization of land, continued to run Sunday discus-sions at the Three Doves under the auspices of the Manhood Suffrage League in the 1870s and 1880s. With strong ties to continental political refugees in Soho, the Manhood Suffrage League was a critical link between Chartism and late Victorian London socialism.[20]

The same intelligent simmer of work, with a significantly diminished political dimension until the 1930s, continued when Berwick Street became a predominantly Jewish center of outwork for the tailoring trade. The building of Regent Street had stimulated a concentration of elite male tailoring in Savile Row, a parallel street located to its west, while "dishonorable" parts of the bespoke trade consolidated in the eastern part of St. James parish. Here, in the Berwick Street area, master tailors employed by Savile Row firms "could locate their burgeoning numbers of outworks, conveniently close and yet out sight of their noble clientele."[21] The dispersal of work into homes and workshops became a major grievance of the "honorable" side of the West End tailoring trade and the source of ethnic tensions. During the 1889 tailors strike, 10,000 West End tailors went out on strike and persuaded 10,000 Jewish tailors in the East End to join them. The strikers demanded sanitary workshops run by employers and "work on-premises." After the West End tailors settled their strike, they left the Jewish East Enders "high and dry," exacerbating already strained relations between Jews and Gentiles in the trade, and between workers in the central area and those located in the East End.[22] Ironically, the strike precipitated the migration of East End Jewish tailors into Soho, thus expanding the ranks of outworkers in the West End.[23] These ethnic tensions were long-lasting and only temporarily resolved in the late 1930s.

A similar expansion of West End outwork in ladies' fashions developed when Oxford Street drapers expanded into department stores for the middle-class mass market, thus establishing some of the industrial conditions under which a Jewish tailoring community emerged in the Berwick Street area.[24] In 1881, one investigator estimated that twenty-five large drapers in the area operated workshops with 4,000 workers in the area north of Oxford Street, a district traditionally the location of the "court dressmaker" who produced individual dresses for a limited public. A new "province of production" was created, to quote geographer Peter Hall, as the private dressmaker often "became a contracting outworker for the big workshop; she found regular work there, she lost no time in fitting customers, she did not have to find her own materials, and she was paid weekly." Initially she produced bespoke dresses for the large emporia, but increasingly her work included ready-to-wear items. In order to keep their workroom staff occupied in the slack season, department stores commissioned their staff to produce simpler, ready-made garments for sale. In the 1890s these included aprons, mob caps, sun bonnets, overalls, cloaks; after the 1900s, they would feature the ready-made blouses and skirts produced in workshops north and south of Oxford Street. Soon, the City and East End clothing factories were opening up outlets around Oxford Circus to be close to the retail stores.[25]

By the 1890s, Berwick Street and its market had emerged as the "high street" for the Jewish tailoring community, a secondary space of settlement in London for Eastern European Jews fleeing from the pogroms of Russia and Poland, and home to the final wave of prewar immigrants to Soho.[26] "The Jews have arrived in the quarter which for 200 years was the French and Italian colony in London."[27] When a sizable Jewish contingent arrived in 1889, they found better work as high-class outworkers for Savile Row firms. By 1900, at a time when only 4 percent of London's population was foreign-born, about 40 percent of St. Anne residents were Jewish (6,000 out of 13,000), while Jews constituted an even higher percentage of residents around Berwick Street in what was becoming known as St. James, Soho.[28] The Jewish settlement had a strong institutional presence in Soho, but it also had permeable boundaries. Jewish Sohoites mixed with all sorts of types in local schools and streets as well as in the mass leisure sites and left political groupings of the interwar years.

Writing about the influx of Jews in the area, Charles Booth declared that "they make a street look bad but their influence has been quieting to the district."[29] They appeared to be an outpost of the "East End in the West End." "It wasn't a ghetto," one Sohoite remembered, "but there was a Jewish community with an infra-structure of some depth"—complete with schools, *shuls*, boys' and girls' club, and street market.[30] By 1900, Jewish businesses accounted for 12 percent of the local street shops in Berwick Street, but shot up to 71 percent by 1931.[31] They included kosher butchers, bakers, fishmongers, restaurants, as well as chandlers, tobacconists, and at least one artificial teeth manufacturer.[32] Despite some commercial diversity, the rag trade dominated, a creative hive of industry reminiscent of Rev. Jones' description of the artisan community of an earlier epoch.[33] Here could be found myriad subsidiary trades of the garment industry: pressing, umbrellas, millinery, embroidery, button-holing, pleating, button-covering, thread, trimmings, and the supply and servicing of sewing machines.[34]

The creation of a garment industry in Soho required coordination among members of the local Jewish diaspora, as the cut-out fabric moved back and forward between the semi-hidden workshops of Soho and the palatial West End "front regions."

> The Jewish tailor's life is a nightmare of trying to satisfy the cutter, who rarely appears in Soho, but sends back the suit or coat, time and again, for alteration. Every other job is a "special," which means express delivery and everybody straining their guts to get it out in time.[35]

Interviews conducted in the 1990s with old Sohoites confirm the hard work and time pressures of this collaboration. Jewish outworkers resented their exploitation at the hands of Savile Row tailors and cutters, the top men in the business. Cutters had their own customers, the "Lords" who patronized Savile Row. "Once you became a cutter in Savile Row you had the power of life or death" over the Jewish tailors of Soho.[36] One ex-tailor likened the relationship to a form of industrial cannibalism. "Beware of Savile Row tailors," he quipped, "they don't need scissors, they only need knife and fork."[37] The industrial pressures weighed heavily on the family. One old Sohoite remembered how as children "we used to have to take the coats to the pressers, pull out the basting, go with the garments to the tailors in Sackville Street and Savile Row and leav[e] them for fittings, and then we had to take the finished garments."[38] The interviews highlighted the mixed use of household space, the coordinated division of labor among men and women and adults and children in the household, the paramount necessity of cooperation among diverse skilled and semi-skilled ethnic workers, and the need for close proximity to West End employers. According to Alfred Marshall, industrial density of this sort had some creative advantages: it generated a valuable social capital, shaped by the face-to-face interactions and knowledge that "people in a place have of each other's skills and resources", so that "if one man starts a new idea it is taken up by others and combined with suggestions of their own."[39] This industrial atmosphere around the market could stimulate innovation while also provoking intense competition. When a retail culture developed as an offshoot of the immigrant tailoring trade, it flagrantly displayed both of these contrasting features.

West End Shopping, the War, and Jewish Traders

Besides labor and social capital, Berwick Street Market's fashion take-off required a set of consumers for its goods: working-class female shoppers who extended their shopping territory to Oxford Street in the years leading up to the Great War. In the Victorian and Edwardian periods, Oxford Street developed its modern reputation as a metropolitan shopping center for the middle-class suburban market. To get in their female customers, Oxford Street traders relied more heavily than their Regent Street counterparts on mass transport (buses and three underground stations), mass media, and mass production. An important benchmark of Oxford Street development was the 1909 opening of Selfridges department store, a massive edifice constructed in neo-baroque "Franco-American" style by the American entrepreneur Gordon Selfridge. Selfridges promoted a cosmopolitanism of commerce that promised middle-class female shoppers freedom of movement independent of men, and visual pleasure untainted by any doubtful associations of libertinism. Selfridges operated a "go as you please," open access policy, and actively recruited casual trade through the "silent salesmanship" of visual display.[40] These policies considerably relaxed the social codes of shopping in the West End, but the genteel ambience and high prices of Selfridges's upper floors effectively excluded working-class customers—the shop girls, clerks, and other service workers who worked in the West End and window shopped along Oxford Street during their lunch breaks.

Two years after its opening, in 1911 Selfridges inaugurated a Bargain Basement, a retail innovation that would attract the kind of consumers who would later make Berwick Street's fortune. Selfridge had earlier pioneered the Bargain Basement in Chicago in order to turn an unattractive area into a "revenue producer."[41] Selfridges intended the Bargain Basement to appeal to the thrifty housewife, concerned with good value and durability of garments, rather than with design.[42] During the First World War, Selfridges explicitly extended a welcome to another set of consumers—the higher echelon of self-supporting working women in search of ready-to-wear bargains. Its advertisements invited members of the "Blue Serge Brigade" to visit the Bargain Basement, a place "in which a girl may wander, meditating on the garments she will buy when her monthly cheque is in her hand."[43] Working women who took up Selfridges's invitation remembered the Bargain Basement as a carnivalesque space of desire and self-fashioning, both safe and dangerous, where typists who existed on small wages descended into the magic of the Basement and engaged in pugilistic disputes over contested dresses and hats. The atmosphere of the Bargain Basement, one woman recalled, was "hot, noisy and colourful": it reminded her and her friend "of what the French Revolution must have been like."[44] It was female customers of this order who made the Bargain Basement the most lucrative space in Selfridges department store during the 1920s. In 1924, when the "B.B." was extended to three and a half acres and advertised the sale of 300 dresses at 10s each, it drew crowds of early morning shoppers, and inspired other Oxford Street stores to follow its example.

Selfridges found a marginal, if profitable, space for scrappy working women in his store, but it was left to Soho tailors and dressmakers-turned-retailers to refashion the Oxford Street end of Berwick Street into a shopping center dedicated to the working girl with a monthly cheque or weekly pay packet in her hand. Berwick Street was able to siphon off traffic from Oxford Street by presenting itself as both an extension of the central shopping zone and yet a sharp contrast to Oxford Street's rigid class codes and lofty prices. In the last days of the war, Jewish residents of Soho watched the guinea gown stores spring up along Berwick Street, opposite the staid Bourne and Hollingsworth emporium on Oxford Street, where employees addressed suburban patrons as "Modom" and the management refused to hire Jewish women as shop assistants.[45]

Like Selfridges's Bargain Basement, Berwick Street's gown shops profited from wartime conditions, in this case the expanding growth and custom of street markets and the increased wages of working women. They were, furthermore, the result of war profits enjoyed by Jewish tailors. Working in small workshops as subcontractors for military uniforms, tailors were able to plough those earnings into retail development of stocking stalls and gown shops, complete with plate glass windows, stainless steel lettering, and even window-dressing.[46]

By 1917 and 1918, Jewish tailors began to strike out on their own as wholesale manufacturers and retailers of ready-to-wear clothes. Some produced ready-to-wear clothes for the quality trade. Others moved down market, using cheap immigrant labor to produce ready-made garments to be sold to working-class consumers. Bankruptcy cases reported in the *Draper's Record* narrated the careers of many of these costumiers, who started off as garment workers and tailors before they set up gown shops after 1915.[47] While their stories did not rival the highly peripatetic careers of Soho's Italian waiters and chefs, who oscillated between London and the Continent, they did reveal a history of migration to London from Russia and Poland and a set of strategic moves across London's social and economic landscape, from east to west. The same columns also documented the considerable economic synergy between the new gown shops and the stocking stalls in Berwick Street Market. Overwhelmingly these proceedings recorded the history of an immigrant family business, involving siblings, parents, children, and in-laws, where women of the family frequently ran the stalls and shops. Israel Kleiner, the Polish-born husband of Madame Ida Kleiner, for example, provided his wife with money to start in trade as a "costumier" in 1916, but he later extracted capital from the shop to pursue other businesses.[48] Female entrepreneurship also resulted from the destabilizing effects of wartime mobilization. Ethel Schatz, for example, came to England in 1910 from Russia, married in 1916, and proceeded to carry on her husband Hyman's business in a hosiery stall in Berwick Street Market while he served in the Russian army between 1917 and 1919.[49]

Berwick Street Market became a prime location for this new hosiery and ready-to-wear immigrant trade. Although there had been street trading in Berwick Street for two hundred years, the market began to expand in the Victorian period, when other markets around Soho, notably Monmouth Market in the 1840s and Newport Market in the 1880s, were eliminated by Victorian street improvements.[50] In 1893, a London County Council report identified 32 stalls in Berwick Street Market; by 1901, the numbers of stalls had increased to 111. By 1930, the market stalls had expanded to 158, while spreading into adjoining Peter Street, Rupert Street, and Pulteney Street.[51] Throughout these years, the Soho market, particularly at its Little Pulteney Street extension, remained a place where thrifty continental housewives still purchased meat and vegetables.

As a whole, however, Berwick Street Market was increasingly identified with Jews and clothes. Its Jewish identity is already suggested in a 1908 photograph of the market, which conveys the impression of an alien proletarian space where children and bearded adults in cloth caps are "caught" standing in the middle of the street, surrounded by stalls that indiscriminately purvey fish and material goods (Figure 13). Like the sellers of durables themselves, the prewar goods available at the market had nothing to do with fashion.[52] But by the 1920s, Berwick Street had become a "cosmopolitan market" with merchandise ranging from fish to fashion.

A Cosmopolitan Mix

In 1922, the travel writer Thomas Burke described Berwick Street Market as "chiefly kept by Jews, but its patrons are cosmopolitan—French, Swiss, Italian,

13 "Berwick Street, circa 1908." From Brian Girling, *The City of Westminster* (Stroud: History Press, 2004), p. 88. This prewar scene conveys the impression of an alien, proletarian space whose occupants are "caught" standing the middle of the street, amidst a jumble of material and food stalls.

Greek and suburban."[53] On Berwick Street, cockney stallholders, with their "racy conversation," who rejoiced in their business and loved to tell the street about it, sold fruit and vegetables in the market, while equally loquacious Jewish traders sold consumer goods in material stalls. Berwick Street not only serviced "work people from near and far, with more wants than their meager earnings could stretch to," but also bargain-hunting metropolitan shoppers.[54] Here Jews and Gentiles, foreigners and English people, gangsters and bohemians, chorus girls and suburban matrons, interacted with female clerical workers and factory girls. The Blue Post, the local market pub, was owned by a Jewish publican, Mr. Joel, whose family had befriended the young Jessie Matthews, the daughter of a stallholder in the market, before she became a star of British stage and screen. One informant claimed to have danced with her as a child in the market, thereby aligning herself to the glamorous world of West End entertainment.[55]

The raffish, low cosmopolitan parts of Soho's economy clustered around the market. There was Eddie Manning's basement café in Berwick Street, where drugs were sold to prostitutes and chorus girls.[56] There was Harry Raymond's homosexual blackmail gang operating out of nearby Lisle Street.[57] Proprietors and employees of Soho's shady nightclubs had close ties to the market. Sam Henry, who introduced the "Bottle Party" as a way to get around licensing restrictions on alcoholic consumption in clubs, started off his working life as a tout for his parents' hosiery and lingerie stall on Berwick Street.[58] At night, Henry's establishments attracted elite pleasure-seekers in motor cars who would disturb the sleep of local residents like Laura Phillips, who remembered the taxis coming and going and saltily characterized the nightclub habitués as "tarts and the Prince of Wales."[59] Daytime shopping in Berwick Street Market also brought out workers tied to the sex trade. On Saturdays, the writer Mrs. Robert Henrey and her mother, a dressmaker, encountered the French maids of the high-class streetwalkers (known locally as "Fifis") who were her mother's regular customers.[60] On Sundays, waiters from the Italian restaurants arrived at the market to sell trinkets, bracelets, and watches picked up in restaurants after closing hours.[61]

Participants in this irregular economy joined more law-abiding members of the public who descended upon the market in search of inexpensive "artificial silk stockings." The display of multicolored stockings drew female shoppers into Berwick Street Market, just as stockings and perfume counters lured them into Oxford Street stores.[62] The *Manchester Guardian* dubbed Berwick Street "The Street of Silk Stockings," where the supply of "nude, peach coloured, and black hosiery appears to be inexhaustible."[63] Phil Franks, whose family moved there from the East End in around 1907 and ran multiple hosiery stalls and a shop at

11 Berwick Street, remembered about fifty stocking stalls open in the market until 9 p.m. on Saturdays and 8 p.m. on weekdays (Jewish Sohoites were "fairly religious," he recalled, but "they had to open Saturdays in order to make a living").[64] In 1921, one writer was struck by the stall-keepers "artless intimacy and reckless confidence in the weather" as they laid out silk stockings, articles of lingerie, along with yards of ribbons and lace, to face the elements. Everything is "open to the world," she observed, even the "little shops on either side of the gutter."[65]

Berwick Street Market stockings were highly prized by the chorus girls of nearby Theatreland, including the young Gertrude Lawrence at the beginning of her career, and by the streetwalkers from Lisle Street, "bold-eyed hussies," who traded bawdy jokes with the cockney stallholders.[66] The stocking stalls even attracted the custom of Virginia Woolf, who loved the market as a space that defied classification and stirred her imagination.

I walked through a narrow street lined on both sides with barrows, where stockings, ironmongery, & candles & fish were being sold. A band organ played in the middle. I bought 6 bundles of coloured tapers. The stir & colour and cheapness [pleased] me to the depths of my soul.[67]

In *Jacob's Room* (1920), Woolf transforms the market into a menacing postwar urban environment of "fierce" light, "raw" meat and "raw" voices, even though her diary accounts recorded her personal delight in mastering the scene and bargaining over "silk stockings (flawed slightly)."[68] Bohemian patrons such as Woolf undoubtedly contributed to the attractions of Berwick Street Market as a tourist destination: they added some cachet to the kinetic, jazz-age street scene. But the bulk of Berwick Street Market's custom came from two other categories of consumers: middle-class shoppers who extended their shopping itinerary on Oxford Street to Berwick Street in search of a bargain, and the large army of female clerical and service workers in and around central London, who found the Oxford Street emporia too grand and expensive for their custom.

The Fashion-Conscious Working Woman of the Twenties

Jewish enterprise and labor facilitated the entry of working women into a new culture of fashion.[69] In 1917 and 1918, the Jewish pioneers of the rag trade were able to capitalize on the wartime expansion of women's average wages, from 13s to 30–35s weekly.[70] At the end of the war, working women would be driven out of many of these well-paid positions, but some of them were able to find reasonable alternatives in the new factories constructed along the outer ring roads around London. Others gained employment in the expanding ranks of female clerical workers, who were determined to look irreproachable in their office settings and appropriately decked out for Saturday night dancing. Despite the Depression in the 1930s, fully employed working-class and middle-class households enjoyed a new level of prosperity, thanks to a lower cost of living. As a consequence, they spent a substantial amount of their increased discretionary income on women's ready-to-wear.[71]

Gown manufacturers who sold their goods in Berwick Street also benefited from the arrival of a simpler tubular style and a shorter skirt. This fashion reduced the material needed to make a woman's complete outfit from twenty yards to ten yards between 1913 and 1925.[72] The loosely fitted *Garconne* look of the early twenties largely overcame sizing problems for mass production.[73] Opportunities presented themselves to "people who built up a flourishing business on a shoestring," who had "a flair for style without being able to put pencil to drawing paper themselves."[74] A self-described "amateur" and "natural" like Laura Phillips of D'Arblay Street was able to get into the ready-to-wear business: "when we first started dresses it was easy. A straight piece with a hole for armholes, it was easy they weren't tailored."[75] By the mid-1920s, the availability of rayon made it possible to sell lightweight dresses in the latest fashions at very cheap prices.[76]

Fueling the demand for inexpensive ready-to-wear was the increased "dress consciousness" among a wide section of the female population, thanks to the circulation of clothing fashion via cheap fashion magazines and the cinema.[77] This dress consciousness signified a cultural sea change and self-confident, urban female style. The flapper look was a visual reminder of the social and bodily transformations of modern femininity: the decline in restrictive dress seemed to signify the loosening of rules of propriety in favor of kinesthetic emancipation. As historian Allison Abra observes, the lighter fabrics, shorter skirts, and loose fit of the flapper dress were deliberately crafted with dancing in mind, and advertisements for cosmetics, fashion, skin care, hair removal, and deodorants introduced dance imagery to promote their products.[78] Fashion, cosmetics, and social dancing prowess in turn underwrote the heterosexual allure of the modern girl "who dared to be herself," who possessed an assertive personality, and who could test out her competence as a young modern by a trip "Up West" to the central fashion district and the West End cinema.[79]

Female consumers especially linked this new look to dance frocks bought in small gown shops. During the interwar period, researchers found that the "fashion hungry section" of the working class preferred ready-to-wear frocks to home-dressmaking. If they wanted something special for Saturday night dancing, they made their purchases at the gown shops rather than at the multiples. Women interviewed by Mass Observation in the late 1930s praised the good value of Marks & Spencer, but also stated that "unfortunately when you buy a frock and come into the street, you see a lot of people who also have the same frock."[80] Small retail outlets, like the Berwick Street shops, offered ready-made frocks produced at a small scale that allowed working women to keep up with fashion.

Keeping up with fashion meant buying a cosmopolitan frock purportedly made in France or America (that is, Hollywood). The same interwar studies found that proprietors of small dress shops claimed to "have gotten our fashions from French and American magazines," or even to have imported "all our dresses from America."[81] Although the clothes they sold were actually produced in London, the guinea gown shops tried to capitalize on the cosmopolitanism of consumption, the fantasies of escape and transformation mobilized by the great department stores of Oxford Street. The schleppers in Berwick Street, recalled writer Stanley Jackson, pressed customers with promises of "a new line just come over from France."[82] Their retailing extended the glamour of imaginative expatriation and privileged mobility, already developed along the great shopping streets, to the working-class mass market.

Interwar guides consistently identified Berwick Street as a fashion destination for independent working women. In Ethel Mannin's jazz-age fiction, a visit to Berwick Street Market signaled the free, adventurous spirit of the young attractive heroine, who lived on her own and bought produce and accessories from the barrows.[83] Berwick Street Market, wrote another journalist, "lives out of doors and doesn't wear hats. It takes strangers into its confidence. It thrusts fur coats, frocks and blouses under your nose."[84] Besides the allure of goods, travel guides also treated the combative relationship between the avid female shopper and smart young Jewish market salesman "with marcelled hair" and "curvilinear noses" as a challenge to be met, even by middle-class shoppers. "Outside each shop [in Berwick Street Market], was a 'tout,'" explained Thelma Benjamin in her *Shopping Guide to London* (1930), "and if you stop to look in the window, you will find a hand on your arm and a persuasive voice in your ear, and, unless you are very firm, you will be led into the shop, from which there seems to be no escape except by purchase!"[85]

A fictional sketch of Berwick Street Market, published in 1926 by H. V. Morton, a columnist on London life for the *Daily Express*, captured the spirit of adventure and the fashion concerns that propelled working women of the jazz age to Berwick Street.[86] This mid-twenties story was an influential and optimistic narrative of Berwick Street's attractions. The story mocks the inauthenticity and pretensions of the "oriental" Jewish stallholders, and it gently satirizes the business girls who buy artificial (rayon) silk stockings from them. Overall it depicts the eponymous Miss Jones, a smart young typist, less as a fashion victim than as a master of urban modernity. Miss Jones repairs to Berwick Street Market after she discovers a "ladder" in her "best pair of non-stop [artificial] silk" stockings—a "tragedy," the narrator adds, for women who try "to dress like a duchess on seventy shillings a week." Stockings were a sign of the working girl's modernity as well as her personal vulnerability: a necessary component of her new emancipated dress, but an accessory in constant need of replenishment. At the end of her workday, as evening approaches, Miss Jones journeys via omnibus to that "Baghdad-in-the-West" known as Berwick Market.[87] Here she sees "dozens of girls like herself ... carefully picking over stalls burdened with every kind of attire, smart, flashy, and slightly elegant." Berwick Street Market's stalls and store awnings effectively establish a bazaar environment: "In sun or rain the shop awnings come down and meet the canvas roofs of a continuous line of street booths, so that when you walk on the footpath you go through a dark tunnel of canvas, just like a Jerusalem *souk* [bazaar]."[88] In a confrontation between East and West, the knowing and up-to-date Miss Jones haggles with a trader over the price of stockings. She mobilizes all her street smarts to talk back to the stallholders, demonstrating a competence that appears to be both ancient and modern. The Jewish traders on Berwick Street do not exactly dress the part of oriental merchants. These children of immigrants are too style-conscious and English speaking. But Morton imagines that "*if*" "all the Jews in Berwick Street would wear long false beards one day, it would be possible to take a photograph which any short-sighted traveller would swear was Jerusalem."[89] Meanwhile, the selling styles of the "ripe young Rebeccas," aided by "their smart younger brothers," mark them as un-English, in a metropolis more insular than prewar London, having "half-closed" its doors to foreigners, thanks to immigration restrictions.[90] Like Virginia Woolf, the gallant Miss Jones triumphantly leaves Berwick Street with the spoils of battle—in her case, stockings—and just enough money left for her "omnibus fare home to England!"[91]

Lest we allow Morton to define the experience of interwar shopping for working-class women, let us look at another optimistic representation, a snapshot of one such customer, circa 1920, standing in front of Phil Franks's shop in Berwick Street (Figure 14). She is dressed up, showing off a tubular frock. Unperturbed by the array of undergarments in the window display to her right, she presents herself as a pleased, confident modern. She stands hand on hip, a posture that was a common motif in Victorian and Edwardian representations of

14 "Woman in Berwick Street Market, 1923." Dressed in a tubular ready-to-wear frock, this young customer of Phil Franks's stalls embodies the new self-confidence and self-possession of the working-class girl of the 1920s.

working women. The hand-on-hip gesture, art historian Kristina Huneault argues, endowed the female subject with an air of self-possession, sometimes undercut by the open space at its core.[92] The posture reveals a girl who can more than take care of herself, who extends her personal space in the picture. Like Miss Jones, she too desires to appear irreproachable, but she does not manifest any of the fashion anxiety, loss of individuality, or even ethnic conflict ascribed by Morton to the crowds of women who descended on "Bagdad-in-the-West."

Both Miss Jones and the anonymous shopper at Franks represented the new breed of fashion-conscious working women, equipped with personality and self-confidence, whom shop touts tried to waylay into the guinea gown shop of Berwick Street. Thanks to these shops, Berwick Street in the twenties became a "hiving ground for Jewish prosperity—and bankruptcies."[93] In 1920, there were three Jewish costumiers on Berwick Street; by 1930, costumier or gown shops accounted for 30 of the 120 Jewish businesses on the street, many of them keeping stalls in the market as a physical extension of the shop, a way of drawing in customers. Street directories also recorded a sizable increase in the number of female proprietors on Berwick Street who were listed under the category costumier or gown shop, with their Parisian fashion pretensions denoted by the title Madame or by their business name, such as Marcelle or Monique.[94] Costumier shops were locally known as guinea gown shops, because each dress they sold cost a guinea, not a cheap price, as dresses could be bought elsewhere for around half of that amount.[95] Designed along the lines of the latest fashions, these guinea gowns were meant for special occasions, to wear to dance halls. Jewish merchants also opened up guinea shops in other parts of London in the early 1920s, but their presence on Berwick Street signaled the arrival of mass market fashion in central London, a decade before Marks & Spencer and C&A established their emporia on Oxford Street.[96]

London's Fashion Center

These shops physically transformed Berwick Street into a plebeian, Georgian version of the Edwardian West End shopping streets. "Nothing impressed me more, as a child," wrote Chaim Lewis, whose father owned a grocery store on Berwick Street, "than the transformation almost overnight of a single street of shabby derelict, Georgian terraced houses which was Berwick Street, into an assemblage of chrome and glass-plated shop-fronts, each competing for the working-class custom. The pace of development was breath-taking."[97] Focusing on the local immigrant environment, Lewis went on to speculate on the social and economic preconditions for this transformation. The conversion of private dwellings into glass-plated shop-fronts required considerable capital, most of it obtained from banks on short-term loans. It required in turn a brisk turnover of stock to cover the loan repayment. This led to cut-throat competition, as neighboring shops, displaying similar dresses in their shop windows, constantly undercut each other by slashing prices.[98]

Competitive conditions gave rise to extraordinary rags to riches tales, ending, not too uncommonly, with a return to rags again. When pressed to account for their business failures before the Board of Trade, bankrupt gown shopkeepers cited bad debts, high interest on borrowed money, lack of working capital, keen competition, stoppage of credit, and losses through burglary and theft. Personal failings also featured in court proceedings: there were confessions of "gambling extravagance" and "unjustifiable extravagance in living." After the Stock Market crash in 1929, additional factors materialized: trade depression, the king's illness, as well as change of fashion, when the short, tubular dresses gave way to longer, fitted styles, cut on a bias, requiring considerably more skill at fitting.[99]

One spectacular case of boom and bust was Solomon Milbourne, already trading on Berwick Street by 1918 as a ladies' tailor.[100] In the inauspicious year of 1929, he declared bankruptcy. He explained to the Board of Trade that he had come from Poland in 1897 and traded as a costumier on several addresses in Berwick Street until 1923. Then he moved to Wardour Street, a more upmarket, secondary West End location, having spent about £500 on the premises. This move evidently did not work out, so Milbourne decided to return to Berwick Street around 1927 and carried on a similar business until June 1929. "Debtor attributed his interest on borrowed money, keen competition, change of fashion, and depreciation in value of lease of 80, Berwick Street."[101] Milbourne's story appeared in the bankruptcy reports of the *Draper's Record* as a sober business history. In the collective memory of Sohoites it has been transmogrified into a comic morality tale. Lewis and others remembered him as the "Turk," a "character larger than life," a Jewish variant of the working-class swell of the music hall.[102] This Yiddisher "Champagne Charlie" was an extravagant spender, the first on Berwick Street to appear with a Rolls-Royce and chauffeur. He "swaggered" along the road, "flaunting a loud check waistcoat across a broad expanse of chest," sporting an ivory-handled walking stick and cigar. He was on friendly terms with the poor residents, never giving any "side," despite his success, until one day he went bust.[103]

Behind the Turk's boom and bust story, Chaim Lewis discerned a driving immigrant ambition which had "no regard for the usual stratifications of class." The new immigrant desired to be a "boss." Once he became one, Sohoites of the next generation reported, he could not bear his children to go out to work for others.

He might well start as a mere felling hand or machinist, move on to become a
small time employer, expand into a dress-shop, in order to provide an outlet for
his own tailored garments, establish still more shops, which in turn entail the
buying of property, so that in time he found himself both head of a chain of
shops and a substantial property owner.[104]

Some historians have linked Jewish retail enterprise to a romance with an abundance of goods among an ethnic group free of puritanical strictures against the
pleasure of things.[105] Other historians criticize this materialist analysis as essential-
izing and encouraging a false notion of Jewish exceptionalism. They have tended
to look to labor sociology to explain the entrepreneurial drive, and have focused
on the outsider status of the Jewish worker that freed him from conservative
artisanal trade discipline and encouraged a competitive spirit, an opportunistic
eye, a "flair for style," and a "fly by night" adaptability.[106]

Like Italian caterers, the Jewish immigrant who extricated himself and his
family from waged work recruited other co-religionists as waged labor for his
expanded business. Oral interviews with Sohoites are largely silent about labor
organizing or strikes among the employees of these small-scale enterprises, with
one exception: Laura Phillips, whose family ultimately ran five shops in and
around the West End, remembered the undue influence of communists on
workgirls in the early 1920s. "Girls that worked for us, in Charlotte Street they
had a lot of communists going on when I was young and we had the shops. Girls
that worked for us ... were busy with communists, this would be the early
20's—22/23." This was a period of innumerable walkouts and lightning strikes
throughout London trades, but Phillips and others also noted that this kind of
agitation seemed to have tapered off.[107] Efforts to regulate the conditions of
employment emanated a decade later from the Labour government rather than
from unions. When Margaret Bondfield became Minister of Labour in 1929, the
newly vigilant Board of Trade tried to crack down on Berwick Street traders who
deprived their shop assistants of half-day holidays.[108]

Meanwhile both Westminster Council and the Metropolitan Police tried to
rein in the market to ensure the free flow of pedestrian and vehicular traffic. This
was part of a general metropolitan trend, but it may have represented a more
determined municipal effort to contain street disorder in Soho.[109] While largely
content to leave Soho in its unimproved state, the Conservatives on the
Westminster Council began to fix their gaze on the western reaches of the
district around Berwick Street as a future parking area for the West End. In 1927,
the Council sold the old St. James workhouse in Poland Street to Lex Garage,
and agreed to plans for the construction of a Green Line Bus station in Little

Pulteney Street. Both projects vastly increased the amount of vehicular traffic entering Soho. To facilitate this traffic, the Council resolved to "progressively reduce" the number of stalls extending into Little Pulteney Street, Rupert Street and Peter Street.[110] Not everyone was pleased by these "improvements." Lovers of Georgian London, already concerned about the demolition of townhouses in Soho Square and Dean Street, deplored the invasion of the western reaches of Soho by "encroaching shops and garages." "Theatreland," the *Observer* told its readers, "is a wealthy country and possesses a high proportion of motor-cars per head of population. Unfortunately, it never seems to know where to put them." Soho, it feared, was going to end its life as "London's garage." It used to be that "you crossed the Channel in crossing Oxford Street, but soon it will be more like crossing the Atlantic," as Soho's "comfortable dirtiness" and garlic aroma was being overlaid with "ferro-concrete." The *Observer* also blamed Soho's Americanization on Jewish Sohoites who had invaded London's Latin Quarter and replaced the continental restaurants on Wardour Street with dress shops. And while Berwick Street was still a market, "every day it becomes an affair of shops instead of stalls."[111]

Berwick Street's variant of American enterprise did not necessarily bring more order and discipline to the locale. Throughout the twenties, the Metropolitan Police endeavored to discipline Berwick Street Market shop touts who interfered with women "foot passengers" and forced them to "go out of their way."[112] Lacking any budget for advertising, shopkeepers employed aggressive shop assistants who received a commission to bring in customers. These schleppers came to national attention in 1922, when the Commissioner of Police issued a warning to proprietors of business who "tout for custom" in the public thoroughfares.[113] By 1927, to deal with the problems of hygiene, disorder, corruption, and traffic control that street markets seemed to present, the London boroughs licensed stallholders and instituted regular inspections of the markets. These licensing procedures were meant to eliminate the sale of pitches in the market previously "controlled by a number of individuals who let them to traders at specific rentals," a practice often controlled by gangsters.[114] Initially, this policy provoked widespread complaints from street traders and by many sectors of the public who accused the councils of trying to eliminate outdoor markets altogether.[115] But it had the opposite effect. Rather than eliminate markets, their licensing actually helped to regularize them as institutions of London life and to enhance their attractions to middle-class consumers as orderly and hygienic spaces.[116] Overall, the markets acquired an appearance of civility and public order. Interwar guides made it clear that street markets were no longer simply the preserve of the poor. Destinations like Berwick Street

Market were now places where middle-class as well as working-class shoppers could go in search of bargains, where they might even obtain luxury goods like "cantaloup" and "pineapple," old antiques (a euphemism for stolen goods), and even some fashionable durables.[117]

However, these measures did not fully end territorial conflicts over pitches in Berwick Street Market. While there was considerable economic synergy between shops and market stalls, relations between shopkeepers and market traders often proved to be conflictual, as the durable goods that they both traded were interchangeable. During the early thirties, the Westminster authorities received many complaints from shop owners (who often operated stalls at other spots on the street) about stallholders who obstructed entrances to their place of business.[118] Nor did authorities succeed in guaranteeing free pedestrian movement through the market. Walker's Court, leading into Berwick Street Market from Little Pulteney Street, became the most treacherous territory for female pedestrians. Covering the "Berwick Street Touting Prosecutions" in 1930, the *Draper's Record* reported that Sidney Weingarten and his son Michael, costumiers in Walker's Court, were fined for engaging in "absolutely intolerable" obstruction and "serious" molesting of women walking through the arcade. Weingarten senior, along with his wife, operated two adjacent shops in the arcade; he denied the charge of obstruction on the grounds that it would be impossible to get customers to buy goods if they were so obstructed. But Laura Phillips remembered otherwise: even though she was a local, she remembered being waylaid into a gown shop by a schlepper in Oxford Street and obliged to leave a deposit on a dress just to escape the premises.[119]

These prosecutions in the thirties coincided with the circulation of highly stereotyped and anti-Semitic visual images of schleppers in the mass media. In Joe Lee's cartoon, "London Laughs: Berwick Market" (Figure 15), appearing in the *Evening News* in 1936, a "marcelled" and well-dressed salesman, sporting a grotesque snout, presses a disdainful female customer to purchase his "chinchilla" fur. Accessorized with electric lights and awnings, Berwick Street appears as a modern fashion street, but the cartoon broadcasts the wide open nature of the market by positioning the sales pitch in the middle of the street and secondarily representing a woman selling items out of her store window.[120]

In the face of media notoriety and loss of trade, the Berwick Street traders tried to band together and mend their ways. At a meeting in March 1932, presided over by the Vicar of St. Luke's, Berwick Street, shopkeepers in Berwick Street and Walker's Court announced a change of practice. Instead of "touts," the newly formed trade association proposed to substitute a "newspaper advertising scheme." To this end, advertisements appeared the following week in the *Daily*

"But I tell you, Madam, it's a genuine chinchilla …
I know the man who shot it!"

15 Joseph Lee, "London Laughs: Berwick Market," *Evening News*, February 20, 1936. This anti-Semitic cartoon mocks the shady commercial practices of the up-to-date schleppers of Berwick Street.

Mirror and the *Daily Express* headlined "Exit the Tout." Patrons were invited to shop at "London's Fashion Centre" "in perfect comfort" and "at your leisure," to enjoy "unparalleled values," "enormous choice," the latest styles, and "highest standard." However, there appears to have been no follow-up to this campaign, and the schlepper continued to dominate the scene along Berwick Street.[121]

By the 1930s, police prosecutions, bankruptcies, and escalating schlepper aggression were interlocking effects of an economic downturn in Berwick Street's fortunes. Not only were Berwick Street traders subject to keen competition and declining property values in the market, but they also found their market niche threatened by the arrival of Marks & Spencer and other multiples on Oxford Street, as well as by guinea gown shops that began to crop up in the eastern parts of the thoroughfare. The multiples sold stockings at a discount, while the gown shops on Oxford Street purveyed the same dance frocks as the shops lining Berwick Street Market. These retail changes along Soho's periphery disrupted the synergy of stockings and frocks that had traditionally drawn customers into Berwick Street Market. To compound its problems, Berwick Street began to lose the custom of the local Jewish community as Jewish families began migrating to the suburbs, even though 7,500 industrial workers were still employed in the Jewish-dominated garment trades in Soho as late as 1938.[122] Spurred on by the availability of cheap, modernized residential housing, low mortgages, and expanding transport systems, this exodus was evident in the shifting residential patterns of Berwick Street Market traders.[123] In 1929, virtually all the material stallholders on Berwick Street still resided in the neighborhood, with one exception: Phil Franks, who had already made it to the "promised land" of Golders Green. By 1937, 40 percent of Franks's colleagues (20 out of 50) had joined him in the exodus out of central London. Most of them were prosperous hosiers who, like Franks, had already opened shops elsewhere.[124]

While no longer residents, Berwick Street traders continued to operate in the market throughout the thirties. All in all, very few alterations were made to Berwick Street's retail culture. But there were signs of a changing political climate. Some members of Berwick Street's Jewish community manifested a new collective spirit of political engagement in the face of fascism abroad and fascism at home. Beginning in the mid-thirties, Berwick Street Market reconnected with its old radical past. In March 1933, Berwick Street merchants were enlisted in a "spontaneous" and "impassioned movement" to boycott German goods to protest Germany's treatment of their co-religionists. Along Berwick Street, bills were distributed with the words "Boycott German Goods."[125] In July 1933, when London's Jews came together in a day of protest against Germany, Berwick Street shops "remained shuttered" with their blinds drawn.[126] In contrast to Greek

Street, where the Italian Fascists held sway, this part of Soho jeered the British Fascists when they paraded through the West End, and its young men and women went off to fight Mosley in Hyde Park and the East End, sometimes in defiance of their parents, who did not want to arouse the hostility of the British.[127] Louis Feldman remembered a number of Communist sympathizers in the Soho community until Stalin's anti-Semitic trials at the end of the thirties. When Communist organizers brought their anti-fascist message to Berwick Street in 1936, they were able to attract a crowd of 300 with a loudspeaker before their leaders were arrested.[128]

The Schlepper and the Shopper in the Age of the Popular Front

Even in decline, Berwick Street Market continued to attract Popular Front writers and artists who represented it as both promising and foreboding. For politically engaged intellectuals committed to a left-wing alliance against fascism, Berwick Street Market became the ambivalent symbol of massed pleasures, calling forth the democratic promise of urban culture, yet also manifesting the degradations of late capitalism. From the aestheticization of goods to the predatory activities of the property market, Berwick Street Market seemed to summon up all the signs of the times.

Many of these conflicting associations appeared in *The Street Markets of London* (1936), a photo-illustrated account of London's street markets, with photographs by the illustrious Bauhaus artist/photographer László Moholy-Nagy, and an accompanying text by journalist Mary Benedetta. *Street Markets* publicized street markets as a tourist destination, but it worked in a different cultural and political register from the middle market, jazz age journalism of "Miss Jones in Baghdad." Instead, it presented its characters and setting in the left-wing humanistic documentary mode of the thirties. Both the text and images of *Street Markets of London* oscillated between two competing interpretations of urban denizens. They celebrated the cockney street seller, into which the Jewish trader was implicitly folded, as a resilient and expressive icon of the nation in hard times, as a public citizen in a public space. At the same time, they still registered the street market and its traders as purveyors of degraded capitalism and as objects of obsessive, subjective meditations.[129]

"I am convinced that the days of the merely 'beautiful' photograph are numbered," declared László Moholy-Nagy in his foreword.[130] This assertion could be taken as a critical judgment on Moholy-Nagy's own aesthetic preoccupations in the 1920s. During the Weimar years, Moholy-Nagy gained his reputation as an avant-garde photographer who tried to capture perceptions and patterns of vision ordered by the new technologies, producing photograms of careful arrangements of line, circles, points, and surface.[131] But in 1936, in the face of political exile, the Depression, and the fascist threat, Moholy-Nagy embraced the goals of documentary realism in his portrayal of London's markets. He hoped that his "pictorial record" of "objectively determined fact" would disabuse the public of "romantic" notions about street markets as the purported settings for "showmen, unorganised trade, bargains, and the sale of stolen goods."[132] Instead, he proposed to reveal markets that operated as a "social necessity," serving as "the shopping-centre . . . for a large part of the working class."[133] Despite this disclaimer, Moholy-Nagy's photographs of Berwick Street Market reproduce many of the romantic notions he disavowed: they show his continued fascination with the happy-go-lucky character of traders, their elementary actors' skill, their impetuosity. Taken with a Leica, the photographs capture their subjects unawares, enabling market personnel to exert little control over their images.[134] Despite his claim to portray objectively determined fact, Moholy-Nagy still participated in the mystique of the street photograph as transparent social documentation.[135] Moreover, the photographs continue to register a preoccupation with geometrically startling images, with surrealist effects, with objects as opposed to human subjects, and with verbal encounters in a claustrophobic, confining space.[136]

Images of Berwick Street Market are interspersed throughout Moholy-Nagy's photo-essay of London's markets. One image follows the conventional rendering of the locale as a bazaar space of awnings and stalls, with a huge mass of customers squeezed into the middle section.[137] Another photograph repeats themes developed by him around other London markets. It features a close-up portrait of one of the stallholders and presents him as good-humored, mouth open, vulgar and energetic in manners, and plebeian in dress.[138] However, a third image (Plate 6) renders the space more insistently modern and less plebeian than other metropolitan markets. A direct view of a stocking stall gives pride of place to the stockings themselves, as a fetishistic sign of modern female desire, as well as a barrier/screen between seller and buyer.

Missing from Moholy-Nagy's portrait gallery of Berwick Street Market are the flashily dressed, racy schleppers of the street. To find them we have to turn to Mary Benedetta's accompanying text. Here the schleppers are not overtly identified as Jews, but as vulgar, style-conscious and aggressive girls of the neighborhood operating in a depressed economy. By the time Benedetta visited Berwick Street Market in 1936, its boom time had clearly passed. Just after the war, Benedetta noted, "Berwick Market did excellent trade, but nowadays it is very quiet." But the hard selling style for which it was famous persisted or even intensified. "You have to be very strong-minded to visit Berwick Market," Benedetta warned her readers. "The stall holders press you much more than in any of the other street markets." This applied especially to the stalls that sold clothing. "Rows of brown eyes try and hypnotise you into buying something, and when you pass by you can feel them darken behind you." But she assured her readers, "this is nothing to worry about—especially if you want a good pair of stockings." When female shoppers ventured into Berwick Street Market they had to be prepared to "bargain with confidence" and to use a "critical eye."[139]

After these preliminary admonitions, Benedetta began her tour of the market. She had a friendly chat with stallholders who sold remnants, useful for lingerie or for "silk jumpers" for a "tailor-made." She also noted the more traditional market strategy of another trader, the corset stall holder, Madame Birnberg, whose striking street cry, "It'll pull yer in duck," "pull yer right in slim," usually "strikes home."[140] And she spent some time interviewing Mrs. Kerners, "a nice, friendly person to buy frocks from," who was "bred and born in the market."[141] Mrs. Kerners had a dozen girls employed in sewing orders in a nearby building for "things made to measure" that were ordered at the stall. "But there is something which makes them feel infinitely more important—electric lights in the street market." Despite these up-to-date retail fittings, "Oxford Street has knocked out Berwick Market," Mrs. Kerners explained with a sad look in its direction.[142]

These friendly exchanges contrasted sharply with Benedetta's unsettling confrontations with the female schleppers of the guinea shops in the Little Pulteney Street arcade. People who entered the Berwick Street Market by Little Pulteney Street were met by "bold-eyed 'girls' of the district" who stood in the doorways. "Watching, waiting," they tried to draw customers into the shops. "Their make-up is crude in daylight, and they have black crimped hair, shiny with brilliantine."[143] Women shoppers had to be prepared to withstand their gaze and taunts, she warned. "Those who go through the arcade a second time, on the way back from that part of the market, are subjected to a certain amount of insolence. The girls fire remarks to each other as you pass that are scarcely complimentary." Benedetta offered a sample of their patter, ranging from "No I've sorted her inside out, already" to "Doesn't look as though she knows what a dress means" to "Too 'igh 'at, dear, anyway" to "I'd sooner put a dress on a scarecrow as put it on 'er." "That," she declared, "is just their charming revenge on you for not visiting their shops when you went by before."[144]

In Benedetta's account, schleppers could penetrate her inside out, question her clothes sense and her body image, and dismiss her as a social snob. They not only resorted to main force but mobilized the heavily gendered advertisements developed by the great stores along the thoroughfares. That is, they played on women's anxious desire to be attractive, stylish, self-fashioning bodies, now that women were equipped with money to spend on themselves and possessed of a new working independence. Benedetta seemed to concur with another contemporary observer who declared that schleppers were "instinctively psychologists" and fully aware of "the individual conceit of the average passers-by."[145]

Two years later, an even darker version of Berwick Street materialized in the 1938 urban fiction of John Pudney and Storm Jameson, who presented the market as a microcosm of England on the edge of a precipice, waiting for war to commence.[146] Instead of close-ups of lively, vivacious schleppers and shoppers, Pudney's *Jacobson's Ladder* and Jameson's *Here Comes a Candle* zoomed in on a region of the metropolis where a long drawn out crisis of capitalism was playing itself out.[147] These Cultural Front novels resembled Soho crime fiction of the period in their portrayal of an urban district that was vulnerable to corruption and ripe for impending disaster.[148] As in crime fiction, Berwick Street served as a meeting place for metropolitan types, many of them social outsiders whose lives were intricately linked to the illicit and licit economy. But in Pudney's and Jameson's novels, what was happening on Berwick Street seemed to represent higher political stakes: behind the manifold petty commerce of the district loomed the international threat of fascism and the financial manipulations of the London property market, a subject that would exercise the popular press in the postwar years.[149]

Pudney's *Jacobson's Ladder* is an urban folk tale, a version of the Berwick Street boom and bust story. Deserted by his girl for a prosperous pugilist, Jacobson asks the Lord to help him to surpass the prosperity of his competitor. He has a small dress-shop, where, beaming and confident, he stands outside to harass women of all shapes and sizes into party frocks. He carefully adjusts his sales pitch to impress different passersby. "Cockney customers like a noise, enjoyed listening to rhetoric. Timid, close-lipped women from the suburbs needed the persuasion of personal appeal. As for the typists and factory hands at lunch time, some sweet music on the radiogram and a few wise-cracks."[150] Jacobson's first commercial move is to slash prices to undercut his fellow traders, who act as a chorus, declaring that "Jacobson's gone crazy," cutting prices as if he were a "chain store."[151] But they admire him, like their non-fictional counterparts admired the "Turk" of popular memory, for enjoying a sudden and incomprehensible success. His second move is to buy cheap goods from Coley, a receiver of stolen goods, who also operates a sleazy nightclub near the market, with a local girl as hostess and stereotypical ex-officer as manager. To save his own skin Jacobson informs the police when Coley is in trouble over selling drugs. Jacobson initially goes from strength to strength, expanding his number of dress shops, venturing into a new plastic product, and gaining ownership of a slum property essential for the construction of a super-cinema on Oxford Street. In the meantime his assistant Mark, an autodidact intellectual and revolutionary who wants to go to Germany and assassinate Hitler, is disgusted with Jacobson's shady business and leaves him to join a counter-demonstration against the fascists. Jacobson begins to have moral qualms of his own and cracks when he learns that the crook Coley is the figure behind the property deal, only to be saved from suicide by the return of the long lost girlfriend.

Similar disreputable characters appear in Jameson's *Here Comes a Candle*. Jameson's novel takes place in New Moon Yard, within a stone's throw of Berwick Street Market, famous for its dress apparel "made especially for under-sized tight bottomed young women."[152] Originally a handsome three-storied house erected in the seventeenth century, New Moon Yard had become a mini-ature slum in the nineteenth century, but since the end of the war it had acquired a "spurious prosperity." Every room on every floor has its tenant or tenants. A relic of Old London, it is now home to an Italian café bar, a cabinetmaker and his workshop, and a sleazy nightclub. Jews, Italians, refugees, ambitious young couples (including a semi-autobiographical portrait of a struggling independent woman working in advertising), old people left behind, two prostitutes, and a poor young working-class family jostle each other for survival. A pair of Jewish arsonists try to entice different occupants with a scheme to burn down the place so that they can collect insurance. Once again the chief beneficiary of this nefarious scheme turns out to be a devious property developer. This time he is an English parvenu and fascist sympathizer, who, like the crook in *Jacobson's Ladder*, plans to use the property as the back end of a site for an Oxford Street cinema. Reviewers at the time recognized *Here Comes a Candle* as an allegory of interwar England on the edge of conflagration. "No longer post war, its charac-ters might be described as ante-bellum, trying to grab something and run before a smash comes."[153]

Wartime

For Berwick Street, the real smash came on September 18, 1940, when a time bomb left a huge crater at the bottom of the street in the market, one of two spots in Soho where the Blitz produced "concentrated damage."[154] *The Times* reported that the day after the bombing, two butchers on either side of the crater had returned to carry on their business.[155] In fact, produce stalls continued to operate throughout the war. The most devastating time bomb for Berwick Street proved to be clothes rationing. When clothes coupons were introduced in June

1940, the first sign of disaster was the padlocking of the furrier's store in Walker's Court. The once-flourishing trade in silk stockings dried up, no longer enticing customers into the street where they would be caught by the arms and shoulders and hustled into dress shops. When *What's On* paid a visit to the market in 1944, it found the street empty and the shops derelict: "the shutters flap before the many little shops which were once full of cheap gowns and where touts used to stand outside and almost drag customers inside to buy."[156] *Kelly's Post Office Directory*'s listings confirmed the decline: whereas in 1940, there were ninety-nine businesses along Berwick Street, only forty-four remained three years later.[157]

Behind this quiet facade, the market enjoyed a partial comeback as a center for black marketeering, where traders sold "coupon-free" stockings to known customers at a price. Their best days arrived when the Americans established their social center, Rainbow Corner, nearby on Shaftesbury Avenue. In the evening, traders would press GIs as they left Rainbow Corner with invitations of "Anything to sell? Anything to sell?" Barter between servicemen and traders ensured "a steady flow of rationed goods to the market" sold undercover.[158] This contraband traffic led to the 1943 arrest and conviction of Hyman Schatz, whom we earlier encountered in Bankruptcy Court in 1930. In the last war, Schatz had left his wife to run the hosiery stall in 1917, while he joined the Russian army. But this time he made a windfall out of coupon-free lingerie and stockings, for which he was sentenced to two months hard labor and fined £500. When detectives went to his flat, they found a wad of cash amounting to £3,000, tangible evidence, observes writer Donald Thomas, of how much the value of trading in Berwick Street had escalated.[159]

Black marketeering dealt a final blow to Berwick Street's already dicey reputation. In 1946, Victor Falber and Sons, one of the Berwick Street hosiers whose multiples had made it up to Oxford Street, asked the Westminster Council to rename Berwick Street.[160] As owners of 12 and 13 Berwick Street, they were finding it difficult to obtain a tenant. For many years, the locality was regarded as a popular shopping center and property was much sought after. Now, Falber noted, that situation was "completely reversed." Berwick Street premises stood vacant and the market was almost deserted. "It is practically impossible to let property in spite of the fact that there is a strong demand, particularly from wholesalers." Falber cited the factors which contributed to its deterioration as a trading center before the war as still representing "a serious handicap to letting the properties." The Council turned him down (it may not have helped that he had been fined for violating labor regulations regarding half-holidays for his shop assistants in the thirties).[161] Until it revived as a sex and records shop center, with high-rise council housing built over the bomb crater, postwar Berwick Street looked, to quote one observer, "rather like a Klondike town after the gold rush."[162]

Remembering the Schlepper

The dress shop schlepper faded from the postwar scene on Berwick Street, but not from the memory of Old Sohoites. Like all historical recollections, the schlepper is a palimpsest: a creation of 1930s subjective and social experience, overlaid by personal history and imaginative associations of subsequent decades. In the late twentieth century, when Jewish Sohoites recalled the schlepper, they did so from the vantage point of émigrés, participants in the exodus to the outer ring of suburbs during the 1930s and 1940s. In 1999, when I interviewed Louis Feldman, a retired furrier, in his flat in North London, he told me, "I get more pleasure speaking about Soho talking to you here than walking through the streets. It's not Soho as it was." Berwick Street Market and its schleppers existed in Feldman's memory as nostalgic icons of a thriving Jewish community where "you could walk around naked and nobody would interfere with you. You could walk around blindfolded . . . you could leave your front door open and nobody would come into rob you . . . nobody had anything."[163] Thanks to the schlepper and other street characters, the raffish flavor of Soho persisted in Feldman's otherwise homely rendition of a safe urban enclave that was simultaneously at the center of things and a magnet for other Londoners. What distinguished the schlepper from other Soho street types was his or her Jewish identity. The schlepper was an ethnic trickster who negotiated the social boundaries of Jew and non-Jew by deploying both old and new resources; he or she was symbolic of the pressures of the back regions and the new commercial pleasures of mass media and fashion.

Not every Jewish Sohoite remembered the schlepper in the same way. Individuals who actually worked as touts and shop assistants on Berwick Street had little to say about the schlepper's dubious salesmanship. And they did not remember themselves as schleppers. They emphasized, instead, the friendliness and openness of the market. "Everybody was friendly . . . it was a good life really . . . we used to meet at night and discuss things, in the street."[164] The narratives of Berwick Street traders detailed the consolidation and intermarriage among families of shopkeepers "who started with nothing, married each other's children, and made money", and ultimately moved their premises from Berwick Street to other parts of London, becoming successful owners of multiple retail and wholesale businesses.[165] Rather than duplicity and aggression, Berwick

Street assistants were remembered for their retail skill and praised for their strategies of personal service and persuasion, so different from the anonymity of the postwar chain stores.[166] Esther Rose, who worked in a milliner's shop in Walker's Court, admired the daughter of Cohen the hosier as "very sharp. I used to watch her dress the window with the hosiery."[167] Some of the Sohoites who worked in the market did not even represent themselves primarily as sellers. While praising the communalism of the market, Phil Franks distanced himself from its retail culture by revealing a secret self devoted to learning: "I was working on the stall during the day" but "secretly joined the Polytechnic evening classes to continue my education." He kept this schooling from his parents, who "didn't believe in education. They thought it would harm my brain or something."[168]

Other Sohoites certainly voiced some disapproval of the schlepper as "very tough," "a bit of a nuisance," a character who "brought the street down" "and "killed the trade."[169] Because of the schlepper, wrote Chaim Lewis, Berwick Street became a "by-word for unethical trading." It brought the "Jewish name into disrepute." "What started out so prominently as a busy shopping centre, attracting shoppers even from fashionable Oxford Street, soon reverted to an insignificant bywater. 'To Let' boards now presided over derelict shops soon to be taken over by petty tradesmen and warehousemen." But, according to Lewis, this was only a temporary setback. "In a matter of a few years they were on their feet again, the wiser for their experience. Now they boldly ventured into Oxford Street, seeing in this busiest of London thoroughfares the greater trading opportunities that were denied them in Berwick Street." By cutting prices they were able to compete with the large stores and attract the working-class shopper. "There was," Lewis went on to state, "no place for the schlepper in Oxford Street: and no one, least of all the Jews of Soho, regretted his going."[170]

As adults, looking back, other Sohoites might share Lewis's moral assessment of the "unethical trading" practices of Berwick Street, but as children, they clearly relished the energetic street theater offered by the schlepper, and in some ways they did regret "his going." Like Benedetta and other interwar journalists, Sohoites remembered schleppers as manipulative street characters, marginal neighborhood figures, entertaining, but tainted by sexual transgression and by racy associations. Another consistent feature of these narrations was the schlepper's status as a second-generation Jewish immigrant who was English speaking, smart, up-to-date, and exemplary of a certain kind of social assimilation and immersion in a world of consumption. Lewis, for example, recalled schleppers as "great talkers, with a leering eye for women and their weaknesses. They were recruited from the local 'smart boys' and gad-abouts, who traded on their vulgar good looks to earn easy money for themselves."

Women walking along Berwick Street, he wrote, needed all their "wits and nerves" to resist their "wordy confidences": "You want to look smart, don't you. Your husband won't recognise you in this frock. You don't need to buy now. Just try it on, that's all."[171]

Others recollected schleppers as larger-than-life, aggressive women. Dennis Turhim remembered his aunt as "the greatest schlapper you have ever seen! She would stand outside and she would get hold of the women including the Jewish women and 'schlap' them in . . . they never came out empty-handed."[172] According to Alex Flinder, Dolly Lewis, the sister of the famous Jewish boxer Kid Lewis, was the "queen of the schleppers in Berwick Street." She was the "brassiest of brassy blonds. You know Bette Midler the actress, she was like her."[173] "When I was very young I remember vividly at the age of about three [Dolly] getting me down on the floor, lying on top of me with her very ample bosom, and saying I love him, I could bite him." In spite of Dolly's flamboyant sexuality, Flinder went on to defend her retail practice as rational and good value. The patter of schleppers like Dolly, he added, "was marvellous . . . technically very proficient. They knew their marketing before marketing as such was even known to be a science . . ."[174]

Clearly, a wide range of cultural resources were attributed to male and female schleppers. Sohoites tended to depict schleppers as masters of plebeian and mass cultural forms. These included vocal performances that were long associated with the fairground cheapjack and the costermonger. Schleppers and stall-holders could be friendly, amusing, and obliging as well as insinuating and aggressive. Female schleppers could also be the tough street girls of the dress arcades who mobilized plebeian women's capacity for public chaffing and verbal commentary, a knowingness amalgamated to modern styles of aggressive, female sexuality.[175] Alex Flinder invoked the example of Bette Midler, but a more historically accurate prototype would be Midler's spiritual ancestor, Sophie Tucker, who regularly performed in interwar London and who made her career by blending "schmalz" and smut. As many commentators have noted, Tucker's outrageous stage persona was inseparable from her exploitation of jazz age, African-American eroticized femininity. Like Tucker, female schleppers such as Dolly Lewis projected "strong personality" and "personal vitality"; they too were buoyant maternalists, with brazen voices.[176]

If female schleppers bore some resemblance to Jewish red hot mamas, the slick, street-smart male schleppers drew some of their fashion inspiration from the music hall swell updated by Hollywood gangster films. They were "vociferously sporty fellows" who traded on their vulgar good looks.[177] Like the fashion-conscious Italian and Jewish gangsters of London's underworld, they had adopted the dress of celluloid criminals. And here they were not completely different from other aspiring Jewish moderns of the East End. In *East End My Cradle* (1944), Willie Goldman recalled his adolescent friend Sol Levine as the best "chatter" of girls among his crowd. Sol wore padded shoulders, swaggered like a gunman, while addressing girls as "Honey" or some other form of American slang, depending on which film star happened to be influencing him at the time.[178] In the early 1990s, when the Museum of Jewish Life mounted an exhibition on "West End Jews," they collected and exhibited a number of family snapshots of Berwick Street traders. The shop assistants, male and female, gaze at the camera with easy familiarity. They are confident moderns as well as modern confidence men, on equal terms with the viewer, aggressively on the alert for the next potential customer (Figure 16). When I showed the photographs of the knowing, cocky young men, hands in their pockets, standing around Franks's stocking stalls to cultural historian Frank Mort, he discerned a local mode of male attire: a Soho style of wide-boy male fashion apparent in pants tighter than the norm, as well as in the cocked and indented trilby hat.

This masculine style leads me to speculate on some covert meanings of the schlepper. The male schlepper bore a strong resemblance to the spiv, the icon of

16 "Phil Franks in Berwick Street Market, 1924." This family snapshot features stylishly dressed Berwick Market traders as knowing, cocky young men on equal terms with the viewer.

1 Postcard of St. Anne, Soho. Based on John Strype's 1754 version of John Stow's *Survey of London* and closely approximating an earlier 1690 parish map. The Soho Society reproduced this early modern map of St. Anne's Soho to demonstrate the persistence of Soho's old urban fabric into the late twentieth century and to defend its integrity against the incursions of the property market and urban planners.

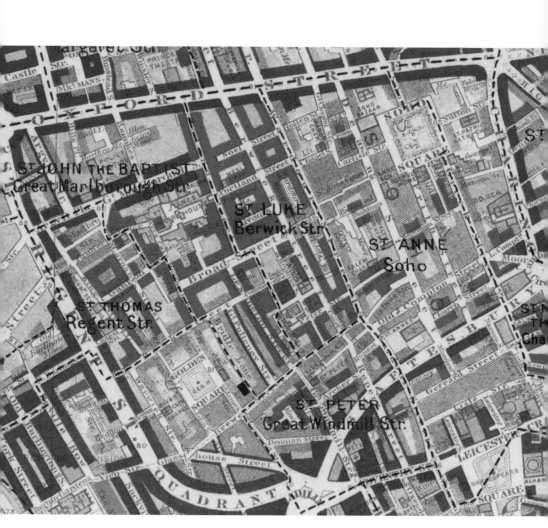

2 "St. James, Westminster and St. Anne, Soho." *Charles Booth Descriptive Map of London Poverty 1889,*
sheet 6 (1). Booth's color-coded map of poverty highlights the relative prosperity of St. Anne, Soho as
compared to the poorer streets of St. James, Westminster to its east that were informally annexed to Soho
after the building of Regent Street.

3 Maud Allan at the Palace Theatre, March 17, 1908. This photograph captures Allan's trancelike stance, evocative of the hysteric, the mystic, and the autoerotic.

Famed for Art as Well as Food

The " Quo Vadis " in Soho

To Celebrate Birthday With " Open House "

The " Quo Vadis "—famous little London restaurant as popular in catering circles as it is among a discerning public—celebrates its tenth birthday next Friday with an " open house " to the friends and customers of its proprietor, Mr. Pepino Leoni.

Leoni, as he is known to everyone, has built up a world-wide and dual reputation for his restaurant. First, it is famed for its food, but, second, for its pictures. For this little Soho restaurant is also a permanent exhibition of modern art.

Its walls are covered with the works of British artists who are given this unusual opportunity of displaying their " wares." To such good effect that in the past few years over a thousand pictures have been sold to customers.

This short article (written by one of the restaurant's oldest customers) reveals some of the secrets of success of the " Quo Vadis."

The " Quo Vadis " is strictly a " one-man show " and has gained its reputation through the personality of its proprietor, Leoni. When an American writer sings the praises of this unpretentious gourmets' paradise to the tune of a column in all the American Hearst newspapers, as he did in August, the reputation of Leoni is advanced to the international class.

This small, young, smiling native of Cannero, a village on Lake Maggiore,

Leoni, proprietor of the " Quo Vadis " Restaurant, Soho, shows customers some of the works of modern art that decorate his walls

came to London when fourteen years old. He was lured by tales of the success here of other Canneresi and by the romance of the mighty Giovanelli, chef of Tzar Nicholas II.

He worked up from *commis* to a better position, then he returned to Italy, voluntarily, to fight in the Great War.

Wounded, he came back to resume his career as waiter until he heard of a derelict restaurant in Dean Street which was going cheap.

Leoni scraped together enough money to acquire this tiny place, never changing its name, because he believed in his rigid policy for success—" to give the best of food and service for the least money."

His first client was the antique dealer, Lionel Harris, whom he strove to please. Then came Clement Bich, one-time manager of the Berkeley and May Fair Hotels. To them he revealed his knack for purveying dishes with character, perfectly cooked and unique for flavour.

The quiet simplicity of " Quo Vadis " and Leoni's own sincere and kindly personality drew gradually a clientele of artists, writers and actors, who wished to escape from the jazz-ridden restaurants of a decade ago. And soon, diplomatic and social circles became aware of this unusual rendezvous.

To Help Artists

Ever on the alert to help others, Leoni donated the walls of his ever-expanding enterprise to Edward Craig, Gordon Craig's son and grandson of the immortal Ellen Terry, for a permanent exhibition of modern art. These paintings were for sale, and not only did the young artists welcome this thriving market-place, but visitors enjoyed the ever-changing pictures.

Other than this, " Quo Vadis " is almost undecorated, except for pink and green walls and ever fresh flowers on the tables.

To Be Enlarged

But Leoni has outgrown the present restaurant, where only two hundred patrons can be served, and when official consent has been given he will take over the neighbouring house.

Plans for this enlargement are being

Continued on page 40

A corner of the " Quo Vadis " Restaurant with its art gallery on the walls. The young chef in the background is an Italian boy who won one of the highest culinary awards in his country—now exchanged for a British student in Italy

4 and 5 "Famed for Art as Well as Food: The Quo Vadis in Soho." *Caterer and Hotel-Keeper*, October 9, 1936, p. 20. Above, Leoni shows patrons the modern artwork of the Grubb Group on exhibit in his dining saloon. Below, he presents the staff and patrons in Quo Vadis's main dining salon. The caption makes special note of the new young chef (seen at the back), who was recruited from Turin by Leoni after he had read *L'Italia Nostra*'s account of him as a talented, unemployed loyal Fascist.

6 László Moholy-Nagy, "Stocking Stall." Moholy-Nagy spotlights a Berwick Street stocking stall as a fetishistic sign of modern female desire and a barrier/screen between buyer and seller.

7 Dennis Turhim, *The Astoria, Charing Cross Road, 1933*. Turhim's watercolor painting of the 1990s recalls the Charing Cross Road as a modern public space open to all, consistent with the democratic spirit of London Transport posters.

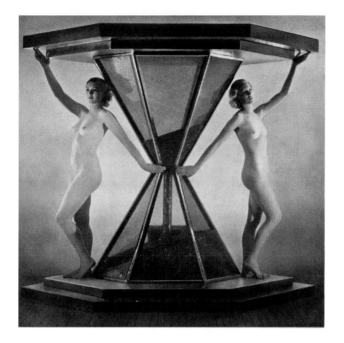

8 "The Hour Glass," *Revudeville 60, from Revudeville, Souvenir of Nos. 57 to 60, c.*1934–5. Revudeville Souvenir photographs were considerably more graphic than the actual stage presentation of tableaux, when medium stage lighting was strategically beamed on the girls' faces and left most of their figures in the shadows.

9 "London Night Life," *London Life*, October 12, 1940, cover. This highly eroticized rendition of the Windmill Girls at War, who are asleep in their dressing rooms yet beautifully made up, glamorizes the wartime genre of shelter scenes where ordinary Londoners survived the war by sleeping.

black-market culture of 1940s London. But the word spiv was around long before the 1940s.[179] The spiv was already a recognized type by the time the schlepper made an appearance in Berwick Street Market. He lived on his wits; he was a cheat and a rogue; he talked fast; and "he got away with it." As Jerry White notes, he was the ice tip of an informal London economy, the connecting link between plebeian London and a well-developed, organized criminal under-world that made interwar Soho its leisure center.[180] As we have seen, wartime conditions actually enabled some schleppers to metamorphose into full-blown wartime spivs, selling "coupon-free" stockings in the market.

Female schleppers also marked a Jewish involvement in this illicit world, an implicit link to the sex trade of the neighborhood. The Berwick Street area was full of male and female sex workers, notably transvestite performers, street-walkers, and dance hostesses employed in the nightclubs in and around Berwick Street. Looking back on their childhood, Sohoites remembered prostitutes as familiar street characters. "There was no escaping the exotic life of these streets," recalled Chaim Lewis. "Much as we tried to look straight ahead of us as we walked to our synagogue in Manette Street . . . we noticed more of the sordid side of life than we dared admit."[181] Streetwise boys could recognize a prostitute from a hundred yards away, recalled one Sohoite.[182] Some Jewish "urchins" even developed personal friendships with the prostitutes who stood at the corner of Greek Street and Manette Street: they remembered one woman nicknamed "Gifty" who gave them hugs, money and sweets.[183] For Feldman, "Gifty" was a second mother: "I used to stand with her till she got a customer. Then she used to give me a peck on the cheek and say, 'I won't be long Louis' and used to disap-pear . . . . She would be back in twenty minutes and we would carry on as if nothing happened." She always gave him sixpence or a shilling, a lot of money at the time. "And I used to go home and give my mother half the money, mother said, in Yiddish, 'where did you get this.' I used to say, 'A very nice lady gave me this.'"[184] For girls it was "different": parents kept a sharp eye on them. Yet, the local economy often required their interaction with street girls. Prostitutes numbered among Esther Rose's best clients for her millinery, when she traded under the name "Madame Hannah."[185]

At the same time, Jewish Sohoites adamantly denied the involvement of local Jewish girls in the trade—"never a local girl," they would say. When pressed, however, Sohoites acknowledged one or two Jewish prostitutes in the area: a "Yiddisher Betty" or a sister of a fighter, but it was "never mentioned."[186] Female informants were equally vehement about their freedom as adolescents to walk unmolested through Soho streets, day and night, although, here again, memories diverged. At least one woman recalled some moments of confusion:

Once I was standing on the corner of Dean Street and Oxford Street waiting for a friend, lunchtime. And one of the girls came up to me and said: "what's it like at this end luv?" And I cannot remember what I answered but I was truly horrified ... but that could happen to you. I mean one could be propositioned ..."[187]

But others insisted that "nobody would interfere with you," a phrase used to signify both the absence of sexual harassment of good women on the street as well as the more general tendency among ethnic groups in Soho to coexist yet maintain social distance.[188] This "absence of disharmony"—a live-and-let-live way of occupying heterogeneous space—closely approximated Sohoites' late twentieth-century understanding of the district's cosmopolitan milieu in the interwar years.[189] Such tolerance also entailed, in their minds, cognitive and physical boundaries. Precisely because women moved among prostitutes, engaged in business transactions with them, observed them at their pitches, it was imperative that the temple of their body, their privacy in public, not be confounded with the public actions of prostitutes.[190] Yet Dolly Lewis, the schlepper, represented exactly that porous boundary and blurring of categories, in sum a cosmopolitan confounding of multiple female sexualities in the locale.

Conclusion

Berwick Street Market's history exemplifies the dynamic interaction between the industrial back regions of central London and the spectacular pleasure zones of the West End boulevards. The landscapes of power along the thoroughfares created the conditions of possibility for the emergence of Berwick Street's industrial economy. Berwick Street Market's subsequent transformation into a retail space also depended on the magnetic appeal of the great shopping streets. Berwick Street tried to siphon off foot traffic from the thoroughfares by offering working-class consumers an alternative to Oxford Street's social exclusions, lofty prices, and class codes.

The cultural practices of Berwick Street Market ratify William Sewell's interpretation of culture not so much as a coherent system as a site of multiplicity, "a sphere of practical activity shot through with willful action, power relations, resistance, and contradiction."[191] Throughout the interwar years, media representations zeroed in on the combative encounters between working-class shoppers and schleppers, treating both sides of the exchange as aspiring moderns who were also counterfeits and upstarts, lacking substance and conviction, ready to stray from the class codes and styles of established English culture.[192]

This ambivalence materialized not only in the middle-market press of the twenties but also surfaced in the writings and documentary photography of Popular Front intellectuals of the thirties. In search of an urban citizenry and democratic urban culture as bulwarks against fascism, Moholy-Nagy, Pudney, and Jameson fixed their gaze on Berwick Street and its denizens. But they also registered Berwick Street as a negative embodiment of capitalist commerce, a back region of the metropolis in terminal decline, both morally and economically. Old Sohoites saw their urban space differently, even though their insider memories also registered uneasiness about the schlepper and his or her unethical practices. By remembering the schlepper, they summoned up memories of a safe and modern space of ethnic settlement that was simultaneously at the center of things and tied to Soho's irregular economy, sexual and gendered nonconformities, and tense, cosmopolitan heterogeneity.

CHAPTER 6

A Jewish Night Out

ON THEIR NIGHTS OUT, JEWISH SOHOITES VENTURED TO THE PERIPHERY OF their neighborhood, to the cinemas, dance halls, and Lyons' Corner Houses that ringed Soho. Here they entered a broader current of London life, yet coexisted with many of the same irregular cosmopolitan elements that gravitated to Berwick Street Market. Rather than decamping entirely from their neighborhood, Sohoites annexed what they imagined to be the safe urban village of Jewish Soho to the outer world of London's commercial thoroughfares. To use the terms of critical geography, they mentally transformed the commercial West End boulevards from a *space* created by finance capital and state rationalities into a quotidian and democratic *place* where they could present themselves as competent moderns.[1]

Moving from dance spaces to massive eateries, this chapter tracks the sequential staging of a night out by Jewish Sohoites along Soho's commercial peripheries of Leicester Square, Charing Cross Road, and Tottenham Court Road. While spotlighting Jewish residents of Soho, I also turn my attention to the social performances of other occupants of these venues, notably professional dance partners, single-sex couples, modern English waitresses, and queer patrons of Lyons'. Jewish Sohoites fashioned their heterosexual destinies amidst a full array of conventional and transgressive bodies.[2] In contrast to theatrical spaces, where nonconformist bodily idioms were spatially marked off from patrons, competing modes of eroticized expression intimately coexisted in these popular venues. At the Astoria Dance Salon, courting couples danced the tango and foxtrot alongside female couples and paid dancing partners who were ambiguously attached to commercialized sex. Jewish Sohoites also found themselves in close proximity to non-normative sexualities when they repaired to the massive

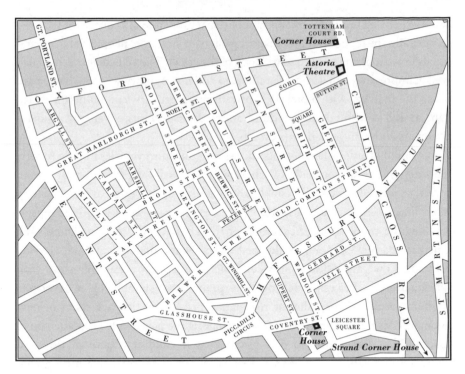

Soho's Eastern Peripheries

Coventry Corner House for "egg mayonnaise" or beans on toast. The Lyons' management relied on its own embodiment of restrained modern femininity, the up-to-date and smartly uniformed waitress known as the Nippy, to manage the mixed crowd. Widely celebrated as a reliable and capable "public servant," the Nippy found her own body subject to intensive managerial surveillance, lest she deviate from the staid variant of modern English womanhood manufactured by her Jewish employers.

The Astoria, Charing Cross Road, 1933

The watercolor painting *The Astoria, Charing Cross Road, 1933* imaginatively captures the annexation of a West End thoroughfare by Sohoites (Plate 7). Painted by Dennis Turhim, a master tailor, after he retired from work in the 1990s, it hangs in Louis Feldman's sitting room in North London. In visual terms, it documents the access of the second generation of Jewish immigrants to new forms of leisure, bodily expression, food culture, and physical settings. Offering a second-story view of the thoroughfare, near its top towards Oxford Street and St. Giles Circus, *The Astoria* records Turhim's memory of the Charing Cross Road.

It is a reassuring image of a modern public space, open to all, consistent with the democratic spirit of London Transport posters. A stream of people, vehicles, and goods flow along the congested roadway of the street. The vehicular traffic is realized in impressive, hyperrealist detail: hand and horse-drawn wagons share space along the roadway with a bicycle, a private car, a delivery van, numerous black cabs, as well as with a double-decker London Transport bus, enveloped in advertisements and with garden seats on top.

Beyond this orderly and democratic array of transport vehicles lies the Astoria Theatre, on the western side of Charing Cross Road at the corner of Sutton Street, its white facade set in relief by the black sea of conveyances passing along its frontage. Financed by Paramount as a showcase for its own productions, it signifies the transnational hegemony of the Hollywood dream machine. The cinema's marquee announces the first-run showing of *Bombay Mail*, starring Edmund Lowe and Shirley Grey.[3] A Dolcis shoe store, a multiple shop with headquarters in Leicester, occupies the premises at street level; it advertises "fashion footwear" for ladies at reasonable prices and displays them in neat geometric fashion.[4] Some pedestrians pass along the pavement; a few are men in work clothes, but most are men, women, and children attired in tidy and contemporary urban street wear. Outside the theater entrance in Sutton Street, men and women queue up to gain entrance to the 8 p.m. performance: they are being entertained by a series of street buskers performing in an empty roadway, who also draw the attention of children further down the pavement who stop and gape.

Besides materializing the global systems of provisioning and distribution that flowed along the roadway, *The Astoria, Charing Cross Road, 1933* also delineates a sedimented landscape of power, laid down through successive cycles of capital accumulation.[5] In 1927, American entrepreneurs built the Astoria Theatre and Dance Salon, constructing it out of the shell of the Crosse & Blackwell warehouse. This warehouse had been erected on the site in 1892, a few years after the Charing Cross Road had opened as a street improvement to facilitate the north–south flow of traffic across the metropolis. When it was converted to a theater, its original brick and stone Gothic front was altered and disguised with a cement facing in a vaguely classical facade.[6] In his careful rendering of the original brickwork on the Sutton Street side of the edifice, Dennis Turhim sustains a visual link to the building's earlier manufacturing use.[7]

The painting also illustrates how social actors transformed large-scale movements of culture and capital into a localized theater of consumption.[8] On Sutton Street, improvising street characters offer free entertainment in an empty roadway leading up to Soho Square. The Sutton Street scene imaginatively stands in for a knowable community of neighbors and pedestrians. In conversation, Louis Feldman drew my attention to the scene, identifying the "real" street characters from the past and detailing their acts, emblematic of individual prowess and cultural invention, not so very different from the positive valuations of schleppers advanced by Alex Flinder and Dennis Turhim. He begins with a pair of entertainers, pictorially represented by a double zigzag in the visual style of the jazz age, who perform a sand dance routine in the street's empty roadway, while a piano player waits his turn, to be followed by a "chap" whose only prop is an umbrella. "In those days," he observed, "buskers were fantastic artists. Each one had something different," a telling contrast, he believes, to the routinized sham of busker culture today, when "everyone plays guitar" and "plays the same tune."[9]

Feldman's memories of pleasure also stretched back to the Astoria Dance Salon, opening in 1927 in the basement of the super-cinema as the first dance hall in central London. Both the Astoria and the Hammersmith Palais were launched by Booker and Mitchell, American pioneers of the postwar dance industry, whose other London establishments included the raffish Rector's Dance Club on the Charing Cross Road.[10] In 1919, the Hammersmith inaugurated the era of palais dancing in Britain, leading to the creation of 11,000 purpose-built dance halls between 1919 and 1926.[11] Decorated in neoclassical, "Renaissance" style, the Astoria repeated the formula that had already made Hammersmith a great popular success: a large, well-sprung maple dance floor lit by revolving colored spotlights, surrounded by chairs and tables for non-alcoholic refreshments, a balcony for viewing, a dais for two excellent bands that ensured continual dance music, a pen for the male and female professional dancers who could be hired as partners for unaccompanied patrons, as well as practice rooms, lavatories, kitchens, and cloakrooms.[12]

Dora Samuel, an ex-milliner who frequented the Astoria in the late twenties and early thirties, personally drew me a floor plan of its interior as she remembered it seven decades later.[13] Her diagram captures many of the Astoria's attractions: it includes a dance floor (supposed to accommodate 1,000 dancers) surrounded by tables and chairs seating two to four couples, where you "go up eight steps" for private sociability and light refreshments. There was also a brilliantly lit band dais where a jazz band played and "stairs to reach above" to the balcony, for non-dancers who wanted to observe those below and have a private tête à tête. At the top of the image, she lists the modest entry fees (2s 6d for the evening, 1s 6d for tea dancing).[14]

Grooming, make-up, and dressing up were essential components of Dora Samuel's preparation for "going to the palais."[15] Like other working-class youth,

Sohoites had to extract the maximum of glamor from limited resources, but their own sartorial skills gave them some fashion advantages.[16] Jewish women like Samuel disdained dresses "off the peg." "Ready-to-wear was a nasty phrase in the Yiddish vocabulary," recalled one East End memoirist.[17] The best dress had to be a garment, sometimes produced out of a material remnant from work, that was expertly fashioned by the wearer or by friends or family.[18] By the late 1920s, Sohoites, like other young women and men of the period, regarded cinema not only as a destination space but as the paragon of glamor to be emulated in other leisure venues. "We grew up with the Hollywood culture of the time" and "aped some of the things they wore," remembered Rachel Goldberg, a clothes designer.[19] The test of cinematic impersonation was the dance floor at the Astoria, although some Sohoites also ventured to the Hammersmith, Carlton (1928), and later to the Paramount (opened in 1936). Beauty culture that was centered on dancing found its enthusiasts among Jewish youth of both sexes. Young men patronized hairdressing salons where they were shaved, hot-toweled, trimmed, oiled and perfumed, while girls went in for perms, hair waving, curling, eyebrow plucking, shampooing, and manicuring. [20]

An evening out not only represented a glamorous break from the arduous labors of the rag trade that consumed their waking hours for six days a week; dance halls also enabled young people to escape the supervision of neighbors and family authorities and engage in a series of heterosexual encounters. It was part of the secularization of the second generation of immigrant Jews. For these reasons, communal authorities regarded mass leisure spaces with considerable disquiet. As with Gentile youth organizations, Jewish clubs vied for the attention and leisure hours of the working-class boy and girl. They continuously waged warfare against the paint and powder that were key elements of the glamorous appearance of tea dancing and cinema-going.[21] Samuel's love of dancing, for instance, brought her into conflict with Miss Lily Montagu, philanthropist, long-time feminist, and director of the West Central Jewish Working Girls' Club (first located in Dean Street, Soho, and then in Alfred Place, Bloomsbury). Through her club, Miss Montagu offered rational recreation and job placement to the Jewish girls of central London, hoping that this social capital would enable them to sustain a Jewish identity while integrating them into English society. Montagu's views of modern womanhood harkened back to the ideals of female chastity and independence promulgated by prewar suffragists like Mrs. Ormiston Chant: the advancement of women through dignified labor and citizenship, coupled with a deep suspicion of commercial entertainments and their sexual dangers for girls.[22] As one Old Girl recalled, the idea of the Girls' Club was "to keep the girls off the street." But, she added, it "snowballed and finished by having proper classes," including a "marvellous dramatic class," even though professional theater workers were barred from membership, on the grounds of dubious respectability.[23]

During the interwar years, Miss Montagu's hold over the leisure time of Jewish working girls was severely challenged by commercial counter-attractions along the West End thoroughfares. Samuel remembered that Miss Montagu was "not terribly keen" on her dancing at the Astoria, particularly when she passed up club meetings to go there instead. Miss Montagu went so far as to visit her widowed mother to complain. A tense conversation ensued, with Miss Montagu speaking "polished" English and Samuel's Yiddish-speaking mother forced to respond in "broken English."[24] As Samuel recounted it seventy years later, the dialogue went like this:

> Miss M.: I don't think [Dora] should [go dancing]
> Mother: But that's what she likes to do
> Miss M.: She should be a good girl
> Mother: She is a good girl![25]

At stake was not only a power struggle between two maternal figures, but also two different modernizing strategies. Miss Montagu's tried to keep Jewish girls within the folds of the Jewish community, while assimilating them to the conventions of English respectability and civic culture. To her, the dance halls smacked of the low cosmopolitan temptations so prevalent on Soho streets. While still remaining within a Jewish crowd, Dora Samuel and her friends chose another route: collective participation in a commercialized dance culture that featured Anglicized versions of American and South American forms and seemed to offer an escape from everyday life.

By going to the Palais, Samuel and her friend simultaneously entered a modern culture of heterosexuality. During the first decades of the twentieth century, historians argue, heterosexuality "stepped out" as a normalized state of erotic pleasure independent of reproduction for both men and women. This modern heterosexual performance depended on a series of modern props— fashion, cosmetics, dancing prowess, and attitude—that were newly available to working men and women through mass commodity culture. Possessing the right look emboldened young working people like Samuel to move beyond their locales into a broader public sphere.[26]

Samuel vividly recalled the bodily preparations necessary for her weekend dancing. She always visited the hairdresser on Friday afternoon to get an "iron wave." Her beauty culture extended to a little rouge, powder and lipstick, which she carefully removed before she returned home in order to avoid a row with her mother. "We always dressed well although we didn't have a lot." To describe her look at age fifteen (1928), she explained that she wore well-pressed clothes, a flared skirt that ended just below the knee, greyish stockings and dancing shoes with short, thin heels. Samuel and her friend Esther Cohen assured me that extreme versions of Hollywood glamour—heavy eye make-up, peroxide-dyed hair, and (later) diamond hair clips—would be deemed unusual or cheap, a view conforming to the standards of Mass Observers who reported on their visits to the halls in the late 1930s.[27] But this was the glamorous appearance cultivated by Rachel Goldberg, living with her parents in Berwick Street: she appeared in her 1936 passport picture as a platinum blonde, with a wavy perm, and she further recalled dressing up "like dogs' dinners" when she went out dancing, wearing heavy mascara, "cupid bow lips," and plucked eyebrows.[28] She also preferred Hammersmith to the Astoria, perhaps because she fancied a more mixed social space where Jews danced alongside of, and sometimes with, Gentiles, and where middle-class patrons were also present. This preference signaled a modest act of cultural nonconformity on Goldberg's part that distinguished her from the usual Soho crowd, indicative of her willingness to test the communal norms of femininity.

Sohoites fondly remembered the Astoria as a meeting place for Jews. "As we got older we went to the Paramount and the Astoria. It was wonderful always packed out with Jewish boys and girls."[29] Sunday nights, recalled Mildred Loss, the widow of Joe Loss, the Astoria's star bandleader, was "almost Jewish night."[30] It would remain a Jewish rendezvous during the Blitz of October 1940, when East End Jews believed it to be a safe underground refuge that "takes you out of yourself": "It's safe there, and we're all together, so don't hear the noise."[31] Within this endogamous category, Sohoites drew some distinctions, between the West End Jews who lived south of Oxford Street within the boundaries of Soho, and those from "the other side" north of Oxford Street, a difference that only Sohoites seemed to care about. A more significant distinction may have prevailed between Jewish denizens of east and west London. Numerous informants remembered the parade of East Enders who would descend on central London on Saturdays, arriving at Portland Place by underground and proceeding by foot to the Astoria.[32] Some East Enders, after attending synagogue in the morning, would arrive in the West End in the afternoon to window shop and stroll around.[33] A larger contingent arrived on Saturday evenings by bus and underground. According to Sonya Birnbaum, East End girls wore black stockings and high-heeled shoes. They were "a different community, a little bit louder than the West End . . . Looked the height of fashion, a little flash."[34]

While some informants insisted there was no difference between the two Jewish communities, other Sohoites claimed more cultural capital for themselves as a result of being able to "walk into culture" into a glittering mixed environment that included the social elite and provided an abundance of pleasures and cultural amenities.[35] "The great thing about the West End at that time . . . was that it was very cosmopolitan," observed Alex Flinder. When Flinder and his friends, including the future filmmaker Michael Klinger, walked around the "block" of Shaftesbury Avenue, Charing Cross Road, Regent Street and Oxford Street, they saw the "smart people" going to the theaters and restaurants, and artists and prostitutes clustered around the stage doors of Charing Cross Road.[36] The influence of the restaurants and the theaters, plus the "personalities" who went to these areas, "rubbed off on us."[37] By contrast, Max Minkoff believed that "the East End community had to entertain themselves more than the West End, who had entertainment on their doorstep."[38] East Enders, declared one Sohoite, were more "cockney," yet the standard of living of the two communities, in terms of wages and housing, did not diverge markedly, a fact that some East End denizens did not fully appreciate.[39] One woman remembered that some East End boys who wanted to make a good "shidduch" (marriage match) mistakenly believed that if "you lived in the West End . . . you were very rich."[40]

The dance floor at the Astoria was the early site of many of these courtships. Sohoites fully participated in the "dancing mad" culture of the twenties and thirties and regarded themselves as avid and adept dancers, a view seconded by various journalists and Mass Observation reports. Dora Samuel, who had received ballet lessons as a young girl, never missed a dance when she went to the Astoria. "They knew I was a good dancer: that's why I had to book the dances ahead."[41] According to Louis Feldman, who regarded himself as a fair dancer, "a woman's dancing skills trumped her looks at the dance hall." "It did not make any . . . difference about her looks. If she was a good dancer she was dancing the whole evening, that's all people wanted." But Feldman did acknowledge that if "there was a good looking girl down there," "they would chat her up hoping there would be an end product to it."[42]

Jewish Sohoites counted dancing prowess as one of the social distinctions that marked them off from Gentiles. In his general study of mid-twentieth century English popular culture, Ross McKibbin notes a chasm between young women's huge enthusiasm for dancing as compared to young men, a result, he believes, of the wider range of sports alternatives available to males. The discrepancy may also be due to women's attraction to dance as a kinesthetic form of expression and to greater attachment to romantic courtship.[43] Beyond physical exercise, women remembered the dance hall as a romantic space that most satisfied female desire, where women established the terms of physical intimacy.[44] Compared to Gentiles, Jewish men seemed to have been exceptional in their dancing enthusiasm. In his East End memoirs, Willie Goldman recalled that when he and his friends ventured to a dance hall frequented by Gentiles, they "didn't like us dancing with their girls," not the least, he claimed, because Jewish youth were so successful at attracting young women. By "combination of good dancing, cheek, and sexual aggressiveness," a Jewish boy could count on being able to "walk home with the most attractive girl in the place," that is, if "they let him get that far."[45] Fearing the effeminate associations of being soft as a dancing boy, Jewish men also felt obliged to supplement dancing with pursuits of a "more manly kind," such as billiards, both of which could be learned at the West Jewish Lads' Club in Fitzroy Square and practiced in more commercial venues.[46] This compensatory strategy informed Leslie Milgrim's quip: "In my day, if a lad was a good dancer and a good snooker player, that was a sure sign of a misspent youth."[47]

Competition and Conflict in the Dance Hall

In 1936, the *Manchester Guardian* proclaimed the Astoria, along with the Hammersmith Palais, to be the home of "serious and competition dancers."[48] Commentators of the period noted the vast gap between palais dancing and what passed for dancing in West End restaurants like the Café de Paris, where society dancers "merely walk" around the dance floor.[49] The standard of dancing at the Astoria was so good, explained the Astoria's manager to a Mass Observer in 1939, that "people from the suburbs are afraid to come here."[50] When asked how they learned to dance so well, Sohoites said that they learned very quickly from each other, from a partner or a friend, without any formal lessons.[51] You "practice with your partner." "Everyone did the same steps." The difference lay in the way individuals "held themselves."[52] Louis Feldman stressed the ability of partners to "click" and "read each other's mind," and respond to the lead of the partner. "Everything," he recalled, "was about keeping in time."[53]

As skilled, competitive dancers, Sohoites embraced the tango as another sign of distinction. When asked about their favorite dance, Dora Samuel, Esther Cohen, and Rachel Goldberg emphatically stated their preference for the tango, a dance that was highly prized by dance professionals but unpopular with the dancing public overall, on account of its perceived difficulty. English dancers, reported dance experts, lacked the temperament for this "most graceful" and "Southern dance."[54] When asked why she liked the tango, Samuel responded that she liked the music. She did not register it as a Latin American form so much as generically foreign, "not from this country."[55] For Samuel, dancing the tango may well have represented a form of "visceral cosmopolitanism," to quote Mica Nava: an imaginative expatriation into a space of kinesthetic pleasure outside the nation.[56] Samuel and others remembered the tango steps as more intricate than, say, the foxtrot. They seemed to have taken as much if not more pleasure in mastering the tango's dance steps in its English edition as in its body-to-body interactions.

Sohoites remembered the Astoria as a space of kinesthetic freedom and improvisation while ignoring the forms of commercial restraints imposed on them. In fact, dancing was not quite the zone of freedom remembered by Samuel and others. Despite the need for empathic communication between partners, popular dancing was highly regulated by the standardized rules of English dancing, particularly for groups and individuals as immersed in the world of competitions as Sohoites. Their recollections of dance were peppered with references to dance competitions and trophies won by themselves or by their siblings. Along with dance lessons and professional dance exhibitions, dance competitions enabled dance teachers to rein in the chaotic, syncopated, "go as you please" popular dancing of the immediate postwar period.[57] By 1924, the Imperial Society of Dance Teachers had established the correct dance steps for four principal dances—foxtrot, quickstep, waltz, and tango. This national codification established the standards by which local competitions were judged. The newly introduced rules of English dancing also imposed strict tempo music on dance bands and prohibited them from indulging in jazz improvisation.[58]

One professional goal of standardization was racial purification of imported dance forms, particularly those believed to be tainted by African-American bodily idioms. Dance professionals managed to reinstate an elite white deportment more reminiscent of the nineteenth century than the jerky syncopations of the jazz age. Standardized rules for the foxtrot, to take the most popular dance form, reintroduced the contrast between the lower body doing all the work and a smooth upper body. Dancers were instructed to give the appearance of "free and flowing and effortless" movement and to exude an air of elegance and class.[59] Similarly, the "un-English" tango, so beloved by the Soho crowd, also underwent a similar process of refinement and standardization.[60] Originally an Argentine dance of the brothels, the tango entered the British dance scene via Paris in 1912–13. In the early twenties, dance professionals introduced an English edition of the Parisian tango, with simplified figures and the elimination of all "objectionable movement" of the crotch, like the "scissors."[61] Through codification, dance professionals established an international as well as national standard for English dancing. As leading dance instructor Victor Sylvester explained to Mass Observation in 1939, "All the continental countries copy the English style because English dancers win competitions."[62] And the most accomplished version of the English style, declared the *Manchester Guardian*, could be found, not among the elite, but among the palais dancers in London halls like the Astoria, where second-generation Anglo-Jews stood out as proficient exponents of the English style.[63]

If controls over dancing remained submerged in Jews' collective memories, so did various forms of sexual license at the Astoria. Memories of going to the palais could be vivid and detailed, but they also evidenced some telling instances of strategic forgetting—particularly when it came to transgressive elements of a dance venue well known to be a "pick-up place."[64] First and foremost, the presence of professional dance partners was notably absent from Sohoites' accounts of dancing at the Astoria. The railed-off enclosure, or pen, for professional dancers, for instance, was tellingly missing from Samuel's otherwise complete diagram of the Astoria's floor plan. Even when asked about paid dancing partners, Sohoites like Samuel could not recall their presence.[65] Yet the pen had been a noted feature of the Astoria dance scene since its opening and was still operating in 1939, when a Mass Observer visited the Astoria and declared the discipline at the pen at the Astoria to be "lax," with men reading newspapers and women knitting.[66] According to McKibbin, the presence of professional dance partners proved to be so "repugnant to those who usually used the palais de danse" that it was eventually abandoned in the late forties. But paid partners were a basic component of the palais scheme before the Second World War.[67] The organization of dance music was structured around the work of professional dancers: a band would play one dance plus a single encore and then pause briefly before changing the rhythm to another dance form, a means of limiting to two dances the time professional partners had to dance with a client for one payment.[68]

Professional pens in dance halls contained roughly equal numbers of men and women. In the Palais, male partners were in particular demand because they serviced female patrons who tended to outnumber their male counterparts. Media accounts often represented male professionals as "gigolos," a term that carried strong implications of commercialized sex.[69] By contrast, female professionals received various treatments in print culture, films, and theater, where they appeared as fallen women, as aggressive "gold diggers," as victims of dancing decadence, or, conversely, as democratic embodiments of the new fashion-conscious, independent working woman.[70] As elsewhere, Astoria dance partners charged sixpence a dance, which they split "fifty-fifty" with the management; they were expected to give lessons from 11 a.m. to 1 p.m., and work as partners for unaccompanied patrons from 3 p.m. to 6 p.m. and then again from 8 p.m. to midnight. The takings of professional partners were modest (£2 to £3 weekly) and their clothing costs, estimated by one dance professional in 1939 at 30–40 percent of his income, very high.[71] Professional dance partners were often drawn from the entertainment world, proud of their showmanship and love of dance. One undercover female journalist writing in the upscale women's magazine *Eve*, who masqueraded as a "sixpenny girl" at the Hammersmith Palais in 1926, gave a positive account of the "romance" of the work. She described her companions in the pen as ex-typists, shop assistants, and other lower middle-class girls "who had to earn their own living and find a pleasant way to do so."[72]

Despite some good press, the professional dance partner remained a morally ambiguous category, blurring the world of entertainment and the sex trade. Paying for dancing, notes Allison Abra, too closely approximated the practice of paying for sex.[73] To compensate, dance partners were expected to present themselves as middle class, "speak in a cultured voice, have a good education, and present faultless references."[74] This class address was meant to ensure the respectability of both the dancers and the dance halls where they were employed. The management was "particular about our reputation," explained the masquerading journalist in *Eve*: "sixpenny girls" were prohibited from smoking on the premises (it was already a teetotal environment), or going to nightclubs after the hall had closed.[75] Nonetheless, throughout this period, professional dancers reported encounters with clients who were not serious dancers, and who wanted to patronize their services "after business hours."[76] Women had to deal with "over-amorous" male clients, while men had to exercise considerable "diplomacy" with married women. Dance partners who were married had to "keep it quiet," in order to sustain the fantasy, if not the actuality, of romantic and erotic availability "after business hours."[77]

If paid partners offered a challenge to Sohoites' model of respectable heterosexuality, so did the presence of female couples on the dance floor. When asked about women dancing together, Dora Samuel could not recall any practice of that sort. She further indicated that such an activity would have been deemed "lowering" for a woman, indicative of her wallflower status.[78] Yet female couples were a highly visible part of the interwar dance hall scene, in part because more women than men patronized the dance halls, even at the Astoria. In 1931, for instance, the *Dancing Times* announced the Astoria's sponsorship of "All Ladies Foxtrot competitions" and, later in the year, an "All Ladies Waltz Competition."[79] Mass Observers, who regarded the dance hall as a "place of sexual enjoyment,"

took note of female couples and included them in their "counts," but regarded them as strangely "out of place" at the halls and in no way indicative of same-sexual desire.[80] Yet, as historian Jenny Taylor observes, Mass Observers' own findings challenged this homogenized picture. One Mass Observer noted that female couples had a special penchant for the rumba, deemed to be a highly sensual Latin dance, while Mass Observation's founder, Tom Harrisson, in his summary report on the halls, observed how "hot dancing was always done by couples of women, and in general, these [couples] dance with notably more freedom and vigour than mixed couples do."[81] Tolerance of female couples did not extend to their male counterparts. For Mass Observation and Palais managers, male couples were a clear sign of sexual perversion, to be prohibited from the dance floor. But they too appeared at the edges of Mass Observation reports on the halls. In 1939, while visiting the Locarno in Streatham, South London (where he noted a strong minority of Jewish patrons), a Mass Observer watched as "a couple of girls started dancing together at 7:55 and from therein on there were always a few female couples on the floor, but never any male couples, until at the end two men began fooling with one another."[82]

Amidst same-sex couples and paid partners, Jewish Sohoites used the Astoria dance floor for Jewish courtship, as a place where we "met our husbands."[83] Compared to Mass Observers, who were on the lookout for "sex" at the dance halls, Sohoites were very circumspect in their 1990s interviews about the physical transactions of courtship, on or off the dance floor. In the thirties, middle-class observers expressed surprise at the open intimacy on display at places like the Astoria, as manifested in the "casual picking" of partners, the numbers of arms round shoulders and hand-holding, the placement of the man's hands on different parts of the woman's body, as well as the degree to which women seemed to govern the conditions of physical intimacy.[84] But such practices were probably normative for Jewish youth. In her retrospective account of her dancing days, Samuel emphasized a polite system of self-introduction and address. When a fellow asked her to dance, no introduction was necessary, but he did have to ask her, "Can I have this dance."[85] Couple dancing, Samuel explained, could then initiate a succession of further encounters later on in the evening or in the week. Dancing set into motion the possibility of unchaperoned, individual dates to the cinema or to a dance or, especially, to refreshments at Lyons' Corner House.

"Meet Me at the Corner House"

Jewish Sohoites regarded the three Lyons' Corner Houses as their special meeting places, an extension of their neighborhood.[86] Each of these massive edifices housed three or four floors of restaurants, the largest room containing around a hundred round tables. Like the Astoria Dance Salon and the Hammersmith Palais, these super-restaurants were industrial sites of leisure, with massive front and back stages, combining catering and musical entertainment, and, in the case of Corner Houses, with no off hours. On Saturday nights, "there would be guest accordionists, jazz musicians, gypsy violinists, sopranos, tenors, double acts, all playing their heads off until past midnight" to the hundreds of East End and West End Jews eating at the tables, while others waited in long queues at the door for their turn to get in.[87] Like the dance halls, Corner Houses provided personal service, sometimes in the form of a waiter and a maître d', but mostly in the figure of the up-to-date Lyons' waitress, affectionately known as the Nippy, who enjoyed an excellent press as a model English girl.

With their "pronounced cosmopolitan atmosphere," Corner Houses were highly syncretic venues, mimicking the architectural splendor of other pleasure palaces along Soho's peripheries, such as the Palace Theatre, while serving inexpensive and plain fare affordable to working-class people.[88] They blended Americanized strategies of consumer democracy with the glamour and attractiveness of continental eateries. Despite their claims to respectability, the Corner Houses were a magnet for the doubtful, low cosmopolitan elements gravitating to Piccadilly and Soho. It was the task of the Lyons' waitress, the Nippy, groomed and trained by the management to be an efficient public servant, to mediate between patrons and the establishment as well as between different classes and tastes serviced in these massive venues.

Located on Coventry Street (1909), the Strand (1915), and the corner of Oxford Street and Tottenham Court Road (1929) (see Figure 17), the Corner Houses were the jewels in the crown of J. Lyons and Company, a food empire that spanned catering, restaurants, hotels, teashops, food processing, food laboratories, and a tea plantation in Africa. Founded by four Anglo-Jews from the north of England in 1887, J. Lyons and Co. started off in exhibition catering. By 1894, J. Lyons had opened its first teashop in Piccadilly, a forerunner of 250 gold and white-fronted teashops that would occupy prestigious sites in London's high streets, suburban towns, and cities throughout Great Britain. Lyons' early history in exhibition catering and teashops helped to shape its restaurant enterprises, encouraging the company to think big in terms of mass provisioning, to publicize its venues through theatrical strategies of showmanship, and to target female customers with promises of light refreshments and a reassuring atmosphere of comfort, cleanliness, efficiency, and respectability. Standardized service, prices, and portion control allowed Lyons to benefit from economies of scale, providing customers with more luxury than the ABC teashops "on razor-thin

LYONS' OXFORD CORNER HOUSE
Oxford Street & Tottenham Court Road, London, W.1.

17 "Oxford Corner House, c.1931." Opened in 1929 at the corner of Oxford Street and Tottenham Court Road, the Oxford Corner House projected the restrained classicism of the Corner House architectural house style. By contrast, its interior public rooms displayed eclectic period styles and were heavily laden with mosaic and marble wall murals.

profit margins."[89] By 1896, Lyons had opened Cadby Hall, a central industrial site near Hammersmith, where the baked goods for the teashops were produced. By appealing to the "fair sex," who might be enjoying a shopping day, as well as the "mere man," the "rampant," "irrepressible" Lyons became a "catering octopus" generating dividends of 600 percent for its investors before the Great War.[90]

In 1896, Lyons diversified into restaurants, opening the Trocadero Restaurant in Shaftesbury Avenue on the site of the notorious Argyll Rooms (1851–78) and the recently defunct Trocadero Music Hall. Like the nearby Café Monico, this site was part of the New London created along Soho's peripheries, a by-product of the construction of Shaftesbury Avenue in 1885–6.[91] Under Lyons management, the Trocadero became a resort, to quote one journalist, "with pretensions to the highest respectability, yet not lacking in the kind of attractiveness that characterized the restaurants abroad."[92] To ensure this "highest respectability," the Trocadero felt obliged to distance itself from its lurid past as well as from the moral laxity of neighboring eateries around Piccadilly, such as the Cavour and the Monico, that were magnets for pimps and foreign prostitutes. Lyons' management instructed its staff that "if a [strange] lady alone should gain admittance she must immediately be surrounded by screens," and that ladies in couples (who are not regular customers) were not to be permitted to take "tables on the balcony."[93] The Trocadero's registration book from the late 1890s contained a list of undesirable male persons to be refused entry. It testified to the challenges faced by the management in its effort to patrol the environment. Villains to be barred included Fraser, "imprisoned for forgery," Neal, who "stole 60 pounds from one of our customers," George English, who "used filthy expressions in New Buffet," as well as Gordon, who was simply "Impossible to satisfy."[94] Despite this vigilance, the Trocadero would continue to attract a mixture of raffish and respectable clientele throughout the interwar years.[95]

The Popular Café in Piccadilly, Lyons' next large venture in central London, represented a prototype for the kind of mass catering that would define the Corner House experience. Opened in 1904 and seating 600, the Popular purveyed a modest version of the Trocadero's luxurious ambience and large menu, also offering continuous music and "magnificent surroundings" at popular prices.[96] The multistoried Corner Houses elaborated the Popular's formula of mass provisioning, glamorous surroundings, and personalized service into a distinctive commercial style that marked, to quote one historian, a "new way of life in London's neon lit West End."[97] And they continued to confound foreign observers by amalgamating different traditions and genres of mass catering: "A Lyons café is a thing by itself, neither a café in the continental sense nor a British teashop nor a restaurant nor a confectioner's, but a little of each," declared German travel writer Paul Cohen-Portheim in 1935.[98]

Like many interwar consumer spaces, the beginnings of the Corner Houses may be traced to the decade before the Great War. The first Corner House opened in 1909, at the corner of Coventry Street and Rupert Street near Leicester Square. Like the Trocadero, it was a site with a past, formerly occupied by the Challis Hotel, "rather a favourite stopping place for racing men," a location that seemed to have possessed a "bad character" as far back as local historians could remember.[99] To start fresh, Lyons commissioned an imposing four-storied edifice of neo-Baroque design. It was so grand that the "public assumed it was to be a new hotel . . . of the expensive West End variety."[100] By 1922, an expanded Coventry Street Corner House could accommodate 3,000 people at one sitting. It was part of the continual physical encroachment on Old Soho in the interwar years.[101] Less flamboyant than the original Corner House, it conformed to an emerging Lyons house style that was already discernable in the Strand Corner House (1915) and would guide the construction of the even more massive Oxford Corner House (1928), at the corner of Tottenham Court Road and Oxford Street.[102] Although the Corner Houses outwardly projected "restrained" classicism, their interior public rooms displayed eclectic period styles and were heavily laden with mosaic and marble wall murals, fancy architectural details, mirrors, and heavy carpeting, all meant to convey an atmosphere of luxury reminiscent of the Palace Theatre and the Savoy.[103] Together, these three super-restaurants could accommodate over 9,000 people at a sitting, but the important statistic, as far as the management was concerned, was how many times a day these places were filled—with a goal of 10–15 daily turnovers.[104]

As early converts to a "corporate image," Lyons adapted standardized techniques to deliver luxury to the millions. The white terracotta facades of the buildings helped to create a useful architectural label for the public, signaling that "the restaurants are under the same management and provide identical bills of fare."[105] The Corner House name itself was deliberately neutral, suggesting uniformity of quality, price, and menu, and underscoring the commercial importance of a corner site, with multiple entrances that could draw in traffic from at least two directions.[106] Economies of scale, achieved through extremely low wages, stable material costs, and vast numbers of customers, contributed to static overheads and allowed two of the three Corner Houses to turn profits before the Second World War (Oxford Corner House evidently never made a "farthing").[107]

At the same time, the Corner Houses promoted glamour, novelty, and personal service. Continuous musical entertainment accompanied the provision of food and drink. The company became one of the largest employers of freelance musicians, most of them Jews from the East End or Soho. In 1932 alone, Lyons spent £150,000 on entertainment. At its zenith, Coventry Street featured seven twelve-piece jazz bands, not to speak of 200 chefs, backed up by a waiting staff of 1,200, who served 400,000 meals a week.[108] During the interwar years, the management continued to introduce new amenities and specialized restaurants, anxious to sustain public interest in the establishments at a time when teashop custom was declining, owing to shorter work hours, suburbanization, and the growth of industrial canteens.[109] On the ground floor of the Coventry Corner House, there was a food hall, a shoeshine parlor, a theater booking office, and a telephone bureau. The All-Night Café in Coventry Street opened in 1922, followed by the Vita Sun Café in 1923; in 1936, the Coventry Street basement was transformed into a brasserie, reminiscent of "somewhere in the Balkans," complete with a courtyard with jade-green and orange aluminum and an orchestra in gypsy costume to recreate the "light-hearted intimate atmosphere of continental restaurants"[110] (Figure 18). Trying to keep up with the vogue for "restaurants of all nations" epitomized by Soho's establishments, as well as the delicatessens opened up by Central European refugees from Hitler, the brasserie purveyed continental delicacies of many nations while its orchestra featured an

18 "Continent in Corner House," *Lyons Mail* 32 (October 1936), p. 115. In 1936, the basement of Coventry Corner House was redecorated as a brasserie, evocative of "somewhere in the Balkans," where patrons were serenaded with gypsy music.

equally ersatz musical diet of Tzigane, Italian, French, Spanish, Cuban, and Viennese numbers.[111] In 1937, the Old Vienna Café opened on the mezzanine floor, while a range of self-service restaurants materialized during wartime, including the "Salad Bowl" on the first floor. The Strand and Oxford Corner Houses followed suit, opening specialized restaurants on different floors, with their own separate menus.[112]

By visiting the Corner Houses, East End and West End Jews entered mainstream commercial culture, where suburban day trippers like Jennifer Wayne took "for granted that to eat in London meant Lyons' Corner House."[113] But Jewish Sohoites claimed a proprietary relationship to the Lyons' Corner Houses as part of their locale. Unlike their East End peers, a visit to the Corner House was not a trip Up West to a world that wasn't yet theirs.[114] Laura Phillips and Esther Rose, for example, remembered the Coventry Corner House as an extension of their work and living space, where they ordered a cheap dish such as "egg mayonnaise," "Corner House code" for a scrimping customer.[115] Esther Rose, an ex-milliner, remembered working late in the evening, taking home hats and paying parents and friends to help her stitch them. As a reward, she took them to the Corner House. "Then we used to go to the Corner House at 10:30 in Oxford Street and I used to pay for their coffees. At 4d each because they helped." Here they would sometimes meet up with Jewish boys: "We used to 'make up' and go, meet some of the boys."[116]

Sohoites also linked Lyons to their dancing forays at the Astoria, as a sequential staging of a night out on the town in the late twenties and thirties that mostly ended—for the girls—around 10:30. "And then the new Corner House opened in Oxford Street, and we used to go eat and then the shoes came off as we had been dancing every dance."[117] Removing shoes under the table was an assertive act on the part of young people who made themselves at home in a public space. Sohoites gravitated to some public rooms as particular meeting places. Dora Samuel's favorite was the "big room in the basement," where you could get beans on toast, the first venue, she believed, where this Americanized form of fast food was on offer in London. Alternatively, Anne Kahn especially remembered the basement space of Oxford Corner House for its continental atmosphere in the redecorated "Brasserie," where she could "listen to the gypsy music."[118] Rachel Goldberg also linked food and music in her wartime memories of the "Salad Bowl" in the Coventry Street mezzanine: "we used to pile up plates" at half a crown, and listen to Ravel's *Bolero*, the signature tune of the room, played over and over again.[119] It was, she recalled, a meeting place for Jewish youth. The Corner House was the "centre for everyone no matter where they came from," remembered Louis Feldman. "Lyons was all within the budget of whatever you earned."[120] Jewish men and women arrived in single-sex groups of friends, from work or from dancing at the Astoria, but they also came on dates. Feldman remembered one disastrous occasion when he brought a girl who "decided to eat." "Between the two of us, it came to 2/6 or 2/4. After ordering it she decided she didn't want it and I was *platzing* [exploding or collapsing inside]."[121]

For dating couples, the evening's entertainment could continue with a visit to the cinema or end with a walk home, with some of the young men hoping for, in Louis Feldman's late twentieth-century phrase, an "end product."[122] Young men would ask a woman if they could "see you home," but if they were hoping for a cuddle or some petting (unless it was in a dark turning on the way), they were in for a rude surprise. When they arrived at Dora Samuel's door in Cleveland Street, located north of Oxford Street, maternal authority reasserted itself.[123] "There was no front garden in Cleveland Street, just a little step at the door, and my mother used to shout out from the window, 'it's time you came up.' I used to say to her, 'Don't ever do that again to me. Please!' "[124]

Jewish Sohoites felt at home in the Corner Houses with their combination of good service, friendliness, and air of classlessness, even if the food was slightly unfamiliar and unkosher.[125] They located the Corner House at the center of an imaginary urban nightscape remembered as strikingly free of other transients. Visits to the Corner House were part of their tale of the urban village when, to quote Kitty Fegan, "it was safe to walk anywhere."[126] "The lamps were lit up," remembered Laura Phillips, "and . . . there were no people walking around in the West End, if they didn't live there because they would go home [by taking] the last tube at 12 midnight."[127]

Wait Staff and Other Patrons

In fact, there were throngs of other urban denizens milling around the West End and frequenting Lyons' at night. Musicians and theater workers gravitated to the Coventry and Strand Corner Houses because of their cheap prices, their all-night cafés, and their convenience to the theater district and Soho's nightclubs. Lyons' Corner House was a place where one could pass the time between performances or between jobs. At the end of the 1930s, Mass Observer Alec Hughes accompanied nightclub musicians to Coventry Street in the early morning hours. While waiting for the Underground to reopen, they horsed around, read newspapers, wrote music, played practical jokes on each other, told dirty stories, and made an instrument out of a cellophane straw.[128] In non-fictional and fictional accounts of espionage activity in London, intelligence spies and double agents visited the Corner Houses to meet with their contacts.[129] The Coventry Street area, far from being regarded as safe, was notorious for being the leisure center of London's underworld.[130] Corner Houses, "open forever," were part of a liminal nighttime itinerary, whose habitués included dance hostesses and their escorts, confidence men, blackmailers, and the like.[131]

Nonetheless, Sohoites were not alone in registering this part of the West End as a Jewish space. Glyn Roberts, a Welsh writer newly arrived in London in the early 1930s, interpreted the Jewish presence at these pleasure palaces on Saturday and Sunday nights as a foreign invasion. To his provincial eyes, the Corner Houses epitomized the disorienting, un-English heterogeneity of the West End. Jews may have numbered only 200,000 among London's huge population, but "if you walk past the Empire [theater] into Piccadilly any Sunday evening you will find it hard to believe there are as many Gentiles as that."[132] According to Roberts, Jews had monopolized the "flashy side of life." They dominated the cinema queues for first-run movies in the West End, they transformed Wardour Street into a "glossy ghetto," and they crowded into Lyons' Corner House as if "the place is reserved for Hebrews."[133] This flashy side was epitomized in their look: Jewish men wore "suits all of a pattern and very new," while Jewish girls had "brilliantly colourful clothes" and "do their utmost to use Art to improve on Nature." Roberts originally thought that "these people" must be wealthy—they seemed to be so self-assured, colorful and glossy—but these early impressions proved to be misleading: "But I found out that they were really very poor and that they invaded the West End in their tens of thousands only twice a week or so."[134]

Mass Observation unearthed similarly negative sentiments linking Lyons' and Jews when it conducted public surveys of anti-Semitism in the late thirties and during wartime. The informants also noted the showy clothes and boisterous manners of Jews who frequented Lyons' Corner Houses on Saturday and Sunday evenings. Some individuals viewed Lyons' as a Jewish firm that had itself monopolized the refreshment trade and the flashy side of life in London.[135] The firm's Jewish associations had already attracted anti-Semitic troublemakers in the mid-thirties: in 1936, fights broke out between Jews and Blackshirts at the Strand Corner House, where Blackshirts were selling Fascist newspapers.[136]

Not everyone regarded the Jewish presence as an invasion. Some patrons were too immersed in their own scene at Lyons' to notice, while others regarded Jews as part of the heterogeneous social backdrop for their own performance. Rupert Croft-Crooke, writer, biographer, and historian of homosexuality, observed Jews at Lyons' Corner House as one of the "worlds within worlds that make any great city complex and fascinating." Like the Palace Theatre in Maud Allan's day, the Corner Houses were a magnet for men looking for homosex who adopted a look of highly sexualized femininity. Croft-Cooke remembered visiting the Coventry Corner House in 1925, during his early exploration of queer London. Here he caught sight of the "obvious" queers, known as "so," the pronoun for "young, indeterminate, arrivals," gifted with the power of mimicry and "dramatic sense of presence." The obvious ones seemed to belong to no particular class, for social distinctions were lost in the masquerade. He found them in the basement floor of the Coventry Corner House, in a room familiarly called the "Lily Pond." While the largest part of the room, entered by the main doors, was given over to the usual customer, including suburban families, typists and clerks, and "happy groups of East End Jews," the Lily Pond was situated at the end of the room, at tables at a slightly higher level, near the far wall. When the room was later redecorated (as the brasserie), he recalled, the queer customers dispersed into discreet drinking clubs in nearby Soho and Mayfair.[137]

Rather than disappear altogether, the Lily Pond may have shifted spaces within the Coventry Corner House. A "Public Servant," interviewed by Jeffrey Weeks and Kevin Porter in the 1980s, recalled the basement brasserie as a meeting place for homosexuals in the thirties. But he located the Lily Pond on the first floor, as did many other queer memoirists and oral history subjects.[138] In any case, the salient features of the queer meeting place remained the same: a mirrored, wide expanse of room where gay men coexisted yet remained socially segregated from other patrons.

The wait staff seem to have been instrumental in managing the boundaries between queers and straights. "The waitresses knew you and if you were a regular they saved a table for you."[139] On the side reserved for gay people, the waitresses "wouldn't let a woman anywhere near," remembers another informant. "No, not this table. It's reserved."[140] At the same time, queer patrons were expected to observe a certain decorum so as not to call attention to themselves: no obvious pick-ups, limited circulation around the tables, not too much flamboyance by way of dress and make-up.[141] When they exceeded these limits, they could be chucked out by a huge commissionaire. But Quentin Crisp and his friends, who sported lipstick and called each other Greta and Marlene, were never deterred from the Lyons' Corner House: "They tried to keep us out but the place was so large and had so many entrances . . . people were always creeping in."[142] Crisp and his "lawless" companions went there during the rush hour and regularly skipped out without paying their bills, evidently unconcerned about the drastic effects of this "petty" crime on the limited income of Lyons' Nippies, who had to make up "shorts" from their own wages.[143]

The smartly uniformed Nippy, who serviced the many publics of the Corner House and managed their sometimes strained interaction, was Lyons' most successful corporate image. As historian Jerry White observes, even more than Priestley's "factory girls looking like actresses," the Nippy was the defining symbol of the feminized world of work that London represented in the 1930s.[144] She inspired plays, film, fancy dress costumes, as well as fictional portraits in the novels of the day. The Nippies, declared the *Westminster Gazette* in 1928, ranked with the "policemen and busmen" as a "body of cheerful and efficient public servants."[145]

This cheerful symbol of public service was a product of extensive publicity and training. Although Lyons' had always employed waitresses in its teashops and Corner Houses, in 1925 it elevated them to iconic status, endowing them with a name, a new uniform, and even a theme song. Nippy was meant to convey modern efficiency and speed; it was "short, expressive, easily remembered."[146] The Nippy's up-to-date image was further enhanced by her black and white uniform, from which all "emblems of servitude," such as high collars and cuffs, and apron strings, had been banished.[147] The Nippy was kitted out as a stylish flapper, in a fitted black alpaca dress, with sixty decorative mother-of-pearl buttons down the front, detachable and starched Peter Pan collar and cuffs, and pinned-on apron.[148] Instead of a maid's cap, Miss Nell Bacon, who was Chief Superintendent of Lyons' Teashops, suggested a black and white coronet that would be suitable for shingled and bobbed hair.[149] Selected for her pleasant personality, memory, deportment, and condition of her hands, the Nippy received special instruction at a training center for six weeks.[150] Here, unskilled working-class women were transformed into "teashop debutantes."[151] The Nippy was taught how to walk and present herself. She was trained in personal grooming and in the art of serving: where to place utensils and condiments on the table; how to serve food from the left and remove plates from the right. She was taught manners, to address customers politely as sir or madam, never to rush their orders or be too familiar. Counseled to leave her troubles at home, she was instructed to project cheerfulness and remember that the customer is always right.[152] Finally, she was given a thorough knowledge of the bill of fare: she had to memorize the prices of hundreds of items and familiarize herself with "foreign cooking expressions," such as "Assiette Anglaise."[153] This training guaranteed uniformity of service from one Lyons' shop to another and rendered Nippies, who wore numbers and often changed their workplace within the Lyons' empire, interchangeable.

The *Lyons Mail* invited Nippies to imagine themselves as glamorous ambassadors, akin to actresses, models, and even journalists "who are to a very large extent dependent upon their power of agreeableness for their living."[154] The in-house magazine further encouraged them to identify with lady customers, who might arrive at Lyons' without escorts, possess a confident knowledge of the menu, and have their own money to spend.[155] To instill team spirit and encourage the pursuit of physical fitness, Lyons management sponsored dancing and sports activities for its staff at the company's sports center in Sudbury.[156]

Like the Jewish girls from Soho, the Nippy's ultimate destiny was marriage rather than Hollywood. The model Nippy performed a restrained femininity in keeping with the era's lower middle-class ideals of conservative modernity.[157] Her feminine appearance was patrolled for evidence of too much paint and artifice. The *Lyons Mail* counseled her against peroxide hair, and company guidelines strictly prohibited the wearing of eye make-up and jewelry on the job, apart from a wedding ring. Lyons' assured the wait staff that a catering career was good preparation for marriage and that Nippies married at a higher rate than the general population.[158] According to some ex-Nippies, Lyons' offered a romantic atmosphere not only for customers but also for Nippies discreetly scouting out potential mates. "We all had admirers," declared one ex-Corner House Girl, "that's where I met my husband," although she also acknowledged that she once caught the eye of a more elevated customer, a Brazilian Consul General who invited her to dinner at the Savoy.[159]

In 1939 *Picture Post* ran "Nippy: The Story of Her Day," with photographs by Bill Brandt (Figure 19), that traced the journey of one Corner House Nippy from home to work to spaces of leisure, figuring her as a vulnerable figure subjected to a harsh bureaucratic discipline but also as self-regulating and intro-spective. This Nippy's pay packet contained 25s, to which would be added 25s in tips (reckoned to be a good week).[160] These earnings would be comparable to assembly line employment along the ring road, in the new electrical industries such as that in the Art Deco Hoover Factory.[161] But ex-Nippies who responded to the company's public call in the 1990s for Nippy reminiscences remembered lower weekly wages than this, plus significant deductions for clothes and other items.[162] More than anything else, managerial surveillance of their bodies summoned up indignant memories. Many correspondents recalled the "daily inspection": standing in line before the manager or manageress and "putting your hands out" to insure their nails were perfectly clean. "What I remember most about being a nippy was the inspection every morning," wrote one corre-spondent.[163] Rosemary Laird detailed the drill: "clean uniform, no missing buttons, clean hands and nails, stocking seams straight, shoes not down at heel, and hair off the collar."[164] "The rules and regulations we had were unbelievable," Kathleen Pittman wrote. "*No* lipstick, not too much powder. *No* fancy

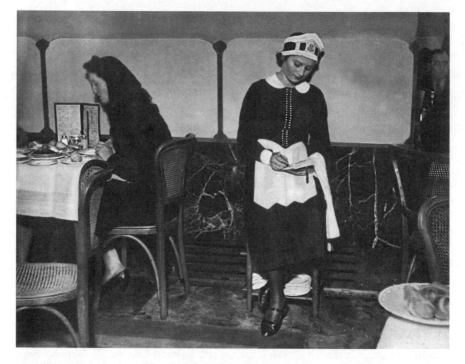

19 Bill Brandt, "A Pause in the Day's Bustle." From "Nippy: The Story of Her Day," *Picture Post*, March 4, 1939. Brandt captures the hard-working, smartly uniformed nippy in an introspective moment, double-checking the customer's bill lest she be charged with "shorts."

shoes—black stockings only. *No* rings (except wedding and engagement)." If a Nippy showed up in a shabby outfit, she had to "go straight off and get a new one & we had to pay and our wages were very small—we had to rely on tips." But the hardest condition for Nippies were the bills: "we had to double check everything & if we forgot to put any item down the discrepancy was ours and every week there was a large list of *shorts* & often we hardly took any wages [home]."[165]

It was the Depression, and "we had to put up with these conditions if we wanted a job," Mrs. Pittman concluded.[166] "It was not so bad for me," declared one ex-Nippy to historical sociologist Miriam Glucksmann in 1990, "because I was living at home with my parents but it was terrible for these girls who came from the depressed areas [of the North]."[167] "If you wanted to stand up for yourself or anything, you just went. You couldn't go to the union to say they dismissed me just because I answered back," recalled Rose Bird in 2000.[168] Lyons had quashed efforts to unionize waitresses in 1920: the firm overcame a lightning strike that broke out when a waitress—with sixteen years of service—was fired for wearing a union badge. Five hundred union members among the Lyons' wait staff walked out; Lyons immediately retaliated by recruiting blacklegs and threatening to sack all strikers who did not return to work the following day.[169]

Customers who luxuriated in Lyons' romantic atmosphere of beautifully starched white tablecloths, sparkling "imitation silver canteen cutlery" and soft, romantic music did not help the Nippies' work situation.[170] "People would come in for a 6d pot of tea and sit there all afternoon listening to the orchestra, and you wouldn't get any tip."[171] Patrons evidently took the management quite literally when it invited the public to make a day of it at Lyons'. To see "John Bull at home," one German guide recommended, "go to Lyons palaces and watch young and old, men and women, shop-assistants and typists, sitting in front of a cold cup of tea and half a sandwich and listening for hours at a time to the trumpet-drowned orchestra which our restaurant king gives his public."[172] Besides availing themselves of the free amenities of the establishment, Corner House customers, many of them new to the restaurant habit, also found the standardized atmosphere to be reassuring: it helped to know "where you stood" and what you were "going to pay."[173]

East End and West End Jews certainly fell into the category of neophyte restaurant patrons. "We might have 6d in our pockets and sit for hours in the Corner House . . . with a small ice cream—much to the chagrin of the waitresses who were waiting for us to move on."[174] These teenage memories tended to treat the Nippy as just one component of the overall service: "When you went into the Corner House, you felt like a film star because someone waited on you and the china matched and the tea was in a tea pot, the milk in a jug and sugar in a jar. This was not to mention the cutlery," remembered one Jewish East Ender.[175]

Conclusion

Jews, Nippies, and queers maintained distinct identities and spatial enclaves within the broad expanse of Lyons' commercial spaces. Keeping their distance, these aspiring moderns nonetheless shared some common features. Like queer patrons, Jews used grooming, make-up and up-to-date fashion to signal their capacity for modern self-fashioning. But some observers of the Lyons' scene registered their social performances more negatively, as transgressions of a staid and restrained Englishness, a view reproduced in Mass Observer's reports on the dance halls. Jews' stylish appearance obscured their poverty and made them seem dangerously unplaced; queers' use of make-up could be read as a defiant act of visibility and alignment with modern femininity.[176] The Lyons' management expected a model English girl, the efficient, clean, and attractive Nippy, to orchestrate the social-sexual traffic of these spaces. Yet it also subjected her body to intense corporate scrutiny, lest she echo her unruly patrons and exhibit a similar flamboyance and sexual sophistication by wearing jewelry, make-up, and nail polish. Like the dance halls, Lyons' palatial establishments enabled some occupants to perform expressive bodily practices, while demanding strict bodily management from others. This interplay of bodies, disciplines, ethnicities, and affective expression also materialized in Soho's more intimate basement night-clubs, with diverse political effects. Moving from the peripheries back into Soho's narrow streets, we turn next to Soho's notorious shady nightclubs, famous for their hot jazz, social masquerades, and cultures of risk.

CHAPTER 7

The Shady Nightclub

In May 1928, the *New York Times* reported that fifty members of Scotland Yard's famous Flying Squad, "who usually devote their energies to making lightning dashes through London in pursuit of murderers, burglars, and car thieves," donned evening dress and raided ten night clubs in the fashionable West End of London. It was the "biggest round-up in years." The *New York Times* and other news outlets emphasized the singularity of the raids and hinted at political intrigue: it was "the first time that the Flying Squad was detailed for such comparatively innocuous [activity]," while "two foreigners prominently associated" with nightclub management have been "deported without the reason being made public." Two of the raided clubs belonged to Mrs. Kate Meyrick, the eminently well-connected "queen of the night clubs," mother-in-law of one peer and the prospective mother-in-law of another.[1]

By all accounts, Mrs. Meyrick was an astonishing individual to emerge as London's "nightclub queen" (Figure 20). Sir Chartres Biron, the Bow Street magistrate who sent her to prison on more than one occasion, remembered her as "a lady, of good appearance and charming manners," who "conducted her various clubs with more decorum than many, but also with a fine contempt for the law."[2] An Irish woman of genteel upbringing, Mrs. Meyrick claimed to have gone into the nightclub business for reasons of "economic security." Before she arrived in London, she had been married for ten years to a medical doctor operating a private mental asylum in Brighton that treated shell-shock patients in the Great War. In 1919, when her husband took up with one of the nurses, she determined to leave him. She went to London to make her proverbial fortune, with six children in tow and only a few pounds in her pocket. Here a "new life" opened up for her. She answered an advertisement to run tea dances at Dalton's in

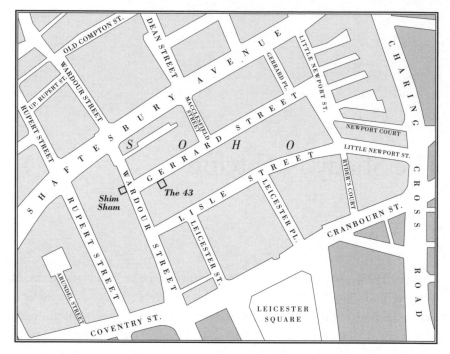

Gerrard and Wardour Street

Leicester Square. Constantly invaded by gangsters, Dalton's was finally raided by the police as a resort of prostitutes and condemned by a magistrate as a "sink of iniquity."[3] In her later memoirs, she represented herself as an innocent who had not even ventured into a nightclub before she ran one. She gradually came to realize an important aspect of human character: that evening clothes and appearance were "no gauge as to a person's character and habits."[4]

Continuing to learn the nightclub business, Mrs. Meyrick entered into a partnership in Brett's Club in the Charing Cross Road, before opening up the 43 Club in a damp cellar in Gerrard Street. The 43 became the "mother house" of her nightclub empire and the most notorious nightclub in London. It was raided by police in February 1922 for selling alcoholic drinks after-hours; one month later, it gained heightened notoriety when Freda Kempton, a dance hostess of the club, died of a cocaine overdose. Kempton had been last seen at the 43 in the company of Brilliant Chang, a Chinese restaurateur who was accused of supplying her with drugs.[5] In 1924, the police again raided the 43 and took into custody thirty-seven "laughing guests," including two Indian Army officers, a lawyer, and an undergraduate, as well as seven women. Variously dressed in evening clothes, fancy dress, and "plus fours," these revelers were bundled into Black Marias and sent to Vine Street police station. "One van drove away with its occupants singing, 'It ain't goin to raid no more,' and another started the refrain, "'We won't get home till morning.'"[6]

Between 1922 and 1924, Meyrick's proprietary clubs were raided and closed many times for serving alcohol without a license and after hours. Her defiance of the licensing regulations made her the rebellious standard bearer of freedom from restrictive drinking regulations.[7] Year after year, she obligingly provided headlines for the tabloid press, who positioned her at the center of sensational changes in the nightlife, hedonistic leisure, body idioms, and sexualized femininities of the Roaring Twenties.[8] Mrs. Meyrick would be imprisoned four times, but she soon surfaced as hostess of another club. The heaviest fines were incommensurate with the profits she made from illegal nightclubs. She went from strength to strength, brazenly operating a chain of Soho nightclubs whose names constantly changed. She reckoned that she made about £500,000 out of her nightclub business, despite the fact that she was supposedly a prime target of a "War on Night Clubs" between 1924 and 1928, conducted by the deeply unpopular and puritanical Home Secretary, William Joynson-Hicks (nicknamed "Jix" by the press). A few of her establishments were subject to police raids, including the Silver Slipper, Meyrick's most sumptuous establishment, off Regent Street.[9] But the 43, her stronghold, continued to operate without interference. When undercover police visited it, they blandly reported the presence

20 "Mrs. Meyrick and Her Girls." From Kate Meyrick, *Secrets of the 43: Reminiscences by Mrs. Meyrick* (London: John Long, 1933), opp. p. 182. Mrs. Meyrick made twenty-five dance hostesses available to male patrons. Her "Merry Maids" were schooled in glamorous standards of dress, conversation, and grooming, as well as in the boundaries of licit commercial sex.

of respectable people in evening clothes consuming fruit cup and orange squash.[10] As early as 1925, the press complained that Jix's aggressive campaign against "night club evils" had devolved into a "one-armed war."[11] Despite their aggressive rhetoric, senior police officials left the oversight of West End clubs, including their sporadic raiding, to the discretion of Sergeant Goddard, attached to the local Savile Row station of the Met's C Division, covering Mayfair, St. James, and Soho. By the end of the decade, they would acknowledge that their confidence in Goddard's probity had been singularly misplaced.[12]

Meanwhile, Mrs. Meyrick's used her nightclub profits to assimilate her children into upper-class social networks, sending them to England's most elite schools. One son went to Harrow, while two daughters attended Roedean before taking up posts as dance hostesses in their mother's clubs. "Known to every strata of London society," Mrs. Meyrick successfully annexed "one aristocratic son-in-law after another."[13] In 1926, her daughter Nancy married the 26th Baron de Clifford; two years later her daughter May married the 14th Earl of Kinnoull. Like the police raids, these aristocratic marriages enhanced Mrs. Meyrick's celebrity, as well as attracting press censure on the social dangers of advanced nightclubs, where the "atmosphere of artificial gaiety" encouraged the "free and easy mingling of classes" and led to "strange matrimonial alliances" in violation of class lines and traditions.[14]

But by 1928, Mrs. Meyrick's luck seemed to be running out. The Flying Squad's raids on two of her clubs in May of that year demonstrated a renewed determination by the government to close her down for good. Following her May arrest, Mrs. Meyrick was sentenced to six months in Holloway for what the magistrate called her inveterate law-breaking. When she exited Holloway Prison on November 28 there was a champagne party at the Silver Slipper to celebrate her release. But three days later, on December 1, she was charged with a more serious crime: the bribery and corruption of Sergeant George Goddard, responsible for supervising nightclubs in central London. Goddard had first arrested Meyrick in 1922; by 1924, he seemed to have worked out a financial arrangement with her, tipping her off before a police raid descended on her establishment. Anonymous complaints and questions in Parliament finally impelled the Police Commissioner and the Home Office to deploy the elite Flying Squad against Mrs. Meyrick. Goddard was accused of amassing over £12,000 in protection money. Some of the banknotes stashed away by Goddard were traced to the bank accounts of Meyrick, and two Italians in the restaurant and brothel business. Meyrick was sentenced to eighteen months' hard labor. Released in 1930, she went on a tour of the continent and returned to run the 43 again. For continuing to run unregistered clubs, she served two more prison sentences. She used the time inside Holloway Prison to write her memoirs (published posthumously in 1933), finally retiring from the nightclub business in 1932 and dying of pneumonia a year later. Her fortune had vanished as a result of the stock market crash and the plummeting value of her clubs while she was in prison.[15] After her death, two of her daughters tried to keep up the family business, but their establishments never enjoyed the same popularity. Meanwhile, Goddard's case led to the wholesale housecleaning of the C Division, under the new regime of Metropolitan Commissioner Byng.[16]

In historical accounts of the twenties, Mrs. Meyrick serves as the fixed point in the shifting terrain of London's hedonistic action environment, to use Erving Goffman's concept of a tightly packed space where individuals immersed themselves in risky social practices to disrupt the routines of daily life.[17] Like New York nightspots of that era studied by historian Lewis Erenberg, Meyrick's clubs were designed to foster a sense of speed. They turned night into day, mixed respectable men and women with a fast crowd, and accelerated bodily sensations through drink and dancing to achieve "new frontiers of experience."[18]

No social group more exemplified this jazz age quest for speed and action than the Bright Young Things (BTYs), a coterie of top-drawer blue bloods and down-at-heel bohemians who were closely aligned to Meyrick's club empire. According to literary historian D. J. Taylor, this small coterie glided through the decade on "a compound of cocktails, jazz, license, abandon, and flagrantly improper behavior", and wielded tremendous influence on popular conceptions of youth out of all proportion to their numbers.[19] The middle-market press regularly carried photographs of glamorous female BYTs as eye candy for male readers, while moralizing over their antics and social transgressions.[20] They were famous for their sexual ambiguity, unquenchable energy, frenetic pace, quest for novelty, and rebellion against the stiff formality of society's old guard. Creatures of publicity, they forged a shrewd relationship to the glamour-hunting press, particularly to newspaper gossip columnists like Patrick Balfour (the son of a Lord and "Mr. Gossip" in *The Sketch*), who were themselves insider members of society. Mrs. Meyrick's clubs occupied a place in the BYT's well-publicized nocturnal landscape, alongside treasure hunts, hoaxes, fancy dress parties, gatecrashing, and practical jokes. According to Taylor, Bright Young novels by Anthony Powell and Evelyn Waugh are filled with "cryptic nods in her direction."[21] These fictional references to Meyrick's "mother house" mimic the truncated and clipped style of the BYT's own private jokes, catchphrases, and one-liners. "I say," asks a naval officer in Anthony Powell's *Afternoon Men*, "do any of you ever go to The 43?" Similarly, when Sebastian Flyte and his friends visit a nightclub in "Sink Street" in Waugh's *Brideshead Revisited*, they arrive at a thinly disguised version of the 43, which becomes a shorthand for the futility, fractured alliances, and dead ends of youthful folly.[22] Other retrospective accounts uniformly invoked Meyrick's downfall as a convenient narrative closure to the jazz age twenties. For these histories, Meyrick's reign epitomized an age begun in the traumatic wake of the Great War that allegedly screeched to a halt with the Wall Street crash, Britain taking its currency off the Gold Standard, and the darkening political and social mood of the Hungry Thirties.[23]

Mrs. Meyrick and her clubs were icons of twenties nightlife, but it would be a mistake to argue, as Patrick Balfour and others have done, that in bringing her down Lord Byng successfully killed the nightlife of London.[24] Having exposed how profitable a certain brand of unregistered club could be, Mrs. Meyrick inspired many imitators in her wake. Shady nightclubs endured into the thirties as lucrative Soho businesses. They became bottle parties, adopting the legal ruse of operating as private parties. Cultural innovation came in the form of "coloured clubs" that heated up the nightlife of London and served as meeting grounds for the left Popular Front.[25] The advent of new media outlets and forms of musical connoisseurship in the thirties represented two necessary preconditions for the popularity of black clubs, and they in turn were interwoven with a radical social and cultural movement forged around anti-fascism.[26] At the same time, black clubs remained sleazy and exploitative spaces, reproducing salient features of Meyrick's twenties action space: a Soho location, a crowded and mixed social scene, a charismatic host, institutionalized spontaneity, multiple forms of gender and sexuality, and a general culture of risk, speed, and dissimulation. In sum, Meyrick's template for the successful shady nightclub would be replicated in the thirties in a changed milieu.

Soho and Louche Cosmopolitanism

Mrs. Meyrick first located her nightclub empire in the southeastern part of Soho, in that "triangle of disillusion, formed by Shaftesbury Avenue, Charing Cross Road, and Leicester Square."[27] By centering her clubs in Soho, Meyrick built on the district's prewar reputation for transgressive nightlife.[28] Just prior to the Great War, Soho's leisure industry vastly expanded from restaurants and cafés to a handful of licit bohemian dance clubs. Located in underground basements or in attics reached by "crazy and steep staircases," they were "small and simple and intimate" spaces where "Montmartre met jazz."[29] A by-product of the renaissance of theatrical and social dancing, they prided themselves on their un-English atmosphere. They were a place to go after the theater and the closing time at the Café Royal. These prewar nightclubs mobilized the elite privileges of private membership clubs—organized by committee, protected by burly commission-aires, unmolested by the police—to mount a rebellion against Victorian respect-ability. They provided a legendary public setting for the collective creative life of modernism, as well as a cultural battlefield among competing and self-indulgent rivals such as Ezra Pound and Wyndham Lewis.[30] Bohemian women such as the young Rebecca West and Jean Rhys, and art school "crop heads" Nancy Cunard and Iris Tree, also inserted themselves into the ranks of revelers at the Cave or the Crabtree.[31] Proudly boasting an anti-bourgeois ethos, the Cabaret Club gave free membership to impecunious artists and writers. Such nonconformist gestures persisted in the closed, high bohemian clubs of the twenties, such as David Tennant's Gargoyle Club in Meard Street, Elsa Lanchester's Cave of Harmony in St. Giles, and the Hambone Club in Ham Yard. Tightly restricted to members, they permitted a range of heterodox practices. At the Hambone, Radclyffe Hall danced cheek to cheek with her lovers, and a notice declared that "Work is the curse of the drinking classes."[32]

Mrs. Meyrick also constructed her market niche in relation to swank supper clubs that began to materialize just before the war in Mayfair or "St James, Soho," just off Regent Street. Like their bohemian counterparts, Murray's and the 400 were private members' clubs dedicated to making night into day and to delivering a cosmopolitan form of bodily pleasure that was simultaneously continental and American.[33] They set the standard for the smart nightclubs of the next decade, such as the exclusive Embassy Club in Old Bond Street (opened 1919), where a couch was reserved for the Prince of Wales, or the Kit Kat Club and the Café de Paris, both operating as supper clubs open to an elite public. During the Great War, hotel ballrooms at the Ritz, the Piccadilly, and the Savoy sponsored late-night dancing, even dispensing with the requirement of evening dress for the duration of the war.[34]

Meyrick's twenties clubs were even more directly linked to the fast life emerging underground in wartime Soho. Wartime conditions accelerated the growth of Soho's illegal nighttime economy. "The parents and begetters" of shady nightclubs, declared bohemian writer Thomas Burke, were repressive laws.[35] By restricting public sociability and prohibiting the serving of drinks after 9 p.m., the 1915 Defense of the Realm Act, or DORA, literally drove late-night drinking and dancing underground. Hundreds of clandestine, unregistered nightclubs opened up in dingy basements. Wartime Soho transmogrified into a "fertile habitat" for transgressive practices, such as gambling, drugs, illegal drinking, and cross-class erotic encounters.[36] The illegal status of nightclubs encouraged the practice of other illicit pleasures, not only gambling but also the cocaine habit ascribed to American and Canadian officers, who passed it on to their girlfriends. In this cultural microclimate, pleasure became "polymorphous," to quote historian Marek Kohn.[37] Meanwhile West End prostitutes, harassed by stringent policing of the blacked-out streets, found refuge in the clubs. Soho's reputation as London's racy cosmopolis only intensified as French, Belgian, and Serbian soldiers headed for it as their leisure center, as did American, Canadian, and African troops.[38]

After the war, a floating population from all countries continued to be attracted to Soho's louche atmosphere, and to the opportunities for work in night clubs and pubs.[39] Wartime restrictions on drinking persisted; in 1921, a new regulation allowed an extension of evening hours until 11 p.m. and, provided some food was served, to 12:30 a.m.[40] Illicit nightclubs, modeled on American speakeasies, proliferated. Prohibition-like conditions proved a gold-mine for twenties proprietors of nightclubs, who attempted to impart an increasingly transatlantic flavor to London's dives, from the spatial arrangements and band music down to the name of the establishment (Florida, Manhattan, Rector's) and the theatrical procedures of gaining entry, including bars on locked doors, peepholes, or a heavily guarded lift.[41] For a time, African-American musicians were heavily recruited en masse to Soho and West End nightclubs to replace the German bands banished during the war.[42] New Orleans jazz entered London in 1919 via the Original Dixieland Jazz Band, an all-white band that played at Rector's Club in Charing Cross Road as well as at the Hammersmith Palais de Danse, both owned by the American Bill Booker.[43] In 1920 even the staid Embassy Club booked the "Jazz Kings," a New Orleans black band whose clarinetist was the legendary Sidney Bechet.[44]

The 43

These were the conditions under which Mrs. Meyrick began her nightclub career. By taking out a lease on 43 Gerrard Street, Mrs. Meyrick chose to remain near the entertainment center of the West End (and not too far from elite Mayfair flats), yet situate her nightspot in a low-rent and unimproved district, relatively immune from careful police surveillance. Her manager, Richard Carlish, described the place as originally a "dingy little joint that looked as if it might sell fish and chips, women, hemp, or all three in a special little package."[45] Gerrard Street was a heterodox zone of mixed economies and sedimented historical associations. In 1922, a blue plaque graced the façade of 43 Gerrard Street to commemorate the fact that it had been the residence of poet John Dryden in 1697.[46] By the 1920s, it was certainly no longer a fashionable address, but some elements of the old artisanal culture were still in evidence.[47] The *Post*

Office Directory recorded that Dillins the swordmaker, Wilkes the gunmaker, and Warner the seal engraver were still plying their trade on the street. Literary restaurants founded at the turn of the century, like the Mont Blanc, continued to operate. Signs of jazz age Soho were equally apparent in the numerous firms associated with the film industry—producers, theatrical agents, suppliers, film importers and distributors—centered in adjacent Wardour Street. Another feature of Soho's industrial economy, the Jewish clothing trades, was also visible: Mr. Gold, a tailor, occupied the top floor of Mrs. Meyrick's building, while Nellie Endelmann, costumier, trading as "Madame Adella," set up shop in 1923 at 23 Gerrard Street.[48]

At the 43, Mrs. Meyrick mostly catered to the conservative elite, but socialist Bohemia and Bloomsbury had already staked out a claim on the street. The 1917 Club, co-founded by Leonard Woolf to establish a conversational community dedicated to world peace, was located across the street, while David Garnett's bookstore soon followed at 30 Gerrard Street.[49] Gerrard Street also attracted a floating population of street sellers, entertainers, and criminals.[50] Last but not least, Gerrard Street was a major red light district for street prostitution, one of three principal spots for soliciting in central London.[51] Frances Partridge, a younger member of the Bloomsbury Group who worked in Garnett's bookstore, remembered "brushing past the prostitutes that haunted that street" starting at 2:30 in the afternoon.[52]

The 43's thug-like doormen, consisting of two ex-policemen and "German Albert," were frontline protection from the police and the villains of the street.[53] Inside the club, Soho's ethnic composition, service economy, and consumer niches materialized in transformed form: Jewish tailors morphed into Jewish musicians; the club had a Jewish manager, Richard Carlish, who also served as host, occasional waiter, and look-out; English streetwalkers and service and theatrical workers blended into dance hostesses, while waiters "with Italian surnames" served the drinks, although they claimed British citizenship when interrogated by raiding police.[54] All these service workers kept the profits and drinks flowing. As the "mechanical background," to quote the *Stage*, they allowed Mrs. Meyrick to perform her character role as eccentric host.[55] Anecdotal evidence also documents the presence of transvestites, lesbians, and "fairies" seated at tables around the dance floor.[56]

Another alignment between the street and the club was the atmosphere of sleaze and seediness.[57] Mrs. Meyrick's bare premises consisted of a front office and lounge with a bar on the ground floor, a basement dancing space, and a ladies' cloakroom on the first floor. The two principal action environments were her office and the basement dance floor. In the office, Mrs. Meyrick sat behind the cash desk, collecting door money (earning her over £100,000 in thirteen years) from non-members as they came in. She vetted the customers and, according to her manager, "discarded those we thought we could do without."[58]

This arbitrary and selective vetting was part of the club's appeal: "To pass through the close-watched door was to feel oneself the victor in a hazardous and honourable encounter," Alec Waugh observed.[59] The basement consisted of a rectangular room, 45 x 15 ft., with wooden chairs and tables around a small dance floor. The band rostrum was under the stairs, and there was a slightly elevated platform for entertainers in an alcove at the back. In 1922, the band consisted of a piano, banjo, and drum with cymbals, instruments suitable for jazz dancing music.[60] Later the band expanded to five pieces, adding trumpet and saxophone. In the wee small hours it would be dark, noisy, and full to capacity with eighty people: "People love crowds," Mrs. Meyrick wrote. "To enjoy themselves thoroughly they must go to some place too full to find a table and too crowded to dance in comfort."[61] Mrs. Meyrick's more luxurious clubs never enjoyed the same popularity as the homely 43, not even the Silver Slipper club off Regent Street, whose glass floor lit from below had a "strange effect on a dress of very thin nature."[62] The crowded dance floor forced people to mix, yet the tables allowed them to return to their own group.[63] There was no further demarcation of space, no proscenium stage separating the performers from the audience. In many ways, the audience was the entertainment.

Mrs. Meyrick as Host

Habitués of the 43 agreed that the main attraction was Mrs. Meyrick herself. She seemed to embody the precise combination of familiarity and novelty, elite decorum, anti-Victorianism and raffish lawlessness that made her clubs attractive venues. Whenever Mrs. Meyrick was incarcerated, the "magic" was gone and her clubs "languished."[64] Memoirists repeatedly fixed on her personal magnetism and the compelling incongruity of her homely traits. They described her as small, middle-aged, shabbily dressed, with knotty "bow-legs and untidy hair," who looked "horribly out of place" in an establishment that catered to sleek, aristocratic guests who mostly arrived in evening dress.[65] The tabloid press summoned up stereotypes of the school matron cum brothel keeper to characterize an individual remembered as rapacious, yet generous, who ruled her girls with an "iron rod," but who paid her band overtime if they had to work an extra hour.[66] According to Carlish, Meyrick's ladylike demeanor enabled her to treat disruptive gangsters with fantastic guile, speaking to them softly. Even when they began to bluster, she usually managed to ease them out without raising her voice.[67] Undercover police marveled at her capacity to discipline crowds of rowdy, drunken students.[68] She flouted the law and asked police to remove their headgear when they conducted a raid.[69]

Mrs. Meyrick's style bore a family resemblance to society hostesses like American-born Lady Cunard and Mrs. Laura Corrigan, who had a flair for mixing blue bloods, stage stars, and exotic novelties at their parties.[70] At the same time, she carefully crafted her action environment as an alternative to the fashionable conventions of entertaining. In contrast to the snooty atmosphere maintained by Luigi of the Embassy Club, who "dressed" his room according to the strict protocols of social exclusion, Mrs. Meyrick was more open to customers with deep pockets and no pedigree.[71] As a self-proclaimed rebel against society conventions and puritanical "kill-joys," Meyrick carved out a niche similar to Rosa Lewis of the Cavendish Hotel, another great favorite of the Bright Young Things.[72] Both exercised a personal and arbitrary style of social management; both were knowledgeable and defiant of elite social codes and protocols; both were post-Victorians who took the side of hedonistic youth against the "grandmotherly limitations set by the authorities on public amusement."[73]

Like Lewis, "Ma Meyrick" was especially indulgent to elite young Guardsmen and university students, whom she occasionally allowed into her clubs for free or whose drinks she charged to visiting plutocrats.[74] She projected a motherliness as part of her business acumen to encourage the illusion of privacy, intimacy, even domesticity.[75] According to journalist Arthur Tietjen, "scions of ancient houses" fought over the opportunity to assist her in vetting the guests at the door: "seated behind the desk they would make a great business of checking and passing in their friends."[76] They helped to serve out ham and eggs for breakfast at 3 a.m. Meyrick also mothered the old guard. Cabinet ministers and members of the Diplomatic Corps may have been stern and official during "business hours," wrote one musician, but at Meyrick's establishment "they acted like children."[77] According to the Sunday tabloids, regressive behavior extended to "hardened Colonels from the East" who liked to dance "Ring o' Roses" with the dancing hostesses.[78] Mrs. Meyrick infantilized and chided her guests, but never upstaged their play or seriously questioned their social prerogatives.

The Social Mix

Mrs. Meyrick established an atmosphere of speed from the right mix of stage and variety, crime, sporting world, and society. Her clubs made no pretense to restrict access to club members. Society men sometimes brought elite women to the 43, who took pleasure in their own spectatorship and their right to look.

The women came attired for dancing, in short tubular dresses, made of thin, almost transparent fabrics, that were class differentiated less by overall design than by exquisite, luxurious fabrics. According to one source, such garments were worn by young women with "white oval faces, small breasts, blue eyes, thin arms, no expression [and] no blood."[79] In the early twenties, these female patrons included the immensely wealthy heiress Lady Mountbatten, who married into the high aristocracy, with her "priceless" jewelry and taste for raffish nightlife. The club also attracted intrepid debutantes.[80] Young Daphne Fielding, a BYT core participant, was entranced with the urban fantasy of slumming represented by a visit to the 43. She would sneak out of her aunt's home to go with her friends to the club and was fascinated by the jingle of the "tinny piano which greeted one on arrival in a dark, smoky atmosphere" and by the hostesses who "became intriguing figures of conjecture."[81] By the end of the decade, Mrs. Meyrick's Silver Slipper, just to the east of Regent Street, became a favorite resort of young debutantes who had superseded married women as front-page news and were the epitome of glamor.[82] In November 1931, for instance, Tom Driberg wrote in his *Daily Express* column of his visit to a club "situated in a basement off Regent-street [Silver Slipper], which is enjoying a remarkable vogue." Here he found Miss Meyrick and other socialites, including two pretty debutantes, "who looked and felt tired, as well as they might, for it was three in the morning and their combined ages amount to about thirty-five."[83]

These representatives of café society constituted Mrs. Meyrick's regulars. Their numbers were augmented by provincial businessmen, rowdy university students, free-spending burglars, film stars, artists and writers like Jacob Epstein and Joseph Conrad, foreign potentates and diplomats, including the "Bolshevik" delegation, as well as "low-minded" members of the 1917 Club who popped across the road for a final "illicit drink."[84] Lower down the social order were the mostly Jewish musicians, attracted by the after-hours visits of American musical celebrities to the club, such as Sophie Tucker and Paul Whiteman, who began dropping in around 1925, adding a "strange excitement to The 43."[85] The late-night visits of these musical celebrities established the 43 as an innovative cultural space, particularly for jazz-minded dance musicians working in West End bands who were bored to a man with the strict tempo, muted orchestrations, and evenly balanced instrumentalism of hotel music.[86]

Sophie Tucker, fresh from an engagement at the Kit Kat Club, brought celebrity talent and a different mode of female embodiment. She was down to earth, Jewish, maternal, self-mocking, and frankly sensual.[87] Paul Whiteman "would bring his band to play for us at the '43' after his theatre performance was over, and the mere rumour of his arrival was sufficient to crowd the club to the point of suffocation," Meyrick recalled.[88] Here you could "hear all of the world's greatest artists at jazz—all for the price of the entrance fee (10 shillings) and a drink," remembered Joe Glicco who played saxophone in Mrs. Meyrick's band.[89] Thanks to Mrs. Meyrick, aspiring young musicians, such as Billy Amstell and Harry Gold, who could not afford £5 to enter the Kit Kat Club, were able to hear and play with these international stars. "Many of the greatest British players of to-day [1952] owe much of their early education to those 'jam sessions' with the great ones under the stairs of the '43,'" Glicco observed.[90] Amstell and Gold remembered Mrs. Meyrick fondly, because she allowed them to have a "blow," to perform the kind of jazz improvisations that were strictly forbidden in smart restaurants.[91]

Meyrick was proud of the diversity of her clientele. She reckoned it to be exemplary of Britain's continued authority as an imperial nation: on certain nights, she claimed, "I have seen my dance-floor scintillating with foreign orders and variegated by faces of every hue from copper to ivory-yellow," a range of difference that excluded the African diaspora.[92] Like other club owners, she also fabricated a transatlantic ambience, encouraging her hostesses to adopt American slang, supporting improvisational jam sessions in the early morning hours, and constructing a secret back exit in the event of a police raid. Nonetheless, elite British metropolitan culture set the tone of the 43, a tone that tolerated slurs and impugned the masculinity of Jews and non-Westerners who arrived on the scene. One Guardsman mistakenly called Michael Arlen, the famous novelist, a "dirty, little Jew" and menaced him, requiring the management to step in to protect Arlen. On another occasion, one of her guests mistook film heart-throb Rudolph Valentino for a waiter. On Boat Race night the undergraduates shouted "Throw the damned nigger out!" when Prince Ghika made an appearance.[93]

There were, moreover, clear limits to the cosmopolitan forms of bodily display that were licensed by Meyrick's establishment: despite Meyrick's early connection with Brilliant Chang, interracial couples were a rare sight on Mrs. Meyrick's dance floor, as were same-sex couples. In Brideshead Revisited, Sebastian Flyte and a friend visit "Ma Mayfield's" and are mistaken for "fairies" by the dance hostesses.[94] But they are the kind of fairies who observe elite class decorum—that is, they do not wear rouge and powder and do not form single-sex couples on the dance floor.[95] Fairy patrons who stayed at their tables did not provoke police suppression of the club on the grounds of disorderly conduct.[96] Unlicensed drinking, rather than "degenerate vice" or "perversion," was the formal police charge laid against Mrs. Meyrick after 1922.[97]

Hostesses and Commercialized Sex

Nonetheless, Meyrick's dance floors still presented a morally ambiguous spectacle of heterosexuality, as elite couples danced in close proximity to those "intriguing figures of conjecture," the paid dance hostesses. Nightclubs were places to go on to, wrote H. V. Morton, because, like gamblers, nightclub habitués "are wound up."[98] By migrating there, young people sought refuge from the dullness of society events and from equally dull smart restaurants. They went on to the 43 to prolong the night and to dance, drink, and socialize in a restricted space. Margaret Whigham (later the Duchess of Argyll), the "Debutante of 1930," remembered sallying forth with one young man to dinner, pleading tiredness and going home at 10:30, only to step out again to meet another beau at the Embassy Club or the Café de Paris. At closing hour, she and her partner would "float on" to late nightclubs such as Meyrick's Silver Slipper.[99] The dancing culture that they brought with them was, by all accounts, neither inspired nor technically proficient. The crowded dance floors of small nightclubs made expressive or acrobatic dancing of, say, the Charleston impossible. Musicians who worked at the Embassy Club described the dancing guests as "moving wallpaper," hardly moving at all.[100] Dance critics frequently observed that in "the smart dancing places of London the dance is the least important . . . in the dance hall it is the only thing that matters."[101] Most of Mrs. Meyrick's guests fell into the category so lamented by dance professionals: those who "decline to take their dancing seriously."[102]

Yet dancing still wrought significant cultural and gender changes in elite circles. Along with shrinking incomes, new forms of housing (Mayfair mews flats) that prohibited large gatherings and encouraged small-group socializing outside the home, and the need for men to go to work, the nightclub habit reordered the intimate practices of society.[103] Dance clubs enabled society debutantes and their beaus, as well as young married couples, to participate in a modernized, "Americanized" variant of elite heterosexuality. The social columnist Patrick Balfour would go so far as to insist that dancing destroyed the gentlemen's clubs of the West End, arguing that men now enjoyed feminine company in the evening because it contained more erotic promise.[104] Thanks to the nightclub, insisted another observer, "women have got the men who escaped them back in their hands."[105]

Despite these claims, nightclubs also sustained older modes of sociability. Socially and legally the fortunes of the nightclub were entwined with West End clubland. Clubs like the 43 operated as arenas of commercialized sex, as late-night supplements to homosocial clubland, akin to the Empire Promenade of the 1890s so deplored by Mrs. Chant (see chapter 2). After an evening at their club, many men moved on to Gerrard Street to engage in cross-class encounters. A typical diary entry by Sir Bruce Lockhart, a society journalist and diplomat who reckoned that he had spent £15,000 on nightclubs and cabarets in the 1920s, went as follows: "Went to club, got drunk, and then to 43."[106] Precisely because the nightclub was aligned with clubland traditions, it was protected from open police surveillance. Anyone with five shillings to spare and a list of twenty potential members could open a proprietary drinking club. However much Home Office and police authorities deplored the shady nightclub, they felt compelled to treat the registered dance club as if it were the legal equivalent of the elite Carlton Club or the myriad workingmen's clubs. Fear of political reprisals made them reluctant to revise the laws on clubs to strengthen police surveillance, or in any way to infringe on manly prerogatives of club privacy.[107] The nightclub would benefit from the hallowed privileges of male homoso- ciality, at the same time that it became the active competitor for the time and money of clubmen.

The management made available twenty-five dance hostesses to clubmen like Lockhart. In contrast to dance halls, Meyrick did not seem to employ male dance instructors, although some of her female patrons brought in their own paid escorts.[108] Sophie Tucker was struck by the large number of "women, more women, and again more women" who decorated the room.[109] They were part of a new profession, the product of dancing schools that opened up for social and theatrical dancing beginning in the years immediately preceding the First World War. Recruits to this new profession were mainly working-class girls, but its ranks included members of the "new poor" from the older middle and even elite rentier classes. Personal advertisements in the *Dancing Times* by lady dancers stressed their refined tastes and "up-to-date dancing," as well as good appearance and "tact, ability and personality." Moreover, female advertisers promised to be "smart and entertaining" and "easy to get on with."[110] Male partners, by contrast, placed considerably less emphasis on appearance and personality, or even on dancing ability, stressing instead the acquired social credentials of a gentleman. Many claimed to be an "officer," a "member of leading West End clubs," a "public school man," or a man possessing "University Education."[111]

Mrs. Meyrick schooled her "Merry Maids" in the forms of self-presentation, dress, and grooming promoted by female partners in the *Dancing Times* notices. She also trained them in the boundaries of licit commercial sex, a feature decid- edly omitted in the advertisements. Her girls were taught to fit themselves into a range of types appropriate to different, but highly stereotyped, erotic codes of whiteness: they were "Blondes, brunettes, and red-heads; slim and Junoesque;

calm of temperament and mercurial . . . girls to suit all sorts of men in all sorts of moods." Meyrick dance hostesses, moreover, were expected to possess charm, good looks, and "have some culture in addition."[112] Some dance hostesses acquired American accents, adding smartness and pep to their conversation, but most tried to project a hygienic form of glamor marked as white and English— clean, slim, well-coiffed and dressed—in the spirit of the cosmetic ads that used dancing themes to attract female readers.[113]

While admitting that women of ill repute had caused her trouble in her early years, Mrs. Meyrick went to some lengths in her memoir to counter reports that her hostesses were prostitutes. As testimony to the moral benefits of her establishments, she cited a number of nightclub marriages between her "Merry Maids" and American millionaires or peers of the realm.[114] She also pointed to the profits a talented hostess could make without "turning to a degraded means of gaining her livelihood."[115] She claimed to have paid her hostesses a weekly salary of £3 (comparable to the earnings of some factory workers, chorus dancers, and the overall takings of dance hall hostesses), but on average, she insisted, they augmented these wages by earning £14 or £15 a week in tips and commissions.[116] "The Meyrick clubs," she insisted, "have always made it worth the while of their dance hostesses to keep straight." Nightclubs were not for all girls, but any girl "suited to the life"—who could "look after herself"—could make a small fortune out of rich men who were "dancing mad."[117]

The reputation of Meyrick's hostesses was certainly subject to dispute. Over the years, undercover police identified the dance hostesses at the 43 as belonging to the prostitute class, a view endorsed by Waugh in his fictional portraits of the 43.[118] But musician Billy Amstell disagreed: interviewed in the 1990s, he remembered how some of his fellow musicians, "the 'good-time' Charlies, used to come down [to the 43] to have a drink with the hope of having one of the girls. But there was no hanky panky, or if it went on I didn't see it."[119] In 1929, the Sunday tabloid *The People* tried to have it both ways: "Some of her girls had forgotten what morals meant; the virtue of others was as impregnable as a nunnery."[120]

Risky working conditions and the ambiguous status of dance partners, who were neither ladies nor street girls but glamorized service workers engaged in cross-class liaisons, partially account for this blurring of sexual boundaries. To accrue the fantastic earnings that Meyrick claimed they made, dance hostesses had to both amuse their patrons and graft them. They had to be "gold-diggers," a resonant term of the period associated with the "surplus" numbers of women after the war who were driven to be flappers on the make, seducing men out of their money.[121] As modern women, they embodied a form of female assertiveness guided by short-term ambitions. According to Carlish, Meyrick's hostesses served two purposes. "In the first place, they attracted free-spending customers, and in the second place they encouraged them to spend even more freely." They helped to "oil the machinery," he went on to explain, and "keep the waiters busy." Yet he also insisted on the management's policy of strict morals. This translated into decorous behavior on the job. "If a girl went away with a man, she was not permitted to return to the club that night. That meant she lost any further hostess fees and commission on sales for the rest of the night."[122]

Carlish did not detail the intense verbal pressure and competitive exchange, or the emotional work, that such women had to perform to earn their living. Hostesses not only learned how to wear their clothes and be peppy, but also to hustle money from tipsy customers. Working on commission and on tips, Meyrick's employees had to persuade customers to buy them champagne at three times the price it cost the management and to purchase chocolates at two guineas (£2 2s) a box, which hostesses sold back to Meyrick at half price. Hostesses were obliged to act as if they were going to deliver sexual favors, to go away with a man even if they did not intend to do so.[123] Fictional accounts of the nightclub scene, from Waugh to urban noirists like Gerald Kersh, zoom in on the intensity of this commodity exchange, particularly on the kind of time/money pressure built into the encounter. In Kersh's *Nights and the City* (1938), set in 1937, Helen, a new club hostess in a Soho dive, is being schooled by her boss in the practices of grafting. "You won't drink much if you've got any sense," her boss tells her. "Get the customer to offer drinks to the band . . . Be hard, but don't look it. Graft. Get yourself some money too . . ." The boss indicates that he does not care if Helen takes men home with her, but "while the club is open you're not allowed to leave the place, not even to go to the door and kiss a man good night." When Helen recounts these instructions to her friend Vi, who really is a street-walker, Vi is appalled at the hypocrisy: "'You more or less promise to go home with the fellers, don't you? Well, that's taking money under false pretenses,' said Vi, with an air of virtue."[124]

Gangster and Police Raids and Undercover Police

If dance hostesses helped to oil the "machinery," gangster and police raids augmented the sense of speed, disrupting the expected rules of social performance and spectacle. During the interwar years, Soho was the leisure center of the underworld as well as the prize location of lucrative criminal protection rackets that especially targeted nightclubs. Soho became the territory of the Sabini gang from Clerkenwell, led by Darby Sabini and his four sons. In the 1920s, the Italian mob dominated the racecourses and demanded protection from street bookies. During the interwar years, they expanded their protection racket to Soho's shady businesses, but not without violent flare-ups. Territorial challenges to their reign from rival gangs from Birmingham and South London sporadically exploded in violent brawls and mayhem.[125] There were "occasions when every window" of the 43 was smashed by the racecourse gangs, Mrs. Meyrick recalled. She also noted that whenever a gang of ruffians appeared, "the policeman would glide around the corner."[126] "Occasionally, boys from the Elephant and Castle mob managed to get past our security system at the door," Carlish recalled. They "absorbed a few crates of Champagne and began to pinch the bottom of the hostess hatcheck girl." At certain times Mrs. Meyrick was driven to organizing her "members into a sort of guard against surprise raids by the hooligans," while Carlish mobilized his own "Italian mob" of waiters.[127] In time, Mrs. Meyrick came to an understanding with Darby Sabini, leader of the Italian mob, who liked and respected her, accepted her protection money, and defended her from the depredations of "the Birmingham mob trying to muscle in on the London rackets."[128]

Police raids simultaneously contributed to the sense of risk in Meyrick's clubs and to the buttressing of class hierarchy. During these raids, Meyrick recalled, regular members showed their good breeding and social discipline under stress.[129] "Most of our male members were officers of distinguished regiments, members of the peerage, experienced Men about Town or rich young City magnates, there was never the slightest sign of panic." The girls took "their cue from the men," as did strangers who derived confidence from the calm nonchalance of the regulars. Because they were only sporadic, police raids contributed to the explosive revelry of Meyrick's nightclub without disrupting its operations.[130] These raids also provided free publicity. After a police raid, Mrs. Meyrick's champagne became even more famous.[131] Her sensational trial in 1928 for bribing the police attracted throngs of curiosity seekers: "we were crowded out night after night, for people would come down to the club out of curiosity," Mrs. Meyrick recalled.[132] Alternatively, Meyrick and her employees openly exploited the fact that she had a financial arrangement with local police to reassure patrons that they need not fear raids: "It's all right now," a dance hostess confided to P.C. Dobree, working undercover at the club in 1931, "we were expecting a raid but it's past the time now."[133]

Police raids were preceded by inside surveillance of the club by plainclothes police like P.C. Dobree, who belonged to yet another ambiguous social grouping in the nightclub: the undercover policeman. Like the dance hostess, he was a figure "of intense conjecture," crossing class boundaries in a social masquerade that set the nightclub apart from everyday life. While keeping watch inside, undercover policemen played a double role. On the one hand, they were rational, observing subjects, who conscientiously recorded a social ethnography of club habitués and their practices, based on surface details and visual stereotyping. On the other hand, plainclothes police mimicked male patrons who fell victim to their own sexual impulses and who were willing to "dance with this class of women and leave accompanied by them to give vent to their sexual passion elsewhere."[134] To gain admission to the club, they also had to transgress class boundaries: arrive in evening clothes, by taxi or private car, and, when inside, dance with aplomb as well as negotiate the complexities and expenses of commercialized sex. Sometimes, as part of their cover, they would escort a female friend or a wife, but not infrequently they arrived with a streetwalker picked up in Piccadilly and paid 10 shillings for her trouble.[135] Alternatively, if they arrived alone, without a female companion, they were introduced to a dance instructress, who kept them spending. This upper-class masquerade was a relatively new and expanded practice for police outside the ranks of Special Branch, and, like undercover duty in lavatories and queer dance halls, it occasioned considerable public criticism and ridicule.[136]

Social challenges of this sort confronted Police Constable Lord, who was engaged in undercover work inside the 43 in April 1931, while Meyrick was still in Holloway Prison. Lord was there to document illegal drinking in the club before a raid took place later in the night. Lord arrived alone without a female escort and was introduced to Rosie the dance instructress, who attached herself to him. Rosie freely ordered champagne, whisky, breakfast, coffee, all at exorbitant rates charged to Lord's tab. After the raid, as Lord prepared to leave, Rosie asked him to pay her a pound. She tried a number of ploys. "I shall have to charge double because after a raid, people don't come and we get nothing." She also emphasized her personal services to him. "'I have been with you the whole evening, this is my living dancing, could you spare a pound?' I said, 'Well I don't know.' She said, 'It is usual.' I said: 'Then I won't transgress or offend.'"[137] At the end of his report, Lord reflected on the pressures and risks occasioned by his assignment. He not only had to engage in petty infractions of the law but also to submit to the lawless impulses of the hostesses. "Dancing instructresses with whom I have been *compelled* to associate have continually *pestered me* for shillings with which to play on the [gaming] machines. On many occasions to avoid suspicion I have been *obliged* to give them money" (emphasis added). Both dance instructresses and waiters told him "they get no pay" but had to rely on the generosity of the patrons. On occasion, dance instructresses had even solicited him: in the case of Rosie, she asked him if he "wanted a lady, I can arrange that with a friend but I don't do that."[138]

Lord's diffident narrative placed him in a favorable moral light, but it also exposed his sense of professional vulnerability. To experience the risky pleasures of the shady nightclub, the well-heeled revelers of the 43 subjected themselves to police raids, physical threat from gangsters, a depletion of their wealth, and some damage to their respectable reputation. For policemen and dance hostesses, risk and masquerade were not so much a part of their leisure as a condition of their daily labor. Pitted against each other, both Rosie and P.C. Lord were both resourceful agents, engaged in dissimulation and in a struggle of wills.

Professional dance partners employed in public dance halls regarded Rosie's working conditions as sordid and deprofessionalizing. "Dorothy," who worked at the Royal Tottenham Palais, reported to a Mass Observer in 1939 that she "used to work in night clubs [and] got out and says she would not return for £20 a week. They don't have to be dancers in these jobs. They get commission on the drinks they sell and what you get out of the patrons."[139] Out of uniform, Lord seemed to have experienced a similar loss of status, at a time when undercover nightclub assignments became a subject of public scandal and media outrage.[140] The cross-dresser, explains historian Matt Houlbrook, is simultaneously the source of cultural anxiety and a figure of humor and intrigue.[141] Certainly the press found undercover police engaged in class cross-dressing to be both doubtful and humorous. Press headlines, such as "Dancing Policeman Calls for Champagne," summoned up the comic figure of a tipsy policeman luxuriating in pleasures above his station. Media accounts judged policemen on nightclub duty to be both humorous and troubling, precisely because they inverted the conventional ideal of the bobby as a highly disciplined, regimented servant of the state.[142] As early as 1925, serious questions were asked in Parliament whether it was not an "undignified proceeding" for police officers to dress up like the frequenters of nightclubs.[143] By the end of the decade, a report of the Royal Commission on Police Powers and Procedure, published just as the Meyrick-Goddard trials were underway, warned against the practice of undercover nightclub work as a source of temptation to young policemen and tending towards their "demoralization."[144]

The great wads of banknotes handed to the jury for their perusal at the Goddard trial did nothing to allay public anxieties on this point.[145] Goddard's was the only case of police corruption to be substantiated in the 1920s, but neither historians today nor knowing contemporaries at the time believed that Goddard was an isolated offender. "The Goddard case has opened the eyes of the authorities to a police scandal that has been common knowledge for years," declared the *Daily Express*, a view echoed by many other publications.[146] The *Daily Telegraph* tartly observed that Goddard "was almost as much in [Meyrick's] regular pay as her musicians and waiters."[147] In the short term, police authorities responded to the Goddard scandal by cutting back on undercover duty in night-clubs and assigning women police as escorts for the men engaged in this kind of plainclothes work. Female officers evidently proved to be more successful than their male counterparts at navigating the sartorial and social codes of the night-club scene.[148] According to the Royal Commission on Police Powers, women could more easily "disguise their appearance" than male constables, who were often "chosen for their youth" and "dressed in clothes to which they were unac-customed." As historian Louise Jackson observes, the Commission evidently presumed women to be more mutable and difficult to locate in the "symbolic order."[149] Besides these reforms, in 1931, Commissioner Byng also instituted an internal shake-up of police personnel: he quietly but thoroughly cleaned ranks in the C Division, suspending twenty-six constables and one inspector and transferring twenty-four others elsewhere.[150] But very little was done to change the conditions that encouraged police corruption and extortion. Police continued to receive low wages and Parliament did not revise the club laws. Nor did the Met fully dispense with undercover work in nightclubs that resulted in public scandal. Throughout the following decade, rumors of police corruption continued to tarnish the C Division's reputation.

Nothing much had changed when Mrs. Meyrick ended her reign as London's nightclub queen, having presided over an action environment that manipulated local resources to produce a culture of speed for metropolitan patrons. For over a decade, her clubs had inverted the meanings of time, turning night into day, encouraging patrons to live for the moment in close proximity to "figures of conjecture" who blurred social hierarchy and class traditions. The cultural and political effects of her club empire were decidedly mixed. Her clubs simultane-ously encouraged wasteful consumption and police corruption as well as modernized forms of gender and heterosexuality in elite circles. They sponsored an innovative culture of musical improvisation, at the same time defending the pre-eminence of empire and establishment values of racial superiority and marked social hierarchy, adapted to include self-made men from the war who were trying to break into society.[151] Meyrick's string of clubs would collapse at her death in 1933, but thirties' nightspots would replicate her business strategies for risky pleasures. Some of them, notably the black clubs of Soho, would do so under radically different political conditions.

The Thirties Scene

Shady nightclubs like Meyrick's did not die in the thirties; they were reborn as the West End's next best thing: the bottle party. The bottle party was originally a social innovation of the Bright Young Things of the twenties for their private parties. In commercial venues, the bottle party worked as follows: individuals were invited to a "party" and would arrange with wine agents to order drinks for themselves in advance. As participants in a private party, revelers were outside the law and could drink as late into the night as they wished. In practice, strangers gained admission to these resorts by paying money at the door; once inside, they could obtain drinks from a hostess who had reserved bottles in advance. Once the legality of bottle parties was upheld in a 1932 court case, they proliferated across the West End by 1934. In 1935, police estimated fifty known bottle parties in and around Soho, but press estimates far exceeded that number.[152] Even swank West End places, such as Mayfair's Old Florida, turned themselves into "bottle parties," effectively becoming shady clubs and expanding the ranks of the illicit.[153] "Night clubs are no more," declared *What's On* in 1937. "These days the private party [operating as a commercial ruse] has taken their place."[154]

Black clubs, popular venues of the thirties that attracted a range of black and white patrons, also turned themselves into bottle parties. Like Soho's foreign restaurants, black dance clubs first opened in the late twenties as enclave businesses, catering to London's small but diverse black diaspora of service workers, merchant seamen, entertainers, and students. By the thirties, they had increased in number and expanded their clientele to include adventurous white patrons. Thirties' clubs included the Nest and Bag o' Nails in Kingly Street (managed by Mildred Hoey, an old hand of Mrs. Meyrick's), Jig's Club in Wardour Street, the Blue Lagoon and Frisco's in Frith Street, and the Big Apple and Cuba Club in Gerrard Street.[155] Blacks and Jews often teamed up to run these nightspots. They were densely localized in Soho basements, below dress shops and Italian cafés, and subject to gangland attacks and police raids. Despite the sleazy ambience, they benefited commercially from a growing interest among white sophisticates who believed black musicians to be the true producers of "pure" jazz.

By the middle of the decade, entertainment guides advertised black clubs as one of the new sights of London, along with wider streets, modernist architecture, and avant-garde store decoration. All these trends signaled London's modernity and renewed prosperity in the mid-thirties, as it seemed to be pulling itself out of the Depression, while Berlin "dropped out" of the running and Paris remained mired in economic depression.[156] London's nightlife sparkled by comparison with the darkening picture across the Channel. By 1937, over £31 million was spent in Britain by tourists, which was not appreciably less than the total profits from coal and woolen exports.[157] A guidebook of 1937 assured readers that they could find all the pleasures of Paris, Vienna and New York in London: "The most bohemian of Parisians, the laughter loving Viennese, and the gayest of Americans come to London and confess it is the grandest city in Europe."[158]

Aiding and abetting this resurgence were a series of royal occasions between 1935 and 1937 that highlighted London as the "metropolis of empire." First there was George V's Jubilee in 1935, followed by his death in 1936. This led to coronation plans for Edward VIII, who abdicated before the coronation date to marry an American divorcée, followed by George VI's coronation in May 1937. These events happened in such quick succession that 1936 was dubbed the "year of three kings" when "David's [Edward VIII's] Coronation became Bertie's [George VI's] Coronation. The Jubilee Committees became the nuclei of the Coronation Committees."[159] George VI's coronation was intended to bind the British people to a new monarch, after the death of one beloved ruler and the shocking abdication of another. It would mobilize "state magic" to dispel the threat of fascism abroad and shift attention away from unrest in its own empire and at home.[160] But the official meanings of the 1937 coronation had to contend with crosscurrents that disputed the legitimacy and centrality of the official spectacle. The coronation became the occasion for the inauguration of Mass Observation, a progressive organization of voluntary social investigators, dedicated to capturing an alternative, people's version.[161]

For their part, nightclubs mounted other, more indecorous counter-spectacles to the royal occasions. Faced with the prospect of "hundreds of thousands of provincial and overseas prospective visitors to London," "Directors of Entertainment" were "cudgeling their brains to gather a good share of the golden harvest," observed *Melody Maker*.[162] Besides the usual fare of late-night drinking and gambling, they came up with two new nighttime attractions: hot jazz and striptease shows (to be discussed in chapter 8), both disorderly bodily performances at some remove from the stately royal pageant snaking its way through London's main thoroughfares.

Royal occasions also affected Soho's nightlife by provoking police crackdowns on its hot spots. In 1936 and 1937, to safeguard the royal pageantry of the coronation, police attempted to cleanse "London's public face" through pre-emptive police raids, plainclothes surveillance, and repression of undesirables in London's cosmopolitan center.[163] "Determined efforts by Scotland Yard and Westminster are stringing out the night life racket of London before Coronation visitors arrive in force," *What's On* declared.[164] A special division of Scotland Yard that "deals with vice in the underworld of London" was planning a "clean up of the London underworld" in the month before the coronation, reported the *New York Times*. "There is no doubt that resorts politely called night clubs . . . where these people congregated, will be closed." These clubs were in "the purlieus of

Soho"—described as the little streets behind Piccadilly Circus, Shaftesbury Avenue, and Regent Street.[165]

Police clamped down on two categories of Soho nightspots. First, they conducted a drive against queer clubs, most of them makeshift spaces with limited financial return that were used, according to the *Evening Standard*, by "men and women of perverted moral sense."[166] They largely catered to working-class custom and, according to historians, attracted very few Jews as patrons or business owners.[167] To expose the indecent practices of places like Billie's Club in Little Denmark Street, undercover policemen impersonated patrons who enjoyed dancing with lipsticked, powdered, and sometimes cross-dressing femi-nized queers, or West End "girls."[168] Keeping observation at such places, declared the *Evening Standard* in 1937, "would not have been a pleasant" duty for the police, especially as "it was admitted that these officers had to pretend that they were of a similar class to the persons frequenting the premises."[169] Simultaneously, police mounted a broad campaign against the far more numerous and profitable bottle parties. In December 1936, twenty-seven West End and Soho bottle parties were raided, including venerable old timers like the 400 and Old Florida.[170] The round-up included many black clubs, such as the Nest, Frisco's, Cuba Club, and the Shim Sham.[171]

Black Clubs

In 1937, the year of George VI's coronation, journalist Maurice Richardson spotlighted the exoticized and democratic spaces of London's black clubs. Surveying the "Bottle Party Belt," he drew a sharp distinction between old and new forms of nightlife in London. Overall, he concluded, "nothing much had changed in the ten years since the Merrick Goddard regime." Complaining that the "higher walks of night-life," often managed by "ex-officers of the chronically unsuccessful type," still conserved "the masochistic traditions of British pleasure-seeking," Richardson enumerated their dreary features: lukewarm dance music that would give "Bojangles of Harlem pneumonia" and "snooty boredom" as "the correct facial expression." The exception to this dismal scene, he noted, were places like the Nest, Frisco's, and the Shim Sham, where "injections of negroes and swing have hotted up the night boxes." All sorts of sophisticates went to Frisco's: intellectuals, businessmen, film stars, the press, and higher bohemia. The Nest was tougher and noisier. A Barbadian looked after the hats and coats, while Mrs. Cohen, the wife of the owner, presided as the "finest specimen of a night-club queen in London." These clubs contained "all colours, sexes, and professions." There were plenty of bandsmen, music hall performers, students,

West Indians, Americans, and Africans, but "very few coloured girls," nearly all of them London-born or from Cardiff. At these clubs, Richardson confided to readers, "you will find the atmosphere ... friendly, quite democratic, very international."[172]

This dichotomized picture of nightlife echoed other press notices by journalists who brought black clubs to the attention of white sophisticates. Leading the musical campaign was *Melody Maker*, the "jazz enthusiast's bible" and trade journal for dance musicians and "semi-pros."[173] Its columns regularly disparaged British hotel jazz as light music in thrall to a sprightly businessman's tempo, while exalting true jazz as the direct expression of African-American race and culture.[174] According to Spike Hughes, an influential reviewer for *Melody Maker*, jazz was "the music of Harlem gin mills, Georgia backyards, and New Orleans street-corners—the music of a race that plays, sings and dances because music is its most direct medium of expression and escape."[175] To further its proselytizing mission, *Melody Maker* not only publicized the records of American stars like Louis Armstrong and Duke Ellington; it organized British tours for them, but only as entertainers who were not allowed to be accompanied by their own bands.[176] The importation of live jazz from America was thwarted by legal restrictions on work visas for American musicians. After 1935, stars like Armstrong could still work in Britain as soloists, but they had to perform with a British band or assemble their own band from musicians in residence.

To satisfy increased consumer demand for American black musicians, the black British community moved in to fill the void.[177] In Soho's clubs, black Britons were not only expected to play jazz like Americans; management required them to impersonate black Americans, adopting American slang, deportment, and dress, despite the fact that most of them hailed from Cardiff, Africa, and the West Indies. Some of them recalled these impersonations as demeaning and exploitative, but the vogue for true jazz provided local musicians of color with new opportunities for work of an irregular sort, musical improvement, and professional networking.

In the black clubs, black and white musicians of all backgrounds played together, attempting to reinvent themselves as a variant of the American musical scene. Featuring hot dancing and music, as well as illicit practices—"weeds," prostitutes, and gambling—these resorts considerably accelerated the culture of risk, dissimulation, and institutional spontaneity that had been on offer at the 43 in the previous decade. The dance scene in these clubs was more acrobatic and eroticized, and less couple-oriented than at West End resorts. Dances ranged from a conga line to a shuffle, trucking, and the jive, as well as a Suzy Q that, on one occasion, ended in an "unrehearsed strip tease."[178] Swing dancing allowed for cooperation and self-expression: with its steady 4/4 beat and horizontal movement, dancers could improvise with their feet and hands, even break away from their partners, or, in the case of back flips, literally "fly."[179]

Unlike New York's Cotton Club which only admitted white patrons, these clubs actually welcomed black and white customers. The social mix exceeded the old 43 or even London's queer resorts of the time: at Jig's, "pale faces" from the suburbs jostled with prostitutes and pimps, single-sex dancing couples, lesbian waitresses who were visited by rich white women, international black stars, black working people, and representatives of high bohemia.[180] The clubs also attracted individuals committed to different forms of political internationalism, from Garveyite pan-Africans to Jewish musicians recruited into a Communist-led union as part of the fight against Nazism.[181]

Two of the best-remembered and longest-lasting black clubs were Jig's Club on Wardour Street, with its "charged atmosphere," and the Nest on Kingly Street in Soho's western reaches, just behind the stately facade of Regent Street, where the proprietor kept a table reserved for visiting and unpaid musicians who wanted to improvise together.[182] At Jig's, white and black locals met up with black American stars such as Armstrong, who would perform in the West End theaters, music halls, and cabarets, and then move on to Soho clubs to socialize, eat West Indian food, and jam.[183] According to Leslie Thompson, a West Indian musician and pan-Africanist, Armstrong was pleased to meet "another coloured fellow" in these clubs "who played trumpet and lived in England."[184] Armstrong and Dizzy Gillespie also patronized The Nest.[185] It came to represent the Americanized nightclub spirit of hot jazz, described by jazz historian Sid Colin as "peroxide hostesses, scruffy waiters, and 'I have an uncle in the Mafia.'"[186] Other members of the black diaspora also gravitated to these clubs. The Nest was a favorite among West African students, such as Ben Nnamdi Azikiwe, pan-Africanist and future Nigerian head of state. Azikiwe incorporated the Nest and Jig's Club into his nighttime itinerary along with more explicitly political venues such as the nearby Florence Mills Social Parlour on Carnaby Street. At Florence Mills, Azikiwe dined with fellow black pan-Africanists, but he liked to frequent the Nest because he was attracted to the casual "confraternity between blacks and whites" that assembled there.[187]

The Nest's confraternity included white bohemians who embraced some combination of jazz, radical politics, and sexual adventure: composer Constant Lambert, who always fell for "exotic girls" and was attracted to the black waitresses at the Nest, as well as philosopher A. J. Ayer, who loved dancing and ventured down the stairs to sniff marijuana, dance, drink, and enjoy the corned beef hash.[188] His wife Renée liked to pick up "negroes" there as well, following in the footsteps of society women like Lady Mountbatten who treated blacks as an exotic accompaniment to their own elite entertainment.[189] Journalistic accounts of the shady nightclub often took note of the fair girl with the "aristocratic name," as a transgressive female hedonist who chose to dance exclusively with "negroes who would dance cheek to cheek with her."[190] Apart from some left-wing intellectuals and radical Jewish musicians, it is doubtful that most of the Nest's white patrons were committed to the principles of democratic internationalism.[191] Black Welsh musician Joe Deniz remembered that "Guard officers, business people . . . used to go there [the Nest] because it was the thing to do."[192] The management of the Nest recognized and exploited the cachet of racial mixing: Mr. Cohen used to pay cab drivers to "siphon-off" black customers on their way to other dives. When they entered the Nest club, they would be given free drinks with the understanding that white customers "could then be free to chat with them."[193]

Gangsters, looking for trouble, comprised another group of low cosmopolitan outsiders who frequented the Nest. Musician Joe Glicco remembered a night when the Hoxton gang came to the Nest looking for another gang. Unlike Mrs. Meyrick, the club management was helpless to manage them or control their violence. "They came in fifteen strong, and looked carefully round the room . . . As they got drunk they made foul remarks about the decent, coloured folks who were there to dance." A fight broke out and the "band, scared to death," played on "while the other customers cleared out as fast as possible."[194] The Nest was finally closed in 1939, after a gang of jewelry thieves were found to be operating there (having stolen diamond clips valued at £2,256 from a Park Lane matron who frequented the club).[195]

The Shim Sham Club

Jack Isow's Shim Sham Club at 37 Wardour Street represented a commercial effort to stabilize this scene and transform the shady black club into an aboveground enterprise with substantial infrastructural investment (Figure 21). The Shim Sham boasted professional lighting, a well-sprung dance floor, and an ambitious decorative scheme.[196] According to police reports, one entered on the second floor, where the office and lavatories were located. From there, one descended to a large main room on the first floor, consisting of a small, elevated bandstand, semi-circular bar (which ostentatiously displayed non-alcoholic drinks of lemon and orange squash), and a 30 x 20 ft. space reserved for dancing, surrounded by forty tables.[197] Behind a swing door, a kitchen prepared snacks appealing to the genteel British palate: smoked salmon, mock turtle soup, fried fillet of plaice, lobster mayonnaise, peach melba.[198] Even when an anonymous

21 The Shim Sham Club. From Rudolph Dunbar, "Harlem in London: Year of Advancement for Negroes," *Melody Maker*, March 7, 1936, p. 2. Progressive journalists praised the Shim Sham as a democratic and international space of hot jazz and interracial dancing. In the photograph at top left, Rudolph Dunbar and Ike Hatch admire Sanderson's murals of "Negro types." In the center, Ike Hatch is depicted as the expressive face of the Shim Sham.

letter writer complained about the Shim Sham to authorities in 1935, the writer advised undercover police to arrive in evening dress with a lady friend to avoid suspicion (evidently lounge suits were primarily worn by the "coloured denizens").[199]

At the Shim Sham, Isow hoped to attract the kind of social mix of high and low that made nightclubs exciting and popular. Reviewers announced sightings of international celebrities and blue bloods at the club, including Douglas Fairbanks and Lady Ashley.[200] The Shim Sham was patronized by all sorts, both "Mayfair" and "Soho," the latter signifying theater workers and musicians, as well as local villains and sexual nonconformists. Homosexuals, lesbians, "men living on the immoral earnings of women," and interracial couples made the Shim

Sham "the talk of London," according to anonymous letters sent to the police. Boxers, black artists, journalists, and members of high bohemia, including *Express* columnist and café communist Tom Driberg, filled out the picture of Shim Sham patrons.[201]

In this enhanced space, black British musicians presented themselves professionally to white patrons and participated in the cultural fusions that resulted in black British swing. In 1935, the Shim Sham opened to rave reviews in the jazz-minded trade and entertainment guides. On March 9, jazz critic Leonard Feather, who was then a fledgling journalist for *Melody Maker*, publicized it as "Another London Harlem Club" in Soho. He presented the club as the venture of black American entertainer Ike Hatch, formerly the MC of the Nest Club and known to BBC audiences for his minstrel program. On the first night, Feather admitted that he arrived there with "mixed feelings, expecting to find just another of those suffocating underground cellars." To his surprise, he found an "expansive and brilliantly lit room," comfortable seating, and a bandstand complete with two pianos. There were also "striking mural decorations" by "Sanderson," a noted travel writer, naturalist, and zoologist, depicting "Negro types." On the stand, Trinidadian drummer George "Happy" Blake and his band swung out "with more percussion than discretion," while American musical star Garland Wilson "idly filled the role of second piano." Adopting a hipster stance, Feather wrote: "Hundreds of people filed in, until I thought that every spade and every jigchaser in London must be among those present. Near beer, weeds, and lounge suits were the order of the night with many." Feather continued in this voice: "Eight hours for work, eight hours for sleep, and eight hours at the Shim Sham. That will be the new daily round for these carefree coloured denizens of London." The *New Amsterdam News*, where Feather regularly appeared as columnist of "London Lowdown," immediately took exception to Feather's condescending reference to "spades" and "jigchasers" (both American slang for blacks). But racial stereotyping and exotic fantasies of "Harlem nights" remained staples of positive reviews of the Shim Sham in London's entertainment media.[202]

Echoing Feather, *London Week* waxed enthusiastic about the jazz scene at the Shim Sham, also noting the physical amenities of the place and the cachet of African-American entertainers as guests. It praised the rhythm combination of the band under the direction of "Happy" Blake, and it identified Ike Hatch, "from Harlem," as the owner/manager who aimed to establish the Shim Sham as London's "Cotton Club." As a further incentive to visit, *London Week* proffered the fact that the "Blackbirds," a popular African-American dance troupe, "were there in force." "Great hoofing, song and playing by such stars as Garland Wilson were witnessed."[203]

Reviewers especially praised Ike Hatch as the expressive face of the Shim
Shim. Hatch was skilled at mediating between black and white cultures in the
metropolis. Born in New York in 1892, Hatch was trained in voice and toured
the States as a vaudeville performer, going to the South as part of a vocal and
piano act. When Hatch arrived in London in 1925, he hooked up with pianist
Elliott Carpenter to play music halls, theaters, and clubs in blackface. By the
mid-thirties, Hatch was regularly performing on the BBC, again as part of a
minstrel program, recording for Parlophone, as well as serving as MC in Soho's
black clubs. He continued to run clubs until the 1960s. Journalists of the thirties
praised Hatch's "talent-spotting ability," but, in the 1990s, one West Indian musician recalled his minstrel style with contempt: according to Louis Stephenson,
Hatch was a "pure hustler," a "real down South darkie, 'Yowsa, yowsa, let's have
some fun.'"[204]

George "Happy" Blake, the "ebony showman" at the Shim Sham, described as
more "Dixieland than Krupa" by *Melody Maker*, drew together other black
musical traditions in interwar Britain.[205] Both "Happy" and his brother Cyril
participated in the first wave of Afro-Caribbean entertainers to settle in London
after the Great War. Hailing from Trinidad, they had served in the Merchant
Marine and arrived in London shortly after the Armistice. As historians have
noted, of all of Britain's non-white colonial subjects, Caribbean migrants were
closest to the mother country in language, religion, and schooling. They came
from a world profoundly shaped by Britishness, but this imperial culture was
part of a rich, internationally open, and distinctively modern cultural mix, one
produced by migrations inside and outside of the Caribbean as well as by extensive racial intermarriage.[206]

As insiders/outsiders, the Blake brothers eventually infused British jazz with
calypso and Latin American elements. They arrived in London with a familiarity
with West Indian string instruments. In 1919, the Southern Symphonic Orchestra
was touring Britain and recruited both brothers as replacements for African-
American members who had departed.[207] During the thirties, both Blake
brothers tried to organize professional black bands. "Happy" Blake's "all-coloured
band" established a residency at the Cuba Club in 1936, one of the first London
nightclubs to feature a Latin American ambience, but it would not be the first
black band to gain bookings in elite West End clubs like the Old Florida and the
Café de Paris.[208] That distinction went to the "West Indian Dance Band," led by
Ken "Snakehips" Johnson, a Guyanese dancer who had perfected a hip-swiveling
dance derived from Earl "Snakehips" Tucker.[209]

"Happy" Blake's band at the Shim Sham included the black Welsh guitarist
Joe Deniz who eventually joined Johnson's band. In a 1993 BBC interview, Joe

recalled the Shim Sham as a space of professional improvement for a black Briton like himself, who possessed little formal musical training and a more attenuated relation to American black traditions than West Indian players.[210] After working in a string of small joints, including the Nest and the Cuba Club, Joe followed Happy Blake to the Shim Sham as his guitarist.[211] Joe remembered the Shim Sham as "the first real effort to make [a black club] look like a place, not thrown together."[212] At the Nest and the Shim Sham, he mixed with legendary guitarist Belgian Django Reinhardt and American artists.[213] Watching and playing with the "visiting fireman" and West End musicians, absorbing techniques and instrumental lore, Joe received his musical education in these Soho clubs, where American, African, and Latin American musical traditions coalesced.

The Shim Sham was also a space of negotiation with the political radicals of Jewish London.[214] Black musicians became friends with some of the Jewish sidemen who visited the premises. Here Deniz made contact with guitarist Ivor Mairants, who told the Deniz brothers that they played guitar very well and encouraged them to move beyond the black club scene of Soho. The club attracted other West End musicians, such as Billy Amstell and Harry Gold, who had frequented the 43 in the twenties, but now sat in with the black musicians and American stars like Coleman Hawkins to play improvised small band swing music, where it was possible to "play in the cracks" and stray from the conventional regularity of strict tempo orchestration.[215] Based on 4/4 (rather than 2/4) beat, swing bands substituted string bass and guitar for tuba and banjo to provide rhythm, stripping away the vertical harmony element to emphasize horizontal flowing rhythms, with greater room for soloists to improvise.[216]

Since their days at the 43, Amstell and Gold had undergone a radical political conversion. Living in the "backwoods" of the East End and working in the West End, these West End musicians were exposed, more than others of their own background, to the disparities between rich and poor.[217] "We musicians," declared Harry Gold, "came from ordinary backgrounds but our music gave us a way into that society environment."[218] Elite nightclubs were forcing grounds for radical Jewish politics. At Ciro's and the Embassy Club, where Billy Amstell played with the Ambrose orchestra, "people used to come and they were well fed and they used to guzzle into their food and drink and only round the corner people were sleeping in doorways, wrapped in paper."[219] According to Amstell, the spectacle of conspicuous consumption in the midst of great hunger in the thirties converted him and others to socialism.[220] "I watched the rich patrons of the Café de Paris and thought about it all politically," Harry Gold recalled in his memoirs. "It reinforced my socialist convictions."[221] Also reinforcing their

left-wing convictions and driving them into Soho after-hours spaces was the
subordinate status they experienced at the swank West End resorts, where they
were required to enter separate doors and were proscribed from mixing with
guests. Class knowledge and class grievances made them receptive to recruitment into the Communist Party. "All those people were beneath contempt,"
remembered Van Phillips of the Savoy Havana Band and major Communist
recruiter. "If you weren't a communist already, you'd be a bloody communist if
you'd seen what we'd seen of the ruling class."[222] Another radicalizing force was
the anti-Semitism they confronted in the East End and in the open-air labor
market for musicians in Archer Street, where the British Union of Fascists
distributed pamphlets.[223]

The gathering in the Shim Sham of Jewish anti-fascists and Communists, as
well as black pan-Africanists, transformed it informally into a "democratic" and
"international" space of the Cultural Front. During their jazz study in 1939, Mass
Observers uncovered links joining Jewish dance musicians, radical politics, and
the Shim Sham. Mingling with the "amazingly cheerful" musicians in Archer
Street, Mass Observer Hugh Clegg met the well-traveled Charles Bohm, a music
union organizer. Bohm invited him back to his flat in Victoria, where his book-
cases were filled with Left Book Club books and the writings of Lenin.[224] Bohm
told him of his successful organizing of dance musicians into a Communist-led
local union: "from being individualists and reactionaries" musicians had become
"politically minded." "You couldn't have talked politics among the rank and file
6 or 7 years ago ... I don't know any part of the population that has changed
quicker."[225] "They provided the largest section of May Day demonstration."
While a staunch supporter of restrictions on American musicians, Bohm
declared himself to be a great enthusiast of the Shim Sham, now defunct. "I used
to work at the old Shim Sham club. It had an international reputation. It was
better known in New York than in Manchester." "All sorts mixed there—Mayfair,
Soho, boxers and friends of Royalty—a whole cross-section of society."[226]

While cataloguing the "cross-section of society" at the Shim Sham, Bohm
failed to mention its racial diversity, perhaps reflecting a brand of Marxism that
regarded jazz as a cosmopolitan mix, the "authoritative people's music," the
music of a class rather than of a race or an ethnicity.[227] He also ignored its raffish
sexualities. Yet Rudolph Dunbar, a noted pan-Africanist, Guyanese clarinetist,
composer, and band leader, identified racial mixing of men and women as *the*
most distinguishing feature of the Shim Sham. Writing in the *Melody Maker* in
1936, Dunbar highlighted the Shim Sham as the capstone of an extraordinary
"year of advancement for Negroes" (Figure 21 above). As notable benchmarks,
Dunbar ticked off Korda's production of *Sanders of the River*, featuring Paul

Robeson and employing hundreds of people of color as extras, the establishment of a new club for black undergraduates in London, the boxing triumph of Joe Louis, and even the Italo-Abyssinian War, which generated much "sympathy and understanding for the negro," despite its horror. He speculated that "it was because of this enhanced status of the Negro that Ike Hatch has had such a remarkable success with his club."[228]

Acknowledging the dynamic musical environment of the Shim Sham, Dunbar was even more impressed with the dancing of "white and coloured people together." He singled out the interracial spectacle of the dance floor as a phenomenon that forced English people to adapt to a new social order. He noted the limitations of some white patrons, including attempts by some "to imitate the Negro style of dancing," as well as their initial resistance to racial mixing on the dance floor, depending on the make-up of the interracial couple. If the female partner was black, "and of that irresistible Creole type of loveliness," the couple might provoke admiration. But a black male partner would be looked upon as "something despicable," and his white partner classed as "trash," a view, as we shall see, adopted by undercover police. Still there were "no unpleasant scenes ever. . . Generally the people who don't like it make their exit—though, more often than not, they return later, having apparently thought it over." For this reason, Dunbar believed, "the Shim Sham represents the new outlook on the colour question."[229]

Jack Isow, co-owner of the Shim Sham, was motivated by more mundane and opportunistic concerns than pan-Africanists and white musicians who integrated jazz into an internationalist left politics. Black musicians remembered Isow as an exploitative owner who cheated Ike Hatch.[230] But he too was an outsider, at a considerable remove from the "snooty boredom" and genteel prejudices of the British elite. Born in Russia in 1899 and arriving in London with his family at age eight, he was characterized in the press and police reports as a stateless person. A ruthless businessman, he evidently possessed a genuine enthusiasm for nightclub life, and became, for a time, a variety manager for Coleman Hawkins, the internationally famous boogie-woogie and stride pianist. But Isow did not share the political views of the leftist musicians in his employ: according to a Special Branch report in 1966 he "had never been a member of any foreign or subversive political organization", nor was he "known to have participated in extreme politics in this country."[231] Isow was, however, not indifferent to the rise of fascism: in the late 1930s, he belligerently stood up to fascists (as well as to gangsters and police) who threatened his enterprises.

In the folklore of Jewish Soho and theatrical London, the rotund, pugnacious Isow looms large as a successful Jewish postwar restaurateur, owner of the famous Isow's, a high-class kosher-style restaurant at the corner of Walker's Court and Brewer Street that was heavily patronized by Hollywood and Broadway stars. Prior to his catering success, he ran a number of shady establishments in the 1920s and 1930s, and had racked up a significant criminal record for operating unlicensed premises where illegal drinking and gambling took place.[232] Isow's leisure empire continued the entrepreneurial strategies of his immigrant father, Isidore Isowitzky. Before the Great War, his father operated a nickelodeon and a billiard club in the East End, as well as a sewing machine repair business. Jack Isow took over his father's clubs and expanded westwards, opening billiard and gaming clubs "of doubtful repute" in Soho in the 1930s. "From the time that he left school," Special Branch reported to Home Secretary Roy Jenkins in 1966, "Isow had a chequered history of employment, ranging over such occupations as commission agent, variety artist manager, mechanical engineer, billiards hall keeper and caterer."[233]

The Shim Sham was Isow's first foray into the nightclub business. By 1935, he was a seasoned businessman with substantial capital and extensive connections with wine suppliers and the entertainment world. In 1935, he owned two clubs, the Majestic Billiard Hall and the Shim Sham, at number 37 Wardour Street, "fifty yards down from Shaftesbury Avenue," in close proximity to the theater, cinemas, and variety theaters.[234] These clubs were situated within Soho's cosmopolitan pleasure zone. During the interwar period, the northern part of Wardour Street had become a "glossy ghetto," the business hub of Britain's film industry. In 1932, the *Evening News* described it as "long and narrow, like a strip of film . . . People jostle one another on the niggardly pavements, little groups of men stride out of door ways, arguing rather intensely."[235] Further to the south, the Gerrard Street part of Wardour Street, where the Shim Sham was located, was the site of other shady nightclubs, plus the Tea Kettle, a queer café decorated in false Tudor. The street was "alive with prostitutes," who patronized the Jewish-owned gown shops and milliner's shops, known for their "commerce of touters and knock offs."[236] Esther Rose, trading under the name of "Madame Hannah," owned a milliner's shop in Wardour Street. She sold hats to Mrs. Meyrick of the 43, as well as to street girls, who "used to walk up and down outside there . . . and always had to have a change [of fashion]."[237]

Standing at the door, welcoming patrons when they entered, or walking up and down the main room, Isow was critically important to the successful operation of the Shim Sham. But he could not prevent the place from being menaced by gangsters. Two months after the Shim Sham opened, a court case involving Isow's Majestic Billiard Hall, located below the Shim Sham, exposed the system of criminal extortion and violence operating in Soho's club world. On May 1, 1935, four men were charged at Bow Street Police Court with willful damage to the Majestic Billiard Hall. They were members of the notorious Sabini gang, engaged in an organized raid and intent on avenging some earlier offense previously committed by Isow against their boss, "Harry Boy Sabini." Windows, crockery, a lampshade, and a table were smashed, while Isow's employees sustained injuries.[238] Initially, witnesses at the scene made statements to the police, but within two weeks, these statements were retracted and the police could find no one willing to testify against the Sabini gang.[239] Reading *The Times* report between the lines, it appears likely that Isow reached some temporary truce with the Sabinis. But the same gang menaced the Shim Sham in 1936, with similar scenes of violent intrusions and dropped court charges.[240] Renowned for his explosive temper, Isow clearly lacked Mrs. Meyrick's capacity to placate and charm the Italian mob.

Police posed an even greater threat to Isow's enterprises than gangsters. As "one of the largest Bottle Party establishments running in the West End, and without doubt the very worst," the Shim Sham became the special target of police animus, at the same time as it was lauded in the entertainment press as a harbinger of London's new cosmopolitanism. As in the case of the 43, anonymous letters, including two that were apparently written by nightclub competitors of Isow, seem to have set a police investigation into motion. Most of the writers signed themselves anonymously, adopting a civic identity, such as "Englishman," "Neighbour," or "Citizen."[241] Letter writers condemned the club as lewd and scandalous, but most of them indicated that they had participated in some of the club's activities. The "patter of the cabaret" was "an absolute scandal" while "the encouragement of Black and White intercourse is the talk of the town," declared one anonymous writer in April 1935. A second anonymous letter, from a "neighbour in the rear of Wardour Street," declared the Shim Sham to be "a den of vice and iniquity": "there is a negro band, white woman [sic] carrying on perversion, women with women, men with men, a second Caravan Club." (This refers to a "queer" club closed in 1934 and was clearly meant as a slur, but it also suggests a pattern of queer migration to black clubs in the late thirties.) Some "obnoxious things" happened in the lavatories, the letter writer added.[242] "One who has been there" alleged that "Snow" and "hashish" were sold in the form of cigarettes.[243]

These complaints, along with reports from agents of the Public Morality Council, led to undercover observations of the Shim Sham between May and October 1935.[244] To prosecute the Shim Sham as an unregistered club, police needed to show that its claim to be a private bottle party was fraudulent. In June 1935, they assigned two young constables, Sweny and Stannard, the task of gaining entry into the club as non-members and obtaining drinks that had not been ordered in advance. Their reports paid particular attention to the activities of Isow and Hatch, documenting their supervision of alcoholic consumption and their collusion with Sam Henry of the Advance Wine Company who provided the intoxicants (via a boy on a bicycle). Arriving with "friends," each constable took note of the "indecent dancing," where participants seemed to gain "sexual pleasure in the dancing," but they did not join in on the dance floor. The activities of the habitués took a back seat to Isow's defiance of the law and the police. Met authorities were most indignant over a conversation that transpired between P.C. Sweny and a Shim Sham waiter. When told that a bottle would cost 23 shillings, Sweny stated, "That is too much for us." The waiter explained, "Our expenses are heavy, what with the orchestra, fines, and *paying the Police*," a remark underlined by senior officials reading the report.[245]

The police raided the club on July 5, 1935. Unlike Mrs. Meyrick, who graciously welcomed the police and asked them to remove their headgear, Isow antagonized police by belligerently resisting their entry with a warrant. He exploded when the inspector asked Isow his position there: "I'm not answering any questions you've already been my teacher—you are taking a fucking liberty with me—it is persecution." He "continually interrupted the conversation using obscene remarks and accusing me of persecuting him." Hatch quietly complied with the police interrogators until Isow told him, "Don't answer his bloody questions."[246]

On October 1, 1935, at Bow Street Court, Isow and Hatch were charged with operating an unlicensed club and fined £200 and £50 in court costs. The "whole of the defence" was that the police were "unreliable."[247] "The result of this case," reported Superintendent Ralphe, is "more than satisfactory."[248] However, by March 1936, local police officials acknowledged that "this Bottle Party establishment is much the same as it was prior to the Police prosecution."[249] Despite heavy legal penalties, the Shim Sham seemed to thrive. On one night, police estimated that the door money brought in over £50. Anonymous letters continued to arrive at Scotland Yard, complaining of personal effects stolen from club patrons as well as disgusting behavior by "niggers and girls of ill repute." The most effective stimulus to police action came from "Pro Bono" in March 1936. "Pro Bono" asked the Commissioner of Police if he was aware that the Shim Sham "is a den of vice run under the guise of a bottle party club." Not only were the hostesses "whores in the employ of the man who runs the club," but the owner bragged that he had the police "squared."[250]

Infuriated by this boasting, the Met once again ordered undercover observation. Because "Isow was no longer taking chances" and declining to serve strangers who did not have an order with a wine company, the police proceeded with an eye to prosecuting the Shim Sham for illegal dancing and music.[251] In May and June 1936, undercover police paid more attention to the habitués of the club and their bodily practices, looking for evidence of indecency.[252] To describe the social crowd, undercover police resorted to the same pathologizing, visual stereotypes contained in the anonymous letters. The police constable assigned to outside duties catalogued the high and low cosmopolitan types entering and leaving the establishment: noting when, for example, "men and women in evening dress arrive," or when two women of the "Lesbian type" departed, or when prostitutes exited with "three men of colour." Inside the premises, P.C. Brunton, who came accompanied by a female "friend," surveyed the dance floor: at 12:40 a.m. there were "12 couples dancing on the floor including six coloured men"; at 2:40 a.m. the dance floor was full, including "several women dancing together." Scanning the room he noted the provocative costume of the "young coloured girl" who sold cigarettes, as well as the presence of "prostitutes, ponces, and lesbians" among a crowd that expanded from 40 persons to 180.[253]

Undercover reports again led to the raiding of the Shim Sham in December 1936, along with twenty-six other clubs, for unlicensed dancing and music. Isow was fined £25, three times the fine imposed on other proprietors. By then he had shifted his attention to a suburban roadhouse near St. Albans, called the Barn, which would soon bring him again into conflict with the police and anti-Semites in late-thirties London. According to his daughter-in-law Hilda Winston, interviewed in the 1990s, Isow purchased the Barn in 1936, in retaliation for being denied entrance there because he was a Jew. A resident of suburban Barnet, Isow went "there for tea one day, and he was barred by the doorman. Because he was a Jew and he said I am going to buy this place and I'm going to sack you—and he did just that. He was a character."[254] Anti-Semitism would continue to haunt him in the suburbs, as it would many Jewish Sohoites who made the exodus to outer London. The *Jewish Chronicle* reported on May 23, 1936 that "hooligans have poured oil and permanganate into 300,000 gallons of water in the swimming pool at the Barn club, the well-known road house on the Barnet by-pass." The same miscreants also nailed up a notice headed by a large swastika and the letters "P.J" (Perish Judea). Isow told the *Chronicle* representative that Jews formed about 75 percent of the visitors to the club since he had taken it over. Renowned for his rough and ready character, he displayed a tough resilience: "Little do the culprits know that they have done me far more good than harm. I have received publicity the value of which more than compensates for the damage they have done . . . and there are some people who were sympathetic towards the Fascists but have since altered their opinion."[255] Nonetheless, by February 27, 1937, Isow had to give up the Barn when he was sent to prison for conducting the club as "a gaming house, permitting dancing, singing, and music without a licence, and selling intoxicating drinks after hours."[256] The press described Isow as an outsider—a "stateless person," a "White Russian," and an alien—but they were also indignant that the police constable, who brought two sisters to dinner with him, left a hefty tip of 12s for the waiter.[257]

Isow returned to Soho, where he was again prosecuted and jailed for running a betting shop in Lisle Street in 1937.[258] His next venture in catering turned out to be his most successful. In 1938, he opened a small café in Walker's Court, near the corner of Brewer Street, amidst the dress shops and their schleppers.[259] Isow's "Jewish style" restaurant started off selling salt-beef sandwiches, but after the first US troops arrived in 1942, "business began to pick up."[260] Isow's expanded to a second building and eventually took over the entirety of Walker's Court and established a frontage on Brewer Street. "All the celebrities came into Isow's Restaurant. All the boxing fraternity—Jack Solomons and the others. All the film actors and actresses [on the recommendation of Lindy's of Times Square]—Danny Kaye, Betty Hutton, Frank Sinatra, and Walt Disney."[261] Isow's became the premiere Jewish restaurant in the West End, the only one to attract many non-Jewish patrons. Underneath the restaurant, Isow operated (in his wife's name) a small basement club, the Jack of Clubs.[262]

Despite his postwar stature as a respectable restaurateur, Isow continued to run into trouble with authorities: in 1946, he was charged with engaging in black market dealings and attempting to bribe the police. A year later the same policemen were convicted of "sundry criminal offences." In telling his version of this story, Isow emphasized the "violent anti-Semitic remarks" of the officers, caught on tape, thanks to an early tape recorder hidden in the fireplace. In the late forties, the Ministry of Labour accused him of "underpayment of wages"; in the mid-fifties, the Board of Trade investigated his attempts "to defraud creditors" when he liquidated his restaurant business.[263] By 1953, Isow had become a large property owner in Soho and leased and eventually sold some of the Walker's Court premises to Paul Raymond, "the porn king," who built a strip club empire in Soho.[264] This was indeed a big transition in the fortunes of Soho's Berwick Street and environs: from a predominantly Jewish immigrant neighborhood, albeit with illicit commerce, it had decisively transmogrified into a non-residential and highly capitalized sex shop and striptease center. Jewish folk memories mark the closing of Isow's in 1972 as part of the end of Jewish Soho and the rise of Soho porn culture. But in doing so, they have obscured recollections of the entrepreneur's own contributions to shady ventures in interwar Soho.[265]

Wartime Black Clubs

The wartime arrival of 130,000 black GIs reshaped the fortunes of Soho's black clubs and sparked considerable public debate.[266] Thanks to the influx of "coloured soldiers and seamen," Soho had begun "to assume the appearance of a coloured quarter," observed *What's On* in 1943.[267] In Soho and elsewhere, the kind of interracial dance scenes lauded by Rudolph Dunbar in 1936 often provoked violent reactions from white GIs and some Britons. Recalling the war, Laurie Deniz stated, "if there were coloured Yanks and white Yanks [in a club], nine times out of ten there would be trouble if coloured Yanks danced with white girls."[268] Even before the arrival of the American troops, government officials worried about the racial tensions that might result from large numbers of black troops who were part of a segregated army on British soil. Although there was no formal color bar in Britain, the "coloured people of the Empire" who visited Britain found themselves excluded from some hotels, restaurants, dance halls, and nightclubs. Employment opportunities for black Britons were bleak, and opposition to interracial marriages in British seaports became widespread in the 1920s and 1930s. These prewar conditions were already a diplomatic embarrassment to officials at the Colonial Office, who feared that ill treatment of African-Americans in Britain would intensify disaffection in the colonies. Some MPs raised objections to the segregationist policies of the US army in Parliament, but the Foreign Office and the War Office, anxious to avoid "friction between the two armies," worried lest British fraternization with black troops damage long-term diplomatic relations between the United States and Britain. This led to a policy of discouraging and disciplining British women who consorted with black soldiers.[269]

If government officials were conflicted in their reaction to black Americans and US segregationist policies, so were British people. In its Home Intelligence reports for 1942, the Ministry of Information concluded that the "British are characteristically against discrimination, though association between these [black] troops and British girls [is] regarded with disapproval." Working for the Ministry of Information, Mass Observation documented similar findings regarding interracial sex. Racial tensions sharpened in 1943, as the number of black troops stationed in Britain swelled, and the media extensively publicized cases of sexual assault involving British women and black Americans.[270] An informal color bar operated in many West End venues: to avoid conflicts between white and black American servicemen, the management of the Paramount Dance Hall on Tottenham Court Road only admitted black GIs if they entered with "coloured partners", and did not attempt to dance with white women.[271] But black troops found a friendlier reception at Soho's "coloured clubs."

22 The international stream at the Bouillabaisse: "The Moment They Have Been Waiting For." From "Inside London's Coloured Clubs," *Picture Post*, July 17, 1943. *Picture Post* featured interracial dancing as the embodiment of the internationalist wartime dancing front.

Picture Post's 1943 photo-essay, "Inside London's Coloured Clubs," represents a pointed intervention in the escalating debate over race and sex (Figure 22). Like Mass Observation, *Picture Post* was an expression of left cultural politics of the late thirties.[272] Founded in 1938, it successfully wedded the English documentary mode of social commentary to revolutionary developments in layout, typography, and photography pioneered by avant-garde magazines on the Continent. Its resiliently cheerful reportage did not shy away from controversy, but, as Stuart Hall observes, it tended to present conflict and dissent as surface images, part of the infinite "active variety" of English life.[273] Its account of London's "coloured clubs" fell into this category. Like other magazine features, this photo-essay provided upbeat wartime propaganda while addressing a wartime experience that disquieted many readers.[274]

"Inside London's Coloured Clubs" displays the attractions of Soho clubs like Frisco's and the Bouillabaisse for the soldiers and seamen who swelled "London's coloured population." The article's text firmly locates these Soho clubs as the successors to the defunct black clubs of the thirties—the Nest, Smokey Joe's, the Shim Sham, and Jig's Club—"most of them casualties of the war" (or, more accurately, wartime police crackdowns).[275] Like their predecessors, the new clubs featured hot jazz and musical improvisation performed by black entertainers such as Joe Deniz and Cyril Blake, who had gained a new public following through their recordings and BBC performances. However, the real stars of black clubs are the new wartime clientele. Images, captions, and text all testify to the liveliness, communal energy, and diversity of occupation, skin color, accents and nationalities of the "international stream." "At the Bouillabaisse," declares one caption, "you see the light-skinned American and the black Nigerian. You hear the accent of Chicago mixing with cockney and Cardiff. Soldiers, Red Cross Workers, students, factory workers, actors, and swing fans—all come to the basement under White London. They all mix in an international stream."[276]

The photographs represent black men laughing and dancing with ordinary English girls. A wide rectangular photo spread extends across two pages of the story to illustrate the international stream of the Bouillabaisse on New Compton Street. The reader is positioned at eye-level with interracial couples on the dance floor: the "dark Nigerian" facing the camera is dancing with a white woman; next to them, a blond English woman with spectacles, in ordinary street attire, is laughing and dancing with the "light-skinned Negro." This dancing scene embodies the internationalist sentiments of the wartime "dancing front," when progressive organs celebrated jazz and jazz dancing as "a potential weapon, and one we possess and Germany doesn't." Voicing a common left-wing perspective at the time, Mass Observation's founder Tom Harrisson hoped that jazz could be a "crystallizer of feeling" on behalf of progressive internationalism; it could further a modern, democratic mythopoesis to counter the "atavism" of Germany and the "revival of racist superstition."[277]

"Inside London's Coloured Clubs" records a young, animated, communal throng, with one exception: a cameo portrait of "The White Girl Who Likes Frisco's" (Figure 23). This photograph spotlights the face and shoulders of an elegantly dressed and groomed young woman. She is looking off into the distance, emotionally detached from her black partner in military uniform, his face and figure in shadows. "She's smart," declared the caption, "apparently well-to-do and is said to hail from Mayfair. She's often here in Frisco's, dancing and talking to celebrities." "The white girl" is not presented as a point of identification for readers, and she stands apart from the happy multitude. Beautiful and unapproachable, she is an elite pleasure-seeker, following in Lady Mountbatten's tradition. However much Picture Post embraced the internationalism of Soho's "coloured clubs," it still registered anxieties about the boundaries of the race and nation through the figure of the detached female hedonist, who already seemed to some to be a traitor to her race and nation as far back as 1918, when Maud Allan and Margot Asquith were accused of being part of a sodomitical Fifth Column during the First World War. There may have been no color bar at Frisco's, but Picture Post's rendering of the scene still fell short of realizing Rudolph Dunbar's utopian dreams of a "new outlook on the colour question."

23 "The White Girl at Frisco's." From "Inside London's Coloured Clubs," *Picture Post*, July 17, 1943, p. 20. Despite its praise for the internationalist wartime spirit of London's black clubs, *Picture Post* registered widespread anxieties over racial mixing by spotlighting the figure of the female hedonist from Mayfair who frequented Frisco's.

Conclusion

While ground-breaking, the black clubs of the thirties were structural variants of the shady nightclub form already on display in Mrs. Meyrick's establishments of the Roaring Twenties. Both the 43 and the Shim Sham were packed spaces that fostered a culture of illegality, while endeavoring to manage social and sexual transgressions and chaotic intrusions from without. They attracted patrons who wanted to see life or partake in "early morning excitement." The right social mix was essential to their appeal, as was the blend of dancing, alcoholic consumption, erotic expression, and social and theatrical performances in an undemarcated space. In each club, a more bounded space was set aside for more clandestine encounters (at the Shim Sham, lavatories for sex and drugs) or for more privileged action (at the 43, Mrs. Meyrick's office, where young bloods assisted her in vetting prospective patrons).

The black clubs also duplicated the same division of labor present in earlier shady nightclubs. Both the 43 and the Shim Sham boasted a proprietor, manager, service personnel, entertainment staff, and cabaret performers, as well as doorman/commissionaire. The service staff was in large part drawn from the racial/ethnic mix of the locale. The Italian waiter/commissionaire seemed to have remained a fixture throughout the period, but now black entertainers, skilled at social mediation, rivaled Jews as masters of ceremonies in Soho's black clubs.[278] A relatively adventurous musical culture also characterized these two spaces. Isow and other proprietors of black clubs continued Meyrick's practice of providing raucous and improvised music that violated the strict tempo of West End hotel bands by drawing on the free services of jamming West End sidemen and visiting firemen from America.

Sex workers, in the form of dancing hostesses, were another fixture of the twenties that carried on into the thirties. Besides paid dance partners, black patrons also filled the "hostess" role: they were recruited to entertain well-heeled white patrons who were eager to see how "coloured people enjoyed themselves" and willing to buy them drinks in exchange for a dance or the promise of sexual favors outside the club. Racial mixing could be interpreted by disgruntled white patrons and law enforcers as another form of sexual enticement, or even "sexual perversion." Adding to the transgressive mix were undercover police whose masquerades and tense exchanges with hostesses undoubtedly contributed to the atmosphere of risk and excitement.

Managing the culture of risk in these establishments depended on the social skills and cultural capital of the host/proprietor, as well as the social make-up of club patrons. Because she possessed a winning way with both gangsters and police, Mrs. Meyrick was by far the most successful entrepreneur of shady resorts. Through print culture, including her own interviews and reports of her court testimonies, Mrs. Meyrick established herself as a personality and folk heroine of pleasure-seeking Mayfair by trading on a combination of gracious hospitality, rapacious greed, and inveterate law-breaking. Her popularity flagged only when it became known that her "fine contempt for the law" extended to bribing the police.

Like Meyrick, Isow tried to attract an exciting mix of "high" and "low" social types, but he never quite solidified Meyrick's loyal society following. Nor did he successfully placate the police. There may have been more than a tinge of anti-Semitism in the Met's palpable hostility towards Isow, the undesirable alien. Harry Daley, a homosexual policeman who was a lover of E. M. Forster, recalled a number of fascist sympathizers in the C Division of the Metropolitan Police and elsewhere.[279] Nine months after Isow's Barn was vandalized by Nazis in 1936, Isow was successfully prosecuted and imprisoned for illegal gambling and infringement of the liquor laws. Once again, the comparison to Meyrick is instructive: when considering whether to prosecute her for returning to night-club management in 1931, authorities worried about her capacity to garner public sympathy as a persecuted "martyr," but they voiced no such concerns regarding Isow.[280] Corruption, racism, and anti-Semitism remained enduring features of police oversight of London's shady nightclubs.

At the Shim Sham, Jack Isow exploited the new cachet of black clubs as innovative spaces of musical and political culture. Progressive media outlets lauded the clubs as vibrant enactments of progressive politics of the nation and the democratic world. As purveyors of interracial dancing and hot jazz, these clubs came to represent the internationalist, utopian spirit of the wartime "dancing front," despite the racism, grafting of patrons, exploitation of staff, and depredations of marauding gangsters that also transpired in these spaces. Yet, even as it endorsed the wartime morale of the clubs, *Picture Post* registered its uneasiness with the interracial scene by spotlighting the elite female hedonist, the girl from Mayfair, whose decadent lineage looped back to Mrs. Meyrick and her BYT patrons, as well as even further back to Maud Allan and the Great War. Meanwhile, another Soho venue offered a safer, more licit and strictly white atmosphere for male suburbanites, keen to see life Up West. For this middle-market niche, we turn next to the Windmill Theatre and its tasteful, erotic entertainments.

CHAPTER 8

Windmill Theatre

In July 1937, Elizabeth Bowen visited the Windmill Theatre, just "off Piccadilly," as theater critic of the magazine *Night and Day*. She reported that the ninety-fourth edition of the Windmill's *Revudeville* was great fun. In this tiny theater, the revue had to be intimate, because the cast was "practically in your lap." Providing the sex appeal were the resourceful Windmill Girls and the "pretty tableau" of nude showgirls in static, artistic poses. These acts were complemented and showcased by two ingenious and physically witty comedians. Bowen credited the Windmill management with fostering an air of domesticated Britishness, citing manager Vivian Van Damm's motto "Britain for the Britisher" and the "cosiness" of owner Mrs. Laura Henderson's name. Even with a nude tableau, the show sustained a firm moral footing, emphatically underwritten by the Metroland suburban homes advertised on the drop-curtain. "Taken all together, this is Britain no doubt."[1]

The terms used by Bowen to describe Windmill entertainments—cozy, intimate, little, resourceful, moral, patriotic—were also used to register an emerging British national fiction in the period between the wars: a movement away from the formerly heroic and imperial rhetoric of national identity towards a more inward-looking, domestic, and homogeneous Little England, interpreted at the time as feminine.[2] This shift in national temperament was most closely associated with middle-class suburbia—that is, with the fake Tudor facades of the Metroland homes advertised on the Windmill fire curtain.[3] However, by 1940, the same qualities of ordinariness and resourcefulness were ascribed to embattled Londoners heroically defending themselves against German bombardment. The friendly, unpretentious Windmill Theatre played a role in transplanting this national imaginary to London's urban core: as the only West End theater to stay

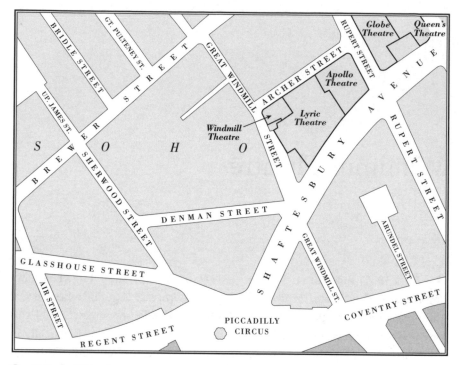

Great Windmill Street

open throughout the Blitz, its motto, "We Never Closed," came to symbolize the resilience of ordinary Londoners improvising to fight off the German Luftwaffe.

Blitz histories commonly acknowledge the Windmill's iconic role during the "Battle of Britain," but they tend to interpret its wartime renown as a straightforward result of its courageous heroism under fire.[4] However, the Windmill's landmark status was not so straightforward. It became a national institution not only by staying open and acquiring a new wartime audience, but also by continuing to embody 1930s middlebrow suburban values in an urban setting—relocating them to central London, the new symbolic heart of the embattled nation. The unpretentious performances at the Windmill sustained a connection with ordinary prewar culture, while transmuting ordinariness into an idealized expression of wartime morale.[5]

This chapter tracks how the Windmill took shape as a middlebrow consumer space that would prove strategic to Blitz propaganda. Let me say a few words about middlebrow. During the interwar period, literary critics such as Virginia Woolf and Queenie Leavis invoked middlebrow as a term of derision—to denote the insular, escapist, feminized literary taste of suburban England.[6] At the same time, other cultural producers, notably the BBC, adopted middlebrow as a more neutral category.[7] They, too, associated middlebrow with lower middle-class suburbanites, with the black-coated (and white collar) workers who were the main beneficiaries of the expanding consumer industries of the 1930s.[8] These cultural outlets treated middlebrow not as a term of reproach but as a market niche they wanted to attract, a cultural product pitched to middling consumers, male or female.

To the well-known list of cultural sites of English middlebrow, we should now add the Windmill Theatre and its ordinary, unpretentious entertainments. As an urban space to "pop into," the Windmill attracted middle-class male commuters, "time-fillers" waiting for their trains.[9] Windmill patrons may have lived in suburbia, but they also resisted the feminized domesticity associated with this place. By visiting the Windmill they sought their own middlebrow entertainment in the form of clean, licensed, healthy, and up-to-date borderline material, in keeping with the streamlined taste of thirties commodity culture.[10]

The Windmill purveyed its borderline erotic material in a border space between the West End and Soho. The Windmill's liminal geography was crucial to its commercial success and political survival. Situated in Great Windmill Street, long renowned for its exhibitions of the "female form divine," the theater benefited from proximity to the theatrical trades and to Piccadilly Circus, the hub of tourist London. In this border space, the Windmill management combined certain features of Soho's commercial hinterland with the labor practices of the more heavily capitalized commerce showcased along its borders. The film industry also cast its shadow over the Windmill: to beat the talkies at their own game, the Windmill adapted the strategies of cinema exhibition on display at the Leicester Square cinemas to present its own version of fast-paced, live entertainment.[11]

The theater's liminal geography also accounts for the official toleration of its erotic exhibitions. The Lord Chamberlain, the theater censor, could be more easily persuaded to license the performance of stationary nude tableaux at a theater tucked into a Soho side street than one prominently situated along a main boulevard of Theatreland. While discreetly located in the backwaters of Piccadilly, the Windmill's building, a five-story "Edwardian wedding cake fantasy" of projecting cornices and ledges, was still visible from Shaftesbury Avenue to the south, allowing easy access to tourists or suburban patrons who lacked knowledge of Soho's more underground and raffish dives.[12]

The Windmill's success also hinged on the savvy marketing strategies of its theater owner and her manager, both of whom were situated at some distance from "middle England."[13] A wealthy widow of an East Indian jute merchant and well-positioned in society, Mrs. Laura Henderson presided over the Windmill as its "fairy godmother" until her death in 1944 (Figure 24).[14] Her photograph graced the first page of Windmill souvenir programs, surrounded by her troupe of performers who consisted of clothed men and scantily attired women. She was also shown pulling the oars of a skiff around the Serpentine or masquerading as a natty German gentleman to test whether foreign visitors received a cordial reception.[15] Mrs. Henderson established her cozy name by supporting child welfare, female patriotism, civic activism, and the performing arts, while more daringly extending her patronage to birth control.[16] She also devoted herself to a range of Conservative political causes, from the National Police Fund to reward police for their work during the General Strike in 1926, to support for the right-wing, pro-appeasement Anglo-German fellowship in 1936. Mrs. Henderson was not unique in blending an interest in the charitable welfare

REVUDEVILLE at THE WINDMILL THEATRE, Piccadilly

is the most famous stage entertainment in London. Mrs. Laura Henderson opened the show over five years ago with the help of Mr. Vivian Van Damm, since when it has gone from success to success, and many famous artists continue to face the footlights at this famous theatre for the first time. ACE FILMS regularly present a forty-minute variety film of the best material in each show, and have already Trade Shown :

"DIGGING FOR GOLD"
4,066 ft.   B.R. 13810

"FULL STEAM"
4,266 ft.   B.R. 13823

"BOTTLE PARTY"
4,156 ft.   B.R. 13892

"PICCADILLY PLAYTIME"
4,510 ft.   B.R. 13988

"SONG IN SOHO"
4,418 ft.   B.R. 14100

"WINDMILL REVELS"
4,194 ft.   B.R. 14188

"CARRY ON, LONDON"
4,188 ft.   B.R. 14355

"WEST-END FROLICS"
4,335 ft.   B.R. 14475

"UP-TOWN REVUE"
4,076 ft.   B.R. 14606

Revudeville Films are now playing successfully everywhere

24 Mrs. Henderson and Vivian Van Damm, late 1930s. Mrs. Laura Henderson and Vivian Van Damm were an odd couple who helped to create a market niche for English middlebrow erotic entertainments.

of women and children with pro-German appeasement politics; such a mixture characterized the position of Nancy Astor, the first Conservative woman MP.[17]

By the 1930s, Mrs. Henderson extended her patronage to the theater. In 1931, she purchased the Great Windmill property, originally constructed as a cinema in 1910. She had it gutted and refitted it as a full-scale theater house in miniature, complete with proscenium stage, lounge, auditorium seating for 320, and dressing rooms in the basement.[18] Initially, she tried to operate the space as a venue for legitimate theater and then as a revival cinema for foreign films. In both instances, the theater failed to attract West End patrons in sufficient numbers. Mrs. Henderson continued to support high cultural performances such as the Independent Theatre and the "All-British" Markova-Dolin Ballet. But her next West End scheme was to turn the Windmill into a variety theater.[19]

When Mrs. Henderson leant her support to non-stop variety, she clearly deviated from the traditional terrain of high-minded female cultural philanthropy.[20] But times had changed, and variety was undergoing a shift in its reputation and cultural value. In 1931, in the depths of the slump, variety appeared to be an endangered British art form threatened by the American talkies. American cinema corporations had already bought up many famous Victorian music halls and variety theaters of central London and transformed them into super cinemas. Variety artistes joined the ranks of the unemployed in droves, leaving only top stars like George Robey and Gracie Fields unscathed. Legitimate theater also suffered from competition with radio and cinema, but the scale and degree of variety's distress were substantially greater. These new threats to the popular arts allowed Mrs. Henderson to embrace variety's homely pleasures as a national, cultural treasure.[21]

To transform her theater into a variety space, Mrs. Henderson turned to Vivian Van Damm, who had established a dazzling reputation in the 1920s as one of "the liveliest go-getters" of Wardour Street, Soho, the business center of the British film industry.[22] Van Damm (or VD as he was known) was the son of a Whitechapel solicitor of Jewish Dutch descent, married to the niece of Joe Lyons of the Lyons catering empire. In his 1952 memoirs, he described himself as a "practical man, with vision, yet something of a gambler."[23] He took pride in being an amateur, not "bound by set conventions and archaic ideals." Compared to the Shim Sham's Jack Isow, VD represented a more upscale and Anglicized version of the Anglo-Jewish entertainment impresario. He was consummately adept at negotiating the genteel protocols of official London. As the former manager of major West End cinemas, many of them converted from music halls, he was already experienced at staging risqué attractions that sailed close to the wind of the censor's code of public decency.[24] His entrepreneurial style attracted the attention of Sidney Bernstein, who offered him a management position in his Granada cinema circuit. VD declined Bernstein's offer in favor of Mrs. Henderson's Windmill, where he was promised a free hand in its creative development. He warned Mrs. Henderson that she might lose as much as ten thousand pounds in the Windmill's early years (this turned out to be a conservative estimate). He was appointed general manager, hiring others to produce individual editions; in 1936, he took over as producer and inherited the theater from Mrs. Henderson on her death in 1944.[25] Over the years, Henderson and Van Damm continually sparred over her attempt to interfere with the shows, but they remained a loyal "odd couple."[26]

As a successful showman, VD knew how to appeal to middlebrow British national taste. Frank Mort argues insightfully that, like other Jewish entrepreneurs of the twentieth century, VD's outsider status enabled him to manipulate the "invented traditions" of Englishness. He was a British variant of the Jewish film moguls who "captured Hollywood," skillful at consolidating the association of certain forms of theatrical female glamour with a national type, in this case with modern, healthy English femininity.[27] Although declining to psychoanalyze himself, Van Damm frequently paraded his command of the new psychology of salesmanship to sell the Windmill's product. Both his later memoir and his writings in the thirties are peppered with Freudian buzzwords like instinct, repression, and the unconscious to assess his own motivations and the "extraordinary psychological" tendencies of the Windmill patrons.[28]

Like many other Anglo-Jews, VD was publicly reticent about his Jewish identity, although he maintained strong Jewish connections. But his 1953 memoirs discuss at length an incident that probably made him vulnerable to anti-Semitic slurs. Rejected for active duty during the Great War on account of his asthma, he was mistakenly arrested for avoiding conscription, and only released from jail when he could document his medical exemption.[29] At a time when the jingoist press fixed on Jewish men as notorious shirkers, Van Damm may well have found himself stigmatized as Jewish and un-English. His daughter Sheila implied this much in her assessment of his heroism during the Blitz. She believed that VD's bitter wartime experience in the Great War bolstered his resolve to keep the theater open to entertain the troops during the Blitz.[30]

Windmill's Early Days

Before the Windmill could redeem VD's honor and emerge as a world-famous London institution, it had to survive the early years of the slump. To promote the Windmill, VD publicized it as philanthropic and "all-British," but also speedy and up-to-date. Stories of Mrs. Henderson's good turn for variety circulated widely in the press. "I only employ British artists," Mrs. Henderson wrote to the *Daily Herald*, "but they are not easy to find, do send me along any you know of."[31] VD assured reporters that the Windmill would be modern and democratic: there would be no star names in the program, and open auditions on Wednesdays would make it a Mecca for new talent. He pledged to "ditch" the "old style variety act" that had declined in popularity and to replace it with intimate revue, calling the show *Revudeville* after a winning contestant coined the name in a competition in the *Star*.[32] An additional sign of modernity was the management's concern for the bodily health and hygiene of its employees: the *Gloucester Echo* reported that a "special medical adviser and physical culture consultant had been retained" at the theater. This was in tune with the interwar national fitness movement to protect and improve the health of citizens; it also replicated the welfare capitalism of West End establishments like Selfridges and J. Lyons that combined steady employment, social and medical benefits, and low wages.[33] Meanwhile Mrs. Henderson mobilized her elite society connections to support her philanthropic venture.[34]

As the Windmill began to catch on, its market niche was threatened by the proliferation of non-stop revues in other West End theaters. Another "trick of showmanship" was necessary to raise the Windmill above the status of "almost-ran."[35] To edge out the competition, VD introduced nude tableaux, or the "bare idea," described by him as a "revolutionary idea in British show-business." Although female nudity was not new to the New York or Parisian stage, it represented a daring departure for London theaters open to the public. It built on a longstanding tradition of apparent or semi-nudity on the British stage that dated back to the static tableaux vivants of Regency London and their revivals as Living Pictures in late Victorian variety theaters. "Charmingly absent-minded about their costumes," the Windmill's showgirls dispensed with the flesh-colored mesh tights previously worn by their theatrical predecessors of the "Naughty Nineties." Their artistic renditions consisted of impersonations of classical art and painting, valorized as dead white art and supplemented by the Windmill's own inventions, such as ship's figureheads, "muses," and Hiawatha.[36] Posers stopped short of the more kinetic exhibition of classical art earlier embodied in Maud Allan's expressive dancing at the Palace Theatre in 1908. Compared to the striptease acts performed in American burlesque they seemed to worldly observers to be passé and sedate.[37]

To realize this "revolutionary idea in British show-business," ·VD had to persuade Lord Cromer, the Lord Chamberlain, to license artistic nude tableaux. A member of the Royal Household and appointed by the king, the Lord

Chamberlain was located at St. James's Palace, in an atmosphere of leather armchairs and impervious calm.[38] Because the Windmill operated as a theatrical revue (with dialogue) rather than as variety, it came under the Lord Chamberlain's jurisdiction and not under the surveillance of municipal authorities.[39] To win Lord Cromer over to the bare idea, Mrs. Henderson cultivated her personal relations with him: ex-Windmill Girls remembered her rushing into dressing rooms unannounced (to the amused embarrassment of undressed chorus girls), occasionally with the Lord Chamberlain in tow.[40]

Both VD and the Lord Chamberlain rationalized the staging of nude displays on two grounds: it was a safety valve to contain disorderly male sexuality, and it offered a tasteful (if slightly dated) British alternative to the foreign license of Paris and New York that would enhance London's reputation as an international tourist attraction. Immediately popular with Windmill theatergoers, the bare idea engendered some controversy in the national and trade press, as well as protests from the Public Morality Council (PMC).[41] But the Windmill managed to weather these complaints and to prevail over its commercial competitors, thanks to its special relationship with St. James's Palace and Mrs. Henderson's generous subsidy.[42] Intended as only a temporary experiment, the Windmill's tableaux were retained as a permanent feature.[43]

By the end of 1932, the essential components of the Windmill's theatrical production were in place. Its intimate revue format was shaped and constrained by state censorship and dynamic marketing techniques; it featured "naughty specialities, gorgeous girls, and comics who are destined to go places."[44] Building on the theatrical strategies developed by theater impresario André Charlot during the Great War, VD centered his intimate revue on a troupe of chorus girls, chosen for their ability to sing and act as well as dance. In the case of *Revudeville*, they were augmented by a handful of skilled ballet dancers and male singers, dancers, and comedians. Careful attention was paid to strict running order and to the use of imaginative, simple, and bold lighting to dress the stage. Non-stop revue meant fast changes, no breaks between turns, and the grouping of artists in half-dozen or so scenes or sketches.[45] The Windmill's "simple recipe" of fourteen turns extending over two hours would be repeated in 340 successive editions of *Revudeville* until its closure in 1964. The theater charged West End theater prices for its tickets: 1s 6d to 6s 6d, roughly the equivalent of first-run West End cinema but cheaper to middle-range tickets in legitimate theater. Throughout the thirties the theater remained in the red and dependent on Mrs. Henderson's financial support.

To facilitate the smooth production of new editions, Van Damm fitted up the Windmill as a self-contained unit that fabricated dresses, lighting technology, and scenery, as well as English dancing girls with self-confident and magnetic "personality."[46] "My aim," declared VD, "has been to show English womanhood under the best possible conditions."[47] Noted for her "freshness and beauty" and her youth, the Windmill Girl tended to be eighteen or nineteen years old and to remain in the Windmill's employment for only a few years. As a "girl," the Windmill's theater worker offered a pliant, unthreatening form of passive, to-be-looked-at femininity, free from any troubling association with reproductive sexuality or cynical sexual knowledge. While modern, she provided a liberal counterpoint to the futuristic, androgynous body machine associated with avant-garde art. The Windmill showgirl displayed the same curvaceous figure—medium breasts, small waists, and long legs—that characterized the idealized chorus girl body of the period, a "specifically Caucasian archetype of erotic appeal."[48] The body type of female performers had to conform to the Lord Chamberlain's specifications that they had a "normal figure," and that women with big breasts would be dismissed.[49]

Recruited for their personality, youth, beauty, and talent—and "normal figure"—Windmill Girls were transformed from "Plain Janes into Personality Girls" who learned to "please and stand out in the crowd."[50] They were rapidly put through the "Mill" of grooming, cosmetics, clothes, plus fitness training and standardized dance instruction. The final product closely resembled Mrs. Meyrick's "Merry Maids."[51] The makeover of Windmill dancers emphasized the precise codes of femininity—of smartness, health, and cleanliness—that were endlessly relayed throughout the thirties to women via advertisements, women's magazines, and Hollywood icons. Such bodily refinements were part of the intricate, extended process of improvement of working-class appearance that visually integrated working women, such as Lyons' Nippies, into a broad-based consumer society.[52] From this makeover, Windmill Girls would emerge as paragons of the theatrical look of the day: in the thirties, smiling faces with plucked, arched eyebrows, permanent wavy hair (or platinum blond wigs), healthy teeth, and red lips; later in the decade and into the forties, a more military glamour, with long hair, swept up or in a page boy bounce, eyes made up with heavy mascara and eye shadow, and deep red lips.

After a short training, Windmill Girls would be sent directly into the productions. With the exception of professionally trained ballet dancers, most members of the chorus demonstrated rudimentary performance skills. They were expected to participate in miniature versions of C. B. Cochran's West End productions, themselves adaptations of Hollywood and Broadway musical spectacles. During the show, they sang and performed jazz, tap, high kicks, and skirt dancing.[53] Their youth and limited skills made them a cheap labor force willing to participate in teamwork and to endure long hours for low pay, roughly the equivalent of a shopgirl's salary. Initially, this grueling work regime provoked journalistic complaints of "sweated labour."[54] In defense, Mrs. Henderson and Van Damm insisted that their chorines only performed a few minutes at a time and benefited from secure and stable employment.[55] Instead of assembling the chorus and other acts for the duration of a show's run, its two permanent companies worked on alternative days for the entire duration of a *Revudeville* show.[56]

Long hours and steady employment fostered a cohesive and insular theatrical culture known for its friendly atmosphere, discipline, and obedience to rules. According to comedian Eric Barker, the workday at the "Treadmill" was "so long and arduous that it [became] a sealed off world like a boarding school, though less colourful in many ways."[57] Yet when interviewed many decades later, ex-Windmill Girls registered fond memories of their days at the theater, especially of the female camaraderie backstage. "The girls I worked with were wonderful," declared Linda Carroll. After sixty years she could still "remember all their names. . . . The place was like a family, it was so friendly."[58] They also recalled a highly paternalist structure, where they were fined for swearing and prohibited from drinking or fraternizing with the audience or stagehands.[59]

Girls and Gags and Windmill Commandos

In performance, Windmill Girls were expected to project an air of youthful inno-cence and health, to be at once glamorous and ordinary. Windmill dance routines reproduced this dichotomy by featuring naughty costumes and restrained erotic movement (Figure 25). Windmill Girls "pranced" around the stage as harem maidens, garage mechanics, or Foreign Legionnaires, attired in shorts, with an open midriff and a diaphanous, net top that left "little to the imagination."[60] Despite exotic costumes, the dance movements were reassur-ingly wholesome and domesticated, not too "French" or "oriental" or "primitive." Jazz productions rarely reproduced the jerky hip movement and shimmy shakes that made contemporary syncopation expressive of both rhythmic and erotic insistence.[61] The cancan, a reminder of the naughty Victorian past, remained a perennial favorite with Windmill patrons. But it was considerably toned down from the frenzied abandon associated with Parisian versions. The Windmill production of the "The Very Naughty Nineties" led one critic to imagine he was at the Folies Bergère. "But it was only a very brief moment, because it seemed to be tinged with an air of Tooting respectability." For all their assumed naughtiness, Windmill Girls "remained quite nice, respectable suburban young ladies."[62]

25 Windmill costumes. From Derek Parker and Julia Parker, *Natural History of the Chorus Girl* (Newton Abbot: David and Charles, 1975). The Windmill Girls tended to be unskilled theater workers whose dance numbers combined risqué costumes and restrained erotic movements.

Theater observers also remarked on the sanitized nature of the nude tableaux. When Barker had his first view of the "phenomenon" in 1932, he saw a goddess of fire standing in an alcove, where the "lights were rather dim," with one arm "gawkishly held above her head as though she were about to shave."[63] To Barker, the "phenomenon" was neither decadent Victorian pornography nor timeless art, but commonplace modern cheesecake: posing this way the goddess was a variant of the highly sanitized, commodified bodily displays already in wide circulation.[64]

The "phenomenon" witnessed by Barker embodied the compromise that had been worked out between the management and the censor. According to their agreement, by remaining motionless under subdued lighting, the poser was art, but if she moved, she was indecent, a distinction recalling the Victorian controversies over tableaux vivants and based on the presumption that the artistic nude transported its beholder into a realm of disinterested contemplation where more mundane feelings and passions would be suspended. Posing showgirls did not possess the dancing skills required of the chorus, but they were better paid, receiving an extra pound a week for each pose performed. Some of them regarded posing as a way to observe stagecraft and break into show business. Posers could not smile, they tended to look off into the distance, "and they had to have their front foot forward so you could not see anything in what they called 'the fork.' "[65] Some looked bored (when one practical "muse" was asked what she thought about when she stood immobile on the stage, she replied that "I always figure my weekly accounts").[66] Posing was a test of endurance and balance, requiring the "muse" to last twelve minutes or longer in an awkward position. Margaret Law remembered that she "wobbled too much to be a muse" and instead developed a specialty as a "can-can dancer."[67]

Not all Windmill employees shared VD's enthusiasm for nude displays. In 1932, VD encountered some resistance when he consulted Windmill dancers about introducing nudes. Doris Barry, one of the first soubrettes, remembered these early discussions:

> When Van Damm first told us he was introducing nudes, we were all going to leave. Nobody wanted to be associated. But he was a persuasive man, a marvellous character. He argued: what was the difference between people coming into the theatre and looking at a naked woman and people going into a picture gallery? The human body was beautiful.[68]

Barry came around to his view, but she was less persuaded by a second argument: "He had also said, it's much better that these men come here than go into brothels and places. We were not at all sure that we agreed."[69] Throughout the thirties, theater workers remained divided on the question of nude posing. Some female performers worried that nude posing would impede their theatrical careers, while others got used to it and even took pleasure in showing off their bodies.[70]

Whatever their private views, showgirls were mobilized to defend nude posing in public. Some reiterated the line of argument advanced by VD and the Lord Chamberlain that they were engaged in artistic display. Others articulated a post-Victorian rejection of bodily shame, and delight in being looked at: "We are told that we are beautiful and we are young—why should we be prevented from displaying ourselves in such delightful surroundings?"[71] When asked about wearing flimsy attire on stage, the girls cited the footlights as an invisible barrier: "After all, we're up on the stage and there is a barrier of none too bright footlights between us and the audience"—a protective device that did not hide them from the audience but vice versa.[72] As a final defense, they detailed the ideal conditions backstage, where they were protected from intruders.[73]

Only one person was allowed to bend the rules prohibiting men from visiting the women's dressing rooms: VD, who "went through the girls a bit. It's common knowledge." Current favorites were always positioned in "dressing room no. 5," close to the "old boy's office." A former stagehand remembered opening a door and finding Van Damm "on top of [a chorus girl] on the dressing table." "It didn't disrupt the show," Peggy Martin insisted, but it is fair to assume that it buttressed VD's patriarchal reputation as a handsome, "sophisticated charming man whose word was law."[74]

In contrast to his own commanding view of female bodies, VD tried to restrict the audience's gaze through "medium lighting," involving the most sophisticated theater lighting technology available at the time. Lighting would be projected from the balconies and strategically beamed on the girls' faces, leaving most of their figure in shadows.[75] Under these conditions, only the outlines of the nude pose would be visible to patrons, who were also instructed that "artificial aids to vision" were prohibited in the auditorium.[76] However, the Windmill provided a less obstructed view of the "phenomenon" in flash photographs that were reproduced on posters outside the theater and in souvenir programs.

Windmill nudes were the chief attraction of souvenir programs printed and distributed to patrons all over the world, a striking affirmation of Britain's status in a world empire.[77] Often encased in art deco structures, the tableaux appeared as smooth, impenetrable, white bodies, reinforced by airbrushing and pink body paint (Plate 8). Souvenir programs expanded the boundaries of "publicly acceptable, mass produced images of semi-nude women" to include sleek "borderline material."[78] They coincided with the pioneering efforts of *Esquire* to stake out this niche for middle-class male consumers in the United States, but in 1934 they were the only publication of their kind in the UK.[79]

The Public Morality Council, already engaged in a campaign against stage nudity, targeted the souvenir programs and their graphic nudes as a clear violation of the Lord Chamberlain's rules. In 1935 the PMC lodged a complaint with the Lord Chamberlain's Office (LCO) against a photograph of the "Hourglass," a nude tableau featured in *Revudeville* 60 that showed two "apparently nude" women facing the audience in two-thirds pose (Plate 8).[80] Characteristically, the theater censor stepped forward to mediate between the Windmill and its purity critics. The Lord Chamberlain's staff publicly defended the Windmill's erotic display as "suitable" and "artistic," but also reminded Mrs. Henderson of her personal assurance that the souvenir photographs and their representations on the walls of the theater would be discontinued. However artistic and inoffensive a tableau might appear in performance, "the draping and lighting was invisible in the photograph" and "gave an entirely false impression of the living representation on the stage."[81]

The Lord Chamberlain's staff suspected that VD used these reproductions to attract theater patrons with very little interest in artistic display, who labored under the false notion that stage nudes would materialize as graphically as they appeared in the photos. The Windmill patrons were impressionistically described by the press as overwhelmingly male, middle-class (an observation supported by the ticket prices), and middle-aged. With the exception of wartime audiences, Windmill patrons remained a public embarrassment to the management, a challenge to its much vaunted patriotic and cultural mission. The Windmill never included the audience in Windmill publicity shots in the thirties, and only rarely in the forties, where they were always represented from the back, an anonymous mass of interchangeable, disconnected bodies.[82]

The vast majority of stall patrons were anxious to gain a seat in the favored front rows, known as the "full sight seats," just under the footlights, where they could ogle and almost touch the girls.[83] "When those in the front two rows leave, the places are eagerly filled by spectators who have been sitting farther back."[84] This was the famous Windmill "steeplechase," a practice that was first observed in American burlesque theaters and eventually migrated to London.[85] Windmill "commandos" were known to queue for hours in the rain for the highest priced seats. Graham Greene described the rites of the Windmill "commandos" as "rather sombre": "It isn't like one of the old-fashioned music-halls with a boisterous bar at the back: there is almost a religious air, of muffled footsteps and private prayers."[86] Each morning, a mechanic had to tighten the bolts on the seats because they had received such a "pounding."[87] When asked about the rush to the front rows in 1940, VD answered censoriously, "they are always dirty old men."[88]

Included in their ranks were the surreptitious masturbators, the "dirty mackintosh" brigade, who disgusted and unnerved many female performers.[89] "The only disagreeable aspect of our work," Pat Ingram told the *Daily Mirror* in 1937, was the presence of "men with base ends in view, sitting in the front rows and the stalls, just watching. To them, it matters not whether you dance or how you dance."[90] Interviewed in the 1990s, sixty years later, Doris Barry could be more explicit:

> For young girls . . . it was not very good to be up there on the stage with an audience full of men with raincoats across their knees, half of them playing with themselves. This is what was going on while you had to sing and dance. You couldn't help but be aware of it. And this opened my eyes certainly, and gave me a rather bad opinion of males in general.[91]

Apart from the exertions of the "dirty mac" brigade, audiences were notoriously unresponsive to the performances. Their reticence was in direct contrast to the traditions of the music hall, where artists cultivated a close rapport and interaction with the audience. It was also a deviation from new forms of British stage comedy cultivated by the Palladium's wildly popular "Crazy Gang," a comic team who would interrupt other acts and descend into the auditorium and dance "Boomps-a-Daisy" with the audience.[92] Some reviewers attributed the studied indifference of Windmill patrons to the fact that the daytime audience was mainly visitors to London sampling the shows or killing time before their train.[93]

VD detected a deeper "psychological" meaning for this unresponsiveness, ascribing it to a culture of restraint and bodily embarrassment that critics have tended to associate with middlebrow. In his program notes, he deplored the fact that the audience failed to show their healthy enjoyment of good "fun."[94] He admonished patrons to clap and laugh "without being afraid of the man sitting next to you, who may think it is 'bad form' or something." He reported that even Windmill Girls complained of "the hardness they met with over the footlights."[95] The atmosphere improved when there were periodic spikes in female attendance, such as during the holiday season. When present, female patrons "seem to really want to enjoy the comedy, whereas the men, especially during the afternoons, seem to take it for granted."[96]

Comedians bore the brunt of audience indifference and hostility. They provided the front-cloth act that occupied the audience during set and costume changes. Windmill comedy appeared in two forms, low and middlebrow. In the first category were "red-nosed comedians" like Gus Chevalier, a robust, bawdy Glaswegian of the old school of music hall comedy. Gus leered at the girls and sported a red facial appendage that signified unruly appetite and broad phallic humor. Sheila Van Damm remembered Chevalier as an "absolute master at hotel bedroom scenes. His timing, with doors opening and slammed and squealing girls running in and out, was perfection."[97] Hotel bedroom and hospital scenes, with "comic songs and the usual business," provided similar opportunities for suggestive meanings and the voyeuristic inspection of body parts and processes that elicited a dual reaction of "desire and disgust."[98] Dirty jokes and verbal innuendoes referenced low body parts and processes. They were peppered with references to "knickers" and "joy stick," and included many "plumbing" and "lavatory jokes."[99] Transgressive street characters also made an appearance, notably the West End streetwalkers whose pitches abutted the Windmill, and effeminate "pansies" who appeared in jokes about men in groups.[100] Like American burlesque, these rude jokes—both heterosexual and perverse—were intended to heat up the atmosphere of sexual suggestiveness to provide more kick.[101] Yet pansy jokes were subject to diverse interpretation by different constituencies in the audience: one ex-Windmill dancer remembered a sizable number of "cranks" and "kinky boys" in the audience who periodically penned marriage proposals to the female impersonator.[102]

The Lord Chamberlain's staff were particularly concerned to smoke out indecent jokes and physical humor that exceeded heterosexual norms and encouraged perversion.[103] They also scrutinized comedy sketches involving comedians in close proximity to girls in skimpy costumes. To their mind, these routines were not only indecent but also a "low-class type of humour." By weeding out salaciousness, the script readers believed they could improve the class tone of the Windmill. However, since the Lord Chamberlain's staff only examined the script dialogues in advance, they could not fully anticipate the visual and kinetic components of the Windmill performances—including the staging of nude poses, the skimpy dancing costumes, the action or "business" of physical comedy, the indecent "raspberries," not to speak of the ad lib propensities of comedians or the effeminate manners on display in female impersonations and comic satires of men in groups.[104]

The LCO not only restricted the sexual content of Windmill productions; it declared God, clergy, royalty, and living persons to be out of bounds for stage representations.[105] Comedians who were subject to this regime would have to exercise considerable ingenuity to produce a skit that would pass the censor's blue pencil, yet have some point. As a result of this censorship regime, the Windmill became an experimental space of middlebrow comedy of everyday life.[106] Two factors facilitated this development: Van Damm's own contempt for the Windmill audience, and the productive consequences of censorship that forced comedians to innovate their comic routines through verbal dexterity.[107] With a "monopoly on stage nudity," Van Damm didn't "give two-pence" what the audience thought.[108] In the 1930s, Windmill comedians John Tilley and Eric Barker pioneered comedy that showed the impertinent side of lower middle-class culture. Their skits built on some of the features of snappy radio comedy developed in the United States. They were full of literary and cultural allusions, demonstrating a knowingness and command of cultural capital beyond the reach of the less educated. At the same time, their acts tended to debunk high culture and intellectual ideals, "as of marginal value in the workaday world in which sensible people lived."[109] They regularly parodied pompous professionals and experts, shady businessmen, traffic controllers, and, most of all, superior BBC presenters.

Affairs of State

Two affairs of state—the coronation of 1937 and diplomatic relations with Mussolini and Hitler—brought the Windmill's formula of "girls and gags" into conflict with the censor. During Coronation Year, the Lord Chamberlain found himself in the awkward position of staging the royal ceremony at the same time as having to defend the Windmill's stage nudity to other government officials, press commentators, and indignant citizens. In the spring of 1937, to cash in on the thousands of international tourists arriving for the royal event, impresarios of London's nightlife introduced American striptease and what they described as continental stage shows. This provoked a "Stop-the-Striptease" scandal, which in turn exposed the conflicting systems of state surveillance operating in relation to erotic entertainments. The advent of striptease threatened the Windmill's stable market niche, while media scandal over stage nudity strained the Windmill's modus vivendi with the LCO.[110]

The first sign of disturbance occurred in early January 1937, when the *Star* carried a front-page advertisement for Dean Street's London Casino, featuring an "almost nude" showgirl. The Casino put on spectacular cabaret shows that were "a London version of the Folies Bergère."[111] *Star* readers were apparently "shocked" at the "almost nude girl staring out" at them on the tabloid's front page. "To many it was news that the night life of the metropolis exhibited anything resembling what many Englishmen regard as continental degeneracy," explained the *News Review*, which then proceeded to clarify some features of this news. First, "having no actual plot," the London Casino's cabaret did not come under the Lord Chamberlain's jurisdiction, but instead received its license from the London County Council. Second, the Casino's showgirl "was actually wearing flesh coloured tights." Although there was counterfeit at the Casino, there was no "welshing" at the Windmill, where the program *was* under the control of the theater censor. Years ago, the *News Review* explained, Lord Cromer had decided to permit tasteful nude statues at Mrs. Henderson's theater, on condition that they didn't "move."[112]

An upmarket venue appealing to "Mayfair" and the "transatlantic crowd," the London Casino on Dean Street was hardly a rival for the Windmill patrons. However, the Windmill soon faced more direct competitors who threatened to entice away its patrons with a more kinetic form of erotic display emanating out of America. In March 1937, impresario George Black announced his plan to feature "American" striptease in *Swing is in the Air* at the Palladium.[113] Van Damm was even more concerned with competition from André Charlot, the inventor of intimate revue, who had rented the Vaudeville on the Strand to stage his own version of non-stop revue, *Strips and Stripes*, and promised "lots of Pretty Girls with very few Clothes." "Swiftly is the atmosphere of New York's 42nd Street invading London," declared the *Illustrated Sporting and Dramatic News*. "It has now reached the Strand. This is almost entirely on the lines of such New York delights as Minsky's 'follies' and of our own Windmill Theatre."[114]

Faced with this competition, VD swung into action. On March 28, 1937, he gave an interview to the *Sunday Dispatch*, where he defended Windmill tableaux as artistic and inoffensive, if not "too original." But tomorrow, he explained, "we are trying out a new idea in fan dancing." "I will admit that such a spectacle could not have been produced in London six years ago. The public is now willing to accept it." VD stressed that whenever the dancer was nude, "she is completely still."[115]

By introducing a fan dance, the Windmill tried to stay within the licit boundaries of nude display, yet compete with the suggestive appeal of striptease. Like striptease, the fan dance's main attraction was its tease factor: it was not so much how much a woman actually exposed but how much she seemed to reveal and how much she provoked the desire to reveal more.[116] By the standards of Chicago and New York, Eileen Cruikshank's fan dance in *Revudeville*'s "Sheik of Araby" represented a restrained homegrown "tease."[117] Wielding a "high, heavy ostrich feather fan," she tried to move with such sleight of hand that the audience could only imagine what the dancer was actually wearing under it. Instead of moving her own body, she manipulated the fans in a manner faintly reminiscent of the light shows innovated by Loie Fuller. Her dance also involved coordination with other more mobile and fully attired dancers, who often manipulated the fans to keep her covered. She wore nothing, apart from "peach-coloured" body make-up, while the rotating spotlights restricted visibility to a "momentary glimpse" of any particular part of her body.[118] *What's On* reported that her fan dance "has to be seen to be believed," although the *Era* was less enthusiastic, deeming her a "very attractive lady" but not a "brilliant dancer."[119] "The fans were heavy," Eileen recalled in 2005, and "some of the girls let them drop by accident—though I never did. I was too professional." This did not imply any qualms about exhibiting her body: "I knew I had a good body . . . and I couldn't wait to show it off."[120]

By April, the Windmill was advertising a second innovation: a "dance of the seven veils," cashing in on the continuing allure of the orientalist body as a site of sensual excess. Once more, the management assured the public it was not "strip-tease." "When she removes the seventh veil, she will be quite immobile." Marie of the Seven Veils is "evidently box office," declared the *Tatler*. "And Marie has the right figure for it, although as dancer she would win no . . . prize." Talented dancer or not, Marie pulled in "packed houses," with the press reporting "middle" applause from the audience "and no one appeared to take any exception to the performance."[121]

The Windmill's new turns fueled public debate over "undress on the stage" that peaked during Coronation Week.[122] On May 7, the *Daily Mirror* published a photograph of the Windmill's "Enchanted Fountain" scene and a caption that read: "Calling in at the Windmill Theatre, Lensman thought he must be in Paris instead of London when he saw this Fountain tableau."[123] Featuring three "apparently" nude women draped around a fountain, with a fully dressed man seated on the side, this image was evidently taken from one of the Windmill souvenir magazines without the permission of the management (Figure 26).[124] While provoking a storm of protest, the "Enchanted Fountain" also represented a milestone in the mass media circulation of female nudes. After its publication, airbrushed female nudes began to appear in mainstream British magazines appealing to middle-class male consumers, as well as on "page three" of the *Daily Mirror*.[125]

The "Stop-the-Strip-tease" scandal provoked tension between the LCO and other regulatory agencies over the migration of Windmill practices and personnel to less salubrious performance sites.[126] Police Commissioner Philip Game (brother of H. C. Game, on the LCO staff) notified the Lord Chamberlain that

Friday, May 7, 1937   THE DAILY MIRROR

★
NYMPHS OF
THE FOUNTAIN

Calling in at the Windmill Theatre, *Lensman* thought he must be in Paris instead of London when he saw this Fountain tableau.

✦ ✦ ✦

The singer is John Stevens, and the statues are posed by some of the lovely Revudebelles who have made the Windmill's artistic tableaux famous.

★

26 "Nymphs of the Fountain," *Daily Mirror*, May 7, 1937, p. 9. The appearance of this *Souvenir* photograph in a daily newspaper provoked a storm of protest. After its publication, air-brushed female nudes began to appear in mainstream British media.

he had received numerous complaints "in regard to the present production at the Windmill Theatre." He especially drew attention to protests over "a photograph of one scene in the *Daily Mirror* of the 7th May." Game was also indignant that "disreputable bottle parties are sheltering behind the Windmill performance."[127] In response, a staff member of the LCO defended the theater censor's policy towards the Windmill, drawing a distinction between a stage performance and an act performed in the boozy intimacy of a nightclub.[128] Scotland Yard countered by documenting the Windmill's influence on more raffish spaces: it cited a recent incident at the Paradise Club, a bottle party on Regent Street, where a fan dance and a striptease were performed by two ex-Windmill dancers, Eileen (most likely the Windmill's featured fan dancer) and Iris Young, who appeared to be quite bare but wore "adhesive tape" to cover their private parts. It further noted that bottle parties defended the introduction of "objectionable shows of this nature" on the grounds that they were openly permitted at the Windmill Theatre.[129] Both the police and the LCO agreed to thrash out their differences once the "Coronation troubles are over."[130]

At the end of May, H. C. Game reviewed the Lord Chamberlain's rationale for nude tableaux in two internal memoranda. These documents exuded a worldly clubman's view of the need to regulate vulgar forces in civil society, including the busybodies of the PMC. Starting with the premise that "commercialization of sex in some form or another on the stage" was a given, Game asserted it was reasonable to "canalize it" through "artistic sex such as tableaux."[131] Static tableaux were acceptable to the censor and the British public, Game insisted, but he proposed to rule out cancan and striptease as disruptive, kinetic performances emanating out of France and America whose aim was "eroticism impure and simple." To distinguish the English traditions of nude tableaux from these foreign practices, Game invoked the old distinction of the nude versus the naked, or the classical as against the grotesque female body, a debate circulating around Living Pictures since they had become a music hall turn in the 1890s. In defending tableaux, the LCO endeavored to contain disorderly female bodies within the bounds of the domesticated, classical form, with its sleek, symmetrical, and closed structure.[132]

To resolve the controversy, the Lord Chamberlain tried to broker a compromise among theater managers, licensing authorities, and purity reformers. First, he called a private meeting with Van Damm and Charlot. To prepare for this meeting, his office prepared an ultimatum threatening to ban nude displays completely if they did not comply with the desired modifications that hewed to Game's specifications. Both men were upset, but the tactful Van Damm followed up his meeting with Cromer in characteristic fashion. He thanked Lord Cromer for "his extreme courtesy at the interview", and apologized for the "extremely difficult position in which I had inadvertently placed you by that picture in the *Daily Mirror.*" He reminded him how much Mrs. Henderson had lost "in running this Theatre and keeping 130 people employed." Once again, he invited him to visit the Windmill to see for himself "if this entertainment offends public decency in any way."[133]

Charlot, by contrast, bitterly reported that he had had to close his show at the Vaudeville Theatre in the first week of June because of a "drop in our taking," owing to the fact that press notices "stated that the show was perfectly respectable and devoid of nudity."[134] He also sent a "long report," dubbed his "Apologia pro vita sua" by the Lord Chamberlain's staff, defending his theatrical practice. The report surveyed post-Victorian displays of the female form and challenged the distinctions of art and impure eroticism marked out by Game. It traced instead the historically shifting boundaries of licit erotic female display on the British stage and elsewhere, from bath scenes in music halls, to turn-of-the-century tableaux vivants, to Maud Allan and beyond. Charlot defended his practice of giving the public what it wants, "providing entertainment for men with tired feet, who did not wish to use their brains." And he raised the problem of the "growing loss" of the public for musical theater.[135]

After that, Charlot moved to Hollywood, never to return to the London stage. One month later, as a "sop" to the purity lobby, Lord Cromer organized a conference in July with theater representatives, which concluded that there was no need for drastic change. Charlot's departure in 1938 left the Windmill in virtual control of the market niche for stage nudes. Until the war, its only theatrical competitor remained the sleazy Prince of Wales Theatre, where, according to Graham Greene, "peroxided" showgirls, as "tall as grenadiers," their eyes "as empty as statues," walked "lazily with a sneer in at one wing and out at the other."[136]

The second affair of state involved political satire of fascist leaders. If the Windmill's new kinetic acts threatened to sully the national image during the coronation period, its comic turns periodically threatened to unsettle diplomatic relations with Europe's dictators. As early as 1935, the LCO's script readers judged Eric Barker's burlesque of the League of Nations ("Intrigue of Nations") during the Abyssinian conflict in 1935 as "needlessly barging in on a delicate situation." Lord Cromer worried that the character of "Signor Whale-Blubber," a clear reference to Mussolini, might offend "sensitive foreigners."[137] After 1937, political censorship of this sort only intensified: the LCO was especially anxious not to embarrass a government that was committed to détente with Germany. Whereas negative depictions of Hitler and Mussolini were routinely deleted, racist satires of non-Europeans easily passed inspection, because these sketches were not deemed to be politically offensive. Witness a scene featuring Gus as a "Chinaman" surrounded by a bevy of attractive Revudebelles that turned on presumed differences of male sexuality between West and East (Figure 27). The LCO's concern with the feelings of "sensitive foreigners" evidently did not extend to subalterns and racial others around the empire.

Political censorship went beyond prohibitions against rude impersonations of living persons: as late as 1939, the management was warned not to make up the soldier dolls as "Nazi" and to cut references to "Nordic" and "Concentration

27 "Gus Chevalier, Eileen, Maureen, and Marie," *Revudeville, Souvenir of Nos. 85–91*, 1937. In the middle picture, Gus impersonates a Chinaman surrounded by a bevy of attractive Revudebelles. The humor of the sketch depends on the presumed distinction between male sexuality in the West and the East. It illustrates the commonplace racial stereotyping of Windmill sketches that easily passed inspection by the Lord Chamberlain's Office. At the same time, LCO readers carefully monitored Windmill scripts for any possible affront to Mussolini and Hitler and their followers, deemed to be "sensitive foreigners."

Camp." While she energetically defended the artistry of the Windmill tableaux, Mrs. Henderson made no effort to protest the suppression of political satire. Nor did Van Damm openly resist political censorship, although the reappearance of offending material in later scripts does suggest some continued efforts on the part of scriptwriters, comedians, and the management to stage anti-Nazi sentiments.[138] Not surprisingly, this low-grade guerrilla warfare between Windmill comics and the censor over Hitler jokes would abate with the commencement of war in 1939. By then, other features of Windmill productions had catapulted it on to the national political stage of an embattled home front.

Windmill at War

In wartime, the Windmill built on its "carrying on" tradition to assume a different, and more iconic, role in national politics. 1939–45 would prove to be the Windmill's "vintage years" when it pulled itself out of the red.[139] Amidst a rising critique of prewar authorities as elitist appeasers, the Windmill became a national institution whose "non-star entertainment" exemplified the new democratic spirit of the Blitz. This populist reputation involved no small irony, since the theater was supported and underwritten by individuals—such as Mrs. Henderson and the Lord Chamberlain—who were deeply implicated in the much disparaged prewar appeasement culture. Publicly, however, the theater presented itself as the embodiment of the "little people" of London, a testimony to their determination and teamwork.

Not only was London the principal and most consistent target of air raids, it was the focus of wartime propaganda by writers, artists, and photographers living in central London for the war's duration. Most of them were working for the Ministry of Information (to the east of Soho) and the BBC (to the west). Under these circumstances, the Windmill was no longer operating in an urban space deemed to be "remote from the British body politic."[140] The Windmill's liminal space "off Piccadilly" had become the heart of the city under siege, damaged by some bombings, yet the nerve center of wartime communication and propaganda. It was a meeting ground for many people increasingly living their private lives in public who did not want to die alone.[141] In the same period, Soho became more foreign than it had been for decades: the rendezvous of the Free French and other foreign servicemen, including white and black GIs after 1942.

Along with the rest of the West End theaters and cinemas, the Windmill was closed by order of the government in the first week of the war in September

1939. This closure provoked a crisis in the West End entertainment industry, leading many actors and entertainers who were not conscripted to join the state-sponsored associations ENSA (Entertainments National Service Association) and CEMA (Council for the Encouragement of Music and the Arts) to perform for the troops and civilian populations around the country.[142] Van Damm kept his company together in Soho, practicing in the theater so that it would be ready to give public performances when the government allowed theaters to reopen shortly thereafter. After his male stagehands and performers were conscripted, Van Damm staffed the non-stop revue with middle-aged stage-hands and seventeen-year-old boys and girls, many of whom were also volunteers in the air raid and fire brigade, and were photographed in their uniforms.[143] *Revudeville* performances continued six days a week; on Sundays, the company frequently traveled to military bases to perform for the troops.[144]

While the Windmill stayed clear of any criticism of the conduct of the war, its own staple offerings of "girls and gags" became woven into public debates over home front discipline, civilian morale, and moral rearmament. During the "phony war" of 1939, the press found inspiration in the familiar traditions of the Windmill.[145] The *Jewish Chronicle*, always a loyal supporter of the Windmill, applauded "the courage, energy, inventiveness and determination of this little theatre."[146] It "needs something more than a war to knock them out of their established course," observed *The Times*, even though "gas-masks for a brief moment or two make their appearance on the stage."[147] Other reviewers also found its revues refreshingly free from allusions to the war: "Revudebelles" disported themselves "mostly on the beaches of islands in the pacific . . . which makes the war seem an h—l of a way off," observed the *Illustrated Sporting and Dramatic News*.[148]

At the same time, the Windmill's familiar routine was again threatened by commercial rivals seeking to heat up the atmosphere of wartime pleasures. The Windmill found its virtual monopoly on nude display challenged by striptease acts and topless continental cabaret routines that proliferated in entertainment venues outside the jurisdiction of the Lord Chamberlain. In cabarets and private bottle parties in Soho and the West End, patrons were treated to floor shows of showgirls dancing bare-breasted or with pasties, while road shows featuring American-style striptease regularly made the rounds of military garrisons in the provinces.[149] In October 1939, when *Picture Post* featured the Cabaret Club's floor show in a photo spread, Home Office authorities were decidedly nonplussed. As in 1937, they worried about the broad dissemination of these risqué images outside the precincts of Soho's raffish pleasure zone.[150] They judged the circulation to be a threat to wartime discipline and morale, citing the many anonymous complaints they had already received against the clubs as unpatriotic, wasteful hideouts for a "Fifth Column."[151]

The pressure on authorities intensified in February and March 1941, when the *Daily Telegraph* published an extensive correspondence on "undress on the stage." Letter writers calling themselves "Vigilante" and "Mother of Sons" denounced stage nudity and blue gags from America as leading to moral laxity and giving "Hitler justification for saying we are a decadent democracy."[152] A distinct minority of correspondents, just enough to keep the debate going, defended wartime hedonism and attacked "moral clean-up" as "one of the most familiar weapons of Totalitarian tyranny."[153] In April 1940, the "public outcry against stage vulgarity" forced Lord Clarendon, the new Lord Chamberlain, to call a "nudity" conference. Attended by licensing authorities, the police, and representatives from all branches of the entertainment industry, the conference resulted in a theatrical ban on "unauthorized" ad lib "gags," "strip-tease, suggestive nudity, and impropriety of gestures."[154]

"Untouched" was "one man at the Conference who had no criticism to meet, no speech to make." He was "Vivian Van Damm, manager and producer of the tiny Windmill Theatre, off Piccadilly Circus who has for eight years been running nonstop Revudevilles with nude 'artistic tableaux.'"[155] "This outcry against so-called strip-tease," VD explained to a reporter, "is the outcome of the fact that I have been copied and badly copied." "Arguments about stage nudity may come and go," observed *What's On*, "but the little Windmill goes on undisturbed forever—so it seems."[156]

Despite this good press, the Windmill's management had to contend with two inconvenient consequences of the conference. First, it was now required to present the Lord Chamberlain with photographs of its nude tableaux in advance of the show. Second, it could also expect regular visits from the LCO's aptly named "Mr. Titman," regarded as their expert on "brassieres and trunks," who tried to attend every new edition of the show.[157] This expanded surveillance heavily intensified the micro-inspections of costumes and the staging of nude poses. During the Blitz of autumn 1940, the correspondence between the censor (who had removed to a tower in Windsor Castle) and the theater manager (who was holding on in Soho) became comically surreal. Over the course of the war, the two parties quibbled over plumbing and pansy jokes, the multiplication and rationing of nudes, details of sightlines, "unpleasant bottoms," giant balloons that failed to cover the breasts of dancing girls, dropped fans, loose brassieres, the problem of working with "poor war materials" that sagged in the crotch, and the misleading nature of flash photographs in reproducing stage nudes.[158]

The LCO's surveillance of Windmill entertainments implicated it in the same voyeuristic scrutiny of female bodies as the dirty mackintosh brigade. In 1944, Mr. Titman visited the theater after receiving a complaint that the "sexual parts" of the girls' bodies were completely exposed during the cancan and another dancing scene. Instead of his usual box seat, he sat in the front stalls, next to the Windmill's "commandos," and discovered a different "line of vision." He ascertained that it was "during the vigorous action and turning that these things are seen," although he admitted that he had to strain "every optical nerve" to see "the things myself." VD promised to add "an extra covering of net" to the nude and put in new elastic to "hold the sides [of the dancers' costumes] down more securely," although he was "unable to trace the slight sign of the genital organs being displayed by any single girl."[159] Men were not the only ones to participate in this surveillance: Mrs. Henderson would pipe up periodically to declare that, seated in her box (and very myopic), she could see "*nothing* that you would object to."[160]

Memoirs of the war tend to confirm the Lord Chamberlain's suspicions that the Windmill's performers exposed more flesh than what was actually licensed. Flimsy costumes and teasing "glimpses of more than was intended" were crucial to the Windmill's success, but Sheila Van Damm believed that mishaps on the stage accelerated as a reckless wartime spirit took hold.[161] It became common for fan dancers to drop their fans deliberately; when the Lord Chamberlain's assistants complained, Van Damm would explain that the girl in question was in training. One male dancer recalled that when the girls cartwheeled in the "wild cancan numbers," "little breasts were popping all over the stage." He ascribed this outcome not so much to shoddy war materials as to the attitude that "it was war, what the hell, here today, gone tomorrow." When the Lord Chamberlain's representative paid a visit, the dancer went on to recount, "brassieres would be put on again, and instead of girls giving a provocative performance, they would become coy and demur."[162] But VD could do nothing to protect a performer named Clare, whose physique seems to have exceeded the requirements of a "normal figure": she ran into the dressing room crying, "I've just been fired . . . the Lord Chamberlain said my tits are too big for this little theatre."[163]

There were other ways in which female performers exceeded the licensed fare of the theater. Dela Lipinska did so by adopting an aggressive style of verbal performance. She was a "diseuse," one of a few foreign artistes on permit who appeared at the Windmill in 1940 and 1941. Script readers objected to her suggestive songs about amateur tarts, even if they were sung in Polish.[164] By contrast, Graham Greene was enthralled with her sultry performance. Young and mischievous, she "woos the man in the mackintosh in the front row, who stares vacantly back at her."[165] Greene's enthusiasm, however, was not shared by the regulars in the front rows. Like the LCO staff, the commandos clearly preferred the passive "naughtiness" of Margaret, the beautiful English blonde, attired in Russian boots, hat, scarlet cloak and nothing underneath, to the "calculated" ribaldry of the fully dressed "genuine Slav."[166]

In this game of censorship, the Windmill acquired an edge by fashioning itself as a powerful political resource during the Blitz. On September 7, 1940, there were forty-two theaters running in London's West End: then came the bombs and "only the little Windmill" was still "on its feet." British papers commended the "giant little Windmill Theatre" for "fearlessly braving the nightly hazards." To protect his theater, Van Damm, the Anglo-Jew and rejected military recruit from the Great War, assumed the role of military commander, turning his theater into a "fortress" and mobilizing his "magnetically attractive garrison" of gorgeous girls.[167] As Sheila Van Damm observed, "He had been rejected for military service in the First World War on medical grounds, and he was not going to be left out of this."[168] VD saw to it that the Windmill was strengthened by sandbags; he organized a fire-watching and bomb-watching brigade. When a bomb was found outside the theater, he was reputed to proclaim, "Hurry up. Get this bloody bomb off my doorstep. I've got a show to put on."[169] To keep the theater open, he arranged for the performers to sleep there. Backstage became a bunker, a dormitory, and a work space, accommodating the performers as well as mothers and other family members. "Naturally their hours have had to be altered and the first show begins at mid-day. The dressing-rooms have been fitted up as dormitories and most of the cast are at presently sleeping on the premises."[170]

As a result the Windmill's theatrical culture became even more regulated and closed than it had been during the thirties. At the same time, postwar memoirs recalled explosive, transgressive episodes. There were trysts between male and female performers in the men's showers. The girls snuck out for late-night suppers with admirers in defiance of VD's curfews. Discreet abortions were purportedly arranged by VD. Performers were not as stoic and determined as VD insisted: there were angry flare-ups over VD's insistence that the show would go on in the face of London's "intensive hell." One ballerina put it this way: "Why doesn't the old bastard close the bloody place? We'll all be killed."[171]

But these were all backstage scenes. For the public, VD went to great lengths to ensure that his glamorous regiment received full media attention as heroic members of London's civilian army. In a BBC broadcast interview, four Windmill Girls told "the pick of the Windmill bomb stories" that displayed their *nerve* and absence of "nerves." They recounted heroic tales of rescuing horses from a burning stable, assisting police when a bomb fell in nearby Berwick Street

Market, and, in one case, barely escaping a bomb that fell on the café across the road. At the end of the show, they sang "Babies of the Blitz."[172]

The press was quick to exploit the visual attractions of the Windmill at war, at once novel and resonant with the broader wartime conditions of the population. For the first time, photographers were allowed backstage at the Windmill, where they took carefully staged shots of the girls that amalgamated home and work, glamour and grit, in service to a "People's War." The Windmill Girls epitomized the home front fighters at the center of the urban war zone, putting aside their private lives and identities, and collectively demonstrating a public resilience.

These backstage scenes operated at different registers. The cover of the racy periodical *London Life* features Windmill Girls asleep in their civilian dugout (Plate 9). They are viewed close up and from above, almost as if the camera mimicked the German bombers descending on them (or the RAF fighters who practiced their new radar equipment by trying to spot the Windmill as they flew over London). Pressed together in bed, apparently undressed under the covers, hair in rollers and headbands, their faces are carefully made up. The nude "four-in-a-bed" photograph evokes the underground pornographic genre of the lesbian brothel scene. Bedtime pictures of Windmill Girls in the popular press are much cozier and more discreet (Figure 28). "Our Daily Life in Air-Raided London" presents three girls asleep on the floor, keeping up appearances, but their bodies are decorously separated and fully clothed. In addition, one Windmill Girl remains awake. When it was published in the *Glasgow Evening News*, under the caption, "The Show Goes On," the same photograph was cropped to highlight the single girl undressing for the night, while smiling invitingly to the reader.[173]

These bedtime scenes blend two genres of wartime photographs, the shelter scene and the pin-up. Although only 5 percent of Londoners sought refuge on the platforms of the London Underground, scenes of these Tube shelters "captured the nation's imagination."[174] Like the people of the shelters, Windmill Girls were supposed to embody ordinary qualities of "patience, cheerfulness, resignation, friendship, and even gaiety." Like the shelter scenes, the civilian dugout at the Windmill reproduced a common visual trope of Londoners surviving and resisting the bombing by sleeping (Figure 29).[175] Yet the representations of the two environments carried different political meanings. In contrast to Bill Brandt's depictions of the unglamorous Tube shelters, there are no details of squalor in the Windmill's dressing rooms. Nor is there any suggestion of the ethnic diversity recorded by Brandt, of the "cosmopolitan cities" of Sikhs, Orthodox Jews, and others who established their own "colonial districts" in "London's Underworld."[176] Brandt's shelter scenes, moreover, foreground an imagery of protective, defiant Cockney mums and their brood to exonerate poor

OUR DAILY LIVES IN AIR-RAIDED LONDON.

The WINDMILL *is the only theatre which remained carrying on in London last week, and at the time of writing, is still going strong. Here's an after-the-show snapshot showing three girls sound asleep on mattresses and one getting ready for bed, for the casts sleeps in the theatre.*

28 "Our Daily Lives in Air-Raided London," *The Sketch*, October 2, 1940. This photograph of the Windmill Girls in their dressing rooms combines two wartime genres: the shelter scene and the pin-up.

mothers from accusations of maternal and civic neglect. By contrast, no class vindication of the disparaged social body materializes in the Windmill's pictures of theatrical beauties at war.

Rather than defend proletarian family values, Windmill photographs more explicitly ratify the imperatives of healthy English heterosexuality. In so doing, they resemble that other popular icon of war: the pin-up (see Figure 28). The Windmill Girl undressing for the night smiles at the camera and is reassuring in her girl-next-door familiarity. She is clean, flawless, and engaged in welcoming flirtation with the viewer. Even at bedtime, she is "keeping up appearances,"

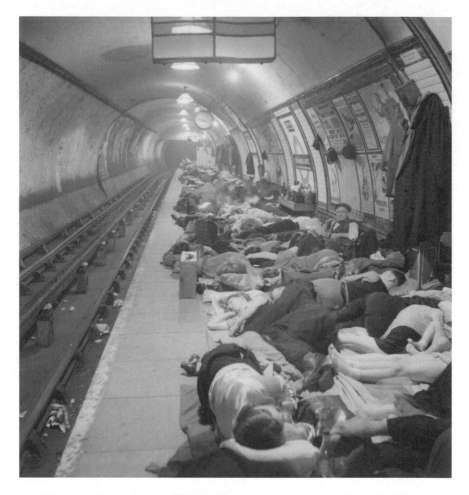

29 Bill Brandt, "Elephant and Castle Tube Station," November 1940. Bill Brandt's Underground shelter scenes present a striking contrast to the glamorized bedtime scenes of the Windmill Girls at War. In this photograph, Brandt highlights masses of undifferentiated bodies that collectively survive bombing raids by sleeping in the Underground under unhygienic and uncomfortable conditions.

following the dictate that "beauty" is wartime "duty."[177] While she represents a resilient, mobile femininity, she is delivered up as an incitement to reinvigorated heterosexuality.[178]

Along with photographic scenes of Underground shelters, images of the gallant Windmill Girls were exported to the United States as propaganda for the Blitz spirit: glamorous testimony that "London can take it," that Londoners had formed a self-sufficient, democratic civilian army to resist Hitler, an army that reconciled class differences.[179] In 1942, the Windmill inspired a Broadway show, *The Heart of the City*, a backstage story of the "little Windmill theatre" that dramatized the performers' tough theatrical dedication to a life and death struggle.[180] One month later, a photo spread of the Windmill Girls, both on Broadway and the West End, appeared in *Life*, with an accompanying text that praised "the little London theatre" as a "monument to the wartime pluck of 31 pretty girls." *Life*'s photo essay faithfully transmits familiar tropes of the Windmill: survival by sleeping, keeping up appearances, female camaraderie backstage, teamwork on stage, and restrained erotic movement. Plans were afoot in Hollywood to film the play, but they were delayed until 1945, when MGM put out a film version in Technicolor, starring Rita Hayworth. (*The Times* observed that the dance turns in the film were generally "more successful than those which actually found their way on to the boards [at the Windmill]".)[181]

A new wartime audience consolidated the Windmill's international reputation. It became the "favourite spot for servicemen," an amusement center for privates and non-commissioned officers in central London. VD weekly distributed 500–600 free tickets to servicemen, but even so the Windmill finally "began to make a profit" because it was able to fill the auditorium for every performance, thanks to the patronage of servicemen milling around Soho throughout the day. As a result, the despised "dirty mackintosh" brigade was marginalized in favor of a more democratic patron, Mr. Everyman, and the commandos had to compete for the front seats with the young men in uniform. Theater workers were delighted. They viewed servicemen as a more responsive audience for their dance routines, and their presence surely encouraged female performers to loosen up their acts. As early as 1942, news stories publicized stage-door romances and marriages between Windmill Girls and uniformed officers. The Windmill's popularity with servicemen led the *Daily Mail* to credit it as "one of three institutions that kept the nation together."[182]

The military news services also noted the popularity of Windmill Girls as "pin ups" and praised their "democratic practice": "Each girl is given ample opportunity of showing her talent, and like in the Army, she has to 'go through the ranks.'"[183] When Mrs. Henderson died in 1944, her will resonated with plans for stable postwar social reconstruction. Under the headline, "Legacies for All at Windmill," the *Star* reported that each employee had been bequeathed £10 (while VD had been given ownership of the theater). It went on to reassure the Windmill's patrons that her death spelled no change in the Windmill's familiar performances.[184]

A new culture of misrule, racial segregation, and energized masculinity materialized with the arrival of white GIs in 1942. One American newspaper calculated that over a million GIs saw the shows and contributed over $200,000 to the Windmill's wartime prosperity. An urban legend circulated around the presence of American servicemen at the Windmill. It involved their breaching of the theater's intensely English decorum. "Young America, raised on Abe Minsky productions with such titles as 'Julius Teaser,' 'Panties Inferno,' 'Anatomy and Cleopatra' . . . took the Windmill to its heart," wrote David Clayton in 1950. For three years and a half, GIs sat in the auditorium, "smoking cigars, chomping their jaws, and yelling 'Take it off, Take it off.' And 'shake it sister.' That was when the seats really got broken."[185] When asked about it in the 1950s, Jill Anstey, a show-girl, remembered the Americans fondly, as "the grandest audiences, much warmer than our English. And they were really very well behaved, after you got used to the shouting."[186]

This exuberant, democratic American presence masked an important social exclusion: race. Neither the popular press nor the Windmill archives contain any mention of "coloured servicemen" in the audience, even though many thousands of black GIs in Britain gravitated to Soho as their leisure center. Nor was there any review of Windmill attractions in the columns of the *New Amsterdam News* and the *Chicago Defender*, two prominent African-American newspapers that regularly covered Soho's hotspots. On this basis, it is fair to assume that an informal color bar operated at the Windmill, as it did elsewhere in sexually charged West End venues.[187] If black GIs had been able to gain entry to the theater, they might well have provoked a riot in the auditorium and a crackdown by the Lord Chamberlain, given the Windmill's provocative display of white showgirls who were "charmingly absent-minded about their costumes" and the explosive relations between white and black servicemen. Black GIs clearly found a friendlier reception at Soho's black clubs, many of them located cheek by jowl with the Windmill. The coexistence of the very white and English Windmill and the international black clubs in Soho's narrow streets testified to the cultural contrasts and different levels of social tolerance in this cosmopolitan locale.

A second urban legend about the Windmill at war spotlighted a posing girl who came to life amidst the raucous crowd and detonating bombs. In his memoir, VD recalled a time (in 1944) when a flying bomb hit the top of the Regent Palace Hotel just across the way. After the explosion, a posing girl wearing a Spanish hat (and nothing more) slowly moved and thumbed her nose at the bomb. For this spontaneous gesture, she received a "tremendous ovation." Reflecting on that special occasion, VD added, "I am sure that the Lord Chamberlain would not have objected to this posing figure moving."[188]

The posing girl who moved epitomized the spirit of the Blitz, when everyday ordinariness was recast as an idealized expression of wartime morale. The

Windmill's courage under fire advanced a democratic nationalist propaganda that was both invented and exclusionary. It staged a form of British popular entertainment that came to the defense of living arts by drawing on industrial methods and by amalgamating performance genres that were "in some ways Transatlantic, in others Continental."[189] Its erotic entertainments were simultaneously wholesome and prurient, civic-minded and cynically commercial, intimate and distant, exhibitionist yet highly disciplined and censored. Windmill publicity celebrated the healthy, heterosexual pleasures of looking at beautiful English girls' bodies, yet the theater attracted "the wrong kind" of patrons whose behavior veered towards the "perverse." While embracing the moral solidarities of interwar middle England, it was able to mutate geographically and politically during wartime, from blandly suburban to newly heroicized urban, from an insular mode of being to a populist expression of collective identity. As a result, the Windmill parlayed its Depression-era middlebrow entertainment into a celebrated act of wartime heroism and pulled itself "out of the red."

Conclusion

Through a series of exclusions, the Windmill sustained a political imaginary of the British people as democratic and homogeneous, and also white. This chapter has delineated some of the political and sexual restraints on Windmill performances, such as the efforts of the censor to prohibit pansy jokes and satirical mocking of dictators, but let us briefly return to the question of race, a vexed issue during the war. Race was certainly an imaginative category shaping Windmill entertainments throughout its history. From its inception, the Windmill showcased indigenous talent, celebrating English womanhood as the embodiment of an idealized form of Caucasian beauty. It satirized racial others by mobilizing commonplace stereotypes. During wartime, in deference to the Anglo-American special relationship, the Windmill seems to have pursued a more deliberate policy of racial exclusion. These racial exclusions reappear in nostalgic reminiscences of the Windmill, including the recent film *Mrs. Henderson Presents* (2005). Popular memory tends to locate the Windmill in a more innocent, communal and distant past, radically detached from the more multiracial London of the twenty-first century. By simplifying and sentimentalizing the wartime moment, these memories also perpetuate the Windmill's own rendering of middlebrow Englishness and the spirit of the Blitz.

Epilogue

Soho has long been a storied place. One legend credits Soho with a timeless essence and effortless capacity to sustain a traditional culture of nonconformity for over three hundred years.[1] Another version, repeated many times over many decades, declares that Soho is not what it was and is in terminal decline. This book challenges both interpretations for the fifty years prior to the Second World War. It chronicles Soho's cosmopolitan makeover at the fin de siècle and tracks its subsequent mutations over succeeding decades. Soho was neither timeless nor unchanging; it was the outcome of mental and material processes converging to produce a cosmopolitan space.

At the dawn of the twentieth century, Soho transmuted from a dingy industrial hinterland into a sophisticated commercial venue renowned for its social diversity, disparate political loyalties, and cosmopolitan pleasures. It served as a strategic location for the brokering of transnational goods and bodily display. A range of social actors contributed to Soho's refashioning. Writers, journalists, artists, and theater people—the well-known cast of bohemian characters associated with Soho—publicized its tasteful and sleazy attractions; they were enthusiastically joined by local ethnic entrepreneurs, who marketed transnational cultural forms adapted to English tastes. To promote Soho, bohemians and local impresarios not only advertised its foreignness but also trumpeted its status as a precious remnant of Old London. Local histories of Soho, advanced by civic-minded reformers like Reverend Cardwell of St. Anne, Soho, provided the historical glamor to refurbish Soho's cosmopolitan reputation.[2] Thanks to local history, the English literary ghosts of the Georgian past continued to haunt Soho's dingy streets and alleys, endowing them with a special atmosphere and aura of literary reminiscence.[3] In the Edwardian years, Old Soho was famous for

being solidly English and at the same time raffishly foreign, elegantly old-fashioned and shockingly modern.

Modern commercial economies of dancing, food, music, fashion, and sex
took hold in this Old London setting. These economies were interwoven with
each other and linked to the heavily capitalized developments along Soho's
peripheries. Theatrical and social dancing were integral to this commercial
synergy. Theatrical dancing had close tie-ins to catering, thanks to after-theater
suppers that made the fortune of Soho's restaurateurs. Dancing created thousands of jobs for dance musicians both in and around Soho. In Soho nightclubs,
dancing overlapped with commercialized sex. Social dancing was even crucial to
the take-off of the ready-to-wear dress trade surrounding Berwick Street Market,
where typists and shop assistants bought stockings and dance frocks—reputed
to be "just in from France"—as necessary accessories to a night out at the palais.
In the words of travel writer Robert Machray, Soho became the place that "holds
more of the night side of London than all of the rest of it put together."[4]

Dancing exemplifies the fractured cultural politics of Soho's cosmopolitan
spaces. *Nights Out*'s story of dance began at Soho's borders, at Leicester Square,
where the Victorian theaters of variety featured spectacular ballets as leg shows
for Men of the World. These cosmopolitan entertainments came under attack
from feminist purity reformers, determined to reshape the metropolis and the
globe according to their own moral vision of orderly circulation. The purity
campaign precipitated some unintended consequences, including the decision
by the management of the Palace Theatre to recruit the North American dancer
Maud Allan to fill the sex appeal slot. The Maud Allan boom was one of the
Edwardian developments that facilitated the entry of respectable women into
the night side of London. Allan's artistic but "nude" cosmopolitan performances
attracted the usual range of male patrons, while also appealing to men looking
for homosex and female patrons compelled by Allan's expressive kinesthesia and
embodiment of "freedom through dance." Twenty years later, at the Astoria
Dance Salon, Jewish residents of Soho also embraced dancing as a form of kinesthetic freedom and imaginative expatriation from the routines of daily life, even
though their dance steps adhered to the standardized rules of English dancing.
The working life of dance professionals exposed more explicit market relations
of power and inequality: in local dance halls, paid dance partners had to contend
with "over-amorous" patrons, while nightclub hostesses were expected to graft
their partners. The daily performances of the cheerful, well-drilled Windmill
Girls involved a grueling work routine. But even the "Treadmill's" theater
workers had breakout moments: they loosened up their routines during wartime
when they acquired a more responsive audience of young servicemen. During

the London Blitz, dancers dropped their fans, and cartwheeling members of the chorus showed glimpses of body parts that were not licensed by the censor. These practices had a specific political dimension: the Windmill Girls at war improvised kinetic movements in service to the heterosexual imperatives of wartime democratic nationalism. A few streets over, interracial dancing in Soho's black clubs materialized a more left-wing expression of international solidarity.

But Soho could also be a space of the extreme right as well as of the left. During the interwar years, the Italian catering trade served as a vehicle for the right-wing takeover of the Italian diaspora. The fiery anarchist and anti-Fascist Emidio Recchioni went so far as to assert that the militaristic labor organization of the catering trade, along with caterers' tendency to pander to conservative social elites, rendered it susceptible to reactionary politics. This accusation seems excessively deterministic, but there is no doubt that Italian Fascists endeavored to penetrate London's Italian colony through the catering trade. To this end, they flattered maître d's and restaurateurs with promises of honors, while also pressuring them to recruit their employees into the local Fascio and refuse to employ anti-fascists. Yet tensions between Italian Fascists and anti-fascists of other ethnicities rarely spilled into the streets. How do we account for the coexistence of extreme political views in Soho, and what does this coexistence suggest about the district's cosmopolitanism? Political tensions and differences may well have contributed to the tension or "edge" associated with Soho's cosmopolitan ambience. But the policy of social segregation pursued by the Fascists seems to have kept these tensions in check. Italian Fascists instructed their London members to obey British laws and stay out of local politics (even though the Fascist government gave financial support to British Fascists).[5] At a time when second-generation Jews were moving beyond their own communal institutions, Fascists endeavored to control Italian immigrants by keeping them within a bounded diaspora, closed off from local London institutions and social groupings. Ironically, the Fascist strategy of segregation enabled Jewish Communist musicians, black pan-Africanists, and English anti-fascists to protest the Abyssinian war and build cultural institutions of the Popular Front in Soho, yet remain unmolested (unlike local *Italian* anti-Fascists) by the local *squadristi* who frequented the Greek Street headquarters of the London Fascio.

This book also documents the mixed effects of government oversight and policing in Soho. Soho club owners and restaurateurs were subject to a widespread pattern of corrupt policing throughout the interwar years, decades before scandals over police protection of Soho's sex trade erupted in the public media. In the twenties and thirties, Sohoites also suffered from the actions of Britain's political police. Special Branch records expose the class and ethnic prejudices of the British political class and the degree to which MI5 colluded with Italian Fascists before 1935. While the Special Branch opposed the naturalization of Italian anti-Fascists, another authority, the theater censor, endeavored to keep Soho's entertainments in line with the official appeasement culture of the thirties. In deference to the government's policy of political détente, the Lord Chamberlain's readers suppressed political satire of Europe's dictators at the Windmill Theatre. The LCO's restrictions on topical political satire and sexual innuendo had some unexpected, even productive, cultural consequences: they not only provoked a low-grade, informal resistance on the part of theater workers and management; they also incited Windmill's comedians to devise new strategies of middlebrow comedy of everyday life.

A Changing Soho

Prior to the outbreak of the Second World War, cosmopolitan Soho was subject to dynamic and sometimes pernicious geopolitical forces, yet two key elements of the local scene remained intact: its old material fabric and its status as a residential immigrant community. These stable features of the local environment came under threat in the postwar decades, when the property market heated up and the residential immigrant community declined to the point of virtual extinction. Soaring property values cemented a corrupt alliance among "bent" coppers, "sex barons," and property developers that threatened to "develop" old Soho, along with its residential community, artisanal crafts and commerce, out of existence.[6]

The first signs of change began to manifest themselves in the late 1930s, as speculators added Soho properties to their portfolios in anticipation of massive rebuilding around Piccadilly Circus.[7] The speculative acquisition of Soho properties considerably escalated during the war, in response to the state's redevelopment plan for the metropolis. Forshaw and Abercrombie's County of London Plan (1943), complete with lavishly reproduced color plates and illustrations, advanced a moral vision of how people should live in cities.[8] Promising a better England for all after the war, it called for rebuilding that ensured low population density, decentralization of congested areas, green spaces, and zoning segregation of residences and businesses. Not surprisingly, it cast a skeptical eye upon Soho: while praising it as a "restaurant area" with "its own peculiar charm," it otherwise treated the district as an example of inner city decay, subject to "deteriorated mixed . . . use."[9]

The County of London Plan would have a complex afterlife in the decades to follow, shaping utopian visions of urban planning at the same time as fueling property speculation in London's central area.[10] In 1946, Westminster Council published the *City of Westminster Plan*; echoing Forshaw and Abercrombie, it called for the wholesale demolition of Soho's 130 or so acres of built environment, including Greek, Frith, Dean, and Old Compton Streets, as well as the small byways, courts, and alleys situated east of Regent Street.[11] The authors regarded Soho as a "misplaced environment," to use Frank Mort's term, its people and industries representing matter out of place.[12] Its narrow, congested thoroughfares were an impediment to the free flow of east-west traffic through central London, while its twelve industrial dwellings were outdated, and green spaces were sadly absent. Apart from the cosmopolitan character of Soho's small restaurants, the Plan's authors could find very little appealing or worth preserving in the area. They took an especially dim view of the district's "far too numerous" small business sites that were mixed in with residences. Based on 1939 data, the authors estimated Soho's residential population at 7,240, a steady decline from the beginning of the century. Outside the catering trade, 10,000 individuals labored in 1,500 industrial workshops, including 406 flats. Many of these workers clearly commuted into Soho to work. Two-thirds of Soho's industrial workforce was still concentrated in the Jewish-dominated garment trades, even though many Jews had already moved their residences to the suburbs. The remaining third were scattered among a myriad of craft industries, ranging from jewelers and silversmiths (647), to printers (942), to wig and hair makers (190), and to cinema film workers (184). The City of Westminster Plan proposed to demolish this crowded, mixed environment and replace it with a clean, hygienic, and specialized business district devoted to restaurants, with a separate area marked out for theaters. Owing to the high land values of the area, the authors envisaged a considerable reduction of the residential population, to 2,500, most of them to be rehoused in "healthy and pleasant" ten-story blocks along a newly rebuilt Old Compton Street.[13]

The City of Westminster Plan did not go unchallenged. The preservationist Georgian Group treated it with contempt, declaring that the plan might as well have been called *Westminster Remangled* and castigating the planners' narrow vision of Westminster as a mere traffic route, a "place on the road to somewhere else ... so arranged that it offers the minimum of obstruction to the 'traffic-flow.'"[14] An article in the *Manchester Guardian* speculated whether the plan might spell the "fin de Soho." The plan would "transform that noisy welter of narrow streets and alleys into an amalgam of [moribund] Mayfair and the Temple," sniffed the paper's "London Correspondent."[15] Unlike the Plan's authors, this reporter did not regard the existence of 1,487 small workshops in the district (not including "the black-market businesses of which one hears so much") to be prima facie evidence of Soho's dereliction. On the contrary, he thought this picture of back-street industry might come as an agreeable surprise to people who tended to think of Soho either as a "pleasure-ground" or more luridly as part of "London's square mile of vice," a common reference to the C Division of the Metropolitan Police encompassing Mayfair and Soho and made infamous by detective memoirs and fiction.[16] Noting that the Council looked with a kindly eye upon "the multitudinous restaurants" of Soho, the "London Correspondent" wondered if these establishments would be able to attract custom once Soho was cleaned up. "Who would want to visit a tidy and hygienic Soho?" he asked, thus summoning up familiar tropes of Soho's double-edged cosmopolitanism that had attracted urban travelers to the district for over fifty years. After all, the quarter's charm lay in the "confusion of odours, nationalities, styles of architecture and decorations." "Its dark and sinister streets, its shady characters, its very squalor are its appeal."[17]

Like many other postwar proposals for urban redevelopment, the City of Westminster Plan was not implemented, but it cast a shadow over Soho and energized an ongoing discourse about it as a dangerous slum. At the same time that Westminster put forward its redevelopment plans, the nation's print culture, noirist films, and television crime detective series were busy demonizing Soho as a claustrophobic world of underworld dens, dingy old alleys and streets that existed "solely for slinking men, prostitutes, perverts, spielers [gamblers] and pimps."[18] But this was not the only kind of publicity to emanate out of postwar Soho. Beginning in the 1950s, local businessmen tried to offset the negative planning culture and media vision of Soho's "vicious circle" with a more pleasing version of Soho's cosmopolitanism.[19]

The Soho Fair

In 1952, the Soho Restaurant Association reached out to ex-soldiers returning from the war, urging them to revisit Soho restaurants and enjoy the same continental atmosphere and reasonable prices that had drawn Londoners to Soho in earlier decades.[20] Between 1955 and 1959, the Soho Association sponsored an annual Soho Fair as a "fiesta" and patch of "uninhibited gaiety" amidst the dull grayness of austerity London.[21] Organizers of the Fair capitalized on Soho's long-standing reputation as the "most cosmopolitan quartre in the world," encompassing "every known trade and profession" and purveying continental food, fashion, and erotic entertainments in a distinctive locale.[22] Besides a waiters' race, talent competitions, nationality days, and gala performances, the Fair even showed off some post-Victorian fleshy delights available in Soho. It staged a parade featuring local models in bikinis who flaunted their "all too solid female flesh."[23]

In 1955, as Frank Mort has observed, Soho certainly needed a favorable publicity boost.[24] Only a few weeks after the Fair's opening, a notorious knife fight broke out on Old Compton Street between two gangsters, Jack Spot and Albert Dimes, over the control of betting pitches.[25] Incidents of this kind seemed to confirm sensational media tales of darkest Soho. Gaston Berlemont, the mustachioed owner of the French House on Dean Street, hoped the Fair would counteract Soho's unsavory reputation as "a square mile of vice."[26] One column in the Soho Fair Programme of 1957 tackled the question directly by asking, "How Wicked Is Soho?" Echoing one conventional view of Soho, the Fair's publicists defended Soho's loucheness as a positive attraction. "As for Soho, it's got everything, casual streetwalking on the largest scale in London, street-betting, brothels, those advertising cards in the windows, a little dope pushing, dirty movies, a great deal of subterranean gambling, and even some illegal weapons trading." While the same writers insisted that the "average Londoner's chances of ever becoming involved with the professional criminal are, conserva-tively, a million to one," they acknowledged that close proximity to these illicit trades proved to be something of a tourist asset: the human animal, being what he is, "likes places with a spicy reputation." So while Soho's respectable busi-nessmen might squirm at the popular equation that "Soho equals Vice," not a few privately admitted that Soho's wicked reputation meant "cash in the till."[27]

Besides wickedness, Fair programs promised visitors a "gastronomical Cook's tour" of a "hundred national cuisines all cheek by jowl in glorious abandon."[28] Soho's food culture would prove critical to the new ways that adventurous postwar Londoners began to cook. Besides old Soho restaurants such as Quo Vadis, Le Petit Savoyard, On Ley, Café Bleu (as well as the Roma, denounced by Sylvia Pankhurst as a hotbed of Italian Fascism in 1940), Fair programs also enumerated the district's Italian food provision shops, such as I Parmigiani and King Bomba. Elizabeth David, who spearheaded the postwar revolution in culinary taste in favor of the Mediterranean diet, recommended these Soho places to readers of her cookbooks as London sources for the ingredients essential to her recipes.[29]

Promising something for everyone, the Soho Fair also reached out to people of color and London's youth. July 17, 1957 was "Commonwealth Day" in Soho, featuring a skiffle contest, a jazz festival, and a calypso ball.[30] Young Londoners, captivated by the electric atmosphere of basement music clubs and espresso bars, flocked to the Fair and transformed it into a week-long hippie street party and "festival of ravers," the first in a series of carnivalesque happenings that amal-gamated youth, music, protest, and identity politics.[31]

The musical activities of Commonwealth Day were an early sign of Soho's place on the map of what would soon be internationally promoted as "Swinging London." In a cover story of *Time* in April 1966, journalist Piri Halasz identified Soho, along with the more upmarket venues of King's Road, Chelsea, and Knightsbridge, as one of Young London's hotspots, a place where London's working-class kids gravitated "to spend what they've got," now that teenage wages were rising.[32] Soho was Swinging London's night scene; during the day it was a hub of boutiques and record shops and the center of male youth fashion.[33] "Perhaps nothing illustrates the new swinging London better than narrow, three-block-long Carnaby Street, which is crammed with a clutch of 'gear' boutiques where the girls and boys buy each other clothes," Halasz reported.[34] Seven years earlier, Colin MacInnes's best-selling *Absolute Beginners* (1959) had already introduced fiction readers to the "mod" teenagers who frequented Soho's streets and establishments.[35] As Frank Mort has observed, this new wave of male adolescents made their social and sexual odyssey to Soho, guided by historically sedimented associations of Soho as a Mecca for male self-invention.[36] Undoubtedly compelled by Soho's notoriety as a wide open place, the tidal wave of young Londoners descending on Soho in the late fifties and sixties were mostly pop culture aficionados, who kept their office day jobs to support their fashion and music habits.[37]

Swinging London built on structural and cultural antecedents of interwar Soho. In Soho's boutiques, music clubs, record shops, and espresso bars, young Londoners encountered some of the Old Sohoites who featured in earlier chapters of this book. In 1961, the young Keith Richards, trying to break into the music scene in Soho, bought a guitar from Ivor Mairants, the West End jazz guitarist who opened a guitar store and music school on the Charing Cross Road after the war.[38] The local Jewish rag trade also played a part in Soho's postwar youth scene. Back in the 1930s, Jewish garment workers catered to fashion-conscious working-class women in Berwick Street Market; thirty years later, Jewish tailors performed a similar service, supplying Carnaby Street merchants with flash clothes to enable young teenagers, in George Melly's words, to "revolt into style."[39]

Pornbrokers and Property Developers

For most of the 1960s, Westminster Council ignored the cultural ferment emerging out of Soho sleaze, although it later tried to capitalize on Carnaby Street's international renown by pedestrianizing the street in 1973. Instead, municipal authorities continued to put forward a range of plans for comprehensive redevelopment of Piccadilly Circus and Soho. Even though none of these plans ever materialized, they set into motion a feeding frenzy among private property speculators. The late 1960s saw schemes for 300,000 square feet of offices around Piccadilly Circus. This meant twenty- or thirty-story tower blocks, with pedestrian walkways 60 feet up in the air extending out towards Regent Street, Soho, and Leicester Square, and six lanes of traffic rushing below.[40] These proposals stalled because of early conservationist protests as well as the astronomical costs and complex traffic logistics involved in their implementation.[41] Aiding and abetting the property grab was Tory legislation that eased rent freezes introduced during the war. The Rent Act of 1957 gave landlords the right to set rents as high as they liked for new tenants. While massive redevelopment schemes never came to fruition, the proposals "left a trail of planning blight," to quote the planning reporter from *The Times*.[42] Grand schemes translated into more modest, piecemeal destruction of Soho streets and properties that were subject to compulsory purchase as slum clearance. As a result, Georgian houses in St. Anne's Court and Livonia Street were pulled down as slums. In the early sixties, Kemp House, a seventeen-story block of council flats built at the bottom of Berwick Street in a Blitz-damaged area, remains a striking reminder of what was intended to be, in Summers's term, a "Brave New Soho."[43]

Meanwhile, private developers cemented a rapacious alliance with Soho "pornbrokers" and "bent coppers." Police collusion with Soho vice racketeers and shady property speculators nearly wrecked Soho and the good name of Scotland Yard. Persistent allegations of police corruption and protection of Soho pornographers culminated in the 1977 arrest and conviction of twelve senior officers of Scotland Yard as well as the resignation and transfer of 400 others.[44]

How was this unholy alliance forged? While waiting to cash in on postwar redevelopment schemes, property speculators let their Soho properties on leases with six-month break clauses. In the 1940s, the Chinese community, fleeing blitzed-out Limehouse, accepted these terms and settled in the Gerrard Street area. The other group of ready tenants were sex merchants. As a fly-by-night, low overhead operation, the sex industry was "best placed" to accept these terms, recalled Bryan Burrough, chair of the Soho Society, in 1994.[45] As we have seen, the use of upper rooms above Soho restaurants as places of assignation was a longstanding practice in Soho, one apparently sanctioned by the police.[46] But the scale and organization of this criminal activity dramatically increased in the postwar years. In the 1930s and 1940s, the Messina brothers, Commonwealth citizens from Malta, developed an extensive ring of prostitutes in Soho, installing around twenty European women in their Soho and Mayfair properties.[47] In 1950, the tabloid *The People* published a sensational exposé of the Messinas that led to the arrest of two brothers for living off the earnings of prostitutes, while the other three escaped to Europe.[48] Their departure opened the way for other criminal entrepreneurs to move into the vice racket in Soho. Bernie Silver, an English Jew who had worked for the Messinas, emerged as the head of a "Syndicate," engaged in Rachman-style "flat farming." During the fifties and sixties, Silver acquired twenty-five to thirty premises in Soho and parts of Mayfair to be used for prostitutes and gambling and illegal drinking clubs. He systematically bribed the police in the "Vice and Clubs offices" to keep these premises open.[49]

Silver's sex-and-property empire mushroomed in the 1960s when newer forms of commercialized sex began to proliferate in Soho, namely strip clubs, sex films, pornography and sex shops. Raymond's Revuebar set the standard for strip clubs, demonstrating just how much money could be made in this enterprise. In 1958, Paul Raymond opened Raymond's Revuebar in Walker's Court, having leased land from Jack Isow, the owner of the defunct Shim Sham Club turned restaurateur. Located a hundred yards from the Windmill Theatre, the Revuebar was ostensibly a members-only private club, but, as in so many other shady nightclubs, memberships were sold at the door. As soon as it opened, the Revuebar was dogged by intensive police surveillance and raids. "The law was on our back all the time. Raiding us all the time," Raymond recalled in a 1983 interview.[50] Raymond aggressively refused to shut down, and defiantly challenged the criminal charges made against him. He insisted that his premises were well conducted, that royalty and women visited his establishment to see continental performances of nudes who moved, and that he was a "prophet of a new liberated sexuality."[51] Within a short time, the Windmill Theatre, which had "never closed" during the war, lost most of its custom to Raymond's Revuebar. Its static nudes and "surreptitious sauciness of a peculiarly English kind" could not compete with Raymond's more cosmopolitan kinetic acts.[52]

Two pieces of legislation in 1959 and 1967 also cleared the way for the aggressive expansion of the sex industry in Soho, enabling "sex barons" to gain a stranglehold on Soho property and control over police operations. The Sexual Offences Act of 1967 not only legalized homosexuality, but partly drove prostitutes off the streets and into the clubs. Meanwhile the Obscene Publications Act of 1959 simply "muddled" the legal status of erotic materials, giving a special unit of the Metropolitan Police extraordinary powers to determine and seize obscene materials.[53] By the early sixties, Bernie Silver had diversified from brothels to strip clubs and pornography. He also managed to place the entire Obscene Publications Squad on his weekly payroll.[54] However, by the early 1970s, the sheer expansion of sex merchants in all branches of the industry meant that

Silver and the police could not keep out competitors. When Silver and some of his corrupt policemen were prosecuted in 1973, the ironic result was the "disappearance of any sort of control over what was displayed in Soho."[55] It took another four years for top brass at Scotland Yard to be prosecuted, but this full sweep merely discredited the police and did not result in a new rule of law. Now, anyone with nerve and financial backing could get into the sex shop business in the district. Aggressive touts, blaring music, and neon signs rendered the sex business much more visible and environmentally offensive than previous forms of commercialized sex. All of this was tacitly sanctioned by Westminster Council's laissez-faire approach until the late 1970s, motivated by a desire to protect ratable income and avoid vacant premises.

Soho Society

This was the state of affairs that led local traders, restaurateurs, and cultural professionals to form the Soho Society as an amenities group in 1972, determined to protect Soho from redevelopment and the depredations of what they called "The Vice." By 1972, Soho's resident population had declined to 3,000; its doctor's surgery was about to be displaced; and plans were afoot to tear down numerous other properties for office development. Something had to be done while remnants of the community still existed.

The Soho Society presented itself as not so much opposed to planning as the advocate of an alternative design for living, embodied in the concept of the urban village.[56] By so doing, it staked a claim about what and who constituted key elements of a dynamic Soho present. It also advanced a generous vision of Soho's usable past. Just as Londoners were beginning to take stock of their multi-ethnic and multiracial city, the Society celebrated Soho's cosmopolitan history as a harbinger of the multicultural future.

The Soho Society was not the first to conceptualize Soho as a friendly urban village, but it was in the forefront of those eager to publicize its village culture as an idealized form of modern urbanity.[57] As a planning concept, the urban village built on early twentieth-century ideals of the garden city, but relocated them in the urban core. The urban village gained academic currency in the 1960s, following sociologist Herbert Gans's study of Boston's West End. Gans argued that behind the appearance of urban decay lay a coherent social community of Italian immigrants, bound together by strong structural hierarchies and dynamically linked to other spaces.[58] In London, exponents of the urban village interpreted it as an extension of London's own history as a series of villages. For journalist Tony Aldous, writing in 1980, the urban village signified a thriving and individualistic small community. It was a mixed-use environment where "thousands happily live and work."[59]

The Soho Society's advocacy of the urban village also derived from its institutional and cultural attachment to the local Anglican parish. Not only was the Society first housed in the tower of St. Anne Church; the Soho Housing Association built homes for Soho residents on church land.[60] Bryan Burrough, the leader and spokesman of the Society and widely regarded as the "man who saved Soho," was a deacon of St. Anne and deeply imbued with a broad church ethos of the social gospel.[61] In talks and interviews, he frequently cited Reverend Cardwell, the reforming vicar of St. Anne at the turn of the century, as a role model and touchstone on anti-vice campaigns, religious toleration, local history, and community building. In 1977, for example, Burrough gave a talk on the church to the local history group. The *Soho Clarion* reported that "of particular interest was the [Victorian] 'Committee against Vice,' which complained bitterly that the 'disorderly houses' could afford to pay very high rents and that restaurants and shopkeepers were consequently being displaced from their premises."[62] Twenty years later, in an interview with me, Burrough claimed to be "thinking a lot about Cardwell," recalling his spirit of toleration, his desire to be a good neighbor to immigrant residents of his parish, his support for reform candidates at the local ward elections of 1903.[63] Like Cardwell, Burrough also believed that local history was important to community morale. "Soho's noble past," he insisted, was reflected not only in its fascinating, irreplaceable Georgian housing stock but in its present occupations.[64] Following this historical logic, Burrough's primary allegiance was to older residents and their skilled trades as the rightful occupants of Soho's material fabric.

While celebrating Cardwell, both Burrough and the Soho Society felt obliged to adapt the Victorian rector's parochial vision for the late twentieth-century urban village. The Society shared Cardwell's high estimation of the artistic, literary, and historical associations of Soho Past, memorialized by the blue plaques affixed to building facades throughout the district. It also shared his regard for Soho's craft traditions, but, unlike Cardwell, it included tailoring and catering among the prized industries of the district. As part of its localism, it embraced Georgian architecture, just beginning to return to favor in Cardwell's day, as a more human scale and English way of living in the city, uncontaminated by modernist (and continental) systems of planning and design. But it departed from Cardwell's focus on historical luminaries by pursuing a more democratic variant of social history: its newsletter circulated life stories of long-term working-class residents, many of them born and raised in Soho, as the active subjects of history. The *Soho Clarion* even incorporated prostitutes into the historic village as lively street characters, part of the passing scene. While retaining Cardwell's argument about rents and vice, the Society tried to dispense with his Victorianism by redefining the boundaries of acceptable sex work. Despite their effort to be up-to-date and worldly, their historical narrative of Soho's village was more than a little sentimental, infused with a little Englander attachment to a stable, bounded, face-to-face community.

"Must Soho Die?" asked the group's newspaper, the *Soho Clarion*, in its inaugural issue of December 1973. Warning that the community was in danger of being "developed out of existence and its present trading and residential communities destroyed forever," the year-old Soho Society launched its media campaign to convince the public, the media, and Westminster Council that Soho was worth saving. Despite a "certain seediness," Soho was a "good place to be," a place of great variety and vitality, drawing its strength and cosmopolitan character from a unique mixture of residents from many lands with traders and artisans of every kind. Yet this "traditional centre of crafts" was in "imminent danger of destruction." [65]

The *Soho Clarion* identified long-term residents and businesses as its principal constituencies in need of protection from municipal planners and private property developers. Tenants in four sites in West Soho had already been notified to vacate at Christmas so that developers could convert their residences into offices, showrooms and luxury maisonettes.[66] In picturesque detail, the *Soho Clarion* tried to render visible both the architectural heritage and the hidden industries under threat. On Broadwick Street, for instance, Sutton Estates intended to tear down the interiors of 45–48 Broadwick Street and only keep the facade of "these very important early Georgian terraces," one of the few remaining examples of the beauty and character of eighteenth-century domestic architecture in Soho. The mixed land use of this block was typical of Soho, while the projected luxury maisonettes and showrooms were out of place in the old Georgian environment. As important, they were beyond the means of the present occupants, which consisted of a doctor's surgery, goldsmiths, silversmiths, the Flute Makers' Guild, and a maker of leather umbrella handles. While acknowledging that these houses lacked electricity and bathrooms, the Society also insisted that they were essentially sound structures. With renovation, they could provide decent homes and working accommodation to meet the "needs of small craftsmen and traders of Soho."[67]

Within a few months the Society had persuaded Westminster Council to repel the "concrete invasion" and make Soho a conservation area, thus ending the widespread threat of demolition.[68] Local activists built alliances with other groups operating in the West End districts, modeling their campaign on the strategy exploited by the Covent Garden Community Association. Instead of comprehensive urban redevelopment, they championed small-scale renovation.[69] The Soho Society's campaign gained instant media attention, not least because its leaders included professionals and cultural entrepreneurs with considerable public relations flair. The Society also benefited from Soho's central location, its fame/notoriety, and its proximity to the headquarters of professional architectural and conservationist groups, and to the media.[70] The "friendly persuaders of Soho are winning a battle to save London's oldest 'village,'" declared the *Evening News*. It noted that the "persuaders" were not "a noisy, militant, angry brigade of students and arty left-wingers," but a small group of mostly middle-aged citizens, who included in their numbers delicatessen managers, restaurateurs, a master tailor, a chef, architects, a literary agent, and a member of the Foreign Office.[71]

As one of its publicity stunts, the Soho Society took Westminster councillors, many of whom did not even realize anyone actually lived in Soho, on a "Soho Walkabout," gaining coverage in five national dailies.[72] "We split them into groups of four, and took them round," Bryan Burrough recalled in 1980. "The group I was with we took to Kettner's basement, then into the kitchen of a Chinese restaurant, then to a drum maker's and a flute maker's and finally gave them all dinner in a 1730s house in Great Pulteney Street with a coal fire burning in the grate. They were amazed to learn there were such places, and quite staggered to be told that every single place they'd been to that night was due for demolition."[73]

Having won this first battle, the Society turned its attention to community activities that could reinforce links between working-class residents and business concerns, many of them run by non-English speakers: it translated notices on threatened trades into Chinese, Greek, and Italian and introduced a history group, a Soho Festival, a youth club, a football team, and a community newspaper. In 1976, it formed the Soho Housing Association; with help from the Council, it renovated residential properties that had been previously slated for demolition. Within twenty years, it would be operating more than 400 flats in the West End worth more than £40 million. During these decades, Soho's population increased from 3,000 to 5,000, and its school was once more full of children.[74]

Despite early successes, the Society failed to stem the loss of artisan businesses or contain the aggressive practices of the sex trade in the 1970s. In 1980, the *Soho Clarion* once again carried the banner headline, "Must Soho Die?" and listed "picture framers, pastry cooks, last makers, book binders, fine print dealers, feather arrangers" among "Soho's Endangered Species." They were all casualties of the insidious economic effects of new and destructive forces, most especially the takeover of Soho properties by the porn trade and the increase in rental values "way above those which any legitimate business can afford."[75]

The Society carefully argued its case against "The Vice" on environmental grounds, although there was a post-Victorian moralism at work in its thinking. The Society crafted its position as follows: Soho had always been a red light district, and Sohoites had always lived with prostitutes as part of its cosmopolitan mix. But this older variant of commercialized sex was different, more decorous and less disruptive of gender norms, than the offensive trade of the present day. At least this was the point of view of Wardour Street film entrepreneur Peter Phillips, a local businessman who was interviewed in the *Soho Clarion*. In common with other long-time Sohoites, Phillips claimed to miss the streetwalkers (now that they were banned from the streets) and their cheerful banter with punters. He also took the occasion to compare the friendly tarts of old with the activities of "today's tattooed touts of indeterminate sex who call out from the doorways of strip joints."[76]

Having staked out an environmentalist position on the sex trade, the Society struggled for years to persuade Westminster Council to change its lax policy towards sex shops. Members regularly attended Licensing Sessions and instituted twenty-three public inquiries against the trade, winning them all.[77] The *Soho Clarion* ran a regular column, "We're Watching," that reported on proposed shifts in land use. In 1976, it protested an unauthorized neon sign on Dean Street as well as a proposed change of business from butcher shop to private club and cinema. In 1977, it challenged another change of business on Dean Street "from auctioneer" to "health studio sauna massage parlour" on the grounds that the existing need for these services was "well catered-for already" in the area. At the same time, the newspaper sadly noted the closing of old businesses and restaurants.[78] The venerable L'Escargot on Greek Street closed its doors after seventy years in business in 1980, because patrons would not walk down the street. Isow's had closed five years previously, in 1975, for environmental as well as financial reasons, a rather ironic denouement to Isow's 1958 leasing and eventual sale of the Walker's Court property to Paul Raymond that enabled him to open up a strip club business in Soho in the first place.[79]

In 1986, after a long campaign, the Society finally persuaded Westminster Council to license a fixed number of sex shops in the district. By 1989, the number of houses used by The Vice had fallen from 185 to 35; by 1994, to 20. All in all, by the end of the 1980s, Soho seemed to have turned a corner as the licensing system stemmed the vast expansion of the sex industry.[80] But the clean-up of Soho had unanticipated consequences, as least as far as the Soho Society was concerned, leading to an outbreak of "designer restaurants" and other symptoms of gentrification.[81] The Society managed to save Soho's built environment, but a new Soho was reborn as a leisure and business center for young professionals and gay men. Rents skyrocketed in the late 1980s, driving out old businesses for good. The escalation of rents was the final nail in the coffin for the old immigrant working community of Soho, facilitated by Westminster's revision of planning regulations that equated offices and light industrial premises as interchangeable forms of land use. Immediately, tailors were forced out of their premises, to be replaced by media offices. In 1988, in one building alone, eighteen tailors were forced out. The landlord, an offshore holding company in the Cayman Islands, intended to upgrade the facilities and rent them out as offices.[82] But the property boom also made the fortune of local entrepreneurs. In the 1970s, Paul Raymond bought up the Windmill Theatre and hundreds of other properties used by the pornography trade in the western part of Soho, all the while insisting that he did not offer sweeteners to the police.[83] Apart from his strip club and pornography magazines, he made heaps of money as a landlord to the porn trade. He then reaped even greater profits from a renewed Soho, thanks to the escalation of land values via gentrification. By 1992, Raymond was named the richest man in Britain, ousting the Duke of Westminster.[84]

Although somewhat contained, the sex industry still continued to diversify and develop global links. Problems persisted with unlicensed shops, many of them owned by Russians and Albanians who recruited illegal migrants from Eastern Europe to work in their businesses. While fighting unlicensed shops, the Soho Society repeatedly came to the defense of self-employed prostitutes working in brothels. Consistent with environmentalism, it joined with the English Collective of Prostitutes in 2005 to protest Westminster Council's decision to buy thirty Soho properties identified as brothels and redevelop them. "We don't have a problem with brothels as such," declared Bryan Burrough, then honorary president of the Society, while Joan Martyr, another active member and a former costume designer for Raymond's Revuebar, declared, "They are so much part of the area. . . . Without them the area would be all office blocks and non-stop clubs."[85]

A Reborn Soho

A reborn Soho became a magnet for the "pink pound," with Old Compton Street transformed into the Champs Élysées of Gay Europe.[86] Building on a gay night-club scene centered around the old Astoria Theatre, now rechristened as Bang, and a few openly gay cafés, Soho became a center of gay consumption. Its first gay shop, Clone Zone, opened in Old Compton Street in 1992. It sold sports-wear, books and gifts, as well as sex toys and body jewelry in the basement.[87] By 1994, the Village Group, an association of local gay businesses, began to adver-tise Soho as Europe's top gay village.[88] Initially, some members of the Soho Society tended to dismiss Soho's queer popularity as transient, believing that gay men would move on "and others will arrive in their place."[89] But the Society soon welcomed gay men and lesbians as part of Soho's multicultural mix and viewed them as an acceptable face of sexual Soho. In 1999, after a horrific nail bombing attack on the Admiral Duncan, a gay pub in Old Compton Street, the *Soho Clarion* took the occasion to reflect on the bomber's "hatred of those who are in any sense identifiably different." "In Soho where being 'different' has been the norm since the 18th century the bomber did not produce the effect he intended."[90]

Coinciding with Soho's rebirth as a gay village was its consolidation as the primary core of the creative industries, the hub of video, music, film, television, advertising, and design for London, spreading from Covent Garden and building on old Soho linkages with music, film and television, and the performing arts. Signs of gentrification included the opening of restaurants dedicated to new British cooking, the founding of the Groucho Club in 1984 as a watering place for literary and new media types, and, most striking, the decision of well-heeled professionals to reside in Soho, purchasing flats in renovated Georgian terraces. They were drawn to Soho's raffish theater of consumption, "to the variety of options in such a compact area, the sense of discovery on finding fun nestled among the strip joints, or buried in a backstreet basement."[91] Creative industries resemble the old garment industry in their tendency to cluster in specific areas, resisting post-Fordist tendencies towards the "putting-out" mode of produc-tion.[92] To quote one geographer, for creative media types, Soho is a "place where one must be" to make it in the industry. It is a place to mix work and play, enabling opportunities for personal contexts and networks in less formal surroundings.[93]

The new business sector appears to be less committed to staying in Soho than the old industries of the district. After all, Soho's cachet depends on its "edge," its deviation from the norm. Recently, observers have warned that the advent of "mega bars" threaten to erode this distinctive atmosphere and demote Soho to an alcohol-fueled, downmarket attraction.[94] The migration of the homeless into the district, following on Thatcherite welfare cutbacks, has also been a subject of concern. In 2010, Soho still remains the hub of media/creative industries, but it has to compete with other creative quarters in London. New small "creative" businesses are moving out to south and east London, attracted not only by cheaper rents, but by the "interesting buildings" and alternative milieu.[95]

This postwar history underscores how relatively protected from incursions of the property market Soho had been before the Second World War. However, it was never quite the safe urban village of tolerance recalled by old Sohoites. Not only did it support contentious forms of commerce; it also became the site for extreme political tensions among Italians over fascism and anti-fascism. Even the black clubs that evolved into progressive sites of Popular Front culture in the thirties remained sleazy and hazardous spaces of labor, racial, and sexual exploitation. The *Manchester Guardian* might declare Soho's "shady characters, its very squalor" to be part of its historic appeal, but these characters and squalor often translated into structural inequalities, corrupt policemen, and marauding gangsters.[96] Postwar Soho's pornbrokers and bent coppers did not materialize out of the blue; they were merely perfecting a system of graft already in place. Alternatively, it could be argued that creative elements of Soho's prewar economy, as well as its heterogeneous, cosmopolitan ambience, paved the way for Soho's dynamic place in postwar British pop culture and consumption. These older formations would include Archer Street's open air labor market for dance musicians, the black clubs of the thirties, and the garment trades of West Soho, not to speak of Soho's bohemian reputation as a destination space for adventurous men trying to find themselves. The new Mediterranean diet advanced by Elizabeth David built on Soho's food culture, while repudiating the hybrid gastronomy of Soho's Franco-Italian restaurants.

In the new millennium, Soho has lost its singularity as London's cosmopolis, a demotion that exposes its vulnerability to changing fashions and global capital. Since the 1960s, the ethnic, racial, and sexual diversity of Londoners has rapidly proliferated elsewhere in the metropolis. It is now possible to find alternative milieux in north, east and south London that can serve as compelling stage sets for a cosmopolitan experience. To quote Jerry White, Soho is now "one jewel among many," and shines out less brightly, while still retaining a unique personality of its own.[97] But how the diffusion of heterogeneity will play itself out in London's new millennium remains to be seen. To gain some insight, contemporary denizens of the metropolis can revisit Soho's cosmopolitan past as one historical precedent of the challenges and pleasures of living with difference.

Abbreviations

BL   British Library
BLSA   British Library Sound Archive
DPP   Records of the Director of Public Prosecutions
HO   Home Office Files
IWM   Imperial War Museum, London
KV   Records of the Security Service, National Archives
LMA   London Metropolitan Archives
LCC   London County Council
MEPO   Metropolitan Police Files, National Archives
MMB   Millennium Memory Bank, British Library Sound Archive
MOA   Mass Observation Archive, University of Sussex
NA   National Archives, London
NYPL   New York Public Library
PMC   Public Morality Council
TM   Theatre Museum, London
WA   Westminster Archives, London
WCC   Westminster City Council
WEJ   West End Jews Oral History Project, Jewish Museum, London

Notes

Introduction

1. Douglas Goldring, *The Nineteen Twenties: A General Survey and Some Personal Memories* (London: Nicholson & Watson, 1945), 145.
2. For a discussion of Woolf's "usual round," see Jean Moorcroft Wilson, *Virginia Woolf's London: A Guide to Bloomsbury and Beyond* (London: Tauris Parke, 2000; orig. 1987), 141. For Woolf's discovery of Berwick Street Market and her observations on rambles in Soho and the 1917 Club, see Virginia Woolf, *The Diary of Virginia Woolf*, vol. 1: *1915–1919*, ed. Anne Olivier Bell (Harmondsworth, UK: Penguin, 1979), 134–5, 148; Virginia Woolf, *The Diary of Virginia Woolf*, vol. 2: *1920–24*, ed. Anne Olivier Bell and Andrew McNeillie (Harmondsworth, UK: Penguin, 1981; orig. 1978), 21.
3. See, for example, Virginia Woolf, *Jacob's Room*, ed. and annotated Sue Roe (London: Penguin, 1992).
4. Thomas Burke, *The London Spy: A Book of Town Travels* (London: Thornton Butterworth, 1922), 158.
5. Virginia Woolf, "Street Haunting," in *Collected Essays* (New York: Harcourt Brace, 1967), 159.
6. James H. Winter, *London's Teeming Streets: 1830–1914* (New York: Routledge, 1993), 214.
7. Virginia Woolf, "Oxford Street Tide," in Woolf, *The London Scene* (New York: F. Hallman, 1975), 20.
8. On enclave entrepreneurs, see Donna Gabaccia and Franca Iacovetta, *Women, Gender, and Transnational Lives: Italian Workers of the World* (Toronto: University of Toronto Press, 2002).
9. Paul Morand, *A Frenchman's London* (London: Cassell, 1934), 188–9.
10. On Soho as a parallelogram, see Arthur Tietjen, *Soho: London's Vicious Circle* (London: Allan Wingate, 1956).
11. On the republican army of street ramblers, see Woolf, "Street Haunting," 155.
12. Soho's 1901 population is based on a survey of the manuscript census for 1901 of the civil parish of St. Anne, Soho and St. James, Westminster east of Regent Street. *Census of England and Wales, 1901* (London: HMSO, 1902), RG13/100–01, RG13/97, RG13/98. For Soho's population in 1939, see Joseph Rawlinson and W. R. Davidge, *City of Westminster Plan* (London: Westminster City Council, 1946), 38.
13. John Eade, *Placing London: From Imperial City to Global City* (Oxford: Berghahn, 2000), 68.
14. On Soho's outlandish population, see Charles Booth, *Life and Labour of the People of London*, vol. 2, 3rd ser., Religious Influences (London: Macmillan, 1902), 185.
15. Ibid.

16. Count E. Armfelt, "Cosmopolitan London" (1902), in G. R. Sims, ed., *Edwardian London*, vol. 1 (London: Village Press, 1990), 241.

17. For an excellent overview of this literature, see Rebecca L. Walkowitz, *Cosmopolitan Style: Modernism beyond the Nation* (New York: Columbia University Press, 2006), Introduction. See also Pheng Cheah and Bruce Robbins, eds., *Cosmopolitics: Thinking and Feeling beyond the Nation* (Minneapolis: University of Minnesota Press, 1998); Martha Nussbaum, "Patriotism and Cosmopolitanism?" in Joshua Cohen, ed., *Respondents, for Love of Country: Debating the Limits of Patriotism* (Boston: Beacon Press, 1996); Carol A. Breckenridge, Sheldon I. Pollock, and Homi K. Bhabha, *Cosmopolitanism* (Durham, NC: Duke University Press, 2002).

18. On cosmopolitanism as "fatally tainted" and elitist, see Timothy Brennan, quoted in Tanya Agathocleous, "Cosmopolitanism and Literary Form," *Literary Compass* 7, no. 6 (2010): 454. On cosmopolitanism as an intellectual program, see Amanda Anderson, *The Powers of Distance: Cosmopolitanism and the Cultivation of Detachment* (Princeton: Princeton University Press, 2001); Jessica Schiff Berman, *Modernist Fiction, Cosmopolitanism, and the Politics of Community* (Cambridge, UK: Cambridge University Press, 2001).

19. Walkowitz, *Cosmopolitan Style*, 4.

20. James Clifford, "Mixed Feelings," in Cheah and Robbins, *Cosmopolitics*, 362–70.

21. Mica Nava, *Visceral Cosmopolitanism: Gender, Culture and the Normalisation of Difference* (Oxford: Berg, 2007).

22. Arjun Appadurai, "Disjunction and Difference in the Global Cultural Economy," *Public Culture* 2, no. 2 (1990).

23. Stuart Hall, "The Social Eye of *Picture Post*," *Working Papers in Cultural Studies* 2 (1972): 71–87. For the United States, see Michael Denning, *The Cultural Front: The Laboring of American Culture in the Twentieth-Century* (London: Verso, 1996); Lewis A. Erenberg, *Swingin' the Dream: Big Band Jazz and the Rebirth of American Culture* (Chicago: University of Chicago Press, 1998).

24. Agathocleous, "Cosmopolitanism and Literary Form," 454.

25. Ibid., 456; Felix Driver and David Gilbert, *Imperial Cities: Landscape, Display and Identity* (Manchester: Manchester University Press, 1999).

26. *The Times*, June 3, 1897, quoted in Tori Smith, "'A Grand Work of Noble Conception': The Victoria Memorial and Imperial London," in Driver and Gilbert, *Imperial Cities*, 25; Felix Driver and Davis Gilbert, "Heart of Empire? Landscape, Space, and Performance in Imperial London," *Environment and Planning D: Society and Space* 16 (1998): 11–28.

27. Judith R. Walkowitz, "Going Public: Shopping, Street Harassment, and Streetwalking in Late Victorian London," *Representations*, no. 62 (1998), 1–30; Judith R. Walkowitz, "The 'Vision of Salome': Cosmopolitanism and Erotic Dancing in Central London, 1908–1918," *American Historical Review* 108, no. 2 (2003), 337–76; Gavin Weightman, *Bright Lights, Big City: London Entertained, 1830–1950* (London: Collins & Brown, 1992); Erika Diane Rappaport, *Shopping for Pleasure: Women in the Making of London's West End* (Princeton: Princeton University Press, 2000). See also chapters 2–4 of this volume.

28. Walkowitz, "'Vision of Salome,'" 337–76.

29. "Newspaper Clippings," 1898–1907, vols. 14–15, WA.

30. Frank Mort, *Capital Affairs* (London: Yale University Press, 2010). On the convergence of mental and material processes to produce a keyword or binding term, see Raymond Williams, *Keywords: A Vocabulary of Culture and Society* (New York: Oxford University Press, 1976).

31. Cheah and Robbins, *Cosmopolitics*; Walkowitz, *Cosmopolitan Style*; Agathocleous, "Cosmopolitanism and Literary Form."

32. "Newspaper Clippings," vol. 15, WA; "A London Terror," *Sun*, Oct. 2, 1895; "Soho Incident," *Sun* [July 1896].

33. John Galsworthy, *The Forsyte Saga* (New York: Dover, 2002; orig. 1920), 360.

34. Thomas Burke, *Nights in London* (New York: Holt, 1918), 175.

35. Alec Waugh, quoted in Jerry White, *London in the Twentieth Century: A City and Its People* (New York: Viking, 2001), 131.

36. Paul Gilroy, *The Black Atlantic: Modernity and Double Consciousness* (London: Verso, 1993).

37. Nigel Fielding, *The Police and Social Conflict: Rhetoric and Reality* (London: Athlone, 1991); Ross McKibbin, *Classes and Cultures: England, 1918–1951* (Oxford: Oxford University Press, 2000).

38. Kate Meyrick, *Secrets of The 43: Reminiscences by Mrs. Meyrick.* (London: John Long, 1933), 44.

39. Lucio Sponza, *Divided Loyalties: Italians in Britain during the Second World War* (New York: P. Lang, 2000).

40. Jim Fyrth, ed., *Britain, Fascism and the Popular Front* (London: Lawrence & Wishart, 1985); Kevin Morgan, "King Street Blues: Jazz and the Left in Britain in the 1930s–1940s," in Andy Croft, ed., *A Weapon in the Struggle: The Cultural History of the Communist Party in Britain* (London: Pluto, 1998).

41. White, *London in the Twentieth Century*; Mort, *Capital Affairs.*

42. Peter Ackroyd, *London: The Biography* (London: Chatto & Windus, 2000); Roy Porter, *London: A Social History* (London: Hamish Hamilton, 1994); D. J. Taylor, *Bright Young People: The Lost Generation of London's Jazz Age* (New York: Farrar, Straus, & Giroux, 2009).

43. Judith Summers, *Soho: A History of London's Most Colourful Neighbourhood* (London: Bloomsbury, 1989); Gerry Black, *Living Up West: Jewish Life in London's West End* (London: London Museum of Jewish Life, 1994).

44. Matt Houlbrook, *Queer London: Perils and Pleasures in the Sexual Metropolis, 1918–1957* (Chicago: University of Chicago Press, 2005); Matt Cook, *London and the Culture of Homosexuality, 1885–1914* (Cambridge, UK: Cambridge University Press, 2003). See also *Walking after Midnight: Gay Men's Life Stories* (London: Routledge, 1989); Frank Mort, *Cultures of Consumption: Masculinities and Social Space in Late Twentieth-Century Britain* (London: Routledge, 1996); Kevin Porter and Jeffrey Weeks, *Between the Acts: Lives of Homosexual Men 1885–1967* (London: Routledge, 1991).

45. See also George Chauncey, *Gay New York: Gender, Urban Culture, and the Makings of the Gay Male World, 1890–1940* (New York: Basic Books, 1994). Chauncey's new volume will address the racial dimensions of Gay New York history.

46. Alessandro Portelli, "What Makes Oral History Different," in Robert Perks and Alistair Thomson, eds., *The Oral History Reader* (London: Routledge, 1998), 63; Ronald J. Grele, "Movement without Aim: Methodological and Theoretical Problems in Oral History," in Perks and Thomson, *The Oral History Reader*, 38–52.

47. Esther Rose, interview 347, Nov. 9, 1993, WEJ; Andrew Miller, *The Earl of Petticoat Lane* (London: Heinemann, 2006).

48. Eade, *Placing London*, 83. See the Epilogue of this volume.

49. Robert Graves and Alan Hodge, *The Long Week-End: A Social History of Great Britain 1918–1939* (New York: Norton, 1994). New directions in interwar studies have focused on the democratization of consumer culture, but most of them identify the suburbs as sites of innovation, not the city center. See D. L. LeMahieu, *A Culture for Democracy: Mass Communication and the Cultivated Mind in Britain between the Wars* (Oxford: Clarendon Press, 1988); Michael T. Saler, *The Avant-Garde in Interwar England: Medieval Modernism and the London Underground* (Oxford: Oxford University Press, 1999); McKibbin, *Classes and Cultures.*

50. Rawlinson and Davidge, *City of Westminster Plan*, 37.

51. "Inside London's Coloured Clubs: The Moment They Have Been Waiting for," *Picture Post* 20 (July 17, 1943), 29–21

52. Tietjen, *Soho.*

53. Sydney Alexander Moseley, *The Night Haunts of London* (London: Stanley Paul, 1920), 41.

54. On the "women of the painted class," see Moseley, quoted in Matt Houlbrook, "'The Man with the Powder Puff' in Interwar London," *Historical Journal* 50, no. 1 (2007): 169.

55. Houlbrook, "'The Man with the Powder Puff,'" 146.

56. Arthur Ransome, *Bohemia in London* (Oxford: Oxford University Press, 1984; orig. 1907), 110–17.

57. Horace Wyndham and Dorothea Saint John George, *Nights in London . . . With Illustrations by Dorothea St. John George* (London: John Lane, 1926), 54–5.

58. Frances Partridge, *Memories* (London: Gollancz, 1981), 87.

59. Robert Machray, *The Night Side of London* (Philadelphia: J. B. Lippincott, 1902), 4.

60. Deborah Epstein Nord, *Walking the Victorian Streets: Women, Representation, and the City* (Ithaca, NY: Cornell University Press, 1995), 4.

61. H. V. Morton, *H. V. Morton's London, Being the Heart of London, the Spell of London, and the Nights of London, in One Volume*, 18th edn (London: Methuen, 1957), 307–9.

62. On the history of artificial lighting, see Wolfgang Schivelbusch, *Disenchanted Night: The Industrialization of Light in the Nineteenth Century* (Berkeley: University of California Press, 1995); Lynda Nead, *Victorian Babylon: People, Streets, and Images in Nineteenth-Century London* (New Haven: Yale University Press, 2000); Chris Otter, *The Victorian Eye: A Political History of Light and Vision in Britain, 1800–1910* (Chicago: University of Chicago Press, 2008).

63. "Minutes of Proceedings," April 14, 1910, 203–6; July 29, 1926, 389, WCC, WA. Westminster Council oscillated in its use of electrical and gas lighting at the turn of the century. In 1910 it revoked its experiment of using electric arc lights to illuminate most of the main thorough-fares of its district and contracted for high pressure gas lamps. See Nigel E. Pollard, "A Short History of Public Lighting in the City of Westminster," *IPLE Lighting Journal: Official Journal of the Institutions of Public Lighting* (1984): 53–8.

64. Quoted in Gavin Weightman and Steve Humphries, *The Making of Modern London* (London: Ebury Press, 2007), 116.

65. Alan Jenkins, *The Twenties* (London: Heinemann, 1974), 23.

Chapter 1: Cosmopolitan Soho

1. Postcard of St. Anne, Soho, Museum of Soho, London. The postcard reproduces an image from Strype's 1754 version of Stow's *Survey*, which was a replica of a map from the 1720 edition and closely approximated a 1690 map of the parish. On mapping in London after the Great Fire, see Cynthia Wall, *The Literary and Cultural Spaces of Restoration London* (Cambridge, UK: Cambridge University Press, 1998), ch. 3; Peter Ackroyd, *London: The Biography* (London: Chatto & Windus, 2000), ch. 23.

2. F. H. W. Sheppard, "General Introduction," in *Survey of London, Volumes 33 and 34: St Anne Soho* (London, 1966), 3. At http://www.british-history.ac.uk/report.aspx?compid=41022 (accessed May 2011).

3. See also "The Plan of St. Anne's Parish before Street Improvements," in John Henry Cardwell, ed., *Two Centuries of Soho: Its Institutions, Firms, and Amusements* (London: Truslove & Hanson, 1898), 138. At http://www.archive.org/details/twocenturiesofso00cardiala (accessed May 2011).

4. Erika Diane Rappaport, *Shopping for Pleasure: Women in the Making of London's West End* (Princeton: Princeton University Press, 2000); Judith R. Walkowitz, "The 'Vision of Salome': Cosmopolitanism and Erotic Dancing in Central London, 1908–1918," *American Historical Review* 108, no. 2 (2003): 337–76.

5. Rappaport, *Shopping for Pleasure*, 7, 146.

6. Jerry White, *London in the Nineteenth Century: 'A Human Awful Wonder of God'* (London: Cape, 2007), 24; John Summerson, *Georgian London*, new edn (London: Pimlico, 1991).

7. White, *London in the Nineteenth Century*, 24; Rappaport, *Shopping for Pleasure*; Judith R. Walkowitz, "Going Public: Shopping, Street Harassment, and Streetwalking in Late Victorian London," *Representations*, no. 62 (1998): 3.

8. Hermione Hobhouse, *A History of Regent Street* (London: MacDonald and Jane's/Queen Anne Press, 1975), 82.

9. Summerson, *Georgian London*, 162.

10. John Nash, quoted in John Summerson, *John Nash, Architect to King George IV* (London: Allen & Unwin, 1935), 124.

11. Thomas H. Sheppard and James Elmes, *Metropolitan Improvements*, quoted in White, *London in the Nineteenth Century*, 24.

12. Harold P. Clunn, *London Rebuilt, 1897–1927: An Attempt to Depict the Principal Changes Which Have Taken Place, with Some Suggestions for the Further Improvement of the Metropolis* (London: Murray, 1927), 115; "London Restaurant," *What's On*, Feb. 12, 1937, 727.

13. Raphael Samuel, "Introduction," in Wolfgang Suschitzky and Raphael Samuel, *Charing Cross Road in the Thirties* (London: Nishen Photography, 1989).

14. John Eade, *Placing London: From Imperial City to Global City* (Oxford: Berghahn, 2000), 65.

15. Gordon Mackenzie, *Marylebone: Great City North of Oxford Street* (London: Macmillan, 1972), 72.

16. George Duckworth, Oct. 21, 1898, in Charles Booth, *Life and Labour of the People of London: The Charles Booth Collection, 1885–1905 from the British Library of Political and Economic Science, London* (Brighton, UK: Harvester Microform, 1988), B355, 89.

17. Rappaport, *Shopping for Pleasure*, 117–18.

18. Thomas Burke, *The Streets of London Through the Centuries*, 4th edn (London: Batsford, 1949), 145.

19. "Meet Me at . . .," Jan. 4, 1915; "The Magnet of the Streets," Sept. 21, 1915, Selfridges Archives (in Selfridges Department Store), London.

20. W. Macqueen-Pope, *The Melodies Linger On: The Story of the Music Hall* (London: W. H. Allen, 1950), 231.

21. Morris B. Kaplan, *Sodom on the Thames: Sex, Love, and Scandal in Wilde Times* (Ithaca, NY: Cornell University Press, 2005); Mark (pseud.) Benney, *Low Company: Describing the Evolution of a Burglar* (London: Peter Davies, 1936).

22. Duckworth, in Booth, *Life and Labour*, B355, 8–11, 86, 87, 108–9.

23. Soho's 1901 population is based on a survey of the manuscript census for 1901 of the civil parish of St. Anne, Soho and St. James, Westminster east of Regent Street. *Census of England and Wales, 1901* (London: HMSO, 1902), RG13/100–01, RG13/97, RG13/98. Note that St. Anne, Soho also "contracted" as a consequence of the building of the Charing Cross Road, with the area around St. Martin's Lane to the east of the new thoroughfare cut off from the body of the parish.

24. "Charing-Cross Road," *Pall Mall Gazette*, Feb. 26, 1887, 21, 22.

25. Jerry White, *London in the Twentieth Century: A City and Its People* (New York: Viking, 2001), 105.

26. Pamela K. Gilbert, *Mapping the Victorian Social Body* (Albany: State University of New York Press, 2004).

27. "In the Slums of Soho: A Chat with Rev. Cardwell," *Cassell's Saturday Journal*, Aug. 8, 1900, "Newspaper Clippings," vol. 14. WA.

28. Gerry Black, *Living Up West: Jewish Life in London's West End* (London: London Museum of Jewish Life, 1994); Judith Summers, *Soho: A History of London's Most Colourful Neighbourhood* (London: Bloomsbury, 1989); Richard Tames, *Soho Past* (London: Historical Publications, 1994).

29. Inspector McKay, testimony, *Report of the Royal Commission upon the Duties of the Metropolitan Police* (1908), vol. 2, Q.5841–4.

30. Ibid., quoted in Summers, *Soho*, 158–9. See also Joseph McLaughlin, *Writing the Urban Jungle: Reading Empire in London from Doyle to Eliot* (Charlottesville: University Press of Virginia, 2000), 136–9; Eade, *Placing London*, 67–8; "Newspaper Clippings," vol. 15, WA.

31. "The Worst Street in London," *Daily Express*, Oct. 20, 1906, "Newspaper Clippings," vol. 14, WA. G. R. Sims leant credibility to McKay's claims in a seven-part series in the *Daily Telegraph*, where he exposed a "foreign syndicate" of bullies and white slavers who frequented Soho gambling clubs. "Violent and lawless," these men were a constant source of "anxiety and trouble, not only to the local police, but to the special department [i.e. Special Branch] which has to guard against the commission of diabolical outrages both here and abroad." George Robert Sims, *Watches of the Night* (London: Greening, 1907), 45. By eliding political exiles with other traffickers in vice, Sims lent support to the anti-alien propaganda targeting "undesirable aliens" for deportation under the Aliens Act of 1905.

32. "Topics of the Day: The Worst Street," *Evening Standard*, Oct. 20, 1906; "News Clippings," vol. 14, WA.

33. "Worst Street," "News Clippings," vol. 14, WA. See also John Henry Cardwell, ed., *Twenty Years in Soho: A Review of the Work of the Church in the Parish of St. Anne's, Soho from 1891 to 1911* (London: Truslove & Hanson, 1911).

34. Rosemary Ashton, *Little Germany: Exile and Asylum in Victorian England* (Oxford: Oxford University Press, 1986), 99.

35. Haia Shpayer-Makov, "Anarchism in British Public Opinion 1880–1914," *Victorian Studies* 31, no. 4 (1988): 487–516.

36. Guy Deghy and Keith Waterhouse, *Café Royal: Ninety Years of Bohemia* (London: Hutchinson, 1955), 54.

37. See "8000 Anarchists in London," *Daily Express*, Dec. 2, 1894, 2. See also *Morning Leader* (London), Feb. 17, 19, 20, 24, 1894; H. Oliver, *The International Anarchist Movement in Late Victorian London* (Beckenham, UK: Croom Helm, 1983), ch. 5. On terrorism and the Special Branch, see Bernard Porter, *The Origins of the Vigilant State: The London Metropolitan Police Special Branch before the First World War* (London: Weidenfeld & Nicolson, 1987).

38. Soho as a "paradise for pimps", quoted in Summers, *Soho*, 155.

39. Conference at St. Anne, quoted in Summers, *Soho*, 157.

40. *Report of the Royal Commission on Alien Immigration, with Minutes of Evidence and Appendix, Volume 1: The Report* (1903), 18. Although he was unable to identify the prior occupational history of foreign prostitutes, Ankur Sherwell characterized British women who frequented Piccadilly Circus and ultimately entered Salvation Army rescue homes as follows: "it is . . . [an] impressive fact, that so many of the girls who regularly frequent Piccadilly, and Regent Street, and the other thoroughfares of the West are drawn from domestic service, where the rigors of the economic struggle are certainly not so severely felt." Arthur Sherwell, *Life in West London: A Study and a Contrast*, 2nd rev. edn. (London: Methuen, 1897), 147. See Judith R. Walkowitz, *Prostitution and Victorian Society: Women, Class, and the State* (Cambridge, UK: Cambridge University Press, 1980).

41. Edward J. Bristow, *Vice and Vigilance: Purity Movements in Britain since 1700* (Totowa, NJ: Rowman & Littlefield, 1977).

42. Stefan Petrow, *Policing Morals: The Metropolitan Police and the Home Office, 1870–1914* (Oxford: Oxford University Press, 1994), 166–74.

43. "Bogus Clubs," *Daily Telegraph*, April 4, 1896, "Newspaper Clippings," vol. 15, WA.

44. *Lloyd's Weekly News*, n.d., "Newspaper Clippings," vol. 15, WA; "A London Terror," *Sun*, Oct. 2, 1895.

45. "Police Campaign against Indecent Postcards," *Vigilance Record*, Feb. 1906, 23; "Improper Postcards," Jan. 1909, 8; "Obscene Picture Postcards," May 1904, 2.

46. "Soho Incident," *Sun* [July 1896], "Newspaper Clippings," vol. 15, WA.

47. McLaughlin, *Writing the Urban Jungle*.

48. "In the Slums of Soho."

49. "The Soho of To-day: A Chat with the Rev. J. H. Cardwell," *Westminster Observer*, Jan. 23, 1903, "Newspaper Clippings," vol. 14, WA.

50. "In the Slums of Soho."

51. Sherwell, *Life in West London*, 35.

52. Ibid., 57. Sherwell subscribed to the late Victorian discourse on sweating, interpreted more along the lines of a moral and biological disorder of bodies and boundaries than a distinctive labor process and mode of industrial organization.

53. "Interview with Reverend J. H. Cardwell, St. Anne's Soho, 14 June 1898," in Booth, *Life and Labour*, B243.

54. Ibid.; "The Soho of To-day."

55. See, for example, Charles Booth, "Maps Descriptive of London Poverty," 1898–9, at http://booth.lse.ac.uk (accessed Sept 24, 2010).

56. See, for example, Melville MacNaghton, report on "Gundersten" in "Disturbances: Foreign Anarchists coming to the UK," July 27, 1894, HO 144/587/62840c, 38, NA.

57. Cardwell, *Twenty Years in Soho*, vi, 152.
58. "Two Centuries of Soho and the Critics," *St. Anne Soho Monthly Paper*, 7 (1898): 15; Cardwell, *Twenty Years in Soho*, 44–6.
59. George Walter Thornbury and Edward Walford, *Old and New London; Illustrated. A Narrative of Its History, Its People, and Its Places*, vols. 1–4 (London, 1873); Henry Benjamin Wheatley and Peter A. Cunningham, *London Past and Present: Its History, Associations, and Traditions. By H. B. Wheatley. Based Upon the Handbook of London by the Late Peter Cunningham* (London: J. Murray, 1891); Edward Francis Rimbault and George Clinch, *Soho and Its Associations, Historical, Literary and Artistic. Edited from the Mss. of . . . E. F. Rimbault by G. Clinch* (London: Dulau, 1895).
60. Andrea Zemgulys, *Modernism and the Locations of Literary Heritage* (Cambridge, UK: Cambridge University Press, 2008), 83.
61. On the dystopic elements of historical memory and space, see Lynda Nead, *Victorian Babylon: People, Streets, and Images in Nineteenth-Century London* (New Haven: Yale University Press, 2000), 5–6; Billie Melman, *The Culture of History: English Uses of the Past, 1800–1953* (Oxford: Oxford University Press, 2006), 6–9. On heritage as a form of nationalist nostalgia, see Peter Mandler, *The Fall and Rise of the Stately Home* (New Haven: Yale University Press, 1997); Raphael Samuel, *Theatres of Memory* (London: Verso, 1994).
62. George Walter Thornbury, *Old and New London: A Narrative of Its History, Its People, and Its Places*, vol. 3 (London: Cassell, 1887), 173.
63. Donald J. Olsen, *The City as a Work of Art: London, Paris, Vienna* (New Haven: Yale University Press, 1986), 306.
64. "The Uglification of London," *Builder* 72 (Mar. 27, 1897): 287–9.
65. Donald J. Olsen, *The Growth of Victorian London* (New York: Holmes & Meier, 1976); "The Architecture of the Shop Front-II," *Builder* 106 (Jan. 30, 1914): 66–7.
66. John Henry Cardwell, *Men and Women of Soho, Famous and Infamous: Actors, Authors, Dramatists, Entertainers and Engravers* (London: Truslove & Hanson, 1903); Cardwell, *Two Centuries of Soho*.
67. Sir Walter Besant, "Preface," in Cardwell, *Two Centuries of Soho*, vii.
68. Ibid., x.
69. Cardwell, *Two Centuries of Soho*, 41.
70. Ibid., 62–5. Most of the charities restricted their efforts to the English poor, but there were some exceptions. The London City Mission hired an Italian missionary to work in Soho, while Mission officials enumerated foreigners from 22 nations in attendance at their services.
71. Summers, *Soho*, 132.
72. Cardwell, *Two Centuries of Soho*, 114.
73. Ibid., 65.
74. Margot C. Finn, *After Chartism: Class and Nation in English Radical Politics, 1848–1874* (Cambridge, UK: Cambridge University Press, 1993); Stan Shipley, *Club Life and Socialism in Mid-Victorian London* (Oxford: History Workshop, Ruskin College, 1971).
75. Cardwell, *Two Centuries of Soho*, 104.
76. Ibid., 223.
77. Ibid., 264, 239.
78. Ibid., 185, 192, 196.
79. Ibid., 158–64.
80. Ibid., 189.
81. Ibid., 188–9. Wardour Street's notoriety for fake antiques engendered the derogatory term "Wardour Street English," to refer to those spurious archaisms in historical novels "which set out to show us how men spoke in a particular age and succeed only in giving us something which men never spoke in any age." Thomas R. Lounsbury, "Wardour Street English," *Harper's Monthly* 119 (June 1909): 87; "Wardour-Street English," *Littell's Living Age*, 179 (1888): 500; John Harris, *Moving Rooms* (New Haven: Yale University Press, 2007).
82. Cardwell, *Two Centuries of Soho*, 67–8.
83. Ibid., 180.

84. Ibid., 208.

85. Ibid., 263.

86. Ibid., 265–94.

87. Ibid., 290–1.

88. "Soho and Its Restaurants," *Caterer and Hotel-Keeper*, June 15, 1906, 262–6; "Soho and Its Restaurants," July 16, 1906, 304–6; "Soho and Its Restaurants: III. Gerrard Street, Dryden, and the Origins of Coffee Houses," Aug. 15, 1906, 338–40; "Soho and Its Restaurants: IV. Gerrard Street (Continued)—the Literary Club and the Italian Element," Nov. 15, 1906, 480–2; "Soho and Its Restaurants: V. Gerrard Street (Continued)—a Notable Cosmopolitan Career," Dec. 15, 1906, 542–4; "Soho and Its Restaurants: VI. Lisle Street," Feb. 15, 1907, 84; "Soho and Its Restaurants: VII. Leicester Square," Mar. 15, 1907, 112–13.

89. "Soho and Its Restaurants," June 15, 1906, 263.

90. While concentrating on the streets within St. Anne, Soho, the *Caterer's* series on Soho also mentioned establishments west of Wardour Street, such as the Florence, and even bakers north of Oxford Street in Charlotte Street.

91. "Soho and Its Restaurants," June 15, 1906, 262.

92. Ibid., July 16, 1906, 304–5.

93. Ibid., June 15, 1906, 265.

94. Robert Machray, *The Night Side of London* (London: John Macqueen, 1902), 98.

95. "Soho and Its Restaurants: III," July 16, 1906, 339.

96. On "wily, handy Italians", see Howard Paul, "A Dinner at Kettner's," *Caterer and Hotel-Keeper*, Feb. 15, 1898, 64.

97. "Soho and Its Restaurants: V," 542–4.

98. On Escoffier, haute cuisine, and London, see Stephen Mennell, *All Manners of Food: Eating and Taste in England and France from the Middle Ages to the Present* (Oxford: Basil Blackwell, 1985), 134–65; John Burnett, *England Eats Out: A Social History of Eating out in England from 1830 to the Present* (New York: Longman, 2004), 151–8; Amy B. Trubek, *Haute Cuisine: How the French Invented the Culinary Profession* (Philadelphia: University of Pennsylvania Press, 2000), 42–51.

99. "Soho and Its Restaurants: V," 543. See also in *Caterer and Hotel-Keeper*: "Italian Cookery and Its Exponents," Mar. 15, 1900, 211–12; "The Italian Caterer's Methods," Feb. 16, 1903, 57; "A Veteran Caterer's Memories, Aug.–Sept. 1928, 54.

100 Peter Barber and Peter Jacomelli, *Continental Taste: Ticinese Emigrants and Their Café-Restaurants in Britain, 1847–1987* (London: Camden History Society, 1997). See chapter 4, this volume.

101. Eade, *Placing London*, 6.

102. "Open-Air Cafés," *Caterer and Hotel-Keeper*, July 16, 1906, 13.

103. Arthur Ransome, *Bohemia in London* (Oxford: Oxford University Press, 1984; repr. of 1907 edn); Frank Mort, *Cultures of Consumption: Masculinities and Social Space in Late Twentieth-Century Britain* (New York: Routledge, 1996).

104. On the transmission of bohemia into English literary culture, see Hugh David, *The Fitzrovians: A Portrait of Bohemian Society, 1900–1955* (London: Michael Joseph, 1988); Peter Brooker, *Bohemia in London: The Social Scene of Early Modernism* (Houndmills, UK: Palgrave Macmillan, 2004).

105. Ransome, *Bohemia in London*, 5.

106. Ibid., 6.

107. Ibid., 124, 110.

108. Ibid., 127.

109. Ibid., 110–17.

110. Old Compton Street had been Soho's main shopping street since the eighteenth century (and was the favored resort of Verlaine and Rimbaud, who gave literary readings there in the 1870s when they were in exile in London). Founded in 1848, Roche's already enjoyed a worldwide reputation for the quality of its cooking at economic prices. David, *The Fitzrovians*, 36.

111. Ibid., 37.
112. Ransome, *Bohemia in London*, 112–13.
113. Ibid.
114. Ibid., 129.
115. "Our Booking Office," *Punch*, Oct. 6, 1907, 288.
116. Brooker, *Bohemia in London*, 6.
117. Rupert Croft-Cooke, *Feasting with Panthers: A New Consideration of Some Late Victorian Writers* (London: W. H. Allen, 1967).
118. Ed Cohen, *Talk on the Wilde Side: Towards a Genealogy of a Discourse on Male Sexualities* (New York: Routledge, 1993), 197; Kaplan, *Sodom on the Thames*, 235.
119. Brooker, *Bohemia in London*, 8.
120. Joseph Conrad, *The Secret Agent* (New York: Bantam Books, 1984; repr. of 1907 edn); A. N. Wilson, *The Faber Book of London* (London: Faber and Faber, 1993); Rick Allen, *The Moving Pageant: A Literary Sourcebook on London Street-Life, 1700–1914* (London: Routledge, 1998), 271–3.
121. Eileen Sypher, "Anarchism and Gender," *Henry James Review* 9, no. 1 (1988): 15.
122. Tames, *Soho Past*, 44–5.
123. On the pastness of *The Secret Agent*, see Wendy Lesser, "From Dickens to Conrad: A Sentimental Journey," *English Literary History* 52, no. 1 (1985): 201.
124. Conrad, *The Secret Agent*, 108.
125. Ibid., 107.
126. Ibid.
127. Ibid., 40, 106.
128. Ibid., 1.
129. On the treatment of the pornography shop, see in particular Brian Shaffer, "The Commerce of 'Shady Wares': Politics and Pornography in Conrad's *The Secret Agent*," *English Literary History* 12, no. 2 (1995): 443–66; Rishona Zimring, "Conrad's Pornography Shop," *Modern Fiction Studies* 43, no. 2 (1997): 319–48.
130. Shaffer, "The Commerce of 'Shady Wares,'" 445.
131. Conrad, *The Secret Agent*, 1.
132. Ibid., 1–2; Rebecca L. Walkowitz, *Cosmopolitan Style: Modernism beyond the Nation* (New York: Columbia University Press, 2006), 47.
133. Conrad, *The Secret Agent*, 2.
134. Ibid. On Winnie and the shopgirl, see Elizabeth Carolyn Miller, *Framed: The New Woman Criminal in British Culture at the Fin de Siècle* (Ann Arbor: University of Michigan Press, 2008), 180. On tableaux vivants, see Zimring, "Conrad's Pornography Shop," 334; Shaffer, "The Commerce of 'Shady Wares,'" 458.
135. Conrad, *The Secret Agent*, 107.
136. Ibid.
137. Ibid.
138. Ibid.
139. Ibid., 108.
140. Ibid., 9.
141. Ibid.
142. Ibid.
143. "A Georgian House in Danger," *The Times*, Jan. 9, 1914, 9.
144. The 1913 Act superseded earlier preservationist Acts of 1882, 1900, and 1910, considerably extending the meaning of historic interest and importance to include vernacular houses like 75 Dean Street. Besides the extensive publications of historical topographies, the cultural effort to document "Vanishing London" inspired the formation of the Society for Photographing Relics of Old London, and the monumental *Survey of London*, under the leadership of the London County Council (LCC). The earliest preservationist society was William Morris's National Society for the Protection of Ancient Buildings, founded in 1877. By 1898, the LCC had obtained authority to purchase or to support the "preservation of

buildings and places of architectural or historical interest." See Hermione Hobhouse, *Lost London: A Century of Demolition and Decay* (London: Macmillan, 1971), 6–8.

145. "The Georgian House in Soho," *The Times*, Jan. 15, 1914, 9.

146. "A Soho House," *Manchester Guardian*, Dec. 16, 1912, 7.

147. "The Georgian House in Soho," Jan. 15, 1914, 9.

148. May Morris, "Arts and Crafts: The Future of 75, Dean-Street," *The Times*, Jan. 26, 1914; C. R. Ashbee, "Introduction," in *The Survey of London* (New York: AMS Press 1971), xxxvi.

149. "A Georgian House in Danger," 9.

150. George Laurence Gomme, *London* (Philadelphia: J. B. Lippincott, 1914), 323.

151. "The Preservation of No. 75, Dean-Street," *The Times*, Jan. 17, 1914.

152. Ibid.

153. Hobhouse, *Lost London*, 27.

154. Harris, *Moving Rooms*, 104.

155. "The Georgian House in Soho," *The Times*, May 23, 1914, 5.

156. "The Hogarth House in Soho: Vandalism Far Advanced," *The Times*, May 3, 1919, 9.

157. John Harris, "What Might Be Called a Frame-Up: The Hogarth House," *British Art Journal* 1, no. 1 (2000): 19–21.

Chapter 2: Battle of the Empire

1. "They All Loved Leicester Square," *Queen* (1950), Empire Theatre File, TM.

2. *The Sketch*, quoted in Barry Faulk, *Music Hall and Modernity: The Late-Victorian Discovery of Popular Culture* (Athens: Ohio University Press, 2004), 77.

3. Robert Machray, *The Night Side of London* (Philadelphia: J. B. Lippincott, 1902).

4. "London County Council: The Licensing Committee," *Music Hall and Theatre Review*, Oct. 12, 1894, 12–14.

5. The "Prudes on the Prowl" correspondence in the *Daily Telegraph* appeared on the following days: Oct. 13, 15, 16, 17, 18, 19, and 20, 1894.

6. "Mrs. Prowlina Pry—I Hope I Don't Intrude," *Punch*, Oct. 27, 1894, 194.

7. Lisa Tickner, *The Spectacle of Women: Imagery of the Suffrage Campaign, 1907–14* (Chicago: University of Chicago Press, 1988), 169.

8. On the visual iconography of the spinster advocate of women's rights, see Charles Harrison, *Theatricals and Tableaux Vivants for Amateurs. Giving Full Directions as to Stage Arrangements, "Making up," Costumes and Acting* (London: L. Upcott Gill, 1882); Tickner, *The Spectacle of Women*, 160.

9. One reading of this image is provided by Faulk, *Music Hall and Modernity*, 88.

10. Tracy Davis, *Actresses as Working Women: Their Social Identity in Victorian Culture* (London: Routledge, 1991), 155.

11. Winston Churchill, *My Early Life: A Roving Commission* (New York: Scribner's, 1930), 156–57; Gareth Stedman Jones, "Working-Class Culture and Working-Class Politics in London, 1870–1900: Notes on the Remaking of a Working Class," *Journal of Social History* 7 (1974): 496; Susan D. Pennybacker, *A Vision for London, 1889–1914: Labour, Everyday Life and the LCC Experiment* (London: Routledge, 1995), 167; Chris Waters, "Progressives, Puritans, and the Council, 1889–1914," in Andrew Saint, ed., *Politics and the People of London: The London County Council, 1889–1965* (London: Hambledon, 1989), 59–60.

12. Henry George Hibbert, "Empire Theatre to Be Closed: Mr. Butt Takes a Step Which Costs Thousands; What the Promenade Was," *Weekly Dispatch*, July 23, 1916.

13. Jones, "Working-Class Culture," 495–6; Penelope Summerfield, "The Effingham Arms and the Empire: Deliberate Selection in the Evolution of Music Hall in London," in Eileen Yeo and Stephen Yeo, eds., *Popular Culture and Class Conflict, 1590–1914: Explorations in the History of Labour and Leisure* (Atlantic Highlands, NJ: Humanities Press, 1981), 209–40; Davis, *Actresses as Working Women*; Edward J. Bristow, *Vice and Vigilance: Purity Movements in Britain since 1700* (Totowa, NJ: Rowman & Littlefield, 1977); John Stokes, *In the Nineties* (New York: Harvester Wheatsheaf, 1989); Amy Koritz, *Gendering Bodies/Performing Art: Dance and*

Literature in Early Twentieth-Century British Culture (Ann Arbor: University of Michigan Press, 1995); Faulk, *Music Hall and Modernity*.

14. Felix Driver and David Gilbert, *Imperial Cities: Landscape, Display and Identity (Studies in Imperialism)* (Manchester: Manchester University Press, 1999); T. C. Barker and Michael Robbins, *A History of London Transport: Passenger Travel and the Development of the Metropolis*, 2 vols. (London: Allen & Unwin for London Transport Executive, 1975–6).

15. On transnational moral purity feminism, see Ian R. Tyrrell, *Woman's World/Woman's Empire: The Woman's Christian Temperance Union in International Perspective, 1880–1930* (Chapel Hill: University of North Carolina Press, 1991).

16. "Mrs. Chant in America," *Vigilance Record*, May 1890, 47, 48.

17. "Mrs. Ormiston Chant: Interview," *Women's Penny Paper* (1888): 1.

18. Sarah Blair, "Local Modernity, Global Modernism: Bloomsbury and the Places of Literacy," *English Literary History* 71, no. 3 (2004): 820.

19. "Mrs. Ormiston Chant: Interview."

20. Marjory Lester, "Family Histories," MS, n.d.; Richard Nickson, "G.B.S. and Laura Ormiston Chant—Man and Superwoman," *Independent Shavian* 37, nos. 1–2 (1999); Joseph W. Donohue, *Fantasies of Empire: The Empire Theatre of Varieties and the Licensing Controversy of 1894* (Iowa City: University of Iowa Press, 2005), 23–4; "Mrs. Chant in America."

21. Nadja Durbach, *Bodily Matters: The Anti-Vaccination Movement in England, 1853–1907* (Durham, NC: Duke University Press, 2005); Gayle V. Fischer, *Pantaloons and Power: Nineteenth-Century Dress Reform in the United States* (Kent, OH: Kent State University Press, 2001); Stella Mary Newton, *Health, Art and Reason: Dress Reformers of the 19th Century* (London: J. Murray, 1974).

22. Chant's political commitments were expressive of her heterodox Christianity and commitment to a universal brotherhood of man (i.e. cosmopolitanism in the Kantian sense). She was a Dreyfusard, theosophist, participant in the 1893 World Parliament of Religions, and head of a delegation of nurses who went behind the lines during the Greek-Turkish conflict in Crete in 1899. See Philippa Levine, "Chant, Laura Ormiston, 1884–1923," in *Oxford Dictionary of National Biography*, at http://www.oxforddnb.com/view/article/49196 (accessed Sept. 14, 2010).

23. "The Plague in India," *Vigilance Record*, Jan. 1889, 140; "Editorial Notes," *Vigilance Record*, Jan. 15, 1888, 55.

24. John P. Burris, *Exhibiting Religion: Colonialism and Spectacle at International Expositions, 1851–1893* (Charlottesville: University of Virginia Press, 2001).

25. Paul A. Kramer, "Empires, Exceptions, and Anglo-Saxons: Race and Rule between the British and the United States Empires, 1880–1910," *Journal of American History* 88, no. 4 (2002): 1315–53.

26. Quoted in Benny Green, *The Last Empires: A Music Hall Companion* (London: Pavilion, 1986), 72.

27. Mary P. Ryan, *Women in Public: Between Banners and Ballots, 1825–1880* (Baltimore: Johns Hopkins University Press, 1990), 78.

28. Lynda Nead, *Victorian Babylon: People, Streets, and Images in Nineteenth-Century London* (New Haven: Yale University Press, 2000); Patrick Joyce, *The Rule of Freedom: Liberalism and the Modern City* (London: Verso, 2003); Miles Ogborn, *Spaces of Modernity: London's Geographies, 1680–1780* (New York: Guilford, 1998); James H. Winter, *London's Teeming Streets: 1830–1914* (New York: Routledge, 1993).

29. Joyce, *The Rule of Freedom*, 64.

30. Some of this logic of governmentality derives from the LCC's primary oversight with regard to the physical safety of buildings, an oversight it extended to music and dancing licenses. The same inspectors sent out to examine the exits and sanitary conditions of the buildings also reported on the entertainment. Waters, "Progressives, Puritans, and the Council," 58–61.

31. Judith R. Walkowitz, *Prostitution and Victorian Society: Women, Class, and the State* (Cambridge, UK: Cambridge University Press, 1980); Judith R. Walkowitz, *City of Dreadful Delight: Narratives of Sexual Danger in Late-Victorian London* (Chicago: University of Chicago Press,

1992); Lucy Bland, *Banishing the Beast: English Feminism and Sexual Morality, 1885–1914* (London: Penguin, 1995); Frank Mort, *Dangerous Sexualities: Medico-Moral Politics in England since 1830*, 2nd edn (London: Routledge, 2000); Donohue, *Fantasies of Empire*.

32. Laura Ormiston Chant, "Women and the Streets," in James Marchant, ed., *Public Morals* (London: Morgan & Scott, 1902), 129.

33. Judith R. Walkowitz, "Going Public: Shopping, Street Harassment, and Streetwalking in Late Victorian London," *Representations* 62 (1998): 11–12.

34. Susan J. Ferry, "Bodily Knowledge: Female Body Culture and Subjectivity in Manchester, 1870–1900," dissertation, Johns Hopkins University, 2003.

35. Laura Ormiston Chant, "Woman as an Athlete, a Reply to Dr. Arabella Kenealy," *Littell's Living Age*, June 1899, 802–6.

36. On feminism and physical culture, see E. M. King, *Rational Dress; or, the Dress of Women and Savages* (London: Kegan Paul, 1882); Newton, *Health, Art and Reason*.

37. King, *Rational Dress*, 26–7; "Notes and Comments," *Rational Dress Gazette*, Jan. 1899, 15; "How Will Dress Reform Affect Trade and the Well-Being of English Work People?" *Rational Dress Gazette*, Oct. 1899, 51–2.

38. King, *Rational Dress*, 13.

39. Ken Montague, "The Aesthetics of Hygiene: Aesthetic Dress, Modernity, and the Body as Sign," *Journal of Design History* 7, no. 2 (1994): 91.

40. Walkowitz, *City of Dreadful Delight*, chs. 1 and 2.

41. Laura Ormiston Chant, "Amused London No. I," *Vigilance Record*, June 1888, 5; "Amused London No. II," *Vigilance Record*, July 1888, 69; "Amused London No. III," *Vigilance Record*, Aug. 1888, 81, 82; "Amused London No. IV," *Vigilance Record*, Sept. 1888, 89; "Amused London No. V," *Vigilance Record*, April 1888, 28.

42. Albert Chevalier, *Albert Chevalier: A Record by Himself. Biographical and Other Chapters by Brian Daly* (London: John Macqueen, 1895), 134.

43. Chant, "Amused London No. I."

44. Susan A. Glenn, "Reflections on 'the Body' in Labor History," *Labor: Studies in Working-Class History of the Americas* 4, no. 2 (2007): 51.

45. Chant, "Amused London No. IV"; Carolyn Steedman, *Strange Dislocations: Childhood and the Idea of Human Interiority, 1780–1930* (Cambridge, MA: Harvard University Press, 1995).

46. Chant, "Amused London No. IV."

47. Chant, "Amused London No. II"; Chant, "Amused London No. III."

48. Chant, "Amused London No. II."

49. Ibid.

50. Davis, *Actresses as Working Women*, 155.

51. Arnold Bennett, *A Man from the North* (New York: George H. Doran, 1911), 11.

52. John Hollingshead, *The Story of Leicester Square* (London: Simpkin & Marshall, 1892), 40.

53. Ibid., 63.

54. Richard D. Altick, *The Shows of London* (Cambridge, MA: Belknap Press, 1978), 229.

55. "Opening of Leicester-Square This Day," Box 3, "Leicester Square/Savile House," in John Johnson Collection, Bodleian Library, University of Oxford.

56. Altick, *The Shows of London*, 489.

57. "Destruction of Savile House," *Illustrated London News*, Mar. 11, 1865, 238.

58. Altick, *The Shows of London*, 345–6.

59. Green, *The Last Empires*, 36; Raymond Mander and Joe Mitchenson, *The Lost Theatres of London* (London: New English Library, 1968; repr. 1976), 17.

60. Donohue, *Fantasies of Empire*, 47.

61. Marvin Colson, *Places of Performance: The Semiotics of Theatre Architecture* (Ithaca, NY: Cornell University Press, 1989); "Bohemian Round the Empire: An Evening with Mr. Slater," *The Sketch*, May 30, 1894, 252.

62. Daniel Joseph Kirwan, *Palace and Hovel: Or, Phases of London Life, Being Personal Observations on an American in London* (Hartford: Belknap & Bliss, 1870), 467.

63. W. Macqueen-Pope, "Old-Time Magic of the Empire," *Everybody's*, Dec. 31, 1949; Tom Taylor, *Leicester Square: Its Associations and Its Worthies* (London: Bickers, 1874), Empire Theatre File, TM.

64. Tom Taylor, "Leicester Square," Leicester Square Scrapbook, St. Martin in the Fields, vol. 1/1, WA.

65. Emily Constance Cook, *Highways and Byways of London* (London: Macmillan, 1907), 286; Justin McCarthy, *Reminiscences*, vol. 1 (London: Chatto & Windus, 1899), 102.

66. Symons, quoted in Peter Brooker, *Bohemia in London: The Social Scene of Early Modernism* (Houndmills, UK: Palgrave Macmillan, 2004), 32.

67. Jane Pritchard, "Genée, Dame Adeline, 1878–1970," in *Oxford Dictionary of National Biography*, at http://www.oxforddnb.com/view/article/33368 (accessed Sept. 14, 2010).

68. Amy Koritz, "Moving Violations: Dance in the London Music Hall, 1890–1910," *Theatre Journal* 42, no. 4 (1990): 428.

69. For commentaries on the working girl who was neither a prostitute nor a lady, but in command of an erotically charged "glamor," see Alexandra Carter, "Over the Footlights and under the Moon: Images of Dancers in the Ballet at the Alhambra and Empire Palaces of Varieties, 1884–1915," *Dance Research Journal* 28, no. 1 (1996): 7–18; Peter Bailey, " 'Naughty but Nice': Musical Comedy and the Rhetoric of the Girl, 1892–1914," in Michael R. Booth and Joel H. Kaplan, eds., *The Edwardian Theatre: Essays on Performance and the Stage* (Cambridge, UK: Cambridge University Press, 1996), 36–60.

70. Gavin Weightman, *Bright Lights, Big City: London Entertained, 1830–1950* (London: Collins & Brown, 1992), 78–9.

71. "They All Loved Leicester Square," *Queen* (1950), 24–6.

72. Beaumont, quoted in Ivor Forbes Guest, *Ballet in Leicester Square: The Alhambra and the Empire, 1860–1915* (London: Dance Books, 1992), 92.

73. Quoted in Green, *The Last Empires*, 72.

74. "Empire Theatre of Varieties, 1889–1904," Theatre and Music Halls Presented Papers, LCC 10, 803, LMA. The "backs of theatres" would remain "sodomite" strongholds throughout the early twentieth century. In the early twentieth century, a German sexologist was astonished to observe "two hundred urnings, soldiers, prostitutes, and pseudohomosexuals crowded shoulder to shoulder" in the parterre of the Empire promenade. Magnus Hirschfield, *The Homosexuality of Men and Women* (Amherst, NY: Prometheus, 2000), 791.

75. "County of London Sessions," *The Times*, July 16, 1892, 16; "Police," *The Times*, July 18, 1902, 13.

76. Donohue, *Fantasies of Empire*, 57. See chapter 3 of this volume.

77. As Stokes has observed, Coote's challenge to the Living Pictures "reinvigorated the old topic of the 'naked' versus the 'nude,' " a dichotomy that depended on a certain representation of the undraped female body. Stokes, *In the Nineties*, 77. See also Alison Smith, Robert Upstone, and Tate Britain, *Exposed: The Victorian Nude* (New York: Watson-Guptill, 2002), 2, 8, 166–8.

78. Mrs. Chant, "Transcript Testimony," Oct. 10, 1894, 11, Empire Theatre of Varieties, LCC MIN 10, 803, LMA; Laura Ormiston Chant, *Why We Attacked the Empire* (London: Horace Marshall, 1895), 5.

79. "London County Council," 12.

80. Mrs. Chant, "Transcript Testimony," 4.

81. Ibid.

82. Donohue, *Fantasies of Empire*, 99.

83. Mrs. Chant, quoted in "London County Council," 13.

84. "A Facer," *Moonshine*, Oct. 24, 1894, 193.

85. Chant, "Transcript Testimony," 13.

86. Ibid., 14.

87. Ibid., 14, 15.

88. Ibid., 16. Mrs. Sheldon Amos, "Transcript Testimony," 1894, 48, 49; Miss Reed, "Transcript Testimony," 1896, 224, 215, 204, LCC MIN 10, 803, LMA.

89. Mrs. Chant, "Transcript Testimony," 7.

90. Ibid.

91. Ibid., 9.

92. "London County Council."

93. Georg Simmel, *Simmel on Culture: Selected Writings*, ed. David Frisby and Mike Featherstone (London: Sage, 1997), 175; Peter Bailey, "Adventures in Space: Victorian Railway Erotics, or Taking Alienation for a Ride," *Journal of Victorian Culture* 9, no. 1 (2004): 1–21.

94. "Englishman to the Editor," *Daily Telegraph*, Oct. 13, 1894, 5.

95. Faulk, *Music Hall and Modernity*; Donohue, *Fantasies of Empire*, 50.

96. G. B. Shaw, quoted in Faulk, *Music Hall and Modernity*, 81.

97. Ibid., 81.

98. Brooker, *Bohemia in London*, 29.

99. Karl E. Beckson, *Arthur Symons: A Life* (Oxford: Clarendon Press, 1987); Brooker, *Bohemia in London*; Stokes, *In the Nineties*.

100. See, for example, the statements of Mr. Gill, the solicitor defending the Empire management. "Transcript," Oct. 14, 1894, LCC MIN 10,803, LMA.

101. "A Facer," Engraving, *Judy*, Oct. 24, 1894, 193.

102. "Suggested New Empire Costume," Engraving, from *Moonshine*, Oct. 27, 1894, 194.

103. Kramer, "Empires, Exceptions, and Anglo-Saxons"; Charles Wentworth Dilke, *Problems of Greater Britain*, 4th rev. edn (New York: Macmillan, 1890).

104. "The Finest Stage Crowd of Recent Years: 'Votes for Women,' " *The Sketch*, May 15, 1907, 13.

105. Katrina Rolley, "Fashion, Femininity, and the Fight for the Vote," *Art History* 13 (1990): 47–71; Angela V. John, *Elizabeth Robins: Staging a Life, 1862–1952* (London: Routledge, 1995); Penny Farfan, "From *Hedda Gabler* to *Votes for Women*: Elizabeth Robins's Early Feminist Critique of Ibsen," *Theatre Journal* 48, no. 1 (1996): 59–78; Laura Winkiel, "Suffrage Burlesque: Modernist Performance in Elizabeth Robins's *The Convert*," *Modern Fiction Studies* 50, no. 3 (2004): 570–94; Susan Torrey Barstow, " 'Hedda Is All of Us': Late Victorian Women at the Matinee," *Victorian Studies* 43, no. 3 (2001): 387–411.

106. Chant, *Why We Attacked the Empire*, 5.

107. Donohue, *Fantasies of Empire*, 236–8.

108. Frank Mort, *Cultures of Consumption: Masculinities and Social Space in Late Twentieth-Century Britain* (London: Routledge, 1996), 187.

Chapter 3: The "Vision of Salome"

1. *New Jersey Telegraph*, Mar. 23, 1908, Maud Allan Clippings, NYPL.

2. On the history of early modern dance and its relation to the ballet, see Ann Daly, *Done into Dance: Isadora Duncan in America* (Bloomington: Indiana University Press, 1995); Linda Tomko, *Dancing Class: Gender, Ethnicity, and Social Divides in American Dance, 1890–1920* (Bloomington: Indiana University Press, 1999); Lynn Garafola, *Diaghilev's Ballets Russes* (New York: Da Capo Press, 1998; orig. 1989); Ivor Guest, *Ballet in Leicester Square: The Alhambra and the Empire, 1860–1915* (London: Dance Books, 1992). Two early histories of turn-of-the-century dance include J. E. Crawford Flitch, *Modern Dancing and Dancers* (London: Grant, Richards, 1912); Troy Kinney and Margaret Kinney, *The Dance: Its Place in Art and Life* (1914; repr. New York, 1935). On the English country dance revival, see Georgina Boyes, *The Imagined Village: Culture, Ideology and the English Folk Revival* (Manchester: Manchester University Press, 1996); Daniel J. Walkowitz, *City Folk: English Country Dance and the Politics of the Folk in Modern America* (New York: New York University Press, 2010).

3. "Maud Allan the Rage in London," *New York World* [1908], Allan Clippings.

4. Critical works on Maud Allan's dancing career include Philip Hoare, *Wilde's Last Stand: Decadence, Conspiracy and the First World War* (London: Duckworth, 1997); Deborah Jowitt, *Time and the Dancing Image* (Berkeley: University of California Press, 1989); Amy Koritz, *Gendering Bodies/Performing Art: Dance and Literature in Early Twentieth-Century British Culture* (Ann Arbor: University of Michigan Press, 1995); Susan Manning, "The Female

Dancer and the Male Gaze: Feminist Critiques of Early Modern Dance," in Gay Morris, ed., *Moving Words: Re-writing Dance* (New York: Routledge, 1996), 153–66; Felix Cherniavsky, *Did She Dance: Maud Allan in Performance*, CD-ROM (Toronto: Arts Inter-Media Canada/ Dance Collection Danse, c.1991); Felix Cherniavsky, *The Salome Dancer: The Life and Times of Maud Allan* (Toronto: McClelland & Stewart, c.1991); Elaine Showalter, *Sexual Anarchy: Gender and Culture at the Fin de Siècle* (New York: Viking, 1990). Works that also focus on her participation in the 1918 libel trial include Hoare, *Wilde's Last Stand*; Lucy Bland, "Trial by Sexology? Maud Allan, *Salome*, and the Cult of the Clitoris Case," in Lucy Bland and Laura Doan, eds., *Sexology in Culture: Labelling Bodies and Desires* (Chicago: University of Chicago Press, 1998), 183–97; Michael Kettle, *Salome's Last Veil: The Libel Case of the Century* (London: Hart-Davis, 1977); Jennifer Travis, "Clits in Court: *Salome*, Sodomy, and the Lesbian 'Sadist,'" in Karla Jay, ed., *Lesbian Erotics* (New York: New York University Press, 1995), 147–63; Laura Doan, *Fashioning Sapphism: The Origins of a Modern English Lesbian Culture* (New York: Columbia University Press, 2000).

5. "Maud Allan's Salome Dance," *New Jersey Sun*, Aug. 9, 1908, Allan Clippings.

6. On the Edwardian variety theater, see Dave Russell, "Varieties of Life: The Making of the Edwardian Music Hall," in Michael Booth and Joel H. Kaplan, eds., *The Edwardian Theatre: Essays on Performance and the Stage* (Cambridge, UK: Cambridge University Press, 1996), 61–85.

7. On Marcel Remy and Ferrucio Busoni, see Maud Allan, *My Life and Dancing* (London: Everett, 1908), 51–69; Cherniavsky, *The Salome Dancer*, 122, 123.

8. Julie Wheelwright, *The Fatal Lover: Mata Hari and the Myth of Women in Espionage* (London: Collins & Brown, 1992), 19–24. For a description of Allan's costume, see Noel Pemberton Billing, *Verbatim Report of the Trial of Noel Pemberton Billing, M.P., on a Charge of Common Libel* (London: Vigilante, 1918), 90.

9. Felix Cherniavsky, "Maud Allan, Part II: First Steps to a Dancing Career, 1904–1907," *Dance Chronicle* 6, no. 3 (1983): 139.

10. Cherniavsky, *The Salome Dancer*, 173, 174; Hoare, *Wilde's Last Stand*, 80.

11. On Margot Asquith, see Colin Clifford, *The Asquiths* (London: John Murray, 2002); Cherniavsky, *The Salome Dancer*, 175, 176, 181, 182. According to Cherniavsky (p. 181), Mrs. Asquith financed Allan's move into West Wing, a sumptuous villa overlooking Regent's Park, a fact that was not public knowledge. On Margot Asquith as a cultural trendsetter, see Daphne Bennett, *Margot: A Life of the Countess of Oxford and Asquith* (London: Gollancz, 1984); "In the Great World: Mr. and Mrs. Asquith," *The Sketch*, June 25, 1913, Arncliffe-Sennett Collection, BL; Pamela Horn, *High Society: The English Social Elite, 1880–1914* (Phoenix Mill: Alan Sutton, 1992). On the mixing of society and the cultural avant-garde before the war, see in particular Lisa Tickner, "Popular Culture of *Kermesse*: Lewis, Painting and Performance, 1912–13," *Modernity/Modernism* 4, no. 2 (1997): 67–120.

12. Cherniavsky, *The Salome Dancer*, ch. 2; Lacy H. McDearmon, "Maud Allan," in *International Encyclopedia of Dance* (New York: Oxford University Press, 1998), 42, 43.

13. *Yorkshire Observer*, May 1918, Wilde Cuttings, Oscar Wilde Collection, Clark Library, Los Angeles.

14. "As I See It," *Imperialist*, Oct. 7, 1916, repr. in Billing, *Verbatim Report*, Appendix 1, 449.

15. Travers Humphreys, in Billing, *Verbatim Report*, 6. On the coverage by *The Times*, see Doan, *Fashioning Sapphism*, 211 n. 5.

16. Lady Diana Cooper, *The Rainbow Comes and Goes* (New York: Hart-Davis, 1958), 82; W. J. Macqueen-Pope, *Carriages at Eleven: The Story of the Edwardian Theatre* (London: Hutchinson, 1947), 179; Leslie Baily, *Scrapbook, 1900 to 1914* (London: Muller, 1957), 232–4.

17. See Jowitt, *Time and the Dancing Image*; Koritz, *Gendering Bodies*; Susan A. Glenn, *Female Spectacle: The Theatrical Roots of Modern Feminism* (Cambridge, MA: Harvard University Press, 2000).

18. Samuel Hynes, *A War Imagined: The First World War and English Culture* (London: Bodley Head, 1990); Hoare, *Wilde's Last Stand*; Noel Annan, *Our Age: Portrait of a Generation* (London: Weidenfeld & Nicolson, 1990). On the prewar Wilde legacy, see Richard Ellmann,

Oscar Wilde (New York: Knopf, 1987); Regenia Gagnier, *Idylls of the Marketplace: Oscar Wilde and the Victorian Public* (Stanford: Stanford University Press, 1986); Ed Cohen, *Talk on the Wilde Side: Toward a Genealogy of a Discourse on Male Sexualities* (New York: Routledge, 1993); Neil Bartlett, *Who Was That Man? A Present for Mr. Oscar Wilde* (London: Serpent's Tail, 1988); Peter Raby, *Cambridge Companion to Oscar Wilde* (Cambridge, UK: Cambridge University Press, 2001); *Oscar Wilde: Interviews and Recollections*, ed. E. H. Mikhail (2 vols., London: Macmillan, 1979); Rupert Hart-Davis, ed., *The Letters of Oscar Wilde* (London: Harcourt, Brace & World, 1962). On the Great War, sex antagonism, and female sexuality, see Cate Haste, *Rules of Desire: Sex in Britain; World War I to the Present* (London: Chatto & Windus, 1992); Susan Kingsley Kent, *Making Peace: Gender Reconstruction in Interwar Britain* (Princeton: Princeton University Press, 1993); Philippa Levine, "'Walking the Streets in a Way No Decent Woman Should': Women Police in World War I," *Journal of Modern History* 66, no. 1 (Mar. 1994): 34–78; Angela Woollacott, "Khaki Fever and Its Control: Gender, Class, and Sexual Morality in the British Homefront during the First World War," *Journal of Contemporary History* 29, no. 2 (April 1994): 325–47; Nicoletta F. Gullace, "White Feathers and Wounded Men: Female Patriotism and the Memory of the Great War," *Journal of British Studies* 36, no. 1 (April 1997): 178–206.

19. Robert Machray, *The Night Side of London* (Philadelphia: J. B. Lippincott, 1902).

20. "The Palace Theatre," *Queen*, Oct. 1, 1958, Prints and Cuttings Collection A134, WA; F. H. W. Sheppard, "General Introduction," in *Survey of London: The Parish of St. Anne's, Soho* (London: Athlone Press, 1966), vol. 33.

21. Its luxuries included a grand staircase, rising from floor to floor, and the use of green cippolino and "black antique" marble to produce a polychromatic effect. Electricity was a feature already introduced by D'Oyly Carte at the Savoy, the first theater to be electrified in London. The *Builder* was also impressed with the absence of supporting columns that might impede viewing from the "back rows," as well as the use of dressing rooms, offices, and cloakrooms to insulate the auditorium from traffic noises (Feb. 14, 1891): 126–7; R. D'Oyly Carte, *Monograph of the Royal English Opera House* (London, 1891), 9–14.

22. See chapter 4.

23. Raphael Samuel, "Introduction," in Wolf Suschitzky and Raphael Samuel, *Charing Cross Road in the Thirties* (London: Nishen Photography, 1989).

24. William Tydeman and Steven Price, *Wilde: Salome* (Cambridge, UK: Cambridge University Press, 1996), 20–4; Hoare, *Wilde's Last Stand*, 73; Sander L. Gilman, "Salome, Syphilis, Sarah Bernhardt and the Modern Jewess," in Linda Nochlin and Tamar Garb, eds., *The Jew in the Text: Modernity and the Construction of Identity* (New York: Thames & Hudson, 1996), 97–120; Showalter, *Sexual Anarchy*, 150.

25. Percy Burton, "How a Variety Theatre Is Run," *Strand Magazine* 37 (May 1909): 515.

26. On the Empire Theatre as a cosmopolitan club, see *Music Hall and Theatre Review* (London) (Feb. 12, 1909): 106. The West End clubs were renowned for their ostentation, spectatorship, and smoking room attitudes. Steve Dillon, "Victorian Interiors," *Modern Language Quarterly* 62, no. 2 (2001): 83–115. On the clubs, see Brian Harrison, *Separate Spheres: The Opposition to Women's Suffrage in Britain* (London: Croom Helm, 1978), ch. 5.

27. Kirsten Gram Holmstrom, *Monodrama, Attitudes, Tableaux Vivants: Studies on Some Trends of Theatrical Fashion, 1770–1815* (Stockholm: Almqvist & Wiksell, 1967); Richard D. Altick, *The Shows of London* (Cambridge, MA.: Belknap Press, 1978), 342–6; *London by Night: or, The Bachelor's Facetious Guide to All the Ins and Outs and Nightly Doings of the Metropolis . . .* (London: William Ward, 1859); Robert C. Allen, *Horrible Prettiness: Burlesque and American Culture* (Chapel Hill: University of North Carolina Press, 1991), 92, 93.

28. Altick, *The Shows of London*, 345–6.

29. Jowitt, *Time and the Dancing Image*, 84; Judy Burns, "The Culture of Nobility/The Nobility of Self-Cultivation," in Morris, *Moving Words*, 203–27. See Daly, *Done into Dance*, 124, 125.

30. See Inspector M. Holyoake's report, Nov. 5, 1893, Palace Theatre, Theatres and Music Halls Presented Papers, LCC MIN 10, 870, LMA. The artistic posturing of tableaux vivants also had its analogue in visual pornography: postcards confiscated as indecent often turned out to

be photo-reproductions of foreign "art works" of the nude on display in museums. Alison Smith, *The Victorian Nude: Sexuality, Morality, and Art* (Manchester: Manchester University Press, 1996), ch. 2.

31. W. A. Coote, *A Romance of Philanthropy* (London: National Vigilance Association, 1916), 71–85.

32. W. A. Coote, quoted in George Bernard Shaw, *Our Theatre in the Nineties*, vol. 1 (New York: W. H. Wise, 1931), 83; Coote, *A Romance of Philanthropy*, 75, 79. The foreign-inspired Living Pictures included the oriental "Moorish Baths," most probably removed because it contained an openly erotic theme.

33. "Monocle," [*Tatler*], Aug. 1, 1894, Palace Theatre Cuttings File, TM; J.M.P., "Tableaux Vivants at the Palace Theatre," *The Sketch* (May 28, 1894): 482. On the brokered, codified sexuality of the music halls, see Peter Bailey, *Popular Culture and Performance in the Victorian City* (Cambridge, UK: Cambridge University Press, 1998), 189, ch. 6; Russell, "Varieties of Life."

34. On the 1907 protest by the National Vigilance Association against Living Pictures, see Minutes 184 (Feb. 26, 1907) and 199 (April 30, 1907), Executive Minutes, Sept. 27, 1904–Sept. 28, 1909, GB/106/4/NVA/194.4, National Vigilance Association Collection, National Library of Women, London.

35. On Isadora's elevation, see Christopher St. John, "All We Like Sheep," *Academy* (London) (May 2, 1908): 736. St. John was an intimate of Edy Craig, the sister of Duncan's lover. For other critical reviews, see Koritz, *Gendering Bodies*, 41; Elizabeth Weigand, "The Rugmaker's Daughter: Maud Allan's 1915 Silent Film," *Dance Chronicle* 9, no. 2 (1986): 238. On Duncan's art of flexion and extension, see Daly, *Done into Dance*; Tomko, *Dancing Class*; Jowitt, *Time and the Dancing Image*. For critical praise of Allan, see J. T. Grein, "The Palace: A New Dancer," *Sunday Times* (Mar. 3, 1908), Allan Clippings.

36. See, for example, Elaine Aston, *Sarah Bernhardt: A French Actress on the English Stage* (Oxford: Berg, 1989), 81. Both Allan and Bernhardt were better received in London than in their home country; both found a place in London society that they did not enjoy at home, while they were permitted a certain license to perform risqué acts that British actresses could not emulate.

37. "The Trail of the Decadent," *Modern Society*, Dec. 8, 1910, vol. 12 of Wilde Cuttings, Clark Library, University of California, Los Angeles. *Salome* was Wilde's only dramatic work not rehabilitated after his death. *Salome's* alignment of sex and violence, its manifest expressions of multiple perversions, became inextricably linked with the disgrace and the "morbidity" of the author. As novelist Pat Barker interprets it, for Wilde's devotees, *Salome* could well have signaled his martyrdom, a dramatization of the eruption of strong emotions denied a legitimate outlet. Pat Barker, *Eye in the Door* (London: Viking, 1993), 78.

38. Robert Ross, quoted in Joseph Donohue, "Distance, Death and Desire in *Salome*," in Raby, *Cambridge Companion to Oscar Wilde*, 118.

39. Strauss Clippings, NYPL; Koritz, *Gendering Bodies*, 84, 85.

40. Wilde's emphasis. Oscar Wilde, *Salome: A Tragedy in One Act; Drawings by Aubrey Beardsley* (Boston: Branden, 1996), 29.

41. On Reinhardt's influence, see Cherniavsky, *The Salome Dancer*, 142; Tydeman and Price, *Wilde: Salome*, 140. In her earlier memoirs, published in the *Weekly Dispatch*, Allan wrote that the basic idea came to her while watching Reinhardt's Berlin production. On Reinhardt's staging, see Tydeman and Price, *Wilde: Salome*, 31–40.

42. Allan, *My Life and Dancing*, 126; W. B. Walkley, "The Drama: The New Dancer," *Times Literary Supplement*, Mar. 25, 1908, 598.

43. *Truth* [1908], Allan Personal Box, TM. Allan's appearance as a visionary Salome drew on Gustave Moreau's pictorial versions, but Moreau's Salome is not depicted dancing around the head or independent of Herod and his servants.

44. "Programme for Miss Maud Allan" (1908), Palace Theatre File, TM; *Truth* [1908], Allan Personal Box; "Palace Theatre," *The Times*, Mar. 10, 1908, 5.

45. See, for example, *Music Hall and Theatre Review* 41 (Feb. 26, 1909): 138; "'Salome' Dancers the Latest Sensation," *Spokane Review* (Aug. 30, 1908), Allan Clippings; Cherniavsky, *The Salome Dancer*, 187, 188 n. 21.

46. *The Times* reviewer recommended that audiences visit the Palace before Allan's featured performance at 10:15 to see the Palace Girls. In their "violent prancing and whirling and high-kicking," they offered a "piquant contrast to the wonderful instrument of expression ... the mysterious power that dance becomes with Miss Maud Allan." Walkley, "Drama: The New Dancer." On the Tiller girls, see Doremy Vernon, *Tiller's Girls* (London: Robson, 1988); Derek Parker and Julia Parker, *Natural History of the Chorus Girl* (Newton Abbot: David & Charles, 1975); Ramsay Burt, "The Chorus Line and the Efficiency Engineers," in Burt, *Alien Bodies: Representations of Modernity "Race" and Nation in Early Modern Dance* (London: Routledge, 1998), 84–100.

47. Koritz, *Gendering Bodies*, 39–41.

48. Walkley, "Drama: The New Dancer."

49. "Miss Maud Allan's Salome Dance," *Academy* (Mar. 21, 1908): 598.

50. See Raymond Blathwayt, "Two Visions of Maud Allan," *Black and White*, July 18, 1908, Allan Clippings. On Anglo-Saxonism, race, and the liberal political heritage, see Paul A. Kramer, "Empires, Exceptions, and Anglo-Saxons: Race and Rule between the British and the United States Empires, 1880–1910," *Journal of American History* 88, no. 4 (2002): 1322.

51. Grace Hodson Boutelle, "Maud Allan and Her Dances," *Pall Mall Magazine* 7 (July 1908): 702.

52. Ibid.; Blathwayt, "Two Visions of Maud Allan." On her public lectures, see "Miss Maud Allan on Dancing," *The Times*, Feb. 22, 1909, 10.

53. On dance as the spiritual expression of the spiritual state, see "Modern Dance Criticized by Maud Allan," *Boston Traveler*, Jan. 19, 1910, Allan Clippings. On Allan's body as an instrument, see Cherniavsky, "Maud Allan, Part II," 146.

54. Blathwayt, "Two Visions of Maud Allan."

55. Burns, "Culture of Nobility," 212, 213; Jowitt, *Time and the Dancing Image*, 77–101, 123–30; Martha Banta, *Imaging American Women: Idea and Ideals in Cultural History* (New York: Columbia University Press, 1987), ch. 5; Shannan E. Egan, "The Imperishable Pose: Delsartean Performance of the Feminine Ideal," BA thesis, University of North Carolina, 1998; Nancy Lee Chalfa Ruyter, "American Delsarteans Abroad," in *American Dance Abroad: Influence of the United States Experience; Proceedings of the Society of Dance History Scholars* (Riverside, CA: Society of Dance History Scholars, 1992), 275–82; Daly, *Done into Dance*, 4.

56. Allan, *My Life and Dancing*, 65.

57. Maud Allan, unpublished diary, quoted in Cherniavsky, *Did She Dance*.

58. J. T. Grein, "Duke of York's Theatre: Isadora Duncan," *Sunday Times*, July 12, 1908, 4.

59. Robert Renaud in *San Francisco Chronicle*, quoted in Felix Cherniavsky, "Maud Allan, Part 4," *Dance Chronicle* 8, nos. 1–2 (1985): 15.

60. "Miss Maud Allan's Salome Dance," *Academy* (Mar. 21, 1908): 599; *New Jersey Sun*, Feb. 3, 1910, Allan Clippings.

61. "Miss Maud Allan at the Palace," *Truth*, Mar. 18, 1908; "Miss Maud Allan's Salome Dance."

62. *Chicago Tribune*, Feb. 7, 1910, quoted in Cherniavsky, *Did She Dance*. On the other hand, Carl Van Vechten observed, "Miss Allan yesterday executed steps and curved her body in contortions which are now conventionally supposed to suggest Salome." Van Vechten, "The Dance Criticisms of Carl Van Vechten, Part 1: Reviews Written for the *New York Times*," *Dance Index* 1 (1942): 148.

63. *The Times*, quoted in "Mystery of Noted Dancer Is Solved: Sister of Slayer," *Cleveland News* [1908], Allan Clippings.

64. Thanks to Janice Ross for these insights.

65. Genevieve Stebbins, one of the most important popularizers of Delsarte, included thirty-two "illustrations from Greek art" to demonstrate Delsartean expression, but she also believed that Delsarte incorporated key elements of orientalist dancing. Stebbins, *Delsarte System of Expression* (New York: Dance Horizons, 1902; orig. 1885), 470. Norman Bryson has observed the intense "cultural charge" and "structure of linkage" when dance forms seem to combine opposing cultural meanings (such as the primitive body and the machine); under these conditions, "elements from one fantasy migrate to the other and back, as though the images that

were involved performed closely related functions in the cultural imaginary." Norman Bryson, "Cultural Studies and Dance History," in Jane C. Desmond, ed., *Meaning in Motion: New Cultural Studies of Dance* (Durham, NC: Duke University Press, 1997), 74.

66. *Observer*, quoted in Fiona MacIntosh, "Dancing Maenads in Early Twentieth Century Britain," in MacIntosh, ed., *The Ancient Dancer in the Modern World: Response to Greek and Roman Dance* (Oxford: Oxford University Press, 2010), 194.

67. The Maud Allan Clippings collection at the New York Public Library contains the following newspaper fragment: "Lady — requests the pleasure of — company to dinner at the Savoy Hotel." "'Afterwards Palace Theatre (Salome seance)' was the wording of an invitation card recently sent out."

68. Matinees were introduced in the 1870s to entice polite society back into the theaters. They were also used for experimental theater, and were overwhelmingly patronized by women. William Armstrong, "The Nineteenth-Century Matinee," *Theatre Notebook* (n.p., n.d.), TM.

69. Walkley, "Drama: The New Dancer"; "The Maud Allan Matinées," *Tatler* (Mar. 1, 1911): 228, Palace Theatre File, TM.

70. "Miss Maud Allan: Palace Crowded with Ladies to See the New Dancer," *Daily Chronicle* (London), June 13, 1908, Allan Clippings.

71. On Poiret, see Norah Waugh, *Corsets and Crinolines* (London: Batsford, 1954); Valerie Steele, *Fashion and Eroticism* (New York: Oxford University Press, 1985); Peter Wollen, "Fashion/ Orientalism/The Body," *New Formations* (1987): 3–55; Palmer White, *Poiret* (London: Studio Vista, 1973); "Mrs. Asquith and French Dresses," *The Times*, May 15, 1909, 13. Margot Asquith was severely condemned for her "indiscretion" at exhibiting Poiret's Parisian fashions at Downing Street, but Poiret's war on the corset was not strictly a high fashion or continental innovation. It owed much to the traditions of the Anglo-American women's health reform and aesthetic dress movement of the late nineteenth century, of which Delsartean physical culture was an integral part. Jill Fields, "'Fighting the Corsetless Evil': Shaping Corsets and Culture," *Journal of Social History* 33, no. 2 (1999): 358, 359; Mary Stella Newton, *Health, Art, and Reason: Dress Reformers of the Nineteenth Century* (London: J. Murray, 1974).

72. Cooper, *The Rainbow Comes and Goes*, 82.

73. "An Earl's Daughter Whose Dancing Has Alarmed a 'Palace': Lady Constance Stewart Richardson," *The Sketch* (Feb. 16, 1910), suppl. 9.

74. On Lady Constance's Greek boy's body, see Cooper, *The Rainbow Comes and Goes*, 82.

75. Elizabeth Robins, Diary entry, April 26, 1908, Box 6, Robins Papers, Fales Library, New York University; Cherniavsky, *The Salome Dancer*, 174, 175; Macqueen-Pope, *Carriages at Eleven*, 179. This was a notorious occasion, remembered in memoirs of the period. See, for example, [Julian Osgood Fields], *Uncensored Recollections* (Philadelphia: J. B. Lippincott, 1924), 318.

76. Jamie Camplin, *The Rise of the Plutocrats: Wealth and Power in Edwardian England* (London: Constable, 1978); Anthony Allfrey, *Edward VII and His Jewish Court* (London: Weidenfeld & Nicolson, 1991). On Cassel as a cosmopolitan financier and his relations with the Foreign Office, see Kurt Grunwald, "'Windsor-Cassel'—The Last Court Jew: Prolegomena to a Biography of Sir Ernest Cassel," *Yearbook of the Leo Baeck Institute* 14 (1969): 119–64; Pat Thane, "Financiers and the British State: The Case of Sir Ernest Cassel," *Business History* 27 (Jan. 1986): 80–99. On anti-Semitism and attacks on Jewish financiers, see Bryan Cheyette, "Hilaire Belloc and the 'Marconi Scandal' 1900–1914: A Reassessment of the Interactionist Model of Racial Hatred," *Immigrants and Minorities* 8, no. 1 (1989): 131–42.

77. Gilman, "Salome"; also Sander L. Gilman, "Strauss and the Pervert," in Arthur Goos and Roger Parker, eds., *Reading Opera* (Princeton: Princeton University Press, 1988); Glenn, *Female Spectacle*, ch. 4.

78. Postcard, addressed to Miss D. K. James, 87 Brudenell Road, Leeds, with a photograph of Miss Maud Allan, with caption "Chopin's Funeral March," 4995 Rotary Photo, Foulham and Banfield, Maud Allan Collection, San Francisco Performing Arts Library and Museum, San Francisco. The letter writer inquires: "Hope you haven't got this p.c. Are still gone on this person?"

79. "Touching Missives from Miss Maud Allan's Letter Box," *Weekly Dispatch* (London), Aug. 30, 1908; "Marriage Offers for Miss Maud Allan," Sept. 6, 1908; "Miss Maud Allan's Last Reminiscences," Sept. 13, 1908, Allan Clippings.

80. "Marriage Offers."

81. Lois Draegin, "After Isadora: Her Art as Inspiration," *Dance Magazine* (July 1977): 68. Linda Tomko's comments on Duncan also apply to Allan: because they incorporated cultural resources that they shared with female spectators, their female following could "bring to bear different sets of reference for making meaning out of the dancer's bodily practice." Tomko, *Dancing Class*, 74.

82. "Building the Body Beautiful," *Woman Worker*, Aug. 14, 1908.

83. "I have this gift of dancing and movement," he added, "which everyone tells me is very graceful, and that no one would be able to tell me from a lady, if they did not previously know I was a man." "Marriage Offers."

84. See the discussion of the Cleveland Street Scandal, "La Lanterne," Jan. 20, 1890, DPP 1/95/7, Public Record Office, London; *The Sins of the Cities of the Plain: or, The Recollections of a Mary-Anne, with Short Essays on Sodomy and Tribadism* (2 vols., London, 1881); Morris B. Kaplan, "Who's Afraid of John Saul? Urban Culture and the Politics of Desire in Late Victorian London," *GLQ: A Journal of Lesbian and Gay Studies* 5, no. 3 (1999): 296–300.

85. Kaplan, "Who's Afraid of John Saul"; also George Chauncey, *Gay New York: The Making of the Gay World* (New York: Basic Books, 1994).

86. Program cover, Palace Theatre of Varieties, Oct. 6, 1913, Museum of London.

87. Flitch, *Modern Dancing and Dancers*, 161. The full respectability of the Palace Theatre was certified by the "first ever Royal Command Performance" there in 1912. Gavin Weightman, *Bright Lights, Big City: London Entertained, 1830–1950* (London: Collins & Brown, 1992), 100.

88. On dancing schools, see Garafola, *Diaghilev's Ballets Russes*, 225, 226; "A Successful Teacher," *Dancing Times* 2 (Feb. 1912): 123; "The Sitter Out," *Dancing Times* 5 (June 1915): 298, 299, 331, 332. Events such as the Post-Impressionist exhibition and the Ballets Russes energized London in the years immediately preceding the First World War, when, in the words of Virginia Woolf, "human nature changed." Quoted in Peter Stansky, *On or about December 1910: Early Bloomsbury and Its Intimate World* (Cambridge, UK: Cambridge University Press, 1996), 2. See also Virginia Woolf, *Roger Fry: A Biography* (1940; repr. New York, 1968).

89. "The British Girl in Paris: Our Most Charming Export Commodity," Nov. 23, 1935, Chorus Girl Cutting File, TM; Vernon, *Tiller's Girls*.

90. Ross McKibbin, *Classes and Culture: England, 1918–1951* (Oxford: Oxford University Press, 2000); Victor Silvester, *Dancing Is My Life: An Autobiography* (London: Heinemann, 1958).

91. Jane Desmond, "Embodying Difference: Issues in Dance and Cultural Difference," *Cultural Critique* 26 (Winter 1994): 33–63.

92. Mica Nava, "Cosmopolitanism of Commerce and the Allure of Difference: Selfridges, the Russian Ballet and the Tango 1911–14," *International Journal of Cultural Studies* 1, no. 2 (1998): 163–96.

93. See Simon Collier et al., *Tango: The Dance, the Song, the Story* (London: Thames & Hudson, 1995), 83; H. R. Wakefield on "Modern Dancing," *The Times*, May 27, 1913, 11; Percy Moenich on "Modern Dancing," *The Times*, May 24, 1913, 43; Peroline Maud Webb on "Modern Dancing," *The Times*, May 27, 1913, 9.

94. Strauss's *Salome* was wildly popular on the Continent but also controversial. However, it was among the "prudish English-speaking world" that it met its "fiercest opposition." After a single performance at the New York Metropolitan Opera, the management felt obliged to terminate the production. Oscar Hammerstein took advantage of the sensation aroused by the performance of Allan and her American competitors to stage Strauss's *Salome* in 1909 at his rival Manhattan Opera House. Tydeman and Price, *Wilde: Salome*, 127–8; Glenn, *Female Spectacle*, 102.

95. "Salome in London," *The Times*, Dec. 9, 1910, vol. 13 of Wilde Cuttings; "Salome Leaves Audience Limp," *Daily Sketch*, Dec. 9, 1910, vol. 13 of Wilde Cuttings.

96. Reviewers regarded the opera as "beautiful art wasted on a vile subject," a "brilliant fungus sprung from decaying genius." "Strauss Opera at Covent Garden," *Daily News*, Dec. 9, 1910, Wilde Cuttings; "Music: Salome," *Spectator*, Dec. 24, 1910, 1184, quoted in Koritz, *Gendering Bodies*, 84; "Comments and Opinions," *Musical Standard*, vol. 12 of Wilde Cuttings.

97. On Mme. Acté's costume, see "Strauss's 'Salome' to Be Produced after Having Been Banned for Years: Mme Aino Acté as Salome," *Illustrated London News*, Dec. 3, 1910, vol. 12 of Wilde Cuttings. On Mary Garden's costume and dance, see "The Princess and Her Dance," Strauss Clippings.

98. "Salome," *Daily News*, Feb. 2, 1911, vol. 14 of Wilde Cuttings. On the earlier productions of *Salome* in London, see Tydeman and Price, *Wilde: Salome*, 40–57.

99. In 1909, Bourne played "Justice" in the Actresses' Franchise League's "Pageant of Great Women," at the La Scala Theatre. She also had a long association with Forbes Robertson's touring company. *The Times* obituary of Bourne identified her performance of Salome as her "most famous role." "Miss Adeline Bourne: Actress and Suffragette," *The Times*, Feb. 10, 1965, 15.

100. "Afternoons at the Play: 'Salome' at the Court," *Referee*, Mar. 5, 1911; "Stageland," *Penny Illustrated Paper*, Mar. 11, 1911.

101. " 'Salome' at the Court Theatre," Feb. 28, 1911; "Salome with Head on the Charger," *Morning Leader*, vol. 14 of Wilde Cuttings.

102. *Globe*, Feb. 28, 1911, vol. 14 of Wilde Cuttings; "Stageland."

103. "The New Players," *Bystander*, Mar. 8, 1911, vol. 14 of Wilde Cuttings.

104. "The New Players," *Votes for Women*, Mar. 3, 1911, 358.

105. On suffrage iconography, see Tickner, *Spectacle of Women*, 151–226. On feminist theater, see Barbara Green, *Spectacular Confessions: Autobiography, Performative Activism, and the Sites of Suffrage* (New York: Palgrave Macmillan, 1997): 75. See also Joel H. Kaplan and Sheila Stowell, *Theatre and Fashion: Oscar Wilde to the Suffragettes* (Cambridge, UK: Cambridge University Press, 1994). Feminist theater had a limited relationship to the avant-garde; it overwhelmingly produced contemporary melodramas of social protest or social satire and rarely adopted strategies of theatrical symbolism.

106. These divisions inform a humorous playlet entitled "Salome and the Suffragettes" that appeared in the weekly magazine *The Referee*. "Salome and the Suffragettes," *Referee*, June 28, 1908. They reappear at the end of Allan's 1908 memoir, where she considers votes for women. Although she insists that "woman is a human being," possessing the "absolute right" to education and opportunities in the professions and other vocations, her rightful destiny remains as a "wife and mother" within the "inner sanctum" of home. At the same time, Allan insists on a "genuine sex difference" that renders women "unsuited" to the legal profession as well as politics. *My Life and Dancing*, 113–17.

107. Tickner, "Popular Culture of *Kermesse*," 95.

108. Tickner, *Spectacle of Women*, 205–10. On Edith Craig and the Pioneer Players, whose experimentation included unconventional subject matter and forms drawn from the drama of many countries, see Katharine Cockin, *Women and Theatre in the Age of Suffrage: The Pioneer Players, 1911–1925* (Houndmills, UK: Palgrave, 2001); Joy Melville, *Ellen and Edy: A Biography of Ellen Terry and Her Daughter, Edith Craig, 1847–1947* (London: Pandora, 1987), ch. 14; Sheila Stowell, *A Stage of Their Own: Feminist Playwrights of the Suffrage Era* (Ann Arbor: University of Michigan Press, 1992), ch. 2.

109. On Salome as a female cultural form, see Jane Marcus, "Salomé: The Jewish Princess Was a New Woman," *Bulletin of the New York Public Library* (1974): 105. In Britain, a group of "maverick suffragists" and "minority feminists" clustered around the *Freewoman* and Freewoman Discussion Circles in 1911 and 1912. See Bruce Clarke, *Dora Marsden and Early Modernism: Gender, Individualism, Science* (Ann Arbor: University of Michigan Press, 1996), ch. 2.

110. See Laura Ormiston Chant, *Why We Attacked the Empire* (London: Marshall, 1895).

111. "Stageland."

112. Anonymous, *Maudie: Revelations of Life in London and an Unforeseen Denouement* (London: The "Chatty" Club, 1909). Before her London appearance, the American press reported on one private performance of *Salome* in Budapest, when Allan found herself the victim of a

macabre practical joke. As she proceeded to embrace the head of the Baptist on stage, she found that the dead head of a man had been substituted for the property head. See Hoare, *Wilde's Last Stand*, 75, 85.

113. "Salome Dinner Dances," *New York Times*, Aug. 23, 1908, Allan Clippings.

114. *San Francisco Call*, April 18, 1908; "Mystery of Noted Dancer Is Solved: Sister of Slayer," *Cleveland News* [1908]; "London's Favorite Dancer Sister of Notorious Durrant," *Detroit News*, May 2, 1908, Allan Clippings.

115. "Maud Allan Scoffs at Story Asquith Was Nice to the Barefoot Dancer," *Los Angeles Examiner*, Mar. 10, 1910; "Most Pestered of Premiers," *Cleveland Leader*, April 10, 1910, Allan Clippings; MacIntosh, "Dancing Maenads," 196.

116. Maud Allan, "How I Startled the World," *San Francisco Call & Post*, chapter 12 (Dec. 24, 1921); chapter 13 (Dec. 26, 1921), Maud Allan Collection, San Francisco Performing Arts Library and Museum. On the fraternization charge, see "Presents for 'Hun' Prisoners," *Globe* [1915], Cuttings Collection, MSS. Eng. c.6713, Margot Asquith Collection, Bodleian Library, University of Oxford.

117. "A Deplorable Scandal," *Daily Telegraph*, June 6, 1918, HO 144/1498/364780, Home Office Papers, NA. Reference was also made to Allan's luxurious "black sealskin coat," with a large sable collar and muff. *Lloyd's Weekly News*, April 7, 1918, Wilde Cuttings.

118. Hume Williams, in Billing, *Verbatim Report*, 51-3, 63.

119. Billing, *Verbatim Report*, 76.

120. Medd, "Cult of the Clitoris"; Trudi Tate, "Propaganda Lies," in Tate, *Modernism, History and the First World War* (Manchester: Manchester University Press, 1998), 42-9; Wheelwright, *The Fatal Lover*.

121. Bland, "Trial by Sexology."

122. "The Honor of England," *Morning Post*, June 6, 1918, HO 144/1498/364780, NA.

123. "Mr. Billing's Trial," *The Times*, April 8, 1918; Billing, *Verbatim Report*, 90.

124. Justice Darling, in Billing, *Verbatim Report*, 444.

125. Billing, *Verbatim Report*, 380.

126. When *The Vigilante* announced its renaming, it actually printed a notice warning the public not to be confounded "with the objects aimed at by the various 'Vigilance' Societies which appear to be limited to the suppression of sexual vice." Hoare and others have noted this announcement (*Wilde's Last Stand*, 59) without recognizing its feminist genealogy.

127. Jacqueline de Vries, "Gendering Patriotism: Emmeline and Christabel Pankhurst and World War One," in Sybil Oldfield, ed., *The Working-Day World: Women's Lives and Culture(s) in Britain, 1914-1915* (London: Taylor & Francis, 1994), 75-89; Nicoletta F. Gullace, *The Blood of Our Sons: Men, Women and the Renegotiation of British Citizenship during the Great War* (Basingstoke: Palgrave Macmillan, 2002), ch. 6.

128. Kent, *Making Peace*; Martin Pugh, *Women and the Women's Movement in Britain, 1914-1959* (London: Macmillan, 1992); Gullace, *The Blood of Our Sons*.

129. On the flapper vote, see Billie Melman, *Women and the Popular Imagination in the Twenties: Flappers and Nymphs* (New York: St. Martin's Press, 1988), 29. In his scathing critique of Margot Asquith's memoirs, Harold Begbie refers to her as the "grandmother of the flappers." Begbie, *The Glass of Fashion: Some Social Reflections* (London: Putnam's, 1921), 52. On the body of the flapper, see C. Sheridan Jones, *London in War-Time* (London: Grafton, 1917), 126. Many contemporaries, including the arch-antisuffragist Lord Curzon, recognized the hypocrisy of the age bar for women. They deplored the presumption that female war workers were too "young" and "undisciplined" to vote. See Lord Curzon's speech, quoted in Gullace, *The Blood of Our Sons*, 192.

130. For London, see Silvester, *Dancing Is My Life*; Philip J. S. Richardson, *A History of English Ballroom Dancing (1910-45): The Story of the Development of the Modern English Style* (London: Herbert Jenkins, 1945). For New York, see Tomko, *Dancing Class*, 22, 23; Lewis A. Erenberg, *Steppin' Out: New York Nightlife and the Transformation of American Culture, 1890-1930* (Chicago: University of Chicago Press, 1984), 20-2; Kathy Lee Peiss, *Cheap Amusements: Working Women and Leisure in Turn-of-the-Century New York* (Philadelphia: Temple University Press, 1986).

131. Jones, *London in War-Time*, 22.
132. Marek Kohn, *Dope Girls: The Birth of a British Drug Underground* (London: Lawrence & Wishart, 1992); Richardson, *History of English Ballroom Dancing*, 17–24; Robert Murphy, *Smash and Grab: Gangsters in the London Underworld, 1920–1960* (London: Faber and Faber, 1993), 7–10; Sally Cline, *Radclyffe Hall: A Woman Called John* (London: J. Murray, 1997), 153, 170; Michael Luke, *David Tennant and the Gargoyle Club* (London: Weidenfeld & Nicolson, 1991); "Clubs: Prosecution of Ciro's Club," MEPO 3/251, 1916–1919; "Miss Kate Evelyn Meyrick or Merrick: Allegations of Irregularities," MEPO 2/4481, 1924–1934; "Policy on Night Clubs and Its Effects on Officers," MEPO 2/4458, 1932–1933; "Night Club Irregularities," MEPO 2/2053, 1922.

Chapter 4: The Italian Restaurant

1. Thomas Burke, *Out and About: A Note-Book of London in War-Time* (London: Allen & Unwin, 1919), 62.
2. James Clifford, "Mixed Feelings," in Pheng Cheah and Bruce Robbins, eds., *Cosmopolitics: Thinking and Feeling beyond the Nation* (Minneapolis: University of Minnesota Press, 1998), 362–70.
3. Donna R. Gabaccia, *We Are What We Eat: Ethnic Food and the Making of Americans* (Cambridge, MA: Harvard University Press, 1998); Donna R. Gabaccia, "Global Geography of 'Little Italy': Italian Neighborhoods in Comparative Perspective," *Modern Italy* 2, no. 1 (2006): 9–24; Carol Helstosky, *Garlic and Oil: Politics and Food in Italy* (Oxford: Berg, 2004).
4. Peppino Leoni, *I Shall Die on the Carpet. With a Forward by Fabian of the Yard* (London: Leslie Frewin, 1966), 18. Leoni's autobiography was clearly ghost-written, but it repeats Leoni's life narrative as already recounted in numerous newspaper accounts. It is full of useful social detail and, at strategic points, it conveys an immigrant's perspective on metropolitan life.
5. Alfio Bernabei, *Esuli ed emigrati italiani nel Regno Unito, 1920–1940* (Milan: Mursia, 1997); "Nationality and Naturalisation; Emidio (Emilio) Recchioni; Request in 1915 for Deportation Rejected; Application for Naturalisation Granted 1930; Alleged Involvement in Attempt in 1932 to Assassinate Mussolini," 1915–1934, HO 144/18949, NA; Pietro Dipaola, "Emidio Recchioni," in Maurizio Antonioli, ed., *Dizionario biografico degli anarchici italiani* (Pisa: BFS, 2004); Alfio Bernabei, "The London Plot to Kill Mussolini," *History Today* 49, no. 4 (1999): 2.
6. "Famed for Art as Well as Food: The *Quo Vadis* in Soho," *Caterer and Hotel-Keeper*, Oct. 9, 1936, 20.
7. See, for example, Thomas Cook and Son, *Cook's Tourist's Handbook to Switzerland* (London: Thomas Cook, 1876), 189.
8. Leoni, *I Shall Die*, 42.
9. Fin-de-siècle Cannero had developed a reputation as the home of émigré chefs: Samuel Butler, who stayed there in 1887, remembered being told that Cannero "is the neighbourhood from which all the best cooks and waiters come." Henry Festing Jones, *Samuel Butler* (London: Macmillan, 1920), 110.
10. Alberto Capatti, Massimo Montanari, and Áine O'Healy, *Italian Cuisine: A Cultural History, Arts and Traditions of the Table* (New York: Columbia University Press, 2003), 143.
11. Leoni, *I Shall Die*, 49.
12. On the monotonous diet of the region, see Peter Jacomelli, June 2000, "NLSC: From Source to Salespoint, 2000," F8235, BLSA; Helstosky, *Garlic and Oil*; Capatti et al., *Italian Cuisine*.
13. Jacomelli, F8235A, BLSA.
14. The Piedmont area was notorious for its high incidence of pellagra because corn-based polenta did not supply the requisite vitamin B12.
15. Capatti et al., *Italian Cuisine*, 23, 24.
16. Ibid.
17. Peter Barber and Peter Jacomelli, *Continental Taste: Ticinese Emigrants and Their Café-Restaurants in Britain, 1847–1987* (London: Camden History Society, 1997), 16–19. Cathy

Ross, "The Twentieth Century," in Edwina Ehrman, *London Eats Out: 500 Years of Capital Dining* (London: Philip Wilson, 1999), 90.

18. W. Macqueen-Pope, *'Goodbye Piccadilly'* (Newton Abbot, UK: David & Charles, 1972), 314.
19. Barber and Jacomelli, *Continental Taste*, 17.
20. Emily Constance Cook, *Highways and Byways in London* (London: Macmillan, 1902), 288.
21. Ibid., 287; Nathaniel Newnham-Davis, *Dinners and Diners: Where and How to Dine in London, A New Enlarged and Revised Edition* (London: Grant Richards, 1901), viii.
22. Cook, *Highways and Byways*, 298.
23. Terri Colpi, *The Italian Factor: The Italian Community in Great Britain* (Edinburgh: Mainstream, 1991), 34.
24. Cook, *Highways and Byways*, 288. In "Cosmopolitan London," Count Armfelt discovered waiters in Soho lodging houses, created out of former mansions that had been partitioned into sparsely furnished and carpetless rooms, where lodgers often slept two in a bed. Count Armfelt, "Cosmopolitan London," in G. R. Sims, ed., *Edwardian London* (London: Village Press, 1990; orig. *Living London*, 1902), 243; Barber and Jacomelli, *Continental Taste*, 10.
25. This assistance undoubtedly placed him in the debt of the family correspondent, but Peppino does not mention this.
26. Patrick Joyce, *The Rule of Freedom: Liberalism and the Modern City* (London: Verso, 2003).
27. Charles Booth, *Life and Labour of the People of London: The Charles Booth Collection, 1885–1905 from the British Library of Political and Economic Science, London* (Brighton, UK: Harvester Microform, 1988), A29, A37, A39.
28. Ibid., A44; Lucia Sponza, *Italian Immigrants in Nineteenth-Century Britain: Realities and Images* (Leicester: Leicester University Press, 1988), 104. Leoni earned a pound a week when he worked as a *commis* at the Savoy, but was earning £20 a week when he was headwaiter there in the 1920s.
29. Charles Pascoe, quoted in Barber and Jacomelli, *Continental Taste*, 16.
30. Cook, *Highways and Byways*, 287.
31. "No suburb worthy of the name was without its Italian restaurant," recalled journalist Fred Willis, "and if one was in funds and of the right social caste one entered this elegant saloon for supper." Frederick Willis, *A Book of London Yesterdays* (London: Phoenix House, 1960), 249–50.
32. Charles Pascoe, quoted in Barber and Jacomelli, *Continental Taste*, 18; "The Development of the Swiss Cafe in London," *Caterer and Hotel-Keeper Gazette*, April 16, 1897, 434–6.
33. Leoni, *I Shall Die*, 66.
34. Amy B. Trubek, *Haute Cuisine: How the French Invented the Culinary Profession* (Philadelphia: University of Pennsylvania Press, 2000), ch. 3.
35. Ibid., 47.
36. Ibid.
37. "Restaurants for Sociability," *Caterer and Hotel-Keeper*, Sept. 15, 1908, 422.
38. Jerry White, *London in the Nineteenth Century: 'A Human Awful Wonder of God'* (London: Cape, 2007), 194.
39. Robert Machray, *The Night Side of London* (London: John Macqueen, 1902), 80.
40. Stanley Jackson, *The Savoy: The Romance of a Great Hotel* (London: Muller, 1979), 23.
41. Davis, *Dinners and Diners*, 73.
42. Leoni soon learned that the silent service was a fiction in which both the staff and clientele colluded. Leoni, *I Shall Die*, 83.
43. A. Escoffier, *Auguste Escoffier: Memories of My Life* (New York: Van Nostrand Reinhold, 1997), 90.
44. Leoni, *I Shall Die*, 66; King Bomba handbills, in "Folio re Food" (n.d.), Box 1, File 2, Radclyffe Hall Papers, Harry Ransom Center, Austin, Texas.
45. Capatti, *Italian Cuisine*, 222.
46. Ella Winter, "Cooking in Italy," *Manchester Guardian*, June 22, 1925, 11; "The So-Called English Fare," *Restaurant*, Dec. 1913, 650.
47. On "little places," see Thomas Burke, *Dinner Is Served* (London: Routledge, 1937), 14. On enclave eating, see Gabaccia, *We Are What We Eat*, 62–4.

48. "Chops and Changes," *Caterer and Hotel-Keeper*, Feb. 15, 1887, 386; "Death of a Noted Italian Restaurateur," *Caterer and Hotel-Keeper*, Sept. 16, 1912, 519. See also "His Lordship of Soho," *Westminster Mail*, Jan. 11, 1908, 1.
49. Nathaniel Newnham-Davis, *The Gourmet's Guide to London* (London: Grant Richards, 1914), 255, 256.
50. "The Palace Theatre Programme," Nov. 25, 1913, Palace Theatre File, TM.
51. Davis, *The Gourmet's Guide to London*, 257.
52. Howard Paul, "A Dinner at Kettner's," *Caterer and Hotel-Keeper*, Feb. 15, 1898, 64.
53. "The Secret of the Cheap Table d'Hôte," *Caterer and Hotel-Keeper*, Oct. 16, 1905, 404; H. G. Wells, *Tono-Bungay: A Novel* (New York: Modern Library, 1908), 115–16.
54. Rupert Croft-Cooke, *Feasting with Panthers: A New Consideration of Some Late Victorian Writers* (London: W. H. Allen, 1967), 267. Kettner's was the first Soho establishment to prosper and gain British clientele after a journalist praised it in the pages of *The Times* in 1870.
55. "So-Called English Fare," 650; Winter, "Cooking in Italy," 11.
56. "Aliens in the Catering Trade," *Caterer and Hotel-Keeper*, Aug. 15, 1905, 321.
57. "Spy Waiters," *Daily Mirror*, May 11, 1905, 10.
58. Panikos Panayi, "Sausages, Waiters, and Bakers: German Migrants and Culinary Transfer 1850–1914," in Stefan Manz, *Migration and Transfer from Germany to Britain, 1660–1914* (Munich: Saur, 2007), 156.
59. Charles Booth, "The Employees of the Victualling Industry," in Booth, *Life and Labour*, A29, A52.
60. Ibid., 52, 43.
61. Booth, quoted in Sponza, *Italian Immigrants in Nineteenth-Century Britain*, 103.
62. Pietro Dipaola, "Italian Anarchists in London 1870–1914," Ph.D. diss., London, 2004, 89–90.
63. Ibid., 226.
64. "An Extra Waiter to *The Revue*," *The Revue*, April 1906, 28.
65. "Registry Offices and Their Fees," *The Revue*, Aug. 1906, 44–5.
66. "Notes and Queries. By the Editor—Why was Oddenino Knighted?," *The Revue*, April 1909, 5.
67. Dipaola, "Italian Anarchists in London," 83.
68. "First Defeat for the Cooks," *Daily Express*, April 2, 1913, 5.
69. "Restaurant War Ends," *Daily Express*, April 3, 1913, 6.
70. H. Llewellyn Smith, ed., *New Survey of London Life and Labour* (9 vols., London: P. S. King, 1930–5), vol. 8, 223.
71. "Chief Office Notes," *Catering Worker*, Sept. 1914, 1.
72. Dipaola, "Italian Anarchists in London," 231.
73. Report of Chief Inspector James O'Brien, 1 July 1915, HO 144/18949/ 286107/1, NA.
74. Ibid.
75. Ibid.
76. Dipaola, "Emidio Recchioni."
77. Inspector Quinn, June 22, 1917, HO 144/18949/ 286107/2, NA.
78. Dipaola, "Italian Anarchists in London," 206.
79. Leoni, *I Shall Die*, 101.
80. Ibid.
81. "Exit the German Waiter—Enter the Englishman," *Caterer and Hotel-Keeper*, Sept. 15, 1914, 520.
82. See Panikos Panayi, *Spicing up Britain: The Multicultural History of British Food* (London: Reaktion, 2008); Gerry Black, *Living up West: Jewish Life in London's West End* (London: London Museum of Jewish Life, 1994).
83. Panikos Panayi, "Anti-German Riots in London during the First World War," *German History* 7 (1989): 193.
84. Patisserie Valerie, the landmark establishment of Old Compton Street, dates from this wartime Belgian migration.
85. "The Year in the Catering Trade," *Caterer and Hotel-Keeper*, Jan. 15, 1917, 17–19.

86. On the Beauty Sleep Order, see Marek Kohn, *Dope Girls: The Birth of the British Drug Underground* (London: Granta, 2001; orig. 1992), 29. The Control Board limited the sale of alcohol to civilians to five and a half hours a day, ending at 10:30. "Exit the late Supper" headlined a 1917 report on the closing of Romano's in the Strand. On Romano, see the following from the *Caterer and Hotel-Keeper*: "Caterer's Notebook," April 16, 1917, 117. On the early effects of the war on catering, see "Hotel and Restaurant Profits," Sept. 15, 1914, 542–3; Jan. 15, 1915, 11; "The Year in the Catering Trade," Jan. 15, 1916, 10–12; "Measures affecting the Trade," Oct. 15, 1915, 472, 473.

87. John Burnett, *England Eats Out: A Social History of Eating Out in England from 1830 to the Present* (New York: Longman, 2004), 184.

88. Stephen Graham, *Twice Round the London Clock and More London Nights* (London: Benn, 1933), 208.

89. "In and Around Soho," *Caterer and Hotel-Keeper*, Oct. 15, 1914, 596–9.

90. "Rambler," "This Morning's Gossip," *Daily Mirror*, May 25, 1915, 12.

91. "A Changed Soho: Recall of Foreign Population," *The Times*, Oct. 4, 1915, 11. On Soho's excitement over successful battles (but no record of their failures), see "This Morning's Gossip," Aug. 11, 1916, 10.

92. "Exit the Waiter," *Caterer and Hotel-Keeper*, June 15, 1915, 271.

93. "The Caterer's Note Book, "*Caterer and Hotel-Keeper*, Dec. 15, 1915, 576.

94. Graham, *Twice Round*, 208.

95. Ibid., 209.

96. Arthur Marwick, *The Deluge: British Society and the First World War* (London: Bodley Head, 1965), 92.

97. Ibid.

98. Burke, *Out and About*, 51. See also Graham, *Twice Round*, 211.

99. *Daily Mirror*, quoted in "Soho's Revival," *Soho Gazette*, Dec. 3, 1921, 4.

100. Mrs. Dorothy Constance Peel, *How We Lived Then, 1914–1918* (London: Lane, 1929), 67.

101. Mrs. Robert Henrey, *An Exile in Soho* (London: Dent, 1952), 148–52.

102. Mrs. Robert Henrey, *London under Fire, 1940–45* (London: Dent, 1969), 66.

103. On postwar changes, see Robert Graves and Alan Hodge, *The Long Week-End: A Social History of Great Britain 1918–1939* (New York: Norton, 1994).

104. Chris Ed Wrigley, *Challenges of Labour: Central and Western Europe, 1917–1920: International Conference on "Labour Movements and Revolutionary Potential in Europe at the End of World War I": Revised Papers* (London: Routledge, 1993), 270–1.

105. Ibid.; Graves and Hodge, *The Long Week-End*.

106. "Chaos in the Hotels," *Daily Express*, Feb. 5, 1919, 1. Their stated grievances were the same as those that precipitated prewar strikes: the long work hours and the "tronc system." The *Express* blamed the strike on "alien waiters who had been living in England and earning good incomes while British soldiers had been fighting abroad."

107. Alec Waugh, quoted in Jerry White, *London in the Twentieth Century: A City and Its People* (New York: Viking, 2001), 131; Alison Light, *Forever England: Femininity, Literature and Conservatism between the Wars* (London: Routledge, 1991).

108. "The 'Soho Gazette': Its Aims and Purposes," *Soho Gazette*, Sept. 30, 1921, 1.

109. Ernest Oldmeadow, "The Honour of Soho," *Soho Gazette*, Oct. 7, 1921, 1. See also "Bon Viveur," *Where to Dine in London* (London: Geoffrey Bles, 1937), 53–5, 65–8, 74.

110. Paul Cohen-Portheim, *The Spirit of London* (London: Batsford, 1950; orig. 1935), 90.

111. Elizabeth Montizambert, *London Discoveries in Shops & Restaurants* (London: Women Publishers, 1924), 117.

112. Cohen-Portheim, *The Spirit of London*, 87.

113. Paul Morand, *A Frenchman's London* (London: Cassell, 1934), 188. According to the *New Survey of London Life and Labour*, German residents in the County of London declined from 31,000 in 1911 to 9,000 in 1921. French residents also declined from 16,000 to 14,000, but the decline among Italians was slighter, from 12,103 to 11,733. Smith, *New Survey of London Life*, vol. 1, 82.

114. Smith, *New Survey of London Life*, vol. 8, 221.
115. Ibid.
116. Ibid., 222.
117. Burnett, *England Eats Out*, 197.
118. "March of Fascisti in London," *The Times*, Nov. 6, 1922, 11.
119. Robin Douglas reported that Gennaro's on New Compton Street included "Lasagne alla Mussolini" on its Saturday evening menu. Robin Douglas, *Well, Let's Eat* (London: Cassell, 1933), 5.
120. See also Eileen Hooten-Smith, *The Restaurants of London* (New York: Knopf, 1928), 15.
121. "Diner-Out," *London Restaurants* (London: Geoffrey Bles, 1924), 81, 82. Martini's "fascistic manners" gestured to Mussolini's reputation as a man of order who made the trains run on time and to an anti-democratic, militaristic model of labor discipline introduced into the restaurant by Escoffier, with its kitchen brigades and stations and equivalent ranks and orders in the restaurant saloon.
122. Ibid., 81, 82.
123. Morand, *A Frenchman's London*, 188, 189.
124. Ibid.
125. Ibid.
126. Lucio Sponza, *Divided Loyalties: Italians in Britain during the Second World War* (New York: P. Lang, 2000), 37.
127. On the Club Cooperativo, see *Il Comento*, April 28, 1923.
128. Sponza, *Divided Loyalties*.
129. Dipaola, "Italian Anarchists in London," 263.
130. Richard Wright, "Italian Fascism and the British-Italian Community, 1928–1943: Experience and Memory," Ph.D. diss, Manchester, 2001, 22.
131. Leoni, *I Shall Die*, 127.
132. Ibid., 131.
133. Marek Kohn, "Cocaine Girls," in Paul Gootenberg, ed., *Cocaine: Global Histories* (London: Routledge, 1999), 108.
134. *Thirty-Third Annual Report of the Public Morality Council, 1932* (London, 1932), LMA, A/PMC/ 98.
135. See chapter 7, "The Shady Nightclub."
136. "There are many who believe that certain Italian proprietors of restaurants round Piccadilly, Soho, and Oxford Street pay the police heavily for their indulgence." Sydney Alexander Moseley, *The Night Haunts of London* (London: Stanley Paul, 1920), 41.
137. Leoni, *I Shall Die*, 134.
138. In 1922, for example, the Westminster Watch Committee received numerous complaints from local businessmen on Gerrard Street about women who frequented Umberto's and paraded along the street at all hours, rendering it "most objectionable for respectable people to go along the street." "Minutes of the Watch Committee," Feb. 9, 1922, 371. WCC, WA.
139. Not all the businesses were restaurants, nor were all the proprietors Italian. Watchers observed women taking men to the upper floors above 39 Lisle Street, where Samuel and Mary L. Davidowitch ran a toy shop on the ground floor and basement. "Minutes of Watch Committee," Feb. 13, 1930, 39, WCC, WA.
140. "Minutes of Proceedings," May 12, 1927, 271, WCC, WA.
141. Leoni, *I Shall Die*, 147.
142. Ibid., 148–55, passim.
143. Hugh Belloni, a waiter in Mrs. Meyrick's club, explained that Mrs. Meyrick wrote out an order for drinks that the staff picked up from Molinari's before work and deposited at another address after the club closed in the early morning hours. Belloni, statement [April 1931], "Mrs. Kate Merrick or Meyrick: allegations of irregularities at The Cecil, The 43, and The Bunch of Keys Club, 1924–1935," MEPO2/4481/2v, NA. A third figure, a Mrs. Gadda, was charged with bribing Goddard and running a brothel in the rooms above her restaurant

on Greek Street, but she fled abroad. Clive Emsley, "The Story of a Rotten Apple or a Diseased Orchard?" in Amy Gilman Srebnick and Reney Lévy, eds., *Crime and Culture: An Historical Perspective* (Aldershot, UK: Ashgate, 2005), 98.

144. Leoni, *I Shall Die*, 154.

145. "Famed for Art," 146.

146. Ibid., 157.

147. Edward Carrick, "The Grubb Group—Edward Craig," in Leoni, *I Shall Die*, 146.

148. Marguerite Steen, *A Pride of Terrys: Family Saga* (London: Longmans, 1962), 349.

149. Carrick, "The Grubb Group," 159.

150. Leoni, *I Shall Die*, 163. Boulestin considerably raised the bar of London modernist restaurant decoration. Here, no struggling British artist was on display, only the best artifacts from Paris: silk velvet curtains designed by Dufy and paneled walls and ceiling by Marie Laurençin and Jean-Emile Laboureur. Brigid Allen, "Boulestin, (Xavier) Marcel (1878–1943)," in *Oxford Dictionary of National Biography* (Oxford: Oxford University Press, 2004), at http://www.oxforddnb.com/view/article/50432 (accessed Aug. 15, 2008).

151. Carrick, "The Grubb Group," 160.

152. "Soho Has Its Own Academy," *Daily Express*, June 16, 1933, 5.

153. "Food, Art and Science," *London Week*, Dec. 27, 1935, Grubb Group Clipping File, Parkin Gallery (http://www.parkinfineart.co.uk/).

154. "Marx Memorial Tablet," "LCC Signed Minutes," Jan. 19, 1925, Item 37/37, LMA, LCC/ O8169 1925. Leoni consistently refused to permit a plaque commemorating Marx's residence to be placed on the facade of his building, but he ultimately relented in 1965 when persuaded by a representative from *Pravda*. John Grigg, "Plaquemanship," *Guardian*, Feb. 8, 1965, 18; English Heritage, at http://www.english-heritage.org.uk (accessed June 14, 2010); Leoni, *I Shall Die*, 165; "The Inside Page: Memo to Moscow. Mission Accomplished in the Plaque Plot," *Daily Mirror*, Aug. 11, 1967, 1.

155. Leoni, *I Shall Die*, 163.

156. Their exhibitions challenge the conventional assumption among recent critics that the years after the war witnessed an "end to the collective life of modernist experiment," to be followed, in Peter Brooker's phrase, by the "modernism of the text." Peter Brooker, *Bohemia in London: The Social Scene of Early Modernism* (Houndmills, UK: Palgrave Macmillan, 2004), 9; Steve Bradshaw, *Café Society* (London: Weidenfeld & Nicolson, 1978), 144.

157. These commercial exchanges varied "from the august John Lane" to the notorious Leonard Smithers, who published Wilde and Beardsley and imported most of the expensive pornography circulating in London. Richard Cork, *Art beyond the Gallery in Early 20th Century England* (New Haven: Yale University Press, 1985), 94.

158. Davis, *The Gourmet's Guide to London*, 194–6.

159. Some of its members, notably Sidney Hunt and Claude Flight, had been aligned with the Seven and Five Society (founded in 1920), which also started off defending the aesthetic expression of individual members against any doctrinaire "theory," but increasingly required exhibitors to submit non-representational art. On the Seven and Five Club, see Stephen Coppel, *Claude Flight and His Followers: The Colour Linocut Movement between the Wars* (Canberra: Australian National Gallery, 1992); Lora S. Urbanelli, *The Grosvenor School: British Linocuts between the Wars* (Providence, RI: Museum of Art, Rhode Island School of Design, 1988); Michael Parkin, *The Seven and Five Society, 1920–1935* (London: Michael Parkin Fine Art, 1979). Flight broke with the group, while Hunt continued to exhibit with them from 1926 to 1932.

160. "Mr. Gossip," "The Grubb Group," *Daily Sketch*, April 14, 1928, 5. See D. J. Taylor, *Bright Young People: The Lost Generation of London's Jazz Age* (New York: Farrar, Straus, & Giroux, 2009).

161. Coppel, *Claude Flight*, 2; Caroline Taylor, "Flight Power," *Antique Collector* 67, no. 3 (1996): 54.

162. "Art and Artists," *Observer*, Dec. 16, 1928, 14; Michael T. Saler, *The Avant-Garde in Interwar England: Medieval Modernism and the London Underground* (Oxford: Oxford University Press, 1999).

163. Edward Craig, *Gordon Craig: The Story of His Life* (New York: Knopf, 1968), 337. See also Olga Taxidou, *The Mask: A Periodical Performance by Edward Gordon Craig* (Amsterdam: Harwood Academic, 1998), 49, 72.

164. "Aroma di una buona cucina," in Grubb Group Clipping File, Parkin Gallery.

165. "A Soho Haunt of Smart Bohemia," *Town and Country News*, June 17, 1932, Parkin Collection.

166. "Famed for Art."

167. Bon Viveur, *Where to Dine in London*, 82.

168. Daniel Farson, *Soho in the Fifties* (London: Michael Joseph, 1987), 91.

169. "Famed for Art," 40.

170. Leoni, *I Shall Die*, 198.

171. "Leoni of Quo Vadis," *London Week*, Dec. 27, 1935, in Grubb Group Clipping File, Parkin Gallery.

172. Douglas, *Well, Let's Eat*, 67.

173. Ben Rogers, "Status Quo; Restaurant: Who Goes There? Damien Hirst, for a Start," *Independent*, Jan. 4, 1997, 33.

174. Valerio Calzolari, quoted in Alasdair Scott Sutherland, *The Spaghetti Tree: Mario and Franco and the Trattoria Revolution* (London: Primavera, 2009), 36.

175. Paolo Monelli, *Il ghiottone errante. Viaggio gastronomico attraverso l'italia* (Milan: Fratelli Trevis, 1935), 219.

176. Within a year it had enrolled 1,000 members. Stephen Mennell, *All Manners of Food: Eating and Taste in England and France from the Middle Ages to the Present* (Oxford: Basil Blackwell, 1985), 279.

177. Ambrose Heath, "Wise Advice in *The Manchester Guardian*," *Wine and Food* 1, no. 4 (1934): 56. By contrast, Heath believed the "cooking of France" to be more successful "in making the best of the products of countries north of the Alps." Ibid., 60.

178. "Sunday Evening Group," *Wine and Food* 3, no. 16 (1937): 88.

179. Christopher Dilke, "Personality in Food," *Wine and Food* 5, no. 17 (1938): 49.

180. "Leoni of Quo Vadis."

181. Leoni, *I Shall Die*, 191.

182. Victoria De Grazia, *The Culture of Consent: Mass Organization of Leisure in Fascist Italy* (Cambridge, UK: Cambridge University Press, 1981); Helstosky, *Garlic and Oil*.

183. Helstosky, *Garlic and Oil*; Elizabeth David and Renato Guttoso, *Italian Food* (London: Macdonald, 1954).

184. Clerkenwell used to be the main Italian area, but many of the residential accommodations had been turned over almost completely to warehouses, precipitating a drift westwards, mostly to Soho. White, *London in the Twentieth Century*, 108. Whereas in 1901 the British census recorded 298 Italian café and restaurant owners and 1,964 waiters, by 1931, there were still 2,000 Italian waiters but 1,183 restaurant owners. Terri Colpi, *Italians Forward: A Visual History of the Italian Community in Great Britain* (Edinburgh: Mainstream, 1991), 80. On the migration from Lombardy and Piedmont, see Claudia Baldoli, *Exporting Fascism: Italian Fascists and Britain's Italians in the 1930s* (Oxford: Berg, 2003), 1.

185. Italian Fascists found France to be a less promising outpost, owing to the hostility of the French government, the integration of Italian emigrants into left-wing movements in France, and the growing numbers of Italian anti-Fascists who found refuge there. Sponza, *Divided Loyalties*, 20.

186. Bernabei, *Esuli ed emigranti*. According to Donna Gabaccia, 80 percent of Italian labor leaders left Italy during the Fascist years, most of them settling in France, Belgium, and Switzerland, where they forged solidarities with local labor organizations. In the United States, where Mussolini was very popular among Italian Americans, there were still thousands of Italian nationals and Italian Americans who openly opposed the Fascist regime. By contrast, the historical literature has not uncovered overt anti-Fascist political activity among Italians in Britain after 1924. See Donna Gabaccia, *Italy's Many Diasporas* (Seattle: University of Washington Press, 2000), ch. 6.

187. Terri Colpi, "The Impact of the Second World War on the British Italian Community," in David Cesarani, ed., *The Internment of Aliens in Twentieth Century Britain* (London: F. Cass, 1993), 169.

188. Wright, "Italian Fascism," 62.

189. David Butler and Garth Butler, *Twentieth-Century British Political Facts 1900–2000* (New York: St. Martin's Press, 2000), 158.

190. "Fascists at Large, Anti-Fascists Interned," *New Times and Ethiopia News*, Aug. 17, 1940, 2.

191. Sponza, *Divided Loyalties*, 41.

192. Claudia Baldoli, "The Remaking of the Italian Community in London: *L'Italia Nostra* and the Creation of a Little Fascist Italy during the 1930s," *London Journal* 6, no. 2 (2001), 23–34.

193. Colonel Sir Vernon Kell, "Note on the Organisation and Activities of the Italian Fascist Party in the United Kingdom, the Dominions and Colonies," in "Disturbances: Italian Fascism in U.K.: Forward Note on the Organisations," April 15, 1936, HO 144/21079/ 699617/7, NA.

194. Baldoli, *Exporting Fascism*, 12.

195. Elena Salvoni and Sandy Fawkes, *Elena: A Life in Soho* (London: Quartet, 1990), quoted in Baldoli, *Exporting Fascism*, 18. See also Sponza, *Divided Loyalties*, 56; Colpi, *Italians Forward*, 118.

196. Sponza, *Divided Loyalties*.

197. See, for example, ibid.; Baldoli, *Exporting Fascism*; Peter Gillman and Leni Gillman, '*Collar the Lot!' How Britain Interned and Expelled Its Wartime Refugees* (London: Quartet, 1980).

198. Wright, "Italian Fascism," 155. This is in contrast to Gabaccia's discussion of France and the United States. See Gabaccia, *Italy's Many Diasporas*, ch. 6.

199. Wendy Ugolini and Gavin Schaffer, "Victims or Enemies? Italians, Refugee Jews and the Reworking of Internment Narratives in Post-war Britain," in Gavin Schaffer and Monica Riera, eds., *The Lasting War: Society and Identity in Britain, France, and Germany after 1945* (Basingstoke, UK: Palgrave, 2008), 215.

200. Recently a few historians of Anglo-Italians have insisted on the need to resist the Italian community's retrospective memory of collective innocence and to identify the small but significant minority who actively embraced Italian Fascism. Following the lead of other historians of the Italian diaspora in the Americas, they have insisted on the need to perform "the difficult but important task of differentiation." Franca Iacovetta, quoted in Ugolini and Schaffer, "Victims or Enemies?" 225.

201. De Grazia, *Culture of Consent*; Helstosky, *Garlic and Oil*.

202. Leoni, *I Shall Die*, 18.

203. Kell, "Note," 12–13.

204. Ibid., 9, 15, 17, 21. The Club was the publishing home of the *British Italian Bulletin*, the English-language supplement of *L'Italia Nostra*, a "new departure" since the outbreak of the Italo-Abyssinian outbreak. The report also complained that British writers belonging to "all walks of life," including Ezra Pound, contributed articles criticizing the League of Nations and stressing "Italy's civilizing mission."

205. "Additional Notes," June 6, 1937, 1–3, HO 144/21079/22, NA; "Association of Italian Café Keepers in London—Formation," in ibid., Dec. 18, 1937, 1–3, HO 144/21079/11, NA.

206. "Association of Italian Café Keepers." By 1939, the *Guida Generale* listed membership in the group as 300, again not a majority of café owners, but a substantial minority. Wright, "Italian Fascism," 186.

207. "Signor Grandi Meets Fascists," *Daily Express*, Oct. 3, 1935, 2.

208. "Soho's Italy Gathers Gold for the Fight," *Daily Express*, Nov. 19, 1935, 2. Historians tend to agree that the London Fascio achieved the greatest degree of support among Anglo-Italians during the time of the Abyssinian war and the League of Nations sanctions against Italy. See, for example, Baldoli, "Remaking of the Italian Community," 30.

209. See, for example, "The Empire Spirit Stirs Britain," *New York Times*, Sept. 15, 1935, SM1; "London Waiters Demand Hotels Fire Italians," *Chicago Daily Tribune*, Oct. 14, 1935; "London's Italians Secret Meetings," *Glasgow Herald*, Oct. 3, 1935, 14.

210. Henrey, *London under Fire*, 22, 23.

211. See Mrs. Henrey's many autobiographical writings, *An Exile in Soho; Young Wife* (London: Dent, 1960); *Julia: Reminiscences of a Year in Madeleine's Life as a London Shop-Girl* (London: Dent, 1971); *A Girl at Twenty; Six Months in the Life of the Young Madeleine* (London: Dent, 1974).

212. "Later On," *What's On*, June 7, 1940, 631; Henrey, *London under Fire*, 66.

213. Henrey viewed these Italians as panderers who catered to a decaying aristocratic order and who schemed to "group the elite and keep the public at a respectful distance." Henrey, *London under Fire*, 26.

214. Ibid., 27.

215. Ibid., 66.

216. Stanley Jackson, *An Indiscreet Guide to Soho* (London: Muse Arts, 1946), 26.

217. Baldoli, "Remaking of the Italian Community."

218. Colpi, *Italians Forward*, 91.

219. "War on Soho Front." *Manchester Guardian*, Oct. 15, 1935, 5; "Italians in London Hotels: British Waiters Protest," *The Times*, Oct. 15, 1935, 11.

220. Quoted in Baldoli, *Exporting Fascism*, 73. Its English language supplement, the *British Italian Bulletin*, used the occasion to denounce the demonstrations as "engineered by Russian Soviet agents, Jews, and Communists", and publicized by newspapers controlled by Jews. This was a more explicit expression of anti-Semitism than was customary in *L'Italia Nostra*; J. Fordyce Thom to the editor, *British Italian Bulletin*, Oct. 25, 1935. This is well in advance of *L'Italia Nostra's* own editorial expression of anti-Semitism. Baldoli, *Exporting Fascism*, 138.

221. "Il camerieri all arrembaggio," *L'Italia Nostra*, Oct. 11, 1936.

222. "Cronaca gastronomica. Il cuoco italiana," *L'Italia Nostra*, Mar. 25, 1938, 2.

223. "Even the youngest Italian cook can contribute to the grandeur of the new Roman Empire by showing that the Italian race is very productive and creative," "Cronaca gastronomica," 3.

224. Ibid.

225. "Maestri gastronomici," *L'Italia Nostra*, Oct. 21, 1938, 4.

226. "Articolo con epilogo," *L'Italia Nostra*, Oct. 2, 1935, 5.

227. Jim Fyrth, "Introduction," in Fyrth, ed. *Britain, Fascism and the Popular Front* (London: Lawrence & Wishart, 1985), 9; Juliet Gardiner, *The Thirties: An Intimate History* (London: HarperPress, 2010).

228. See chapter 7 in this volume.

229. Montague Slater, "Artist International Exhibition 1935," *Left Review* 2 (1936): 161. See also Tony Rickaby, "Artists' International," *History Workshop*, no. 6 (1978): 154–68.

230. Slater, "Artist International Exhibition 1935," 161.

231. Ibid., 162.

232. They ranged from Clifford Rowe's social realist *Canvassing the Daily Worker*, to Augustus John's *Portrait of King Faisel*, to Laura Knight's undraped female adolescents in *Dawn*, to Moholy-Nagy's ultramodernist *Aluminum 12*. On the Popular Front of artistic styles, see Donald Drew Egbert, *Social Radicalism and the Arts: Western Europe; A Cultural History from the French Revolution to 1968* (New York: Knopf, 1970), 501.

233. Rickaby, "Artists' International," 158.

234. See, for example, Martin Pugh, *The Pankhursts* (London: Allen Lane, 2001); Ian Bullock and Richard Pankhurst, eds., *Sylvia Pankhurst: From Artist to Anti-Fascist* (Basingstoke, UK: Macmillan, 1992).

235. "Fascists at Large, Anti-Fascists Interned," *New Times and Ethiopia Gazette*, Aug. 17, 1940, 2.

236. On Emidio Recchioni, see Dipaola, "Emidio Recchioni"; Bernabei, *Esuli ed emigranti*, 38–48. On Special Branch's investigation into Recchioni and the assassination attempts, see Bernabei, "London Plot," 2; "Nationality and Naturalisation; Recchioni," HO 144/18949, NA.

237. In *Adam's Breed* (1926), Radclyffe Hall based her fictionalized Casa Basalli on King Bomba. Hall's portrayal also brought into relief Italian women's role in the Soho family enterprise, juxtaposing the tough business acumen of the signora to the exquisite taste of her husband.

Radclyffe Hall, *Adam's Breed* (London: Virago, 1985), 28, 86. See also "Nationality and Naturalisation; Recchioni."

238. Bernabei, "London Plot." King Bomba brochures (c.1925), in "Folio re Food," Box 1, Folder 2, Radclyffe Hall Papers, Harry Ransom Center, Austin, Texas.

239. King Bomba handbills (c.1925), in ibid.

240. Ibid.

241. As late as 1950, Soho's Italian provision shops remained the main suppliers of Continental delicacies. See Elizabeth David, *A Book of Mediterranean Food* (London: John Lehmann, 1950), 151; Bernabei, *Esuli ed emigranti*, 46.

242. Vernon Richards, quoted in Bernabei, *Esuli ed emigranti*, 103.

243. Inspector Hawkins, Report, June 11, 1929, "Nationality and Naturalisation; Recchioni," HO 144/18949/ 286107/7, NA.

244. Ibid.

245. Robert Williams to Alfred Short, M.P., May 23, 1930, "Nationality and Naturalisation; Recchioni," HO 144/18949/ 286107/11, NA.

246. O'Brien, addendum to Report, June 11, 1929, "Nationality and Naturalisation; Recchioni," HO 144/18949/ 286107/7, NA.

247. John Pedder to Col. Carter, Sept. 18, 1930, "Nationality and Naturalisation; Recchioni," HO 144/18949/ 286107/11, NA.

248. John Pedder, HO 144/18949/ 286107/7, Aug. 1, 1929, NA.

249. Quoted in Bernabei, "London Plot."

250. MacDonald had cold-shouldered Mussolini in his first term of office in the early 1920s, but by the late 1920s, he tried to maintain cordial relations. See Bernabei, *Esuli ed emigranti*, 80, 81.

251. Bernabei, "London Plot."

252. On *L'Italia Nostra*'s coverage, see "Al Bando," *L'Italia Nostra*, June 24, 1932, 1; "Nella colonia di Londra," *L'Italia Nostra*, July 1, 1932, 4.

253. Dipaola, "Emidio Recchioni."

254. "Anti-fascist Libel Action," *Daily Telegraph*, July 5, 1933, in "Nationality and Naturalisation; Recchioni," HO 144/286107/14, NA.

255. Bernabei, "London Plot."

256. Sponza, *Divided Loyalties*, 176–80.

257. "High Court of Justice," *The Times*, Mar. 16, 1934, 4.

258. Roger Squillario, "Dean Street Past," *Soho Clarion*, Summer 2009, 12.

259. On Soho's visibility as a center of Fascism, see Wright, "Italian Fascism," 151.

260. "Little Italy in London," *Observer*, June 16, 1940, 10.

261. On the "Battle of Soho," see *Manchester Guardian*, June 12, 1940, 4; "Anti-Italian Riots in Soho," in *The Tom Harrisson Mass Observation Archive* (Brighton, UK: Harvester Press Microfilm Publications, 1983), microform, File Report 184, June 11, 1940; see also Lucio Sponza, "The Anti-Italian Riots, June 1940," in Panikos Panayi, ed., *Racial Violence in Britain in the Nineteenth and Twentieth Centuries* (London: Leicester University Press, 1996); Tony Kushner, *We Europeans? Mass Observation, 'Race' and British Identity in the Twentieth Century* (Aldershot, UK: Ashgate, 2004), 177–85.

262. "Anti-Italian Riots in Soho."

263. Zinna Bulmore, quoted in Judith Summers, *Soho: A History of London's Most Colourful Neighbourhood* (London: Bloomsbury, 1989), 182, 83.

264. Kushner, *We Europeans?*, 183.

265. John Boswell, "Memo. To the Home Office," *Daily Mirror*, April 27, 1940, 6; Baldoli, *Exporting Fascism.*

266. Kushner, *We Europeans?*, 185.

267. "1600 Italians Detained: Soho Round-up Scenes," *Daily Telegraph and Morning Post*, June 12, 1940, 5.

268. Kushner, *We Europeans?*, 185.

269. Sponza, *Divided Loyalties*, 97.

270. See Kushner, *We Europeans?*, 178; "Italians Weep as They Leave London: Want to Return Here," *Daily Herald*, June 14, 1940, 4.

271. Sponza, "The Anti-Italian Riots," 144–5, quoted in Kushner, *We Europeans?*, 178. But some journalists also recognized the mixed ethnic population of the area.

272. "Italian Desks at Information Agency Are Searched," *Daily Herald*, June 12, 1940, 13.

273. "Go Slow—You've Arrested Too Many Italians," *Daily Express*, June 12, 1940, 5.

274. "Little Italy in London."

275. Hannen Swaffer, "The Day Comes to Soho," *Daily Herald*, June 12, 1940, 7.

276. Ibid.

277. "Anti-Italian Riots in Soho," 2.

278. George Trevelyan, "Italy, June 10th," *Spectator*, no. 5842 (1940): 803.

279. Ibid.

280. "A London Diary," *New Statesman and Nation*, June 14, 1940, 742.

281. "I have had this restaurant twenty-seven years," Bertorelli told him. "I am a very bad friend of Mussolini ever since 1914. He has changed his shirt four times. First it was red, then green, then black. Now it is yellow." "Go Slow."

282. On the "poor, sad women" of Soho, see Marie Immaculate Antoinette Woodruff, taped interview, 1992, 12927, IWM; Jackson, *An Indiscreet Guide to Soho*, 27.

283. Lionel Hale, "Life Goes On: *Signori* of Soho," *News Chronicle*, June 12, 1940.

284. Ibid.

285. Bernabei, *Esuli ed emigranti*, 210, 211.

286. He had been on a Special Branch file and the "blue label" [i.e. Fascist] had been mistakenly put on his file. Anzani V. Date of Birth: Anzani, D. Date of Birth: 10.07.1882," Letter, Sept. 18, 1940, HO 405/1961, NA.

287. Sponza, *Divided Loyalties*, 101–21.

288. Summers, *Soho*, 182.

289. Leoni described the new tenants as Indian, but *What's On* lists a Mrs. Choy as tenant from February 1943 to December 1944. See, for example, the advertisement for "Choy's Chinese Restaurant," *What's On*, Aug. 13, 1943, 298.

290. Leoni, *I Shall Die*, 21.

291. Ibid., 17.

292. On Erminia and the restaurant, see Leoni, *I Shall Die*, 15.

293. Loretto Santarelli, statement before War Tribunal, Oct. 23, 1940, "War: Loretto Santarelli, Manager Savoy Hotel Restaurant London, well known and hugely respected person; detention, 1940–1941," HO 45/23695/ 840939/C, NA.

294. Leoni, *I Shall Die*, 24.

295. Ibid., 17, 27. In Italy and in the UK, a higher percentage of southern Italians were strong supporters of Fascism than northern Italians.

296. Wright, "Italian Fascism," 202, 203.

297. Sylvia Pankhurst, "Fascist and Nazi Spies and Propagandists in London," *New Times and Ethiopia News*, June 22, 1940, 1, 2.

298. See, for example, "Fascists at Large, Anti-Fascists Interned," *New Times and Ethiopia News*, Aug. 30, 1940, 2. Pankhurst, "Fascist and Nazi Spies," 1, 2. On the government's hostility to Pankhurst, see A. J. Kellar to Lt. Colonel G. E. Kirk, Feb. 2, 1953, "Sylvia Pankhurst, alias Sylvia Estelle Pankhurst: British, Jan. 1, 1914–Dec. 31, 1953," Feb. 2, 1945, KV2/1570/55a, NA.

299. Silvio Corio, "A Call to Italian Anti-Fascists," *New Times and Ethiopia News*, June 15, 1940, 2.

300. "Italian Fascist Penetration in London," *New Times and Ethiopia News*, Aug. 24, 1940, 4.

301. Sylvia Pankhurst, "Ethiopia Must Be Recognized as Our Ally," *New Times and Ethiopia News*, June 15, 1940, 4.

302. Bullock and Pankhurst, *Sylvia Pankhurst*, 169; "Italian Fascist Penetration in London"; "Fascists at Large," Aug. 24, 1940, 4.

303. "Italian Fascist Penetration in London."

304. Sylvia Pankhurst, "The Anglo-Ethiopian Alliance," *New Times and Ethiopian News,* July 20, 1940, 4.

305. Pankhurst, "Fascist and Nazi Spies."

306. The letters were published in *New Times.* See Rita Pankhurst, "Sylvia Pankhurst in Perspective," *Women's Studies International Forum* 11, no. 3 (1988): 253.

307. "Fascists at Large, Anti-Fascists Interned," Aug. 30, 1940.

308. "Fascists at Large, Anti-Fascists Interned," *New Times and Ethiopia News,* Sept. 14, 1940, 1.

309. "Fascists at Large. Anti-Fascists Interned," Sept. 28, 1940.

310. Sylvia Pankhurst, "The Big Why in Soho" (1940), in E. Sylvia Pankhurst, *Women, Suffrage, and Politics: The Papers of Sylvia Pankhurst, 1882–1960, from the Internationaal Instituut Voor Sociale Geschiedenis, Amsterdam* (based on the original inventory prepared by Wilhelmina H. Schreuder and Margreet Schrevel) (Reading, UK: Adam Matthew, 1991), microform reel 22, no. 155.

311. Summers, *Soho,* 186.

312. "Who Eats in Soho?" *Manchester Guardian,* Mar. 4, 1941, 4.

313. "A few houses are 'down' here and there, among them a famous international chemist's shop at the corner of Greek street, and there is a nasty gap a little farther south [on Dean Street] where a famous church and a theatre have been wrecked." Ibid.

314. Dorothy Shipley White, *Seeds of Discord: De Gaulle, Free France and the Allies* (New York: Syracuse University Press, 1964), 93. David Blacktop, who worked in the Fire Service and was stationed in Soho, also recalled that there was no concentrated damage in Soho, just the "odd building." David Blacktop, interview, Mar. 23, 1992, 12501/3/1–2, IWM.

315. "Town Talk," *London Off Duty,* Winter 1942.

316. When customers complained about the horsemeat served at the Savoy, Chef Latry dismissed their grumblings: "Tell them it's steak or ships," he told the waiter. Latry, quoted in Jackson, *The Savoy,* 176.

317. Salvoni and Fawkes, *Elena,* 56.

318. "Who Eats in Soho?"

319. Mervyn Jones, *Chances: An Autobiography* (London: Verso, 1987), 61.

320. White, *Seeds of Discord,* 98.

321. "Famous Chefs Cook for Free Frenchmen," *Caterer and Hotel-Keeper,* Oct. 25, 1940, 5.

322. Summers, *Soho,* 186.

323. "Who Eats in Soho?"

324. *Manchester Guardian,* Sept. 10, 1943, 4.

325. Inspectors H. Williams and C. Allen, April 30, 1942, "Disturbances: Italian Anti-fascist Federation: Activities in United Kingdom, 1941–1945," HO 144/22491/ 868617/3, NA. On Bossi's partner, see Salvoni and Fawkes, *Elena,* 58. It is notable that Salvoni makes no distinction between Bossi as a known anti-Fascist and Serefino Pini. Whereas Pankhurst identified Pini as a rabid Fascist, Salvoni merely described him in her memoir as a victim of British military violence when interned (*Elena,* 66). By contrast, novelist Lilie Ferrari memorializes a different, but also romanticized, version of the thirties Anglo-Italian political experience. Her historical novel of Soho and Clerkenwell's Italians features a female protagonist from Clerkenwell who makes common cause with Recchioni and his anti-Fascist friends on Old Compton Street. Lilie Ferrari, *Fortunata* (London: Michael Joseph, 1993), 40.

326. Salvoni and Fawkes, *Elena,* 32, 33.

327. "War 70 Years On," *Camden New Journal,* Nov. 5, 2009, at http://www.thecnj.com/ camden/2009/110509/war110509_02.html (accessed May 2011).

328. Rudolph Dunbar, "Harlem in London: Year of Advancement for Negroes; Significance of the Shim-Sham," *Melody Maker,* Mar. 7, 1936, 2.

Chapter 5: Schleppers and Shoppers

1. Alec Waugh, "Round about Soho," in Arthur St. John Adcock, ed., *Wonderful London: The World's Greatest City,* vol. 1 (London: Educational Book Co., 1927), 131.

2. "Threat to London's Glory," *Evening Standard*, Sept. 17, 2001; "All-Conquering Superstores Drive out Street Market," *Independent*, April 14, 1996; "Sex, Fruit and a Soho Scandal," *Evening Standard*, Oct. 24, 1994. On the concept of the market and the spectacle, see Don Slater, "Going Shopping: Markets, Crowds, and Consumption," in Chris Jenks, ed., *Cultural Reproduction* (London: Routledge, 1993), 188–209.

3. On markets during the eighteenth century, see Colin Smith, "The Wholesale and Retail Markets of London, 1660–1840," *Economic History Review* 55, no. 1 (2002): 31–50. On the linkages between retail channels of shop and market, see J. Benson and G. Shaw, *The Evolution of Retail Systems c.1880–1914* (Leicester: Leicester University Press, 1992).

4. Mary Benedetta, *The Street Markets of London*, 156, quoted in Jerry White, *London in the Twentieth Century: A City and Its People* (New York: Viking, 2001), 252; Marjorie Edwards, *Up the Cally: The History and Recollections of London's Old Caledonian Market* (London: Marketprompt, 1989); H. Llewellyn Smith, ed., *The New Survey of London Life and Labour*, vol. 3 (London: P. S. King, 1932), 290–9.

5. On the dichotomous organization of urban modernity, see Georg Simmel, *Simmel on Culture: Selected Writings*, ed. David Frisby and Mike Featherstone (London: Sage, 1997); Erving Goffman, *The Presentation of Self in Everyday Life* (Garden City: Doubleday, 1959); Erving Goffman, *Interaction Ritual: Essays in Face-to-Face Behavior* (New York: Anchor Books, 1967). On recent historical scholarship that applies Goffman to interwar leisure and consumer industries, see Lewis Erenberg, *Steppin' Out: New York Nightlife and the Transformation of American Culture 1890–1930*, 2nd edn. (Chicago: Chicago University Press, 1984); Tracy C. Davis, *Actresses as Working Women: Their Social Identity in Victorian Culture* (London: Routledge, 1991). On the West End shopping scene, see Erika Diane Rappaport, *Shopping for Pleasure: Women in the Making of London's West End* (Princeton: Princeton University Press, 2000), 30; Christopher Breward, "Fashion's Front and Back: 'Rag Trade' Cultures and Cultures of Consumption in Post-War London c.1945–1970," *London Journal* 31, no. 1 (2006) 15–40; Amy de la Haye, "The Dissemination of Design from Haute Couture to Fashionably Ready-to-Wear during the 1920s," *Textile History* 24, no. 1 (1993): 39–48.

6. See Breward's discussion of Goffman, Breward, "Fashion's Front and Back," 16, 17.

7. On urban journalism and guidebooks, see, for example, Mary Benedetta, *The Street Markets of London*, photographs by László Moholy-Nagy (New York: B. Blom, 1972 repr.); Thomas Burke, *The London Spy: A Book of Town Travels* (London: Thornton Butterworth, 1922); Alec Waugh, "Round about Soho"; H. V. Morton, "Miss Jones in Baghdad," in Morton, *The Spell of London* (London: Methuen, 1926), 92–112; Alan Stapleton, *London's Alleys, Byways, and Courts* (London: John Lane, 1924); R. Thurston Hopkins, *This London: Its Taverns, Haunts and Memories* (London: C. Palmer, 1927); Florence Kirkpatrick, "Shopping East and West," in Adcock, *Wonderful London*, vol. 1, 240; Thelma H. Benjamin, *London Shops and Shopping* (London: Herbert Joseph, 1934). For retrospective memories of Jewish Sohoites, see Chaim Lewis, *A Soho Address* (London: Gollancz, 1965); Gerry Black, ed., *Living Up West: Jewish Life in London's West End* (London: London Museum of Jewish Life, 1994). The extensive oral histories of Sohoites have been collected by the Museum of Jewish Life and augmented by my own interviews. Complaints about shop touts also appear in *The Times, Daily Mirror, Draper's Record*, and other news outlets.

8. *Oxford English Dictionary*, at http://dictionary.oed.com.

9. Alfred Rubens, *A Jewish Iconography* (London: Jewish Museum, 1954).

10. On the Jewish pedlar in London, see Betty Naggar, *Jewish Pedlars and Hawkers, 1740–1940* (Camberley, UK: Porphyrogenitus, 1992); Todd M. Endelman, *The Jews of Georgian England, 1714–1830: Tradition and Change in a Liberal Society* (Ann Arbor: University of Michigan Press, 1999); Rubens, *A Jewish Iconography*; Israel Zangwill, "A Bearer of Burdens," in *Selected Works of Israel Zangwill: Children of the Ghetto, Ghetto Comedies, Ghetto Tragedies; a Golden Jubilee Volume* (Philadelphia: Jewish Publication Society of America, 1938), 59–101.

11. J. B. Priestley, quoted in Sally Alexander, "Becoming a Woman in London in the 1920s and 1930s," in David Feldman and Gareth Stedman Jones, eds., *Metropolis London: History and Representations since 1800* (London: Routledge, 1989), 245.

12. Richard Tames, *Soho Past* (London: Historical Publications, 1994), 15.
13. Strype, quoted in "Broadwick and Peter Street Area," *Survey of London, Volumes 31 and 32: St James Westminster, Part 2* (1963), 219–29, at http://www.british-history.ac.uk/ (accessed May 2011).
14. Fanny Burney, quoted in Tames, *Soho Past*, 24.
15. Rev. Harry Jones, "Working Men: Some of Their Ways and Their Wants," *Macmillan's Magazine* (1866), 243.
16. Rev. Harry Jones, *Fifty Years, or Dead Leaves and Living Seed* (London: Macmillan, 1895), 23; John Hollingshead, *Ragged London in 1861* (London, 1861), 116–18.
17. Jones, *Fifty Years*, 23.
18. Jones, "Working Men," 244.
19. Ibid.
20. E. P. Thompson, *William Morris: Romantic to Revolutionary*, rev. edn (London: Merlin Press, 1977), 281.
21. Richard Walker, *Savile Row: An Illustrated History* (New York: Rizzoli, 1989), 32.
22. James A. Schmiechen, *Sweated Industries and Sweated Labor: A History of the London Clothing Trades, 1860–1914* (London: Croom Helm, 1984), 110.
23. Ibid., 104–28; Black, *Living Up West*, 20.
24. On the mass middle-class market, see Rappaport, *Shopping for Pleasure*.
25. Peter Geoffrey Hall, *The Industries of London since 1861* (London: Hutchinson, 1962), 41–70; *Annual Report of the Chief Inspector of Factories and Workshops, Pt. II, vol. VII*, Cd. 1300 (1902), 176; Margaret Wray, *The Women's Outerwear Industry* (London: Duckworth, 1957), 18. On the movement of East End clothing firms into the West End, see Anne J. Kershen, *Off the Peg* (London: London Museum of Jewish Life, 1988).
26. Black, *Living Up West*, 14,20.
27. *Church and Synagogue*, quoted in ibid., 21.
28. On London's foreign-born population, see H. Llewellyn Smith, *The New Survey of London Life and Labour*, vol. 1: *Forty Years of Change* (London: P. S. King, 1930), 82.
29. Charles Booth, *Life and Labour of the People of London: The Charles Booth Collection, 1885–1905 from the British Library of Political and Economic Science, London* (Brighton, UK: Harvester Microform, 1988), B355, 14.
30. Quoted in Black, *Living Up West*, 39.
31. Ibid., Appendix 3, 269.
32. "Moving Here," NA, at http://www.movinghere.org.uk/stories/story359/ (accessed Sept. 25, 2010).
33. Black, *Living up West*, Appendix 3.
34. Hall, *Industries of London*, 65.
35. Stanley Jackson, *An Indiscreet Guide to Soho* (London: Muse Arts, 1946), 147.
36. Dennis Turhim, interview, Aug. 25, 1993, interview 366, WEJ.
37. Leslie Milgrim, "Interview," 1999, interview C/900/01520A and 20B, MMB, BLSA.
38. Quoted in Black, *Living Up West*, 58.
39. Alfred Marshall, quoted in Hall, *Industries of London*, 64, 65. See also Breward, "Fashion's Front and Back," 25.
40. See Gordon Honeycombe, *Selfridges: Seventy-Five Years: The Story of the Store 1909–1984* (London: Park Lane Press, 1984); Mica Nava, "The Cosmopolitanism of Commerce and the Allure of Difference: Selfridges, the Russian Ballet, and the Tango 1911–1914," *International Journal of Cultural Studies* 1, no. 2 (1998): 164–98; Rappaport, *Shopping for Pleasure*.
41. Susan Benson, quoted in N. Wrigley and Michelle Lowe, *Reading Retail: A Geographical Perspective on Retailing and Consumption Spaces* (London: Arnold, 2002), 176.
42. "News from the Bargain Basement," Sept. 21, 1911, Advertising, Book II, Selfridges Archive, Selfridges, London.
43. "The Significance of Selfridges' Bargain Basement," Nov. 11, 1915, Book II, 1915–1917, Selfridges Archives, London. According to historian Sally Alexander, only working women in a "supervisory position" would receive a monthly cheque. Thanks to her for this information.

44. Mrs. K. A. Philpotts, remembering the early years of the Bargain Basement, quoted in Honeycombe, *Selfridges*, 205; Mrs. Valerie Ranzetta, remembering the 1920s, ibid., 208.

45. Elena Salvoni and Sandy Fawkes, *Elena: A Life in Soho* (London: Quartet, 1990), 38; Dora Samuel (pseudonym), interview with author, June 22, 1999, London.

46. On the "Khaki boom," see Todd M. Endelman, *The Jews of Britain, 1656 to 2000* (Berkeley: University of California Press, 2002), 196.

47. "This Week's Bankruptcy Proceedings," *Draper's Record*, Nov. 9, 1929, 316. We also learn of the hopes and tribulations of Israel Freede, arriving from Poland in 1907, naturalized in 1923, who worked as a tailor in the City before he branched out to manufacture costumes in 1920. *Draper's Record*, May 17, 1930, 379, 380.

48. *Drapers Record*, Aug. 1, 1925, 252.

49. *Draper's Record*, Mar. 29, 1930, 768. In returning to Russia, Mr. Schatz was one of 2,000 Russian Jews who chose to fight for the post-revolutionary government rather than enter the British army. On Jewish men who returned to Russia in 1917, see Mark Levene, "Going against the Grain: Two Jewish Memoirs of War and Anti-War . . ." in Michael Berkowitz, Susan L. Tananbaum, and Sam W. Bloom, eds., *Forging Modern Jewish Identities: Public Faces and Private Struggles* (London: Vallentine Mitchell, 2003), 86. According to Levene, of 29,000 to 30,000 Russian Jews in Britain of military age, only 8,000 were known to have served in British military units. Also Louis Feldman, interview with author, June 20, 1999, London.

50. Alec Forshaw and Theo Bergstrom, *Markets of London*, rev. edn (Harmondsworth, UK: Penguin, 1986), 38.

51. H. Llewellyn Smith, *The New Survey of London Life and Labour*, vol. 3 (London: P. S. King, 1932), 324.

52. "The Street of Silk Stockings," *Manchester Guardian*, Sept. 2, 1925, 6.

53. Burke, *The London Spy*, 158.

54. Lewis, *A Soho Address*, 83.

55. David Vaughan, "Jessie Matthews," *Ballet Review* 24, no. 2 (Summer 1996): 33–6; Jeffrey Richards, *The Age of the Dream Palace: Cinema and Society in Britain, 1930–1939* (London: Routledge, 1989; orig. 1984), 39; "Dora Samuel" and "Esther Cohen," interview with author, June 22, 1999, London.

56. Robert Murphy, *Smash and Grab: Gangsters in the London Underworld 1920–60* (London: Faber and Faber, 1993), 15, 17.

57. Angus McLaren, *Sexual Blackmail: A Modern History* (Cambridge, MA: Harvard University Press, 2002), ch. 2; "Blackmail Charge: Alleged Demand for £5000," *The Times*, Oct. 23, 1927, 9.

58. "Night Club Man Made a Vow," *Daily Express*, Dec. 17, 1946, 5.

59. Laura Phillips, interview with author, June 22, 1999, London.

60. Mrs. Robert Henrey, *Madeleine Grown Up* (New York: Dutton, 1953), 100.

61. Leopold Wagner, *More London Inns and Taverns* (London: Allen & Unwin, 1925), 87.

62. Jan Gordon, *We Explore London* (New York: R. M. McBride, 1933), 204.

63. "The Street of Silk Stockings."

64. Phil Franks, interview, April 21, 1993, interview 346, WEJ.

65. Sophie Cole, *The Lure of Old London* (London: Mills & Boon, 1921), 138.

66. Benedetta, *The Street Markets of London*; Hopkins, *This London*, 3; "Dora Samuel," interview with author, June 22, 1999, London.

67. Virginia Woolf, *The Diary of Virginia Woolf*, vol. 1: *1915–1919*, ed. Anne Olivier Bell (Harmondsworth, UK: Penguin, 1979), 135.

68. Virginia Woolf, *Jacob's Room*, ed. and annotated Sue Roe (London: Penguin, 1992), 83; Virginia Woolf, *The Diary of Virginia Woolf*, vol. 2: *1920–24*, ed. Anne Olivier Bell and Andrew McNeillie (Harmondsworth, UK: Penguin, 1981, 1978), 92.

69. Before the Great War, working women made their own clothes, bought them secondhand, or patronized the cheapest tailors and dressmakers who made garments to order.

70. Gail Braybon and Penny Summerfield, *Out of the Cage: Women's Experiences in Two World Wars* (New York: Pandora Press, 1987).

71. Elizabeth Wilson and Lou Taylor, *Through the Looking Glass: A History of Dress from 1860 to the Present Day* (London: BBC Books, 1989), 78; Martin Pugh, *'We Danced All Night': A Social History of Britain between the Wars* (London: Bodley Head, 2008); Juliet Gardiner, *The Thirties: An Intimate History* (London: HarperPress, 2010), 12, 535.

72. New fabrics and new styles were more important for mass manufacturing than technological developments within the clothing manufacturing process, although the invention of the Hoffman press and machinery for blind stitching facilitated mass manufacturing. De la Haye, "Dissemination of Design," 40.

73. Ibid., 38.

74. Jackson, *Indiscreet Guide*, 132.

75. Laura Phillips, interview, Feb. 11, 1993, 306, WEJ. Phillips indicates that she later received some training in design.

76. David Moslyn, a skilled tailor working for West End firms, estimated that the guinea gown manufacturers made about 2–3 shillings per item. Quoted in Amy de la Haye, "The Role of Design within the Commercialisation of Women's Ready to Wear Clothing in Britain during the Inter-war Years, with Specific Reference to the Cheapest Levels of Products," diss., Royal College of Art, 1986, 138.

77. On the factors increasing working-class demand for fashionable clothes, see James Bavington Jefferys, *Retail Trading in Britain, 1850–1950* (Cambridge, UK: Cambridge University Press, 1954); de la Haye, "Role of Design."

78. Allison Jean Abra, "On with the Dance: Nation, Culture and Popular Culture, and Popular Dancing in Britain, 1918–1945," Ph.D. diss., University of Michigan, 2009, 113–16.

79. Carol Dyhouse, *Glamour: Women, History, Feminism* (London: Zed Books, 2010), 100. On trips Up West, see Jean Rhys, *Voyage in the Dark* (1934), quoted in Mica Nava, *Visceral Cosmopolitanism: Gender, Culture and the Normalisation of Difference* (Oxford: Berg, 2007), 84.

80. Quoted in de la Haye, "Role of Design," 138. The Co-op, selling utilitarian goods, did not arrive in Oxford Street until after the Second World War. According to David Moslyn, anyone with any fashion sense avoided the Co-op, where "utilitarian" goods could be obtained. Quoted in ibid., 160.

81. J.40, Mass Observation Files, quoted in ibid., 140.

82. Quoted in Jackson, *Indiscreet Guide*, 44.

83. Ethel Mannin, *Men Are Unwise* (London: Severn House, 1976), 41.

84. Cole, *The Lure of Old London*, 21.

85. Thelma Benjamin, *A Shopping Guide to London* (New York: R. M. McBride, 1930), 180. See also Kirkpatrick, "Shopping East and West," 238–48.

86. H. V. Morton, "Miss Jones in Baghdad," in Morton, *The Spell of London* (London: Methuen, 1926), 92–3.

87. Ibid, 92.

88. Ibid.

89. Ibid.

90. Alec Waugh, quoted in White, *London in the Twentieth Century*, 104.

91. Morton, "Miss Jones in Baghdad," 95.

92. Kristina Huneault, *Difficult Subjects: Working Women and Visual Culture, Britain 1880–1914* (Aldershot, UK: Ashgate, 2002), Epilogue.

93. Lewis, *A Soho Address*, 83.

94. Black, *Living Up West*, Appendix 3.

95. De la Haye, "Role of Design," 138.

96. Honey Summers, interview with author, Sept. 23, 2002, London. On Oxford Street, see Gordon Mackenzie, *Marylebone: Great City North of Oxford Street* (London: Macmillan, 1972); H. P. Clunn, *London Rebuilt, 1897–1927: An Attempt to Depict the Principal Changes Which Have Taken Place, with Some Suggestions for the Further Improvement of the Metropolis* (London: John Murray, 1927).

97. Lewis, *A Soho Address*, 83.

98. Ibid., 84–5.

99. "This Week's Bankruptcy," see the case of Emmanuel Cohen, *Draper's Record*, June 1925, 139; also Fanny Rodes, Mar. 1, 1930, 490; Mrs. B. Myers, Oct. 18, 1930, 163.

100. *The Post Office London Directory* (London: Kelly's Directories, 1918), 198.

101. "This Week's Bankruptcy," *Draper's Record*, Oct. 26, 1929, 316.

102. Peter Bailey, "Champagne Charlie and the Music Hall Swell Song," in Bailey, *Popular Culture and Performance in the Victorian City* (Cambridge, UK: Cambridge University Press, 1998), 101–27.

103. On the Turk, see Dora Samuel and Esther Cohen (pseudonym), interview with author, June 22, 1999, London; Jackson, *Indiscreet Guide*, 131; Lewis, *A Soho Address*, 83–88.

104. Lewis, *A Soho Address*, 84.

105. Andrew R. Heinze, *Adapting to Abundance: Jewish Immigrants, Mass Consumption, and the Search for American Identity* (New York: Columbia University Press, 1990). For a spectacular argument for Jewish exceptionalism, see Yuri Slezkine, *The Jewish Century* (Princeton: Princeton University Press, 2004).

106. Jackson, *Indiscreet Guide*, 132; Breward, "Fashion's Front and Back."

107. Interview with Phillips, interview 306, WEJ.

108. "Berwick Street and the Shops Act," *Draper's Record*, Aug. 30, 1930, 377.

109. Stefan Slater, "Containment: Managing Street Prostitution in London, 1918–59," *Journal of British Studies* 49, no. 1 (2010); Stefan Slater, "Pimps, Police, and Filles de Joie: Foreign Prostitution in Interwar London," *London Journal* 32, no. 1 (2007): 53–74.

110. "Minutes of Proceedings," Nov. 13, 1930, items 661, 662, WCC, WA.

111. "The Invasion of Soho," *Observer*, April 1, 1928, 11.

112. "The Touting Nuisance," *Draper's Record*, Mar. 22, 1930, 701, noted that these touts "occupy such a large amount of time almost daily at Marlborough street [police court]." The *Draper's Record* reported multiple summonses against Berwick Street touters. "Berwick Street Touting Nuisance," *Draper's Record*, April 5, 1930, 19. Westminster City Council was also concerned that the spread of the street market to Rupert Street, Little Pulteney Street, and Peter Street obstructed vehicular traffic. See "Minutes of Works Sub-Committee Re Street Trading 1930–1931," item 62, 63, 153, WCC, WA. These complaints of obstructions persisted. Many shopkeepers lodged complaints about stallholders who hung their goods on their stall "in such a way as to obstruct the view of the shop from the roadway." "Minutes of Works Sub-Committee Re Street Trading 1934–1935," Nov. 13, 1934, 96, WCC, WA.

113. A. H. Dacombe, "Street Trading," *The Times*, Sept. 12, 1923, 6.

114. "Minutes of Works Sub-Committee re Street Trading," Jan. 7, 1930, 3, WCC, WA.

115. Evidently, in the prewar period, all "the pitches in street were controlled by a number of individuals who let them to traders at specific rentals; that the police stopped these payments and compiled a register of traders." Ibid.

116. Mrs. Percy, to the Editor, "Berwick-Street Costermongers," *The Times*, April 4, 1927, 10; White, *London in the Twentieth Century*, 247–52.

117. "London Street Markets: Paradoxes of Fruit Prices," *The Times*, Aug. 4, 1928, p. 14.

118. "Minutes of Works Sub-Committee re Street Trading," Jan.7, 1930, 4, WCC, WA.

119. "Berwick Street Cases," *Draper's Record*, July 19, 1930, 107; "Berwick Street Touting Prosecution," *Draper's Record*, July 26, 1930, 143; Laura Phillips, interview 306, WEJ.

120. Joseph Lee, "London Laughs: Berwick Market," *Evening News*, Feb. 20, 1936.

121. See, for example, "Exit the Tout in Berwick Street," *Daily Mirror*, March 5, 1932, 5.

122. Joe Gilbert, interview, Oct. 14, 1991, interview 327, WEJ; Alexander Flinder, interview, 17 Jan. 1994, interview 371, WEJ. On the number of workers in the Jewish-dominated garment trades of Soho in 1938, see Joseph Rawlinson and William Robert Davidge, *City of Westminster Plan* (London: Westminster City Council, 1946), 40.

123. On middle-class suburbanization, see Alan Arthur Jackson, *Semi-Detached London: Suburban Development, Life and Transport, 1900–39* (London: Allen & Unwin, 1973); Simon Gunn and Rachel Bell, *Middle Classes: Their Rise and Sprawl* (London: Cassell, 2002). On Jewish migration to the London suburbs, see Endelman, *The Jews of Britain*, 197–8.

124. "Minutes of Proceedings," Nov. 28, 1929, 722–4, WCC, WA; "Standing Committee on Expenditure," 1937–1939, WCC, WA, 171–2.

125. *Manchester Guardian*, Mar. 25, 1933, 12.
126. "London Jews' Day of Protest," *Manchester Guardian*, July 21, 1933, 3.
127. "Fascist Parade in London," *Manchester Guardian*, Oct. 7, 1935, 14.
128. "A Communist Fined," *The Times*, Aug. 22, 1936, 14; Feldman, interview with author, June 20, 1999, London.
129. In the same year, Hitchcock's *Sabotage* featured a sado-masochistic crowd in a street market. Gillian Rose, "Engendering the Slum: Photography in East London in the 1930s," *Gender, Place and Culture* 4, no. 3 (1997): 277–300.
130. László Moholy-Nagy, "Foreword," in Benedetta, *The Street Markets of London*, vii; R. Sachesse, "The Disfunctional Leica: Instrument of the German Avant-Garde," *History of Photography*, no. 17 (1993): 301–4; Jeffrey L. Schnapp, "The Mass Panorama," *Modernism/ Modernity* 9, no. 2 (2002): 243–81.
131. Klause Scherpe and Mitch Cohen, "Modern and Postmodern Transformation of Metropolitan Narrative," *New German Critique*, no. 55 (1992): 77.
132. Moholy-Nagy, "Foreword," vii.
133. Ibid.
134. Ibid., viii.
135. Joel Meyerowitz, quoted in Rose, "Engendering the Slum," n. 4.
136. Ibid.
137. László Moholy-Nagy, "Berwick Market: General View," in Benedetta, *The Street Markets of London*.
138. László Moholy-Nagy, "Berwick Street: A Family Business—Flower Sellers," in Benedetta, *The Street Markets of London*.
139. Benedetta, *Street Markets of London*, 53.
140. Ibid., 56.
141. Ibid., 55.
142. Ibid.
143. Ibid., 56–7.
144. Ibid.
145. George Thomas, *A Tenement in Soho* (London: Cape, 1931), 49.
146. John Pudney, *Jacobson's Ladder: A Novel* (London: Longmans, 1938); Storm Jameson, *Here Comes a Candle* (New York: Macmillan, 1939).
147. Jennifer Birkett and Chiara Briganti, *Margaret Storm Jameson: Writing in Dialogue* (Newcastle: Cambridge Scholars, 2007), 169.
148. By comparison, Soho crime novels tended to focus on the murderous machinations of an organized criminal underworld engaged in the trafficking of women. Walter Greenwood, *Only Mugs Work: A Soho Melodrama* (London: Hutchinson, 1938); Sydney Horler, *The House in Greek Street* (London: Hodder & Stoughton, 1935); Grierson Dickson, *Soho Racket* (London: Hutchinson, 1935); John Gordon Brandon, *Murder in Soho* (London: Wright & Brown, 1937). Gerald Kersh managed to inflect a political critique within the crime formula: Gerald Kersh, *Night and the City* (London: Michael Joseph, 1938).
149. Pudney had worked as a property agent in the area. On Jews and the property market, see Stephen Aris, *The Jews in Business* (London: Cape, 1971). See also Frank Mort, *Capital Affairs* (London: Yale University Press, 2010), 290–2. See also "Epilogue," this volume.
150. Pudney, *Jacobson's Ladder*, 68.
151. Ibid., 23.
152. Jameson, *Here Comes a Candle*, 10.
153. Norah Hoult, "Awaiting the Fire," *The Nation*, Mar. 4, 1939, 275.
154. David Blacktop, 12520/3/ 1–2, Imperial War Museum, London.
155. "Damage to West End Stores," *The Times*, Sept. 19, 1940, 2.
156. "Around Town," *What's On*, Sept. 29, 1944.
157. *The Post Office London Directory* (London: Kelly's Directories, 1940), 177; *The Post Office London Directory* (London: Kelly's Directories, 1943), 119.

158. Donald Serrell Thomas, *An Underworld at War: Spivs, Deserters, Racketeers and Civilians in the Second World War* (London: John Murray, 2003), 229.

159. Ibid., 149–50. Thomas lists Schatz as "Schnatz," but Hyman Schatz was the only trader in hosiery approximating that name to appear in the Post Office Directories and in the records of the Street Trading Subcommittee of the Westminster City Council.

160. Victor Falber, letter, "Minutes of Proceedings," Nov. 28, 1946, Street Trading, WCC, WA.

161. "Berwick Street and the Shops Act"; Falber, letter, "Minutes of Proceedings."

162. Jackson, *Indiscreet Guide*, 131.

163. Louis Feldman, interview with author, June 20, 1999, London.

164. Phil Franks, interview 346, WEJ.

165. Ibid.; Laura Phillips, interview 306, WEJ.

166. See Frank Mort, *Cultures of Consumption: Masculinities and Social Space in Late Twentieth-Century Britain* (London: Routledge, 1996).

167. Esther Rose, interview, Nov. 9, 1993, interview 347, WEJ.

168. Phil Franks, interview 346, WEJ.

169. Honey Summers, telephone interview with author, Sept. 23, 2002, London; Esther Cohen and Dora Samuel, interview with author, June 22, 1999, London.

170. Lewis, *A Soho Address*, 87.

171. Ibid., 85.

172. Dennis Turhim, interview 366, WEJ.

173. Alex Flinder, interview, Jan. 17, 1994, interview 351, WEJ.

174. Ibid.

175. On plebeian knowingness, see Peter Bailey, "Conspiracies of Meaning: Music-Hall and the Knowingness of Popular Culture," *Past & Present*, no. 144 (1994): 139–70.

176. Susan A. Glenn, *Female Spectacle: The Theatrical Roots of Modern Feminism* (Cambridge, MA: Harvard University Press, 2000), 50–3; F. Mooney Hughson, "Songs, Singers and Society, 1890–1954," *American Quarterly* 6, no. 3 (1954): 221; June Sochen, "From Sophie Tucker to Barbra Streisand," in Joyce Antler, ed., *Talking Back: Images of Jewish Women in American Popular Culture* (Hanover, NH: Brandeis University Press, 1998), 68–84.

177. Lewis, *A Soho Address*, 85. On the appeal of Hollywood for popular British audiences, see Ross McKibbin, *Classes and Cultures: England, 1918–1951* (Oxford: Oxford University Press, 2000), ch. 11. On London criminals' emulation of the Hollywood gangster, see Murphy, *Smash and Grab*. On Soho criminals, see Mark Benney, *Low Company: Describing the Evolution of a Burglar* (London: Peter Davies, 1936).

178. William Goldman, *East End My Cradle* (London: Faber and Faber, 1940), 82.

179. See, for example, John Worby, *The Other Half: The Autobiography of a Spiv* (London: Dent, 1937); John Worby, *Spiv's Progress* (London: Dent, 1939).

180. White, *London in the Twentieth Century*, 245.

181. Lewis, *A Soho Address*, 132.

182. Milgrim, "Interview," 1999, MMB.

183. Louis Feldman, interview with author, June 20, 1999, London.

184. Louis Feldman, interview, June 22, 1993, interview 337, WEJ.

185. Esther Rose, interview 347, WEJ.

186. Kenneth Brown, interview, Oct. 31, 1990, interview 336, WEJ; Louis Feldman, interview with the author, June 15, 2001, London.

187. Rachel Goldberg (pseudonym), interview with author, June 27, 1999, London.

188. Louis Feldman, interview with author, June 22, 1999.

189. On the "absence of disharmony," see Black, *Living Up West*, 40. Quoted in Ellen Ross, "Missionaries and Jews in Soho: Strangers within Our Gates," *Journal of Victorian Literature* 15, no. 2 (Aug. 2010): 226–38.

190. Susan J. Ferry, "Bodily Knowledge: Female Body Culture and Subjectivity in Manchester, 1870–1900," Ph.D. diss., Johns Hopkins University, 2003.

191. William Sewell, quoted in Gabrielle M. Spiegel, "Introduction," in Spiegel, *Practicing History: New Directions in Historical Writing after the Linguistic Turn* (New York: Routledge, 2005), 20.

192. See Judy Giles, *Women, Identity, and Private Life in Britain, 1900–50* (Houndmills, UK: Macmillan, 1995); Maggie Winship, "New Disciplines for Women and the Rise of the Chain Stores in the 1930s," in Mary Talbot and Maggie Andrews, eds., *'All the World and Her Husband': Women in Twentieth-Century Consumer Culture* (London: Cassell, 2000), 23–45.

Chapter 6: A Jewish Night Out

1. Henri Lefebvre, *The Production of Space* (Oxford: Blackwell, 1991), 87; Michel de Certeau, *The Practice of Everyday Life* (Berkeley: University of California Press, 1984); Derek Gregory, *Geographical Imaginations* (Oxford: Blackwell, 1994); Phil Hubbard, Rob Kitchin, and Gill Valentine, eds., *Key Thinkers on Space and Place* (London: Sage, 2004).
2. On the "invention" of heterosexuality, see Jonathan Katz, "The Invention of Heterosexuality." *Socialist Review* 20 (1990): 7–34.
3. *Bombay Mail* was an American talkie—actually a Universal film—but it adhered to the pattern established by Paramount's *Shanghai Express*, featuring a group of Calcutta-bound passengers thrust into a life-and-death situation bound up with the "political and business life of British India." "Bombay Mail," *New York Times*, Jan. 6, 1934, at http://movies.nytimes.com (accessed Jan. 25, 2010).
4. Richard Davenport-Hines, "Clore, Sir Charles (1904–1979)," in H. C. G. Matthew and Brian Harrison, eds., *Oxford Dictionary of National Biography* (Oxford: Oxford University Press, 2004), at http://www.oxforddnb.com/view/article/30943 (accessed Jan. 25, 2010).
5. According to historical geographers, these sedimented landscapes denote the knife-edge tension within capitalism towards "preserving the values of past commitments made at a particular time place and time, or devaluing them to open up fresh room for accumulation." See Derek Gregory's discussion of Harvey and Zukin, in Gregory, *Geographical Imaginations*, 91–3, 153–9.
6. F. H. W. Sheppard, "General Introduction," in Shepherd, gen. ed., *Survey of London, Volumes 33 and 34: St. Anne, Soho* (London, 1966), at http://www.british-history.ac.uk/report.aspx?compid=41022 (accessed May 2011).
7. Over the next seventy years, the Astoria would change hands many times and acquire new social and cultural associations: in 2002 it became the "biggest live music venue for rock in central London" and a raucous adjunct to Soho's glitzy gay nightlife, hosting a "G.A.Y." dance night on Saturdays, while still proudly advertising its early origins as a "pickle factory." At http://www.festivalrepublic.com/venues/#Astoria (accessed Jan. 25, 2010). In 2009, despite public outcry and petitions, the Astoria was bulldozed to make way for the Tottenham Court Road station for the new Crossrail network.
8. Frank C. Mort, "Cityscapes: Consumption, Masculinities, and the Mapping of London since 1950," *Urban Studies* 35, no. 5–6 (1998): 891.
9. Louis Feldman, interview with author, June 20, 1999, London.
10. Frances Rust, *Dance in Society: An Analysis of the Relationship between the Social Dance and Society in England from the Middle Ages to the Present Day* (London: Routledge & Kegan Paul, 1969), 393.
11. Allison Jean Abra, "On with the Dance: Nation, Culture and Popular Culture, and Popular Dancing in Britain, 1918–1945," Ph.D. diss., University of Michigan, 2009, 134.
12. On the general design of the dance floor, see ibid., 134–5. The Astoria's neoclassical decor most closely resembled the elite Kit Kat Club in Haymarket, opened in 1925. "A Round of the Night Clubs," in Arthur St John Adcock, ed., *Wonderful London*, vol. 3 (London: Amalgamated Press, 1926), 951.
13. Dora Samuel is a pseudonym. Letter to the author, June 22, 1999, London.
14. Ibid.
15. James J. Nott, *Music for the People: Popular Music and Dance in Interwar Britain* (Oxford: Oxford University Press, 2002), 171.
16. On glamor and the dance hall, see Juliet E. McMains, *Glamour Addiction: Inside the American Ballroom Dance Industry* (Middletown, CT: Wesleyan University Press, 2006).

17. Harry Blacker, *Just Like It Was: Memoirs of the Mittel East* (London: Vallentine Mitchell, 1974), 68.

18. Dora Samuel and Esther Cohen (pseudonym), interview with author, June 22, 1999, London; Mrs. Hannah Myers, interview, July 28, 1972, Family Life and Experience before 1918, C707/401/1, BLSA.

19. Rachel Goldberg is a pseudonym. Interview with author, June 27, 1999, London.

20. Abra, "On with the Dance," 113–16.

21. Basil L. Q. Henriques, *Club Leadership Today* (Oxford: Oxford University Press, 1951), 138; Basil L. Q. Henriques, *The Indiscretions of a Warden* (London: Methuen, 1937), 86.

22. Lily H. Montagu, *My Club and I: The Story of the West Central Jewish Club* (London: Herbert Joseph, 1941); "Tribute from Past Club Members," *Orbit Magazine*, May 1968. On Mrs. Chant, see chapter 2.

23. Irene Glausius, interview, n.d., interview 353, WEJ.

24. See Rebecca L. Walkowitz, *Cosmopolitan Style: Modernism beyond the Nation* (New York: Columbia University Press, 2006), ch. 5.

25. Dora Samuel, telephone interview with author, Oct. 30, 1999, London.

26. See Katz, "The Invention of Heterosexuality"; Chrys Ingraham, *Thinking Straight: The Power, the Promise, and the Paradox of Heterosexuality* (London: Routledge, 2005); Adrian Bingham, *Gender, Modernity, and the Popular Press in Inter-war Britain* (Oxford: Clarendon Press, 2004); Sally Alexander, *Becoming a Woman and Other Essays in 19th and 20th Century Feminist History* (London: Virago Press, 1994); Alys Eve Weinbaum, ed., *The Modern Girl around the World: Consumption, Modernity, and Globalization* (Durham, NC: Duke University Press, 2008); Claire Langhamer, "Love and Courtship in Mid-Twentieth-Century England," *Historical Journal* 50, no. 1 (2007): 173–96; Anna Clark, *Desire: A History of European Sexuality* (New York: Routledge, 2008); Carol Dyhouse, *Glamour: Women, History, Feminism* (London: Zed Books, 2010).

27. Esther Cohen and Dora Samuel, interview with author, June 22, 1999, London. "Big Apple Ball," n.d., includes a reference to Jewish women in "flashy blouses and short skirts," plus diamond clips. The Locarno, Streatham, 38/1/A, MOA. See also "First Visit to the Locarno, April 27, 1939, 38/1/A, MOA; "Royal Tottenham," April 23, 1939, 38/1/C, MOA.

28. Rachel Goldberg, interview with author, June 27, 1999, London.

29. "Living Up West: Jewish Life in London's West End," Exhibition, Museum of Jewish Life, London, 1994.

30. Mildred Loss, interview, Dec. 14, 1993, interview 465, WEJ.

31. "Second Weekly Report on Home Intelligence," 440, Oct. 1940, MOA.

32. Irene Glausiuz, interview 353, n.d., WEJ.

33. J. Green, *A Social History of the Jewish East End in London, 1914–39: A Study of Life, Labour and Liturgy* (Lewiston, NY: E. Mellen 1991), 340.

34. Sonya Birnbaum, interview, Jan. 6, 1993, interview 299, WEJ.

35. On Sohoites who claimed "no difference," see Sidney Diamond, interview, Feb. 10, 1993, interview 339, WEJ. On "walking into culture," see "Living Up West." For Sohoites who made use of the high and low cultural resources of the West End, see interviews with Alex Flinder, Jan. 17, 1994, interview 351; Anne Kahn, Aug. 27, 1992, interview 342; and writers Benny Green, Feb. 3, 1993, interview 336, and Chaim Lewis, Jan. 12, 1993, interview 298. WEJ. This group often came from families with businesses such as hairdressing, public houses, or the theatrical trades that brought them into contact with elite customers, or they went on to higher education and became theatrical professionals and intellectuals. For these individuals, the West End extended to the British Museum, the galleries of the Old Vic and West End theaters, the concert hall at the Queen's Hall, and even, in one case, visits to the bohemian Gargoyle Club and some of Soho's foreign eateries.

36. Manis Goldberg, interview, Nov. 9, 1993, interview 348, WEJ.

37. Alex Flinder, interview 351, WEJ.

38. Max Minkoff, interview, Mar. 21, 1993, interview 812, WEJ. Working-class autodidacts from the East End, such as Joe Jacobs and Harry Blacker, also claimed to have taken advantage of the

cultural opportunities of the West End, but they were a minority group among East Enders going "Up West." Blacker, *Just Like It Was;* Joe Jacobs, *Out of the Ghetto: My Youth in the East End: Communism and Fascism, 1913–1939* (London: Janet Simon, 1978).

39. Gerry Black, ed., *Living Up West: Jewish Life in London's West End* (London: London Museum of Jewish Life, 1994), 26.
40. Rose Friedman, June 6, 1992, interview 363, WEJ.
41. Dora Samuel, interview with author, June 22, 1999, London.
42. Louis Feldman, interview with author, June 22, 1999; interview 377, WEJ.
43. Ross McKibbin, *Classes and Cultures: England, 1918–1951* (Oxford: Oxford University Press, 2000), 395. On kinesthetic expression and the dance renaissance, see chapter 3.
44. Jenny Taylor, "Sex, Snobs, and Swing: A Case Study of Mass Observation as a Source for Social History," in *Mass Observation Online* (Marlborough, UK: Adam Matthew Digital, 2007), at http://www.amdigital.co.uk/collections/Mass-Observation-Online.aspx (accessed Sept. 30, 2010).
45. William Goldman, *East End My Cradle* (London: Faber and Faber, 1940), 94.
46. Ibid.; Leslie Milgrim, interview, Mar. 16, 1999, C/900/01529A and C/900, 01520B, MMB. According to the president of the Imperial Society of Dance Teachers, women learned dancing "quicker than men," because of male "fears of being effeminate." "Dance Teachers," June 19, 1939, 38/6/G, MOA.
47. Leslie Milgrim, interview, MMB.
48. "Our Ballroom Dancing," *Manchester Guardian* 1936, 9.
49. Henry Jacques, "Restaurant Dancing," *Dancing Times* 22 (Dec. 1931): 298, 299.
50. Astoria, Dec. 5, 1939, 38/5/D, MOA.
51. Manis Goldberg, interview 348, WEJ.
52. Dora Samuel, telephone interview with author, Oct. 30, 1999, London.
53. Ibid.; Louis Feldman, telephone interview with author, June 15, 2001, London.
54. Santos Casini, quoted in Abra, "On with the Dance," 234.
55. Dora Samuel, telephone interview with the author, Oct. 30, 1999, London.
56. Mica Nava, *Visceral Cosmopolitanism: Gender, Culture and the Normalisation of Difference* (Oxford: Berg, 2007); Judith R. Walkowitz, "The 'Vision of Salome': Cosmopolitanism and Erotic Dancing in Central London, 1908–1918," *American Historical Review* 108, no. 2 (2003): 337–76.
57. "Our Ballroom Dancing," 9.
58. Philip John Sampey Richardson, *A History of English Ballroom Dancing, 1910–45: The Story of the Development of the Modern English Style ... Illustrated* (London: Herbert Jenkins, 1946), 90.
59. Helen Thomas and Nicola Miller, "Ballroom Blitz," in Helen Thomas, ed., *Dance in the City* (Houndmills, UK: Palgrave Macmillan, 1997), 101.
60. "Non-Mecca Dancing," July 15, 1939, 38/5/F, MOA.
61. "A New Tango," *Manchester Guardian*, Oct. 3, 1920, 10; "Dancing in 1925," *Manchester Guardian*, Jan. 11, 1925, 9; "The Tango and Its Chances," *Manchester Guardian*, Nov. 1, 1925, 9, in "Non-Mecca Dancing," July 15, 1939, 38/5/F, MOA.
62. "Dance Instructors," May 30, 1939, 38/5/G, MOA.
63. "The British Ballroom," *Manchester Guardian*, Jan. 1, 1938, 15.
64. Alan Charles Jenkins, *The Twenties* (London: Heinemann, 1974), 19.
65. Dora Samuel and Esther Cohen, interview with author, June 22, 1999, London.
66. "Song Writers," Dec. 5, 1939, 38/5/D, MOA; Helen B. Josephy and Mary Margaret Macbride, *London Is a Man's Town, but Women Go There* (London: Coward-McCann, 1930), 274.
67. McKibbin, *Classes and Cultures*, 281.
68. Lyndon B. Wainwright, *The Story of British Popular Dance* (Brighton, UK: International Dance, 1997), 34.
69. Abra, "On with the Dance," 204, 205. For one positive media version of the male dancer, see "Sixpenny Partners," *Weekly Telegraph*, Feb. 25, 1939, 17–20; "Professional Partners," 38/3/G, MOA.

70. Most of the media scandals related to dance hostesses involved employees of nightclubs rather than the Palais. However, news stories of lawless activities at the dance halls, including violence, theft, prostitution, and adultery, appeared throughout the interwar years. See, for instance, the following articles in *The Times*: "Dancing Partners Rings Stolen," Mar. 3, 1920, 14; "High Court of Justice," Dec. 20, 1922, 4; "High Court of Justice," Oct. 23, 1923, 5; "Alleged Assault in a Dance Hall," Sept. 17, 1926, 9; "Man's Death in Car Crash," Jan. 13, 1934, 7; "£360 Damages for Assault at a Dance Hall," Mar. 5, 1938, 9.

71. "Dance Professionals," Dec. 12, 1939; June 25, 1939, 38/3/G, MOA.

72. J. Orde Kennedy, "A Sixpenny Girl," *Eve*, April 7, 1926, 35. See also "Professional Dancers," 38/3/G, MOA.

73. Abra, "On with the Dance," 204.

74. "Sixpenny Partners," quoted in ibid., 216.

75. Kennedy, "A Sixpenny Girl," 35.

76. Ibid., 48.

77. "Professional Dancers," May 5, 1939, 38/3/G, MOA; Kennedy, "A Sixpenny Girl," 48. See also "Cyril" at the Locarno, "Professional Dancers," June 25, 1939.

78. Dora Samuel, telephone interview with author, Oct. 30, 1999. On wallflowers at the Astoria, see Anne Kahn, interview, Aug. 27, 1992, interview 368, WEJ.

79. See, for example, "London Dance Notes," *Dancing Times* 22 (Oct. 1931): 109, 213.

80. "Locarno, Streatham," April 27, 1939, 38/1/A, MOA.

81. Taylor, "Sex, Snobs, and Swing," 15; Harrisson, quoted in ibid, 16.

82. "Locarno, Streatham," April 27, 1939, 38/1/A, MOA.

83. Dora Samuel, interview with author, June 22, 1999, London.

84. On Mass Observation's view of sexual intimacy, see "Locarno, Streatham," Nov. 4, 1939, Mar. 18, 1939, 38/1/A, MOA; Taylor, "Sex, Snobs and Swing," 9.

85. Dora Samuel, phone interview with author, June 30, 2000. Louis Feldman also remembered the "Excuse Me's," the practice of "cutting in" to dance with a girl who was a good dancer. Louis Feldman, interview with author, Mar. 31, 2000, London.

86. *Lyons Mail*, quoted in Matt Houlbrook, *Queer London: Perils and Pleasures in the Sexual Metropolis, 1918–1957* (Chicago: University of Chicago Press, 2005), 85. Untitled cutting, *Caterer and Hotel-Keeper*, Jan. 1909; "Front of the House," *Lyons Journal*, Dec. 1949; John Kings, "The Four Corners of London," n.d., J. Lyons archive, Acc 3527/233, LMA.

87. Green, *A Social History*, 342.

88. "Front of the House," J. Lyons, LMA.

89. Peter J. Bird, *The First Food Empire: A History of J. Lyons & Co.* (Chichester: Phillimore, 2000), 107.

90. "Lyons Still Rampant," *Caterer and Hotel-Keeper*, Oct. 15, 1903, 419; S. J. Adair Fitz-Gerald, "Chats with Caterers, No. II—Mr. Joseph Lyons, of Lyons (Limited)," *Caterer and Hotel-Keeper*, June 15, 1904; "Chops and Changes," *Caterer and Hotel-Keeper*, Dec. 15, 1910, 613; "Lyons Less Rampant," *Caterer and Hotel-Keeper*, June 15, 1915, 273.

91. "Great Windmill Street Area," in *Survey of London, Volumes 31 and 32: St James Westminster, Part 2* (1963), 41–56. At http://www.british-history.ac.uk/source.aspx?pubid=290 (accessed May 2011).

92. T. P. O'Connor, "The Trocadero—The Old and the New," J. Lyons archive, Acc. 3527/232, LMA; "Trocadero," in *J. Lyons and Company*, LMA.

93. Alfred Salmon, "Regulations re Ladies," Sept. 19, 1898, J. Lyons archive, Acc. 3527/232, LMA.

94. "Trocadero Reference Book," n.d., J. Lyons archive, Acc. 3527/186, LMA.

95. The Trocadero's Long Bar would remain a popular meeting place for well-heeled homosexuals throughout the interwar period. Houlbrook, *Queer London*, 87.

96. "Activities of the Company—Corner Houses and Restaurants," "Corner House." n.d., J. Lyons archive, Acc. 3527/233, LMA.

97. Gavin Weightman and Steve Humphries, *The Making of Modern London, 1914–1939* (London: Sidgwick & Jackson, 1984), 42.

98. Paul Cohen-Portheim, *The Spirit of London* (London: Batsford, 1950; orig. 1935), 79.
99. "Lyons and Co.," *Caterer and Hotel-Keeper*, Oct. 15, 1906, 439.
100. John Kings, "The Four Corners of London," in "Corner House," J. Lyons archive, Acc. 3527/233, LMA.
101. "Great Windmill Street Area."
102. Ibid.
103. The public rooms of the Oxford Corner House, for example, were decorated in the styles of Pergolesi, Louis XIV, Empire Adam, and Louis XVI, with the requisite "cartouches, raised and sunken panels . . . scrolls, swags, columns, pilasters, and sun-bursts." Bird, *First Food Empire*, 104–5; Julian Salmon, "J. Lyons and Co., Ltd," in J. Lyons archive, Acc. 3527/2227, LMA.
104. Salmon, "J. Lyons and Co., Ltd."
105. "The New Oxford Corner House, London," *Building*, June 1928, 273, in "Corner House," J. Lyons archive, Acc. 3527/233, LMA.
106. Bird, *First Food Empire*, 99; D. J. Richardson, "J. Lyons and Co., Ltd.: Caterers and Food Manufacturers, 1894–1939," in S. B. Miller and Derek J. Oddy, eds., *The Making of the Modern British Diet* (London: Croom Helm, 1976), 166.
107. Bird, *First Food Empire*.
108. Ibid., 103–7.
109. Weightman and Humphries, *The Making of Modern London*, 41–2. See also Stephen Mennell, *All Manners of Food: Eating and Taste in England and France from the Middle Ages to the Present* (Oxford: Blackwell, 1985).
110. "Front of the House," "Corner House," J. Lyons archive, Acc. 3527/286, LMA; "Continent in Corner House," *Lyons Mail*, Oct. 1936, 115.
111. "Continent in Corner House."
112. Catherine Ross, *Twenties London: A City in the Jazz Age* (London: Museum of London and Philip Wilson, 2003), 45.
113. J. Wayne, *The Purple Dress: Growing up in the Thirties* (London: Gollancz, 1979), 101.
114. Blacker, *Just Like It Was*, 174; Andrew Miller, *The Earl of Petticoat Lane* (London: Heinemann, 2006), 15–16.
115. Laura Phillips, interview, Feb. 11, 1993, interview 306; Esther Rose, interview, Nov. 9, 1993, interview 347, WEJ; Miller, *The Earl of Petticoat Lane*, 15.
116. Esther Rose, interview 347, WEJ.
117. Dora Samuel, interview with author, June 22, 1999, London.
118. Anne Kahn, interview 368, WEJ.
119. Rachel Goldberg, interview with author, June 27, 1999, London.
120. Louis Feldman, interview 377, WEJ; telephone interview with author, Mar. 31, 2000, London.
121. Louis Feldman, interview 377, WEJ.
122. Ibid.
123. See Willie Goldman's discussion of the "sex hunt," in Goldman, *East End My Cradle*, 187–9.
124. Rose Friedman, interview 363, WEJ.
125. Ibid.; Louis Feldman, interview 377, WEJ.
126. Kitty Fegan, interview, June 6, 1992, interview 363, WEJ.
127. Laura Phillips, interview 306, WEJ.
128. "Night Clubs," June 4, 1939, 38/4/C, MOA.
129. On spies, see " 'Secrets' Case," *The Times*, Feb. 4, 1938, 8; "Espionage Charge," *The Times*, Jan. 18, 1928, 5; John Cairncross, *The Enigma Spy: An Autobiography: The Story of the Man Who Changed the Course of World War Two* (London: Century, 1997), 54; Nicholas Booth, *Zigzag: The Incredible Wartime Exploits of Double Agent Eddie Chapman* (London: Portrait, 2007), 152; Grace Stoddard, *No Cloak No Dagger* (Tucson: Wheatmark, 2008), 107, 178–9.
130. See chapters 4 and 7; Stefan Slater, "Pimps, Police, and Filles de Joie: Foreign Prostitution in Interwar London," *London Journal* 32, no. 1 (2007): 53–74.

131. See, for example, "A Blackmailer Sentenced," *The Times*. Jan. 7, 1914, 3; "Struggle with an Armed Man," *The Times*, Dec. 27, 1932, 7; "Shooting Affray in London Café," *The Times*, April 21, 1945, 4; "Night Clubs," June 4, 1939, 38/4/C, MOA. See also Gerald Kersh, *Night and the City* (New York: Simon & Schuster, 1946), 25, 30, 216.

132. Glyn Roberts, *I Take This City* (London: Jarrolds, 1933), 272.

133. Ibid., 97, 273–4.

134. Ibid., 275.

135. "Anti-Semitism Survey," Dec. 1938, A12, 34, MOA.; "Morale in Sept. 1942," Report 1431, Aug. 1942, MOA; "Public Opinion as a Means of Overcoming Anti-Semitism," File Report 1669L, April 3, 1943, MOA.

136. Frederic Mullally, *Fascism inside England [with Plates]*. (London: Claud Morris, 1946), 26; "Magistrate and a Police Constable," *The Times*, Feb. 10, 1936, 14.

137. Rupert Croft-Cooke, *The Numbers Came* (London: Putnam, 1962), 32–4.

138. Kevin Porter and Jeffrey Weeks, *Between the Acts: Lives of Homosexual Men 1885–1967* (London: Routledge, 1991), 111.

139. "John," in ibid., 139.

140. Alkarim Jivani, *It's Not Unusual: A History of Lesbian and Gay Britain in the Twentieth Century* (London: Michael O'Mara, 1997), 53.

141. Frank Oliver, *Walking after Midnight: Gay Men's Life Stories* (London: Routledge, 1989), 12.

142. Quentin Crisp, quoted in Jivani, *It's Not Unusual*, 53.

143. Quentin Crisp, *The Naked Civil Servant* (London: Fontana, 1977), 37.

144. Jerry White, *London in the Twentieth Century: A City and Its People* (New York: Viking, 2001), 195.

145. "Fleet Street Looks at *Lyons Mail*," *Lyons Mail*, Feb. 1928, 24.

146. "Nippy: The Story of Her Day," *Picture Post*, Mar. 4, 1939, 29, 30.

147. Bird, *First Food Empire*, 114; "Nippy," 29.

148. Mrs. B. Summerly, "Letters of Reminiscence from Former Nippies," Jan. 12, 1990, J. Lyons, Acc. 3527/235, LMA.

149. "Brighton Women's Part in Big Undertaking," *Brighton Review*, June 1948; "Photographs of and Articles on Miss Nell Bacon, Chief Superintendent of Lyons' Teashops, 1897–1957," J. Lyons archive, Acc/3527/231, LMA.

150. "Preparing Teashop Debutantes," *Lyons Mail*, May 1939, 12–13; "Nippy."

151. "Preparing Teashop Debutantes."

152. "Hints to Waiters and Waitresses," n.d., J. Lyons archive, Acc/3527/200, LMA.

153. Bird, *First Food Empire*, 117; "Hints to Waiters and Waitresses."

154. "Mainly for Ladies," *Lyons Mail*, April 1920, 124–5.

155. "Mainly for the Ladies," *Lyons Mail*, Feb. 1920, 179.

156. "Showing You the Sudbury Stroll," *Lyons Mail*, Nov. 1938, 130–1. These sports centers were key features of the welfare capitalism of chains and superstores like Marks & Spencer and Selfridges.

157. Alison Light, *Forever England: Femininity, Literature and Conservatism between the Wars* (London: Routledge, 1991), 8, 154.

158. "Nippies Lead the Marriage Walk (1937)," "Nell Bacon," in "Nippy," J. Lyons archive, Acc. 3527/231, LMA.

159. Weightman and Humphries, *The Making of Modern London*, 42.

160. "Nippy," 31.

161. Miriam Glucksmann, *Women Assemble: Women Workers and the New Industries in Inter-war Britain* (London: Routledge, 1990), 138. It would also put Corner House Nippies in the high median of wage earnings for waitresses. H. Llewellyn Smith, ed., *The New Survey of London Life and Labour*, vol. 8 (London: P. S. King, 1935), 215.

162. Mrs. Margaret Butler, n.d.; Mrs. A.W., Jan. 21, 1990; Mrs. Down, n.d.; Mrs. D. Hugh, Jan. 1, 1990, Nippy Reminiscences, J. Lyons archive, Acc. 3527/233, LMA. These correspondents reported wages that varied from 12s 6d (presumably a young starter) to 27 shillings with a share of the tips. Peter Bird states that Nippies' salaries (including teashop workers, whose

salaries were higher because their tips were lower), averaged £1 16s 4d or 36s 4d in 1920. Bird, *The First Food Empire*, 111.

163. W. Back, n.d., "Nippy Reminiscence," J. Lyons archive, Acc. 3527/233, LMA.

164. Rosemary Laird, Jan. 1, 1990, ibid.

165. Kathleen Pittman, Feb. 10, 1990, ibid.

166. Ibid.

167. Doris, quoted in Glucksmann, *Women Assemble*, 30.

168. Rose Bird, interview, 1999, MMB.

169. Glucksmann, *Women Assemble*, 30.

170. Green, *A Social History*, 341; Rosemary Laird, "Nippy Reminiscence," J. Lyons archive, Acc. 3527/233, LMA.

171. Doris, quoted in Glucksmann, *Women Assemble*, 30.

172. Silex, *John Bull at Home* (London: Harrap, 1931), 53. In contrast, Cohen-Portheim believed the massified atmosphere of the Corner Houses rendered it more Soviet than English. Cohen-Portheim, *Spirit of London*, 79.

173. "Mr. Taylor," "Making of Modern London, 2," letter, Sept. 11, 1983, 46.6, Museum of London.

174. "Jewish East End of London Photo Gallery and Commentary," at http://www.jewisheastend.com/eastendtalk.html (accessed Feb. 7, 2010).

175. Quoted in Vivienne Woolf, *Capturing Memories: The Art of Reminiscing* (London: Vallentine Mitchell, 2002), 102.

176. See, especially, Houlbrook, " 'The Man with the Powder Puff' in Interwar London," *Historical Journal* 50, no. 1 (2007): 145–71.

Chapter 7: The Shady Nightclub

1. "Scotland Yard Raids West End Night Clubs: Closes Two Owned by Lord de Clifford's Mother-in-Law in Biggest Round-up in Years," *New York Times*, May 25, 1928, 5.

2. Sir Henry Chartres Biron, *Without Prejudice: Impressions of Life and Law* (London: Faber and Faber, 1936), 61.

3. Kate Meyrick, *Secrets of the 43: Reminiscences by Mrs. Meyrick* (London: John Long, 1933), 22.

4. Ibid., 27.

5. Ibid., 53–8. See also Alan Charles Jenkins, *The Twenties* (London: Heinemann, 1974); Robert Murphy, *Smash and Grab: Gangsters in the London Underworld, 1920–60* (London: Faber and Faber, 1993); Marek Kohn, *Dope Girls: The Birth of the British Drug Underground* (London: Granta, 2001, 1992).

6. " '43' Club Raid Disclosures," *Evening News*, Oct. 20, 1924; "Liquor Licensing: Kate Evelyn Meyrick: Notorious Night Club Owner, 1924–1933," HO 144/17667, NA.

7. "Secret History of Mrs. Meyrick," *Daily Express*, Jan. 30, 1929, HO 144/17667, NA.

8. On the interwar media and gender, see Adrian Bingham, *Gender, Modernity, and the Popular Press in Inter-war Britain* (Oxford: Clarendon Press, 2004), ch. 5.

9. Andrew Barrow, *Gossip: A History of High Society from 1920 to 1970* (London: Pan, 1978), 36.

10. Guy R. Williams, *The Hidden World of Scotland Yard* (London: Hutchinson, 1972), 148.

11. "Mr. Joynson Hicks: One Armed War on Night Club Evils," *Evening News*, Jan. 26, 1925, "Entertainments: Police Supervision of Night Clubs, 1924–1935," HO 45/16205, NA.

12. Clive Emsley, "The Story of a Rotten Apple or a Diseased Orchard?" in Amy Gilman Srebnick and René Lévy, eds., *Crime and Culture: An Historical Perspective* (Aldershot, UK: Ashgate, 2005), 85–104.

13. "Scotland Yard Raids."

14. "Shocking Revelations of London's Night Clubs," *Washington Post*, Nov. 28, 1926, SM1.

15. Barrow, *Gossip*, 65.

16. Emsley, "Story of a Rotten Apple," 98.

17. Erving Goffman, "Where the Action Is," in Goffman, *Interaction Ritual; Essays on Face-to-Face Behavior* (Garden City, NY: Anchor Books, 1967), 149–270.

18. Lewis A. Erenberg, *Steppin' Out: New York Nightlife and the Transformation of American Culture, 1890–1930* (Chicago: University of Chicago Press, 1984), 140, ch. 7.
19. D. J. Taylor, quoted in Dwight Garner, "The Mahvelous and the Damned," *New York Times,* Jan. 23, 2009, C33; D. J. Taylor, *Bright Young People: The Lost Generation of London's Jazz Age* (New York: Farrar, Straus, & Giroux, 2009), 59.
20. Bingham, *Gender, Modernity,* ch. 5.
21. Taylor, *Bright Young People,* 54.
22. Evelyn Waugh, *Brideshead Revisited: The Sacred and Profane Memories of Captain Charles Ryder: A Novel* (Boston: Little, Brown, 1979), 113–15.
23. For example, see Patrick Balfour, *Society Racket: A Critical Survey of Modern Social Life* (London: John Long, 1933); John Collier and Iain Lang, *Just the Other Day: An Informal History of Great Britain since the War* (London: Hamish Hamilton, 1932); Jenkins, *The Twenties*; Robert Graves and Alan Hodge, *The Long Week-End: A Social History of Great Britain 1918–1939* (New York: Norton, 1994).
24. Balfour, *Society Racket,* 119.
25. On the Popular Front and culture, see Michael Denning, *The Cultural Front: The Laboring of American Culture in the Twentieth Century* (London: Verso, 1986).
26. Stuart Hall, "The Social Eye of *Picture Post,*" *Working Papers in Cultural Studies* 2 (1972): 87.
27. H. V. Morton, *The Nights of London* (London: Methuen, 1926), 99.
28. In the early twenties, Soho nightclubs were notorious for their "alien waiters, negro musicians, 'dirt, unbridled rapacity,' grafting dancing partners, and general tawdriness." Horace Wyndham and Dorothea Saint John George, *Nights in London ... With Illustrations by Dorothea St. John George* (London: John Lane, 1926), 15, 16.
29. "Cabaret Theatre Club: The Cave of the Golden Calf," Brochure, May 1912, TM.
30. Peter Brooker, *Bohemia in London: The Social Scene of Early Modernism* (Houndmills, UK: Palgrave Macmillan, 2004), 8, 53, 87.
31. Jean Rhys, *Smile Please: An Unfinished Autobiography* (Harmondsworth, UK: Penguin, 1981; orig. 1979); Hugh Wyndham, *Nights in London.*
32. Ethel Mannin, *Young in the Twenties: A Chapter of Autobiography* (London: Hutchinson, 1971), 32. On the Cave of Harmony, see Elsa Lanchester, *Elsa Lanchester Herself* (New York: St. Martin's Press, 1983), 54–9. On Radclyffe Hall, see Michael Baker, *Our Three Selves: The Life of Radclyffe Hall* (New York: Morrow, 1985), 20; Douglas Goldring, *The Nineteen Twenties: A General Survey and Some Personal Memories* (London: Nicholson & Watson, 1945), 147.
33. By 1914, *The Sketch* could point to the 400, Murray's and the Lotus as a sign that "London is in the midst of another new movement", and "desires to keep later hours." "Later London: The New Supper Clubs I: The Lotus," *The Sketch,* Jan.–April 1914, 83.
34. To compete with nightclubs in the early 1920s, these hotels introduced midnight cabarets. See Balfour, *Society Racket,* 113, and articles in the *Stage*: "L.C.C. Licensing," Nov. 10, 1921, 21; "Cabaret," Oct. 24, 1927, 22.
35. Thomas Burke, *English Night-Life: From Norman Curfew to Present Black-Out* (London: Batsford, 1943), 135.
36. Marek Kohn, "Cocaine Girls," in Paul Gootenberg, ed., *Cocaine: Global Histories* (London: Routledge, 1999), 108.
37. Ibid., 108, 113.
38. Catherine Ross, *Twenties London: A City in the Jazz Age* (London: Museum of London and Philip Wilson, 2003), 107. On prostitutes' migration into Soho, see Jerry White, *London in the Twentieth Century: A City and Its People* (New York: Viking, 2001), 333.
39. Ross, *Twenties London,* 107.
40. John Burnett, *England Eats Out: A Social History of Eating out in England from 1830 to the Present* (New York: Longman, 2004), 197.
41. Ivor Patrick Gore, "Cabaret," *Stage,* Mar. 14, 1926, 14.
42. White, *London in the Twentieth Century,* 107.
43. Ibid., 119. After he performed at the Hippodrome, the Jamaican guitarist Dan Kildare remained at Ciro's until 1916, when it was closed for selling drinks after hours. See also

Howard Rye, "Fearsome Means of Discord: Early Encounters with Black Jazz," in Paul Oliver, ed., *Black Music in Britain: Essays on the Afro-Asian Contribution to Popular Music* (Milton Keynes, UK: Open University Press, 1990), 45–57.

44. The "Jazz Kings" had splintered off from the Southern Symphonic Orchestra to play at the Philharmonic Hall. Ross, *Twenties London*, 31; George McKay, *Circular Breathing: The Cultural Politics of Jazz in Britain* (Durham, NC: Duke University Press, 2005), 102.

45. Richard Carlish, *King of Clubs. Richard Carlish as Told to Alan Bestic.* (London: Elek Books, 1962), 45.

46. Meyrick, *Secrets of the 43*, 31–44.

47. *The Post Office London Directory* (London: Kelly's Directories, 1923), 133.

48. "Soho Shopbreaking," *The Times*, Jan. 1, 1926, 9. See chapter 5.

49. On the 1917 Club, see Leonard Woolf, *Beginning Again; An Autobiography of the Years 1911 to 1918* (New York: Harcourt, 1964), 207; Goldring, *The Nineteen Twenties*; Douglas Goldring, *Odd Man Out: The Autobiography of a "Propaganda Novelist"* (London: Chapman & Hall, 1935), 208; Christine Stansell, *American Moderns: Bohemian New York and the Creation of a New Century* (New York: Metropolitan Books, 2000), 83.

50. On blackmailers, see Angus McLaren, *Sexual Blackmail: A Modern History* (Cambridge, MA: Harvard University Press, 2002), 113. On transvestites, see Laura Phillips, interview, Feb. 11, 1993, interview 306, WEJ.

51. On the red light districts, see *Thirty-Third Annual Report of the Public Morality Council* (1932), 32, Public Morality Council Archive, A/PMC/98, LMA.

52. Frances Partridge, *Memories* (London: Gollancz, 1981), 87.

53. Carlish, *King of Clubs*, 35.

54. Report of Inspector Frank Smith to the Superintendent, April 25, 1931; "Mrs. Kate Evelyn Meyrick or Merrick; Allegations of Irregularities at the Cecile, the 43, and the Bunch of Keys Club," 1924–1935, MEPO 2/4481/2, NA.

55. "Dancing Instructresses," *Stage*, Nov. 18, 1926, 27.

56. Meyrick, *Secrets of the 43*, 143; Waugh, *Brideshead Revisited*, 115.

57. Unlike the cabaret restaurants in Mayfair and the Haymarket, the decor of the 43 did not evoke all the fantasies that money could buy. See, by contrast, Lewis A. Erenberg, "From New York to Middletown: Repeal and the Legitimization of Nightlife in the Great Depression," *American Quarterly* 38, no. 5 (1986): 761–88.

58. Carlish, *King of Clubs*, 61.

59. Alec Waugh, *Kept: A Story of Postwar London* (New York: A. & C. Books, 1931), 24.

60. Sid Colin, *And the Bands Played On* (London: Elm Tree Books, 1977), 60.

61. Meyrick, *Secrets of the 43*, 120.

62. Jenkins, *The Twenties*, 23.

63. Erenberg, *Steppin' Out*, 124.

64. Carlish, *King of Clubs*, 51; "How 43 Electrified London; and the Woman," *People*, Feb. 3 1929, 5.

65. Michael Harrison, *London beneath the Pavement* (London: P. Davies, 1971), 255; Frederick Dew Sharpe, *Sharpe of the Flying Squad* (London: John Long, 1938), 319.

66. "How 43 Electrified London;" Jack Glicco, *Madness after Midnight* (London: Elek Books, 1952), 21.

67. Carlish, *King of Clubs*, 35.

68. Robert Fabian, *London after Dark* (New York: British Book Centre, 1954), 20.

69. Carlish, *King of Clubs*, 47.

70. B.B., "People and Parties," *Evening Standard*, Jan. 22, 1937, 16.

71. Barbara Cartland, *We Danced All Night* (London: Robson, 1994), 244.

72. Meyrick, *Secrets of the 43*, 118.

73. Victor MacClure, *How to Be Happy in London* (London: Arrowsmith, 1926), 107.

74. Arthur Tietjen, *Soho London's Vicious Circle* (London: Allan Wingate, 1956), 134.

75. Ibid., 131.

76. Ibid.

77. Glicco, *Madness after Midnight*, 24.
78. "How 43 Electrified London."
79. Amy de la Haye, "The Role of Design within the Commercialisation of Women's Ready to Wear Clothing in Britain During the Inter-war Years, with Specific Reference to the Cheapest Levels of Products," diss., Royal College of Art, 1986, 39; Elizabeth Wilson and Lou Taylor, *Through the Looking Glass: A History of Dress from 1860 to the Present Day* (London: BBC Books, 1989). On the physiognomy of debutantes, see Michael Arlen, quoted in Frances Lonsdale Donaldson, *Child of the Twenties* (London: Hart-Davis, 1959), 79.
80. Meyrick, *Secrets of the 43*, 161.
81. Daphne Fielding, *Mercury Presides* (London: Eyre & Spottiswoode, 1954), 96–7.
82. Margaret Campbell, Duchess of Argyll, *Forget Not: The Autobiography of Margaret, Duchess of Argyll* (London: W. H. Allen, 1975), 49.
83. "Talk of the Town," *Daily Express*, Nov. 12, 1931, 17.
84. Goldring, *The Nineteen Twenties*, 145.
85. Meyrick, *Secrets of the 43*, 78.
86. Colin, *And the Bands Played On*, 21; James J. Nott, *Music for the People: Popular Music and Dance in Interwar Britain* (Oxford: Oxford University Press, 2002), 233.
87. June Sochen, "From Sophie Tucker to Barbra Streisand," in Joyce Antler, ed., *Talking Back: Images of Jewish Women in American Popular Culture* (Hanover, NH: Brandeis University Press, 1998); Susan A. Glenn, *Female Spectacle: The Theatrical Roots of Modern Feminism* (Cambridge, MA: Harvard University Press, 2000), 50–3.
88. Meyrick, *Secrets of the 43*, 146.
89. Glicco, *Madness after Midnight*, 23.
90. Ibid.
91. Billy Amstell, quoted in Sheila Tracy, *Talking Swing: The British Big Bands* (Edinburgh: Mainstream, 1997), 74.
92. Meyrick, *Secrets of the 43*, 47.
93. Ibid., 117, 137, 154.
94. Waugh, *Brideshead Revisited*, 115.
95. Matt Houlbrook, *Queer London: Perils and Pleasures in the Sexual Metropolis, 1918–1957* (Chicago: University of Chicago Press, 2005), ch. 3; Matt Houlbrook, "'The Man with the Powder Puff' in Interwar London," *Historical Journal* 50, no. 1 (2007): 145–71.
96. Waugh, *Brideshead Revisited*, 113–14.
97. On the suppression of queer clubs as disorderly spaces of perversion, see Houlbrook, *Queer London*, ch. 3; "Billie Joyce and Others (Billie's Club): Conspiracy to Corrupt Morals," 1936, DPP2/ 355, NA; "Neave, Jack Rudolph and Others: Disorderly House, 'Caravan Club,'" 1934, DPP2/ 224, NA.
98. Morton, *The Nights of London*, 71.
99. Argyll, *Forget Not*, 49.
100. Colin, *And the Bands Played On*, 21.
101. H. V. Morton, *H. V. Morton's London, Being the Heart of London, the Spell of London, and the Nights of London, in One Volume*, 18th edn. (London: Methuen, 1957), 413.
102. "Thirty Years in the Ballroom: The Editor Looks Back," *Dancing Times*, Dec. 1940, 138.
103. Gavin Weightman and Steve Humphries, *The Making of Modern London 1914–1939* (London: Sidgwick & Jackson, 1984); Balfour, *Society Racket*.
104. Balfour, *Society Racket*, 120.
105. Paul Morand, *A Frenchman's London* (London: Cassell, 1934), 197.
106. Robert Hamilton Bruce Lockhart, *The Diaries of Sir Robert Bruce Lockhart*, vol. 1: *1915–1938*, ed. Kenneth Young (London: Macmillan, 1973), 115.
107. "Policy on Night Clubs and Its Effects on Officers Detailed for This Work. Commissioners' Observations and Suggested Legislative Amendments," Jan.18, 1933, MEPO 2/4458/A, NA.
108. Meyrick, *Secrets of the 43*, 143.
109. Sophie Tucker, *Some of These Days: The Autobiography of Sophie Tucker* (Garden City, NY: Garden City, 1946), 213.

110. For a sample of these letters, see the following issues of the *Dancing Times*: Feb. 1922, 549; April 1922, 667; June 1922, 844.
111. See the *Dancing Times*: Oct. 1921, 79; Dec. 1921, 326; May 1922, 751. Occasionally both women and men advertisers noted the financial difficulties that motivated employment in this "new profession," stating they were "hard up" or members of the "Old Army–New Poor." See also Morton, "A Night Club," in Morton, *The Nights of London*, 167–72.
112. Meyrick, *Secrets of the 43*, 210.
113. On the English glamor girl, see Doremy Vernon, *Tiller's Girls* (London: Robson, 1988). See chapter 8, this volume.
114. Meyrick, *Secrets of the 43*, 148–50.
115. Ibid., 211.
116. Ibid., 213–14. By contrast, in 1932, Mrs. Cecil Chesterton estimated that a female worker in an electric bulb factory would make £2 15s a week. Mrs. Cecil Chesterton, "British Work for British Women: The Filament Girl," *Daily Express*, June 6, 1932, 6.
117. Meyrick, *Secrets of the 43*, 89.
118. Waugh, *Brideshead Revisited*, 115; Evelyn Waugh, *A Handful of Dust* (Boston: Little, Brown, 1977).
119. Billy Amstell, quoted in Tracy, *Talking Swing*, 34.
120. "Where Mrs. Meyrick's Huge Profits Come From," *The People*, Feb. 10, 1929, 5.
121. Louise A. Jackson, *Women Police: Gender, Welfare and Surveillance in the Twentieth Century* (Manchester: Manchester University Press, 2006), 108.
122. Carlish, *King of Clubs*, 36.
123. Ibid.
124. Gerald Kersh, *Night and the City* (New York: Simon & Schuster, 1946), 137–9, 228–9.
125. Arthur Harding and Raphael Samuel, *East End Underworld: Chapters in the Life of Arthur Harding* (London: Routledge & Kegan Paul, 1981), 338; Murphy, *Smash and Grab*, 30–4.
126. Meyrick, *Secrets of the 43*, 44.
127. Carlish, *King of Clubs*, 57.
128. Ibid., 69.
129. Meyrick, *Secrets of the 43*, 88–9.
130. On nightclubs as spaces of institutional spontaneity, see Erenberg, *Steppin' Out*, 132.
131. Carlish, *King of Clubs*, 43.
132. Meyrick, *Secrets of the 43*, 207.
133. Carlish, *King of Clubs*, 122; Williams, *The Hidden World*, 155.
134. Inspector Frank Smith to the Superintendent, Feb. 3, 1930, "Mrs. Kate Evelyn Meyrick," MEPO 2/4481/1a, NA.
135. "Police Notes 'Destroyed,'" *Daily Express*, Jan. 23, 1929, 1.
136. Louise Jackson, "'Lady Cops' and 'Decoy Doras': Gender, Surveillance, and the Construction of Urban Knowledge in Britain 1919–1950," *London Journal* 27, no. 1 (2002): 63–83. On queer impersonations, see Houlbrook, *Queer London*, part 3.
137. Williams, *The Hidden World*, 152.
138. P.C. Lord to the Superintendent, April 25, 1931, MEPO 2/4481/52C/1759, NA; Williams, *The Hidden World*, 147–51.
139. "Dance Professionals, Royal Tottenham," interview with Dorothy, May 5, 1939, 38/3/6, MOA.
140. On the troubled reputation of police during the late 1920s, see Stefan Slater, "Containment: Managing Street Prostitution in London, 1918–59," *Journal of British Studies* 49, no. 1 (2010): 332–57; Emsley, "Story of a Rotten Apple."
141. Houlbrook, quoted in Nadja Durbach, *Spectacle of Deformity: Freak Shows and Modern British Culture* (Berkeley: University of California Press, 2009), 4.
142. "Dancing Policeman Calls for Champagne," *Daily Express*, Jan. 24, 1929, 3.
143. Parliamentary debate, clipping, Feb. 27, 1925, "Clubs and Night Clubs, 1922–1935," ILS/C/16/03/008, LMA.
144. Quoted in Jackson, *Women Police*, 108.

145. Barrow, *Gossip*, 43.
146. "Secret History of Mrs. Meyrick," *Daily Express*, Jan. 30, 1929, in "Police: Ex-Station Sergeant George Goddard: Sentenced in 1929 to 18 Months Imprisonment and a Fine of 2,000 Pounds on Charges of Conspiracy and Accepting Bribes in Connection with Night Clubs. Crown's Right to Retain Moneys Found in Goddard's Possession (Rowlatt J Decision), 1928–1930," HO 144/12266/598822/7, NA.
147. "Night Clubs and the Police," *Daily Telegraph*, Jan. 30, 1929; *Daily Herald*, Jan. 30, 1929; "The Goddard Case," *Daily News*, Jan 30, 1929; "Police Ex-Station Sergeant George Goddard," HO 144/12266/532055/7, NA.
148. Jackson, " 'Lady Cops' and 'Decoy Doras,' " 73.
149. Royal Commission on Police Powers, quoted in Jackson, *Women Police*, 111. On the symbolic order, see ibid.
150. Emsley, *Story of a Rotten Apple*, 98.
151. Donaldson, *Child of the Twenties*, 71.
152. "Report of the Police of the Metropolis for the Year 1935" (1935/36), in "Liquor Licensing Bottle Parties, 1932–1938," HO 45/18488. See also "Guests Fleeced by 'Hostesses': Bottle Party Ruses." *Daily Mail*, Aug 21, 1935, HO 45/18488/598822/21, NA. The *Daily Mail* estimated 170 bottle parties in the West End.
153. By the end of the decade, even indignant proprietors of hotels and restaurants joined the ranks of purity reformers and the Home Office, and declared a War on Night Clubs. See the Home Office's meeting with the Restaurant and Hotel Delegation, "Liquor Licensing," Nov. 2, 1938, HO 45/18488/598822/49, NA.
154. *What's On*, July 16, 1937, 15. Police fought back by persuading the London County Council in 1936 to agree to prosecute nightclubs that violated its statutory licensing laws regarding public dancing and music. "Minutes of the Entertainment Committee, Dec. 2, 1936," LCC MIN 4401, LMA.
155. On Frisco's see "Bottle Party Belt", and "London Night and Day," *Night and Day*, July 22, 1937, 3; on the Bag o' Nails, see Argyll, *Forget Not*, 49.
156. *Modern Architecture in England* (New York: Museum of Modern Art, 1937), 26. On New London, "A New London," *Vogue*, Aug. 5, 1936, 13, quoted in Bronwen Edwards, "Making the West End Modern: Space, Architecture, and Shopping in 1930s London," Ph.D. diss., University of the Arts, London, 2004, 2; Alan Jenkins, *The Thirties* (London: Heinemann, 1976). By the middle of the decade, according to Alan Jenkins, "everybody but the unemployed . . . regarded the worst of the Depression as over." Jenkins, *The Thirties*, 149.
157. Juliet Gardiner, *The Thirties: An Intimate History* (London: HarperPress, 2010), 605.
158. *London, the Wonder City: Being a Concise Pocket Reference of Events Both Social & Sporting and a Gazetteer and Guide* (London: Pullman Car Co., 1937), 21.
159. Jenkins, *The Thirties*, 156.
160. On state magic, see B. Malinowski, "A Nation-wide Intelligence Service," in Mass Observation, *First Year's Work, 1937–38*, ed. Charles Madge and Tom Harrisson (London: Lindsey Drummond, 1938), 112, quoted in David Cannadine, "The British Monarchy, c.1820–1877," in Eric Hobsbawm and Terence Ranger, eds., *The Invention of Tradition* (Cambridge, UK: Cambridge University Press, 1983), 149. On the crises of the 1930s, see Ronald Blythe, *The Age of Illusion: England in the Twenties and Thirties, 1919–1940* (London: Hamish Hamilton, 1963); Samuel Lynn Hynes, *The Auden Generation: Literature and Politics in England in the 1930's* (New York: Viking Press, 1977); John Baxendale and Christopher Pawlin, *Narrating the Thirties: A Decade in the Making, 1930 to the Present* (Houndmills, UK: Macmillan, 1996).
161. Humphrey Jennings and Charles Madge, eds., *May the Twelfth: Mass-Observation Day-Surveys 1937 by over Two Hundred Observers* (London: Faber and Faber, 1937).
162. "Mushroom Growth of Bottle Parties is First Sign of Jubilee Plans," *Melody Maker*, Mar. 30, 1935, 1.
163. Houlbrook, *Queer London*, 251.
164. "London Lore: Night Club Racket," *What's On*, April 9, 1937, 1017.

165. "22,000 to Preserve Coronation Peace," *New York Times,* April 25, 1937, 35.
166. "Scotland Yard Makes a Drive against Vice Haunts: A Clean-up before the Coronation," *Evening Standard,* Jan. 27, 1937, 13. These raids were conducted by a "special [vice] squad of picked detectives" operating outside of special divisions. The Met had set up the "vice squad" around 1930; during the mid-thirties, it focused on "disorderly houses," prostitution and white slavery rings, and pornography shops as well as homosexuals. Intensified police activity also resulted from prodding on the part of purity reformers, notably the Public Morality Council. On the Clubs and Vice Squad, see Houlbrook, *Queer London,* 34; Martin Fido and Keith Skinner, *The Official Encyclopedia of Scotland Yard* (London: Virgin Books, 1999); "Making London Safe for the Coronation," *News of the World,* Oct. 4, 1936, 18. See the Annual Reports of the Public Morality Council for 1932, 1933, 1935, A/PMC/98, LMA.
167. On the relative absence of Jewish workingmen in "queer" urban venues, see Houlbrook, *Queer London,* 187–8; George Chauncey, *Gay New York: Gender, Urban Culture, and the Making of the Gay Male World, 1890–1940* (New York: Basic Books, 1994), 72.
168. D. S. Murray, cross-examination, Nov. 26, 1936, 14, "Defendant: Joyce, Billie Joyce ..." CRIM 1/ 903, NA; D. S. Dorey, report on Nov. 14, 1936, 6, CRIM 1/ 903; "Billie Joyce and Others (Billie's Club): Conspiracy to Corrupt Morals," DPP 2/ 355, NA; Houlbrook, *Queer London,* part 3.
169. "Summing Up in Billie's Club Case at Old Bailey," *Evening Standard,* Jan. 26, 1937, 5.
170. "Bottle Parties: L.C.C. Regulations, Unlicensed Music and Dancing," *The Times,* Jan. 29, 1937. See "27 'Bottle Parties' Raided," *Morning Advertiser* 3, Oct. 5, 1936, HO 45, 18488.
171. "Bottle Parties in 'C' Division: Licensing Offences 1932–1936," MEPO 2/ 4482, NA; "Liquor Licensing Bottle Parties" May 7, 1932–Nov. 3, 1938: HO 45/ 184888, NA; Colin, *And the Bands Played On,* 64; "Bottle Parties: New Style: Light Shed on Nightlife within the Law," *Morning Post,* Mar. 7, 1934; "The Old Florida and Victors: Bottle Parties and Evasion of Licensing Laws by Advance Catering," MEPO 2/4499, NA; "London on the Bottle," *New York Times,* April 8, 1934, RE 11.
172. Maurice Richardson, "The Bottle Party Belt," *Night and Day,* July 1, 1937, 23.
173. John Chilton, *Louis: The Louis Armstrong Story, 1900–1971* (Cambridge, MA: Da Capo Press, 1988), 163.
174. "Mike," "British Bands Have No Individuality," *Melody Maker,* Feb. 6, 1937, 6. On *Melody Maker,* see Godbolt, *History of Jazz,* passim.
175. Spike Hughes, "Meet the Duke" (1933), reprinted in Mark Tucker and Duke Ellington, *The Duke Ellington Reader* (Oxford: Oxford University Press, 1993), 73.
176. On Armstrong and Ellington's visits, see Godbolt, *History of Jazz,* chs. 6, 7. On the history of the gramophone record industry, see Nott, *Music for the People,* part 2.
177. On West Indians in the Southern Syncopated Orchestra, see Rye, "Fearsome Means of Discord," 53.
178. Glicco, *Madness after Midnight,* 132.
179. Lewis A. Erenberg, *Swingin' the Dream: Big Band Jazz and the Rebirth of American Culture* (Chicago: University of Chicago Press, 1998), 49–50.
180. On black clubs, see Godbolt, *History of Jazz,* 189–91; Colin, *And the Bands Played On,* 66; Glicco, *Madness after Midnight;* Tracy, *Talking Swing;* Rye, "Fearsome Means of Discord"; Andy Simon, ed., *Headnotes, Black British Swing: The African Diaspora's Contribution to England's Own Jazz of the 1930s and 1940s* (London: Topics Records, 2001); McKay, *Circular Breathing.* In addition to Richardson's piece on bottle parties, another notice in *Night and Day* describes Frisco's as "the real thing (Dress optional)", run by an "astonishingly well-preserved West Indian Negro" (July 22, 1937, 3). The same note commented on the "cheerful vocal staff (black) and clientele of exquisite young men (white)" at the Nest, where dress was also optional. On lesbian waitresses at Jig's Club, see Glicco, *Madness after Midnight,* 132.
181. On pan-Africanism, see Jeffrey Green, "Trumpet Player from the West Indies," *Black Perspectives in Music* 12, no. 1 (1984): 98–127. On Jewish musicians who frequented the black clubs, see Godbolt, *History of Jazz.*

182. Colin, *And the Bands Played On*, 66.
183. Ibid., 134.
184. Leslie Thompson, quoted in Alyn Shipton, *A New History of Jazz* (New York: Continuum, 2001), 367.
185. Denied a solo at the Palladium, Gillespie "sat in" at the Nest. See Godbolt, *History of Jazz*, 118.
186. Colin, *And the Bands Played On*, 65.
187. Nnamdi Azikiwe, *My Odyssey: An Autobiography* (New York: Praeger, 1970), 203. The Florence Mills Social Parlour is mentioned in Alison Donnell, "Una Marson: Feminism: Anti-colonialism, and a Forgotten Fight for Freedom," in Bill Schwarz, *West Indian Intellectuals in Britain* (Manchester: Manchester University Press, 2003), 128–9. Azikiwe identified the Nest with the same exotic fantasy of pleasure as the entertainment press: in his 1970 autobiography, he declared that "Hatch's singing and dancing coupled with the bevy of beauties who flocked there transformed it into 'a second Harlem.'" Azikiwe, *My Odyssey*, 197.
188. On Lambert, see "Humphrey Searle: Memoir," at http://www.musicweb-international.com/searle/500.htm (accessed May 2011); on Ayer and his wife, see Ben Rogers, *A. J. Ayer: A Life* (New York: Grove Press, 1999), 128.
189. Rogers, *A. J. Ayer*, 128; Barbara Bush, *Imperialism, Race, and Resistance: Africa and Britain, 1919–1945* (London: Routledge, 1999), 211.
190. Hugh Ross Williamson, "In a Negro Night Club," *Listener*, July–Dec. 1936, 250–1.
191. Simon Gikandi, "Pan-Africanism and Cosmopolitanism: The Case of Jomo Kenyatta," *English Studies in Africa* 43, no. 1 (2000): 3.
192. Joe Deniz, interview, 1993, Stephen Bourne Interview Collection, intended for use in BBC Radio @ Ladbroke Radio Series, C1019/3, BLSA.
193. Simon, *Headnotes*, 13. Simon is drawing on the oral history of jazz interviews of the British Library Sound Archives.
194. Glicco, *Madness after Midnight*, 131.
195. "Alleged Theft of Jewelry," *The Times*, April 25, 1939, 5; "'The Nest' Club Raided: Described as a Haunt of Criminals," Aug. 19, 1939, 7.
196. Simon, *Headnotes*, 11; P.C. John Dunbar Brunton, May 11, 1936, "Shim Sham or Rainbow Roof Unregistered Clubs. Bottle Parties and Sales of Liquor Out of Hours," MEPO 2/4494/44, NA.
197. A photograph of the Shim Sham in *Melody Maker* records white musicians in band uniform, white patrons in evening dress who were dancing or sitting at tables covered with starched white tablecloths and cutlery and attended by formally attired waiters. Rudolph Dunbar, "Harlem in London: Year of Advancement for Negroes, *Melody Maker*, Mar. 7, 1936, 2.
198. Shim Sham cabaret menu, "Shim Sham," MEPO 2/ 4494./12d, NA.
199. "An Englishman to County Clerk," June 2, 1937, "Shim Sham," MEPO 2/4494/12g, NA.
200. Leonard Feather, "London Lowdown," *New Amsterdam News*, Oct. 19, 1935, 6.
201. On Driberg, see Francis Wheen, *Tom Driberg: His Life and Indiscretions* (London: Chatto & Windus, 1990), 92.
202. "It's Now 'Spades and Jig-Chasers,'" *New Amsterdam News*, April 13, 1935, 10.
203. *London Week*, Mar. 15, 1935, 41.
204. On Hatch's talent-spotting ability, see Rudolph Dunbar, "Harlem in London: Year of Advancement for Negroes," *Melody Maker*, Mar. 7, 1936, 2; "Elliott Carpenter," interview in Chris Goddard, *Jazz away from Home* (London: Paddington Press, 1979), 297. See also Arthur Badrock, "Hatch and Carpenter in England," at http://www.vjm.biz/articles6.htm (accessed May 2011); Louis Stephenson, interview, Oct. 28, 1987, London, "Oral History of Jazz in Britain," C122, BLSA; Michael Pickering, "The BBC's Kentucky Minstrels, 1933–1950: Blackface Entertainment on British Radio," *Historical Journal of Film, Radio and Television* 16, no. 2 (1996): 161–96. It may well be that Hatch's minstrel style provoked Feather's hipster references to "spades" and "jigchasers" at the Shim Sham. See Val Wilmer, "Appreciation: Leonard Feather," *Guardian*, Oct. 6, 1994, A15.
205. "Dixieland Drummer Happy Blake for the Stage," *Melody Maker*, Mar. 7, 1936, 12.

206. Bill Schwarz, "Crossing the Seas," in Schwarz, *West Indian Intellectuals*, 1–30; Stephen Howe, "C. L. R. James: Visions of History, Visions of Britain," in ibid., 159.

207. See McKay, *Circular Breathing*, 145

208. Howard Rye, "Cyril McDonald Blake (1897–1951)," in *Oxford Dictionary of National Biography* (Oxford: Oxford University Press, 2004), at http://www.oxforddnb.com/view/article/74921 (accessed April 17, 2006); John Cowley, "'Cultural Fusions': Aspects of British West Indian Music in the U.S. and Britain, 1918–51," *Popular Music* 5 (1985): 81–96. On the Blake Brothers, see Rye, "Fearsome Means of Discord," 50, 57; Cowley, "London Is the Place: Caribbean Music in the Context of Empire," in Oliver, *Black Music in Britain*," 64, 66, 76. As Andrew Simon notes, "Happy" Blake was a "key but under-documented advocate of black British jazz." *Headnotes*, 11.

209. On "Snakehips Johnson" see Rye, "Fearsome Means of Discord," 56, 57; "All British-Coloured Band Scores," *Melody Maker*, Aug. 8, 1935, 7; "British Band Delivers the Rhythmic Goods," *Melody Maker*, Aug. 22, 1936, 3; Val Wilmer, "First Sultan of Swing," *Independent*, Feb. 24, 1991, 10. Johnson took lessons from African-American choreographer Buddy Bradley, who had been brought over to London by theater impresario C. B. Cochran. Simon, "Headnotes," 9.

210. Joe Deniz, interview, 1993. They grew up to "the sound of fado as their father played violin and mandolin for Portuguese-speaking compatriots." They also heard calypsos performed locally by the Bay's West Indian guitarists. Val Wilmer, "Troubadour from Tiger Bay," *Guardian*, May 3, 1994, 18.

211. Better clubs, Joe stated, "rarely if at all employed black people." Nor did he see "much advantage" to the music at posh clubs, where Cole Porter tunes like "Night and Day" were the staple fare. Joe Deniz, interview, 1993.

212. Ibid.

213. Wilmer, "Troubadour from Tiger Bay."

214. Frank Deniz, interview, Aug. 18, 1989, London, Oral History of Jazz in Britain, NSA: C1221/81–82, BLSA; Wilmer, "Frank Deniz, Gentle and Gifted Musician Who Survived in an Age of Discrimination," *Guardian*, July 30, 2003, 25; Leslie Thompson, *Leslie Thompson: An Autobiography, as Told to Jeffrey Green* (Crawley, UK: Rabbit Press, 1985), 57, 84. On Jews, blacks, and jazz, see Mark Slobin, "Some Intersections of Jews, Music, and Theater," in Sarah Blacher Cohen, ed., *From Hester Street to Hollywood: The Jewish-American Stage and Screen* (Bloomington: Indiana University Press, 1983), 29–44.

215. Rye, "Fearsome Means of Discord," 55; Wilmer, "First Sultan of Swing."

216. Erenberg, *Swingin' the Dream*, 29.

217. On the "backwoods" of the East End, Ivor Mairants, interview, July 23, 1996, London, Oral History of Jazz in Britain, C122/2923–294, BLSA.

218. Harry Gold, *Gold, Doubloons and Pieces of Eight: The Autobiography of Harry Gold*, ed. Roger Cotterrell (London: Northway, 2000), 52.

219. Amstell, quoted in Kevin Morgan, "King Street Blues: Jazz and the Left in Britain in the 1930s–1940s," in Andy Croft, ed., *A Weapon in the Struggle: The Cultural History of the Communist Party in Britain* (London: Pluto, 1998), 125.

220. Billy Amstell, interview, Mar. 16, 1993, London, Oral History of Jazz in Britain, C122/188–189, BLSA. On the politics of hunger, see James Vernon, *Hunger: A Modern History* (Cambridge, MA: Belknap Press, 2007), ch. 8.

221. Gold, *Gold, Doubloons*, 52.

222. Phillips, quoted in Morgan, "King Street Blues," 125.

223. Ibid.

224. Ibid., 124.

225. Bohm, quoted in ibid., 128.

226. Hugh Clegg, "M.U. Officials in Archer Street," May 15, 1939, 38/4/B, pt. 10, MOA. See also Morgan, "King Street Blues," 124, 128.

227. See Morgan, "King Street Blues,"132.

228. Dunbar, "Harlem in London," 2.

229. Ibid.
230. Thompson, *Leslie Thompson*, 57, 84.
231. "Confidential Report" [1966], "Isow, J. A. Aka Isowitzsky Date of Birth 21/01/1897," HO 405/24361, NA.
232. In 1937, when Isow was charged with illegal activities at the Barn, Isow's prosecutor stated that in 1922 he was fined £10 for keeping an unlicensed billiard hall, £40 for assisting in the management of a betting house, £100 for keeping a betting house in Shaftesbury Avenue, and, in 1935, fined £20 and ordered to pay £52 10s costs for selling intoxicating liquor after hours at an unregistered club, the Shim Sham. He would serve two more prison sentences, one in 1938, for keeping a betting club in Lisle Street. "Raid on Barn Club: Manager Sent to Prison," *The Times*, Feb. 27, 1937, 9.
233. "Special Branch," Mar. 31, 1966, "Isow, J. A.," HO 405/24361/17, NA.
234. Joe Deniz, interview, 1993.
235. James A. Jones, "Village Streets of London," *Evening News*, Mar. 4, 1932, 9.
236. Patrick Hamilton, *Midnight Bell* (London, 1929), quoted in White, *London in the Twentieth Century*, 314. See chapter 5.
237. Esther Rose, interview, Nov. 7, 1993, interview 347, WEJ. On Wardour Street, see *The Post Office London Directory* (London: Kelly's Directories, 1935), 1050.
238. "Scene in a Soho Club: Four Men Charged with Willful Damage," *The Times*, May 2, 1935, 4.
239. Ibid., and *The Times*: "Alleged Riot at a Soho Club: Witness's Retraction of Previous Evidence," May 14, 1935, 13; "Scene of a Soho Club: Alleged Terrorizing of Witnesses," May 21, 1935, 13; "Scene at a Soho Club: Conspiracy Charge Dismissed," June 15, 1935, 9.
240. On the Sabini gang and their move into Soho, see Murphy, *Smash and Grab*, 30-3; White, *London in the Twentieth Century*, 260, 261; Harding and Samuel, *East End Underworld*, 182-5, 328; Tietjen, *Soho London's Vicious Circle*, 42-6. See also "Publichouse Brawl in Soho," *The Times*, Feb. 13, 1930, 9; "Gang Rivalry in Soho," April 3, 1930, 11. On the 1936 brawl, see, "Club Menaces," *The Times*, Feb. 8, 1936, 9, and a similar outcome, "Charges Dismissed," Mar. 3, 1936, 4.
241. "Shim Sham," MEPO 2/ 4494, 44b, NA.
242. Anonymous letter, Jan. 27, 1937, MEPO 2/4494/52, NA.
243. Ibid.; Anonymous, April 23, 1935; "A Neighbour of Wardour Street," May 14, 1935; "A Citizen," May 5, 1935; "An Englishman" to Chief Clerk, LCC, June 3, 1935; Anonymous to Lord Trenchard, June 6, 1935, MEPO 2/ 4494/5, NA.
244. The reports from the Public Morality Council (PMC) are not in the Shim Sham files of the Metropolitan Police, but Matt Houlbrook believes they were crucial to police identification of queer resorts and shady nightclubs. The PMC concentrated its "patrol work" in central London, particularly in Soho. Houlbrook, *Queer London*, 78. The annual reports of the PMC certainly credited its own investigations with providing the necessary information and incentives for police closure of illicit nightclubs and bottle parties, where violations of the licensing laws and unnatural practices took place. It particularly focused its attention on resorts "catering for the scum of Soho," that collected "undesirable persons," including "women in male attire, effeminate men and coloured people." Public Morality Council, Annual Reports for 1929–33, 1935, 1939, 1940. *Thirty-Third Annual Report of the Public Morality Council* (1932), 32; *Fortieth Annual Report* (1939), 24, 25; *Thirty-Sixth Annual Report* (1935), 26, A/PMC/98, LMA.
245. P.C. Sweny, report June 3, 1935, July 1, 1935, "Shim Sham," MEPO 2/4494/18, NA; P.C. Stannard, July 1, 1935, "Shim Sham," MEPO 2/4494/12B, NA.
246. Inspector Deller to Superintendent Ralphe, July 12, 1935, "Shim Sham," MEPO 2/4494/18B, NA. On Hatch's response to the raid, see ibid.
247. Ibid.
248. Ibid.
249. Inspector Batson to Superintendent Ralphe, Mar. 28, 1936, "Shim Sham," MEPO 2/4494/39A, NA.

250. "Pro Bono" to Commissioner of Police, Mar. 18, 1936, "Shim Sham," MEPO 2/4494, 36, NA.
251. Inspector Batson to Superintendent, Mar. 13, 1936, "Shim Sham," MEPO 2/4494/44A, NA.
252. They did not seek out the services of the hostesses, nor did they mingle with other guests. Because they were preparing to raid multiple establishments, the Met had dispensed with the kind of costly, intensive undercover work required to identify and document "indecent" practices by specific patrons. Houlbrook, *Queer London*, 77.
253. Inspector Batson to Superintendent, Mar. 13, 1936, "Shim Sham," MEPO 2/4494/44A; P.C. Brunton, report, Mar. 11, 1936, /44B; P. S. Gowan to Superintendent, May 11, 1936, /44D; P.C. Graves, report, April 6, 1936, /44C, NA. Other reports document the size of the crowd, the "objectionable manner" in which the couples danced, the continuing presence of the "rubber sheath machine" in the lavatory.
254. Hilda Winston, interview, Jan. 24, 1994, interview 372, London, WEJ.
255. "The Barn Club: Swimming Bath Polluted at Night: Typical Anti-Semitic Hooliganism," *Jewish Chronicle*, May 23, 1936, 25.
256. "Raid on Barn Club: Manager Sent to Prison," *The Times*, Feb. 27, 1937, 9.
257. "Policeman's 12/- tip for Waiter," *Evening Standard*, Jan. 29, 1937. The press also highlighted the indulgences of undercover policewomen. "Roadhouse Nights of Two Policewomen with Dinner, Wine, Cabaret, Etc.," *Evening News*, Jan. 19, 1937. "Women P.C. at the Barn Club," *Evening News*, Jan. 18, 1937, p. 1 photo of Mr. Jack Isow, unattributed, MEPO 2/4494, NA.
258. "Bottle Parties: Court Proceedings," *The Times*, Jan. 22, 1937, 11; "Bottle Parties: L.C.C. Regulations," 11. The limited liability company that owned the Shim Sham declared bankruptcy in June 1937. "Law Notices," June 22, 1937, 4; "Report on Successful Prosecutions of 16 Bottle Parties," "Liquor Licensing," HO 45/184888, NA.
259. On Isow's subsequent businesses, Nosher Powell with William Hall, *Nosher* (London: Blake, 1999), 96–146, passim; "Isow, J. A," HO 405/24361, NA.
260. "'Flash' Isow leaves the West End – for 18 Months," *Daily Mail*, Mar. 15, 1946; "Isow of the Shim Sham Gets 18 Months Jail," *Daily Express*, Mar. 15, 1946; "Isow, J. A.," HO 405/24361/9, NA.
261. Quoted in "Moving Here," "Hotels, Pubs, and Restaurants," at http://www.movinghere.org.uk/stories/story361, NA. During the war, the restaurant became so profitable that Isow could afford to rent Joseph Kennedy's palatial eleven-room flat in Manchester Square, complete with an "illuminated cocktail cabinet" and "sunken marble bathtub." "£100 in Sergeant's Pocket," *Daily Herald*, Mar. 18, 1946, "Isow, J. A.," HO 405/24361/8, NA.
262. Hilda Winston, interview, Jan.24, 1994.
263. Michael Winner, "Selfridges: If There's One Thing That Gets My Beef . . ." *Sunday Times*, Mar. 4, 2007; Mrs. M. E. Nichol, M.P., n.d. [1966], "Isow, J. A.," HO 405/24361/11, /12; "Isow's Restaurant Ltd," J148/11; "Isow's Ltd., Underpayment of Wages: 1949–1956," Aug. 30, 1950, LAB 11/2742; "Isow's Ltd v. D. Demetriades, 1972," J148/11, NA.
264. Powell, *Nosher*, 97.
265. See Louis Feldman, interview with author, June 20, 1999, London; Peter Phillips, quoted in "Stayers," *Soho Clarion*, 82 (Summer 1983), 15. See also Martin Tomkinson, *The Pornbrokers* (London: Virgin Books, 1982).
266. For numbers, see David Reynolds, *Rich Relations: The American Occupation of Britain, 1942–1945* (London: Phoenix, 2000), 227
267. "Around Town: Harlem in London," *What's On*, June 4, 1943, 89.
268. Laurie Deniz, interview, C122/93, BLSA.
269. On the color bar before the war, Jennings and Madge, *May the Twelfth*, 61, 62. On bleak employment prospects for black Britons, see Joe Deniz, interview, 1993. On interracial marriage, see Laura Tabili, *"We Ask for British Justice": Workers and Racial Difference in Late Imperial Britain* (Ithaca, NY: Cornell University Press, 1994), ch. 7; Chris Waters, "'Dark Strangers' in Our Midst: Discourses of Race and Nation in Britain, 1947–1963," *Journal of British Studies* 36, no. 2 (1997): 207–38.

270. On Home Intelligence Reports, see Reynolds, *Rich Relations*, 307. On Mass Observation and race, see Tony Kushner, *We Europeans? Mass-Observation, "Race" and British Identity in the Twentieth Century* (Burlington, VT: Ashgate, 2004), ch. 2; and "Bulletin and Directives, August 1943," File Report 1885, MOA. On rising tensions in 1943, see Sonya Rose, "Girls and GIs: Race, Sex and Diplomacy in Second World War Britain," *Journal of International History* 19, no. 146-60 (1997): 154. On government debates, see Reynolds, *Rich Relations*, ch. 14; Christopher Thorne, "Racial Issues and Anglo-American Relations," *New Community* (Summer 1974): 262-71.

271. Roma Fairley, *Come Dancing, Miss World* (London: Neame, 1966), ch. 9. Many thanks to Allison Abra for this reference.

272. Hall, "Social Eye of *Picture Post*," 90; Joshua Esty, *A Shrinking Island: Modernism and National Culture in England* (Princeton: Princeton University Press, 2004), 45. On new forms of knowledge, see Hall, "Social Eye of *Picture Post*." On Mass Observation, see Peter Gurney, " 'Intersexual' Dirty Girls: Mass Observation and Working-Class Sexuality in England in the 1930s," *Journal of the History of Sexuality* 8, no. 2 (1997): 259-90; James Buzard, "Mass-Observation, Modernism, and Auto-Ethnography," *Modernism/Modernity* 4, no. 3 (1997): 93-122; Penny Summerfield, "Mass-Observation: Social Research or Social Movement," *Journal of Contemporary History* 20, no. 3 (1985): 439-52; Ben Highmore, *Everyday Life and Cultural Theory: An Introduction* (London: Routledge, 2002); Dorothy Sheridan, Brian V. Street, and David Bloome, *Writing Ourselves: Mass-Observation and Literacy Practices* (Cresskill, NJ: Hampton Press, 2000).

273. See, for example, the coverage of nightclubs in 1939, in "The First War-Time Night Club," *Picture Post*, 5 (Oct. 28, 1939): 36, 37. The publication of images of semi-nude dancers in "The First War-Time Night Club" set off alarms at the Home Office because they appeared in a family magazine. On the government's response, see Sir Alexander Maxwell to the Secretary of State, Oct. 31, 1939, "Clubs and Bottle Parties: Correspondence Leading up to the Introduction of the Licensing Act, 1949, 1939-1954," MEPO 2/8512/2A, NA. The nightclub story also provoked outcries of "indecency" from readers as well as a defense of cabaret dancers by a "glamour girl's father." "Indecency," Nov. 25, 1939, 48, 59, in ibid. See also Christina Baade, " 'The Dancing Front': Dance Music, Dancing, and the BBC in World War II," *Popular Music* 25, no. 3 (2006): 347-68.

274. Hall, "Social Eye of *Picture Post*," 109.

275. "Inside London's Coloured Clubs," 20. On the closure of disreputable bottle parties, see S.D. Gavin, report, Nov. 7, 1939, "Clubs and Bottle Parties," MEPO 2/8512/3, NA.

276. Captions of conversations "overheard" at the club, such as a French officer telling a "coloured seaman" about the absence of a color bar in France, offer a sharper political intervention than the editorial voice of the text.

277. Baade, "The Dancing Front"; Tom Harrisson, "Whistle While You Work," *New Writing*, n.s. 1 (Autumn 1938), 47-67; "Dancing Through," in Tom Harrisson and Charles Madge, eds., *War Begins at Home. By Mass Observation* (London: Chatto & Windus, 1940), 222-53, esp. 249-50; "Doing the Lambeth Walk," in Tom Harrisson and Charles Madge, *Britain, by Mass-Observation* (London: Cresset, 1986; orig. 1939), 139-84. See Highmore, *Everyday Life*, 107-9. On the response of dance musicians, see Colin, *History of Jazz*, 75. On Harrisson's early dismissal of popular music, see Nott, *Music for the People*, 215. On combating Nazi atavism, see Angus Calder, "Mass-Observation 1937-49," in Martin Bulmer, *Essays in the History of British Sociological Research* (Cambridge, UK: Cambridge University Press, 1985), 128.

278. Specific individuals linked these new spaces to the old 43: Mildred Hoey, who "covered" for Mrs. Meyrick as the putative owner of the club in Gerrard Street in 1932, went on to become the proprietor of the Bag o' Nails in the thirties. Hoey kept a table for West End musicians, including veterans of jamming sessions at the 43 like Billy Amstell and Ivor Mairants, who had moved on to black clubs after Mrs. Meyrick's establishments closed down.

279. Daley, *This Small Cloud*, 168.

280. Minute 24, Feb. 2, 1930, "Mrs. Kate Evelyn Meyrick," MEPO 2/4481, NA.

Chapter 8: Windmill Theatre

1. Elizabeth Bowen, "The Theatre," *Night and Day*, July 29, 1937, 29.
2. Alison Light, *Forever England: Femininity, Literature and Conservatism between the Wars* (London: Routledge, 1991), 8, 154. On conservative modernity and the 1930s, see also Chris Waters, " 'Dark Strangers' in Our Midst: Discourses of Race and Nation in Britain, 1947–1963," *Journal of British Studies* 36, 2 (April 1997), 211; Chris Waters, "The Americanization of the Masses: Cultural Criticism, the National Heritage, and Working-Class Culture in the 1930s," *Social History Curators* 17 (1989–90): 22–3; Raphael Samuel, "Exciting to be English," in Raphael Samuel, ed., *Patriotism: The Making and Unmaking of British National Identity*, vol. 1 (London: Routledge, 1989); Ross McKibbin, *Classes and Cultures: England 1918–1951* (New York: Oxford University Press, 1998): xviii–lxvii.
3. On Metroland, see A. A. Jackson, *Semi-Detached London: Suburban Development, Life, and Transport 1900–1939* (London: Allen & Unwin, 1973), 203, 235–8.
4. There are endless casual references to the Windmill in popular histories of the Blitz and mid-century London. The only sustained scholarly assessment of the Windmill is Frank Mort, "Striptease: The Erotic Female Body and Live Sexual Entertainment in Mid-Twentieth-Century London," *Social History* 32, no. 1 (2007), 27–53. On the "myth of the Blitz," see Angus Calder, *The Myth of the Blitz* (London: Pimlico, 1992), 212–20. On sex and nationalism, see Sonya Rose's discussion, "Sex, Citizenship, and the Nation in World War II Britain," *American Historical Review* 103, n. 4 (1998): 1159, 1160; Geoff Eley, "Finding the People's War: Film, British Collective Memory and World War II," *American Historical Review* 106, no. 3 (June 2001): 818–38; John Baxendale, *Narrating the Thirties: A Decade in the Making, 1930 to the Present* (Houndmills, UK: Macmillan, 1996); Robert Mackay, *Half the Battle: Civilian Morale in Britain during the Second World War* (Manchester: Manchester University Press, 2002).
5. Thanks to Ian Burney for insight into ordinariness and wartime morale.
6. Light, *Forever England*, 8, 154. For Queenie Leavis and Virginia Woolf, middlebrow lacked the sophistication of the highbrow and the vitality of the traditionally popular. Its consumer targets were the women readers of suburbia, noted for their minute attention to class differences and domestic interiors. Queenie Leavis, *Fiction and the Reading Public* (London: Chatto & Windus, 1932); Virginia Woolf, "Middlebrow," in *The Death of the Moth and Other Essays* at http://ebooks.adelaide.edu.au/w/woolf/virginia/w91d/chapter22.html (accessed July 2011).
7. The *OED* also noted that *Punch* immediately adopted the term "middlebrow" to deride the pretentious offerings of state broadcasting. At http://dictionary.oed.com (accessed Sept. 30, 2010), now http://www.oed.com/.
8. On middlebrow as a literary form and market niche, see Nicola Humble, *The Feminine Middlebrow Novel from the 1920s to the 1950s: Class, Domesticity, and Bohemianism* (Oxford: Oxford University Press, 2001), 9; R. M. Bracco, *Merchants of Hope: British Middlebrow Writers and the First World War, 1919–1939* (Oxford: Berg, 1993); Joan Shelley Rubin, *The Making of Middlebrow Culture* (Chapel Hill: University of North Carolina Press, 1992). On middle-class suburban consumerism on the part of public servants, teachers, bank and insurance officials, technicians and many clerical workers in private industries, see John Stevens, *British Society, 1914–1945* (London: Penguin, 1984), ch. 4; McKibbin, *Classes and Culture*; J. Stevenson and C. Cook, *Britain in the Depression: Society and Politics 1929–1939* (London: Longman, 1994).
9. "We Are Amused," *News Review*, June 27, 1940, Windmill Cuttings. vol. 42, TM.
10. Kenon Breazeale, "In Spite of Women: Esquire Magazine and the Construction of the Male Consumer," *Signs* (Autumn 1994): 1–22; Joanne Meyerowitz, "Women, Cheesecake, and Borderline Material: Responses to Girlie Pictures in the Mid-Twentieth Century U.S.," *Journal of Women's History* 8, no. 3 (Fall 1996): 9–36; Liz Conor, *The Spectacular Modern Woman: Feminine Visibility in the 1920s* (Bloomington: Indiana University Press, 2004).
11. Dan Farson, *Soho in the Fifties* (London: Michael Joseph, 1987), 8. On the Windmill, the "Talkies," and Wardour Street, see "Woman-Land," *Exeter Press*, Mar. 24, 1932, Windmill Revudeville Cuttings, vol. 23, TM.

12. See Mort, "Striptease"; "Staid Burlesque," *Los Angeles Times*, June 29, 1952, L12; Sheila Van Damm, *We Never Closed: The Windmill Story* (London: Robert Hale, 1967), 31.

13. On middle England, see Calder, *The Myth of the Blitz*.

14. On "fairy godmother," see W. J. Bishop, " 'Revudeville': Variety's 'Fairy Godmother' and the Windmill," *Era*, April 13, 1932, Windmill Cuttings, Box 23, TM. For more on Mrs. Henderson, see Sheila Van Damm, *We Never Closed*, ch. 2; Vivian Van Damm, *Tonight and Every Night. [the Story of the Windmill Theatre. With Plates Including Portraits]* (London: Stanley Paul, 1952), ch. 7, Windmill Scrapbooks, vol. 23, TM; *Belfast Telegraph*, April 1, 1932; "Obituaries," *The Times*, Nov. 30, 1944, 8. According to one article, her father was physician to the royal family, and this may have been one basis for her friendship with the royal princesses.

15. *Revudeville* 20 souvenir program, 1933; Windmill souvenir program, 1937, Windmill Programmes, TM.

16. The press reported on her lecture to the Cardiff branch of the Women's Guild of Empire as its president in May 1932, and it noted her support for the Hyde Park Babies' Club, the Docklands Settlement, and the Marie Stopes Mothers' Clinic. See Windmill Scrapbooks, vol. 23, TM; *South Wales Echo*, May 7, 1932. On Mrs. Henderson's philanthropies, see *The Times* "National Police Fund," May 18, 1926, 5; "Court Circular," May 26, 1932, 17; Nov. 23, 1932, 17; "Anglo-German Fellowship," July 15, 1936, 19; "Sir R. Storr's Appeal for Women's Orchestra," April 21, 1937, 14; *Revudeville* 65, Feb. 4, 1935, "Revudeville Clippings and Programs," NYPL. On independent theater between the wars, see Maggie Gale, *West End Women: Women and the London Stage* (London: Routledge, 1996), 38–53.

17. On appeasement and the Anglo-German Fellowship, see Frank McDonough, *Neville Chamberlain and the British Road to War* (Manchester: Manchester University Press, 1998), 143–51; Scott Newton, *Profits of Peace: The Political Economy of Anglo-German Appeasement* (Oxford: Oxford University Press, 1996), chs. 3 and 4; Richard M. Griffiths, *Fellow Travellers of the Right* (Oxford: Oxford University Press, 1983), 182–6; Terence Rogers, "The Right Book Club," *Journal of Contemporary History* (Autumn 2003): 1–15. On Nancy Astor's contradictions and participation in the right-wing, pro-Hitler Cliveden Set, see Norman Rose, *The Cliveden Set: Portrait of an Exclusive Fraternity* (London: Cape, 2000) and the following reviews of it: Thomas Pakenham, "The Other Conspiracy," *Times Literary Supplement*, no. 5086 (2000): 26; Ian Gilmour, "Termagant," *London Review of Books* 22, no. 20 (2000): 12.

18. "Piccadilly, South Side," in *Survey of London: Volumes 29 and 30: St James Westminster, Part 1* (1960), 251–70, at http://www.britishhistory.ac.uk/ (accessed Sept. 30, 2010).

19. See Sheila Van Damm, *We Never Closed*; Kathrine Sorley Walker, "The Markova-Dolin Ballet, 1935–1937," *Dance Now* (Spring 1998–Winter 1999/2000): 66–86; Ian Vevar, n.t., *The Outspar* (South Africa), Feb. 20, 1953, Windmill Cuttings, vol. 55, TM; *Star*, Feb. 22, 1937, Windmill Cuttings, vol. 33, TM.

20. See Gale, *West End Women*.

21. On the interwar stage, revues, and variety, see Philip Godfrey, *Back-Stage: A Survey of the Contemporary English Theatre from behind the Scenes* (London: Harrap, 1933); Roger Wilmut, *Kindly Leave the Stage: The Story of Variety* (London: Methuen, 1985); Clive Barker and Maggie B. Gale, eds., *British Theatre between the Wars* (Cambridge, UK: Cambridge University Press, 2000).

22. Sheila Van Damm, *We Never Closed*, 32.

23. Vivian Van Damm, *Tonight and Every Night* (London: Stanley Paul, 1952), 12.

24. *Sunday Dispatch*, Mar. 28, 1937, Windmill Cuttings, vol. 33, TM.

25. In the mid-thirties, he would return to the cinema by producing film shorts of *Revudeville*, used as "fillers" by cinemas to satisfy domestic film quotas.

26. See Vivian Van Damm, *Tonight and Every Night*, ch. 7; Sheila Van Damm, *We Never Closed*, ch. 2; and extant correspondence.

27. Mort, "Striptease"; Neil Gabler, *An Empire of their Own: How the Jews Invented Hollywood* (New York: Crown, 1989).

28. On Freudianism without Freud, see Rachel Bowlby, *Shopping with Freud* (London: Routledge, 1993). See also Robert Graves and Alan Hodge, *The Long Week-End: A Social History of Great*

Britain, 1918–1939 (New York: Norton, 1994), 90–2; "Windmill Sails," no. 27, June 1933, Windmill Programmes, TM.

29. Vivian Van Damm, *Tonight and Every Night*, 23, 36. He was subsequently able to sign on as an instructor on the combustion engine for a short time.

30. See Todd M. Endelman, *The Jews of Britain 1656 to 2000* (Berkeley: University of California Press, 2002), 196. Sheila Van Damm, *No Excuses* (London: Putnam, 1957), 25. She did not mention the strong anti-fascism that animated many other Anglo-Jews. On one occasion, Van Damm wrote of his perceived marginality in his program notes. *Revudeville* 17 (Nov. 14, 1932), Windmill Programmes, TM. For Van Damm's obituary, see "Mr. Vivian Van Damm," *The Times*, Dec. 15, 1960, 13.

31. Mrs. Henderson to the *Daily Herald*, April 13, 1932, Windmill Cuttings, vol. 23, TM.

32. Van Damm, quoted in *Daily News and Chronicle*, Dec. 16, 1931, *Edinburgh Evening News* Dec. 17, 1931, Windmill Cuttings, vol. 23, TM.

33. See Gordon Honeycombe, *Selfridges: Seventy-Five Years* (London: Park Lane Press, 1984); Peter Bird, *First Food Empire: A History of J. Lyons and Co.* (Chichester, UK: Phillimore, 2000).

34. Richinda Power, "Healthy Motion: Images of 'Natural' and 'Cultured' Movement in Early Twentieth Century Britain," *Women's Studies International Forum* 19, no. 5 (1996): 551–65; Mrs. Henderson to the editor, *Daily Herald*, May 17, 1932; A. R. Thomas, "Stage Gossip," *Star*, Feb. 1, 1932; "Dancing Girls," *Gloucester Echo*, Jan. 29, 1932, Windmill Cuttings, vol. 23, TM.

35. Sheila Van Damm, *We Never Closed*, 60, 61.

36. Oden and Olivia Meeker, "London's Prim Burlesque," *Los Angeles Times*, June 29, 1952, 112; "The Audience is the Joke," *Sunday Mail* (Rhodesia), May 12, 1957, Windmill Cuttings, vol. 60, 1957–8, TM; Peter Bailey, "Musical Comedy and the Rhetoric of the Girl, 1892–1914," in Bailey, *Popular Culture and Performance in the Victorian City* (Cambridge, UK: Cambridge University Press, 1998), 128–50; Vivian Van Damm, *Tonight and Every Night*, 86, 87.

37. On Maud Allan and the tradition of erotic display, see chapter 3, this volume; Judith R. Walkowitz, "The 'Vision of Salome': Cosmopolitanism and Erotic Dancing in Central London, 1908–1918," *American Historical Review* 108, 2 (April 2003): 236–76. On Living Pictures, see Joseph Donohue, *Fantasies of Empire: The Empire Theatre of Varieties and the Licensing Controversy of 1894* (Iowa City: University of Iowa Press, 1995); Brenda Assael, "Art or Indecency? Tableaux Vivants on the London Stage and the Failure of Late Victorian Moral Reform," *Journal of British Studies* 4 (2006): 744–58.

38. The Lord Chamberlain's duties included the organization of royal events like weddings and coronations, but also theater censorship. Sheila Van Damm, *We Never Closed*, 162.

39. On the Lord Chamberlain's Office, see in particular, Steve Nicholson, *The Censorship of British Drama 1900–1968*, vol. 2: *1933–1952* (Exeter: Exeter University Press, 2005), chs. 1, 2, 6.

40. Jean Kent, quoted in "How I Was Shocked – By the Lord Chamberlain," *Sunday Dispatch*, Jan. 6, 1957, Windmill Cuttings, Miscellaneous Box, TM; "There Once Was a Windmill," *Knight* 6, no. 1 (July 1967): 71–3, 97, Theatre Clipping Collection, NYPL.

41. "Variety" (Nov. 17, 1932), Public Morality Council, Annual Reports 1932, 1933, Public Morality Council archive, A/PMC/98, LMA.

42. Until 1937, the Windmill's only non-stop competitor was the Prince of Wales. Eric Barker, *Steady Barker: The Autobiography of Eric Barker* (London: Secker & Warburg, 1956), 128.

43. Windmill Cuttings, vol. 31, TM; "Theatre: Night Time Nudes," *News Review*, Jan. 14, 1937.

44. David Clayton, "All Change at the Windmill," *Lilliput* 26 (Jan.–June 1950): 48.

45. On Charlot, see James Ross Moore, "Crazy Girls," in Barker and Gale, *British Theatre between the Wars*, 92–5; James Ross Moore, *Andre Charlot: The Genius of Intimate Musical Revue* (Jefferson, NC: McFarland, 2005). On the Windmill's format, see "Variety Theatres," *The Times*, Jan. 3, 1933, 1; Vivian Van Damm, *Tonight and Every Night*, 112, 113, 12.

46. VD also insisted that his productions depended on "tons" of scenery created on site, stored away and delivered to the theater every morning at 8 a.m. He was more than a manager or "impresario" but something of an "engineer, something of an architect, a practical man, with vision, yet something of a gambler." Vivian Van Damm, *Tonight and Every Night*, 12.

47. "Famous 'Windmill' Grinds out Starlets for Screen and Stage," *News Service*, July 19, 1943; see also Mort, "Striptease."
48. On the Windmill girl's ideal statistics, see Sheila Van Damm, *We Never Closed*, 155. On burlesque audiences and their taste, see Kathleen Spies, " 'Girls and Gags': Sexual Display and Humor in Reginald Marsh's Burlesque Images," *American Art* (2004): 33–57. On the whiteness of this erotic image, see Breazeale, "In Spite of Women," 12.
49. See Nicholson, *The Censorship of British Drama*, 203.
50. "Mrs. Henderson's House of Delights," *Guardian*, Nov. 18, 2005. At http://www.guardian.co.uk/film/2005/nov/18/2 (accessed May 2011).
51. See chapter 7.
52. Pat Kirkham, "Fashioning the Feminine," in Christine Gledhill and Gillian Swanson, eds., *Nationalising Femininity: Culture, Sexuality, and Cinema in World War Two* (Manchester: Manchester University Press, 1996); Pat Kirkham, "Beauty Is Duty," in Pat Kirkham and David Thomas, eds., *War Culture: Social Change and Experience in World War Two* (London: Lawrence & Wishart, 1996), 13–28.
53. Windmill chorines tended to be, in the words of one reviewer, "hard-working, cheery young ladies" who "sang with more spirit than talent." *The Times*, July 19, 1938, 12.
54. Complaints of sweated labor summoned up images of overworked and unhealthy laboring bodies at variance with the Windmill girl's purported "freshness and beauty." See, for example, Daniel Bender, *Sweated Work, Weak Bodies: Anti-Sweatshop Campaigns and Languages of Labor* (New Brunswick: Rutgers University Press, 2004); Kristina Huneault, *Difficult Subjects: Working Women and Visual Culture* (Aldershot, UK: Ashgate, 2003). Sheila Van Damm's memoirs lend credence to these rumors of sweated labor. She noted that in 1936, "statistically inclined" girls estimated that, "at a weekly wage of £2 10s they were being paid only 1s 8d per performance." Sheila Van Damm, *We Never Closed*, 85, 87.
55. Vivian Van Damm, to the Entertainment Committee, Mar. 16, 1932, GLC/DG/EL/3/E22, LMA.
56. Hannen Swaffer, "I Heard Yesterday," *Daily Herald*, April 13, 1932, Windmill Cuttings, vol. 23, TM; "Anon" to the Entertainment Committee of the GLC, Feb. 23, 1932, GLC/DG/EL/E/E 22, LMA; Sheila Van Damm, *We Never Closed*, 85, 87.
57. Barker, *Steady Barker*, 120.
58. Michelle Stanistreet, "How the Windmill Girls Kept the Blitz at Bay," *Sunday Express*, Nov. 20, 2005. See also Charmian Innes, account of the thirties in ibid.
59. They also passed comment on the long working days. "We used to work all morning, all day and at evening," one former Windmill girl told Sheila Van Damm. "I didn't get home until eleven-thirty all night. I'd eat a meal and go straight to bed. Then I had to be back at the theatre for ten o'clock rehearsal next morning. If it was a dress rehearsal I arrived at nine in order to be made up by ten." Sheila Van Damm, *We Never Closed*, 86.
60. *The Times*, July 19, 1938, 12.
61. I have found only one occasion, March 1937, for a revue entitled "Sunday in Harlem," when the Windmill showcased an African-American dancer; Windmill Cuttings, vol. 31, TM; "Sunday in Harlem," *Evening News* [1937]. See Mica Nava, *Visceral Cosmopolitanism* (Oxford: Berg, 2007), ch. 5; Rebecca A. Bryant, "Shaking Things Up: Popularizing the Shimmy in America," *Popular Music* 20, no. 2 (Summer 2002): 168–87.
62. Windmill Press Cuttings, vol. 40, TM; "*Daily Film Renter*, July 18, 1940.
63. Barker, *Steady Barker*, 122.
64. Meyerowitz, "Women, Cheesecake, and Borderline Material."
65. Kathryn Johnson, quoted in "Sex, Censorship, and the Real Mrs. Henderson," *Independent*, Nov. 12, 2005, 3.
66. Quoted in "Staid Burlesque."
67. Margaret Law, in "Memories of the Windmill," in "Mrs. Henderson Presents," at http://www.writingstudio.co.za/page1069.html (accessed Sept. 30, 2010).
68. Doris Barry, "A Song and Dance Girl," in Mavis Nicholson, ed., *What Did You Do in the War, Mummy? Women in World War II* (London: Pimlico, 1996), 196.

69. Ibid., 196, 197.
70. Margaret McGrath's comments to Charles Graves, in Graves, *Off the Record* (London: Hutchinson, 1941), 56, 79; contrast with Eileen Cruikshank's memories, in Glenys Roberts, "I Was Britain's First Nude Dancer," *Daily Mail*, Nov. 26, 2005.
71. "A Very Arch Bishop," *Era*, Aug. 7, 1935, Windmill Cuttings, vol. 26, TM.
72. "We feel we gain in respect rather than lose it by the work we do," Jan Foreman told the *Era* in 1935. "With the superb lighting and colour effects provided for us," declared Bobbie Bradshaw, "we are enabled to represent to the public a beautiful picture. Thousands go to our art galleries to see the paintings, and we maintain that our work is in the same artistic vein." "A Very Arch Bishop"; "Other People's Jobs: How it Feels to be a Windmill Girl," Mar. 19, 1952, Windmill Cuttings, vol. 54, 1952–3, TM. See also Michael Bentine, *The Long Banana Skin* (London: Wolfe, 1975), 150. Thanks to Tracy Davis for the observation about lighting. See also C. Harold Ridge, *Stage Lighting: Principles and Practice* (London: Pitman, 1935).
73. Foreman, quoted in "A Very Arch Bishop."
74. Ronnie Bridges, quoted in "Mrs. Henderson's House of Delights"; Kenneth More, *More or Less* (London: Hodder & Stoughton, 1978), 61; Jean Kent, in "Memories of the Windmill"; Peggy Martin, quoted in "Mrs. Henderson's House of Delights." These reminiscences of VD's sexual exploits began to surface in published memoirs in the 1970s, and were rehearsed in the press again with the production of "Mrs. Henderson Presents" in 2005.
75. Many thanks to Tracy Davis for an explanation of interwar theatrical lighting systems.
76. Sheila Van Damm, *We Never Closed*, 154; Vivian Van Damm to George Titman, Oct. 28, 1940, *Revudeville* 138, Lord Chamberlain's Play Correspondence, File 3680, BL.
77. VD claimed that annual sales of *Revudeville* programs soon numbered around 40,000 and cleared £150. Windmill Programmes, no. 20 (1933), TM.
78. Borderline was the contemporary category commonly deployed in the United States to signal the inclusion of nude visual imagery within the category of licit. See Meyerowitz, "Women, Cheesecake, and Borderline Material," 9–10.
79. Bill Osgerby, "A Pedigree of Masculinity ..." in Bethan Benwell, ed., *Masculinity and Men's Lifestyles* (Oxford: Blackwell, 2004): 57–88; Jill Greenfield, Sean O'Connell, and Chris Reid, "Fashioning Masculinity: Men Only, Consumption and the Development of Marketing in the 1930s," *Twentieth-Century British History* 10, no. 4 (1999): 457–76.
80. Howard Tyrer to Major Gordon, June 15, 1935, Lord Chamberlain's Play Correspondence, File 14368, Folder 1, BL. Tyrer deemed this two-thirds pose to be more graphic and objectionable than the actual stage pose.
81. Memorandum by "C.L.," May 20, 1935, Lord Chamberlain's Play Correspondence, File 14368, Folder 1, BL.
82. The press characterized Windmill patrons as "tired businessmen" and "time-fillers" waiting for trains, provincial and international visitors. See, for example, "Revudeville," *Era*, April 13, 1932, Windmill Cuttings, vol. 42; "We Are Amused"; Clayton, "All Change at the Windmill," 49; Andre Charlot thought the Windmill catered to the "middle and cheaper theatre public." Andre Charlot to Lord Chamberlain, May 1937, Lord Chamberlain's Collection, Deposit 10387, 2nd Series, File 512–37 (1), no. 38, BL.
83. Major Gwatkin to VD, quoted in Nicholson, *The Censorship of British Drama*, 62.
84. "Life Goes On," *News Chronicle* [1940], Windmill Collection, Box 40, TM.
85. Spies, "Girls and Gags"; Andrea Friedman, *Prurient Interests: Gender, Democracy and Obscenity in New York City, 1909–1945* (New York: Columbia University Press, 2000).
86. Graham Greene, "The Theatre," *Spectator* 166 (June 6, 1941): 607.
87. Rop Zone, "Taking a (Nude) Stand against Air Raids," *Seattle Times*, Jan. 8, 2006, J3.
88. Windmill Cuttings, vol. 40, TM; "These Names Make Nudes," *News Chronicle*, Mar. 28, 1940.
89. More, *More or Less*, 55.
90. Pat Ingram, "How Much I Earn," *Daily Mirror*, July 8, 1937, Windmill Cuttings, vol. 32, TM.
91. Barry, "A Song and Dance Girl," 197.

92. W. J. Bishop, "Bright Spots," *Daily Sketch*, Feb. 29, 1940, Windmill Cuttings, vol. 40, TM. On the Crazy Gang, see David Sutton, *A Chorus of Raspberries: British Film Comedy 1929–1939* (Exeter: Exeter University Press, 2000), 49.

93. "We Are Amused."

94. *Revudeville* 27, June 1933, Windmill Programmes, TM.

95. *Revudeville* 119, Mar. 27, 1939; 120, April 17, 1939, Windmill Programmes, TM.

96. Vivian Van Damm, "Windmill Sails," *Revudeville* 63 (1935), Revudeville Programs, NYPL.

97. Sheila Van Damm, *We Never Closed*, 122.

98. "Variety," *Stage*, April 8, 1937; *Revudeville* 60, May 20, 1935, Lord Chamberlain's Play Correspondence, File 145368, BL; Lord Chamberlain's Play Correspondence, File 15166 and 15356, BL. On low comedy, see Spies, "Girls and Gags," and its British variant, see Sutton, *A Chorus of Raspberries*.

99. Report by G. S. Street, Sept. 18, 1934, *Revudeville* 48, Lord Chamberlain's Play Correspondence, File 13204, BL; Report, Mar. 5, 1935, Lord Chamberlain's Play Correspondence, File 13773, BL. On the plumbing and W.C. jokes, see Report by H. C. Game, Sept. 11, 1936, *Revudeville* 82, Lord Chamberlain's Play Correspondence, File 15309, BL; and *The Times*, Feb. 1937, Windmill Press Cuttings, vol. 33, TM.

100. Anne Mitelle, VD's assistant, was told that the skit about "ex-Windmill girls" and "30 bob" earned immorally had better "go." Report of G. S. Street, Mar. 5, 1935, *Revudeville* 57, Lord Chamberlain's Play Correspondence, File 13850, BL. Similarly, when a skit included a fairy or pansy character who impersonated an effeminate male and expressed homoerotic desire, "alterations" were required, as in the case of a police training school skit and another about the Foreign Legion. Gwatkin to VD, April 16, 1937, *Revudeville* 91, Lord Chamberlain's Play Correspondence, File 387, BL; Report by H. C. Game, Sept. 11, 1936.

101. Report from H. C. Game, Oct. 8, 1941, *Revudeville* 148, Lord Chamberlain's Play Correspondence, File 4041, BL.

102. "There Once Was a Windmill."

103. Mort, "Striptease"; Van Damm to Mr. Titman, Nov. 28, 1941, *Revudeville* 148, Lord Chamberlain's Play Correspondence, File 4041, BL.

104. See Lord Chamberlain's Play Correspondence, BL.

105. Nicholson, *The Censorship of British Drama*; Nicholas de Jongh, *Politics, Prudery, and Perversion: The Censoring of the British Stage, 1901–1968* (London: Methuen, 2000).

106. David Cardiff, "Mass Middlebrow Laughter," *Media, Culture, and Society*, 10 (1988): 41; Paddy Scannell and David Cardiff, *A Social History of British Broadcasting*, vol. 1: *1922–1939* (Oxford: Blackwell, 1991).

107. On the productive consequences of censorship, see Annette Kuhn's Foucauldian readings of cinema censorship: *Cinema, Censorship and Sexuality, 1909–1925* (London: Routledge, 1988).

108. Sheila Van Damm, *We Never Closed*, 151; Barker, *Steady Barker*, 123.

109. Cardiff, "Mass Middlebrow Laughter," 44.

110. On the 1937 dispute, see Louise Jury, "Sex, Censorship, and the Real Mrs. Henderson," *Independent*, Nov. 12, 2005, 3; "Censorship: Correspondence, Memoranda, Reports, Press cuttings . . . on the Subject of Nudity on the Stage, Culminating in the Meeting Held by the Lord Chamberlain on the 24th June [1937]," Lord Chamberlain's Collection, Deposit 10397, File 512–37 (1), BL: Thanks to Kathryn Johnson for access to this file.

111. Patrick Balfour, "Midnight Folly," *Night and Day*, Nov. 11, 1937, 28; "Folie d'Amour," advertisement in *Star*, Jan. 1, 1937, presented to Entertainment Committee, Feb. 3, 1937, LCC Entertainment Committee minutes, LCC MIN/4477, LMA; "London Night and Day," *Night and Day*, July 22, 1937, 3. It was opened by Poulsen of the Café de Paris; "London Backchat," *What's On* (April–June 1936), 19.

112. "Theatre: Night Time Nudes,"*News Review*, Jan. 14, 1937, Windmill Press Cuttings, vol. 32, TM.

113. Black literally imported a stripper, Diane Raye, from America, but at the last minute decided not to include her "disrobing act." Gordon W. Halsey, San Marco Restaurant, to the Lord

Chamberlain, April 3, 1937, and "Report on Strip-tease Act as Seen at Victoria Palace," forwarded by Howard Tyler to Major Gwatkin, April 26, 1937, Lord Chamberlain's Collection, Deposit 10387, File 512–37 (1), BL; "Variety," Stage, April 8, 1937.

114. "Plays of the Week," Illustrated Sporting and Dramatic News [1937]; Sporting Life, Mar. 5, 1937, Windmill Cuttings, vol. 33, TM.

115. "More Nudity for Stage Shows," Sunday Dispatch, Mar. 28, 1937, vol. 31, News Review, Jan 14, 1937, Windmill Cuttings, vol. 33, TM.

116. Friedman, Prurient Interests, 67.

117. Brought up in Ealing by her grandmother, while her mother worked in New York at the Ziegfeld Follies and in Paris at the Folies Bergère, Eileen Cruikshank began work at the Prince of Wales until the Windmill hired her as a showgirl. Roberts, "I was Britain's First Nude Dancer."

118. Chief Inspector Martin to Police Commissioner, May 11, 1937, 'Paradise' 189 Regent Street: Anon, complaint re indecent performance, 1937:/10, MEPO 3/941, NA.

119. Roberts, "I was Britain's First Nude Dancer"; "Variety," What's On, May 1937; W. J. Bishop, "Fan Dancer at the Windmill," Era, April 1, 1937, Windmill Cuttings, 33, TM.

120. Cruikshank, quoted in Roberts, "I was Britain's First Nude Dancer."

121. Tatler, Star, Stage, April 29, 1937, Windmill Cuttings, TM.

122. "These 'Strip Shows,'" Daily Telegraph, April 29, 1937; "LCC Drive against Shows in West End," Daily Sketch, May 5, 1937, Lord Chamberlain's Play Correspondence, File 11387, BL.

123. "Nymphs of the Fountain," Daily Mirror, May 7, 1937, Lord Chamberlain's Play Correspondence, File 11387, BL.

124. Theater reviews of Revudeville 91 had already drawn attention to the daring stage version of the tableau: even under dim atmospheric lighting, it "carries the presentation of nudity upon the London stage to . . . the ultimate point permissible by the authorities." Daily Mail, April 27, 1937, Windmill Cuttings, vol. 33, TM.

125. Osgerby, "A Pedigree of Masculinity"; Greenfield et al., "Fashioning Masculinity." The "success" of the Windmill and the Mirror were "coeval," editor Hugh Cudlipp recalled in 1953; the type of audience who goes to the Windmill is "the type of the audience . . . which made the Mirror." Hugh Cudlipp, "Exclusive: The First Nude in Fleet Street," British Journalism Review 3, no. 5 (1994): 17–19; Windmill Cuttings, vol. 55 (1952), TM; James Thomas, "Reflections on the Broken Mirror: The Rise and Fall of Radical Journalism Re-considered,' Media History 9, no. 2 (2003): 103–21; Kevin Williams and Michael Bromley, "Tales of Transformation: The Daily Mirror 100 Years On," Media History 9, no. 2 (2003), 99–106; Michael Bromley, "Was It the Mirror Wot Won It?" in Nick Hayes and Jeff Hill, eds., 'Millions like Us'? British Culture in the Second World War (Liverpool: Liverpool University Press, 1999), 97.

126. Lord Chamberlain's Play Correspondence, File 10387, BL; "Stop This Strip-tease Scandal," Pearson's Weekly, May 1, 1937.

127. Police Commissioner Philip Game, "Minute," May 18, 1937, "Alleged Indecent Dance Act and Bottle Parties at 'Paradise' 189, Regent Street," 1937, MEPO 3/941, NA.

128. Lord Chamberlain to H. T. C. Runge, "Private and Confidential," May 21, 1937, Lord Chamberlain's Collection, File 10387, BL.

129. H. C. Runge to Comptroller, May 30, 1937, ibid.

130. Lord Chamberlain to H. T. C. Runge, "Private and Confidential," ibid.

131. "More Nudity for Stage Shows," Sunday Dispatch, Mar. 28, 1937, Windmill Cuttings, vol. 33, TM; H. C. Game, Memorandum: Stage Nudity [1937] and "Memorandum," May 25, 1937, Lord Chamberlain Collection, Deposit 10387, BL. As Davis observes, Van Damm drew on the cultural logic and "mise en scène" of the Victorian Living Pictures, but extended the repertoire of poses beyond the imitation of classical statuary and art works. Tracy Davis, Actresses as Working Women: Their Social Identity in Victorian Culture (London: Routledge, 1991), 131.

132. On nude vs. naked, see chapters 2 and 3, this volume. On burlesque, see Spies, "Girls and Gags"; "Memorandum," May 25, 1937, Lord Chamberlain's Play Correspondence, File 10387, BL.

133. The Lord Chamberlain then met with Tyrer of the Public Morality Council, who was "quite non-plussed by the Lord Chamberlain's argument" as to the "beneficial effects of the sun and the human body." Evidently Cromer had tried to echo Charlot and contextualize tasteful stage nudity in light of contemporary standards of bodily exposure during sunbathing. VD to Lord Cromer, May 26, 1937, Lord Chamberlain's Play Correspondence, File 10387, BL. In late May, Cromer attended the performance, with Lady Cromer, and VD was "satisfied with his reaction" Cromer to VD, May 27, 1937; VD to Lord Cromer, May 29, 1937, ibid.

134. André Charlot to Major Gwatkin, June 8, 1937, Lord Chamberlain's Collection, File 10387, BL.

135. H. C. Game, "Reflection on Meeting and Charlot's 'Apologia pro vita sua' [1937]" André Charlot, "Report" [1937], Lord Chamberlain's Collection, File 10387, BL.

136. Like Bowen, Greene preferred the good-humored tattiness of the Windmill to the cynical worldliness of the Prince of Wales. Grahame Greene, "The Theatre," *Spectator* 166 (Mar. 7, 1941): 251; 166 (June 27, 1941): 677; 166 (June 6, 1941): 771.

137. Report of G. S. Street, Jan. 14, 1936, *Revudeville* 71, Lord Chamberlain's Play Correspondence, File 14649, BL.

138. Van Damm dutifully oversaw these alterations, while noting in his account book a mounting concern over fascism and war. Sheila Van Damm, *We Never Closed*, ch. 15; Windmill Records, No. 2 account book Sept. 1935–May 1939, Windmill Collection, TM; de Jongh, *Politics, Prudery, and Perversion*; Nicholson, *Censorship*, ch. 1.

139. Sheila Van Damm, *We Never Closed*, 89.

140. On Soho as remote from the "British body politic," see John Galsworthy, *The Forsyte Saga* (New York: Dover, 2002), 450.

141. Geoff Field, "Nights Underground in Darkest London: The Blitz, 1940–1941," *International Labor and Working-Class History*, no. 62 (Fall, 2002): 12. See also Calder, *The Myth of the Blitz*; Tom Harrisson, *Living through the Blitz* (London: Collins, 1976). On the intelligentsia and central London, see Andrew Sinclair, *War like a Wasp: The Lost Decade of the "Forties"* (London: Hamish Hamilton, 1990), 15, 16.

142. For wartime entertainment, see Richard Fawkes, *Fighting for a Laugh: Entertaining the British and American Forces 1939–1946* (London: Macdonald/Jane's, 1978).

143. Windmill Cuttings, vol. 39, TM; *Sketch*, Oct. 4, 1939.

144. Sheila Van Damm, *We Never Closed*, ch. 8.

145. "New Revudeville," *Illustrated Sporting and Dramatic News*, Mar. 8, 1940, Windmill Cuttings, vol. 40, TM; Field, "Nights Underground," 12, 13.

146. Windmill Cuttings, vol. 40, TM; "New Revudeville," *Jewish Quarterly*, Feb. 2, 1940.

147. "Windmill Theatre 'Revudeville,' " *The Times*, Oct. 3, 1939, 6.

148. "New Revudeville," Windmill Cuttings, vol. 40, TM.

149. Nicholson, *The Censorship of British Drama*, ch. 6; Philip Purser and Jenny Wilkes, *The One and Only Phyllis Dixey* (London: Futura, 1978). LCC authorities complained that the poison of stage nudity was spreading from the West End to suburban theaters. J. A. Sharpe to the Editor, *Daily Telegraph*, Mar. 27, 1940, 6.

150. This was a similar kind of official response to the *Daily Mirror's* reproduction of the Windmill's publicity photograph of "Enchanted Fountain" in 1937.

151. Sir Alexander Maxwell to Secretary of State, Oct. 31, 1939, "Clubs and Bottle Parties: Correspondence Leading up to the Introduction of the Licensing Act, 1949, 1939–1954," MEPO 2/ 8512, NA.

152. *Daily Telegraph*, Mar. 29, 1940, 6, and Mar. 30, 1940, 6.

153. E. M. Forster, quoted in Nicholson, *The Censorship of British Drama*, 210.

154. Sir Alexander Maxwell to Secretary of State, Oct. 31, 1939, MEPO 2/ 8512, NA.

155. "Entertainment," *News Review*, April 1940, Windmill Cuttings, vol. 42, TM.

156. "Revudeville," *What's On*, May 10, 1940, Windmill Cuttings, vol. 42, TM.

157. Nicholson, *The Censorship of British Drama*, 228.

158. H. C. Game "Report 8," and Mr. Titman, Nov. 7, 1941, *Revudeville* 148, Lord Chamberlain's Play Correspondence, File 4041, BL; VD to Mr. Titman, Nov. 28, 1941, ibid.; Complaint

from Mr. Nevill Francis, Aug. 3, 1944, *Revudeville* 176, Lord Chamberlain's Play Correspondence, File 5684/44, BL; Mr. Tomlinson, general secretary of the Public Morality Council to the Lord Chamberlain, Aug. 15, 1944, *Revudeville* 176, Lord Chamberlain's Play Correspondence, File 5684/44, BL; George Titman to Vivian Van Damm, Aug. 15, 1944, and Van Damm to Mr. Titman, Aug. 15, 1944, *Revudeville* 176, Lord Chamberlain's Play Correspondence, File 5684/44, BL.

159. Mr. Nevill Francis, Aug. 3, 1944, Mr. Tomlinson, Aug. 15, 1944, George Titman to Vivian Van Damm, Aug. 15, 1944, and Van Damm to Mr. Titman, Aug. 15, 1944, *Revudeville* 176, Lord Chamberlain's Play Correspondence, File 5684/44, BL.

160. Mrs. Henderson to Lord Clarendon, Nov. 6, 1940, *Revudeville* 138, Lord Chamberlain's Play Correspondence, File 3640, BL.

161. Sheila Van Damm, *We Never Closed*, 129. Eileen Cruikshank, one of the first fan dancers, remembered that some girls "let them drop . . . I never did. I was too professional." Roberts, "I Was Britain's First Nude Dancer."

162. "There Once Was a Windmill," 97.

163. Ibid.

164. H. C. Game, Sept. 4, 1940, *Revudeville* 137, Lord Chamberlain's Play Correspondence, File 3656, BL.

165. He commended her as an "artist of the very first rank", and declared that it "doesn't matter at all that you can't always understand the words of her Polish songs—an enchanting gleam in the bawdy eyes, a lift of the delicious nose, and we know at once on what game her Polish soldier is engaged." Graham Greene, "The Theatre," *Spectator* 166 (June 6, 1941), 607.

166. Windmill Cuttings, vol. 42, TM; "Betty Askwith and Theodora Benson," "Theatres of Wartime London," *Sketch*, July 17, 1940.

167. Sheila Van Damm, *We Never Closed*, 94.

168. Sheila Van Damm, *No Excuses*, 25. She does not mention the strong anti-fascism that animated many other Anglo-Jews. For Van Damm's obituary, see "Mr. Vivian Van Damm," *The Times*, Dec. 15, 1960, 13.

169. "There Once Was a Windmill," 73.

170. Windmill Cuttings, vol. 42, TM; "Sleeping on the Job," *Belfast Telegraph*, Sept. 28, 1940.

171. Sheila Van Damm, *No Excuses*, 27; "There Once was a Windmill," 73.

172. Sheila Van Damm, *We Never Closed*, 96; "London under Fire," C704/78C1, BLSA. On the absence of "nerves," see Graves, *Off the Record*, 56.

173. Windmill Cuttings, vol. 42, TM; "Our Lives in Air-Raided London," *Sketch*, Oct. 2, 1940; "The Show Goes On," *Glasgow Evening News*, Sept. 25, 1940.

174. Field, "Nights Underground," 16.

175. Stephen Brooke, "War and the Nude: The Photography of Bill Brandt in the 1940s," *Journal of British Studies* 45 (Jan 2006): 118–38.

176. On the cosmopolitan cities of London's Underworld, see Audrey Smith, "Tube Shelters," in *Seven* 22 (1941): 35, reproduced in Mass Observation Reports, Aug. 1941, 853A, MOA.

177. Kirkham, "Beauty Is Duty."

178. Antonia Lant, "Prologue: Mobile Femininity," in Gledhill and Swanson, *Nationalising Femininity*, 14–32.

179. See Calder, *The Myth of the Blitz*.

180. Burns Mantle, "'Heart of a City': Grim but Heroic," *Chicago Daily Tribune*, Feb. 22, 1942, G8.

181. "London's Windmill Theatre," *Life*, no. 12 (1942): 57–60; "To-night and Every Night," *The Times*, Mar. 9, 1945, 6.

182. "Admiral's Son Marries Windmill Girl," n.p., Oct. 1, 1942, Windmill Cuttings, vol. 45, TM; Harry Miller, *Service to the Services: The Story of the Naafi* (London: Newman Neame, 1971). For reports on parties between Windmill Girls and RAF officers, see Charles Graves, *A Londoner's Life* (London,: Hutchinson, 1942), 82.

183. *Orkney Blast*, Nov. 26, 1943, Windmill Cuttings, vol. 45, TM.

184. "Legacies for All at Windmill," *Star*, April 10, 1944, Windmill Cuttings, vol. 45, TM.
185. Clayton, "All Change at the Windmill," 50.
186. On GIs in London, see Norman Longmate, *The GIs: Americans in Britain, 1942–45* (London: Hutchinson, 1975); Juliet Gardiner, *'Over Here': The GIs in Wartime Britain* (London: Collins & Brown, 1992); David Reynolds, *Rich Relations: The American Occupation of Britain 1942–1945* (London: Phoenix, 1995); Sonya Rose, "Girls and GIs: Race, Sex, and Diplomacy in Second World War Britain," *International History Review* 19, no. 1 (Feb. 1997): 59; Jill Anstey, quoted in Alvin Steinkopf, "Burlesque is a Lady," *Washington Post*, Mar. 6, 1949, L1; Vivian Van Damm, *Tonight and Every Night*, 199.
187. Roma Fairley, *Come Dancing Miss World* (London: Neame, 1966), ch. 9.
188. Vivian Van Damm, *Tonight and Every Night*, 189, 190.
189. Ibid., 199.

Epilogue

1. Peter Ackroyd, *London: The Biography* (London: Chatto & Windus, 2000), 528.
2. "Two Centuries of Soho and the Critics," *St. Anne Soho Monthly Paper* 7 (1898): 15.
3. Arthur Ransome, *Bohemia in London* (Oxford: Oxford University Press, 1984; orig. 1907), 6.
4. Robert Machray, *The Night Side of London* (Philadelphia: J. B. Lippincott, 1902), 4.
5. Claudia Baldoli, *Exporting Fascism: Italian Fascists and Britain's Italians in the 1930s* (Oxford: Berg, 2003), 25, 42.
6. On the postwar property market, see Oliver Marriott, *The Property Boom* (London: Hamilton, 1967); Simon Jenkins, *Landlords to London: The Story of a Capital and Its Growth* (London: Constable, 1975).
7. "London of the Future: The Bressey Plan, Traffic Needs for 30 Years," *The Times*, May 17 1938, 217.
8. Steen Eiler Rasmussen, *London, the Unique City*, rev. edn. (Cambridge, MA: MIT Press, 1982), 427.
9. A. H. Forshaw and Patrick Abercrombie, *County of London Plan* (London: Macmillan, 1943), quoted in Frank Mort, *Capital Affairs* (London: Yale University Press, 2010), 100.
10. Mort, *Capital Affairs*. On the postwar property boom, see Jenkins, *Landlords to London*.
11. The Westminster Plan was produced in compliance with requests from the national government. Sir Joseph Rawlinson and W. R. Davidge, *City of Westminster Plan* (London: Westminster City Council, 1946).
12. Ibid.; Mort, *Capital Affairs*.
13. *City of Westminster Plan*, 36–42.
14. Georgian Group, *Report, 1946* (London: Georgian Group, 1946), 5.
15. This was a dismissive gesture, lumping a cleaned-up Soho with two central areas notoriously devoid of residential population and cultural vitality.
16. See, for example, Robert Fabian, *Fabian of the Yard: An Intimate Record* (New York: British Book Centre, 1953).
17. *Manchester Guardian*, Jan. 28, 1948, 4.
18. Arthur Tietjen, *Soho London's Vicious Circle* (London: Allan Wingate, 1956), 129.
19. Ibid.
20. On the Soho Fair, see Mort, *Capital Affairs*, 197–201.
21. Neville Barker, "Soho Fair," *The Listener*, Mar. 17, 1955, 466.
22. Gaston Berlemont, quoted in ibid. Peter Noble, "Eating Out in Soho," in *Soho Fair Programme* (London: Soho Fair Association, 1955), 23.
23. Edward Hyams, "Pretending to Be Soho," *New Statesman and Society*, July 2, 1955, 66. See Mort, *Capital Affairs*, 199–200.
24. Mort, *Capital Affairs*, 197–201.
25. Peter Noble, "A Stomach in Soho," in *Third Annual Soho Fair Programme* (London: Soho Fair Association, 1957), 26.

26. *Manchester Guardian*, Mar. 11, 1955, 6.

27. Charlotte Plimmer and Denis Plimmer, "How Wicked Is Soho?" in *Third Annual Soho Fair Programme*, 25, Westminster Pamphlets, WA.

28. Westminster Pamphlets, WA; Noble, "Eating Out in Soho," 23; Noble, "A Stomach in Soho," 29.

29. See Mort, *Capital Affairs*, 239–40.

30. Skiffle was an English variant of blues, involving "acoustic but very rhythmic blues, somewhere between older-style Mississippi blues and modern amplified city blues." John Platt, *London's Rock Routes* (London: Fourth Estate, 1985), 9.

31. Ibid., 7–8.

32. Piri Halasz, "Great Britain: You Can Walk Across It on the Grass," *Time Magazine*, Apr. 15, 1966 (web version); Jeff Nuttall, *Bomb Culture* (New York: Delacorte Press, 1969), 38.

33. Raphael Samuel, *Theatres of Memory* (London: Verso, 1994), 87.

34. Halasz, "Great Britain."

35. Colin MacInnes, *Absolute Beginners* (Harmondsworth, UK: Penguin, 2000; orig. 1959).

36. Frank Mort, *Cultures of Consumption: Masculinities and Social Space in Late Twentieth-Century Britain* (London: Routledge, 1996), 155.

37. Shawn Levy, *Ready, Steady, Go! Swinging London and the Invention of Cool* (London: Fourth Estate, 2002).

38. Jim Godbolt, *A History of Jazz in Britain 1919–1950* (London: Quartet, 1984), 189–91; Levy, *Ready, Steady, Go!*, 89; Victor Bockris, *Keith Richards: The Biography* (New York: Da Capo Press, 2003), 30.

39. Levy, *Ready, Steady, Go!*, 106–7; George Melly, *Revolt into Style: The Pop Arts in Britain* (London: Allen Lane, 1970).

40. Bryan Burrough, quoted in Judith Summers, *Soho: A History of London's Most Colourful Neighbourhood* (London: Bloomsbury, 1989), 218; Peter Geoffrey Hall, *Great Planning Disasters* (Berkeley: University of California Press, 1982), 9; Terence Bendix, "A Promenade Plan for Piccadilly Circus," *The Times*, Aug. 5, 1966, 18.

41. "Piccadilly Circus Symbol," *The Times* [1966], Westminster Cuttings and Newspaper Clippings, D133, WA. Peter Hall also suggests that by the 1970s the property boom had declined and the government had changed policy and now desired to limit traffic into central London. Hall, *Great Planning Disasters*, 9.

42. John Young, "Conservation Area Proposed for the Whole of Soho," *The Times*, Sept. 23, 1975, 17.

43. Summers, *Soho*, 218.

44. Martin Tomkinson, *The Pornbrokers* (London: Virgin Books, 1982).

45. Bryan Burrough, "Floreat Soho," in Richard Tames, *Soho Past* (London: Historical Publications, 1994), 137.

46. See chapter 4, this volume.

47. Stefan Slater, "Pimps, Police, and Filles de Joie: Foreign Prostitution in Interwar London," *London Journal* 32, no. 1 (2007): 53–74.

48. Robert Murphy, *Smash and Grab: Gangsters in the London Underworld, 1920–60* (London: Faber and Faber, 1993), 112.

49. On flat-farming, see Peter Gueston, "The Filthy Five," *Guardian*, Aug. 30, 1997, C15; Tomkinson, *The Pornbrokers*, 22.

50. Paul Raymond, interview, BBC Radio 2, 1983, ST. 5447 BW, BLSA.

51. Obituaries of Raymond, quoted in Mort, *Capital Affairs*, 264.

52. "The Charm of Innocence," *Manchester Guardian*, Feb. 1, 1962, 9.

53. Summers, *Soho*, 215.

54. Tomkinson, *The Pornbrokers*, 91.

55. Ibid.

56. On the urban village concept, see David Bell and Mark Jayne, eds., *City of Quarters: Urban Villages in the Contemporary City* (Aldershot, UK: Ashgate, 2004).

57. See John Eade, *Placing London: From Imperial City to Global City* (Oxford: Berghahn, 2000), ch. 2.
58. Herbert J. Gans, *The Urban Villagers: Group and Class in the Life of Italian-Americans* (New York: Free Press, 1969).
59. Tony Aldous, quoted in Eade, *Placing London*, 69.
60. Ibid., 67, 68.
61. "The Man Who Saved Soho," *Soho Clarion*, 127 (Winter 2006/2007), 7–9.
62. "History Group," *Soho Clarion*, no. 20 (Jan.–Feb. 1978), 4.
63. Bryan Burrough, interview with the author, June 1997.
64. Bryan Burrough, "Soho," *Soho Clarion*, no. 1 (Dec. 1973), 1. On Cardwell, see chapter 1.
65. Thelma Seear, "Must Soho Die?" *Soho Clarion*, no. 1 (Dec. 1973), 1. With the exception of one or two listed buildings, only Greek Street, Dean Street, Frith Street and Old Compton Street, together with Soho Square, were protected.
66. Endangered buildings tended to be located in St. James, Soho, increasingly referred to as "West Soho."
67. Seear, "Must Soho Die?"
68. Burrough, "Floreat Soho," 137.
69. Hall, *Great Planning Disasters*, 9.
70. Eade, *Placing London*, 69.
71. "The 26," *Soho Clarion*, 2, no. 3 (June–July 1975), 2.
72. Tony Aldous, *The Illustrated London News Book of London's Villages* (London: Secker & Warburg, 1980), 238.
73. Bryan Burrough, quoted in ibid., 245.
74. "Soho 1973/1984. The Score," *Soho Clarion*, no. 52 (Spring 1985), 9; Burrough, "Floreat Soho."
75. "Must Soho Die?" *Soho Clarion*, no. 33 (Christmas 1980), 1–2; "Soho's Endangered Species," ibid., 6–7.
76. "Stayers, Philms of Peter Phillips," *Soho Clarion*, no. 82 (Summer 1993), 15.
77. Burrough, "Floreat Soho," 137.
78. "We're Watching," *Soho Clarion*, no. 7 (Mar.–April 1976), 8.
79. "Why Soho Is Naughty but Not Very," *Guardian*, Dec. 30, 1980, 3. "Trimmings," *Soho Clarion* 2, no. 2 (April 1975).
80. Summers, *Soho*, 224; Burrough, "Floreat Soho."
81. Summers, *Soho*, 222.
82. "Tailors Forced Out," *Soho Clarion*, no. 64 (1988).
83. Paul Raymond, BLSA; "Save Our Soho," *Evening Standard Magazine*, Jan. 1989, 10–15; "Strip Shows/Sex/Pornography," Westminster Cuttings, A13, WA.
84. Adam Edwards, "The Heiress to London's West End," *Daily Express*, June 12, 2010 (web version); Michael Horsnell, "Paul Raymond Becomes Britain's Richest Man," *The Times*, Nov. 30, 1992 (web version).
85. "Save Our Soho," *Independent*, Mar. 9, 2005, 9; " 'We'll Fight Evictions,' Say Soho's Sex-Strike Prostitutes," *Evening Standard*, Mar. 13, 2000 (web version).
86. Pamela Buxton, "Go West One: Scene Makers: Will Westminster Council Be the Death of Soho?" *Time Out*, July 4, 2001, 24 (web version).
87. Mort, *Cultures of Consumption*, 165.
88. Lynn Wallis and Lynne Eaton, "Gay Businesses Band Together to Promote Soho Abroad," *Independent*, July 20, 1994 (web version). According to Mort, this commercial development was less a continuation of interwar gay consumption in Soho than a new democratization of the gay market and its relocation from west London. Mort, *Cultures of Consumption*, 164–70.
89. Bryan Burrough, quoted in "Swinging Soho—London's Sleaziest Streets in Fashion Again," *Deutsche Presse Agentur*, Dec. 4, 1996 (web version).
90. *Soho Clarion*, no. 100 (Summer 1999).
91. Jonathan Downey, quoted in Buxton, "Go West One."

92. John Montgomery, *The New Wealth of Cities: City Dynamics and the Fifth Wave*, 2nd edn. (Aldershot, UK: Ashgate, 2008), 79.
93. Ibid., 76–7.
94. Buxton, "Go West One."
95. Montgomery, *The New Wealth of Cities*, 70.
96. *Manchester Guardian*, Jan. 28, 1948, 4.
97. Jerry White, email to the author, Aug. 1, 2010.

Selected Bibliography

Archives and Manuscript Collections

Bodleian Library, University of Oxford
British Library, London
Clark Library, University of California, Los Angeles
Fales Library, New York University
Harry Ransom Center, Austin
Imperial War Museum, London
Jewish Museum, London
Library of the Performing Arts, New York Public Library, New York
London Metropolitan Archives, London
London School of Economics Archive, London
Museum of London
National Archives, Public Record Office, London
Parkin Gallery
Selfridge's Archive, London
Theatre Museum, London
Westminster Archives, London
Women's Library, London
San Francisco Performing Arts Library and Museum, San Francisco

Microfilm Collections of Archives

Charles Booth, *Life and Labour of the People of London: The Charles Booth Collection, 1885–1905 from the British Library of Political and Economic Science, London*. Brighton, UK: Harvester Press Microform Publications, 1988.

Mass Observation, *Papers from the Mass Observation Archive at the University of Sussex*. Marlborough, UK: Adam Matthew, 2000.

E. Sylvia Pankhurst, *Women, Suffrage, and Politics: The Papers of Sylvia Pankhurst, 1882–1960, from the Internationaal Instituut Voor Sociale Geschiedenis, Amsterdam*. (Based on the original inventory prepared by Wilhelmina H. Schreuder and Margreet Schrevel.) Reading, UK: Adam Matthew, 1991.

Dorothy Sheridan, *The Tom Harrisson Mass Observation Archive*. Brighton, UK: Harvester Press Microform Publications, 1983.

Unpublished Papers and Theses

Abra, Allison Jean. "On with the Dance: Nation, Culture and Popular Culture, and Popular Dancing in Britain, 1918–1945." Ph.D. diss., University of Michigan, 2009.
de la Haye, Amy. "The Role of Design within the Commercialisation of Women's Ready to Wear Clothing in Britain during the Inter-War Years, with Specific Reference to the Cheapest Levels of Products." M.A. thesis, Royal College of Art, London, 1986.
Dipaola, Pietro. "Italian Anarchists in London 1870–1914." Ph.D. diss., London, 2004.
Edwards, Bronwen. "Making the West End Modern: Space, Architecture, and Shopping in 1930s London." Ph.D. diss., University of the Arts, London, 2004.
Egan, Shannan E. "The Imperishable Pose: Delsartean Performance of the Feminine Ideal." M.A. diss., University of North Carolina, 1998.
Ferry, Susan J. "Bodily Knowledge: Female Body Culture and Subjectivity in Manchester, 1870–1900." Ph.D. diss., Johns Hopkins University, 2003.
Wright, Richard. "Italian Fascism and the British-Italian Community, 1928–1943: Experience and Memory." Ph.D. diss., University of Manchester, 2001.

Magazines, Newspapers and Serials

The Academy
British Italian Bulletin
The Builder
Bystander
The Caterer and Hotel-Keeper
Chicago Defender
Daily Chronicle
Daily Express
Daily Herald
Daily Mirror
Daily News
Daily Telegraph
Dance Index
Dance Magazine
Dancing Times
Draper's Record
Eve
Evening News
Evening Standard
Financial Times
Il Comento
The Independent
Jewish Chronicle
Jewish Graphic
Journal of the Royal Statistical Society
Lilliput
The Listener
L'Italia Nostra
London Off Duty
Los Angeles Times
Lyons Mail
Manchester Guardian (Guardian from 1959)
Melody Maker
Moonshine
Music-Hall and Theatre Review
The New Amsterdam News

New Statesman
New Times and Ethiopia Gazette
New York Times
News Chronicle
News of the World
Night and Day
Observer
Pall Mall Gazette
Penny Illustrated News
People
Picture Post
Punch
Queen
Rational Dress Gazette
The Referee
The Revue
Reynolds News
The Sketch
Soho Clarion
Soho Gazette
Spectator
St. Anne Soho Monthly Paper
Stage
Strand Magazine
Sunday Express
Sunday Times
Tatler
The Times
Truth
Vigilance Record
Weekly Dispatch
Westminster Chronicle
What's On
Wine and Food
Women's Penny Paper

Government Reports

Census of England and Wales, 1901. London: HMSO, 1902.
"Minutes of Proceedings." In *City of Westminster.* Westminster Archives, London, 1910.
"Minutes of Proceedings." In *City of Westminster.* Westminster Archives, London, 1926.
Report of the Police of the Metropolis for the Year 1935. Parliamentary Papers, London, 1935/36.
Report of the Royal Commission on Alien Immigration, with Minutes of Evidence and Appendix, Volume 1: The Report. Parliamentary Papers, London, 1903.
Report of the Royal Commission upon the Duties of the Metropolitan Police. Parliamentary Papers, London, 1908.

Books and Articles

Abot, Henry Aimes. *Eating My Way through Italy.* San Francisco: Golden State, 1936.
Ackroyd, Peter. *London: The Biography.* London: Chatto & Windus, 2000.
Agathocleous, Tanya. "Cosmopolitanism and Literary Form." *Literary Compass* 7, no. 6 (2010): 452–66.
Aldous, Tony. *The Illustrated London News' Book of London's Villages.* London: Secker & Warburg, 1980.
Alexander, David. *Retailing in England during the Industrial Revolution.* London: Athlone, 1970.
Alexander, Sally. "Becoming a Woman in London in the 1920s and 1930s." In David Feldman and Gareth Stedman Jones, eds., *Metropolis London: History and Representations since 1800,* 245–71. New York and London: Routledge, 1989.
———. *Becoming a Woman and Other Essays in 19th and 20th Century Feminist History.* London: Virago Press, 1994.
Allan, Maud. *My Life and Dancing.* London: Everett, 1908.
Allen, Rick. *The Moving Pageant: A Literary Sourcebook on London Street-Life, 1700–1914.* London: Routledge, 1998.
Allfrey, Anthony. *Edward VII and His Jewish Court.* London: Weidenfeld & Nicolson, 1991.
Altick, Richard D. *The Shows of London.* Cambridge, MA and London: Belknap Press of Harvard University Press, 1978.
Anderson, Amanda. *The Powers of Distance: Cosmopolitanism and the Cultivation of Detachment.* Princeton: Princeton University Press, 2001.
Annan, Noel Gilroy. *Our Age: Portrait of a Generation.* London: Weidenfeld & Nicolson, 1990.
Antler, Joyce. *Talking Back: Images of Jewish Women in American Popular Culture.* Hanover, NH and London: Brandeis University Press, 1998.
Argyll, Margaret, Duchess of. *Forget Not: The Autobiography of Margaret, Duchess of Argyll.* London: W. H. Allen, 1975.
Aris, Stephen. *The Jews in Business.* London: Cape, 1971.
Ashbee, C. R. "Introduction." In C. R. Ashbee, ed., *The Survey of London.* New York: AMS Press, 1971.
Ashton, Rosemary. *Little Germany: Exile and Asylum in Victorian England.* Oxford and New York: Oxford University Press, 1986.
Assael, Brenda. "Art or Indecency? Tableaux Vivants on the London Stage and the Failure of Late Victorian Moral Reform." *Journal of British Studies* 45, no. 4 (2006): 744–58.
Aston, Elaine. *Sarah Bernhardt: A French Actress on the English Stage.* Oxford: Berg, 1989.
Atkin, Nicholas. *The Forgotten French: Exiles in the British Isles, 1940–44.* Manchester: Manchester University Press, 2003.
Ayer, A. J. *Part of My Life.* London: Collins, 1977.
Azikiwe, Nnamdi. *My Odyssey: An Autobiography.* New York: Praeger, 1970.
Baade, Christina. "'The Dancing Front': Dance Music, Dancing, and the BBC in World War II." *Popular Music* 25, no. 3 (2006): 347–68.
Bailey, Peter. "Adventures in Space: Victorian Railway Erotics, or Taking Alienation for a Ride." *Journal of Victorian Culture* 9, no. 1 (2004): 1–21.
———. *Popular Culture and Performance in the Victorian City.* Cambridge, UK and New York: Cambridge University Press, 1998.

Baker, Michael. *Our Three Selves: The Life of Radclyffe Hall*. New York: Morrow, 1985.

Baldoli, Claudia. *Exporting Fascism: Italian Fascists and Britain's Italians in the 1930s*. Oxford: Berg, 2003.

——— . "The Remaking of the Italian Community in London: L'Italia Nostra and the Creation of a Little Fascist Italy during the 1930s." *London Journal* 26, no. 2 (2001): 23–34.

Balfour, Patrick. *Society Racket: A Critical Survey of Modern Social Life*. London: John Long, 1933.

Barber, Peter, and Peter Jacomelli. *Continental Taste: Ticinese Emigrants and Their Café-Restaurants in Britain, 1847–1987*. Occasional Paper, Camden History Society. London: Camden History Society, 1997.

Barker, Clive, and Maggie B. Gale. *British Theatre between the Wars, 1918–1939*. Cambridge, UK: Cambridge University Press, 2000.

Barker, Eric. *Steady Barker! The Autobiography of Eric Barker*. London: Secker & Warburg, 1956.

Barker, T. C., and Michael Robbins. *A History of London Transport: Passenger Travel and the Development of the Metropolis*. 2 vols. London: Allen & Unwin for the London Transport Executive, 1975–6.

Barrow, Andrew. *Gossip: A History of High Society from 1920 to 1970*. London: Pan, 1978.

Barry, Doris. "A Song and Dance Girl." In Mavis Nicholson, ed., *What Did You Do in the War, Mummy? Women in World War II*, 194–9. London: Pimlico, 1995.

Barstow, Susan Torrey. "'Hedda Is All of Us': Late Victorian Women at the Matinee." *Victorian Studies* 43, no. 3 (2001): 387–411.

Bartlett, Neil. *Who Was That Man? A Present for Mr. Oscar Wilde*. London: Serpent's Tail, 1988.

Baxendale, John, and Christopher Pawlin. *Narrating the Thirties: A Decade in the Making, 1930 to the Present*. Houndmills, UK: Macmillan, 1996.

Beckson, Karl E. *Arthur Symons: A Life*. Oxford: Clarendon Press, 1987.

Begbie, Harold. *The Glass of Fashion: Some Social Reflections*. New York: Putnam's, 1921.

Bender, Daniel E. *Sweated Work, Weak Bodies: Anti-Sweatshop Campaigns and Languages of Labor*. New Brunswick, NJ: Rutgers University Press, 2004.

Benedetta, Mary. *The Street Markets of London*, photographs by László Moholy-Nagy. New York: B. Blom, 1972.

Benjamin, Thelma Hilda. *A Shopping Guide to London*. New York: R. M. McBride, 1930.

Bennett, Arnold. *A Man from the North*. New York: George H. Doran, 1911.

——— . *The Pretty Lady: A Novel*. London: Cassell, 1918.

Bennett, Daphne. *Margot: A Life of the Countess of Oxford and Asquith*. London: Gollancz, 1984.

Bennett, Tony, Lawrence Grossberg, Meaghan Morris, and Raymond Williams. *New Keywords: A Revised Vocabulary of Culture and Society*. Malden, MA: Blackwell, 2005.

Benney, Mark (pseud.). *Low Company: Describing the Evolution of a Burglar*. London: Peter Davies, 1936.

Benson, John. *The Penny Capitalists: A Study of Nineteenth-Century Working-Class Entrepreneurs*. New Brunswick, NJ: Rutgers University Press, 1983.

Bentine, Michael. *The Long Banana Skin*. London: Granada, 1975.

Berman, Jessica Schiff. *Modernist Fiction, Cosmopolitanism, and the Politics of Community*. Cambridge, UK and New York: Cambridge University Press, 2001.

Bernabei, Alfio. *Esuli ed emigrati italiani nel Regno Unito, 1920–1940*. Testimonianze fra cronaca e storia: guerre fasciste e seconda guerra mondiale. Milan: Mursia, 1997.

——— . "The London Plot to Kill Mussolini." *History Today* 49, no. 4 (1999): 2.

Besant, Walter, and G. E. Mitton. *London, North of the Thames*. The Survey of London. London: A. & C. Black, 1911.

Billing, Noel Pemberton. *Verbatim Report of the Trial of N. P. Billing, on a Charge of Criminal Libel . . . At the Central Criminal Court, Old Bailey*. London: Vigilante, 1918.

Bingham, Adrian. *Gender, Modernity, and the Popular Press in Inter-war Britain*. Oxford: Clarendon Press, 2004.

——— . "Review Essay: 'An Era of Domesticity'? Histories of Women and Gender in Interwar Britain." *Cultural and Social History* 1, no. 2 (2004): 225–33.

Bird, Peter J. *The First Food Empire: A History of J. Lyons & Co*. Chichester, UK: Phillimore, 2000.

Biron, Sir Henry Chartres. *Without Prejudice: Impressions of Life and Law*. London: Faber and Faber, 1936.

Black, Gerry. *Living Up West: Jewish Life in London's West End*. London: London Museum of Jewish Life, 1994.

Blacker, Harry. *Just Like It Was: Memoirs of the Mittel East*. London: Vallentine Mitchell, 1974.

Blair, Sarah. "Local Modernity, Global Modernism: Bloomsbury and the Places of Literacy." *English Literary History* 71, no. 3 (2004): 813–38.

Bland, Lucy. *Banishing the Beast: English Feminism and Sexual Morality, 1885–1914*. London: Penguin, 1995.

——. "Trial by Sexology? Maud Allan, Salome, and the Cult of the Clitoris Case." In Lucy Bland and Laura L. Doan, eds., *Sexology in Culture: Labelling Bodies and Desires*, 183–97. Chicago: University of Chicago Press, 1998.

Blythe, Ronald. *The Age of Illusion: England in the Twenties and Thirties, 1919–1940*. London: Penguin, 1964.

Bockris, Victor. *Keith Richards: The Biography*. New York: Da Capo Press, 2003.

Bolton, Arthur T. "The Possibilities of an Eighteenth Century Revival." *Journal of the Royal Institute of British Architects* 5 (1898): 245–7.

Bon Viveur (pseud.). *The Daily Telegraph Book of Bon Viveur in London*. London: Daily Telegraph, 1953.

Booth, Charles. *Life and Labour of the People of London*, vol. 2, 3rd series, Religious Influences. London: Macmillan, 1902.

Booth, Michael R., and Joel H. Kaplan. *The Edwardian Theatre: Essays on Performance and the Stage*. Cambridge, UK: Cambridge University Press, 1996.

Bourdieu, Pierre. *Distinction: A Social Critique of the Judgement of Taste*. Cambridge, MA: Harvard University Press, 2000. (Originally published 1984.)

Bowlby, Rachel. *Shopping with Freud*. London and New York: Routledge, 1993.

Bracco, Rosa Maria. *Merchants of Hope: British Middlebrow Writers and the First World War, 1919–39*. Providence, RI: Berg, 1993.

Braybon, Gail, and Penny Summerfield. *Out of the Cage: Women's Experiences in Two World Wars*. London and New York: Pandora Press, 1987.

Breazeale, Kenon. "In Spite of Women: 'Esquire' Magazine and the Construction of the Male Consumer." *Signs* 20, no. 1 (1994): 1–22.

Breckenridge, Carol A., Sheldon I. Pollock, and Homi K. Bhabha. *Cosmopolitanism*. Durham, NC: Duke University Press, 2002.

Breward, Christopher. "Fashion's Front and Back: 'Rag Trade' Cultures and Cultures of Consumption in Post-war London c.1945–1970." *London Journal* 31, no. 1 (2006): 15–40.

Bristow, Edward J. *Vice and Vigilance: Purity Movements in Britain since 1700*. Dublin: Gill and Macmillan; Totowa, NJ: Rowman & Littlefield, 1977.

Brooke, Stephen. "War and the Nude: The Photography of Bill Brandt in the 1940s." *Journal of British Studies* 45 (2006): 118–38.

Brooker, Peter. *Bohemia in London: The Social Scene of Early Modernism*. Houndmills, UK: Palgrave Macmillan, 2004.

Bryson, Norman. "Cultural Studies and Dance History." In Jane C. Desmond, ed., *Meaning in Motion: New Cultural Studies of Dance*. Durham, NC: Duke University Press, 1997.

Buckley, Cheryl, and Hilary Fawcett. *Fashioning the Feminine: Representation and Women's Fashion from the Fin de Siècle to the Present*. London: I. B. Tauris, 2002.

Bullock, Ian, and Richard Pankhurst, eds. *Sylvia Pankhurst: From Artist to Anti-Fascist*. Basingstoke, UK: Macmillan, 1992.

Bulmer, Martin. *Essays on the History of British Sociological Research*. Cambridge, UK: Cambridge University Press, 1985.

Burke, Thomas. *Dinner Is Served*. London: Routledge, 1937.

——. *English Night-Life: From Norman Curfew to Present Black-Out*. London: Batsford, 1943.

——. *The London Spy: A Book of Town Travels*. London: Thornton Butterworth, 1922.

——. *Nights in London*. New York: H. Holt, 1918.

—— . *Nights in Town*. London: Allen & Unwin, 1919.

—— . *Nights in Town: A London Autobiography*. London: Allen & Unwin, 1915.

—— . *Out and About: A Note-Book of London in War-Time*. London: Allen & Unwin, 1919.

—— . *The Streets of London through the Centuries*. 4th edn. London: Batsford, 1949.

Burnett, John. *England Eats Out: A Social History of Eating out in England from 1830 to the Present*. Harlow, UK: Pearson; New York: Longman, 2004.

Burris, John P. *Exhibiting Religion: Colonialism and Spectacle at International Expositions, 1851–1893*. Charlottesville: University of Virginia Press, 2001.

Burton, Antoinette M. *At the Heart of the Empire: Indians and the Colonial Encounter in Late-Victorian Britain*. Berkeley: University of California Press, 1998.

—— . *Burdens of History: British Feminists, Indian Women, and Imperial Culture, 1865–1915*. Chapel Hill: University of North Carolina Press, 1994.

Bush, Barbara. *Imperialism, Race, and Resistance: Africa and Britain, 1919–1945*. London and New York: Routledge, 1999.

Butler, David, and Garth Butler. *Twentieth Century British Political Facts, 1900–2000*. New York: St. Martin's Press, 2000.

Buzard, James. "Mass-Observation, Modernism, and Auto-Ethnography." *Modernism/Modernity* 4, no. 3 (1997): 93–122.

Caffin, Caroline, and Charles Henry Caffin. *Dancing and Dancers of Today: The Modern Revival of Dancing as an Art*. New York: Da Capo Press, 1978.

Cain, P. J., and A. G. Hopkins. *British Imperialism: Crisis and Deconstruction, 1914–1990*. London and New York: Longman, 1993.

—— . *British Imperialism: Innovation and Expansion, 1688–1914*. London and New York: Longman, 1993.

Calder, Angus. *The Myth of the Blitz*. London: Pimlico, 1992.

—— . *The People's War: Britain 1939–45*. London: Cape, 1969.

Camplin, Jamie. *The Rise of the Plutocrats: Wealth and Power in Edwardian England*. London: Constable, 1978.

Cannadine, David. "The British Monarchy, c.1820–1877." In E. J. Hobsbawm and T. O. Ranger, eds., *The Invention of Tradition*, 101–64. Cambridge, UK and New York: Cambridge University Press, 1983.

—— . *Ornamentalism: How the British Saw Their Empire*. London: Allen Lane, 2001.

Capatti, Alberto, Massimo Montanari, and Aine O'Healy. *Italian Cuisine: A Cultural History*. New York: Columbia University Press, 2003.

Cardiff, David. "Mass Middlebrow Laughter: The Origins of BBC Comedy." *Media, Culture, and Society* 10 (1988): 41–60.

Cardwell, John Henry. *Men and Women of Soho, Famous and Infamous: Actors, Authors, Dramatists, Entertainers and Engravers*. London: Truslove & Hanson, 1903.

—— . *The Story of a Charity School: Two Centuries of Popular Education in Soho, 1699–1899*. London and New York: Truslove, Hanson, & Comba, 1899.

Cardwell, John Henry, ed. *Twenty Years in Soho: A Review of the Work of the Church in the Parish of St. Anne, Soho from 1891 to 1911*. London: Truslove & Hanson, 1911.

—— . *Two Centuries of Soho: Its Institutions, Firms, and Amusements*. London: Truslove & Hanson, 1898. At http://www.archive.org/details/twocenturiesofso00cardiala (accessed May 2011).

Carlish, Richard, with Alan Bestic. *King of Clubs: Richard Carlish as Told to Alan Bestic*. London: Elek Books, 1962.

Carter, Alexandra. "Over the Footlights and under the Moon: Images of Dancers in the Ballet at the Alhambra and Empire Palaces of Varieties, 1884–1915." *Dance Research Journal* 28, no. 1 (1996): 7–18.

Cartland, Barbara. *We Danced All Night*. London: Robson, 1994.

Certeau, Michel de. *The Practice of Everyday Life*. Berkeley: University of California Press, 1984.

Chant, Laura Ormiston. *Why We Attacked the Empire*. London: Horace Marshall & Son, 1895.

—— . "Women and the Streets." In James Marchant, ed., *Public Morals*, 128–34. London: Morgan & Scott, 1902.

Chauncey, George. *Gay New York: Gender, Urban Culture, and the Makings of the Gay Male World, 1890–1940*. New York: Basic Books, 1994.

Chauncey, George, Martin B. Duberman, and Martha Vicinus. *Hidden from History: Reclaiming the Gay and Lesbian Past*. New York: New American Library, 1989.

Cheah, Pheng, and Bruce Robbins, eds. *Cosmopolitics: Thinking and Feeling beyond the Nation*. Minneapolis: University of Minnesota Press, 1998.

Cherniavsky, Felix Benjamin. *The Salome Dancer: The Life and Times of Maud Allan*. Toronto: McClelland & Stewart, 1991.

Chevalier, Albert. *Albert Chevalier: A Record by Himself. Biographical and Other Chapters by Brian Daly*. London: John Macqueen, 1895.

Cheyette, Bryan. "Hilaire Belloc and the Marconi Scandal." *Immigrants and Minorities* 8, no. 1 (1989): 131–42.

Chilton, John. *Louis: The Louis Armstrong Story, 1900–1971*. Cambridge, MA: Da Capo Press, 1988.

Churchill, Winston. *My Early Life: A Roving Commission*. New York: Scribner's, 1930.

Clark, Anna. *Desire: A History of European Sexuality*. New York and London: Routledge, 2008.

Clifford, Colin. *The Asquiths*. London: John Murray, 2002.

Clifford, James. "Mixed Feelings." In Pheng Cheah and Bruce Robbins, eds., *Cosmopolitics: Thinking and Feeling beyond the Nation*, 362–70. Minneapolis: University of Minnesota Press, 1998.

Cline, Sally. *Radclyffe Hall: A Woman Called John*. London: J. Murray, 1997.

Clippinger, D. A. *The Elements of Voice Culture, a System of Exercises Designed for the Use of Choirs, Choruses, Rudimental Classes*. Cincinnati and New York: Fillmore Music House, 1905.

Clunn, H. P. *London Rebuilt, 1897–1927: An Attempt to Depict the Principal Changes Which Have Taken Place, with Some Suggestions for the Further Improvement of the Metropolis*. London: John Murray, 1927.

Cockin, Katharine. *Women and Theatre in the Age of Suffrage: The Pioneer Players, 1911–1925*. Houndmills, UK: Palgrave, 2001.

Cohen, Deborah. *Household Gods: The British and Their Possessions*. New Haven: Yale University Press, 2006.

Cohen, Ed. *Talk on the Wilde Side: Towards a Genealogy of a Discourse on Male Sexualities*. New York: Routledge, 1993.

Cohen-Portheim, Paul. *The Spirit of London*. London: Batsford, 1950. (Originally published 1935.)

Cole, Sophie. *The Lure of Old London*. London: Mills & Boon, 1921.

Colin, Sid. *And the Bands Played On*. London: Elm Tree Books, 1977.

Collier, John, and Lain Lang. *Just the Other Day: An Informal History of Great Britain Since the War*. London: Hamish Hamilton, 1932.

Collier, Simon, Artemis Cooper, Maria Susana Azzi, and Richard Martin. *Tango! The Dance, the Song, the Story*. London: Thames & Hudson, 1995.

Colpi, Terri. "The Impact of the Second World War on the British Italian Community." In David Cesarani, ed., *The Internment of Aliens in Twentieth Century Britain*, 172–87. London: F. Cass, 1993.

——. *The Italian Factor: The Italian Community in Great Britain*. Edinburgh: Mainstream, 1991.

——. *Italians Forward: A Visual History of the Italian Community in Great Britain*. Edinburgh: Mainstream, 1991.

Colson, Marvin. *Places of Performance: The Semiotics of Theatre Architecture*. Ithaca, NY: Cornell University Press, 1989.

Conor, Liz. *The Spectacular Modern Woman: Feminine Visibility in the 1920s*. Bloomington: Indiana University Press, 2004.

Conrad, Joseph. *The Secret Agent*. New York: Bantam, 1984. (Originally published 1907.)

Cook, Emily Constance. *Highways and Byways in London ... With Illustrations by Hugh Thomson and F. L. Griggs*. London: Macmillan, 1902.

Cook, Matt. *London and the Culture of Homosexuality, 1885–1914*. Cambridge, UK and New York: Cambridge University Press, 2003.

Cooper, Diana. *Autobiography* [*of*] *Diana Cooper*. Salisbury, UK: Michael Russell, 1979.

——. *The Rainbow Comes and Goes*. London: Hart-Davis, 1958.

Coote, William Alexander. *A Romance of Philanthropy*. London: National Vigilance Association, 1916.

Coppel, Stephen. *Claude Flight and His Followers: The Colour Linocut Movement between the Wars*. Canberra: Australian National Gallery, 1992.

——. *Linocuts of the Machine Age: Claude Flight and the Grosvenor School*. Aldershot, UK: Scholar Press, 1995.

Cork, Richard. *Art beyond the Gallery in Early 20th Century England*. New Haven: Yale University Press, 1985.

Cowley, John. " 'Cultural Fusions': Aspects of British West Indian Music in the U.S. and Britain, 1918–51." *Popular Music* 5 (1985): 81–96.

Craig, Edward. *Gordon Craig: The Story of His Life*. New York: Knopf, 1968.

Crisp, Quentin. *The Naked Civil Servant*. London: Fontana, 1977.

Croft, Andy. *A Weapon in the Struggle: The Cultural History of the Communist Party in Britain*. London: Pluto, 1998.

Croft-Cooke, Rupert. *Feasting with Panthers: A New Consideration of Some Late Victorian Writers*. London: W. H. Allen, 1967.

——. *The Numbers Came*. London: Putnam, 1962.

Daley, Harry. *This Small Cloud: A Personal Memoir*. London: Weidenfeld & Nicolson, 1986.

Daly, Ann. *Done into Dance: Isadora Duncan in America*. Bloomington: Indiana University Press, 1995.

David, Elizabeth. *A Book of Mediterranean Food*. London: John Lehmann, 1950.

David, Hugh. *The Fitzrovians: A Portrait of Bohemian Society, 1900–1955*. London: Michael Joseph, 1988.

Davis, Tracy. *Actresses as Working Women: Their Social Identity in Victorian Culture*. London: Routledge, 1991.

Deghy, Guy, and Keith Waterhouse. *Café Royal: Ninety Years of Bohemia*. London: Hutchinson, 1955.

De Grazia, Victoria. *The Culture of Consent: Mass Organization of Leisure in Fascist Italy*. Cambridge, UK: Cambridge University Press, 1981.

De Groot, Gerard J. *Blighty: British Society in the Era of the Great War*. London: Longman, 1996.

De Jongh, Nicholas. *Politics, Prudery and Perversions: The Censoring of the English Stage, 1901–1968*. London: Methuen, 2000.

de la Haye, Amy. "The Dissemination of Design from Haute Couture to Fashionably Ready-to-Wear during the 1920s." *Textile History* 24, no. 1 (1993): 39–48.

Denning, Michael. *The Cultural Front: The Laboring of American Culture in the Twentieth-Century*. London and New York: Verso, 1996.

Desmond, Jane. "Embodying Difference: Issues in Dance and Cultural Difference." *Cultural Critique* (Winter 1994): 33–63.

——. *Meaning in Motion: New Cultural Studies of Dance*. Durham, NC: Duke University Press, 1997.

Dilke, Charles Wentworth. *Problems of Greater Britain*. 4th rev. edn. London and New York: Macmillan, 1890.

Dillon, Steve. "Victorian Interiors." *Modern Language Quarterly* 62, no. 2 (2001): 83–115.

Diner-Out. *London Restaurants*. London: Geoffrey Bles, 1924.

Doan, Laura L. *Fashioning Sapphism: The Origins of a Modern English Lesbian Culture*. New York: Columbia University Press, 2001.

Donaldson, Frances Lonsdale. *Child of the Twenties*. London: Hart-Davis, 1959.

Donohue, Joseph W. "The Empire Theatre of Varieties Licensing Controversy of 1894." *Nineteenth Century Theatre* 15, no. 1 (1987): 50–60.

——. *Fantasies of Empire: The Empire Theatre of Varieties and the Licensing Controversy of 1894*. Iowa City: University of Iowa Press, 2005.

Douglas, Robin. *Well, Let's Eat*. London: Cassell, 1933.

Downes, Mollie Panter. *London War Notes, 1939–1945*, ed. William Shawn. London: Longman, 1972.

Driver, Felix, and Gilbert Davis. "Heart of Empire? Landscape, Space, and Performance in Imperial London." *Environment and Planning D: Society and Space* 16, (1998): 11–28.

——. *Imperial Cities: Landscape, Display and Identity*. Studies in Imperialism. Manchester and New York: Manchester University Press, 1999.

Durbach, Nadja. *Bodily Matters: The Anti-Vaccination Movement in England, 1853–1907*. Durham, NC: Duke University Press, 2005.

——. *Spectacle of Deformity: Freak Shows and Modern British Culture*. Berkeley: University of California Press, 2009.

Dyhouse, Carol. *Glamour: Women, History, Feminism*. London: Zed Books, 2010.

Dyos, H. J. *Exploring the Urban Past: Essays in Urban History by H. J. Dyos*, ed. David Cannadine and David A. Reeder. Cambridge, UK and New York: Cambridge University Press, 1982.

Eade, John. *Placing London: From Imperial City to Global City*. Oxford: Berghahn, 2000.

Egbert, Donald Drew. *Social Radicalism and the Arts, Western Europe: A Cultural History from the French Revolution to 1968*. New York: Knopf, 1970.

Eley, Geoff. "Finding the People's War: Film, British Collective Memory, and World War II." *American Historical Review* 106, no. 3 (2001): 818–38.

Emsley, Clive. "The Story of a Rotten Apple or a Diseased Orchard?" In Amy Gilman Srebnick and René Levy, eds., *Crime and Culture: An Historical Perspective*, 85–104. Aldershot, UK: Ashgate, 2005.

Endelman, Todd M. *The Jews of Britain, 1656 to 2000*. Berkeley: University of California Press, 2002.

——. *The Jews of Georgian England, 1714–1830: Tradition and Change in a Liberal Society*. Ann Arbor: University of Michigan Press, 1999.

Erenberg, Lewis A. "From New York to Middletown: Repeal and the Legitimization of Nightlife in the Great Depression." *American Quarterly* 38, no. 5 (1986): 761–78.

——. *Steppin' Out: New York Nightlife and the Transformation of American Culture, 1890–1930*. Chicago: University of Chicago Press, 1984.

——. *Swingin' the Dream: Big Band Jazz and the Rebirth of American Culture*. Chicago: University of Chicago Press, 1998.

Esty, Joshua. *A Shrinking Island: Modernism and National Culture in England*. Princeton: Princeton University Press, 2004.

Fabian, Robert. *Fabian of the Yard: An Intimate Record by Ex-Superintendent Robert Fabian*. London: Naldrett Press, 1950.

Fabian, Robert. *London after Dark*. New York: British Book Centre, 1954.

Fairley, Roma. *Come Dancing, Miss World*. London: Neame, 1966.

Farfan, Penny. "From *Hedda Gabler* to *Votes for Women*: Elizabeth Robin's Early Feminist Critique of Ibsen." *Theatre Journal* 48, no. 1 (1996): 59–78.

Farson, Daniel. *Soho in the Fifties*. London: Michael Joseph, 1987.

Faulk, Barry. *Music Hall and Modernity: The Late-Victorian Discovery of Popular Culture*. Athens, OH: Ohio University Press, 2004.

Fawkes, Richard. *Fighting for a Laugh: Entertaining the British and American Armed Forces, 1939–1946*. London: Macdonald and Jane's, 1978.

Feldman, David, and Gareth Stedman Jones. *Metropolis London: Histories and Representations since 1800*. History Workshop Series. London and New York: Routledge, 1989.

Ferrari, Lilie. *Fortunata*. London: Michael Joseph, 1993.

Fido, Martin, and Keith Skinner. *The Official Encyclopedia of Scotland Yard*. London: Virgin Books, 1999.

Field, Geoff. "Nights Underground in Darkest London: The Blitz, 1940–1941." *International Labor and Working-Class History*, no. 62 (2002): 11–49.

Fielding, Daphne. *The Duchess of Jermyn Street: The Life and Good Times of Rosa Lewis of the Cavendish Hotel*. London: Eyre & Spottiswoode, 1964.

——— . *Mercury Presides*. London: Eyre & Spottiswoode, 1954.

Finn, Margot C. *After Chartism: Class and Nation in English Radical Politics, 1848–1874*. Past and Present Publications. Cambridge, UK and New York: Cambridge University Press, 1993.

Fischer, Gayle V. *Pantaloons and Power: Nineteenth-Century Dress Reform in the United States*. Kent, OH: Kent State University Press, 2001.

Flitch, J. E. Crawford. *Modern Dancing and Dancers*. London: Grant Richards, 1912.

Forshaw, A. H., and Patrick Abercrombie. *County of London Plan*. London: Macmillan, 1943.

Forshaw, Alec, and Theo Bergstrom. *Markets of London*. Rev. edn. Harmondsworth, UK: Penguin, 1986.

Foster, Susan Leigh. *Reading Dancing: Bodies and Subjects in Contemporary American Dance*. Berkeley: University of California Press, 1986.

Foucault, Michel. "Practices of Spaces." In Marshall Blonsky, ed., *On Signs*, 122–45. Oxford: Basil Blackwell, 1985.

Fraser, W. Hamish. *The Coming of the Mass Market, 1850–1914*. London: Macmillan, 1981.

Friedman, Andrea. *Prurient Interests: Gender, Democracy, and Obscenity in New York City, 1909–1945*. New York: Columbia University Press, 2000.

Gabaccia, Donna. "Global Geography of 'Little Italy': Italian Neighborhoods in Comparative Perspective." *Modern Italy* 2, no. 1 (2006): 9–24.

——— . *Italy's Many Diasporas*. Seattle: University of Washington Press, 2000.

——— . *We Are What We Eat: Ethnic Food and the Making of Americans*. Cambridge, MA: Harvard University Press, 1998.

Gabaccia, Donna, and Franca Iacovetta. *Women, Gender, and Transnational Lives: Italian Workers of the World*. Toronto: University of Toronto Press, 2002.

Gabler, Neal. *An Empire of Their Own: How the Jews Invented Hollywood*. New York: Crown, 1988.

Gale, Maggie B. *West End Women: Women and the London Stage, 1918–1962*. London and New York: Routledge, 1996.

Galsworthy, John. *The Forsyte Saga*. New York: Dover Publications, 2002. (Originally published 1920.)

Garafola, Lynn. *Diaghilev's Ballets Russes*. Repr. edn. New York: Oxford University Press, 1989.

Gardiner, Juliet. *The Thirties: An Intimate History*. London: HarperPress, 2010

Garelick, Rhonda K. *Rising Star: Dandyism, Gender, and Performance in the Fin de Siècle*. Princeton: Princeton University Press, 1998.

Georgian Group. *Report, 1946*. London: Georgian Group, 1946.

Gershon, Ruth. "A Life in Clothes." *Granta*, no. 65 (1999): 79–102.

Gikandi, Simon. "Pan-Africanism and Cosmopolitanism: The Case of Jomo Kenyatta." *English Studies in Africa* 43, no. 1 (2000): 3–27.

Gilbert, Pamela K. *Mapping the Victorian Social Body*. Studies in the Long Nineteenth Century. Albany: State University of New York Press, 2004.

Giles, Judy. *Women, Identity, and Private Life in Britain, 1900–50*. Women's Studies at York. Houndmills, UK: Macmillan, 1995.

Gillman, Peter, and Leni Gillman. *"Collar the Lot!" How Britain Interned and Expelled Its Wartime Refugees*. London: Quartet, 1980.

Gilman, Sander L. *The Jew's Body*. New York and London: Routledge, 1991.

Gilroy, Paul. *The Black Atlantic: Modernity and Double Consciousness*. London: Verso, 1993.

Gledhill, Christine, and Gillian Swanson. *Nationalising Femininity: Culture, Sexuality and British Cinema in the Second World War*. Manchester: Manchester University Press, 1996.

Glenn, Susan A. *Female Spectacle: The Theatrical Roots of Modern Feminism*. Cambridge, MA and London: Harvard University Press, 2000.

Glicco, Jack. *Madness after Midnight*. London: Elek Books, 1952.

Glucksmann, Miriam. *Women Assemble: Women Workers and the New Industries in Inter-war Britain*. London and New York: Routledge, 1990.

Godbolt, Jim. *A History of Jazz in Britain 1919–1950*. London: Quartet, 1984.

Goddard, Chris. *Jazz Away from Home*. New York and London: Paddington Press, 1979.

Godfrey, Philip. *Back-Stage: A Survey of the Contemporary English Theatre from behind the Scenes.* London: Harrap, 1933.

Goffman, Erving. *Interaction Ritual; Essays on Face-to-Face Behavior.* Garden City, NY: Anchor Books, 1967.

———. *The Presentation of Self in Everyday Life.* New York: Anchor Books, 1959.

Gold, Harry, and Roger Cotterrell. *Gold, Doubloons and Pieces of Eight: The Autobiography of Harry Gold.* London: Northway, 2000.

Goldman, William. *East End My Cradle.* London: Faber and Faber, 1940.

Goldring, Douglas. *The Nineteen Twenties: A General Survey and Some Personal Memories.* London: Nicholson & Watson, 1945.

———. *Odd Man Out: The Autobiography of a "Propaganda Novelist."* London: Chapman & Hall, 1935.

Goldsmith, Margaret. *Soho Square.* London: Sampson Low, Marston, 1947.

Gomme, George Laurence. *London.* Philadelphia and London: J. B. Lippincott, 1914.

Goodway, David. *London Chartism, 1838–1848.* Cambridge, UK: Cambridge University Press, 1982.

Gordon, Jan. *We Explore London.* New York: R. M. McBride, 1933.

Gossman, Lionel. "Anecdote and History." *History and Theory* 42, no. 2 (2003): 143–68.

Gowing, Laura. *Common Bodies: Women, Touch and Power in Seventeenth-Century England.* New Haven: Yale University Press, 2003.

Graham, Stephen. *London Nights: A Series of Studies and Sketches of London at Night.* London: Hurst & Blackett, 1925.

———. *Twice Round the London Clock and More London Nights.* London: E. Benn, 1933.

Gram Holmstrom, Kirsten. *Monodrama, Attitudes, Tableaux Vivants: Studies on Some Trends of Theatrical Fashion 1770–1815.* Stockholm: Almqvist & Wiksell, 1967.

Graves, Charles. *Londoner's Life.* London: Hutchinson, 1942.

———. *Off the Record.* London: Hutchinson, 1942.

Graves, Robert, and Alan Hodge. *The Long Week-End: A Social History of Great Britain 1918–1939.* New York: Norton, 1994.

Green, A. I., M. Follert, K. Osterlund, and J. Paquin. "Space, Place and Sexual Sociality: Towards an 'Atmospheric Analysis.' " *Gender, Work and Organization* 17, no. 1 (2008): 7–27.

Green, Benny. *The Last Empires: A Music Hall Companion.* London: Pavilion, 1986.

Green, J. *Social History of the Jewish East End in London, 1914–39: A Study of Life, Labour and Liturgy.* Lewiston, NY: Mellen, 1991.

Green, Jeffrey. "Trumpet Player from the West Indies." *Black Perspectives in Music* 12, no. 1 (1984): 98–127.

Greenfield, Jill, Sean O'Connell, and Chris Reid. "Fashioning Masculinity: Men Only, Consumption and the Development of Marketing in the 1930s." *Twentieth-Century British History* 10, no. 4 (1999): 457–76.

Greenwood, Walter. *Only Mugs Work: A Soho Melodrama.* London: Hutchinson, 1938.

Gregory, Derek. *Geographical Imaginations.* Oxford: Blackwell, 1994.

Grele, Ronald J. "Movement without Aim: Methodological and Theoretical Problems in Oral History." In Robert Perks and Alistair Thomson, eds., *The Oral History Reader*, 38–52. London and New York: Routledge, 1998.

Griffiths, Richard. *Fellow Travellers of the Right: British Enthusiasts for Nazi Germany, 1933–9.* Oxford: Oxford University Press, 1983.

Grossman, Lloyd, and Edwina Ehrman. *London Eats Out: 500 Years of Capital Dining.* London: Museum of London and Philip Wilson, 1999.

Guest, Ivor Forbes. *Ballet in Leicester Square: The Alhambra and the Empire, 1860–1915.* London: Dance Books, 1992.

Gullace, Nicoletta. *The Blood of Our Sons: Men, Women, and the Renegotiation of British Citizenship during the Great War.* Basingstoke, UK: Palgrave, 2002.

Gunn, Simon, and Rachel Bell. *Middle Classes: Their Rise and Sprawl.* London: Cassell, 2002.

Gurney, Peter. "'Intersexual' Dirty Girls: Mass Observation and Working-Class Sexuality in England in the 1930s." *Journal of the History of Sexuality* 8, no. 2 (1997): 259–90.

Hall, Lesley A. *Sex, Gender, and Social Change in Britain since 1880.* New York: St. Martin's Press, 2000.

Hall, Peter Geoffrey. *The Industries of London since 1861.* London: Hutchinson, 1962.

Hall, Radclyffe. *Adam's Breed.* London: Virago, 1985.

Hall, Stuart. "The Social Eye of *Picture Post.*" *Working Papers in Cultural Studies* 2 (1972): 71–87.

Harding, Arthur, and Raphael Samuel. *East End Underworld: Chapters in the Life of Arthur Harding.* London and Boston: Routledge & Kegan Paul, 1981.

Hare, Kenneth. *London's Latin Quarter.* London: Bodley Head, 1926.

Harris, John. *Moving Rooms.* New Haven and London: Yale University Press for the Paul Mellon Centre for Studies in British Art, 2007.

——— . "What Might Be Called a Frame-Up: The Hogarth House." *British Art Journal* 1, no. 1 (2000): 19–21.

Harrison, Brian Howard. *Separate Spheres: The Opposition to Women's Suffrage in Britain.* London: Croom Helm, 1978.

Harrison, Charles. *Theatricals and Tableaux Vivants for Amateurs. Giving Full Directions as to Stage Arrangements, "Making up," Costumes and Acting.* London: L. Upcott Gill, 1882.

Harrison, Michael. *London beneath the Pavement.* London: P. Davies, 1971.

Harrisson, Tom. *Living through the Blitz.* Harmondsworth: Penguin Books, 1979.

——— . Harrisson, Tom. "Whistle While You Work." *New Writing* n.s. 1 (1938): 47–67.

Harrisson, Tom, and Charles Madge. *Britain by Mass-Observation.* London: Cresset, 1986.

Harrisson, Tom and Charles Madge, eds. *War Begins at Home. By Mass-Observation.* London: Chatto & Windus, 1940.

Hart-Davis, Rupert. *The Letters of Oscar Wilde.* New York: Harcourt, Brace & World, 1962.

Hayes, Nick, and Jeff Hill. *'Millions Like Us'? British Culture in the Second World War.* Liverpool: Liverpool University Press, 1999.

Heath, Ambrose. "Wise Advice in the *Manchester Guardian.*" *Wine and Food* 1, no. 4 (1934): 56–62.

Heinze, Andrew R. *Adapting to Abundance: Jewish Immigrants, Mass Consumption, and the Search for American Identity.* New York: Columbia University Press, 1990.

Helstosky, Carol. *Garlic and Oil: Politics and Food in Italy.* Oxford: Berg, 2004.

Henrey, Mrs. Robert. *An Exile in Soho.* London: Dent, 1952.

——— . *Julia: Reminiscences of a Year in Madeleine's Life as a London Shop-Girl.* London: Dent, 1971.

——— . *London under Fire, 1940–45.* London: Dent, 1969.

——— . *Madeleine Grown Up.* London: Dutton, 1953.

——— . *Madeleine, Young Wife.* London: Dent, 1960.

Henriques, Basil. *Club Leadership Today.* Oxford: Oxford University Press, 1951.

——— . *The Indiscretions of a Warden.* London: Methuen, 1937.

Highmore, Ben. *Everyday Life and Cultural Theory: An Introduction.* London: Routledge, 2002.

——— . *The Everyday Life Reader.* London: Routledge, 2002.

Hill, B. *Boss of Britain's Underworld.* London: Naldrett Press, 1955.

Hirschfield, Magnus. *The Homosexuality of Men and Women.* Amherst, NY: Prometheus, 2000.

Hoare, Philip. *Noël Coward: A Biography.* New York: Simon & Schuster, 1996.

——— . *Oscar Wilde's Last Stand: Decadence, Conspiracy, and the Most Outrageous Trial of the Century.* New York: Arcade, 1998.

Hobhouse, Hermione. *A History of Regent Street.* London: MacDonald & Jane's, Queen Anne Press, 1975.

——— . *Lost London: A Century of Demolition and Decay.* London: Macmillan, 1971.

Holledge, Julie. *Innocent Flowers: Women in the Edwardian Theatre.* London: Virago, 1981.

Hollingshead, John. *The Story of Leicester Square.* London: Simpkin & Marshall, 1892.

Honeycombe, Gordon. *Selfridges, Seventy-Five Years: The Story of the Store 1909–1984.* London: Park Lane Press, 1984.

Hooten-Smith, Eileen. *The Restaurants of London.* New York: Knopf, 1928.

Hopkins, R. Thurston. *This London: Its Taverns, Haunts, and Memories.* London: C. Palmer, 1927.

Horn, Pamela. *High Society: The English Social Élite, 1880–1914.* Phoenix Mill, UK: Alan Sutton, 1992.

Houlbrook, Matt. "'The Man with the Powder Puff' in Interwar London." *Historical Journal* 50, no. 1 (2007): 145–71.

——— . *Queer London: Perils and Pleasures in the Sexual Metropolis, 1918–1957.* Chicago: University of Chicago Press, 2005.

Hughson, F. Mooney. "Songs, Singers and Society, 1890–1954." *American Quarterly* 6, no. 3 (1954): 221–32.

Humble, Nicola. *The Feminine Middlebrow Novel, 1920s to 1950s: Class, Domesticity, and Bohemianism.* Oxford: Oxford University Press, 2001.

Humphries, Stephen, and John Taylor. *The Making of Modern London, 1945–1985.* London: Sidgwick & Jackson, 1986.

Huneault, Kristina. *Difficult Subjects: Working Women and Visual Culture, Britain 1880–1914.* Aldershot, UK: Ashgate, 2002.

Hussey, Mark. *Virginia Woolf A to Z: A Comprehensive Reference for Students, Teachers, and Common Readers to Her Life, Work, and Critical Reception.* New York: Facts on File, 1995.

Hynes, Samuel. *The Auden Generation: Literature and Politics in England in the 1930's.* New York: Viking Press, 1977.

——— . *A War Imagined: The First World War and English Culture.* London: Bodley Head, 1990.

Ingraham, Chrys. *Thinking Straight: The Power, the Promise, and the Paradox of Heterosexuality.* New York and London: Routledge, 2005.

Jackson, Alan Arthur. *Semi-Detached London. Suburban Development, Life and Transport, 1900–39.* London: Allen & Unwin, 1973.

Jackson, Louise A. "'Lady Cops' and 'Decoy Doras': Gender, Surveillance, and the Construction of Urban Knowledge in Britain 1919–1950." *London Journal* 27, no. 1 (2002): 63–83.

——— . *Women Police: Gender, Welfare and Surveillance in the Twentieth Century.* Manchester: Manchester University Press, 2006.

Jackson, Stanley. *An Indiscreet Guide to Soho.* London: Muse Arts, 1946.

——— . *The Savoy: The Romance of a Great Hotel.* London: Muller, 1979.

Jacobs, Joe. *Out of the Ghetto: My Youth in the East End: Communism and Fascism, 1913–1939.* London: Janet Simon, 1978.

Jameson, Storm. *Here Comes a Candle.* New York: Macmillan, 1938.

Jefferys, James Bavington. *Retail Trading in Britain, 1850–1950.* Cambridge, UK: Cambridge University Press, 1954.

Jenkins, Alan. *The Thirties.* London: Heinemann, 1976.

——— . *The Twenties.* London: Heinemann, 1974.

Jenkins, Simon. *Landlords to London: The Story of a Capital and Its Growth.* London: Constable, 1975.

Jennings, Humphrey, and Charles Madge, eds. *May the Twelfth; Mass-Observation Day-Surveys 1937 by over Two Hundred Observers.* London: Faber and Faber, 1937.

Jivani, Alkarim. *It's Not Unusual: A History of Lesbian and Gay Britain in the Twentieth Century.* London: Michael O'Mara, 1997.

John, Angela V. *Elizabeth Robbins: Staging a Life, 1862–1952.* London: Routledge, 1995.

Jones, C. Sheridan. *London in War-Time.* London: Grafton, 1917.

Jones, Gareth Stedman. "Working-Class Culture and Working-Class Politics in London, 1870–1900: Notes on the Remaking of a Working Class." *Journal of Social History* (1974): 460–508.

Jones, Harry. *Fifty Years, or Dead Leaves and Living Seeds.* London: Smith Elder, 1895.

Jones, Mervyn. *Chances: An Autobiography.* London: Verso, 1987.

Josephy, Helen B., and Mary Margaret Macbride. *London Is a Man's Town, but Women Go There.* London: Coward-McCann, 1930.

Jowitt, Deborah. *Time and the Dancing Image.* Berkeley: University of California Press, 1989.

Joyce, Patrick. *The Rule of Freedom: Liberalism and the Modern City.* London: Verso, 2003.

Kaplan, Joel H., and Sheila Stowell. *Theatre and Fashion: Oscar Wilde to the Suffragettes.* Cambridge, UK: Cambridge University Press, 1994.

Kaplan, Morris B. *Sodom on the Thames: Sex, Love, and Scandal in Wilde Times.* Ithaca, NY: Cornell University Press, 2005.

——— . "Who's Afraid of John Saul? Urban Culture and the Politics of Desire in Late Victorian London." *GLQ: A Journal of Lesbian and Gay Studies* 5, no. 3 (1999): 296–300.

Katz, Jonathan. "The Invention of Heterosexuality." *Socialist Review* 20 (1990): 7–34.

Kent, Susan. *Making Peace: The Reconstruction of Gender in Interwar Britain.* Princeton: Princeton University Press, 1993.

Kersh, Gerald. *Night and the City.* London: Michael Joseph, 1938.

Kershen, Anne J. *Off the Peg.* [London]: [London Museum of Jewish Life], 1988.

——— . *Uniting the Tailors: Trade Unionism among the Tailoring Workers of London and Leeds, 1870–1939.* Ilford, UK: F. Cass, 1995.

Kettle, Michael. *Salome's Last Veil: The Libel Case of the Century.* London: Hart-Davis, 1977.

King, E. M. *Rational Dress; or, the Dress of Women and Savages.* London: Kegan Paul, 1882.

Kinney, Troy, and Margaret West Kinney. *The Dance; Its Place in Art and Life.* New York: Tudor, 1935. (Repr. of rev. edn. 1914.)

Kirkham, Pat. "Fashioning the Feminine." In Christine Gledhill and Gillian Swanson, eds., *Nationalising Femininity: Culture, Sexuality and British Cinema in the Second World War,* 152–71. Manchester: Manchester University Press, 2010.

Kirkham, Pat, and David Thoms. *War Culture: Social Change and Changing Experience in World War Two Britain.* London: Lawrence & Wishart, 1995.

Kirkpatrick, Florence. "Shopping East and West." In Arthur St. John Adcock, ed., *Wonderful London: The World's Greatest City,* vol. 1 (London: Educational Book Co., 1927), 238–48.

Kirwan, Daniel Joseph. *Palace and Hovel: Or, Phases of London Life, Being Personal Observations on an American in London.* Hartford: Belknap & Bliss, 1870.

Klein, Jennifer. *For All These Rights: Business, Labor, and the Shaping of America's Public-Private Welfare State.* Princeton: Princeton University Press, 2003.

Knepper, P. "The Other Invisible Hand: Jews and Anarchists in London before the First World War." *Jewish History* 22, no. 3 (2008): 295–315.

Kohn, Marek. "Cocaine Girls." In Paul Gootenberg, ed., *Cocaine: Global Histories,* 105–22. London: Routledge, 1999.

——— . *Dope Girls: The Birth of the British Drug Underground.* London: Granta, 2001, 1992.

Koritz, Amy. "Dancing the Orient for England: Maud Allan's 'the Vision of Salome.'" *Theatre Journal* 46 (1994): 63–78.

——— . *Gendering Bodies/Performing Art: Dance and Literature in Early Twentieth-Century British Culture.* Ann Arbor: University of Michigan Press, 1995.

——— . "Moving Violations: Dance in the London Music Hall, 1890–1910." *Theatre Journal* 42, no. 4 (1990): 419–31.

Kramer, Paul A. "Empires, Exceptions, and Anglo-Saxons: Race and Rule between the British and the United States Empires, 1880–1910." *Journal of American History* 88, no. 4 (2002): 1315–53.

Kuhn, Annette. *Cinema, Censorship, and Sexuality, 1909–1925.* Cinema and Society. London and New York: Routledge, 1988.

Kushner, Tony. *We Europeans? Mass-Observation, "Race" and British Identity in the Twentieth Century.* Aldershot, UK and Burlington, VT: Ashgate, 2004.

Kushner, Tony, and Kenneth Lunn. *The Politics of Marginality: Race, the Radical Right, and Minorities in Twentieth Century Britain.* London: F. Cass, 1990.

Kynaston, David. *The City of London,* vol. 1: *A World of Its Own, 1815–1890.* London: Chatto & Windus, 1994.

Lanchester, Elsa. *Elsa Lanchester Herself.* New York: St. Martin's Press, 1983.

Langhamer, Claire. "Love and Courtship in Mid-Twentieth-Century England." *Historical Journal* 50, no. 1 (2007): 173–96.

Leavis, Q. D. *Fiction and the Reading Public.* London: Chatto & Windus, 1932.

Lefebvre, Henri. *The Production of Space.* Oxford: Basil Blackwell, 1991.

LeMahieu, D. L. *A Culture for Democracy: Mass Communication and the Cultivated Mind in Britain between the Wars*. Oxford and New York: Clarendon Press, 1988.

Leoni, Peppino. *I Shall Die on the Carpet. With a Forward by Fabian of the Yard*. London: Leslie Frewin, 1966.

Lesser, Wendy. "From Dickens to Conrad: A Sentimental Journey." *English Literary History* 52, no. 1 (1985): 185–208.

Levene, Mark. "Going against the Grain: Two Jewish Memoirs of War and Anti-war. . ." In Michael Berkowitz, Susan L. Tananbaum, and Sam W. Bloom, eds., *Forging Modern Jewish Identities: Public Faces and Private Struggles*, 88–106. London and Portland, OR: Vallentine Mitchell, 2003.

Levine, Philippa. "'Walking the Streets in a Way No Decent Woman Should': Women Police in World War I." *Journal of Modern History* 66, no. 1 (Mar. 1994): 34–78.

Levinson, André. *André Levinson on Dance: Writings from Paris in the Twenties*, ed. Joan Ross Acocella and Lynn Garafola. Hanover, NH: Wesleyan University Press, 1991.

Levy, Shawn. *Ready, Steady, Go! Swinging London and the Invention of Cool*. London: Fourth Estate, 2002.

Lewis, Chaim. *A Soho Address*. London: Gollancz, 1965.

Liebknecht, Wilhelm. *Karl Marx; Biographical Memoirs*. trans. E. Untermann. Chicago: C. H. Kerr, 1901.

Light, Alison. *Forever England: Femininity, Literature and Conservatism between the Wars*. London: Routledge, 2000. (Originally published 1991.)

Lockhart, Robert Hamilton Bruce. *The Diaries of Sir Robert Bruce Lockhart*, ed. Kenneth Young. London: Macmillan, 1973.

London by Night, or the Bachelor's Facetious Guide to All the Ins and Outs and Nightly Doings of the Metropolis. London: William Ward, 1857.

London, the Wonder City: Being a Concise Pocket Reference of Events Both Social & Sporting and a Gazetteer and Guide. London: Pullman Car Co., 1937.

Looker, Ben. *Exhibiting Imperial London: Empire and the City in Victorian and Edwardian Guidebooks*. London: Goldsmith's College, 2002.

Luke, Michael. *David Tennant and the Gargoyle Years*. London: Weidenfeld & Nicolson, 1991.

Lunn, Kenneth, and Richard C. Thurlow. *British Fascism: Essays on the Radical Right in Inter-war Britain*. New York: St. Martin's Press, 1980.

MacClure, Victor. *How to Be Happy in London*. London: Arrowsmith, 1926.

Machray, Robert. *The Night Side of London*. Philadelphia: J. B. Lippincott, 1902.

MacInnes, Colin. *Absolute Beginners*. Harmondsworth, UK: Penguin, 2000. (Originally published 1959.)

Mack, Joanna, and Steve Humphries. *London at War: The Making of Modern London, 1939–1945*. London: Sidgwick & Jackson, 1985.

Mackay, Robert. *Half the Battle: Civilian Morale in Britain during the Second World War*. Manchester: Manchester University Press, 2002.

Mackenzie, Gordon. *Marylebone: Great City North of Oxford Street*. London: Macmillan, 1972.

Macpherson, Heather. "Sarah Bernhardt: Portrait of the Actress as Spectacle." *Nineteenth-Century Contexts* 20 (1999): 409–54.

Macqueen-Pope, W. *Carriages at Eleven: The Story of the Edwardian Theatre*. London and New York: Hutchinson, 1947.

——— . *'Goodbye Piccadilly'*. Newton Abbot, UK: David & Charles, 1972.

——— . *Haymarket: Theatre of Perfection*. London: W. H. Allen, 1948.

——— . *The Melodies Linger On: The Story of Music Hall*. London: W. H. Allen, 1950.

Mandler, Peter. *The Fall and Rise of the Stately Home*. New Haven: Yale University Press, 1997.

Mannin, Ethel. *Men Are Unwise*. London: Severn House, 1976.

——— . *Sounding Brass*. 2nd edn. New York: Duffield, 1926.

——— . *Young in the Twenties: A Chapter of Autobiography*. London: Hutchinson, 1971.

Manning, Susan. "The Female Dancer and the Male Gaze: Feminist Critiques of Early Modern Dance." In Gay Morris, ed., *Moving Words: Re-writing Dance*, 153–66. London and New York: Routledge, 1996.

Marriott, Oliver. *The Property Boom*. London: Hamilton, 1967.

Marwick, Arthur. *The Deluge: British Society and the First World War*. London: Bodley Head, 1965.

Mass Observation. *First Year's Work, 1937–38*, ed. Charles Madge and Tom Harrisson. London: Lindsey Drummond, 1938.

Matthews, Jessie, with Muriel Burgess. *Over My Shoulder: An Autobiography, as Told to Muriel Burgess*. London: W. H. Allen, 1974.

McCalman, Iain. "Unrespectable Radicalism: Infidels and Pornography in Early Nineteenth-Century London." *Past and Present* 104, no. 1 (1984): 74–110.

McCarthy, Justin. *Reminiscences*, vol. 1. London: Chatto & Windus, 1899.

McClelland, E. M. "Sidelights on Universal Benevolence, 1789–1820." *Comparative Studies in Society and History* 9, no. 4 (1967): 349–61.

McKay, George. *Circular Breathing: The Cultural Politics of Jazz in Britain*. Durham, NC: Duke University Press, 2005.

McKibbin, Ross. *Classes and Cultures: England, 1918–1951*. Oxford: Oxford University Press, 2000.

McLaren, Angus. *Sexual Blackmail: A Modern History*. Cambridge, MA: Harvard University Press, 2002.

——— . "Smoke and Mirrors: Willy Clarkson and the Role of Disguises in Inter-war England." *Journal of Social History* 40, no. 3 (2007): 597–618.

McLaughlin, Joseph. *Writing the Urban Jungle: Reading Empire in London from Doyle to Eliot*. Charlottesville: University of Virginia Press, 2000.

Medd, Jodie. " 'The Cult of the Clitoris': Anatomy of a National Scandal." *Modernism/Modernity* 9, no. 1 (2002): 21–49.

Melly, George. *Revolt into Style: The Pop Arts in Britain*. London: Allen Lane, 1970.

Melman, Billie. *The Culture of History: English Uses of the Past, 1800–1953*. Oxford and New York: Oxford University Press, 2006.

——— . *Women and the Popular Imagination in the Twenties: Flappers and Nymphs*. New York: St. Martin's Press, 1988.

Meltzer, Albert. *The Anarchists in London, 1935–1955*. Sanday, Orkney: Cienfuegos Press, 1976.

Melville, Joy. *Ellen and Edy: A Biography of Ellen Terry and Her Daughter, Edith Craig, 1847–1947*. London: Pandora, 1987.

Mennell, Stephen. *All Manners of Food: Eating and Taste in England and France from the Middle Ages to the Present*. Oxford: Basil Blackwell, 1985.

Meyerowitz, Joanne. "Women, Cheesecake, and Borderline Material: Responses to Girlie Pictures in the Mid-Twentieth Century U.S." *Journal of Women's History* 8, no. 3 (1996): 9–36.

Meyrick, Kate. *Secrets of the 43 Club*. Dublin: Parkgate, 1994.

Mikhail, E. H., ed. *Oscar Wilde: Interviews and Recollections*. London: Macmillan, 1979.

Miller, Andrew. *The Earl of Petticoat Lane*. London: William Heinemann, 2006.

Miller, Elizabeth Carolyn. *Framed: The New Woman Criminal in British Culture at the Fin de Siècle*. Ann Arbor: University of Michigan Press, 2008.

Mitchenson, Joe, and Mander Raymond. *The Lost Theatres of London*. London: New English Library, 1968. (Repr. 1976.)

Mitford, Jessica. *Hons and Rebels*. London: Gollancz, 1960.

Mizejewski, Linda. *Divine Decadence: Fascism, Female Spectacle, and the Makings of Sally Bowles*. Princeton: Princeton University Press, 1992.

Monelli, Paolo. *Il ghiottone errante. Viaggio gastronomico attraverso l'Italia*. Milan: Fratelli Trevis, 1935.

Montagu, Lily H. *My Club and I: The Story of the West Central Jewish Club*. London: Herbert Joseph, 1941.

Montague, Ken. "The Aesthetics of Hygiene: Aesthetic Dress, Modernity, and the Body as Sign." *Journal of Design History* 7, no. 2 (1994): 91–112.

Montgomery, John. *The New Wealth of Cities: City Dynamics and the Fifth Wave*. 2nd edn. Aldershot, UK: Ashgate, 2008.

Montizambert, Elizabeth. *London Discoveries in Shops and Restaurants*. London: Women Publishers, 1924.

Moore, James Ross. *André Charlot: The Genius of Intimate Musical Revue*. Jefferson, NC: McFarland, 2005.

Morand, Paul. *A Frenchman's London*. London: Cassell, 1934.

More, Kenneth. *More or Less*. London: Hodder & Stoughton, 1978.

Morgan, Kevin. "King Street Blues: Jazz and the Left in Britian in the 1930s–1940s." In Andy Croft, ed., *A Weapon in the Struggle: The Cultural History of the Communist Party in Britain*, 123–41. London: Pluto, 1998.

Morris, Christopher. *Reading Opera between the Lines: Orchestral Interludes and Cultural Meaning from Wagner to Berg*. New Perspectives in Music History and Criticism. Cambridge, UK and New York: Cambridge University Press, 2002.

Morris, Ira. *The Glass of Fashion*. London: Pilot Press, 1947.

Mort, Frank. *Capital Affairs*. London: Yale University Press, 2010.

——. *Cultures of Consumption: Masculinities and Social Space in Late Twentieth-Century Britain*. London: Routledge, 1996.

——. *Dangerous Sexualities: Medico-Moral Politics in England since 1830*. 2nd edn. London: Routledge, 2000.

——. "Striptease: The Erotic Female Body and Live Sexual Entertainment in Mid-Twentieth-Century London." *Social History* 32, no. 1 (2007): 27–53.

Morton, H. V. *H. V. Morton's London, Being the Heart of London, the Spell of London, and the Nights of London, in One Volume*. 18th edn. London: Methuen, 1957.

——. *The Nights of London*. London: Methuen, 1926.

——. *The Spell of London*. London: Methuen, 1926.

Moseley, Sydney Alexander. *The Night Haunts of London*. London: Stanley Paul, 1920.

Mullally, Frederic. *Fascism inside England*. London: Claud Morris Books, 1946.

Murphy, Robert. *Smash and Grab: Gangsters in the London Underworld, 1920–60*. London: Faber and Faber, 1993.

Museum of Modern Art. *Modern Architecture in England*. New York: Museum of Modern Art, 1937.

Naggar, Betty. *Jewish Pedlars and Hawkers, 1740–1940*. Camberley, UK: Porphyrogenitus, 1992.

Nava, Mica. *Visceral Cosmopolitanism: Gender, Culture and the Normalisation of Difference*. Oxford: Berg, 2007.

Nead, Lynda. *Victorian Babylon: People, Streets, and Images in Nineteenth-Century London*. New Haven: Yale University Press, 2000.

Nevill, Ralph, and Charles Edward Jerningham. *Piccadilly to Pall Mall, Manners, Morals, and Man*. London: Duckworth, 1908.

Newnham-Davis, Nathaniel. *Dinners and Diners: Where and How to Dine in London*. Enlarged and rev edn. London: Grant Richards, 1901.

——. *The Gourmet's Guide to London*. London: Grant Richards, 1914.

Newton, Scott. *Profits of Peace: The Political Economy of Anglo-German Appeasement*. Oxford: Clarendon Press, 1996.

Newton, Stella Mary. *Health, Art and Reason: Dress Reformers of the 19th Century*. London: J. Murray, 1974.

Nicholson, Steve. *The Censorship of British Drama, 1900–1968*, vol. 1: *1900–1932*. Exeter, UK: University of Exeter Press, 2003.

——. *The Censorship of British Drama, 1900–1968*, vol. 2: *1933–1952*. Exeter Performance Studies. Exeter, UK: University of Exeter Press, 2003.

Nicholson, Virginia. *Among the Bohemians: Experiments in Living, 1900–1939*. New York: William Morrow, 2004.

Nickson, Richard. "G.B.S. and Laura Ormiston Chant—Man and Superwoman." *Independent Shavian* 37, nos. 1–2 (1999): 21–4.

Nicolaievsky, Boris. *Karl Marx: Man and Fighter*. London: Methuen, 1936.

Nochlin, Linda, and Tamar Garb, eds. *The Jew in the Text: Modernity and the Construction of Identity*. New York: Thames & Hudson, 1996.

Nord, Deborah Epstein. *Walking the Victorian Streets: Women, Representation, and the City*. Ithaca, NY: Cornell University Press, 1995.

Nott, James J. *Music for the People: Popular Music and Dance in Interwar Britain*. Oxford Historical Monographs. Oxford and New York: Oxford University Press, 2002.

Nussbaum, Martha. "Patriotism and Cosmopolitanism?" In Martha Nussbaum and Respondents, *For Love of Country: Debating the Limits of Patriotism*, ed. Joshua Cohen, 2–20. Boston: Beacon Press, 1996.

O'Byrne, Alison. "The Art of Walking in London: Representing Urban Pedestrianism in the Early Nineteenth Century." *Romanticism* 14, no. 2 (2008): 94–107.

Ogborn, Miles. *Spaces of Modernity: London's Geographies, 1680–1780*. New York: Guilford, 1998.

Oldfield, Sybil. *This Working Day World: Women's Lives and Culture(s) in Britain, 1914–1945*. Gender and Society. London: Taylor & Francis, 1994.

Oliver, H. *The International Anarchist Movement in Late Victorian London*. Beckenham, UK: Croom Helm, 1983.

Oliver, Paul. *Black Music in Britain: Essays on the Afro-Asian Contribution to Popular Music*. Milton Keynes, UK: Open University Press, 1990.

Olsen, Donald J. *The City as a Work of Art: London, Paris, Vienna*. New Haven: Yale University Press, 1986.

——. *The Growth of Victorian London*. New York: Holmes & Meier, 1976.

Osgerby, Bill. "A Pedigree of Masculinity." In Bethan Benwell, ed., *Masculinity and Men's Lifestyle Magazines*, 57–88. Oxford and Malden, MA: Blackwell, 2003.

Otter, Chris. *The Victorian Eye: A Political History of Light and Vision in Britain, 1800–1910*. Chicago: University of Chicago Press, 2008.

Panayi, Panikos. *Racial Violence in Britain, 1840–1950*. Leicester: Leicester University Press, 1993.

——. *Spicing up Britain: The Multicultural History of British Food*. London: Reaktion, 2008.

Pankhurst, Rita "Sylvia Pankhurst in Perspective." *Women's Studies International Forum* 11, no. 3 (1988): 245–62.

Parker, Derek, and Julia Parker. *Natural History of the Chorus Girl*. Newton Abbot: David & Charles, 1975.

Parsonage, Catherine. *The Evolution of Jazz in Britain, 1880–1935*. Aldershot, UK: Ashgate, 2005.

Partridge, Frances. *Memories*. London: Gollancz, 1981.

Pascoe, Charles Eyre. *London of To-day: An Illustrated Handbook for the Season*. 8th annual edn. London, 1892.

Peel, Mrs. Dorothy Constance. *How We Lived Then, 1914–1918*. London: Lane, 1929.

Peiss, Kathy Lee. *Cheap Amusements: Working Women and Leisure in Turn-of-the-Century New York*. Philadelphia: Temple University Press, 1986.

Pennybacker, Susan D. *A Vision for London, 1889–1914: Labour, Everyday Life and the LCC Experiment*. London: Routledge, 1995.

Petrow, Stefan. *Policing Morals: The Metropolitan Police and the Home Office, 1870–1914*. Oxford: Oxford University Press, 1994.

Pickering, Michael. "The BBC's Kentucky Minstrels, 1933–1950: Blackface Entertainment on British Radio." *Historical Journal of Film, Radio and Television* 16, no. 2 (1996): 161–95.

Platt, John. *London's Rock Routes*. London: Fourth Estate, 1985.

Pollard, Nigel E. "A Short History of Public Lighting in the City of Westminster." *IPLE Lighting Journal: Official Journal of the Institutions of Public Lighting Engineers* 1984, 53–8.

Port, M. H. *Imperial London: Civil Government Building in London 1850–1915*. New Haven: Yale University Press, 1995.

Portelli, Alessandro. "What Makes Oral History Different." In Robert Perks and Alistair Thomson, eds., *The Oral History Reader*, 63–74. London and New York: Routledge, 1998.

Porter, Bernard. *The Origins of the Vigilant State: The London Metropolitan Police Special Branch before the First World War*. London: Weidenfeld & Nicolson, 1987.

Porter, Kevin, and Jeffrey Weeks. *Between the Acts: Lives of Homosexual Men, 1885–1967*. London and New York: Routledge, 1991.

Porter, Roy. *London: A Social History*. London: Hamish Hamilton, 1994.

Powell, Nosher, with William Hall. *Nosher*. London: Blake, 1999.

Power, Richenda. "Healthy Motion: Images of 'Natural' and 'Cultured' Movement in Early Twentieth Century Britain "*Women's Studies International Forum* 19, no. 5 (1996): 551–65.

Pudney, John. *Jacobson's Ladder: A Novel*. London: Longmans, 1938.

Pugh, Martin. *The Pankhursts*. London: Allen Lane, 2001.

Raby, Peter. *The Cambridge Companion to Oscar Wilde*. Cambridge, UK: Cambridge University Press, 1997.

Radford, Robert. *Art for a Purpose: The Artists' International Association, 1933–1953*. Winchester, UK: Winchester School of Art Press, 1987.

Ransome, Arthur. *Bohemia in London*. Oxford and New York: Oxford University Press, 1907. (Repr. 1984.)

Rappaport, Erika Diane. *Shopping for Pleasure: Women in the Making of London's West End*. Princeton: Princeton University Press, 2000.

Rasmussen, Steen Eiler. *London: The Unique City*. Rev, edn. Cambridge, MA: MIT Press, 1982.

Rawlinson, Joseph, and W. R. Davidge, *City of Westminster Plan*. London: Westminster City Council, 1946.

Reynolds, David. *Rich Relations: The American Occupation of Britain, 1942–1945*. London: Phoenix, 2000.

Rhys, Jean. *Smile Please: An Unfinished Autobiography*. Harmondsworth, UK: Penguin, 1981. (Originally published 1979.)

Richards, Jeffrey. *The Age of the Dream Palace: Cinema and Society in Britain, 1930–1939*. London: Routledge, 1989, 1984.

Richardson, D. J. "J. Lyons and Co., Ltd.: Caterers and Food Manufacturers, 1894–1939." In S. B. Miller and Derek J. Oddy, eds., *The Making of the Modern British Diet*, 161–72. London: Croom Helm, 1976.

Richardson, Philip John Sampey. *A History of English Ballroom Dancing (1910–45): The Story of the Development of the Modern English Style*. London: Herbert Jenkins, 1945.

Rickaby, Tony. "Artists' International." *History Workshop* no. 6 (1978): 121–38.

Ridge, Cecil Harold, and Frederick Samuel Aldred. *Stage Lighting: Principles and Practice*. London: Pitman, 1935.

Rimbault, Edward Francis, and George Clinch. *Soho and Its Associations, Historical, Literary and Artistic. Edited from the Mss. Of . . . E. F. Rimbault by G. Clinch*. London: Dulau, 1895.

Ritchie, J. Ewing. *The Night Side of London*. London: W. Tweedie, 1857.

Roberts, Glyn. *I Take This City*. London: Jarrolds, 1933.

Rogers, Ben. *A. J. Ayer: A Life*. New York: Grove Press, 1999.

Rogers, Meyric R. "Notes on Some Recent Accessions for the Richard T. Crane Jr. Memorial." *Bulletin of the Art Institute of Chicago* 44, no. 2 (1950): 27–35.

Rogers, Terence. "The Right Book Club." *Journal of Contemporary History* (2003): 1–15.

Rolley, Katrina. "Fashion, Femininity, and the Fight for the Vote." *Art History* 13 (1990): 47–71.

Rose, Gillian. "Engendering the Slum: Photography in East London in the 1930s." *Gender, Place and Culture* 4, no. 3 (1997): 277–300.

Rose, Norman. *The Cliveden Set: Portrait of an Exclusive Fraternity*. London: Cape, 2000.

Rose, Sonya. "Girls and GIs: Race, Sex and Diplomacy in Second World War Britain." *Journal of International History* 19, no. 1 (1997): 146–60.

——— . "Sex, Citizenship, and the Nation in World War II Britain." *American Historical Review* 103, no. 4 (1998): 1147–76.

Ross, Catherine. *Twenties London: A City in the Jazz Age*. London and New York: Museum of London and Philip Wilson, 2003.

Ross, Ellen. "Missionaries and Jews in Soho: 'Strangers within Our Gates.'" *Journal of Victorian Culture* 15, no. 2 (2010): 226–38.

Rubens, Alfred. *A Jewish Iconography*. London: Jewish Museum, 1954.

Russell, Dave. "Varieties of Life: The Making of the Edwardian Music Hall." In Michael R. Booth and Joel H. Kaplan, eds., *The Edwardian Theatre: Essays on Performance and the Stage*. Cambridge, UK: Cambridge University Press, 1996.

Rust, Frances. *Dance in Society: An Analysis of the Relationship between the Social Dance and Society in England from the Middle Ages to the Present Day*. London: Routledge & Kegan Paul, 1969.

Ruyter, Nancy Lee Chalfa. "American Delsarteans Abroad." In Christena L. Schlundt, ed., *American Dance Abroad: Influence of the United States Experience; Proceedings of the Society of Dance History Scholars: Fifteenth Annual Conference, University of California, Riverside, Ca, 14–15 February 1992*, 275–82. Riverside, CA: Society of Dance History Scholars, 1992.

Ryan, Mary P. *Women in Public: Between Banners and Ballots, 1825–1880*. Johns Hopkins Symposia in Comparative History. Baltimore: Johns Hopkins University Press, 1990.

Rye, Howard. "Fearsome Means of Discord: Early Encounters with Black Jazz." In Paul Oliver, ed., *Black Music in Britain: Essays on the Afro-Asian Contribution to Popular Music*, 45–57. Milton Keynes: Open University Press, 1990.

Sackville-West, V. *The Edwardians*. Garden City, NY: Doubleday, Doran, 1930.

Saint, Andrew. *Politics and the People of London: The London County Council, 1889–1965*. London: Hambledon, 1989.

Sala, George Augustus Henry Fairfield. *London up to Date*. London: A. & C. Black, 1894.

Saler, Michael T. *The Avant-Garde in Interwar England: Medieval Modernism and the London Underground*. New York and Oxford: Oxford University Press, 1999.

Salmon, Eric. *Bernhardt and the Theatre of Her Time*. Contributions in Drama and Theatre Studies. Westport, CT: Greenwood Press, 1984.

Salvoni, Elena, and Sandy Fawkes. *Elena: A Life in Soho*. London: Quartet, 1990.

Samuel, Raphael. *Theatres of Memory*. London: Verso, 1994.

Samuel, Raphael, ed. *Patriotism: The Making and Unmaking of British National Identity*. 3 vols. History Workshop Series. London and New York: Routledge, 1989.

Sansom, William. *The Blitz: Westminster at War*. Oxford: Oxford University Press, 1990. (Originally published 1947.)

Scannell, Paddy, and David Cardiff. *A Social History of British Broadcasting*. Oxford and Cambridge, MA: Basil Blackwell, 1991.

Schivelbusch, Wolfgang. *Disenchanted Night: The Industrialization of Light in the Nineteenth Century*. Berkeley: University of California Press, 1995.

Schmiechen, James A. *Sweated Industries and Sweated Labor: A History of the London Clothing Trades, 1860–1914*. London: Croom Helm, 1984.

Schnapp, Jeffrey L. "The Mass Panorama." *Modernism/Modernity* 9, no. 2 (2002): 243–381.

Schneer, Jonathan. *London 1900: The Imperial Metropolis*. New Haven: Yale University Press, 1999.

Schwartz, Joan M., and James M. Ryan. *Picturing Place: Photography and the Geographical Imagination*. London: I. B. Tauris, 2003.

Schwarz, Bill. *West Indian Intellectuals in Britain*. Manchester: Manchester University Press, 2003.

Segre, Claudio G. *Italo Balbo: A Fascist Life*. Berkeley: University of California Press, 1987.

Sewell, William H. "Historical Events as Transformations of Structure: Inciting Revolution at the Bastille." *Theory and Society* 25, no. 6 (1996): 841–81.

Shaffer, Brian W. "'The Commerce of Shady Wares': Politics and Pornography in Conrad's *The Secret Agent*." *English Literary History* 62, no. 2 (1995): 443–66.

Sharpe, Frederick Dew. *Sharpe of the Flying Squad*. London: John Long, 1938.

Shaw, George Bernard. *Our Theatre in the Nineties*. New York: W. H. Wise, 1931.

Shellard, Dominic, Steve Nicholson, and Miriam Handley. *The Lord Chamberlain Regrets–: A History of British Theatre Censorship*. London: British Library, 2004.

Sheppard, F. H. W., "General Introduction." In F. H. W. Sheppard, gen. ed., *Survey of London, Volumes 33 and 34: St Anne Soho*. London, 1966. At http://www.british-history.ac.uk/report.aspx?compid=41022 (accessed May 2011).

———. gen. ed., *Survey of London, Volumes 33 and 34: The Parish of St. Anne, Soho*. London: Athlone Press, 1966.

Sheridan, Dorothy, Brian V. Street, and David Bloome. *Writing Ourselves: Mass-Observation and Literacy Practices*. Cresskill, NJ: Hampton Press, 2000.

Sherwell, Arthur. *Life in West London: A Study and a Contrast*. 2nd rev. edn. London: Methuen, 1897.

Shipley, Stan. *Club Life and Socialism in Mid-Victorian London*. Oxford: History Workshop, Ruskin College, 1971.

Shipton, Alyn. *A New History of Jazz*. New York and London: Continuum, 2001.

Showalter, Elaine. *Sexual Anarchy: Gender and Culture at the Fin de Siècle*. New York: Viking, 1990.

Shpayer-Makov, Haia. "Anarchism in British Public Opinion 1880–1914." *Victorian Studies* 31, no. 4 (1988): 487–516.

Sigel, Lisa Z. *Governing Pleasures: Pornography and Social Change in England, 1815–1914*. New Brunswick, NJ: Rutgers University Press, 2002.

Silex, Karl. *John Bull at Home*. London: Harrap, 1931.

Silvester, Victor. *Dancing Is My Life: An Autobiography*. London: Heinemann, 1958.

Simmel, Georg. *Simmel on Culture: Selected Writings*, ed. David Frisby and Mike Featherstone. London: Sage, 1997.

Simon, Andy, ed. *Headnotes, Black British Swing: The African Diaspora's Contribution to England's Own Jazz of the 1930s and 1940s*. London: Topics Records, 2001.

Sims, George Robert. *Watches of the Night*. London: Greening, 1907.

Sinclair, Andrew. *War like a Wasp: The Lost Decade of the Forties*. London: Hamish Hamilton, 1989.

Slater, Don. "Going Shopping: Markets, Crowds, and Consumption." In Chris Jenks, ed., *Cultural Reproduction*, 188–209. London: Routledge, 1993.

Slater, Montague. "Artist International Exhibition 1935." *Left Review* 2 (1936): 161–4.

Slater, Stefan. "Containment: Managing Street Prostitution in London, 1918–59." *Journal of British Studies* 49, no. 1 (2010): 332–57.

——— . "Pimps, Police, and Filles de Joie: Foreign Prostitution in Interwar London." *London Journal* 32, no. 1 (2007): 53–74.

Slobin, Mark. "Some Intersections of Jews, Music, and Theater." In Sarah Blacher Cohen, ed., *From Hester Street to Hollywood: The Jewish-American Stage and Screen*, 29–44. Bloomington: Indiana University Press, 1983.

Smith, Alison. *The Victorian Nude: Sexuality, Morality, and Art*. Manchester: Manchester University Press, 1996.

Smith, H. Llewellyn, ed., *The New Survey of London Life and Labour*. 9 vols. London: P. S. King, 1930–5.

Soho Hospital for Women, *Soho Centenary: A Gift from Artists, Writers and Musicians to the Soho Hospital for Women*. London: Hutchinson, 1944.

Spies, Kathleen. "'Girls and Gags': Sexual Display and Humor in Reginald Marsh's Burlesque Images." *American Art* 18, no. 2 (2004): 33–57.

Sponza, Lucio. "The Anti-Italian Riots, June 1940." In Panikos Panayi, ed., *Racial Violence in Britain in the Nineteenth and Twentieth Centuries*, 227. Leicester: Leicester University Press, 1996.

——— . *Divided Loyalties: Italians in Britain during the Second World War*. Bern and New York: P. Lang, 2000.

——— . *Italian Immigrants in Nineteenth-Century Britain: Realities and Images*. Leicester: Leicester University Press, 1988.

Stansell, Christine. *American Moderns: Bohemian New York and the Creation of a New Century*. New York: Metropolitan Books, 2000.

Stansky, Peter. *On or about December 1910: Early Bloomsbury and Its Intimate World*. Studies in Cultural History. Cambridge, MA: Harvard University Press, 1996.

Stapleton, Alan. *London Alleys, Byways and Courts*. London: Bodley Head, 1924.

Stebbins, Genevieve. *Delsarte System of Dramatic Expression*. Rev. and enlarged edn. New York: Dance Horizons, 1902. (Originally published 1885.)

Steedman, Carolyn. *Strange Dislocations: Childhood and the Idea of Human Interiority, 1780–1930*. Cambridge, MA: Harvard University Press, 1995.

Steele, Valerie. *Fashion and Eroticism: Ideals of Feminine Beauty from the Victorian Era to the Jazz Age*. New York: Oxford University Press, 1985.

Steen, Marguerite. *A Pride of Terrys: Family Saga*. London: Longmans, 1962.

Stevenson, John, and Chris Cook. *Britain in the Depression: Society and Politics, 1929–1939*. London and New York: Longman, 1994.

Stokes, John. *In the Nineties*. New York: Harvester Wheatsheaf, 1989.

Stowell, Sheila. *A Stage of Their Own: Feminist Playwrights of the Suffrage Era*. Ann Arbor: University of Michigan Press, 1992.

Suleiman, Susan. "Bataille in the Streets: The Search for Virility in the 1930s." *Critical Inquiry* 21, no. 1 (1994): 61–79.

Summerfield, Penny. "Mass-Observation: Social Research or Social Movement." *Journal of Contemporary History* 20, no. 3 (1985): 439–52.

Summers, Judith. *Soho: A History of London's Most Colourful Neighbourhood*. London: Bloomsbury, 1989.

Summerson, John. *Georgian London*. New edn. London: Pimlico, 1991.

—— . *John Nash, Architect to King George IV*. London: Allen & Unwin, 1935.

Suschitzky, Wolfgang and Raphael Samuel. *Charing Cross Road in the Thirties*. London: Nishen Photography, 1989.

Sutherland, Alasdair Scott. *The Spaghetti Tree: Mario and Franco and the Trattoria Revolution*. London: Primavera Books, 2009.

Sweeney, John, *At Scotland Yard: Being the Experiences during Twenty Seven Years' Service of John Sweeney*, ed. Francis Richards. London: Alexander Moring, 1905.

Symons, Arthur. *Cities and Sea-Coasts and Islands*. London: W. Collins, 1918.

Tabili, Laura. *"We Ask for British Justice": Workers and Racial Difference in Late Imperial Britain*. Ithaca, NY: Cornell University Press, 1994.

Tames, Richard. *Soho Past*. London: Historical Publications, 1994.

Tate, Trudi. *Modernism, History and the First World War*. Manchester: Manchester University Press, 1998.

Taxidou, Olga. *The Mask: A Periodical Performance by Edward Gordon Craig*. Contemporary Theatre Studies. Amsterdam: Harwood Academic, 1998.

Taylor, Caroline. "Flight Power." *Antique Collector* 67, no. 3 (1996): 54.

Taylor, D. J. *Bright Young People: The Lost Generation of London's Jazz Age*. New York: Farrar, Straus, & Giroux, 2009.

Taylor, Tom. *Leicester Square: Its Associations and Its Worthies*. London: Bickers, 1874.

Thane, Pat. "Financiers and the British State: The Case of Sir Ernest Cassel." *Business History* 27 (Jan. 1986): 80–99.

Thomas Cook & Son. *Cook's Tourist's Handbook to Switzerland, Via Paris*. London: Thomas Cook & Son.

Thomas, Donald Serrell. *An Underworld at War: Spies, Deserters, Racketeers and Civilians in the Second World War*. London: John Murray, 2003.

Thomas, George. *A Tenement in Soho*. London: Cape, 1931.

Thomas, Helen, and Nicola Miller. "Ballroom Blitz." In Helen Thomas, ed., *Dance in the City*, 89–110. Houndmills, UK: Macmillan, 1997.

Thompson, E. P. *William Morris: Romantic to Revolutionary*. Rev. edn. London: Merlin Press, 1977.

Thompson, Leslie, and Jeffrey P. Green. *Leslie Thompson: An Autobiography*. Crawley, UK: Rabbit Press, 1985.

Thornbury, George Walter, and Edward Walford. *Old and New London: A Narrative of Its History, Its People, and Its Places*. 6 vols. London, 1873–8.

Thurlow, Richard C. *Fascism in Britain: A History, 1918–1985*. Oxford: Blackwell, 1987.

Tickner, Lisa. "The Popular Culture of Kermesse: Lewis, Painting and Performance, 1912–13." *Modernity/Modernism* 4, no. 2 (1997): 67–120.

—— . *The Spectacle of Women: Imagery of the Suffrage Campaign, 1907–14*. Chicago: University of Chicago Press, 1988.

Tietjen, Arthur. *Soho: London's Vicious Circle*. London: Allan Wingate, 1956.

Tomkinson, Martin. *The Pornbrokers*. London: Virgin Books 1982.

Tomko, Linda J. *Dancing Class: Gender, Ethnicity, and Social Divides in American Dance, 1890–1920*. Bloomington: Indiana University Press, 1999.

Tracy, Sheila. *Talking Swing: The British Big Bands*. Edinburgh: Mainstream, 1997.

Travis, Jennifer. "Clits in Court: Salome, Sodomy, and the Lesbian 'Sadist.'" In Jay Karla, ed., *Lesbian Erotics*. New York: New York University Press, 1995.

Trubek, Amy B. *Haute Cuisine: How the French Invented the Culinary Profession*. Philadelphia: University of Pennsylvania Press, 2000.

Tucker, Sophie. *Some of These Days: The Autobiography of Sophie Tucker*. Garden City, NY: Garden City, 1946.

Tydeman, William, and Steven Price. *Wilde: Salome*. Cambridge, UK: Cambridge University Press, 1996.

Tyrrell, Ian R. *Woman's World/Woman's Empire: The Woman's Christian Temperance Union in International Perspective, 1880–1930*. Chapel Hill: University of North Carolina Press, 1991.

Ugolini, Wendy, and Gavin Schaffer. "Victims or Enemies? Italians, Refugee Jews and the Reworking of Internment Narratives in Post-war Britain." In Gavin Schaffer and Monica Riera, eds., *The Lasting War: Society and Identity in Britain, France, and Germany after 1945*, 207–25. Basingstoke, UK: Palgrave, 2008.

Van Damm, Sheila. *No Excuses*. London: Putnam, 1957.

——— . *We Never Closed: The Windmill Story*. London: Robert Hale, 1967.

Van Damm, Vivian. *Tonight and Every Night*. London: Stanley Paul, 1952.

Vernon, Doremy. *Tiller's Girls*. London: Robson, 1988.

Vernon, James. *Hunger: A Modern History*. Cambridge, MA: Belknap Press, 2007.

Viveur, Bon. *Where to Dine in London*. London: Geoffrey Bles, 1937.

Wagner, Leopold. *More London Inns and Taverns*. London: Allen & Unwin, 1925.

Wainwright, Lyndon B. *The Story of British Popular Dance*. Brighton, UK: International Dance 1997.

Walker, Richard. *Savile Row: An Illustrated History*. New York: Rizzoli, 1989.

Walkowitz, Daniel J. *City Folk: English Country Dance and the Politics of the Folk in Modern America*. New York: New York University Press, 2010.

Walkowitz, Judith R. *City of Dreadful Delight: Narratives of Sexual Danger in Late-Victorian London*. Women in Culture and Society. Chicago: University of Chicago Press, 1992.

——— . "Cosmopolitanism, Feminism, and the Moving Body." *Victorian Literature and Culture* 38, no. 2 (2010): 427–49.

——— . "Emergence of Cosmopolitan Soho." In Sophie Watson and Gary Bridge, eds., *The New Blackwell Companion to the City*, 419–30. Oxford: Blackwell, 2010.

——— . "Going Public: Shopping, Street Harassment, and Streetwalking in Late Victorian London." *Representations* 62 (1998): 1–30.

——— . "The Indian Woman, the Flower Girl, and the Jew: Photojournalism in Edwardian London." *Victorian Studies* 42 (1999): 3–46.

——— . *Prostitution and Victorian Society: Women, Class, and the State*. Cambridge, UK and New York: Cambridge University Press, 1980.

——— . "The 'Vision of Salome': Cosmopolitanism and Erotic Dancing in Central London, 1908–1918." *American Historical Review* 108, no. 2 (2003): 337–76.

Walkowitz, Rebecca L. "Conrad's Adaptation: Theatricality and Cosmopolitanism." *Modern Drama* 44 (Fall 2001): 318–36.

——— . *Cosmopolitan Style: Modernism beyond the Nation*. New York: Columbia University Press, 2006.

Wall, Cynthia. *The Literary and Cultural Spaces of Restoration London*. Cambridge, UK and New York: Cambridge University Press, 1998.

Waller, Maureen. *London 1945: Life in the Debris of War*. London: John Murray, 2004.

Walsh, Michael J. K. *C. R. W. Nevinson: This Cult of Violence*. New Haven and London: Yale University Press, 2002.

Waters, Chris. "The Americanization of the Masses: Cultural Criticism, the National Heritage, and Working-Class Culture in the 1930s." *Social History Curators* 17 (1989–90).

——— . "'Dark Strangers' in Our Midst: Discourses of Race and Nation in Britain 1947–74." *Journal of British Studies* 36, no. 2 (1997): 207–38.

——— . "Progressives, Puritans, and the Council, 1889–1914." In Andrew Saint, ed., *Politics and the People of London: The London County Council, 1889–1965*, 49–70. London: Hambledon, 1989.

Watt, Ian, ed. *Conrad: The Secret Agent. A Casebook*. London: Macmillan, 1973.

Waugh, Evelyn. *Brideshead Revisited: The Sacred and Profane Memories of Captain Charles Ryder; A Novel*. Boston: Little, Brown, 1979.

——— . *A Handful of Dust*. Boston: Little, Brown, 1977.

Waugh, Norah. *Corsets and Crinolines*. London: Batsford, 1987. (Originally published 1954.)

Wayne, Jenifer. *The Purple Dress: Growing up in the Thirties*. London: Gollancz, 1979.

Webb, Thomas Duncan. *Crime Is My Business*. London: Frederick Muller, 1953.

Webster, Charles. "Healthy or Hungry Thirties." *History Workshop* 13 (1982): 110–29.

Weightman, Gavin. *Bright Lights, Big City: London Entertained, 1830–1950*. London: Collins & Brown, 1992.

Weightman, Gavin, and Steve Humphries. *The Making of Modern London, 1815–1914*. London: Sidgwick & Jackson, 1983.

——— . *The Making of Modern London, 1914–1939*. London: Sidgwick & Jackson, 1984.

——— . *The Making of Modern London*. London: Ebury Press, 2007.

Weinbaum, Alys Eve. *The Modern Girl around the World: Consumption, Modernity, and Globalization*. Durham, NC; London: Duke University Press, 2008.

Wells, H. G. *H. G. Wells in Love: Postscript to an Experiment in Autobiography*, ed. G. P. Wells. London: Faber & Faber, 1984.

——— . *Tono-Bungay: A Novel*. New York: Modern Library, 1908.

Westminster, Loelia, Duchess of. *Grace and Favour: The Memoirs of Loelia Duchess of Westminster*. London: Weidenfeld & Nicolson, 1961.

Wheatley, Henry Benjamin, and Peter Cunningham. *London Past and Present: Its History, Associations, and Traditions. By H. B. Wheatley. Based Upon the Handbook of London by the Late Peter Cunningham*. London: J. Murray, 1891.

Wheelwright, Julie. *The Fatal Lover: Mata Hari and the Myth of Women in Espionage*. London: Collins & Brown, 1992.

Wheen, Francis. *Tom Driberg: His Life and Indiscretions*. London: Chatto & Windus, 1990.

White, Dorothy Shipley. *Seeds of Discord: De Gaulle, Free France and the Allies*. New York: Syracuse University Press, 1964.

White, Jerry. *London in the Nineteenth Century: 'A Human Awful Wonder of God'*. London: Cape, 2007.

——— . *London in the Twentieth Century: A City and Its People*. London and New York: Viking, 2001.

White, Palmer. *Poiret*. London: Studio Vista, 1973.

Wilde, Oscar. "Oscar Wilde at the Vale." In *Oscar Wilde, Interviews and Recollections*, ed. E. H. Mikhail. London: Macmillan, 1979.

——— . *Salome: A Tragedy in One Act; Drawings by Aubrey Beardsley*. Boston: Branden, 1996.

Williams, Emlyn. *Emlyn: An Early Autobiography 1927–1935*. London: Bodley Head, 1973.

Williams, Guy R. *The Hidden World of Scotland Yard*. London: Hutchinson, 1972.

Williams, Raymond. *Keywords: A Vocabulary of Culture and Society*. Rev. edn. New York: Oxford University Press, 1985.

Willis, Frederick. *A Book of London Yesterdays*. London: Phoenix House, 1960.

Wilmut, Roger. *Kindly Leave the Stage! The Story of Variety 1919–1960*. London: Methuen, 1985.

Wilson, A. N. *The Faber Book of London*. London: Faber and Faber, 1993.

Wilson, Elizabeth. *Bohemians: The Glamorous Outcasts*. London: I. B. Tauris, 2000.

Wilson, Elizabeth, and Lou Taylor. *Through the Looking Glass: A History of Dress from 1860 to the Present Day*. London: BBC Books, 1989.

Wilson, Jean Moorcroft. *Virginia Woolf's London: A Guide to Bloomsbury and Beyond*. London: Tauris Parke, 2000. (Originally published 1987.)

Wilson, Trevor. *The Myriad Faces of War: Britain and the Great War, 1914–1918*. Cambridge, UK: Polity Press, 1986.

Winkiel, Laura. "Suffrage Burlesque: Modernist Performance in Elizabeth Robins's *The Convert*." *Modern Fiction Studies* 50, no. 3 (2004): 570–94.

Winship, Maggie. "New Disciplines for Women and the Rise of the Chain Stores in the 1930s." In Mary Talbot and Maggie Andrews, eds., 'All the World and Her Husband': Women in Twentieth-Century Consumer Culture, 23–45. London: Cassell, 2000.

Winter, James H. London's Teeming Streets: 1830–1914. London and New York: Routledge, 1993.

Wohl, Anthony S. The Eternal Slum: Housing and Social Policy in Victorian London. Studies in Urban History. London: Edward Arnold, 1977.

Wollen, Peter. "Fashion/Orientalism/the Body." New Formations (1987): 3–55.

Woolf, Leonard. Beginning Again: An Autobiography of the Years 1911 to 1918. New York: Harcourt, 1964.

Woolf, Virginia. The Diary of Virginia Woolf, vol. 1: 1915–1919, ed. Anne Olivier Bell. Harmondsworth, UK: Penguin, 1979.

——. The Diary of Virginia Woolf, vol. 2: 1920–1924, ed. Anne Olivier Bell and Andrew McNeillie. Harmondsworth, UK: Penguin, 1981. (Originally published 1978.)

——. The Diary of Virginia Woolf, vol. 5: 1936–1941, ed. Anne Olivier Bell and Andrew McNeillie. London: Hogarth, 1984.

——. Jacob's Room, ed. and annotated Sue Roe. London: Penguin, 1992.

——. The Letters of Virginia Woolf, vol. 3: 1923–1928, a Change of Perspective, ed. Nigel Nicolson and Joanne Trautmann. London: Hogarth Press, 1977.

——. The Moment, and Other Essays, ed. Leonard Woolf. New York: Harcourt, 1948.

——. "Oxford Street Tide." In Virginia Woolf, The London Scene, 16–22. New York: F. Hallman, 1975.

——. "Street Haunting." In Virginia Woolf, Collected Essays, 155–66. New York: Harcourt Brace, 1966.

Woollacott, Angela. "Khaki Fever and Its Control: Gender, Class, and Sexual Morality in the British Homefront during the First World War." Journal of Contemporary History 29, no. 2 (April 1994): 325–47.

Worby, John. The Other Half: The Autobiography of a Spy. London: Dent, 1937.

——. Spiv's Progress. London: Dent, 1939.

Wray, Margaret. The Women's Outerwear Industry. London: Duckworth, 1957.

Wyndham, Horace, and Dorothea Saint John George. Nights in London. With Illustrations by Dorothea St. John George. London: John Lane, 1926.

Yeo, Eileen, and Stephen Yeo. Popular Culture and Class Conflict, 1590–1914: Explorations in the History of Labour and Leisure. Brighton, UK: Harvester Press; Atlantic Highlands, NJ: Humanities, 1981.

Zemgulys, Andrea. Modernism and the Locations of Literary Heritage. Cambridge, UK and New York: Cambridge University Press, 2008.

Zimring, Rishona. "Conrad's Pornography Shop." Modern Fiction Studies 43, no. 2 (1997): 319–48.

Index

Page numbers in italics refer to illustrations.

professional dance partners in, 192–3; styles of dancing in, 190–2
Au Petit Savoyard, 116, 292
Ayer, A. J., 234
Azikiwe, Nnamdi, 234, 359n187

Bacon, Miss Nell, 204
Bag o' Nails, 230, 363n178
Balfour, Patrick ("Mr. Gossip"), 117, 213, 214, 222
Bankruptcy, 154, 163
Barker, Eric, 262, 263, 268, 273
Barry, Doris, 264, 266
BBC, 140, 238–9, 248, 254–5, 268, 275, 279–80
Beardsley, Aubrey, 56, 78
Beaumont, Cyril, 56
Beauty culture, 186, 188. *See also* Social dancing: dress and grooming for
Beecham, Thomas, 83
Benedetta, Mary, 169, 170–2, 176
Benjamin, Thelma, 159
Berlemont, Gaston, 292
Berlemont, Victor, 142
Bernabei, Alfio, 131–2, 135
Bernhardt, Sarah, 71, 72, 81, 89, 321n36
Bernstein, Sidney, 258
Bertorelli, David, 134, 141
Berwick Street area, 139, 143, 148–52, 246, 294; and remapping of Soho, 2. *See also* Berwick Street Market
Berwick Street Market, 1–2, 7, 13, 108, 144–8, 279–80; cosmopolitanism of, 148, 155–7, 159; decline of, 168, 173–5; female proprietors in, 154, 162; Jewish identity of, 154, 157, 160, 163–4, 166; left politics and, 143, 168–72; middle-class shoppers in, 165–6; municipal authorities and, 164–5, 166, 343n112; stockings sold in, 1, 156–7, 160, 170, 171, 173–4; and West End emporia, 153–4, 168, 176; working women as customers of, 12, 153–4, 171–2, 287, 293
Besant, Sir Walter, 28
Billie's Club, 232
Billing, Noel Pemberton, 68, 87–9
Bird, Rose, 205
Birnbaum, Sonya, 189
Biron, Sir Chartres, 209
Bissell, George, 117
Black, George, 269
Black, Gerry, 9
Black Britons, 7, 127, 233, 247, 362n269. *See also* Blake, Cyril; Blake, George "Happy";

Deniz, Joe; Deniz, Laurie; Thompson, Leslie
Black jazz clubs, 7, 12, 230, 232–5, 251–2; interracial dancing in, 12, 235, 236–7, 241, 247–9, *250*, 252, 288; Jews and, 7, 12, 230, 241–2 (*see also* Isow, Jack); and left politics, 12, 127, 239–41; musicians in, 7, 233, 234, 237–40; and pattern set by 43 Club, 214, 251; rise of, in 1930s, 11, 12, 230; in wartime, 247–50. *See also* Shim Sham Club
Black marketeering, 174, 178–9, 290–1
Blackshirts (British Union of Fascists), 11, 202, 240
Blake, Cyril, 238, 248
Blake, George "Happy," 237, 238–9
Blitz, the, 139–40, 142, 173, 188; Windmill Theatre during, 253–4, 258, 275, 277, 279–80, 282–4, 287–8
Bloomsbury, 49, 217
Blue Post pub, 156
Bohemia, 32, 33–7, 101, 117, 217, 237
Bohemia in London (Ransome), 33–7, 38
Bohm, Charles, 240
Bondfield, Margaret, 164
Bond Street, 147
Booker, Bill, 185, 216
Booth, Charles, 3, 20, 22, 26, 98, 103, 151
Booth, J. B., 56
Bottle parties, 229–30, 232, 272; origins of, 156, 229; in Soho, 156, 214, 230, 232. *See also* Black jazz clubs
Bouillabaisse club, 248, 249
Boulestin, Marcel, 115, 332n150
Boulogne Restaurant, 32–3
Boundaries of Soho, 2–3, 17, 20, 22, 23, 26, 148–9
Bourdin, Martial, 24, 37–8
Bourne, Adeline, 84–5, 325n99
Bourne and Hollingsworth, 154
Bowen, Elizabeth, 253
Brandt, Bill, 205, *206*, 280–1, *282*
Breckenridge, Carol, 4
Brideshead Revisited (Waugh), 213–14, 221
Bright Young Things, 13, 117, 213, 219, 230
British Union of Fascists, 111, 202, 240
Broadwick Street, 298
Brooker, Peter, 36, 37
Brothels, 24, 301. *See also* Prostitutes
Bulmore, Zinna, 132–3
Burke, Thomas, 108–9, 155–6, 215
Burlesque, American, 259, 266, 267
Burnett, John, 108
Burney, Fanny, 148